THE WANDERER

Whose farthest footstep never strayed
Beyond the village of his birth
Is but a lodger for the night
In this old wayside inn of earth.

To-morrow he shall take his pack
And set out for the ways beyond
On the old trail from star to star,
An alien and a vagabond.

—Richard Hovey

Camper's & Backpacker's Bible

Edited by
C. B. Colby

SUPERVISORY EDITOR:
Irene Hinds
COPY EDITOR:
Alice Roberts

CHIEF EDITORIAL RESEARCHER:
Marleen Anderson
EDITORIAL RESEARCHERS:
Carol Altman
Judith E. Cohen
Mary Kannar
Gay E. Riedel
Cheryl Wanner
Gritli Wolbach

ART DIRECTOR:
Maria Barranco Opiela
ASSISTANT ART DIRECTOR:
Nancy Jensen

MANAGING EDITOR:
George M. Horn
ASSISTANT MANAGING EDITOR:
John C. Rhodes
PRODUCTION EDITOR:
Bob Dana
ASSISTANT PRODUCTION EDITOR:
Jeff Arnold
PUBLISHER:
Robert F. Scott

Stoeger Publishing Company

Copyright © 1977 by Stoeger Publishing Company

All rights reserved

Published by Stoeger Publishing Company

Library of Congress Catalog Card No: 76-54415

International Standard Book No.: 0-88317-033-7

Manufactured in the United States of America

Distributed to the book trade by Follett Publishing Company, 1010 West Washington Boulevard, Chicago, Illinois 60607 and to the sporting goods trade by Stoeger Industries, 55 Ruta Court, South Hackensack, New Jersey 07606

In Canada, distributed to the book trade and to the sporting goods trade by Stoeger Trading Company, 900 Ontario Street East, Montreal, Quebec H2L 1P4

Contents

Foreword

Why do we camp or backpack?

Ever since the ancestors of man tentatively came down from the trees to lay dubious claim to the savannas and grasslands, the earth has been a place of mystery and adventure. Ever since that time, thanks to the discovery of the uses of tools and weapons and the knowledge of fire making, man has also ventured farther and farther afield.

It is no surprise, therefore, that man has always been something of a gypsy. The lookout has always been on distant horizons from which at any time another and stranger siren song may come calling and take the heart, to love or to kill, with treasure or with ashes.

Camping and backpacking are two forms of recreation (which happily have not been relegated to the role of lost arts) that genuinely link us with our long past. Despite the inroads made by the advancing tides of urbanization, the wilderness still beckons us.

Only a camper or backpacker can follow the trail of Coronado across the Staked Plains in search for the Seven Cities of Cibola, the legendary cities of gold. For more than a thousand miles of unexplored mountains and plains Coronado's expedition had marched, always being told by the ragged Indians from their mud hovels that what they sought lay *"Más allá"*—farther on.

In the end, Casteñada, chronicler of the expedition, summed up its results with an exquisite comment: "Granted that they did not find the riches of which they had been told, they found a place in which to search for them." Had they but known, a fortune in gold, silver, copper and other minerals lay just beneath their feet.

A place in which to search!

No motorist can know the Lake Erie-Ohio River portages of the pre-Revolutionary border as can the hiker. Or the tortuous road followed by Rogers' Rangers to Canada and back. Who is not susceptible to the lure of such romantic names as the Bozeman Trail, Hastings' Cutoff, Lassen's Route, the trail taken by the Mormon Battalion, the Natchez Trace, the Trail of Tears of the exiled Cherokees, or the pioneering route of the hard-riding Pony Express?

We are never alone when we set out into the wilderness; a host of silent companions is at our side. Scale Mount Marcy in New York's Adirondacks, and it is 1837 and veteran guides John Cheyney and Harvey Holt, the first to climb it, are at your elbow. Stand at the Sycamore Shoals of

the Watauga and it is 1775 once again. A treaty is being signed by the Cherokee Nation which cedes to the Transylvania Company the vast territories of Kentucky and Tennessee. Find Kaskaskia, Logtown or South Pass and you are in the presence of the past. A camper and backpacker can make time turn backwards in its flight and experience emotions that are as old as mankind in what is once again "the forest primeval."

Hiking and camping in wild and silent places can be a genuinely rewarding and renewing experience, a way to recharge one's batteries, so to speak. Unfortunately, it can sometimes be a miserable, even perilous interlude, sometimes fraught with fatal hazards.

This CAMPER'S & BACKPACKER'S BIBLE, edited by my friend C.B. Colby, the country's foremost authority on camping and hiking, is intended to be a practical, authoritative and comprehensive handbook and guide for the beginner or the experienced hiker. Here is a book that not only tells you how and where to hike and camp, but describes in detail the various kinds of gear and equipment available.

This is a book that will enable you to hit the trail or open road secure in the knowledge that your equipment is the very finest you can select (paradoxically, the most elaborate or expensive equipment is not always the best) and that you are in the hands of competent guides and advisors. The nearly-three-dozen authors whose expertise has been tapped by Mr. Colby are each nationally known experts in their respective fields.

The CAMPER'S & BACKPACKER'S BIBLE offers trail-tested advice on boots, socks, the care of the feet, walking clothes and even raingear. You will learn to be able to choose the best in packs, tents, sleeping bags, stoves, and cooking and eating utensils. You will learn how to plan meals and to cook them, how much food and water to carry, what to take in the way of flashlights, lanterns, binoculars, cameras, first-aid kits and toilet gear. Whether you are a first-timer or an experienced and adventurous hiker or camper, it is no exaggeration to say that there is something of value here for everyone.

In this remarkable new volume, you may discover

"Roads that are straight and that end at a gate
  Are not half so enticing to follow
As are long roads that twist and are lost in the mist
  Like the path of the south-flying swallow."

—ROBERT F. SCOTT

Articles

Before You Begin
by C.B. Colby

Since my first overnight "camp" well over a half century ago (on top of a New Hampshire railroad embankment so as not to miss the before-dawn unloading of a circus train), camping has been not only my favorite vacation but my favorite vocation. For almost two decades I was camping editor of *Outdoor Life* magazine. I have authored, co-authored and edited several books on camping and along the way camped, backpacked and hiked from Newfoundland and Labrador to Alaska, and from Hudson Bay to Hawaii and Mexico, and in a host of pleasant places in all directions in between. The Colbys are still at it.

How camping has changed, and generally for the better in every way! No longer is it a battle of the bugs, bumpy sleeping and bad weather, and—unless you insist upon roughing it—you can be as comfortable as at home in almost any situation or under any circumstances. It is all in knowing how, and the CAMPER'S & BACKPACKER'S BIBLE will provide that know-how in time-tested and highly palatable formulas.

Even camping guides and information have changed. One of my century-old camping manuals

suggests that all campers should wear their drawers inside out to prevent the seams from chafing; to rid a tent's interior of unwanted insects all that is required is to "flash a little black powder." Today we can do quite a bit to make a camping family comfortable.

To the uninitiated the subject of camping or backpacking can be bewildering, if not a little awesome, but actually camping today can be simple and as comfortable as a stay at a resort, but at a fraction of the cost with a lot of fringe benefits you never will find in a resort folder. The main fringe benefit from investing in camping equipment is that once that first vacation under canvas has been paid for, your entire accommodations can be used year after year at no additional cost except for minor repairs and maintenance. Some of my own gear is still perfectly serviceable after a quarter of a century of pitching and breaking camp in hundreds of campsites.

For those who are taking up camping for the first time and those who are comparative old-timers in the craft yet want to improve their camping skills, we have assembled some of the nation's out-

standing experts and asked them to share their knowledge on as many different phases of the subjects of camping and backpacking. These are not armchair experts but men and women who have earned their reputations the hard and exciting way on wilderness trails in all kinds of weather from coast to coast and around campfires in a thousand different parts of the continent and beyond. There is something for everyone who enjoys the glow and curling smoke from a campfire, the challenge of a high trail, or the sounds and neighborly chatter of a public campground.

If you are contemplating camping or backpacking as a new way to spend your vacation, you will thoroughly enjoy *Camping: The Economy Vacation,* by Glenn Sapir; *Planning a Family Camping Vacation Is Easy* and *Fringe Benefits of Camping,* both by Pete Czura; or *Hike the Long Trails,* by Dave Richey. If you are already a cycle rider, Jim Elder tells you how to camp on two wheels in *Two-Wheel Camping,* and Herb Williams makes *Station-Wagon Travel Camping* simple and inviting for the "wagon master" and his family.

Should you already be a boater and enjoy the quiet of a lake, river or stream, Vin Sparano introduces you to canoe tenting in *A Look at Canoe Camping,* and Homer Circle reveals the double fun you have been missing if you are a non-fishing camper or a non-camping fisherman in his article *Fishing/Camping Has It All.* You will find that you have been missing a lot of fine fun by leaving out either half of this delightful vacation combination.

Perhaps you are asking "But where can I camp?" Ken Heuser tells you in *Where to Find out about Camping Areas,* and Bill Vogt gives still more help in *Public and Semi-Public Camping.* Once you have selected the area for your vacation and picked a campground or destination point, *Choosing the Right Site,* by Glenn Sapir, will help you pick the best spot for your family to set up your tent or camping trailer from all the other sites in the campground. Glenn gives many tips to assure that your site will provide for a comfortable and convenient stay. If you have been debating going north of the border to try Canadian hospitality and camping, by all means go, for it is one of my favorite camping destinations. *Camping in Canada* by my Canadian friend Jerry Knap will make it all so simple.

For the backpacking enthusiasts who may want to try a change and yet not lose the adventure of the high country, *Horse Packing—The Best of Two Worlds,* by Ed Park, may offer an enticing alternative. If you have tried camping and now want to try backpacking, Jim Bashline in his article *Pick a Pack and Pack It* will get you started correctly. Sheila Link's tips and suggestions for better trail meals, *Meals along the Trail,* will do much to make your hiking vacation a double treat at chow time with a minimum of fuss and equipment.

Fortunately family campers who plan to stay awhile in a campground can set up a convenient and efficient kitchen for family meals, thanks to modern gas appliances, stove stands, refrigerators and what not, and many first-hand tips from an expert. Sylvia Bashline's *Setting Up a Camp Kitchen* will help you plan a cooking area as convenient as your home kitchen and perhaps even more pleasant. Maybe you have talked with the "chefs" who camp with a camping trailer with many built-in conveniences for family living and would like to investigate that kind of "tow-tent" camping. You'll find a lot of good, sound pros and cons on the subject by Bruce Brady in his article *Tent or Pop-Up Tent Trailer.* Even if it does not settle the matter for your family for good, it will cue a lot of campfire conversation on an intriguing subject, including the art of maneuvering such a small trailer. Just to help you decide to at least try trailering, Katie McMullen makes the hardest maneuver easy in her fine piece *How to Back a Trailer.* Anyone who can drive a car with reasonable skill can learn the knack of trailering a lot easier than learning to drive the family vehicle.

Of course, if you are a rabid tenter or backpacker, picking your shelter can be as exciting as putting your name on the dotted line for your first house. Jim Elder's *No Best Tent* explains why every camper must pick the best tent for his particular requirements, and how to make that choice and get full value for your camping-home dollar. This is a very valuable article for the tenter, whether he is buying a two-man packing tent or a two-room family tent for a destination vacation of several weeks.

If you are already a camper but have never tried fall camping, a most informative article, *After Labor Day,* by Bob Gooch, may start an entire new habit. Late fall camping has many advantages including no bugs, snakes or thunderstorms, no crowds, no unbearably hot nights in a tent, and

much more that Bob makes completely alluring. The Colbys have always been attracted to fall camping and *After Labor Day* covers the highlights in a way you'll enjoy.

For those campers with youngsters that have to return to school, where to store all that equipment becomes a possible Labor Day chore every season's end. Dick Smith's article *Winter Storage of Camping Gear* will offer some new suggestions as to where and how to pack it away safely and compactly so that it will be ready for emergency use or another season at a moment's notice. Tips on cleaning, repairing and packing make this an important article for campers of any type.

Old-time campers pore over catalogs and haunt sporting goods stores and outfitters right along with the tyro—perhaps even more so—and such articles as *The Advantages of Buying Quality Equipment,* by Thayne Smith, and *Selecting Quality Clothing,* by Cam Sigler, will steer you around some of the common pitfalls. These two articles point out the best ways to check for quality in all kinds of camping equipment from stoves to jackets and gives practical tests to let you know just what your dollar is buying. Good quality equipment will pay you back in many years of satisfaction and these two experts will quickly prove to you that no matter what you pay, you may not always get what you pay for. Sometimes, if you know quality, you may get a lot more than what the price tag suggests.

If you would be interested in a camping and backpacking vacation except for the youngsters, be sure to read Lue Park's reassuring article *Kids As Campers.* Don't wait until the children are "old enough" or you may lose them forever as camping companions. Mrs. Park will make you think differently for she makes camping with kids entirely practical, an exciting adventure for them as well as the parents, and something to look forward to with extra special pleasure and anticipation for all members of your family. And what if they bring up the subject of their pets?

Dog expert Dave Duffey covers this topic in *Pets in Camp* for the veteran as well as inexperienced camper. He gives suggestions and a lot of pointed information as to how to keep your family pet from becoming the family pest and the bane of any campground. An untrained and unreliable dog can be a dangerous hazard in bear country as many backpackers have discovered. If you are a dog lover, be sure to read this informative article.

Camp pests can range from ants and ticks to porcupines and bear and the camper must expect to encounter some of these, for they were there first. John Malo covers these natives of camping areas in his article *Camp Pests* and not once does he mention loud hi-fi and all-night card games.

Some of the things the wilderness backpacker may encounter besides wildlife can be almost any small emergency from a hornet sting to a sudden vicious storm. The latter can be a real danger in high country and two experts give plenty of sound advice when an unexpected storm catches you on a high trail. *Be Ready for Sudden Storms*, by Herb Williams, and *On Your Own . . . And Still Alive*, by Gene Kirkley, are two articles hikers and backpackers should remember well. They are packed with first-hand information that can turn a dangerous situation into merely an exciting experience to talk about around the campfire. You may expect the worst, but these two outdoorsmen will help you prevent the worst from ever happening.

The focal point for many campers is the campfire, yet it is amazing how few people really know how to select proper fuel, build a fireplace for cooking or sitting-and-staring, or use an ax or hatchet properly. Vin Sparano takes away the mystery in *Tips on Campfires, Woods and Axes* so that you can build the best fire for what you need—cooking, warmth or simply enjoyment before you head for the sleeping bags.

With that in mind, Gene Kirkley's article *Put the "Good" in "Good Night"* can teach even the veteran a few tricks to ensure a good night's sleep no matter how you camp. He covers bags, mattresses of all kinds, clothing and all the other things that make for restful sleeping or restless hours in the dark. Read it and really enjoy your camping nights.

The author of the highly acclaimed book *Knives and Knifemakers*, Sid Latham introduces you to a *New Breed of Blades*. He covers all types of the favorite companion of the outdoorsman, his sheath knife, from blade steel to sheath, and gives expert advice for selection of size, shape and sheath for your particular purpose. The article is illustrated with outstanding photos of many new and interesting types of knives as seen through his camera.

As an expert photographer, Sid also covers cameras and outdoor photography in his article on cameras for the camper and backpacker. These range from the inexpensive to the complex. His article *Outdoor Photography* will do much to make your photo-journal of your next camping trip exceptional because of your new understanding of cameras, film, lenses and how to combine them for surprisingly professional results.

A short, but expertly covered, illustrated course in keeping your sheath knife keen winds up the articles. Sid Edmund shows in fine detail how to dress the blade for any chore from making a fuzz stick for starting a campfire to skinning a trophy or carving steak. To serve you well, a good sheath knife must be cared for, kept clean and keen and protected. *Keep Your Knife Sharp* shows you how to do just that.

Looking back over the list of articles and the men and women who have contributed them, I am proud indeed to have been able to gather this collective outdoorsman's know-how for this first edition of CAMPER'S & BACKPACKER'S BIBLE. I have known all of these fine folks for many years and talked across campfires to many of them in many places. To them a hearty "thank you" and I commend to you their skills and suggestions. If you can pass along some of this to other campers across your future campfires, it will serve to keep alive the traditionally friendly feeling that glowing embers and the presence of other woodsmen always seem to engender. May your campfires always burn brighter for such sharing.

Camping:
The Economy Vacation
by Glenn L. Sapir

Think back to your last vacation. If you hadn't gotten "into" camping by then, you spent a lot more money than you had to. To take liberties with an advertising slogan, if your vacation did not include camping, you may have been "spending more and enjoying it less."

"Wait a minute," you say. "I was thinking of getting into camping, taking my wife and two kids on a camping vacation, but after looking through a supply catalog, I was overwhelmed with all the gear I had to buy and the price it would have cost me."

Sorry, fella. That you might have gotten the impression you would need tons of gear is understandable. But the truth is that you could have bought most of the basics cheaply. In fact, the money you ultimately spent on your noncamping vacation could have been your entire stake for making your necessary camping-supply purchases.

Let's take a look at what you really need for a camping vacation for a family of four and see how much this equipment will cost. Let's see what other costs you can expect to incur as a result of going the camping route. And let's see what you spent on your noncamping vacation. You may be surprised at the comparative figures.

Where was it you went? Oh, you, your wife and two kids spent a week on the Maine coast. You stayed in a motel from Saturday night through the following Sunday morning. You needed two rooms each night, one for you and your wife and one for the children. You think each room cost about $27 per night, so you were spending $54 per day to shelter your family. If my calculations are close to being right, you spent about $430 for beds to lie on and a roof to cover your family. And when you turned in the keys to the two rooms that last Sunday morning, you were relinquishing any claim to those rooms. If you wanted to come back again, you would have to pay the same price.

If you had invested that in the camping gear you had been thinking about, what would you have needed to parallel your motel room?

You would have needed a tent large enough for four people. According to one supplier's catalog, you could have bought a good 9- by 12-foot cabin tent for $120. If you had wanted to go as luxuriously as this catalog could equip you to do, you could have purchased a really roomy 16- by 10-foot two-room tent for $300.

Of course, with just a tent, you're still sleeping on the ground, so let's get you four cots or air mattresses

Typical motel where rates run as high as $25 a night or even more, depending upon location, facilities and equipment.

and four sleeping bags. That same catalog shows that you could have had four adequate summer sleeping bags for a total of $64, cots for as little as $13 each, and air mattresses for as little as $8 apiece. Of course, you would have had to pay for a site, but many beautiful, quiet and isolated Maine campgrounds have sites available for $4 per night. For eight nights, the site fee would have been $32. Are you a little bit surprised?

Do you remember that you weren't particularly thrilled with the food you ate, except for those fantastic—and expensive—lobster dinners? But even if the food wasn't prepared exactly the way you like it, you did have to eat, and eat you did, three times a day, for eight days. You paid for a total of ninety-six meals. Breakfast averaged about $2 per person, lunch about $3 per person and dinner about $10 per person. So, you spent about $60 per day on food, or almost $500 for the week. Your room and board cost over $900!

If you had decided, instead, to invest in camping gear, you would have bought a stove, some camp dishes, cutlery, and pots and pans—that is, if you didn't want to take any of these things from your home kitchen. That investment, according to the same catalog, might have cost you $70. You surely would have wanted to bring a charcoal grill, even though many campgrounds feature permanent grills at every site. For an hibachi-type grill, deluxe model, you'd spend a maximum of $15. Of course, you'd have to have equipment that would keep your food in good condition, so you would need an ice chest and an insulated jug. For a family of four, you would want large units. Together, the two items should cost you about $50.

What else would you have needed—besides food, of course? You would have wanted aluminum foil, plastic bags and plastic wrap, all minimal-expense items and all the things you would have had at home anyway.

You would have had to buy food. Assuming that you're not going to feed yourself with any of the sport fish that might swim just yards from your site, you would have had to buy enough food for thirty-two meals. Figuring on generous portions, your breakfast might have consisted of eggs, coffee, milk, orange juice, bacon, ham and toast. Lunches would have been beverages and sandwiches: cold cuts such as ham, turkey, roast beef. Dinners would have varied. Along with a vegetable dish every night, you could have had steak, chicken, hamburgers, hot dogs, lamb chops, ribs, and for a special treat, lobster once or twice. You could have gone out to one of the crowded lobster restaurants, for you certainly were not bound to your site, but you would have easily spent $40 on the meal. Or you could have dined at the site, boiling your own lobsters, sitting under the stars as you sip a glass of Chablis from the bottle you had brought from home.

Quiet, starlight and privacy—that's what restaurants call ambience and you pay for it—yet here you would have had five-star ambience at your own site, and the meal would have cost half of what you would have spent in a commercial lobster house. Your total food bill for the vacation could have been between $80 and $100. Compare that to the $500 you spent during your conventional vacation.

There are a few other miscellaneous items you would have needed for your camping comfort, but they would have been minimal in cost. And as you accumulate camping experiences and camping gear, you would find yourself purchasing accessories such as electric air pumps, canopies for shade and rain protection while dining, and similar comforts.

But when you've added up the cost of that first camping vacation, if you chose that catalog's most luxurious items—a two-room tent, for instance—and added lots of food and all those finer things in life—you will find that the total comes to no more than $725.

Resort restaurants are expensive when a family of four has three meals a day.

Your conventional vacation cost over $900.

A saving of at least $175 is indeed impressive, but the real value of camping as an economy vacation will become much more obvious when your family takes its second camping vacation, for then you'll realize how much of your initial expenses were capital investments. The second time around, all you have to pay for is food, fuel and a few cooking essentials, and of course your campsite. Generously apportioning the food budget again, you spend about $150. On the other hand, if you decided to take a similar motel-restaurant vacation the next year, you'd have to pay $900 again—even if inflation doesn't take its toll. You will have saved over $750, enough to finance five more weeks of vacation—if you can figure out how to get all that vacation time. Problems, problems!

That, future camper, in easily understood black and white, and even better understood green—as in dollar bills—is why camping is called the economy vacation.

EXPENSES FOR AN EIGHT-DAY VACATION FOR A FAMILY OF FOUR—THE FIRST YEAR

Motel-Restaurant-Type Vacation

2 motel rooms at $27 each	$432
32 breakfasts at $2 each	64
32 lunches at $3 each	96
32 dinners at $10 each	320
Total	**$912**

Camping Vacation

9- by 12-foot cabin tent	$120
or	or
16- by 10-foot two-room tent	$300
4 air mattresses at $8 each	32
or	or
4 cots at $13 each	52
4 sleeping bags at $16 each	64
2-burner propane stove	35
4 sets of four-piece cutlery	16
4-party cookset (includes 4-quart pot, 2-quart pot, coffee pot and cover, fry pan, handle, 4 compartmented plates, and 4 cups)	14
outdoor grill	15
insulated 3-gallon jug	13
19-gallon ice chest	39
campsite rental at $4 per day	32
food	80 to 100
propane lantern	19
fuel (propane, charcoal)	25
Total	**$504 to $724**

EXPENSES FOR THE SAME TRIP THE SECOND YEAR

Motel-Restaurant-Type Vacation

2 motel rooms at $27 each	$432
32 breakfasts at $2 each	64
32 lunches at $3 each	96
32 dinners at $10 each	320
Total	**$912**

Camping Vacation

campsite rental at $4 per day	$32
food & miscellaneous kitchen items	100
fuel	25
Total	**$157**

If you prefer stove cooking, there are many one-, two- and three-burner stoves fueled by gasoline, propane, butane or even alcohol, which will provide the chef with at-home cooking convenience. Modern iceboxes, stove stands and other kitchen items help to make the modern camp cook feel at home, even when roughing it in the wilderness.

Where to Find out about Camping Areas

by Ken Heuser

More people are camping now than ever before, and the prospects for increased participation are big. Increasing right along with the demand are camping areas. The time to plan for camping is before you go on the trip. It's almost as much fun to plan as to be there. There are many different types of campgrounds so you'll want to pick the one that suits your type of camping best. The farther off the road you plan to go the fewer facilities you'll find. There are campgrounds for nearly everyone's needs, from full-service facilities to barebones places that make you wonder if anyone had ever been there before.

The U.S. Forest Service has eighty-six wild areas and 14,500,000 acres of land in fourteen states for you to camp on. There are literally hundreds of these federal campgrounds at lakes, along streams and in the mountains. Some charge a fee, some are free, depending on the demand and the season. The majority of these fine campgrounds are located in western states. There are thousands of miles of foot trails for the backpacker to investigate. Some of the most beautiful scenery in the world is on U.S. Forest Service land—our land. On most Forest Service land camping is not restricted to designated campgrounds. Some of the most memorable camping we have had has been outside such sites. Leave your campsite the way you found it, and don't violate the rules for staying on designated roads with your vehicles. For information regarding U.S. Forest Service campgrounds, see Sources of Information at the end of this article.

Another major federal agency operating almost exclusively in the West is the Bureau of Land Management (BLM). The Bureau's lands are at lower elevations than the Forest Service lands. The Bureau manages federal lands such as the vast sagebrush country of Nevada, southern Idaho, Utah, western Colorado and various parts of other western states. Some of these lands are also full of juniper and cedar and are absolutely delightful for exploring and camping, especially along small creeks and watercourses. BLM campgrounds are usually not well appointed, and since they are mainly in arid country, very few even have water. For information on BLM campgrounds, see Sources of Information.

With a possibility of water and an outdoor privy, the primitive-type campground will offer the camper a place to camp with more privacy.

The National Park Service is another federal agency that is important to campers. Many and varied services are offered. It is wise to check in advance on the availability of spaces in the rush season. For complete information see Sources of Information.

These three agencies are well known throughout the country, but they are not the only federal agencies that have public campgrounds. The Army Corps of Engineers has some of the best accommodations found anywhere. Some of the facilities are downright plush, featuring heated restrooms with showers, wood for campfires, solid picnic tables and more room per camper than is usually found. These campgrounds are not well known, so you have to seek them out. See Sources of Information.

The National Wildlife Refuges are managed by the U.S. Fish and Wildlife Service. Some of the refuges have excellent campsites, some have very marginal ones, and others have none at all. The refuges are always very interesting, as there are animals and birds in quantities to observe. If you like this sort of thing, I highly recommend you look into the possibilities. Follow the rules in the refuges; don't go into prohibited areas. See Sources of Information.

Indian tribes are fast developing camping areas on their reservations. Some of these areas are organized, some primitive, but all are interesting. Tribal cultures may be observed, gifts bought and crafts studied. To find out which areas are being opened up, you must contact the tribal council at each reservation. The addresses of the councils and other information on reservation camping can be obtained from the Bureau of Indian Affairs, Interior Building, South,

1951 Constitution Avenue, N.W., Washington, D.C. 20240.

If you plan to spend a lot of time in federal areas, it will be well worth your while to buy a Golden Eagle Passport. This can be secured for $10.00 at any designated fee area. It entitles you to enter all federal recreational fee areas. This permit applies to entrance fees only and not to overnight camping fees. For senior citizens (62 years or older) a Golden Age Passport is available. It takes the place of the Golden Eagle, is free of charge, covers the same services, and in-cludes a 50-percent reduction on overnight camping at almost all federal camping areas. This in-cludes National Park, National Forest, Corps of Engineers and Bureau of Land Management lands. To obtain this passport, you must present yourself at any area where the passport may be used and carry reasonable proof of your age.

These campgrounds are only the tip of the iceberg. Thousands of public campsites are built and maintained by lesser governmental agencies—town, county, city and state. It is these campsites that can delight the casual traveler, as they are not usually as crowded as the big popular sites and not as well known. If you are interested in town or city camping areas, check well in advance with the local Chamber of Commerce to find out what kind of facilities are available. If you don't have a pre-planned route, service stations, businesses, tourist information offices and po-lice stations can give you informa-tion right on the spot. County parks dot the landscape like pepper on a fried egg. They are usually

KOA campgrounds with all facilities, such as this one at Dowd Junction, Colorado, are ideal for those who desire lots of company and most of the comforts of home: water, electricity hookups, sewer, laundry facilities, general store, television antennae, playground and paved roads.

scenic and well kept but have only basic facilities, such as water and toilets. County courthouses or county parks departments will be happy to give you the information.

State parks are the salvation of campers east of the Mississippi, where there is comparatively little federally owned land. The states compete actively for the favor of campers. You may have to make reservations in advance for a state-owned campground, as they run full during the summer and especially on weekends. States generally provide listings and maps of state parks indicating what facilities are available. A letter to the State Division of Parks and Recreation of whatever state you are interested in will be routed to the right people. All departments are in the state capitals. Fees vary considerably but are never prohibitive.

Reservations at most state parks are accepted two weeks in advance and must be accompanied by the full fee plus a small service charge. Stays are usually limited to a two-week period. Be sure to check with the state you wish to camp in, because without reservations you'll be out of luck. State and federal camp fees are so low that they hardly pay for maintenance, much less the cleanup and policing the areas; that's why they require payments in advance.

There are several good publications on the market that are worth their weight in freeze-dried ice cream. Rand McNally publishes a campground and trailer park guide that lists 20,000 public and private campgrounds, RV (recreational vehicle) parks and backpacking areas in the East and West. It sells for

Shoshone National Forest in Wyoming affords campers plenty of privacy, but make sure your gas tank is full and your larder is stocked. Easily accessible, but not usually close to towns, National Forest campgrounds involve small or no fees and are usually near places of interest and fishing and hunting opportunities.

$6.95. The company also issues a *National Forest Guide* for $4.95, plus regional guides for less money. *Woodall's Mobile Home and Park Directory* can be purchased at most book and magazine stores and is sometimes available at libraries. It pays to get a good reference source that tells you what to expect in physical environment, elevation, size of campground, number of spaces available for both tenting and trailers (and the fees for both), what months it is open, the maximum trailer size permitted, time limits, whether pets are permitted, what facilities are available (electric, water, sewer, showers, laundry and so forth), whether there are special activities (playgrounds, boating, swimming and the like) and also lists telephone numbers.

Surprises are no fun when you arrive dog-tired and ready to flop down for the night and discover, for instance, that there is no water. You'll be a lot happier if you have a good idea of what you are getting into.

There are thousands of private campgrounds across the country, and they are filling a void between federal government and lesser government accommodations. Private campgrounds, like gold nuggets, are where you find them. Most of them are listed in the aforementioned directories, but a lot of them must be sought out in the area you want to camp in, through businessmen, filling stations, newspapers and other local sources. Private campground fees are usually slightly higher than public

grounds, but they do need to make a dollar, as they are not subsidized as the public areas are. All of us pay toward the public grounds whether we use them or not. In the private grounds there is usually a friendly atmosphere and they are certainly more personal (except the few huge ones that are assembly-line oriented). You can find out easily about any special events or celebrations that could be fun. Some of the private grounds are quite primitive, offering space along a river on the farm to park your rig or put up your tent; others have every possible facility. Make sure you always know what you are getting into and what you will be required to pay for. In some places there will be a small store. If you buy there, you will probably

A county park campground experience includes opportunities for fishing, boating, swimming, hiking, hunting and even resting.

have to pay a little more for items, but it will still beat driving into town for the same things.

Don't be afraid to look the campground over before you commit yourself for the night or week. If it's not what you need or want, move on. Kampgrounds of America (KOA) is the largest chain in the country. Each campground is privately owned but is franchised by KOA, so each must maintain certain high standards of facilities. We've found these grounds to be neat, clean and well equipped. KOA publishes a directory that lists all of their campgrounds (almost 900). These may be picked up at any KOA campground, or by writing the national headquarters at P.O. Box 30558, Billings, Montana 59114. Reservations at private campgrounds are optional, but remember to stop early in the afternoon, don't push on too long. "Early to rise and early to bed" will get you a lot less hassles on the highway, and a lot more enjoyment in the campgrounds.

Besides regular designated campgrounds with facilities of some kind, there are lots of others for the more adventuresome. *The Dictionary of American Slang* defines legs as "a means of transportation, walking as opposed to riding, ride shank's mare—to walk." Getting out of our accustomed bailiwicks of civilization and onto nature's own turf has a lot going for it. Backpacking is a spiritually and physically rewarding pastime. Each trip can be as short or long as you want, as lazy or rigorous, as challenging or benign, as social or antisocial. It's entirely up to you, since you carry your camp on your back. It is a different ball game as far as finding a campsite is concerned.

Check with the local conservation officers in the area you want to visit. They'll come up with a wealth of information, as they know their territory like a cottontail knows his brier patch. They can direct you to trails and places that are not listed or shown on maps. They will tell you what to expect, where the best places are to camp, and how long it will take you to get there. U.S. Forest Service personnel are another rich source of information for the backpacker. Look them up; you'll get cooperation like you never knew existed.

For your first forays, pick an area that has a rather well defined trail. The order of the day again is to stop early. Stay away from areas that have dead trees. Storms in the mountains can be viciously windy, so don't camp where a tree could blow over on you or where dead branches fly around like javelins. Select rock-free, fairly level places if you want to be comfortable, and that's the name of the game. Do not camp near lone trees that might attract lightning.

Never camp at the bottom of a dry wash or creek, as water can rise rapidly from rain high above your camp. If you're at a lake, pick a treeless finger that juts out into the lake if you can find one. It will be cool and comfortable. Hollows always are the coldest spots, as cold air settles down into low places. Campsites on the leeward side and just under the top of a ridge are usually the best. A lot has been said about the rigors of a "dry" camp, but if your canteen is full when you camp, and you washed up at the last water, it's not dry—right? Make sure you pick a well-drained spot, so if it rains you won't wake up lying in an inch or two of water. Insects are always fewer in these locations and the view is always better. Even in rugged country, it's usually easy to find small fairly level spots. Don't settle for a miserable night, do it right. If you intend to stay for more than a day, position your camp so the morning sun will warm it and it will be in the shade in the after-

Western state campgrounds, such as Starr Springs in Utah which is south of Green River on the way to Lake Powell, are usually in very scenic areas. Uncluttered and off the beaten path, such campgrounds are jumping-off points for a multitude of activities.

noon. Always let someone know where you plan to go and when you expect to return. That's very important. Never go alone into a wild or primitive area. Some wild and primitive areas require you to register and some are restricted as to numbers of backpackers these days, so check before you make plans and avoid disappointment. In some primitive areas you are required to pack out all of your trash, so do it! Summing it up: For backpackers, water, fuel and shelter are all you need to keep you happy. Be choosy about location, so your memories will be pleasant ones.

There are times when you can combine several ways of camping on a single trip, for example establishing a base camp in a designated camping area, then taking off on a backpack trip for a few days. Look into these possibilities when you plan your trip. Include something for everyone.

U.S. Forest Service Campgrounds

Region 2—Rocky Mountains
Federal Center Building
Denver, Colorado 80225
303-234-3131

Region 3—Southwestern
Federal Building, 517 Gold Avenue S.W.
Albuquerque, New Mexico 87101
505-843-2401

Region 4—Intermountain
Federal Office Building, 324 25th Street
Ogden, Utah 84401
801-399-6201

Region 5—California
630 Sansome Street
San Francisco, California 94111
415-556-4310

Region 6—Pacific Northwest
319 S.W. Pine Street
Portland, Oregon 97208
503-221-3625

Region 10—Alaska
Federal Office Building, Box 1628
Juneau, Alaska 99801
907-586-7263

U.S. Forest Service
Department of Agriculture
14th and Independence Avenue S.W.
Washington, D.C. 20250
202-447-3957
(general information)

Bureau of Land Management Campgrounds

Alaska
555 Cordova Street
Anchorage 99501
907-277-1561

Arizona
Federal Building, Room 3022
Phoenix 85025
602-261-3873

California
Federal Office Building, Room E-2841
2800 Cottage Way
Sacramento 95825
916-484-4676

Colorado
Room 700, Colorado State Bank Building
1600 Broadway
Denver 80202
303-837-4325

Idaho
398 Federal Building
550 West Fort Street
Boise 83724
208-342-2401

Montana
Federal Building
316 North 26th Street
Billings 59101
406-245-6463

Nevada
Federal Building, Room 3008
300 Booth Street
Reno 89502
702-784-5451

New Mexico
Federal Building
South Federal Place
Santa Fe 87501
505-988-6216

Oregon and Washington
729 N.E. Oregon Street
Portland, Oregon 97208
503-234-4001

Utah
Federal Building
125 South State
Salt Lake City 84111
801-524-5311

Wyoming
Federal Center
Cheyenne 83001
307-778-2326

All other states
7981 Eastern Avenue
Silver Springs, Maryland 20910
301-427-7500

National Parks

Rocky Mountain
P.O. Box 25287
Denver, Colorado 80225

Western
450 Golden Gate Avenue
San Francisco, California 94102
415-556-4196

Pacific Northwest
Room 931, 1424 Fourth Avenue
Seattle, Washington 98101
206-442-5565

All other states
National Parks Service
Interior Building
18th and C Streets N.W.
Washington, D.C. 20240
202-343-1100

Army Corps of Engineers

North Pacific Division Office
210 Custom House
Portland, Oregon 97209

South Pacific Division Office
630 Sansome Street
San Francisco, California 94111

Southwestern Division Office
1114 Commerce Street
Dallas, Texas 75202

Army Corps of Engineers
Washington, D.C. 20250

National Wildlife Refuges

East of the Mississippi
Public Affairs Officer
U.S. Fish and Wildlife Service
Washington, D.C. 20240

Pacific Region
(covers Hawaiian Islands, California, Idaho, Nevada,
    Oregon, Washington)
Public Affairs Officer
P.O. Box 3737
Portland, Oregon 97208
503-234-3361, ext. 4056

Southwest Region
(covers Arizona, New Mexico, Oklahoma, Texas)
Public Affairs Officer
Federal Building, U.S. Post Office and Court House
500 Gold Avenue S.W.
Albuquerque, New Mexico 87103

Alaska Area
813 D Street
Anchorage, Alaska 99501
907-265-4868

Denver Region
(covers Colorado, Iowa, Kansas, Missouri, Montana,
    Nebraska, North Dakota, Utah, Wyoming)
Public Affairs Officer
10597 6th Avenue
Denver, Colorado 80225
303-234-4616

Hike the Long Trails

by David Richey

Hiking North America's long trails is rapidly becoming one of our more popular outdoor pastimes. The thrill and personal enjoyment of conquering all or part of a major trail are dominant factors in causing more individuals and families to turn to this type of recreation.

There are three major long trails in the United States and Canada: the Appalachian Trail (AT), the Pacific Crest Trail (PCT) and the Bruce Trail (BT). All are tailor-made for the backpacking hiker with a yen for long-distance hiking and living next to nature.

Possibly the most famous long trail is the Appalachian Trail, which transverses 2000 miles in a twisting track from Mount Katahdin in Maine through fourteen states and winds up at Springer Mountain in northern Georgia. This wilderness foot trail is generally well marked with blazed marks in white (titanium-oxide) paint along its entire length. Blue blazes designate side trails, while two blazes, one above the other, signify a trail change or a turn that could be overlooked. Fewer than fifty people have accomplished the feat of hiking the entire length of the Appalachian Trail. Much of the work needed to maintain the AT is done by various member hiking clubs along the way.

Information on this long trail can be obtained by writing the Appalachian Trail Conference, 1718 N St. N.W., Washington, DC 20036.

The Pacific Crest Trail (PCT) is a continuous route of 2400 miles which extends from British Columbia south to Mexico and includes the states of Washington, Oregon and California. This trail offers the backpacker wide extremes of elevation changes from tidewater to lofty peaks in the Sierra Nevadas. The highest point along the PCT is 13,200 feet, near Forrester, California. The trail incorporates seven previously established trails: the 514-mile Cascade Crest Trail in Washington; the Oregon Skyline Trail which covers 436 miles; and in California the Lava Crest Trail, Tahoe-Yosemite Trail, John Muir Trail, Sierra Trail and the Desert Crest Trail which combine to cover 1454 miles. This series of western trails meanders through twenty-five national forests and six national parks.

Information on hiking and backpacking the PCT can be obtained from the following sources: Pacific Crest

Walt Sandberg

Getting ready for a backpacking trip along one of North America's long trails entails a lot of work and gear.

Club, Box 1907, Santa Ana, California 92702; Pacific Northwest Region (for Washington and Oregon), Regional Forester, P.O. Box 3623, Portland, Oregon 97208; California Region, Regional Forester, 630 Sansome Street, San Francisco, California 94111.

The least used of the three long trails is Ontario's Bruce Trail (BT). This 430-mile trail extends along the rugged Niagara escarpment from Niagara to Tobermory. It begins near Lake Ontario, travels straight north to Nottawasaga Bay, swings along the Bruce Peninsula, skirts Georgian Bay and finally terminates near Lake Huron. Information on this scenic trail can be obtained from the Bruce Trail Association, 33 Hardale Crescent, Hamilton, Ontario, Canada L8T 1X7.

Hiking and backpacking authorities are often asked exactly what is needed to tackle the long trails. The primary consideration for most backpackers is the length of time on the trail; most hikers simply do not have the time or stamina to spend a great amount of time on the venture.

Most hikers spend anywhere from 2 to 7 days on a specific section of trail. Most of the hikers who have completed the entire Appalachian Trail, which is the longest continuously marked trail in the world, have done so over a period of years.

First determine which section of which trail you wish to hike. The previously listed sources will provide information on the location of overnight shelters. Shelters are spaced every 5 to 10 miles along the AT

These backpackers are working up a section of the Pacific Crest Trail.

Walt Sandberg

and are maintained by local clubs.

Maps of the area being hiked and camped can be obtained from various sources. For trails in the West contact the U.S. Geological Survey, Denver Federal Building, Building 41, Denver, Colorado 80225. For maps showing trails east of the Mississippi, contact the U.S. Geological Survey, Map Information Office, Washington, D.C. 20242.

Once armed with maps of the area to be hiked, you should next outfit yourself with the essentials for hiking and spending a night or nights along the trail. Many backpackers prefer the solitude and independence of making their own overnight camp instead of staying in one of the established shelters.

One of the most important and often overlooked factors in backpacking the long trails is physical conditioning. Too many hikers leave an air-conditioned office, don their hiking boots, throw some clothing and food haphazardly into a backpack and head out. Two hours later, trail-weary and footsore, they realize that conditioning is a step they forgot about.

Preconditioning of legs, feet, back and lungs is necessary before tackling anything as strenuous as parts of the long trails. The terrain often varies from low-lying meadows with trails through small rocks and downed timber to more rugged, boulder-studded trails winding through high peaks. Changes in elevation and terrain place the utmost stress on physical fitness.

I often begin training for hiking mountain trails with easy hiking around home, always using the same footwear needed in the mountains. After your hiking boots feel comfortable on easy hikes, begin a more strenuous regimen.

Office workers who don't mind comments and stares can wear hiking boots to work and use the stairs to build leg muscles. Forget the elevator and climb the stairs to and from work and lunch breaks. An alternative is the football stadium at a nearby school. Several trips up and down these stairs every day is good exercise.

Jogging is an excellent method of getting legs and lungs into shape for strenuous hiking activity. I frequently begin by jogging a half mile and increase the activity every week by a half mile. Once you can jog for 2 miles you are generally ready for any exertions of climbing and carrying a backpack full of gear.

Deep knee bends and leg raises aid the hiker, particularly if you wear hiking boots while doing these exercises. Besides strengthening the legs, this will increase the muscle tone in your lower back and firm up stomach muscles. The lower back carries a tremendous load when the packsack is full and heavy and the travel is uphill.

Proper backpacking for long-trail use means the purchase of good serviceable equipment. Shoddy merchandise often breaks down on the trail many miles from an outfitter or store and is the ruination of many trips. No hiker or backpacker is any better than the boots he's wearing. Good hiking boots are normally manufactured from top-quality leather, either chrome- or oil-tanned. A good boot should be quite stiff in the heel and toe areas and about 7 or 8 inches in height.

Better-grade boots will have a soft collar at the top

A map of the area is important, as is a good compass.

Walt Sandberg

In many cases the going can get rough. This is where quality footwear is important.

Good hiking boots with speed laces and eyelets are needed for hiking.

to prevent chafing. Select a boot with either eyelets or eyelets and speed-lace hooks. The lug sole (such as is manufactured by Vibram) is far superior to any other type. For most hiking trips where the terrain isn't too rugged, most authorities opt for lightweight boots. Choose sturdier boots for rugged country.

A pair of quality wool socks over a lightweight pair of cotton socks is generally all that is needed. Seasoned backpackers usually carry at least one change of socks.

Many backpackers plying the long trail rely on knickers for hiking apparel. They are good because they are cut below the knee which allows for increased freedom of movement.

Clothing should be selected for the weather, although many veteran backpackers include raingear and heavier clothing every time they hit the trail. I often use a nylon windbreaker (which is virtually weightless) over a wool sweater; this combination keeps me warm in all except freezing weather.

A packsack should be made of nylon, with heavier-weight material preferred where climbing and pack weight is going to place greater demands upon it. Look for good stitching; a good-quality packsack will have seven to ten stitches per inch.

Shoulder straps must be padded with either foam rubber or felt and any zippers on packsacks should be made of nylon. Packsacks come in either multicompartmented models or with just one large pocket. Take your choice.

From the standard choice of boots and packsacks for daytime long-trail hiking we can progress to equipment needed for overnight jaunts or week-long hikes. To make life reasonably comfortable on an extended backpacking trip, much more complex gear is required. A sleeping bag for most spring, summer or fall hiking trips can be Dacron Fiberfill II or Dacron 88. Down bags are too bulky and too warm for most trips. Select a bag with a nylon shell and nylon zippers. A waterproof ground cloth is lightweight and keeps your bag dry when you are camping under the stars.

Thomas Huggler

This father and son team of hikers are making camp and cooking supper along Ontario's Bruce Trail.

The easiest type of camp is made by stretching a sheet of nylon over a length of nylon rope between two trees, laying out your ground cloth and sleeping bag and turning in for the night. At the other extreme are those hikers who pack a lightweight tent into their packsacks. A backpacker's tent or a tube tent is ideal for long-trail hikers; these range from 4 to 7 pounds in weight, and the cost varies from $70 to $150. Be sure to select a well-constructed nylon tent with strong stitching.

Freeze-dried food is nutritional and also economical, both in cost and weight. Sporting goods stores have a vast array of ready-made meals. Some of the better brand names are Chuck Wagon Foods, Rich-Moor and Trail Chef.

Anyone tackling a trail such as the Appalachian, Pacific Crest or Bruce should plan to carry one of the lightweight single-burner cookstoves for preparing a noon or evening warm meal. The Optimus IIIB or Primus IIIB is a logical choice for this task. Take a tip from seasoned hikers: Plan your meals so that only one pan is needed for cooking. This eliminates the extra weight of additional pans.

There is an endless variety of things other than hiking to do on a long hike. Some of my most memorable backpacking hikes along the Pacific Crest Trail have revolved around side trips to various high mountain lakes. Rainbow, cutthroat and brook trout are found in many lakes, and small streams draining these lakes often contain one of those varieties of trout. A small spinning or fly rod and reel doesn't weigh much and will increase your enjoyment on a long-trail excursion.

Many backpackers delight in game viewing, rock collecting, bird watching or viewing abandoned homesteads or farm dwellings. Hikers are reminded that most abandoned homes are on private property and mustn't be vandalized or disturbed.

There is a definite challenge for backpackers in hiking the long trails. First of all, these trails have not been traveled by very many hikers, and, second, they offer a combination of breathtaking beauty and rugged excitement that is difficult to duplicate in today's outdoor world.

These hikers along the Appalachian Trail have their camp all set up.

Two-Wheel Camping
by Jim Elder

Puffing uphill pedalers and helmeted two-stroke motorcyclists may think they have nothing in common except a two-wheel vehicle. While you can meet some nice people on motorcycles, and the most purist of bicyclists have been known to accept rides and even themselves drive in automobiles, these are not the meeting grounds discussed here. Both types of two-wheel riders sometimes camp, and they share the freedoms and the problems of two-wheel camping.

The freedoms are self-evident, so we need not elaborate on the back-road, secluded-streamside, seldom-visited camping opportunities open to those who forsake the motor home and motels. All problems can be solved, save one. That is the hazard of inconsiderate, even murderous, motorists who refuse to give two-wheelers their legal and practical rights on the road. Education and legislation may remove this eventually, but will take time.

Two camping problems which threaten both bicycle and motorcycle freedom are weight and bulk. Motorized cyclists can perhaps get by with a pound here and some bulk there—weight size they don't really need but carry "just in case." Leg-power cyclists soon become extremely disciplined about unnecessaries.

With either power source, extra weight affects handling, performance, comfort and safety. How about lightening your load before the first trip? The easiest place to start is by leaving out the things you don't really need, and these are not just obvious luxuries. Of course the stereo cassette player, the ice chest, tripod, CB radio, pocket calculator and hair dryer stay home. But how about those beautiful multibuckle cycling boots? Do you really need them *and* hiking shoes? Not unless you are camping your way to a motocross. If you do not intend to walk any side trails, the big boots and a pair of soft mocassins for camp use will do. Bicyclists will want a pair of cycle shoes or light running shoes for pedaling, and maybe a pair of heavier shoes for walking. In any case, two pairs are enough for either kind of two-wheel tripping.

Many campers carry too much food. Unless the entire route is away from civilization and supermarkets, there is no need to carry more than one or two days' rations. Some campers scratch the noon meal off the packing list completely—they treat themselves to a café stop once a day and save cooking and clean-up time as well as weight. Staples such as sugar, salt and coffee are hard to buy in one-day portions, and nice to have along for that midafternoon break, or flat tire, so you carry them, along with quick-energy trail snacks, such as the traditional "gorp"—nut-candy-raisin-and-variations mix.

Canned goods and liquids are tasty, inexpensive and heavy. Freeze-dried dinners can be palatable but are expensive. Dry-mix foods and drinks are an acceptable compromise in weight and price. When geography works with you, you can hit the market late in the afternoon, buy the fixin's for the evening meal and breakfast with little regard for weight and dine as well as any four-wheel V-8 camper. Just don't plan to buy foods that require you to carry larger and heavier cooking utensils.

Weight and bulk can be trimmed as you choose your kitchen. Why carry a plate and a bowl when a large flat-bottomed dish will serve both needs? We use the inexpensive soft-plastic bowls usually sold for feeding pets—they keep food hot longer than metal dishes do. One medium-sized spoon will handle both cooking and

eating, and the folding Buck or a Swiss Army knife is all anyone needs for preparing and cutting up food. Fastidious campers do take a fork. Even if you eat with your fingers, forks are handy to turn bacon.

Unless you are into one-dish dinners or two-hour dining, you will want at least two nesting cookpots with matching lids. The lids should be heavy enough to double as frying pans and should have some kind of detachable handle which also fits the pots. Do not take an aluminum cup. If the coffee is hot enough to drink, the cup will be hot enough to sear your lips. The overrated Sierra cup of steel is a bit better, but the cheap plastic cups next to the dog-food dishes at the discount store are best. Cut the handles off so they will nest together.

What else should you not take along? Too much extra clothing. One change of riding gear and protection from whatever the season promises in inclement weather are enough. If you must appear as a guest of honor at a Best Bike Campers of the Year Banquet

Motorcycles and bicycles have more in common than just two wheels, especially when it comes to camping. They both need lightweight and compact equipment, for safe riding and comfortable camping.

midway in your camping trip, ship your tux ahead—don't try to pack it. Long-distance bike campers might mail basic clothing and equipment ahead and return-mail the dirties. But give United Parcel Service and the U.S. mail plenty of time to fit into your touring-camping schedule. When you pay the postage, remember how nice it will be not to carry the stuff cross-country.

Too many two-wheel campers carry too many tools and parts. Ten years ago for motorcyclists and five years ago for bicyclists good parts and service were hard to come by. Not now. All you need is spares to get you to the next town and enough tools to install them. An accurate tire-pressure gauge is not unnecessary extra equipment, however. Service-station gauges are often not to be trusted. Five pounds too much pressure can burst a bicycle tire, and a five-pound error can seriously affect motorcycle handling.

Enough of what you do not need. In addition to that good air gauge, what should a two-wheel camper carry? Shelter. But not a tent designed to protect mountain climbers on winter ascents. Most bikers are fair-weather campers, so they need only protection from rain and insects. In bug-free country, a simple coated-nylon fly used as ground cloth and/or rain tarp will be enough. Tents should be chosen for ventilation and lightness. Figure five pounds with stakes and poles, and find a tent which will roll up very compactly. Long pole sections are a bother on a bike.

Down used to be the only practical lightweight filling for sleeping bags. But modern synthetics such as Dacron II and Polarguard have proved their worth even to backpackers who fight for every ounce saved. Synthetics weigh a bit more for the same "loft," or warmth, but cost much less and do not retain moisture. Fifty dollars invested in Dacron II or Polarguard will buy as much spring, summer and fall camping comfort as $100 or more in goose down.

Under the bag you will need a pad. Few campers now use air mattresses—they are heavy, cold and prone to leak when you are prone. Open-cell pads, with or without covers, are too bulky for cycle camping. Again, take a lead from the backpackers, who have gone to the Ensolite and Superlite closed-cell body pads, or to the "self-inflating" insulated pad sold by Eddie Bauer.

Daytime riding protection for the body should not be ignored. If you have done any touring, you know that you will need clothing that will keep you covering miles when conditions are not perfect. Both sun and rain, in excess, is an enemy. Light raingear, tougher for motorcyclists because of wind-whip, a compact down vest for nights and chilly days and some kind of

won't-blow-off hat or visor for bicyclists are enough. We'll get into safety and helmets later. For now, just figure that pedalers want to wear as little as possible for comfort and motorized bikers want as much as possible within comfort. And both need the minimum extras for rain and sun.

That's for on the body. In it goes food, and that means preparation and serving, even if you eat with your fingers. While discussing what you don't need, we suggested what you do. Two pots with plate/pan lids, a cup and bowl, spoon, sharp knife and fork (optional). Fish catchers might want to include one of the lightweight wire grills for use where fires are permitted. Don't forget a potholder, a can opener and a water bottle.

Keep the load as far forward as possible, and pack the lighter gear—sleeping bag and pad—above the panniers. These Eclipse bags help keep the heavier items low and as far forward as pedal clearance will allow. Note the flasher taillight for day and night safety.

Handlebar bags must be designed to allow full use of brakes, yet carry a share of the load and especially the items needed along the way. The removable map case is handy, as are the side pouches for sunglasses, bug repellent or whatever.

The old image of the camper as Paul Bunyan, hacking through with an ax, is fading. We don't strip trees for "bough beds" and most of us use only dead wood for cooking and esthetic fires. Since not every campsite is equipped with convenient lodgepole pines full of easy-to-reach "squaw-wood" snags, small camping stoves are an essential part of the outdoor living kit. For fuel, you can choose gasoline, kerosene, LP (Liquefied Petroleum) gas, or solid and gel fuels, such as Sterno and Heattabs. The last-mentioned are cheap and light but a bit short on heat. LP gas is convenient, but replacement canisters come in many shapes and sizes. Be sure to buy a stove which uses an easy-to-find-anywhere refill.

The smallest and lightest LP stoves can sometimes introduce a hazard. Unless some pressure-regulating device is built in, hot sun can cause wild flare-ups when you light the stove. Unfortunately the regulated models are usually larger and heavier. For this reason,

and because naphtha and white-gas fuels are easy to buy anywhere, many campers prefer "gasoline" stoves, such as the Svea and Optimus. New this year is a Coleman backpack stove which has a pump—no external-flame priming necessary—and a flame regulator just like the good old green two-burner camp stoves. It looks like a winner for cycle campers.

Hot stew inside you and a warm bed and tent for you to get inside—what more can you need? Not much. A small flashlight for late camp chores and roadside emergencies. Compact first-aid kit and bug repellent. Sun lotion, personal toilet items, towel, tissue and some matches. Plus plastic bags to pack out your garbage; if you leave it, I will personally someday catch up with you and give it all back, ripe.

Those who possess the leg power or the space may want a few luxuries. A lightweight candle lantern can cozy up a dark camp. A small transistor radio can bring you the top forty and tomorrow's weather report. Perhaps fishing tackle, a camera and a paperback book. Now to get it all on the bike.

Backpackers carry all items listed, plus food for several days, in a pack frame and never complain—much. Properly balanced, even the lightest touring bicycles will carry the same load, and on motorcycles the only problem is where and how to stow the stuff to keep it on, and dry, and away from the high exhaust pipes of some Enduro-type bikes. Let's tackle the bicycle packing first.

Not too long ago, loading a bike meant loading yourself with a rucksack, then tying the leftover stuff to a rear "luggage rack" better suited for schoolbooks. Then the engineers and entrepreneurs and exploiters got on the bike bandwagon and almost buried us in bicycle luggage. You can buy packs for the handlebars, packs which hang inside the frame, saddlebags (panniers), bags which fit over the saddlebags and seat bags. You can even buy bicycle trailers.

Most bike shops and many backpack suppliers sell bike luggage in several price ranges. There are too many brands and styles to cover fairly here, so let's make do with some general guidelines and a look at one system that we have tested recently. First, biggest is not best. Winne's Law, which says that equipment will proliferate to fill any available space, is unamendable. So buy the smallest handlebar and pannier outfit which will carry your minimum camping needs. Pay as much as you can afford for quality and long life. Look for good fabric, zippers, straps and buckles. Insist on rain-flap closures over access openings. Make sure that the mounted packs do not compromise your riding comfort or handling safety.

Before we outfit a motorcycle, let's pack the bike,

because the packing tactics apply to both vehicles. You want to keep weight low and between the axles as far as possible considering the fact that you already occupy most of that optimum space. Relatively heavy items should go low in the panniers (saddlebags), and some, for balance, forward. Motorcyclists can pack the bigger and heavier supplies in a tank bag, but pedalers should not load the handlebar bag so heavily that steering is affected. The tent should ride on the rear rack, under the sleeping pad and bag, which are in a rainproof cover—this can be a plastic garbage bag.

Items which will be needed during the day's ride are most conveniently carried in the handlebar bag or, on a motorcycle, the side pockets of the tank bag.

Except for engines on long upgrades, the one thing bicyclists most envy the motorcyclist is the tank bag. Since the best one is made by Eclipse, a company mostly known for fine bicycle luggage, this doesn't seem fair. But before Eclipse brought out its nylon cordova tank bag, motorcyclists had only two choices: expensive—make that very expensive—Spanish or Italian leather tank bags which were not water-resis-

All this camping gear on a two-wheeler? Not quite, but all the camping equipment will fit in and on a bicycle using the Eclipse cycle panniers, seat, and handlebar bag, plus the Eddie Bauer duffel bag shown in the upper right. With a motorcycle, the same items will fit in the Bauer saddlebags, Eclipse duffel, and Eclipse tank bag grouped at the upper left. Two helmets for motorcyclists are shown—the full-face Bell, best for high-speed highway travel, and the Can-Am Motocross bucket with visor, which gives a little less protection but is less confining and is pleasant for summer back-road motoring. For pedalers, we recommend the Bell helmet for highway and steep downhill travel and a visor for side trails and bike paths. Note the use of stuff sacks for toilet kit and clothing—easier to pack than rigid containers; the very compact tent under the towel, and the Can-Am Motocross gloves with back-hand protection, good for both modes of two-wheel cycling.

Ready for the road, with a well-balanced load securely attached. Many long-distance riders use toe clips for pedaling efficiency, and more and more cyclists are wearing helmets, such as this light but strong Bell.

A brand new type of two-wheeler camper transportation, the Puch (pronounced *Pook*) "moped." Called a bicycle by most states, it usually requires no license or registration. Can be pedaled or powered by its tiny engine. Gets 150 miles per gallon and has a speed of about 20 miles per hour. Ideal for exploring around a campground or pleasure travel near camp.

tant, or cheap vinyl tank bags which didn't resist anything. The Eclipse bag fits over the gas tank on a foam pad, lifts easily for refueling access and comes off quickly when you want it off. One detachable pocket for wallet, keys and such and two fixed sidepockets give extra capacity and keep sunglasses, gloves, snacks, and whatever away from the oil, stove fuel, stove, tools, chain lube and other heavy/dirties carried inside. On top is a nonglare map pocket.

We mentioned high exhaust pipes as a packing hazard. Our solution is a duffel bag strapped on the luggage rack, in line with the machine, and panniers attached over the duffel bag. This raises the center of gravity a bit, but it lowers the temperatures of the packs and cargo. Low pipes make for easier packing, but the rider has to stay on the smoother roads. Many bigger-bore owners use fairings (extended windshields), some of which have storage space for small items. Users of fairings often go for streamlined plastic or metal saddlebags and boxes. These are great, if your gear will squeeze inside. But tent poles cannot be bent to fit.

There are those who lash a packframe and bag upright to the "sissybars." Many fast miles have been ridden that way, but the higher weight placement is bound to affect handling. It can really hurt in one of those jackpot situations where the rider needs every bit of skill, luck and whatever stability the designers sold him.

This brings up the question of safety. Perhaps it is not part of bike camping, but you have to live through the day and the road before you can enjoy the stew and the stars. Regardless of state laws, most motorcyclists wear helmets. No need to revive that controversy here. And they have lights and turn signals and the speed to keep up with four-wheel traffic.

Pedalers, of course, cannot keep up. And they need every possible help to keep healthy. On a busy two-lane road in a national park, we have sometimes wished for flashing lights, Day-Glow triangles, tall flags, and an ax to remove fender-mount mirrors from trailer tow-cars. Many of the cyclists who rode cross-country during the Bicentennial used the bright cloth triangles, attached to the load on the rear or to their shirtbacks. Vertical flags seem to alert motorists, but they add wind resistance and bother some riders. In Scandinavian countries we have seen short horizontal flags, extending a few inches to the left of the rider and attached to the rear carrier. The effect is mostly psychological, but motorists do seem to swing a bit wider when passing bikes so equipped.

New on the market are battery-powered electronic flashers. Mounted on the carrier or on the rider's belt, they alert overtaking drivers. We have found them more effective and certainly less bother than the battery-powered leg-strap lights. As for headlights, the generator models dim as you slow and are a drag on the wheels, and therefore on your legs. A flashlight mounted on the handlebars or on a headband is better, and not riding at night is best of all.

Can't procrastinate any longer. Don't want any bureaucrats to read this and get ideas to limit further the ways we entertain and injure ourselves. But many bicycle riders are looking at helmets. Some are wearing them. Usually after a bad crash last week. We decided to try bike helmets before the fall, figuring that if racing cyclists—who usually do not have to contend with fender-mount trailer-mirror station wagons and drunks and all the other hazards of the highway—wear helmets, they must know something we didn't.

Our initial tests were not encouraging. One helmet was too hot. Another too heavy. A third too lacking in protection. Then we tried the Bell. No need for details here—we like it. In traffic, and on fast downgrades and even on tricky surfaces, we now wear Bell bicycle helmets. And light, tough Motocross gloves.

So motorcyclists and bicyclists do have things in common: helmets, gloves and two-wheel camping. The problems are solvable, the packing is possible and the touring freedom, the outdoor experience and enjoyment, too good for two-wheelers to miss.

Station-Wagon Travel Camping

by C. Herb Williams

Station-wagon camping has come to be looked on by some as a spartan type of travel that is cramped, uncomfortable and somehow unnecessary in this day of self-contained motor homes and travel trailers. However, it has a lot going for it for those who like low cost and simplicity and want to get from one place to another in a convenient and economical way.

As to cost, the original price of equipment is far less for a wagon than for other types of traveling rigs. The gasoline bill will also be a lot less.

A station wagon has the maneuverability and pick-up of a passenger car. This lets you work your way through traffic more easily and not find yourself boxed in nearly as often behind a semi-truck and trailer or other slow-moving rig on crowded highways or long hills.

This can increase your overall milage per day by as much as 5 or 10 miles per hour, which can mean as much as 100 miles in a 10-hour driving day. So if covering distance is important, a station wagon has advantages. The wagon is also far easier to drive and park in town when you stop to pick up supplies. It's easier to park at night because of its shorter length. You can use spots that longer rigs have to pass up.

For these advantages you do have to do without extra space, more cargo capacity and the ability to ignore nasty weather as you cook, eat and shower in a dry, windless motor home or trailer. But with a little thought and effort these problems can be kept to a minimum in a wagon.

One of the best things to help keep station-wagon traveling convenient, comfortable, clean and simple is also free. It's that work horse of our packaged culture, ordinary cardboard, or corrugated paperboard, as it's called in the trade. The foundation for a well-equipped wagon can be a large piece, such as a carton used to ship ranges, bicycles or other bulky products.

Cut it to size so it covers the entire rear floor of your rig and folds up a few inches on either side. This serves several purposes. First, it's good insulation, protecting you from the cold of the car's steel in cold weather. It's also more padding. Lay a couple of inches of foam rubber on top and, along with a sleeping bag, you're set for soft and cozy sleeping. If you decide to sleep on the ground, the corrugated board makes good insulation as well as padding.

This cardboard also protects your rig from scratches, dents and spills. It will absorb outboard-

This ice chest looks nearly new, yet it has seen several years of use, including two cross-country trips. The original shipping container it came in is battered and has been taped up a time or two, yet it protected the ice chest from nicks, punctures and general wear.

motor oil, ketchup, maple syrup and fish scales. Without the unbroken surface of this corrugated board, these would filter or soak down into the cracks of the wagon and be nearly impossible to remove later.

When the cardboard gets dirty, simply get a new piece. You can even lay a spare on top of the first one. Then if one gets too battered or dirty, you can burn it in a campfire and start fresh the next day. Two layers will hardly be noticed as they take up less than half an inch.

When you get home and have unloaded everything, slide the cardboard out and with it will come most of the dust, sand, bits of potato chips and other debris that collect in a car that is used for transportation and living.

The corrugated shipping containers that your stoves, lanterns and ice chests come in should be used. They were designed to protect the merchandise when it was shipped and will continue to protect your equipment for years. For instance, simply leave the ice chest in its corrugated box. The protective box can come to look as if it's been in the middle of a cat-and-dog fight, but the ice chest, lantern or other appliance will look nearly new. The cardboard can take a blow that would damage an ice chest.

Paperboard or plastic milk cartons are a boon for ice chests. Freeze water in them at home and you have ice for the first few days of a trip, plus a supply of pure water as the ice melts. Use the gallon size if possible since a large piece of ice lasts longer than small ones. When the home-frozen ice melts you have a container large enough to hold a bag or block of ice that you buy along the way. This makes for a far neater ice chest, because the melting ice is contained and doesn't fill up the ice chest with water. Here again you can carry a spare, using an empty carton to hold items such as lettuce, tomatoes or fruit, which you want to keep cold but which will bruise or crush if put in the chest with no protection.

The corrugated board is good for at least one more thing—storage. A number of pieces can keep separate and easy to find such things as clean clothing, dirty

A well-organized station wagon or van is quite convenient. Note the simple built-in cupboard in the rear of the van, with the ice chest beside it. The window on the right has a home-made screen. The lightweight table folds up and slides in beside the ice chest for traveling. The camp cook is pulling some things out of the pillowcase she uses to hold dishtowels, pot holders and a number of other things used in cooking.

This jar of peanut butter was allowed to bang around loose and tipped over. The mess was minimized because of a layer of cardboard which was put down in the station wagon before anything else went in.

clothing, reading material, extra shoes, tent stakes or canned goods.

The heavy-gauge cardboard such as is used to ship whiskey or wine are best since they are rugged enough to stand up under the stresses of travel.

There are doubtless many other uses for corrugated paperboard, but one final one is to convert a container into a "ready box" for both camping and day trips. This can carry all sorts of little things such as a selection of nails, screws and bolts, a small screwdriver, a cutting knife, rubber-patching kit, needle and thread, buttons, aspirin, Dramamine, digestive tablets, plastic tableware, Styrofoam cups, string, masking tape, electrician's tape, plastic bags, rubber bands, drinking-water bottle, notebooks, pencils, pens, clothespins, heavy cord, toilet paper, tissues, first-aid kit, paper plates, napkins, bottle and can openers, salt and pepper, and numerous other things. Leave these in the box, and when it comes time for a trip, short or long, put the box in the car and all those useful items are there.

This can prevent a minor problem from becoming a near-disaster. It's surprising how important a button can be if it's missing and there's no way to replace it.

To make the ready box last longer, select one made of heavier paperboard, with good flaps, and paint it inside and out with an enamel paint. Give it a couple of coats and you then have a lightweight but sturdy box that will last for years.

The ready box makes a secure and handy place to carry vacuum bottles with the day's coffee, tea, milk or cold drinks while traveling.

Another free item that is almost a necessity is a supply of the plastic jugs that bleach, soap or milk come in. Six or eight gallons of water in these jugs make you independent of local water at either meal stops or sleep stops.

These containers help take care of two of the important aspects of happy station-wagon traveling: organization of gear and comfort at night.

Of equal importance is the way the kitchen is set up for the cook. Usually this is done out of the rear of the wagon and there are a number of ways to build in shelves, drawers, storage space and compartments. For starters, it's best to go simply and then check out other rigs to find what you ultimately want. A simple plywood box which is like a cupboard with compartments for a stove, cook kit, plates and some canned goods works well. If it's small, it can be lifted out entirely and used on a camp table if the cook wants a little more room or you're going to stay at one spot for a day or two. The main thing is to have everything handy so it can be reached quickly.

A lightweight folding table is extremely handy, for it gives you the independence of being able to stop and cook a meal almost anywhere, whether or not there is a picnic table available.

This built-in or portable kitchen should have some system to keep things in place, for there's nothing more disheartening than to open the back of the

Corrugated paperboard and foam rubber help provide for cozy sleeping in a station wagon. The paperboard also helps keep a wagon clean.

A few of the many small but useful items which can be carried in a "ready box" for sometimes vital use. These items are left in the box between trips and are always there when you're ready to go.

Corrugated shipping containers to organize storage, a large piece of corrugated board for the floor of the wagon, foam rubber and plastic jugs for water are basic items for comfortable station-wagon camping. The dark box in the center is the "ready box" freshly painted. Note that it has hand holes for easy carrying.

wagon and find ketchup spilled and running everywhere.

An old pillowcase can also help organize a wagon. In it you can carry dishtowels, hand towels, tableware, tablecloth, can and bottle openers, sponge, pan holders, cooking utensils, matches and other things used in cooking meals.

A simple overhand knot ties the pillowcase closed and keeps the things inside clean and together. It will store in a number of places in the back and have these frequently used items always handy.

One of the main secrets of making this system work is to have a place for everything and always put each item back in the same place—just where various items should go will suggest itself as you get your rig shaken

down. If this rule isn't followed, organization can become chaos as you hunt for the can opener, your other hiking boot or the can of spaghetti and meat balls. A couple of minutes to put something in its right place after it is used can save several times that at the end of the day or when you're looking for something at night.

As for equipment, the basic items for the camp cook are a portable gas or propane stove, a good-quality ice chest and a cook kit of the nesting kind. Add plastic dishes and cups, tableware, a plastic bucket, plastic dishpan and dish drainer and you're ready to roll. To save space, use paper towels both as towels and as napkins.

Equipped in this way, you can pull into a spot, have

the kitchen in order and be cooking anything from a bowl of soup to a full meal in a matter of minutes.

A portable washing machine can be made of a large, heavy-duty plastic pail which has a tight-fitting lid. Put in dirty clothes, add detergent or soap and fill halfway with water. Close the lid snugly when you start, and the motion of the car while you're traveling will wash the clothes. At the end of the day, all you have to do is rinse them out.

If you prefer to use a laundromat, have each member of your crew put his dirty clothing in a large-mesh bag such as the ones onions come in. Toss bag and all into the washer and then into the dryer. When finished, there's no sorting and no possibility of leaving a single sock stuck against the side of the washer, not to be missed until you're a hundred miles down the road.

Unless you plan to eat at a restaurant whenever it rains, a tarpaulin should be a part of every station-wagon outfit. Good plastic tarps with grommets in place and reinforcements are available for a few dollars. You can also buy a heavier, more rugged one made of fabric. Add three or four poles from the lumberyard. Screw either eye bolts or open hooks into one end of each pole to hold guy ropes and you can make a dry and secure stop in the rain. The tarp can be put up vertically for a windbreak.

A car-top rack and box can carry gear such as the tarp, a tent if you want one, extra food, fishing-rod cases, tackle boxes and other things, including firewood. These boxes can be highly complicated affairs, but a simple box of plywood will do while you're casing fancier rigs.

One thing that greatly increases the usefulness of a

A station wagon or similar vehicle with water jugs and a stove will let campers get off into some magnificent country.

Why be crowded? If you carry your own water in your station wagon you can camp on the other side of the lake instead of where all the people are.

The lonely spots of Mexico's Baja Peninsula are open to station-wagon campers, or in this case, Volkswagen Bus campers, who also carry a tent for extended stays. This kind of camping requires enough water for several days.

box is to have the back end open out like a cupboard, in which you can place some of the cooking items.

The car-top box has a fringe benefit in hot weather. It's like the double wall of a tent and keeps much of the top of your wagon in shade all the time, helping keep the temperature down.

How to keep the bright sun out of your eyes at 5 a.m. or keep the eyes of other campers out of your bedroom at night can be handled in several ways.

Most campers buy flexible stretch-type wire cable and string curtains on it. Make the curtains of material dark enough to keep out much of the light or the early sun will wake you.

Mosquitoes in hot weather can be overcome. You need every bit of breeze you can get, yet if you open the windows you will be eaten alive. One of the simplest ways is to carry mosquito netting. Drape the netting over an open door and then close the door on the netting to hold it in place. Thus you can have ventilation on a hot night yet keep the mosquitoes at bay. Put the netting on the outside of the doors so you can close the windows in a sudden shower. You can build screens that fit your windows. They are great, except they take up more room, and that's one of the things you don't have an oversupply of in a station wagon.

Showers are no problem, even if you're using campgrounds without such facilities. Most campgrounds will let you use the showers for a small fee, less than you would be charged for an all-night stay. A number of motels will do the same if you stop in the morning before they've made up the units for the day.

Many of the things described here are the do-it-yourself kind. This is part of the fun and helps keep down the cost of getting equipped, which is one of the basic advantages of station-wagon camping. There's no end to the innovations you can discover before you settle on the system that suits your own needs best.

One place to keep discovering new twists is in campgrounds you use. When you pull in and set up, you find yourself looking around at the other rigs nearby, while the people at the other rigs are also looking at yours. It's like women at a party checking out the dresses of the other women. One difference, however, is that most of the other campers are very willing to share their discoveries with you, just as you are proud to show them how you solved a particular problem.

It's all part of the fun of station-wagon traveling, which can be convenient, clean, economical and simple in a day when everything else seems to get constantly more complicated.

Choosing the Right Site
by Glenn L. Sapir

Choosing a campsite can be likened to selecting a motel room. If you are traveling, on vacation perhaps, the motel can serve one of two purposes: it can be your base of operations or merely a stopover in a longer journey. In the first case, a poor choice can ruin your whole vacation; in the second, it could put a damper on at least part of your trip.

So there are special qualities to look for in the motel you'd like to stay in, and likewise there are features to look for in the campground upon which you finally decide. Carrying the comparison a little further, you'll realize that there are not only particular features you'd like in your motel, but in your motel room, too; similarly, there are qualities you'll look for in your site as well as in your campground.

Some of the preferred campsite qualities vary from person to person, but there are other features that rate top priority with all campers. Since a campsite is your home away from home, you'll want to have some household conveniences—you might call them necessities—close by.

Most campers learn from experience the importance of selecting a site that is flat and level. Your bed at home is on a level; your dining table is not on a slant; and the surface of your stove is even. A lumpy or slanted bed would be uncomfortable to sleep upon, if you could sleep on it at all. A sloping table would bring out acrobatic skills at mealtime. And a slanted stove surface could facilitate omelette making but would wreck just about any other kind of meal.

Assuredly, a bumpy, lumpy, rocky, hilly piece of ground is not going to make for good sleeping, be it in a bedroll, a sleeping bag or whatever else you're calling "the sack." Trying to cook on an outdoor grill that slopes will be as difficult as trying to eat the resultant meal on an incline.

Flatness, indeed, is a top priority. But flatness in itself is not enough, for if the piece of turf you've selected for your camp is at the bottom of a hill, or perhaps in a small clearing at the base of two joining hills, you will find during the first rainstorm that what comes down, comes down on you—that is, the rain will naturally run off downhill. So selecting a high spot that permits good drainage away from your site is important. Low ground can even be dangerous in flash flood conditions.

A pleasant site with good drainage, plenty of shade trees and no standing dead trees that might be a hazard in a storm. This site has plenty of room for a dining fly, parking and a play area.

One of man's necessities is drink, and the most available type of liquid refreshment in the outdoors is, of course, water. If you've selected a commercial campground, you will find that pure running water has been piped in either to every site or to a central location, thus clean drinking water presents no problem. If, however, you're camping in a more primitive area, you must find your own water supply. So you want your site to be near running water—a stream, a river or a spring. You'll have to treat this water, either by boiling or employing chemical additives. Be sure, however, that your campsite is not near enough to your water source to be swamped if heavy rains cause flooding.

In almost all cases, you'll need an evening fire for warmth and/or for cooking, and the most readily available source of fuel is firewood. Therefore, select a site that has a convenient supply of dead wood—blown-down trees, dead limbs, and the like, or, if at a commercial campground, wood for sale.

There are other criteria you'll insist upon meeting. You'll want to be in a comfortable setting, and desirable ventilation, dryness and temperatures can all contribute to the comfort of your camping adventure. A campsite in a relatively open area is susceptible to the excessive heat that comes with a summer hot spell. But by selecting a site which has trees on its western fringe, you will enjoy the morning's warm-

If you pick a site near water, such as this one, be sure you are well above any flood marks on the bank or driftwood caught in shoreline trees. This site apparently has plenty of small wood available for starting fires and is level and well drained. Camp by running water if possible; it is less likely to produce mosquitoes.

If your site is near stagnant water, you may expect mosquitoes. Watch out for boggy areas, stands of tall grass, and if there are any, check for insects. If you camp there, be sure to keep your tent screens closed at all times and use plenty of insect repellent. Keep food covered.

ing—and drying—sunlight and then the late-afternoon shade.

Other factors can contribute to your comfort—or discomfort. For instance, mosquitoes can prove to be a camper's nemesis, and while manufactures' repellents can help to reduce the annoyance, avoiding the little rascals is the best dope of all. Mosquitoes breed in low-lying wet areas—swamps, marshes, partially dried-up streambeds,—and these are areas that you should avoid.

These are the basics then, the necessities and near-necessities you should look for in selecting a campsite. But when all is said and done, many campers will agree that the reason they're out camp-

ing is to be away from people and close to nature. Privacy is their most immediate need. If that's the case, one should realize that while the family man wants to be at the fringe of the commercial camp-ground, it is father who will have to make the long walk with little children each time they have to go to the bathroom. On the other hand, the family that decides on convenience over privacy and accordingly sets up camp near the restroom or the campground store must expect noise by the "doorstep" at all hours of the day and night! To return to the motel compari-son, selecting such a site can prove to be as regretable a decision as choosing a motel room opposite the ice machine during a liquor convention. So you must take

This is a convenient site if there are children in the party, as the washroom is handy. However, bear in mind the other children may have to make frequent trips to the washrooms, even during the night. Balance the convenience against the drawbacks in noise and traffic.

all factors into consideration, and you'll probably have to compromise on your final choice.

The telephone company, in advertising its Yellow Pages, made famous a slogan. "Let your fingers do the walking" became a household phrase that made sense. In selecting your campsite, the expression is valid and wise. Some campgrounds offer maps on which the number and location of each site are indicated. By writing for brochures and maps, you can do your pretrip planning. After all, if you were planning a motor trip, you probably would be careful in plotting your lodging selections.

The campsite has been compared to the motel room, but before you can select the room, you must choose the motel, and likewise you must pick a campground before choosing a site. What are some of the things you would look for in selecting a motel? Do you want a resort that offers its own activities, or do you merely want a satisfactory lodging from which to operate? This same question should be applied to your choice of campgrounds.

If you decide that what you want is a site located in a resort-type campground, you must focus on what facilities you'll insist on. Perhaps a swimming area rates tops on your list of priorities. Or, possibly, fishing water is your most important desire. Maybe you want a campground that has a common recreation area within its property.

By checking publications such as *Woodall's Trailering Parks and Campgrounds,* you can learn about campgrounds near your various stopping-off points. You'll find valuable information on location, facilities and seasons. And so, in picking your campground and your site, you will have let your fingers do the walking.

Your selection of a campsite is motivated by personal preferences, but by recognizing what you are looking for in your site, then utilizing the advice given here, you can feel assured that your final choice will be a good one.

This site, although level and smooth, is just below a rocky slope. In a heavy storm the run-off may wind up under or on your tent floor unless the floor is completely waterproof and has a waterproof storm strip part way up the tent walls.

Tent or Pop-Up Tent Trailer?

by Bruce Brady

So, you've been bitten by the camping bug and the time has come to decide which type of shelter will best suit your purposes.

At the outset you should understand that no one has yet developed the perfect camping shelter. There are advantages and disadvantages to all types. Perhaps the two most popular at the present time are the ever-reliable tent and its thoroughly modern, and mobile, cousin, the pop-up tent trailer.

First, let's consider the advantages, starting with a look at tents. Today there is an almost endless variety of tents available, from featherweight two-man backpacker jobs to family-sized cottage tents that are almost large enough to accommodate a small circus and an assortment of animals.

Prices for these tents range from less than $25 to more than $500, depending upon material, size, weight, appearance and assorted accessories, such as flies, awnings, screened porches and side rooms. A well-made wall-type tent or umbrella tent large enough to accommodate a family of four can be purchased for about $100. This is certainly the most economical way to go.

Virtually all family-sized tents can be easily carried in the trunk of the family car, or on top of it if a roof-top luggage carrier is used.

The tents found in today's marketplace are almost maintenance-free. They are chemically waterproofed and will turn rain for about five years of normal use if proper care is given them. In addition, it is unnecessary to insure your tent, attach lights to it or purchase license plates in order to move about the country—all of which are required for pop-up tent trailers.

At home, tents are easy to store and occupy little space in the hall closet or storeroom. They do not have to be left outdoors, or parked in a garage as many communities require for storing campers on wheels.

Out on the road, with your tent and cooking appliances safely tucked away, you are free to roam wherever you can drive your vehicle. With tent trailers this is not always the case. In some areas, especially on big turnpikes, motorists are not permitted to tow anything which may encumber mobility. Also there are many tunnels through which trailer-sized gas bottles cannot be taken. Alternate routes of travel must be taken in these instances, which may cause inconvenience to the travelers.

Tents like this one are often preferred by families that have a tight camping budget. Many experienced campers prefer tent camping over all other types. The advantages are numerous.

Depending upon their size, all tents are to some degree portable. If they are small and lightweight, they can be backpacked for miles, and for short distances even if they are large family-sized tents. The campsite is therefore not necessarily dictated by the "end of the road," as is usually the situation when pop-ups are used.

Ask any camper with several years of experience which type of camping shelter provides the greatest freedom and the closest return to nature, and almost invariably he will tell you that tent living is tops. Now that most tents are equipped with mesh nylon screens at the doors and windows and have sewn-in floors to keep out snakes, bugs and other unwanted wildlife, tents offer all the good aspects of indoor living coupled with the sights, sounds and moods of nature.

Only a few years ago tents were almost windowless. Cross-ventilation was unheard of, and to sleep was to bake oneself like the proverbial potato. No longer is this true. Nowadays all family-sized tents are designed with generous windows and screens and with storm flaps which are zippered closed from the inside. (Remember those midnight dashes into an unexpected rainstorm to close the windows from the outside?)

Tent poles used to be the bane of campers. Now most poles are constructed of sturdy, durable lightweight aluminum. Many are of telescoping design, locking into position with spring-loaded snap catches.

Fastest to erect and to strike are the umbrella tents. These are by far the most popular on campgrounds coast to coast. They range in size from 8 feet to 12 feet square. No guy ropes are required. The floor is staked into place and you raise the frame from the inside, just as you would an umbrella. Models with center poles are the easiest to erect, but the pole inhibits movement inside and can be a nuisance.

Cottage-type umbrella tents utilize outside poles and provide maximum inside space for campers. They are also the most expensive. A number of models have dividers which provide two- and even three-room floor plans. Because of the size of these tents, more poles are required, and erecting them can be a problem at night, when it is windy and under other adverse circumstances.

Okay, a tent sounds as though it's just what the doctor ordered. But there are other important considerations. For example, how many campers must your tent accommodate? Will there be kids along? Will you use cots or air mattresses? Remember that your tent must provide ample space for clothing, personal gear, equipment and also room enough to move about comfortably. Sleeping space

Tents such as this go up quickly, and the exterior frame provides maximum living space inside. The picnic tables found in most campgrounds are perfect spots for cooking and eating delicious outdoor meals. A couple of folding lawn chairs complete a very comfortable and economical camping outfit.

is one thing, but adequate space for sitting around on a rainy day is quite another.

It is not a bad idea to go out into the backyard and arrange equipment, cots, sleeping bags, clothing and other essentials into a space which you consider adequate. Then, measure this space, and allow additional room all around. (Most campers soon discover there is seldom enough room for everything and everybody.) When measurements are taken you may realize that what you actually need is two smaller tents rather than one large one, especially if there are young children in the family.

In almost every case, an inexpensive tarpaulin will add greatly to the pleasures of tent camping by providing additional room for storing gear, working, cooking and just generally moving about.

If you plan to travel to a predetermined point and camp for a week at the same site, a large tent which requires a little special effort to erect and to strike is no great chore. If, however, you intend to travel about a great deal, making a series of overnight stops over a couple of weeks, you should consider tentage which goes up and down with a minimum of time and effort.

It is a wise camper who buys the best tent he can afford. Check zippers to be sure they are top quality and close all door and window openings from the inside. There should be double stitching and reinforcement strips along the ridges, corners, grommets, stake loops and all other points of stress and tension. All seams should be lap-felled and double-stitched.

Look for tents made from high-quality, lightweight material such as poplin. Army duck is more rugged but, alas, is much heavier. Light colors reflect more heat and light, but soil more quickly than do dark colors. Green is always a good choice.

It is of great importance to select a tent which is flame-retardant. It is not a wise practice to have any type of open flame in a tent. Nevertheless, the time will come when fire, in one form or another, will be in or near your tent. It's good insurance to be certain that your shelter is flame-retardant should an unexpected accident occur.

If you intend to cook inside your tent, then by all means select one designed for that purpose, with special features such as insulated stovepipe holes.

In recent years the camping shelter that has taken the country by storm is the pop-up tent trailer. On campgrounds nationwide this is the shelter seen most often. It does, unfortunately, entail a much larger investment than does the purchase of a tent. These handy rigs are a cross between a tent and a camping trailer. They vary in price from about $400 for an economy model which sleeps four to more than $3000 for a roomy, self-contained eight-sleeper.

The advantages of a pop-up rig are numerous. First, they do not have to be erected—at least not in the same sense that a tent must be erected. Most of the pop-ups offered today have a variety of built-in features, such as full-sized double beds with comfortable foam-rubber mattresses, refrigerators or ice chests, stoves and ovens, sinks, water tanks, and even commodes and holding tanks. Most are equipped with both 110- and 220-volt electrical systems.

Many of the rigs are now equipped with folding and collapsible solid-state roof and sides. These parts are made of plastic, which eliminates the care and maintenance that must be given to fabrics. The plastic also makes the shelter far easier to heat in winter and to cool in hot weather. Solid-state walls even make it possible to install air conditioners.

Pop-up umbrella tents like these are good choices for campers on the move. They can be erected and taken down in a jiffy. Many camping families, especially those with small children, find that two smaller tents suit their needs better than one large one.

In campgrounds coast to coast, the pop-up tent trailer is the big news. These rigs can be set up in minutes. They offer a variety of built-in features including stoves, refrigerators, water systems and full-sized foam-rubber mattresses.

These Florida campers are in the process of collapsing their pop-up tent trailer. Their camping neighbors, in the background, prefer a pop-up umbrella tent with exterior fiberglass poles.

Tents must be pitched on relatively level ground for campers to be comfortable. With a pop-up rig the wheels can be leveled on a considerable slope.

Tent trailers are light in weight compared with travel trailers of the same square-footage. They are easily towed by a car, and because of their low profile they have minimum wind resistance. Most of them can be used without the special rearview mirrors usually required when pulling a travel trailer.

Many of these pop-up tent trailers are small enough to be unhitched and manhandled into the out-of-the-way camping slots we all seem to draw now and then. When expanded they occupy no more space than a fair-sized tent, and setting up camp takes no more than a few minutes.

A couple of summers ago our family of five had planned a late-afternoon arrival at a campground on the scenic Little Red River in Arkansas. Car trouble delayed our arrival until 10 p.m., at which time we had to select a suitable campsite for our cottage-type tent by flashlight to avoid unduly disturbing other campers nearby. After locating level ground and clearing away sticks, stones and other debris, we set about driving tent stakes and positioning exterior side poles and ridge poles.

Since we were trying to be as quiet as possible and use only such light as we required to do our various jobs, the task took longer than usual. By the time we had unfolded cots, got out the sleeping bags, pillows and other necessities, we had spent almost an hour getting settled for the night.

About the time we finished, another late-arriving family pulled into the campground. Since I was still up and dressed I took my light, went over to our newly arrived neighbor and offered my assistance in setting up his camp. He politely declined my offer, and then while his wife and children watched, he pulled out and cranked up his pop-up rig in less than five minutes. The beds were already made and the kids safely tucked in for the night before I had walked the short distance back to our tent.

While pop-up tent trailers range in price from about $400 to more than $3000, this one is relatively economical and still offers off-the-ground sleeping comfort on foam-rubber mattresses. The large, fully screened windows provide cross-ventilation.

The next morning they prepared their breakfast of ham and eggs on their built-in stove and ate on a foldaway table. Breaking camp took no more time than erecting it—five minutes at the most—and then they were on their way to their next preselected campsite 400 miles away.

This experience points up the convenience of the pop-up camper. For traveling campers these rigs are almost ideal.

Still, there are disadvantages even to these modern contraptions. We've mentioned that you must have insurance coverage to protect your investment (which is substantial) and that you must purchase license plates. You also have to pay taxes on pop-up tent trailers. You must have and maintain brake lights and running lights and carry a spare tire and wheel and an adequate jack for possible flat tires.

Other complications can occur with this kind of rig. Last summer while camping in Colorado we met a fellow traveler with a pop-up tent trailer. In a freak accident on the highway he had ruined an axle and was losing some four days of his vacation while he waited for a replacement part to be shipped from the manufacturer's nearest distribution point. The next morning we struck our tent in about half an hour and when we left the campground he was sitting in the shade hoping he would soon be on his way again.

These convertible campers require some routine maintenance. Tires must be checked and properly inflated and balanced. Wheel bearings must be regularly greased. Pipes and water systems must be winterized or drained in very cold weather. The wiring in complex electrical systems must be periodically checked and maintained. If the roof and sides are made of fabric they must be given the same care and maintenance that tents receive, and eventually they must be replaced with new fabric, which can be costly.

Certainly the greatest thing to be said for the pop-up camper is that its convenience, relative luxury and ease of operation have enticed into camping thousands of families that would otherwise not have discovered the great pleasures this wonderful activity can provide. (For example, most people relish having their beds high off the ground where moisture, animals and insects are never problems.)

Finally, whether you select a tent or a pop-up tent trailer, resolve to buy the best equipment your budget will allow. Aside from saving yourself the aggravations that shoddy, bargain-priced equipment is sure to bring, you will in the long run save yourself some dough, and nowadays this is pretty important to most families.

A pop-up tent trailer that sleeps four campers, sets up in minutes and with its low profile is a snap to tow.

This pop-up tent trailer sleeps six comfortably and can accommodate eight if need be. It has water and electrical hookups on the trailer body. The roof is solid-state, while the sides feature large windows which are all fully screened. (Note the state stickers at the rear of the trailer.)

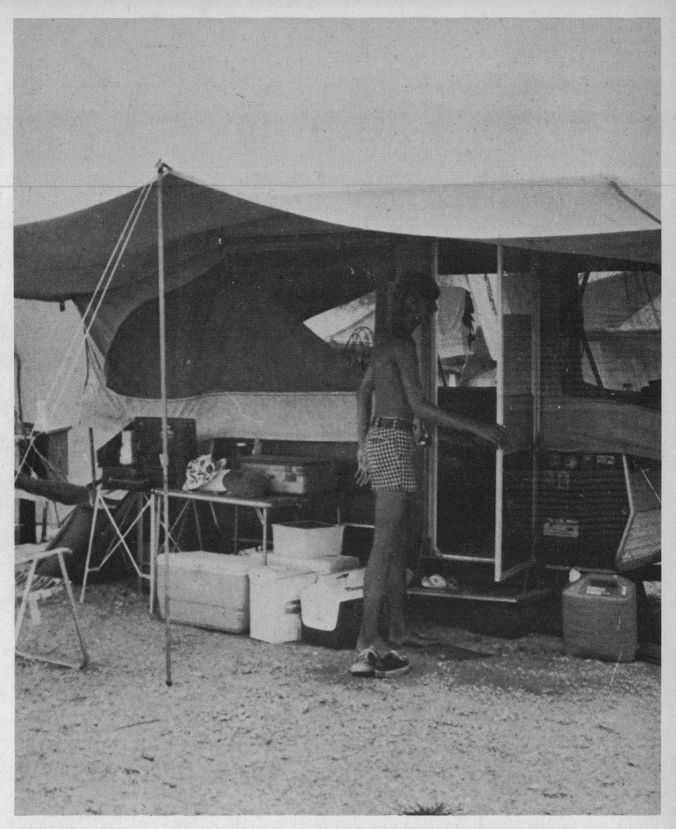

Many campers find pop-up tent trailers such as this one made to order for modern-day camping. They are quickly set up and feature foam-rubber mattresses and a variety of other built-ins. The nylon fly attached to this pop-up extends the living space considerably, providing shade and a protected storage area as well.

Planning a Family Camping Vacation Is Easy

by Pete Czura

Last year, a happy angler was driving home with his family after a two-week camping trip in the Tensleep area of Wyoming, where he had fished for trout every day. But while he was enjoying himself, his family was bored stiff, because the camp, in a remote area, lacked activities in which they could participate.

As the family neared home, Sarah, his wife, commented casually: "Next year, Sam, it will be different. Before we leave we are going to have a family conference and find out exactly what each one of us would like to do on our camping trip."

Sam stared at Sarah in surprise. "She's always been easy going," he thought. "I wonder what's bothering her."

"I know something for certain," Sarah continued. "We won't be fishing every darn day next year."

Sam got the message. And before you and your family head out this summer on a family camping adventure, be sure to have a conference with your clan to find out exactly what all of you want and like to do. If you are an angler, like Sam, that's fine, but don't hog the entire vacation by insisting that everyone go fishing. Even if you are a fishing fanatic, there are other activities afield that you may also enjoy.

There are many interesting activities a family can share on a camping trip if it is planned properly, and collectively, in advance.

What do you and your family like to do? Fish? You'll have to head for the lake and river country. Swim? A lake shore or ocean beach. Hike? You can choose among mountains, valleys, plains, rolling hills, or tackle the beautiful Appalachian Trail which wanders from Maine to Georgia or the John Muir Trail in California. Some of the most popular activities among campers are visiting museums, historical sites, battlefields, scenic regions; attending auctions; wandering into antique shops; exploring caves; river floating. One friend of mine actually goes searching for dinosaur tracks. Others enjoy ethnic festivals, rodeos, Indian powwows, country-fireman water battles, concerts and stage plays. It all depends upon each individual's hobbies, age, physical ability and the size of your budget, which can affect your family camping vacation.

A month or so before your next planned departure date, hold a family council to discuss in a leisurely manner what each member would like to do on this summer's camping trip.

Big Piney Creek is one of the beautiful streams that flows through Arkansas's Ozark National Forest. Fine campsites and a swimming beach lie in the shadow of towering limestone bluffs.

A friend of mine suggests an idea which you may wish to adopt. About a week before the family council meeting, have each member of the family make a short list of favorite activities. However, if the destination has already been selected by majority vote, advise each one to list activities which would be compatible with the areas where you plan to camp. For example, no one would list visiting Civil War battlefields if the family is heading into the mountain country of Montana.

Next, prune the list of activities to a workable number. No one should be allowed to list more than three, and two would be better, so that a family of four persons would have at most eight different types of activities to engage in. Then haul out the road maps to plan your routes.

Routes remind me that many camping vacations have ended on a sour note of disharmony, sometimes even in heated squabbles, because a family set up an overly ambitious schedule and tried to maintain it no matter what happened. If you are towing a camper trailer, or driving a pick-up camper or motor home, don't overdrive. Too many people drive so far that they don't have time to see anything along the way. Be flexible. If you tarry longer at one spot than you had planned, omit some other scheduled stops. As you and the family plan your camping vacation, make sure you don't try to see and do too much in too short a span of time.

When you are seeking the locations of good camping spots along your chosen route, it is a good idea to designate one member of the family to write to the tourist development departments of the states you intend to visit, asking for their free lists of camping locations. Write at least a month before your planned departure date.

Four of the country's largest private campground operators offer free directories of their campground locations. These are Kampgrounds of America (KOA), Box 30558, Billings, Montana 59114 (ask for their *Handbook and Directory for Campers*); United Safari, 1111 North Shore Drive, Knoxville, Tennessee 37919 (list of 154 campgrounds in thirty-four states and five Canadian provinces); Cutty's, 525 6th Avenue, Des Moines, Iowa 50309; Holiday Inn Trav-L-Park, 3742 Lamar Avenue, Memphis, Tennessee 38118.

You can also obtain camping data from chambers of commerce and national park offices along your route. As maps, folders, brochures and other information accumulate, put them into a three-ring binder. Put a few blank pages into the binder for a log of the trip, and make one person responsible for chronicling all

A long-skirted woman demonstrates yarn dyeing at Fort Boonesborough, south of Lexington, Kentucky. The park, on the edge of the Kentucky River, offers a new 182-site campground, open all year.

With top-notch fishing and hundreds of fine camping areas, Florida leads the parade.

Nebraska's northwest corner is a famous region called Pine Ridge. Here prehistoric animals roamed, Indian battles were waged and rockhounds converge. The campground at Fort Robinson State Park is one of the best in the area.

Trailer owners enjoy clean, spacious sites such as this one at Indian Acres, between Washington, D.C., and Richmond, Virginia. Campers are near many historical attractions at Washington, Richmond and Alexandria.

the events of each day. This bonus part of every camping trip gives you a chance to relive some of your funny, sad, exciting experiences.

Where shall you go this year? Anywhere in America, or, if you prefer, wander and camp in some foreign country. If you do go abroad, use the same system I recommend for planning a camping trip in America.

Perhaps this is the point at which to explain how the Swanson family of Lincoln, Nebraska, plans family trips. This is a family of seven persons, Gus and Jean (father and mother), and five children. Each has different interests: Gus, fishing; Jean, history; Eric, rodeos; Kirk, wildflowers; Mark, Indian powwows; Chris and Julie, rockhounding and collecting fossils.

Starting from Lincoln and heading west on highway I-80, the Swanson clan began its odyssey by stopping in Grand Island to visit the Stuhr Museum of the Prairie Pioneers, drove to Kearney to see the restored Fort Kearney, paused at Gothenburg to visit the original Pony Express Station, saw a rodeo and toured the Buffalo Bill Ranch, a state historical park, in North Platte. Next stop was at Lake McConaughy, Nebraska's largest lake, where Gus spent the day fishing while the family explored the replica of Front Street, a frontier cowtown, in nearby Ogallala. Next came a tour of famous landmarks around Bridgeport: Courthouse and Jailhouse Rocks, and Chimney Rock, a towering landmark which the covered-wagon immigrants used as a guide while heading westward. The day ended with a glorious sunset at Scott's Bluff National Monument, at Scottsbluff.

The girls' turn came at the Agate Fossil National Monument, where fossils of animals dating back to the Pliocene and Miocene ages have been and still are being found. Next, the girls rockhounded at Sugarloaf Hill, north of Crawford, while Gus spent an afternoon fishing for trout in Soldier Creek. The rest of the family explored Fort Robinson State Park, once the hangout of the fierce Sioux chief Crazy Horse. A restored jailhouse has been erected at Fort Robinson where Crazy Horse was slain.

On the homeward stretch, the Swansons stopped at the Chadron Museum of Fur Trade, and at Fort Niobrara National Wildlife Refuge to see and photograph Texas longhorns, buffalo and elk. The last stops were at Macy and Winnebago to see Indian powwows.

The entire trip lasted 10 days and covered approximately 1340 miles, which meant that the Swansons averaged about 130 miles of travel per day, leaving plenty of time for activities. They were always just minutes away from private and public campgrounds at the end of each day.

This trip was made in Nebraska, but similar trips

Indian ceremonials can be a welcome change of pace for camping families. Fine camping areas are near many Indian reservations.

can be made in many other parts of the United States. Here is one to consider if you are heading south this summer or autumn.

Georgia's Stone Mountain Park, just east of Atlanta, is a place for all seasons, offering year-round family recreation and a variety of historic restorations. The huge granite mountain has the world's largest piece of sculpture, showing the President of the Confederacy, Jefferson Davis, and Generals Robert E. Lee and Stonewall Jackson riding across the granite monolith. A short trail leads to the top of the mountain, which can be climbed by the average hiker in 45 minutes.

Nature lovers can enjoy seeing and taking pictures of the thousands of hollies, azaleas, crape myrtles and camellias, along with the many deciduous and evergreen trees. There are also rare trees and plants, which grow nowhere else in the world.

Rowboats are available for fishing, and a paddle-wheel riverboat makes excursions around the lake. Other features are an antique auto museum, a scenic railroad with an old steam locomotive which makes a 5-mile trip around the base of the mountain, a game ranch with many free-roaming animals, a War in Georgia exhibit with miniature soldiers re-creating Sherman's devastating march to the sea, and daily concerts on a 732-bell carillon.

Best of all, there are 500 campsites on the all-year family camping area at Stone Mountain Park. Each

The rugged, picturesque wilderness of Wildcat Hills, near Scott's Bluff National Monument, Nebraska, is a must for visitors. Elk and buffalo roam in nearby areas.

site is equipped with a picnic table, electricity and running water. Hot showers and restrooms are within easy walking distance. Cost? A $2 per vehicle admission to the park, which includes a bumper sticker allowing free entry for the rest of the year.

If you are the adventurous type, some western camping ideas may appeal to you. Why not consider exploring ghost towns and Indian rock-art sites? True, this may mean camping in a primitive manner, but I assure you the rewards are worth the slight inconvenience.

I have stood in the lonely silence of a ghost town and with a little imagination heard through a broken window of a sagging saloon the laughter of men and women from a century ago, the happy shouts of a miner who had struck it rich, the clinking of whiskey glasses and the echoes of shots from some long-forgotten feud between gunslingers.

If you are an architecture buff, you will enjoy seeing the various buildings in the ghost towns. If you prefer picture taking, this is an area where you can let loose your imagination as you focus on the tumbledown buildings through the view finder of a camera. Be sure to have plenty of color film.

This year, or a few years from now, may provide your last chance to see some of the finest ghost towns still standing; many are vanishing as a result of ruthless attacks by so-called souvenir collectors, or vandals. At the last count, there were reported to be about 400 ghost towns in twelve Western states.

To view the works of long-vanished Indian rock artists, you will have to hike into canyons or remote areas. Contact some of the Western states' tourism departments to obtain brochures, information and the locations of ghost towns and Indian rock art. Norman Weis's book *Ghost Towns of the Northwest* which contains much valuable data, is available from Caxton Printers, Caldwell, Idaho 83605.

The chief drawback to exploring ghost towns and Indian rock art is that it usually means camping in a primitive area. But there is an extra thrill in pitching your tent in the middle of a ghost town or near an Indian rock-art site. My solution to camping this way has been a Thermos Pop-Up tent, which can be set up and taken down in minutes. Of course, if you have a recreation vehicle, there is no problem with camping.

Perhaps the words of Ernest F. Schmidt, executive director of the American Camping Association, best express what family camping can mean. "A family camping trip," he said, "can strengthen the bonds between yourself and your children. One thing for sure, every family benefits in various ways from spending a short time in our great outdoors."

All it takes is some simple preliminary planning.

A Look at Canoe Camping
by Vin T. Sparano

Last summer I paddled a canoe deep into a Louisiana bayou, emerging 3 days later 12 miles from my starting point. My friends and I had the satisfaction of knowing that we had traveled, camped and fished in areas that could not possibly be reached any other way. These backwater havens are inaccessible even to the backpacker, who can usually navigate any terrain. Canoes, once again, proved to be the most versatile craft a sportsman can use.

A sportsman who owns or rents a canoe but has never used the craft for a trip of a night or more is missing a rare wilderness camping experience. Canoe cruising or camping can also mean better hunting and fishing, since these silent boats can take you deep into remote areas where fish and game have not been spooked by too many people.

Is it difficult to get started in canoe camping? Is it expensive? The answer to both questions is no. If you already have a canoe in the 16- to 17-foot range, it should work fine. And if you're already a camper, you probably have enough gear in your garage for a canoe cruise. Remember, you carry less equipment on a canoe trip than you do when you head for a state forest or park with a station wagon or camp trailer.

The canoe camper, however, doesn't have the equipment limitations of the backpacker; he can afford some luxuries.

Let's start with the canoe. A double-ender, in the 16- to 20-foot range, is best for canoe camping. I use a 17-foot aluminum canoe, and it's an ideal size for canoe cruising. It weighs 60 pounds and holds 755 pounds of gear and people. I weigh 180 and, if another 180-pounder joins me, I can still carry 395 pounds of camping gear. This means my 17-footer can carry two campers and enough gear and food for a couple of weeks.

Bigger canoes are available, but they present weight problems for portaging or car-topping. Canoes smaller than 16 feet, especially the 13-footers and the one-man models, are a joy to use for fishing, duck hunting and exploring, but they are not practical for canoe cruising.

The canoe you eventually select should have a keel which will help you paddle in a straight line over long distances. A canoe that has no keel or a very shallow keel is a white-water model, designed for fast maneuverability; it is for white-water use—not for cruising. A cruising canoe should also have a beam of at least 36

A family, wearing life preservers, leaves a campsite to explore another arm of a Canadian lake.

inches and a center depth of 12 to 13 inches. It should have low ends with the beam carried well into the bow and stern. A 17-foot canoe with this kind of full beam can carry two paddlers, their camp gear and up to a 2-week supply of food.

My canoes are aluminum because I do not have time to pamper them. I want something that I don't have to paint, wash, wax or whatever. I keep my canoes outside all year in a climate that ranges from summer heat to sub-zero ice storms, and the canoes take it in stride. Some of the newer fiberglass canoes have a Kevlar-cloth-laminate layer, which makes the craft extremely tough and resistant to the hard knocks of canoe cruising. ABS (acrylonitrile-buta-diene-styrene) is another modern material that will stand up to the rigors of canoe travel.

Wood-and-canvas canoes, which seem to be making a nostalgic comeback in some areas, are not a good choice for the canoe camper. These handsome craft look beautiful on small lakes and ponds, but I would not want to use one for extended river travel on unfamiliar waters, which is the goal of every serious canoe camper or voyageur. Wood and canvas cannot be expected to withstand occasional scrapes on submerged rocks and gravel beaches.

Canoe equipment is minimal. You'll need two paddles and one spare. Wood paddles are inexpensive, but they also break. The new square-tipped fiberglass paddles are unbelievably tough and a better choice. I've read at least three different rules for choosing paddle length, but the one I use is simple and works fine: For both bow and stern select a paddle that is chin-high on the paddler. You'll also need some kind of folding anchor with 50 feet of 1/4-inch nylon line, life jackets for everyone in the canoe, and a patch kit that matches the material of the canoe. Grumman sells an excellent patch kit for all aluminum boats.

The next biggest expense in putting together a canoe camping outfit is a tent. This is an area in which the canoe camper can afford a luxury that the backpacker must pass up. The backpacker must keep his tent small and light, usually about 6 pounds, and this

The canoe catamaran that provided a good fishing platform for four men and got us safely across a 4-mile lake with 3- to 4-foot waves. Note how the small outboard motor is mounted.

means a tent height of about 4 feet—not very comfortable. The canoe camper, though he should avoid 50- to 60-pound cottage tents, can choose among any number of tents designed for compact camping and canoe cruising. These modern tents weigh 25 to 35 pounds, an acceptable weight for a canoe tent.

My favorite is Eureka's Great Western, a nylon tent with a floor size of 9¼ by 9½ feet and a height of 7 feet. There's enough room in this tent for four campers. Its total weight is 25 pounds and it rolls into a 30-inch by 9-inch package. There are many similar tents available today and finding one that appeals to you should be no problem. The ideal tent for canoe camping should also have a sewn-in floor that extends partway up the wall. This feature is especially important when setting up camp along riverbanks and shorelines.

On occasion, when I've wanted to travel unusually light, I use a Gerry Camponaire II, a less-than-10-pound model that will sleep three canoeists and makes an extremely small package.

During my Louisiana trip, an experienced bayou paddler solved his sleeping problem quickly and easily.

A wood fire built on a riverbank with plenty of driftwood makes a great stove. The sooted grill will be carried in a plastic trash bag to the next campsite.

At night, he would string a hammock, complete with rain tarp and mosquito net, between two trees. His hammock rolled into a tiny stuff bag, and he never had to worry whether the ground under him was wet, lumpy or rocky.

One of the first facts you'll learn to live with on your first canoe cruise is that your gear will constantly get doused with rain, spray, wet paddles and tackle. Unless it is protected, you'll have problems with wet gear the first night. One of the most important rules for the canoe camper is to keep all gear and food dry and lashed securely to the canoe—your survival could depend on it.

I prefer a frameless day pack for my canoe trips. It's waterproof nylon and I fasten it with the shoulder straps to the thwart in front of me. It has a pocket in the top cover for maps and two side pockets for quick access to raingear, matches, candy bars and anything else I want to reach easily. My sleeping bag goes into a waterproof stuff bag and then into a large plastic trash bag, which is also tied to a thwart.

A box of plastic trash bags is an invaluable item on any trip. I've used them to protect equipment, hold trash and carry a dirty fireplace grill. They've also filled in as a makeshift poncho or ground cloth. But, don't depend on them for absolute protection of your important gear and supplies.

In addition to a waterproof bag for my sleeping bag and a waterproof day pack for smaller items, I also use two double-lined waterproof bags. These are designed for canoeists and kayakers. They're guaranteed and will even float in case of a capsize. In one bag, I keep

A good folding anchor is light and convenient to use and store. It's especially useful when you want to stop to fish a quiet pool. This one is made by Grumman.

nonperishable foods, such as freeze-dried items and canned goods. In the other, I keep additional personal gear, such as sweaters, towels, socks, moccasins and such.

Freeze-dried foods make it possible for a single canoe to carry enough food for several weeks, but a week-long diet of freeze-dried meals can have a depressing effect on appetites—especially mine. Canoe campers can and should take along a small cooler. I load my cooler with a couple of steaks, some fresh vegetables, bacon and eggs. If you pack the cooler with a block of ice (not ice cubes), the food will stay fresh for several days. Fresh food does wonders for the morale after three days of canoe travel. When the cooler is empty, it can be used as an additional waterproof container.

For most cooking chores, I prefer a wood fire. Any waterway will have its share of driftwood, so fuel is rarely a problem. A steel grate, carried in a plastic trash bag, is all you need to put together a wilderness stove. Braced across two stout logs or large rocks, a grate will give you a good cooking surface for pots or grilling steaks.

While I think it's unnecessary to take along a big camp stove, I suggest you find a place in your canoe for a small single-burner gasoline or propane stove for quick hot lunches or snacks. There will also be times when you're too tired to build a wood fire for cooking, or you may find that a storm has soaked all available fuel.

If you already have a camp cook kit, it will probably work fine for canoe cruising, but you can reduce the number of pots. You can put together most meals with one 8-quart pot, one 4-quart pot, two frying pans and a coffeepot. Add a plate, plastic cup and utensils for each camper. Cooking utensils should include carving and paring knives, a long fork, a ladle, and a spatula. A pair of cotton gloves will save the cook from burned fingers. The items listed constitute a basic kit. After a few trips, you'll be able to adapt it to suit your own preferences.

Camp lighting is rarely a problem. You should take along a good flashlight and a lantern, either gasoline or propane. I prefer propane in summer when warm temperatures maintain a constant pressure in a low-pressure cylinder. In winter, I use a Coleman gasoline lantern. If the pressure drops in freezing weather I can always pump pressure manually in the tank.

Fishing tackle should always be a part of your canoe equipment. If you dislike long rod cases sticking out of your canoe, get a trail or backpack rod that breaks down into pieces about 15 inches long. A reel to match your rod and a pocket-size tackle box loaded with

Never leave your canoe if you capsize. Remember that it will still keep afloat the maximum capacity for the craft. Even if it is swamped, you can paddle it back to shore, as shown here.

Here's the backpack spinning tackle I keep taped to the thwart on most of my canoe trips.
The rod breaks down into five pieces and fits into an 18-inch case.

spoons, spinners and an assortment of bait hooks are all you'll need. Any riverbank can provide a variety of fresh bait.

You'll discover after one or two canoe trips that these silent boats can open a new wilderness for you. Learn to respect a canoe, but never fear it. The canoe is frequently and unjustly labeled as a dangerous and unstable craft. This is not so. In competent hands, a canoe and perhaps a rubber raft are the only craft capable of traveling treacherous stretches of white water. How, then, can it be called dangerous and unstable? As with any boat, a certain amount of common sense will keep you out of trouble.

Last summer, I fished a large Canadian lake with friends, using two canoes. When the wind picked up in the afternoon or when we had to make a crossing, we lashed the two canoes together and mounted a small outboard motor between them. On one occasion, we used our makeshift canoe catamaran to cross the lake when it was churning up 3- to 4-foot waves.

If you should capsize, remember that your canoe will not sink. Modern canoes have enough flotation to keep their maximum capacity afloat until help arrives. Or you can sit in a swamped canoe and paddle it toward shore with your hands or a paddle. *Never* leave your canoe and try to swim to shore.

One final word to all would-be canoe campers. You will be joining the ranks of the voyageurs who explored the North American continent. Let us preserve, protect and defend from waste and litter the wilderness areas they charted for us, so that our children can also enjoy them. Leave nothing behind—not even your footprints.

No canoe, regardless of material or construction, is indestructible. Always carry a patch kit. This Grumman kit, designed for canoes, will work on any aluminum boat.

I supplement my wood fires with a single-burner propane stove. They are sometimes more convenient to use for quick lunches, a pot of coffee or trail snacks.

Horse Packing
The Best of Two Worlds
by Ed Park

Backpacking is undoubtedly the least expensive and least complicated way to see wild areas. You simply fit all your gear—food, clothing, sleeping bag, tent and so on—into a backpack and start hiking. And for some areas, such as officially designated wilderness areas, backpacking is one of only a few legal ways to go. Since motors of any kind are taboo for most such areas, you must either walk or take a horse.

There are times, however, when backpacking is either impractical or undesirable from one of many standpoints. If you are going a great distance into high-altitude, thin-air mountains, you might not have enough time to haul yourself and your gear to your destination and back. Or you need to take along more gear than usual, being currently vitally interested in photography, fishing, rock hounding or something else that you think requires about 100 pounds of equipment. For big-game hunters, especially if they are after a large species such as elk, backpacking is logical only for a few very strong and very determined hikers. The weight problem is just too staggering.

Maybe the weather, creeping middle age or other factors make it too close to impossible to accomplish what you want to do. What then?

Then, dear camper, is when you consider the horse.

Now, before you rear back, think of old jokes about "How can anything full of hay be so hard" and utter an emphatic "No!" let's give some serious thought to the advantages—and some of the disadvantages—of taking a horse-packing camping trip. In other words, let's look at all sides of horse packing and see if you don't also agree that there are times when it is the best way to go.

To begin with, a string of horses can carry just about any amount of gear you wish to take. If necessary, a string of horses can number in the dozens, with each horse capable of carrying over 100 pounds all day. You can take along those extra camera lenses, a tripod, heavy binoculars, more than one fishing rod, a couple of extra pairs of boots, sufficient clothing for any conceivable weather, a large roomy tent and even a few books to read in your roomy tent if you have to sit out a storm. You can take a cast-iron skillet for efficient campfire cooking, instead of one of those flimsy aluminum pans that always seem to burn things. You can take a wider variety of foods than are normally found in the dried and freeze-dried packets. In other words, you definitely can take more and

Packer/outfitter Sid Simpson of Harmel's Ranch Resort, Gunnison, Colorado, adds a rock to packsaddle to even up the weight.

better things on horses than you can possibly carry on your back.

There are other advantages, too. All of us are getting older with each passing day. At fifty, the hiking and climbing miles go by much more slowly than they did at twenty. This is another good reason to consider a horse-packing trip. You may still want to visit the high country, the remote places, the back country, as you did on foot many years ago. But logic tells you that the only way you'll get there now is by horse. It is not uncommon to see persons well past retirement age sitting smartly in a saddle, enjoying rough country travel. At the other end of the scale, the wee ones may not be old enough or big enough to be taken on a strenuous hike, but even small youngsters can go on a horse-packing trip.

An advantage which we thoroughly enjoy is being able to ride along and look at the scenery, without having to watch constantly where you are putting your feet. Once you've learned to trust your horse, you can relax and enjoy the passing scenes, watch for wildlife or merely absorb the contentment that comes with getting back into the bush.

So horse packing does have definite advantages in many types of situations. But in all fairness, I must mention a few of the disadvantages also.

Somehow, many of us feel that man was just not constructed properly to fit around the back of a horse.

Long fishing rods aren't the best, but they are safer in sturdy cases than packed loose. This is Sid Simpson of Harmel's Ranch Resort.

We were not made to sit, legs sprawled out as if we were trying to do the split, and be subjected to a constant spanking.

Before going on a horse-packing trip, it is highly advisable to get in as much riding practice as possible, if stables are available near your home. Even riding lessons are a good idea; you will learn to mount and dismount, adjust stirrup length, control your horse—making him turn, stop, slow down at your pleasure—

and become more comfortable around horses.

If it is not possible to take lessons or do some riding beforehand, you can make your ride much less painful if you'll do a few things during the trip. First, if you are really a beginner and fear you cannot stand a long ride, be honest with your outfitter and tell him so. He'll plan the trip so that it is short enough each day to stay within the physical limits of all riders. This might mean taking a couple of days to get where he'd normally go in one, but you are not out there to set an endurance record.

Second, if you frequently get off and walk for short distances, the strain of riding will be greatly diminished. There is no stigma attached to walking, and even veteran horsemen do it from time to time, merely for a change of activity.

Walking, leading your horse, is also a good idea in extremely rough or steep places, or if you get cold and need the exercise to warm up.

A problem for some is the annoyance of having horses to fuss with. They need to be saddled, groomed, fed, tied up, untied, hobbled, watered and in general taken care of. But if you hire the services of an outfitter, he will attend to all this, leaving you more time to fish, hunt, hike or relax around camp.

If you are now convinced that a horse-packing trip is a logical and proper thing to consider, we can discuss what you should take along and what you should leave behind.

To begin with, you should come to a firm understanding with your outfitter about just what he is furnishing and what you are expected to furnish. There are many possibilities, ranging all the way from a situation in which you furnish everything except horses and tack to the opposite extreme where the outfitter furnishes everything, including sleeping bags and other personal items.

Since the arrangements can vary so greatly, be sure an agreement is made before you start. It might not be funny to arrive at your campsite, miles from the end of the road, just about dinner time, and have both you and your outfitter insist, "But *you* were supposed to bring the food!"

You should also learn how your equipment is to be packed, to aid you in selecting what to take. Some packers use solid pack boxes, some use heavy canvas sacks, while others wrap gear in sheets of canvas called mantas. If your packer is going to use the solid pack boxes or sacks, find out the inside dimensions. A 6-foot

Packing uncased fishing rods in a packsaddle is a good way to invite broken rods and a ruined fishing trip.

fly rod will not fit inside a pack box whose greatest inside dimension is 4 feet without something giving.

Once there is understanding about who brings what and how things will be packed, you can consider the items that you will almost always have to provide for yourself—personal items, clothes, special equipment such as cameras and fishing tackle and such necessities as medicines.

If your gear is to be packed in solid pack boxes, delicate items such as cameras can easily be packed without risking damage. If you'll be putting your gear into soft pack sacks or having it wrapped in mantas, you should provide some protection yourself.

Long objects such as rifles, shotguns, fishing rods, bows and arrows, or even tent poles can present a problem. A long item sticking out of a pack can catch on limbs and brush, possibly causing a horse to panic and bolt.

I've seen anglers pack long fishing rods into pack sacks with a couple of feet of rod sticking out and the rods not in a case of any kind. Carrying fishing rods outside of a case might be all right in a car, but on a horse you're asking for a broken rod and a ruined fishing trip. If you must take a long rod, be sure it is in a sturdy case. Better yet, invest in some pack rods—those that take down into lengths of less than 2 feet each and come packaged in a strong case.

Firearms, bows and arrows, and tent poles present more of a problem. If you are going on a horse-packing big-game hunt and will be hunting from the horses, you'll need a saddle scabbard for your rifle. If you do much of this, you'll want to purchase your own, though most big-game guides furnish them. However, this is another item to check in advance.

If scabbards are available, a shotgun will usually fit in one of these also. On one horse-packing big-game hunt into the mountains of Idaho, we wanted to take my archery gear. The arrows could be carefully packed without much trouble, but the 6-foot-long bow was a real problem. If I did this often I would certainly buy one of the take-down models, but that time I had only the one bow. My guide and outfitter, Bob Crick of Victor, Montana, had met many such problems in his years of outfitting and he came up with a logical solution. He put the bow in his rifle scabbard along with the rifle. It looked a bit odd, but it worked.

Long tent poles, being sturdy, can usually be stuck in some place, though shorter poles would be better.

Your packer will put things in the best locations, since he's had experience, but if you have to do the

Guide and outfitter Bob Crick, of Victor, Montana, taking the author on a bear and mountain goat hunt in the wilds of Idaho. The horse in the rear with the empty saddle is the author's.

A horse-packing trip is a great way to visit the back-country wilderness.

packing yourself, for whatever reason, there are things to keep in mind. High on this list is the importance of packing the long items so the end that sticks out will not catch on limbs and brush. If possible, have anything that is protruding point back, not forward.

Weight should be equally divided, so the pack is not lopsided. An experienced packer can judge this merely by lifting the packs. Unless you know you are good at it, use a scale. If the loads are a few pounds different, either move items from the heavier to the lighter pack, or put a few rocks in the lighter one.

Everything should be tied down, even after being packed in boxes or sacks. It doesn't happen too often, but now and then a horse will bolt from something like a flushing grouse or balk at crossing a stream or muddy place or for some reason decide to buck. If loads are tied securely, they will probable ride out the storm.

Besides the items discussed, what else should you take on a horse-packing trip?

Clothing is important. You need comfortable boots for riding and sturdy boots for hiking. Western-style riding boots are ideal, but since most of us wouldn't

invest in boots for just one trip, the next best bet is good hiking boots. These will be warm, comfortable, and will protect your feet and ankles against sticks and tree trunks. For pants, again take note of what western horsemen wear: jeans. They are ideal for riding, being both tough and comfortable. From there on it's up to you—flannel or wool shirts, and whatever hat you feel comfortable in.

Probably the most important items of clothing will not be worn most of the time but will ride along with you, tied immediately behind your saddle. This is where you'll keep your rain gear and warmer jacket or coat. Don't make the mistake of glancing at the sky, seeing it is a crystal blue, and packing your warm coat and rain suit in with the other gear. Weather in the mountains can change abruptly, with showers coming and going within minutes. You'll want that weather gear where you can get at it quickly.

What about weather? How much of a problem is it anyway?

That depends, of course, on time of year, altitude and location. Since we often think of the western mountains for horse packing, we need to think of heat,

By packing horses (or mules, as in this case) you can enjoy a deluxe camp, with large, comfortable tents, in remote areas.

cold, wind, rain, even snow, at most any time. Days are apt to be quite warm, even hot, with nights chilly or downright cold. The sky is usually clear, but afternoon and evening thunderstorms are not uncommon, though they are usually brief. If you have any doubts about the weather, ask your outfitter what you can expect for extremes, then go fully prepared for all those extremes.

Finally, where does a person go to find out about qualified outfitters? Many organizations feature such pack trips as part of their programs, and one does not have to belong to the organization in order to participate. Check with the Wilderness Society, 1901 Pennsylvania Avenue, N.W., Washington, D.C. 20006; Sierra Club, 530 Bush Street, San Francisco, California 94108; American Forestry Association, 1319 18th Street, N.W., Washington, D.C. 20036; Trail Riders of the Canadian Rockies, Box 448, Banff, Alberta, Canada. Since many states require packers and outfitters

to be licensed, a letter to the fish and wildlife agency of any state will probably bring you information on licensed packers in that state.

The various outdoor magazines carry advertisements by guides and outfitters and are excellent places to look, especially if you are planning a fishing or hunting trip.

Finally, the Chambers of Commerce of various towns, counties or states can provide information on horse packers in their areas.

We've been on many horse-packing trips—for big-game hunting, for fishing or just for a way of camping away from swarms of other people—and have enjoyed them all. For an excellent way to camp in remote wilderness areas, plus having the conveniences of many creature comforts not available to the backpacker, horse packing definitely is the best of two worlds.

Horse packing allows a fisherman (the author) to get back into the mountains to sample uncrowded fishing—such as is found in the West Elk Wilderness of Colorado.

ARTICLES

After Labor Day

by Bob Gooch

Post-season camping is the subject here—camping during those glorious autumn days after Labor Day when the crowds disperse, campgrounds are suddenly full of empty sites and the concessionaire in the state park turns off his jukebox.

Elsewhere in this book the camper has been told the fundamentals: how to pitch and ditch a tent, build a campfire and cook over an open fire.

The long fall camping season can be divided into three periods: early September, when summerlike conditions still reign; Indian summer, brought on by the first frost; and cold weather, when ice, snow and freezing temperatures discourage all but the hardiest campers. The emphasis here is on the middle period, true autumn in the minds of most campers.

Why camp in the fall? Primarily because it is the most glorious season of the year—flaming autumn foliage that draws millions to the outdoors, thin air that improves visibility, wildlife populations at their annual peaks of abundance, birds migrating south and the dry season that renders lakes and streams clear and sparkling as they reflect the brilliant reds and golds of the season.

And there are other advantages: an absence of insects, few if any snakes or other poisonous reptiles, the end of the season for thunder-and-lightning storms, an invigorating atmosphere that encourages outdoor activity and dry firewood that burns merrily on a brisk autumn evening.

Theoretically, the post-season begins after Labor Day, when the vacation season ends and children go back to school. Because the demand for their facilities is curtailed sharply, most campground operators shift into an off-season pace. The schools and colleges also claim many campground staff members. An early advantage is the sudden availability of almost unlimited camping space and those choice waterfront sites that were always full in August. In early September the insects still buzz, poisonous snakes sun on the trails, the foliage is still green and ominous black clouds accompanied by thunder and lightning may roll over the ridges. But the jukebox across the lake is now usually silent.

Because campground services are often reduced sharply, the camper should go prepared with adequate food, fuel for stoves and lanterns, insect repellent and

The author and his wife enjoying their campfire on a post-season camping trip.

an ax or saw for gathering firewood. Primitive facilities may replace flush toilets and hot showers.

Even though the weather may be hot during the day, September evenings tend to be cool. A light jacket will feel good around the campfire.

While Labor Day changes the camping picture, it is the first frost that signals the beginning of the fall season for veteran campers. That frost sends the insects scurrying, and the snakes and ticks suddenly disappear. The nights are cold, and skim ice may form along the edges of lakes and streams and on water left overnight in a pan or pail.

The foliage responds to the season in flaming reds and golds and duller browns. Leaf by leaf it drifts to the forest floor. Through the bare woods the hills and mountains, the lakes and streams, suddenly become clearly visible from the campsite, the trail, the lake or stream.

While many campers may be out through September, the first frosty dawn seems to spell the end of the season for most, so the fall camper will find even more room in campgrounds.

My wife and I spent an October week in an almost vacant KOA campground on the Current River in the Missouri Ozarks a few years ago. Much of the time we had all the campground facilities, including a spacious shower room, to ourselves. Other campers, most en route for some distant point, set up for one-night stays.

Inexperienced fall campers, accustomed to the summer chatter of happy children and camping families, may experience an initial feeling of loneliness, but soon the beauty of the autumn season takes over and they find contentment in the solitude and the quiet beauty of the Indian summer days.

Whether the fall camper is hiking along the Appalachian Trail, camping in a state park or making the KOA circuit, he will have his choice of sites, an unheard-of luxury in this modern day of camping to the tune of a reservations system.

Most privately operated campgrounds are open on some basis all year. Depending upon the climate, region and demand for their facilities, most publicly owned ones are also open, though often on a limited

This provident fall camper has stacked plenty of firewood.

facility basis. Seasonal information on campgrounds is available in most directories.

While shelter becomes more important during a season that claims a little of both summer and winter, the usual summer tents, soft-top campers and travel trailers will serve well in the fall. Tents with smaller windows are more suitable for cold-weather camping than well-ventilated summer tents, however. All windows should have snug-fitting drop flaps for storm protection.

Small catalytic heaters will quickly warm the area of a tent, and if electrical outlets are available, ordinary electric heaters will serve well. Gasoline lanterns put out a fair amount of heat, but for safety reasons the tent should be well ventilated.

Many campers dislike heaters. They spend the evenings around a campfire and slip quickly into warm sleeping bags, enjoying the opportunity to sleep in cold quarters. If the door flap is opened to admit heat, a campfire will warm a tent.

For most people, getting up in a cold tent is the critical time for cold-weather camping. Then a catalytic heater or an electric heater can be put into operation from the warm comfort of a sleeping bag if adequate preparations have been made the evening before.

The down sleeping bag that was too warm for summer camping may be just the thing for those nippy autumn nights. If the down bag becomes uncomfortable on an unseasonably warm fall night try unzipping it and sleeping between the folds. This seems to permit enough body heat to escape—or cool air to seep in—to permit sleeping in comfort. If it gets cold toward dawn the bag can be zipped up again. Then its warmth will be really appreciated.

Open-fire cooking, uncomfortable in hot or muggy weather, can be a real joy in the fall, particularly for preparing big evening meals. Summer campers, well experienced with gasoline or propane stoves, may need to remember a basic outdoor-cooking rule: cook mostly on coals. It takes a campfire a while to build a good bed of coals, so the fire should be started well in advance of cooking time. Hickory, oak and other hardwoods make the best coals. The wood should be dry and well seasoned.

If fireplaces are not available in the campground,

build a crude one of rocks and small boulders, or even of green logs. The fireplace will hold the coals and provide a resting ledge for utensils.

While the summer camper may choose a site that offers prevailing breezes for protection from heat and insects, the fall camper will fare better if he sets up camp away from the wind, which may become cold in the autumn. At this season there are no insects and hot weather is rare. The thunderstorm season is over, but the hurricane threat rears its ugly head in much of the country. Select a site away from the threat of wind and falling trees. Check weather reports every day for comfort and safety.

Firewood, which can be purchased at the camp store in the summer, may be unavailable in the fall. The camper is on his own with respect to wood gathering. An ax or saw is a necessity. A buck saw, or a hand saw

with pulp blades, is a good choice. Some campers take small chain saws, but they are noisy.

As a rule, firewood in the form of fallen or standing dead timber is not far away. Standing timber is best because it is usually dry and well seasoned. Don't forget to check with the nearest ranger station about the regulations which govern cutting firewood in national and state forests. Although most permit it, it is wise to check. A letter or telephone call to the forest headquarters prior to a trip will save time later on.

The evening campfire is one of the real joys of fall camping. No longer a mere luxury, it becomes necessary for protection against the chill of a long fall evening. A good supply of wood is needed to keep it going.

Most fall campers keep their fires burning from early morning to bedtime, since a fire is particularly

A chain saw is handy for gathering campfire wood, but noisy.

McCullough Corporation

Fall camping coincides with the opening of hunting seasons.

inviting on a frosty morning. Many fall and winter campers keep their fires burning continuously until it is time to strike camp.

My grandmother taught me the secret of banking a fire in order to keep it alive through the night. The fireplace fire in her living room glowed from the first frost until the frogs were chirping in the spring. Her method will work for a campfire. Toward bedtime she let the fire flicker away to a bed of red coals which she covered with ashes. The timing is important for comfort, but the heat from the coals will provide warmth long after the flames have died. The coals, protected by a good cover of ashes, will stay alive all night. In the morning it is a simple matter to rake away the ashes, exposing the hot coals, and pile on a fresh supply of wood. A campfire is best banked when enclosed in a fireplace. If the supply of ashes is low, add some light, dry soil.

Some campers keep their fire going by getting up once or twice during the night to add more fuel. But an unattended fire is dangerous, and who wants to leave a warm sleeping bag on a cold night?

What do you do on a fall camping trip? True, it is too cold for swimming, but canoeing on an autumn stream or lake can be a unique experience. The water is usually deserted, and there is an abundance of wildlife to observe, not to mention the fall foliage in all its glory. Fishing is usually fine in the fall, much better than during the hot summer months, and the angler will usually find no competition on the lake or stream.

Hiking, too, can be invigorating. The thin, cool air puts new life into tired lungs and spring into lazy muscles. The foliage, still colorful in the lowlands, will be gone from the higher mountains. Visibility is better. The hazy mugginess of the summer air has been replaced by crisp clear air that permits the hiker to see for miles.

Wildlife populations have been building up all summer and are at their annual peaks. Food is abundant, and the animals and birds will thrive for a few weeks before food shortages, predators and the ravages of winter take their toll.

The fall bird migrations are also at a peak. There is more bird activity in the fall and spring than at any other time of the year. Bird watching can be all-consuming.

The hunter can combine fall camping with the hunting seasons which are planned to catch the peak of the game crops. Some of the writer's most memorable camping trips have taken him west in the fall as the hunting seasons opened across the land. A fall hunting camp in good game country can be a rewarding experience. The best game country is often the most beautiful country. Because cool weather and early frosts have driven away the bugs, snakes and other pests, wilderness camping is more pleasant in the fall. The best fall hunting often calls for wilderness camping.

In the northern regions an early snow may dust the fall campground. This presents few problems and adds a rich new dimension to the outing. Try studying the myriad of tracks that wild creatures put down in a fresh blanket of snow.

If snow or other inclement weather is forecast it is wise to collect a good supply of wood and put it in the tent or some other place where it will keep dry. A snug camp and an ample supply of firewood makes camping in the snow an unforgettably pleasant experience.

A ground cloth in front of the tent becomes even more important when snow is on the ground, as it prevents tracking in snow to melt and cause discomfort.

Snow does not always mean colder weather, so the cold-weather precautions already discussed cover this situation also. Last fall an unseasonably early snow hit my campground in North Dakota. Strong winds accompanied the storm, but the snow that settled and built up on the canvas tent actually served as insulation against the cold. It disappeared quickly, as most early snows do.

Pitching camp in the snow does present a few problems, but they are not insurmountable. Before putting down the ground cloth, clear away the snow, otherwise it will melt and cause dampness on the tent floor. The snow should also be cleared from in front of the tent and around the fireplace. If snow-laden tree branches extend over the campsite, shake the branches to clear the snow before pitching the tent. Otherwise, heat from the campfire or the sun will melt the snow, which will shower the campers and their equipment.

Wet boots and outer clothing should not be stored in the tent at night if there is some other place they can be placed to dry.

Some avid winter campers select a good campsite convenient to their homes and cover the tent area with a large piece of canvas or plywood. Then, when they want to camp, they simply remove the ground covering and pitch their tent on dry ground.

If the forecasts indicate freezing weather, the camper should take a few cold-weather precautions. For example, empty all water pails, coffee pots or other containers holding freezable liquids before going to bed. I neglected to do this one cold October night in Wyoming and awoke to find an inch of ice in the water pail. Also, beware of leaving saws, axes or other equipment lying in the snow overnight. By morning they may be solidly frozen in.

In most of the country, snow is not a risk in early autumn, but if it does come a little common sense will keep the camper out of trouble. Once you learn to cope with it, camping in the snow can be a top outdoor experience—just as is all post-season camping.

A small heater will quickly warm a tent or camping trailer.

Gloy's.

Fringe Benefits of Camping

by Pete Czura

A minister wrote a letter to a friend extolling the beauties of the Grand Canyon in Arizona. He related how enthralled he felt as he gazed at one of nature's greatest and most impressive creations.

A young lad, the same day, wrote a postcard to his parents, saying: "Today, I stood on the edge of the Grand Canyon and spit a mile down!"

Two entirely different viewpoints, but would it stretch your imagination if I compared campers to the boy and the minister? The minister probed the depths of his heart and soul to express how he felt about the Grand Canyon; the boy barely scratched the surface. It's the same with campers. Some are enjoying the many extras in fun and pleasure that camping provides, but many others are overlooking them entirely.

With a little imagination and very little effort, you can enjoy more fun via a hobby you already are proficient in, or one you can begin on your next camp-out.

Sit back a moment, relax and think. Have you ever unknowingly passed up chances to participate in such activities as ghost-town exploring, rockhounding, hiking along trails that lead into primitive wilderness areas, cave exploring, photographing wildlife or beautiful wildflowers, panning for gold or sapphires, horseback riding, climbing mountains, taking a wild-river float trip, collecting antlers shed by animals, attending Indian ceremonials, making a collection of tree leaves, water skiing, or fishing for elusive trout?

Some of these, of course, are spectator activities, but you don't have to be an expert to participate in any of the bonus pursuits mentioned. Best of all, most of them can become a family venture, bringing more spice and fun to your next camping trip.

Hobbies that are rapidly gaining popularity with campers are rockhounding (collecting semiprecious stones or unusual rocks) and artifact or fossil collecting. The western states contain mother lodes of such stones and rocks and are also sources of Indian and frontier artifacts and fossils.

A friend of mine, Stanley Grzywana of Hammond, Indiana, was camping near a Montana stream last summer when he spotted something protruding out of the water. A few kicks with his boot revealed the perfect fossil remains of a pair of buffalo horns. Today, the horns, mounted over the fireplace mantle in

Tools you'll need to go rockhounding: small hammers, sacks to carry your finds, books to identify them. A small shovel and crowbar will come in handy to pry out big rocks.

Grzywana's home, are the subject of much comment when friends drop in.

However, if you plan to do some "digging," be careful where it's done, as private and certain federal lands are off limits to you.

Artifact hunters who prowl for arrowheads or American antiquities for their private collections are cautioned to be sure that they have permission from land owners to engage in such an activity before venturing on private lands. On public lands, federal law specifically prohibits the removal of any artifacts from lands administered by the U.S. Departments of Interior, Defense and Agriculture.

Rockhounds who search the hills and plains for semiprecious stones or unusual rocks are likely to find a bonanza in Arkansas, Minnesota, Wyoming, Montana, Wisconsin and Nebraska. Agate, rose quartz, jasper, petrified wood, chalcedony, (stones of light gray, blue and milky-white varieties), green jade and others reward their search. Most rockhounding areas are near excellent public and private campgrounds. Contact the tourism department of the state you plan to visit for a listing of public campgrounds.

Equipment needed to pursue this hobby is simple and inexpensive. Some use a stout stick about four feet long, to scratch the earth's surface. This helps avoid a

Women also enjoy panning for gold or sapphires along the Missouri River in Montana.

sore back from bending too many times to examine rocks. A small hammer or prospector's pick comes in handy, too. Bring along a small sack to tote your finds back to camp. To help you identify them, there is an inexpensive book *Field Guide to Rocks & Minerals* by Frederick H. Pough.

A couple of years ago, while camping in the Gates of the Mountain region a few miles north of Helena, Montana, I was accidentally introduced to a new bonus camping sport. Bill Browning, an old friend from Helena, and I were fishing for trout on the Missouri River. After lunch Browning suggested we try our hand at panning for gold and sapphires. At first I thought he was kidding, but when he hauled out a prospector's pan I knew he was serious. So I gamely went prospecting.

We didn't find any gold at Prickly Gulch but we did pan out about $11 worth of commercial sapphires. So if you would like to strike it rich, a prospector's pan will put you in business in any of the western states. However, be prepared to rough it, as only primitive camping prevails at the best panning spots.

Another fascinating activity of the West is attending Indian ceremonials. There are over 350 such ceremonials held each year. Most of the powwows are held during the spring, summer and autumn, when the visitor can easily turn back the pages of American history by observing colorful Indian pageants dating back to the time when there were millions of buffalo and the Indians roamed as free as the wind.

Five of the best-known Indian ceremonials are Intertribal Ceremonials, Gallup, New Mexico; American Indian Exposition, Anadarko, Oklahoma; Winnebago Powwow, Winnebago, Nebraska; Sioux Sun Dance, Pine Ridge, South Dakota, and the All-American Days, Sheridan, Wyoming. New Mexico has the largest number of yearly Indian ceremonials, 75; Oklahoma ranks second with over 50.

If you camp in pristine wilderness areas, your chances of coming upon wild creatures unexpectedly are good. You may be able to "bag," with your camera and an ordinary lens, bear, elk, moose, mountain sheep, goat, deer, hawks, eagles, ducks, geese or busy beavers.

A word of advice: When you do spot a critter, don't move too quickly. If you have to move to obtain a better picture, do it slowly, step by step. You can easily spook your intended subject away if you move too quickly or too much.

If you love wildflowers, many areas in our country still have wildflowers growing in profusion. Remember, they are yours for looking and picture-taking, but *please* don't touch or take!

Purple ink flowers and wild grass grow around Beartooth Lake, Wyoming. In the Midwest and Great Plains areas you can find wild roses with their dainty fragrance. In other places you can see bull dodgers with their prickly centers and saffron petals, and wild sunflowers nodding in the wind. There are about 15,000 species of flowering plants in North America.

Last summer, while camping at Dworshak Lake, about 45 miles east of Lewiston, Idaho, I found a five-acre patch of superb wildflowers. I spent a whole morning photographing these wildflowers with color film and obtained some spectacular close-ups of Indian paintbrush, wild pink, columbine, fireweed, loosestrife, pasque flowers and others.

The subject of cameras always starts up some chin music. Everyone has a favorite. However, one of the ideal cameras to use afield is a 35-millimeter. My choice is the Nikon, which has a bayonet-type mount for fast and easy switching of lenses. I find the Nikon 50-millimeter macro lens one of the sharpest, allowing one to focus from about 3 inches to infinity. It's a fine tool for photographing wildflowers and insects.

There's fun and adventure in cave exploring, cliff-dwelling exploring or searching for Indian rock drawings, called pictographs, in remote canyons. Some sites that I recommend if you are camping in their neighborhood and in an exploring mood, are listed in the following paragraph.

Echo Amphitheatre, at Carson National Forest, New Mexico, has a trail which leads to a natural echo amphitheater carved by wind from the colorful cliffs. Oak Creek Canyon, in Coconino National Forest, near Sedona, Arizona, has a setting of unparalleled beauty with a lazy trout stream meandering amid world-famous red rock formations. You can obtain horses at Sedona if you wish to horseback into this strange world. In the same area there is Montezuma's Castle National Monument, an ancient Indian cliff dwelling. About ten miles northwest of Thermopolis, Wyoming, near Hamilton Dome and along Cottonwood Creek, you will find cliffs containing ancient Indian drawings. John Lumley, the chief of police at Thermopolis, knows the route and sometimes guides people to the cliffs. Several fine campgrounds are near Thermopolis.

Did you know you could cross the Grand Canyon, from rim to rim, on foot? You can. As the crow flies, it is only 12 miles across, but the Kaibab Trail will test your hiking ability to the tune of 21 miles. If you wish, you can ride down Bright Angel Trail to the bottom of the canyon on a sure-footed mule.

Perhaps your hikes may take you into forests which are the homes of deer and elk. An unusual hobby, which may appeal to you, is collecting racks (antlers),

All kinds of wildlife can be captured on film when you camp in remote wilderness areas.

which are shed annually by these animals. Impressive moose antlers can be found near the edge of bogs, where moose go to dine on their favorite food—water plants, twigs and leaves.

Maybe you would like to take a fling at hiking and backpacking to a camp in a remote wilderness area? One of the best locations for such an expedition is the Pacific Crest Trail system. It winds through national forests from Mexico, along the snow-capped skyline of the North Cascades in Washington and Oregon, and down the John Muir Trail in the high Sierras.

For eastern and southern camping and hiking buffs, there is the Appalachian Trail, a footpath extending from Maine to Georgia. It begins at Mount Katahdin, Maine, and after wandering 2500 miles along the crest of the Appalachian mountains, terminates at Mount Oglethorpe, Georgia. This path is used by many vacationing hikers and campers who enjoy roughing it. Of course, you will need proper hiking gear and boots.

How about including explorations of ghost towns on your next camping trip? Or old mines?

Uncompahgre National Forest offers a beautiful view of Ouray, Colorado, and old mines and rustic cabins to wander through. St. Elmo, one of the best-preserved ghost towns in Colorado, is on highway 162, west of Salida.

Montana is rich in ghost towns. My favorites are Elkhorn, Marysville, Bannack and, of course, Virginia City, queen of Montana's ghost towns. Good campsites can be found at nearby towns. Virginia City has a couple of campgrounds just minutes away.

One of the easiest of hobbies is bird watching, and millions of campers have become ardent bird watchers. Some travel a thousand miles just to add one new bird to their life list. Hundreds of people from all over the country converge on Nebraska each spring to see one of America's greatest bird spectacles, when over 250,000 sandhill cranes gather on the mud flats of the Platte River for a five-week stay before heading north. The area between Grand Island and Kearney contains the greatest concentration of cranes. And it seems as if every cottonwood tree along the river harbors a bird watcher.

There are excellent private and public campgrounds at Grand Island and Kearney, along highway I-80. The 329 National Wildlife Refuges in America are also great spots for bird watching. Glacier National Park is host to many golden eagles each fall.

The requirements for bird watching are simple. You'll need a good pair of binoculars, of about seven power, and a guide book to help you identify the birds you see. Your local reference librarian or the Audubon Society can give you the titles of the best bird-watching guides for your area.

Interested in mountain climbing? Don't laugh!

Try backpacking on horseback to remote areas to find little-known camp spots.

Each spring hundreds of bird watchers converge on Nebraska where over 250,000 sandhill cranes spend five weeks on the mud flats of the Platte River before migrating north.

Waterfowl can be seen and photographed at many National Wildlife Refuges.

Bird watchers can see and "bag" osprey and red-tailed hawks with their cameras.

Angling could be one of your most exciting fringe benefits.

There are easily climbed mountains in many parts of the United States.

Many campers are tackling the easy-to-climb mountains. You don't have to be an Edmund Hillary (first to scale Mount Everest), to enjoy mountain climbing. There are peaks scattered throughout the United States which can be tackled by the rankest tyro—and scaled. Among them Mount Marcy in New York state, Blood Mountain in Georgia, Old Rag in Virginia, Telescope Peak in California, Mount Katahdin in Maine, Pinnacle Mountain in Arkansas, Pinnacle Peak in Washington, Fremont Peak in Wyoming and Mount Audubon in Colorado.

No special type of climbing gear is needed to climb any of these mountains. Sneakers or ordinary hiking boots (waffle-design bottoms) will be fine.

Would you believe that Kentucky is still a source of prehistoric animal bones? Scientists are digging up the bones of mammoths and mastodons at Big Bone Lick, 23 miles southwest of Cincinnati, Ohio. The old salt springs there have been called "the nation's outstanding prehistoric boneyard." (Some authorities, however, believe that Agate, Nebraska, is the site of the last place where the largest animals roamed on this continent.)

But since Big Bone Lick was discovered in 1729, it has yielded relics of mammoths and mastodons to collectors and souvenir hunters without letup. By 1840 it was estimated that bones of 100 mastodons, 20 Arctic elephants and innumerable smaller animals had been carried away. Some specimens wound up in European museums. On some Sundays, the public may view the digs, and the Big Bone Lick Historical Society is making plans for guided tours on Sundays during the summer of 1977. There are several excellent campgrounds nearby.

Angling could be one of your most rewarding and exciting fringe benefits. This sport gives you an opportunity to provide fresh fish for dinner, along with a chance to enjoy the tranquility the activity offers. Best of all, entire families can go fishing together. Fish are not particular about what you use to entice them to your hooks. Bait or artificial lures score well. Refined tackle may help you to catch more fish, but not necessarily. I've seen camping anglers use a cut-down tree branch, a bit of string, a No. 8 hook and some active worms to fool trout and bass.

I hope I have convinced you that there is more to camping than just pitching a tent for an overnight stay, then taking off the next morning on a tight traveling schedule. Plan to spend at least a couple of days of your next camping vacation at some spot which offers you a chance to enjoy some other activity. The rewards could be great.

I have only skimmed the surface of what you can enjoy to obtain the maximum fun and pleasure out of camping. With a little ingenuity you can find other equally exciting fringe benefits. I've put you on the path, so to speak; the rest is up to you.

Fishing/Camping Has It All

by Homer Circle

Having spent nearly a half-century in the outdoors, fishing and camping, I feel especially sorry for two outdoor types: campers who never fish and fishermen who never camp.

To make up for these benighteds, I have striven to do far more fishing/camping than I should. In the process I have worn myself to a nub—the healthiest, happiest nub you ever saw!

Now I have decided that there is far more fishing/camping than I can ever take care of, and because I can't stand to see good things go to waste, I'm calling for help.

I'm ready to make a deal. I'll let you fishermen in on my camping know-how and tell you campers how to catch more fish than you can eat. In return, you have to help me enjoy all the fun which otherwise will go begging.

To make it easy, I'll take each group separately and introduce you to time-proven tactics guaranteed to add to your enjoyment. I promise to keep it simple enough even for first-timers. Let's start with the campers.

Fishing Tips for Campers

Every wise camper, whether he is a family tenter or a backpacker, critically appraises each item he carries with him, because space is always at a premium. So fishing gear has to be compacted and chosen for general fishing needs for specific species.

The more basic fishing gear can be as simple as a cut pole, such as a willow branch; some monofilament; No. 10 long-shank hooks; and whatever natural bait you can find, such as crickets, grubs, worms or grasshoppers.

Such primitive gear can be very effective unless the fish are farther out than such a line and pole can reach. This is where modern sporting tackle comes in.

For the beginner, an all-around, hard-to-foul-up outfit is one for spin casting. This consists of a tubular glass rod and a close-face reel filled with monofilament line.

Because these rods are made in telescoping or sectional styles, they can be collapsed to no more than 15 inches. And they still have fine action.

The close-face reel has a push-button release for the

All the equipment for a camping/fishing trip can be carried in an ordinary broad-beam canoe. Pack everything in waterproof containers or sealed plastic bags securely lashed to the canoe, and carry extra paddles. Non-swimmers should wear approved flotation jackets at all times. Watch out for sudden squalls and storms.

line and is so simple to master that with less than an hour of practice you can cast your lure up to 75 feet from shore with acceptable accuracy. Thus you increase your range of operation and the number of species of fish you can catch.

Here are tips on catching the popular species you may encounter as you move around the country camping near water. These can be divided into panfishes and sport fishes.

Panfishes are so called because they fit into a frying pan—for example, bluegill, crappie and catfish. Try these tactics if you want to keep a frying pan happy. *Bluegill.* This fish represents a large family of sunfishes. What fools it also works for its country cousins—rock bass, warmouth, green sunfish, redear, pumpkinseed and longear. All are excellent to eat.

Fish for them at the edge of weed beds, near brush or fallen trees, under docks, in eddies below riffles, around lily pads or along grassy shores. They usually are around such cover because that is where their natural foods are found and it provides both shelter and protection from larger predators.

The two best live baits are crickets and worms. Keep moving and dunking the lure until you find fish. When you find one, there usually are others around, because these are all schooling fish.

The most productive artificial lures are tiny spinners, jigs and poppers. The tiny spinners should be cast near cover and retrieved steadily.

Try a worm or a piece of bacon on the hook of the spinner lure. The whirling, flashing blade attracts the fish and the smell of the meat will cause it to strike.

The jig is a lead head on a single hook, with a body made of feathers, hair or soft plastic. Fish these just over the bottom with occasional twitches.

The popper is a cork head on a single hook and it floats high on the water. Because it is too light to spin cast, you must use a plastic float with it. Attach the float, preferably one 1¼ inches in diameter, about a foot above the popper, and cast near cover.

Let the float lie motionless for 10 to 15 seconds, then twitch ever so slightly. Too much commotion will spook wary fish. A bit of worm on the hook of the popper can work magic at times, too. Popper fishing is exciting and can be most productive.

Crappie. This is a crazy fish with puzzling habits. It is fast moving when feeding on small minnows, its favorite food, yet it wants a lure moved as slowly as possible. It is one of the sweetest and tenderest of fresh-water species.

Crappie are found especially around heavy weed concentrations and brush piles, because that's where minnows hide and these are the crappie's main diet. But you can also find them at times in open water with no cover around at all.

Tiny white or yellow jigs, worked very slowly around weeds or brush, just over the bottom, are most effective. Just keep moving until you find a clustering because they're a clannish fish.

If a boat is available, try drifting with the wind across the open part of a lake. Try jigs or live minnows below a bobber at depths from one foot to several feet. When you catch one crappie, repeat your drift over the same spot and you often can take a stringer full.

Catfish. This family of bewhiskered, ugly fishes numbers over 1000 species around the world. In America the most popular are bullheads and channel, blue, and flathead catfish.

Despite their looks, they are among our most prized food fishes. And they eat anything, alive or dead.

Fish for them along any shore that drops off sharply into deeper, darker water, or in streams where a riffle disappears into deep, quiet holes.

Any smelly lure is good because catfish have taste buds in their whiskers. Among the better baits are cheese, worms, aged shrimp, chicken livers, grubs and leeches.

Impale any of these on a No. 4 hook, cast it out and let it sink to the bottom. Watch your line like a hawk eyeing a mouse hole. When you see the line grow taut, slack, twitch, act nervous or do anything abnormal; set the hook and hang on.

Sport fishes are the larger, more prized species which grow to trophy sizes. Among them are bass, trout, pike, walleye, muskie and many inshore salt-water fish. Whole books could be written on how to fish for each of these, but here, in brief, are some dependable techniques.

Bass. Use a minnow-shaped floater about 4 inches long with two or more treble hooks. Cast near weeds, logs, cattails, lily pads and the like and twitch life into the lure, teasingly, tantalizingly, as if it were injured and expiring.

Trout. Cast a small silver or gold spinner upstream in fast water, quickly reel slack out of your line and keep the spinner working just over the bottom. Concentrate on eddies behind large boulders or at the edge of riffles. You won't need to guess when you have a strike—the bucking rod will tell you.

Pike. Keep casting and retrieving a wobbling red-and-white spoon near weed beds bordering dark water. Sooner or later a toothy pike will try to take it away from you.

Walleye. This is a bottom-hugging fish, and a jig fished slowly just over the bottom is bound to find action. Watch your line and rod tip. When either shows tautness or slackness, set the hook—a prize has inhaled your jig!

Muskie. One of the most prized of all sport fishes, the muskie is also one of the hardest to catch. But if you cast out a noisy spinner-type surface lure, with spinners fore and aft, and keep it moving steadily near weedy cover, you could get the hassle of your lifetime.

Salt-water species. Watch the local fishermen and see what baits or lures they use. Use the same and also ask questions, especially of those locals who are catching the most fish. Fishermen are a friendly lot and usually glad to give you tips.

The foregoing should get you campers into the fishing scene. Just stay with it; fish especially during the hours embracing dawn and dusk, and you'll add fun and good fare to your outings.

Camping Hints for Fishermen

As all veteran fishermen know, historically the prime times of a fishing day are the hours around dawn and dusk. And there's no better way to make the most of them than by camping overnight where you are fishing

Not only will you catch more and bigger fish, but you'll never eat fresher or more delectable fish. There's no doubt about it; the shorter the time between catching and cooking, the more savory the flavor.

So, fishermen, if you haven't tried camping you've been missing some of life's finer outdoor moments. Here are some suggestions that will ease you into it gradually, according to your own peculiarities.

Oversimplified, camping is living outdoors with minimal gear to maintain creature comforts. Some of us can get by with a backpack and 40 pounds of gear. Others prefer to "rough it" in a 30-foot van with all the comforts of a motel room, which by no stretch of the imagination can be described as camping. But, as veteran campers know, there are many options between those extremes.

Because they differ in nature and needs, let's separate camping/fishing on rivers or streams from the same on ponds or lakes.

There are beautiful rivers and streams all over our nation, and the majority of them are slow flowing and safe for a float trip if it is properly planned.

My favorite way to make such a trip is to have someone drop my wife and me with our equipment at an upstream bridge and park our station wagon downstream where we expect to land. In this way you can plan for an overnighter or a float of several days.

The boat should be light but sturdy and roomy enough to hold camping gear. A lightweight outboard motor is handy for moving quickly through static stretches, but not absolutely necessary. Carry extra fuel and such basic tools as slip-joint pliers and a screwdriver.

Plan to phone your car-handling friend within an hour or so after you leave the stream. Thus, if you do not phone by an agreed time, he will know you are in trouble and take appropriate action.

Now about creature comforts and ways to ensure them. Remember that these have to be kept at a minimum because of limited space in the boat.

Packing the boat. Because it might rain or you could upset, everything should be packed in plastic watertight bags or watertight containers. All should be lashed down after the boat is balanced, so that with two of you aboard the bow rides slightly high. Always carry a spare paddle or pair of oars, which can be mounted outside the boat.

Bodily comfort. Your body is comfortable when you are neither too hot nor too cold. Dress in layers. Start off on a cold morning with slacks, shirt, pullover sweater, windbreaker jacket and lightweight rain suit. As the day and you grow warmer, start shucking garments.

Foodstuffs. Keep food simple at first. There is nothing much simpler than preparing meals ahead, packing them in foil, and then heating them over a campfire. Perishables should be eaten first, saving canned foods for the last days of the trip. If you cool canned goods in

The camper who fishes or the fisherman who camps enjoys the best of two sports. You can fish while moving from one tenting site to another. While one partner fishes, the other should paddle, steer and watch for water hazards.

Camping on a lake shore will enable you to be at your favorite spot at dawn or to stay on the lake after dusk with your camp within easy reach. Whether camping on a lake or a stream, be sure your boat or canoe is securely pulled up and fastened for the night.

water, secure the labels with rubber bands or mark the contents on the end of the can with waterproof ink or a marking pen.

Canned goods are easy to open (if you remember to bring a can opener) and may be heated near the fire while hamburgers, steaks or wieners are grilling, and served out of the can to save soiling containers.

Perishables should be carried on ice in an insulated chest. A 2-gallon jug of water, frozen, will help keep things cold and will slowly thaw to provide drinking and cooking water.

Because you usually can catch all the fish you want to eat, if you're the fisherman I think you are, all you need for cooking them is vegetable oil, a skillet and seasoned flour. Man, fresh fish never taste better.

Overnighting. If you, your spouse and your brood have never slept outdoors before, you'll sleep better in the security of an enclosure of some type, such as under a tarpaulin or in a tent.

Instead of buying a tent at the outset, you can perhaps borrow one from a camping friend or rent one from a camping outfitter. You can also fashion one quite easily. Stretch a rope or a clothesline taut between two posts or trees. Over this drape a large sheet of canvas, plastic or any lightweight sheeting material handy.

Make tie-downs at the four corners and sides and you have an acceptable makeshift tent. A plastic sheet for a ground cloth will keep out cold and dampness.

A sleeping bag will keep you warm, and a foam padding or an inflated air mattress will provide sufficient comfort after you get used to it. All these can also be rented from camping outfitters at a very reasonable price. Blankets can be used for cover and mattress.

Choosing the tent site. Keep in mind that it might rain and therefore you should be on high ground where water will drain away, not collect around you or flow through your tent like a mini-river.

Building a campfire. The first essential is a metal grill. Almost anyone can manage to build a fire to cook over, but without something to cook on, the meal can be a real disaster. Grills are inexpensive to buy, or you can use an old refrigerator shelf for the purpose. Find four flat rocks and use these to suspend the grill at its corners about 6 inches above the ground. Then remove the grill and build your fire between the four corner rocks.

Small twigs, paper, and dry sticks will start a fire, but larger pieces of hardwood are needed to provide the coals you need for cooking after the flames have died down. With dry kindling and patience your first camp-cooking fire should give you no serious problems, but if you have doubts you can buy or rent a small camp stove.

Picking a stream campsite. Remember to plan for drainage. If it rains the stream may rise, so either make your camp on sufficiently high ground or be prepared for a quick move if necessary. Be sure your boat is securely moored, in case of flooding or rising water that might carry it away.

You'll have less trouble with mosquitoes if you locate where a breeze blesses you and away from brush, long grass and trees—preferably in the open on a gravel bar. A good supply of insecticide is a must. If you rent a tent, be sure it has screened doors and windows.

Most of what has been said about stream camping also applies to lake camping. The biggest difference is that you can use your vehicle as a sort of catchall at your bare camp.

Station wagons and some cars can become a sleeper for two adults, and a pup tent will suffice for the kids. If you have a lightweight boat, it can serve in place of a pup tent. Lean it against a tree or support it by forked limbs and prop one side on rocks. Make up beds beneath its shelter.

As your experience broadens and you become a seasoned camper, you'll settle on the best camping style for your family. Talk with your camping friends who may have worthwhile suggestions for more camping comfort.

These camping tips should be enough to get you fishermen into the act. Your cumulative knowledge as outdoorsmen will quickly fill the gaps. If you don't catch more and bigger fish than you did before you tried camping, you're not the angler I think you are.

In conclusion, here is my favorite recipe for frying those fresh-caught fish.

Fillet the fish in thumb-size chunks and air-dry for 30 minutes. Dip in buttermilk. Dredge in flour seasoned with Lawry's seasoned salt, one-half teaspoon to a cup. Drop the pieces into piping-hot oil and fry until just done, no more—you can tell by sampling. Then try to get the family to stop eating.

If there are any leftovers, holler for Uncle Homer. I've been known to show up on a remote rocky point in Alaska when the aroma of fresh-fried fish was wafted on the evening breeze.

Camping in Canada
by Jerome Knap

Stories on camping in Canada are fairly common in the outdoor press. By and large, they are accounts of wilderness canoe-camping or backpacking adventures in the Canadian Rockies.

Yet this is not always the information that any serious camper planning his first camping trip to Canada wants. He or she is likely to be more interested in the nitty-gritty of traveling and camping north of the border, or even in the routine of crossing into Canada.

How much red tape is involved in crossing the border? What documents do I need? What are the highways like? Must I know French? Are there many campgrounds? This type of practical information seldom appears in articles on camping in Canada.

The laws and regulations of Canada customs don't make exciting reading. But for the first-time-in-Canada camper, such an article is needed.

Crossing into Canada, in most cases, is not much more difficult than crossing boundaries from one state to another. It just takes a bit more time. Automobiles and baggage, even at airports, are seldom searched. The traveler usually has to answer only a few simple questions, such as: Where were you born? Where do you live? Where in Canada are you going? How long will you remain in the country? What is the purpose of your visit? Are you bringing any gifts for anyone?

You may or may not be asked to show proof of American citizenship. However, you should have identification papers with you in case you are.

American citizens and permanent residents of the United States do not need passports for entry into Canada. For native-born citizens, a birth, baptismal or voter's certificate is ample proof of citizenship. Naturalized United States citizens should carry a naturalization certificate. An Alien Registration Receipt Card (U.S. form 1-151) is needed by permanent residents of the United States who are not American citizens.

Many Americans have the idea that the French language is spoken universally in Canada. Although it is one of the official languages of the country, it is widely spoken only in Quebec and in some portions of the Maritime Provinces. Even in these places, many people and especially people associated with the tourist trade speak English.

Campers intending to drive to Canada should know that some Canadian provinces require the driver of a

One of the best ways to see the real Canada is by boat-cruising along the shores of some of its many lovely lakes. Obtain maps and suggestions for routes from Canadian tourist offices.

car to provide proof of financial responsibility if he is involved in an automobile accident. The easiest way to do this is to obtain a Canadian Non-resident Interprovince Motor Vehicle Liability Insurance Card. This pale yellow card is available only in the United States through the insurance company that insures your car. Your insurance agent can obtain one for you. A valid driver's license from any state is recognized in Canada.

In general the highways in Canada are good. There are, however, fewer four-lane expressways. Speed limits and directions are generally well marked. The secondary and back roads are much like those on the rest of the continent.

At first glance the price of gasoline may seem quite high, but the Canadian gallon (Imperial measure) is 20 percent larger than the American gallon. In some remote backwoods areas, it may be impossible to obtain non-leaded or even high-octane gasoline.

Other campers' questions concern currency, weather and biting insects.

Canada has its own dollars. The value of the Canadian dollar is approximately that of the U.S. dollar. It can be slightly higher or slightly lower, depending on the vagaries of the international money market. Most Canadian stores, restaurants and hotels accept U.S. dollars, but they may not give you the best exchange rate. Exchange rates fluctuate daily and businesses tend to make sure that they don't lose out by underexchanging. Only banks keep abreast of the daily fluctuations in value. Consequently you can get the best rate of exchange in a bank. Banks in Canada are generally open on working days from 10:00 a.m. to 4:30 p.m.

Canadian weather seems to be misunderstood by many American campers. Visitors with skis on the roof racks on their automobiles sometimes arrive in Canada in July and August and ask how far north they would have to drive to find snow. Even the northern provinces have no snow in summer.

By and large you can expect summer weather in Canada to be similar to that of Maine or Minnesota. Newfoundland may be a bit cooler and get more rain, and southern Ontario will be a bit warmer. Southern Alberta, particularly near the mountains, will be dry and sunny almost every day.

Altitude and latitude, of course, play an important role in daily average temperatures. The mountains may be cool, particularly at night. The weather in the northern provinces may vary from the low 40's to the high 80's and can change within 48 hours.

Insects, particularly blackflies and mosquitoes, can be troublesome during the bug season. This begins in mid-May in southern Canada and a bit later as you progress northward. Even in the far north, the peak of the season is usually past by late July. The peak of the blackfly season lasts about 3 weeks, shortly after spring run-off. And the peak of the camping season tends to occur after that of the blackflies.

Anyone going on a Canadian camping trip should bring plenty of insect repellent and be sure his tent is tightly screened.

What can a camper bring into Canada duty free? Almost any piece of equipment can be brought in, as long as it is for the camper's own use. This includes camping equipment of all types, canoes, boats, motors, fishing tackle, cameras, binoculars, and even shotguns and rifles, but not handguns.

If your vehicle is equipped with a licensed Citizen's Band radio (CB), you must have a valid Canadian Citizen's Band Radio License in order to use it in Canada. This also applies to operation of a walkie-talkie unit or a mobile unit in any vehicle or boat of any size. If you have a U.S. FCC license for such a unit you can obtain a Canadian license by submitting proof (such as a photostat copy) of your own license, including call letters and expiration date. The Canadian complimentary license is valid for the life of your own FCC license. Don't try to operate your CB set in Canada without such a certificate!

These Canadian licenses may be obtained by writing to the Superintendent, Telecommunications Regulations Branch, Department of Communications, at any of the following addresses: Room 320-325, Granville Street, Vancouver, British Columbia; Room 300, Financial Building, 10621 100th Avenue, Edmonton, Alberta; Room 600, General Post Office Building, 266 Graham Avenue, Winnipeg, Manitoba; Ninth Floor, 55 St. Clair Avenue East, Toronto, Ontario; Port of Montreal Building, Wing No. 2, Cité du Havre, Montreal, Quebec; Terminal Center (Moncton), Ltd. Building, 1234 Main Street, Moncton, New Brunswick.

In an emergency, Channel 9 is used in Canada, as it is in the United States, for obtaining help, although you can use any channel on which you can contact another CBer for assistance. Similar rules about courtesy, obscenity and profanity are enforced.

In bringing valuable equipment into Canada, the first step is to make certain you can get it back into the United States without arousing suspicion at the U.S. customs office. An official there may think that you are trying to bring Canadian-purchased goods into the

United States without paying duty. To prevent this, make a list of all valuable items—cameras, lenses, binoculars, guns, outboard motors and so on. Take this list to the U.S. customs officer at the border just before you enter Canada. He may or may not look at the actual items, but he will either issue a certificate listing all the items or simply stamp your own list.

If you have guns on the list, don't feel that this certificate constitutes any sort of registration. You have the only copy. The customs certificate is simply proof that you had the items with you before entering Canada. All the empty spaces on the customs certificate will be crossed out by the officer so that you cannot add any items to it. Be sure to keep the certificate in a safe place.

When you cross the Canadian border, Canada customs may ask you what items you have with you. Tell them. If you have any firearms, tell them even if they don't ask. If requested, show them the description list or the U.S. customs certificate. The Canada customs official may issue a Temporary Admissions Permit to cover these items. The sole purpose of this permit is to ensure that the items are taken back into the United States and not sold or given away in Canada. If you want to leave an expensive item as a gift, you must pay import duty, excise tax and sales tax on it.

About the only time I've seen the Temporary Admissions Permit used is when a Canada customs official suspects that a person might be planning to leave something behind. For example, if a pair of campers had half a dozen sleeping bags with them, suspicion might be aroused. A Temporary Admissions Permit is used more often for firearms, but that is because firearms tend to arouse anxiety.

My advice would be to leave guns at home. You won't really need them for protection from bears or wolves. And most hunting seasons are closed during the peak camping months of June, July and August. In fact, during the closed season guns in wilderness areas inhabited by game are evidence of intent to hunt and are subject to seizure by conservation officers.

Handguns are strictly taboo. There is a special provision for the temporary importation of handguns when a visitor is traveling to a bona-fide handgun-shooting competition, but this does not apply to the average camper and does entail some red tape. However, American campers traveling to Alaska via the Alaska Highway may temporarily import handguns into Canada under special permit. The handguns must be enclosed in a case or container which is sealed with a lead seal by Canada customs officers at the point of entry.

It is possible to hunt during a Canadian camping

There are hundreds of splendidly planned, equipped and serviced campgrounds from Newfoundland to Canada's west coast. Many of those along main highways have all the latest hook-ups and recreation facilities.

trip in September or October if the camper has the proper hunting license. Separate fishing and hunting licenses are needed for each province. A camper who wishes to hunt may bring with him as personal luggage 200 rounds of ammunition duty free.

There are import limits on certain other items— food, cigarettes and other tobacco products, alcoholic beverages, film, and flashbulbs. A visitor to Canada may bring with him a "reasonable amount of film and flashbulbs appropriate to the non-resident's visit." The definition of "reasonable" is rather fluid, and Canada customs officials are generous in their interpretation of the term. A camper with a dozen rolls of film would not encounter any problem. The visitor may also bring with him, duty free, 40 ounces of liquor or wine or 24 pints of beer, up to 50 cigars, 2 pounds of tobacco, and 200 cigarettes. He may also bring food for two days.

Bringing dogs into Canada also entails a bit of red tape. A dog being brought or shipped from the United States must be accompanied by a certificate signed by a licensed veterinarian stating that the dog has been vaccinated against rabies during the preceding 12 months. The certificate must have on it a good, clear, legible description of the dog. If the dog has a registry tattoo on its ear or inner thigh, it's a good idea to quote this on the certificate as well. If you're traveling with the dog, keep this certificate with your personal identification. In order for the certificate to be valid, the dog must have been vaccinated at least a week before being brought in. It takes a week for the vaccination to immunize the dog. Hunters entering Canada with hunting dogs vaccinated less than a week prior to entry have been turned back at the border. So don't leave the vaccination until the last minute if you plan to take your dog along.

Dogs must be tied up in campsites in all provincial and national parks. If the dog is allowed to roam, you may be subject to prosecution and fined. Dogs are not allowed on swimming beaches.

Unless they are well trained, dogs can be a hazard on a backpacking trip. More than one dog has run ahead and encountered a bear. Grizzlies usually don't run from a dog; they chase it. And where does the dog run? Right back to his master or mistress for protection. If you take a dog on a backpacking trip, keep him at heel and preferably on a leash.

Incidentally, it is against Canadian game laws to allow a dog to chase deer or other big game. A conservation officer or a forest ranger is allowed to shoot any dog seen chasing big game.

But let's get down to the subject of camping. Specific information on where to camp in Canada is

Canoe trips into the Canadian wilderness offer real adventure and a chance to fish and to see wildlife close up for study and photography.

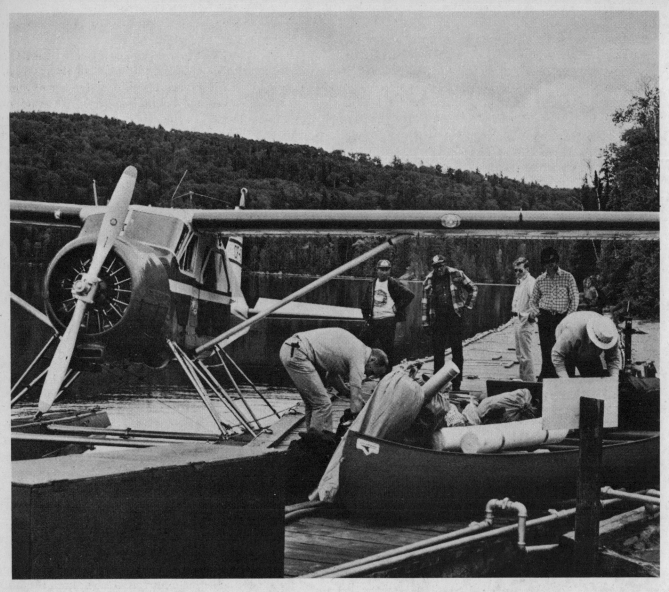

There are many guides who will fly you into a fabulous fishing spot where you can camp and fish completely on your own until the pilot returns for you at the end of your stay. Everything must be flown in and out, even the boats.

beyond the scope of one short article. But here are a few hints on planning your first Canadian camping trip.

One of your first steps should be to acquaint yourself with Canadian geography. The simplest way to do this is with a map. Write to the Canadian Government Office of Tourism, 150 Kent Street, Ottawa, Canada, and ask for a copy of the Canada Highway Map, even if you intend to fly to Canada. This map shows the major highway network over the entire country as well as through the northern United States. From it you can tell which parts of Canada

contain many towns and cities and which are largely wilderness.

Camping is a popular pastime among Canadians. There are literally thousands of campgrounds in Canada, and camping information can be obtained from the sources listed at the end of this article. You can camp in provincial parks, of which there are several hundred; the province of Ontario alone has over 100 provincial parks. These parks vary in size from 60 or 70 acres to 2900 square miles. Many of the parks offer fully serviced campsites with electricity, water and sewage hookups, but a few have absolutely primitive campsites where even a privy is not provided.

Much the same situation exists in the national parks. Then there are parks operated by various cities and by commissions such as the Niagara Falls Commission or the St. Lawrence Seaway Commission. In Ontario there are also parks operated by various conservation authorities, who are responsible for water conservation and flood control on Ontario watersheds.

As if this were not enough, there are hundreds of commercial, privately owned campgrounds. These include such well-known franchise chains as Kampgrounds of America. Most of the private campgrounds are found near large cities.

Camping fees vary from province to province and vary according to the services provided. Generally, $2 per day would be the low for unserviced sites while $6 would be the high for a fully serviced site with electricity, sewage and water hookups. Average costs run $3 to $5 per day.

Canada offers vacations to satisfy a wide range of interests. Some provincial and national parks are known for their outstanding fishing, their abundance of wildlife, unusual and abundant wild flowers, and fine swimming beaches. Some parks have golf courses with very reasonable green fees. Some, such as Ontario's Serpent Mounds Provincial Park, have archeological sites of ancient Indian villages and burial grounds.

Many of the national and provincial parks have extensive nature programs. These include guided natural-history and ecological hikes, guided bird-watching trips, and illustrated lectures on local wildlife and ecology in the evenings. In the famous Algonquin Provincial Park, park naturalists take people out in the evenings on "wolf howls" to hear the spine-tingling howls of wild timber wolves around them in the darkness.

Many provincial and national parks have well-laid-out hiking and backpacking trails and canoe routes. But the Canadian camping story doesn't end there. In wilderness areas you can camp on "Crown Land," as public land is called in Canada. If you are a novice camper who hesitates to tackle a wilderness camping trip, there are outfitters who will take you. Ontario, Manitoba and Quebec have many canoe-tripping outfitters who take campers on wilderness canoe-camping expeditions. They provide knowledgeable guides and all gear except sleeping bags. The costs are reasonable—$200 to $300 per week.

In the western mountains there are outfitters who take campers on backpacking and horseback trips. The cost for horseback trips generally runs about $50 per day. Backpacking trips are, of course, much cheaper.

If the rigors of canoeing or backpacking into the wilderness are too much for you, you can always fly in with a pontoon-equipped aircraft. A number of bush airlines offer fishing-camping packages to Canadian wilderness lakes. The outfitters maintain big, roomy wall tents and canoes or boats on wilderness lakes, and for a package price of $200 to $300 per week, they will fly you in and out and allow you to use the tent, boats and canoes. You must bring your own food, bedding and miscellaneous camping gear, such as stove, lantern, dishes, ax and so forth. The price of these packages is largely determined by the flying distance—how far into the wilderness you want to go.

If you want to camp in the Arctic islands, perhaps in one of the national parks, even that can be arranged through Ecoventures Incorporated, 737 King Street West, Kitchener, Ontario. A camping trip into the Arctic is not cheap—about $700 for a 10-day trip—but the price includes the flight from Montreal.

Getting information on camping in Canada is easy. All of the provincial tourist departments have booklets on camping and travel which list and describe campgrounds. They can also supply you with highway maps and fishing information. For detailed information on the various provincial and national parks, you must write to the parks department concerned. For example, Parks Canada publishes brochures on each of the national parks, which describe the park's history, geography, geology and natural history and list the services available. This organization also publishes two master booklets called *Accommodation in National Parks,* one for eastern Canada and one for the west. These briefly describe each of the national parks and their services. Some provinces have similar publications on their provincial parks.

The Canadian Government Office of Tourism is a good source of general travel information. The booklet *Travel Information Canada* is invaluable to anyone who plans a Canadian vacation. The Office of Tourism does not have detailed camping information, but it does list campgrounds along the Trans-Canada Highway for those who want to motor and camp across Canada. This office maintains branch offices in a number of American cities.

There is no secret, no shortcut, to a successful camping trip in Canada—or anywhere else, for that matter. If there were, it would be planning. Over the years I have noticed that the campers who do their homework and plan everything carefully before embarking on a trip are generally the ones who have the best time.

SOURCES OF INFORMATION

CANADIAN GOVERNMENT OFFICES OF TOURISM IN THE UNITED STATES

R.D. Palmer, General Manager, Eastern U.S.A.
Room 1035, 1251 Avenue of the Americas
New York, New York 10020
212-581-6395

Miss Georgia Maclean, Manager
260 Peachtree Street, Ninth Floor
Atlanta, Georgia 30303
404-577-6810

R. Desjardins, Manager
545 Boylston Street, 6th Floor
Boston, Massachusetts 02116
617-536-1730

A.C. Pascal, Manager
One Marine Midland Centre, Suite 3550
Buffalo, New York 14203
716-852-7369

Roger Cloutier, Manager
Winous-Point Building
1250 Euclid Avenue
Cleveland, Ohio 44115
216-861-2559

Mecheal Wondergem, Manager
1900 First Federal Building
1001 Woodward Avenue
Detroit, Michigan 48226
313-963-8686

F.H. Galipeau, Manager
Exxon Building, Room 1030
1251 Avenue of the Americas
New York, New York 10020
212-757-4917 or -3583

Pierre Bourgon, Manager
Four Gateway Center
Pittsburgh, Pennsylvania 15222
412-391-4160 or -4747

Donald E. Alexander, Manager
Suite 1616, 600 Stewart Street
Seattle, Washington 98101
206-477-3811

Serge Emelyanov, Manager
Suite 1810, 8 Parkway
Philadelphia, Pennsylvania 19102
215-563-1708

David Moilliet, Manager
N.A.B. Building, Suite 200
1771 N Street, N.W.
Washington, D.C. 20036
202-483-5505

Peter D. Hann, Manager
Chamber of Commerce Building
15 South Fifth Street, 12th Floor
Minneapolis, Minnesota 55402
612-332-4314

A.R. Peers, General Manager, Western U.S. and Pacific Area
Suite 1140, Alcoa Building
One Maritime Plaza
San Francisco, California 94111
415-981-8517

Wayne Mercer, Manager
510 West 6th Street
Los Angeles, California 90014
213-622-1029

S. McKelvey, Manager
Suite 410
332 South Michigan Avenue
Chicago, Illinois 60604
312-782-3760

John R. Bunt, Manager
Suite 1160, Alcoa Building
One Maritime Plaza
San Francisco, California 94111
415-981-8515

CANADIAN NATIONAL PARKS OFFICES

Parks Canada
Ottawa, Ontario, K1A 0H4
613-995-6131

Parks Canada—Atlantic Region
Historic Properties, Upper Water Street
Halifax, Nova Scotia B3J 1S9
902-426-3457

Parks Canada—Quebec Region
P.O. Box 10275
Ste. Foy, Quebec G1V 4H5
418-694-4177

Parks Canada—Ontario Region
P.O. Box 1359
Cornwall, Ontario K6H 5V4
613-933-7951

Parks Canada—Prairie Region
114 Garry Street
Winnipeg, Manitoba R3C 1G1
204-985-2110

Parks Canada—Western Region
134—11th Avenue S.E.
Calgary, Alberta T2G 0X5
403-231-4440

CAMPING ASSOCIATIONS

(Source: Canadian Camping Official Publication, Canadian Government Office of Tourism, Reference Unit)

Canadian Camping Association
Suite 203, 102 Eglinton Ave. East
Toronto, Ontario M4B 1E1

Alberta Camping Association
332—6th Avenue S.W.
Calgary, Alberta T2P OR1

British Columbia Camping Association
633 West 8th Avenue
Vancouver, British Columbia V5Z 1C7

Manitoba Camping Association
385 St. Mary Avenue
Winnipeg, Manitoba R3C ON1

New Brunswick Camping Association
P.O. Box 5
Bath, New Brunswick E0J 1E0

Newfoundland and Labrador Camping Association
P.O. Box 4188
St. John's, Newfoundland A1C 5S5

Nova Scotia Camping Association
P.O. Box 3243S
Halifax, Nova Scotia B3J 3H5

Ontario Camping Association
Suite 203, 102 Eglinton Ave. East
Toronto, Ontario M4P 1E1

L'Association des camps du Quebec and Québec Camping Association
1415 est rue Jarry
Montreal, Quebec H2E 1A7

Saskatchewan Camping Association
P.O. Box 823
Regina, Saskatchewan S4P 3B1

TRAVEL AND CAMPING INFORMATION

Alberta
Travel Alberta
10255—104th Street
Edmonton
T5J 1B1

British Columbia
Department of Travel Industry
1019 Wharf Street
Victoria
V8W 2Z2

Manitoba
Tourist Branch
Department of Tourism, Recreation and Cultural Affairs
200 Vaughan Street
Winnipeg
R3C 0P8

New Brunswick
Department of Tourism
P.O. Box 1030
Fredericton
E3B 5C3

Newfoundland
Newfoundland Tourist Services Division
Department of Tourism
5th Floor, Confederation Building
St. John's
A1C 5R8

Northwest Territories
TravelArctic Division of Tourism
Department of Economic Development

Yellowknife
X0E 1H0

Nova Scotia
Nova Scotia Department of Tourism
P.O. Box 456
Halifax
B3J 2M7

Ontario
Tourism Marketing Branch
Ontario Ministry of Industry and Tourism
3rd Floor, Hearst Block
900 Bay Street
Toronto
M7A 1T3

Prince Edward Island
Tourist Information Center
Department of the Environment and Tourism
P.O. Box 940
Charlottetown
C1A 7M5

Quebec
Quebec Department of Tourism, Fish and Game
Place de la Capitale
150 East Boulevard
Saint-Cyrille
Quebec City
G1R 2B2

Saskatchewan
Tourist Branch
Department of Tourism and Renewable Resources
Government Administration Building
Regina
S4S 0B1

Yukon Territory
Yukon Department of Tourism and Information
P.O. Box 2703
Whitehorse
Y1A 2C6

INFORMATION ON PROVINCIAL PARKS, FISHING AND HUNTING REGULATIONS

National Parks of Canada
Parks Canada Division
Public Information Bureau
Department of Indian Affairs and Northern Development
400 Laurier Avenue West
Ottawa, Ontario K1A 0H4

Alberta
Department of Lands and Forests
Natural Resources Building
109 Street and 99 Avenue
Edmonton
T5K 2E1

British Columbia
Fish and Wildlife Branch
Department of Recreation and Conservation
Parliament Buildings
Victoria
V8V 1X4

Small tents complete with their own poles and/or frames are ideal as they save carrying heavy frames and cutting poles to replace them. Canada has hundreds of isolated campgrounds where you can really get away from civilization.

CAMPER'S & BACKPACKER'S BIBLE

Manitoba
Tourist Branch
Department of Tourism, Recreation and Cultural Affairs
Provincial Library and Archives Building
200 Vaughan Street
Winnipeg
R3C 0P8

New Brunswick
Department of Tourism
P.O. Box 1030
Fredericton
E3B 5C3

Newfoundland
Wildlife Division
Department of Tourism
St. John's
A1C 5R8

Northwest Territories
TravelArctic Division of Tourism
Department of Economic Development
Yellowknife
X0E 1H0

Nova Scotia
Department of Lands and Forests
P.O. Box 698
Halifax
B3J 2T9

Ontario
Ministry of Natural Resources
Parliament Buildings
Toronto
M7A 1W3

Prince Edward Island
Fish and Wildlife Division
Environmental
Control Commission
Charlottetown
C1A 7N8

Quebec
Department of Tourism, Fish and Game
Place de la Capitale
150 East Boulevard
Saint-Cyrille
Quebec City
G1R 2B2

Saskatchewan
Public Information Services
Department of Tourism and Renewable Resources
Administration Building
Regina
S4S 0B1

Yukon Territory
Yukon Department of Travel and Information
P.O. Box 2703
Whitehorse
Y1A 2C6

No Best Tent

by Jim Elder

The best tent does not exist. But there are many different tents for many different tenting needs. Most of them are good tents, some are excellent and a few are bad. You can find *your* best tent, expensive or economy, if you approach the choice and the purchase properly.

Your shopping does not start at the store. Cut and serve a homemade pie, pour the coffee and milk and open the family forum. The first order of business is: *How will you use a tent?* Are you car campers or backpackers or ski tourers or canoe paddlers? Is yours a fair-weather family or do you like to stretch the seasons? How much tent can you afford and still have a few bucks left over for a camp stove, a cooler and sleeping bags? Until your primary uses are defined, you are not ready to consider the next question.

That is *size*. Count heads around the table, in case you haven't lately. Size is also a function of time—a tent large enough for an overnight trip might seem to shrink after a rainy week, even if the yardstick says it is still 6 by 9 feet. How you carry a tent—big car, little car, packframe, boat—should also be considered. Big tents have a habit of staying big even when they are rolled up. How long are the poles in the take-down

position? Three-foot sections are small for a station wagon and large on a bicycle. Will you want to cook inside? How about heating—do you need room for a catalytic heater or a sheepherder stove? This suggests another size factor: flies or porches. A spacious rain shelter outside can make a tent bigger, and the bacon grease doesn't go on the tent floor.

Privacy should be considered in choosing a tent size. Does your 8-year-old daughter always bring her best girl friend? Maybe one base tent and one or more smaller satellite tents would make a happier camp and give you and your wife some personal life. Don't ignore individual habits and tastes. Some folks just cannot get dressed unless they stand up; others are good wiggle-squirmers. There are families that are owned by large dogs who are afraid of thunder.

If you put the kids to bed before you got into the privacy problem ("Why can't we sleep with you and Mommy, huh, why, huh?"), don't wake them up for the next round of deliberations. You will want no extra confusion when you tackle tent *type*. Every catalog or brochure throws another term at you: spring bar, modified A-frame, pop-up, pyramid, umbrella, pup, mountain, mushroom, cantilever, flex-

The basic pup tent has been neglected in the rush to lightweights and new pole engineering. But where backpack weight is not a factor, as in boat-beach camping, Coleman's modernized pup, the Mountain model, is a good choice. With full ridge pole, it has the strength to serve as a drying rack for bags and wet suits, plenty of interior space and full screening at each end.

ridge, yurt (yurt? yes), cabin, tunnel, chalet, cabana, cottage—and no doubt cabbage. Then there are the names—Everest, Sierra, Himalaya, Teton, Alp. When the tentmakers run out of mountains they go north and west—Polar, Yukon, Northwest, Klondike. Never a name like Missouri Bogswamp, which is where you really need a tent with good insect screens. Once you have waded through the swamp of names, you can get serious about types.

Tents differ in structure, shape, door and window size, rain shedding, and warmth. Interrelated are wind resistance and ease of erection. But modern tents finally divide into two types, regardless of size, price, shape, color or creed: they are either self-supporting or dependent on guys. ("Guy" is a tent term for a rope that goes from somewhere on the tent or pole to a stake outside, where you strike a rock while trying to drive the stake or trip over the rope in the dark.) Self-supporting tents will stand alone because of the way the poles and fabric are engineered, but some have to be staked down to make the pole-engineering work or to keep the tent from blowing away if you are not inside to hold it down.

Your choice of tent type should be based on where you will use the tent. If you camp on the no-topsoil rock islands of northern Minnesota or on sand beaches, a self-supporting tent is essential. You can always pile stones or canned soup in the corners to hold it down and bury deadmen (short sticks tied to the guy or corner loop, then buried in the sand or snow) for better wind resistance. You don't want a tent which must have seventeen stakes, securely driven, to make it stand. Multitudinous guylines, as suggested, are also a hazard.

If you camp in windy areas, you may need all the tie-downs you can get, guys and all. Just remember to bring a flat-back hatchet or a hammer to drive the stakes. Big rocks are hard to find when you need them to pound stakes, and they get slippery and smash fingers in the rain. Which brings up the next tent-type factor. Tall tents with straight walls that your head and shoulders will not touch are usually of heavy fabric and need no fly—second roof. Lighter fabrics and smaller tents need a fly for rainy-weather or rain-country camping.

The final consideration on type is temperature. If

you camp in the winter or on top of high mountains, you need a tent that will retain heat from you or your supplementary heat source. That means door and window openings which close by zipping or tying, securely. But buttoned up, your tent will sweat—condense body and cooking moisture on the walls and ceiling and then drip it into your soup or sleeping bag—unless you have ventilation, even in the winter or in a rainstorm. That gets us back to flies or vent tubes and into materials.

Next on your decision list is *material*. Some materials are light and strong, and expensive. Others are light and fragile, and still expensive. Then we have heavy and strong and not quite as costly; waterproof and sweaty; water repellent and breathable; canvas, nylon, cotton and blends. Some fabrics will rot or mildew if stored wet. Others will wear through if carried next to the spare tire for 3 miles on a rough road. Figure that light means fragile and expensive, heavy, tough and more modest in cost. Reputable tent makers will offer fabrics and blends suited to the way a particular tent should properly be used.

One last decision before you put out the cat and sleep on your deliberations. Tomorrow you are going tent shopping, but tonight you should decide, realistically, how much you can afford to spend. Now, before the salesman gets you by the left wrist and tells you that this is the tent which withstood three Abominable Snowman assaults on the summit of Annapurna. Remember, you are not climbing Annapurna or Everest or even Mount Washington. And you want some bucks left for an icebox. Or you want two tents,

A bit heavier and folding only to 30 by 10 inches, this Compact III offers generous floor space and kneeling headroom. It is a good choice for overnight or weekend car campers, especially those with smaller automobiles.

for privacy or for two different types of camping. Good shelter can be had for $20 to $200. Make a budget decision and stick to it.

Saturday morning, and down to the store. No matter what your dollar limit, you are entitled to *quality*. You know, more or less, the size and type of tent you need. Maybe you know what material you want. Now you look for lapped seams, double-stitched (the finer the stitching the better the tent—at a price), good zippers, waterproof floors but not walls, and poles which are not too soft. Try to bend the poles with moderate pressure. If they bend, the salesman may throw you out, but you don't want his tent anyway. Even moderately priced tents should have alloy poles.

Look for smooth assembly and disassembly of pole joints, reinforced stress points in the fabric, and flame-retardant fabric. Check the seams for run-off stitches, the screens for snags, and look for an instruction sheet.

That last item you will need. Plus a guarantee in writing that you can take the tent back for a full refund if you find sloppy stitching or other defects, and also if it is hard to set up the second time. The initial attack does not count—some of the best tents are nightmares the first time out of the box. But once you understand the principles, you should be able to erect it on a dark rainy night in a gale, with no more than one assistant and that assistant a travel-weary person. Never buy any tent that does not have this guarantee.

Now you have all the basic information necessary to begin shopping for your best tent, or tents. But we left out a few considerations which didn't fit the categories. One is ventilation. Too many medium- and high-priced two-man tents designed for high-altitude severe-weather use are sold to lake-level summer campers. For an Ozark canoe camper, big, airy but bugproof windows are more important than hurricane-shedding design. Awnings could be important to

This Coleman Olympic tent has been used for four-season camping by a family of six, and too many borrowers to count, for four years. It spent one summer at a tree-planting camp, being lived in and cooked in by two teenage girls. The Olympic now sells for $150 upward, but this veteran shows no signs of fatigue.

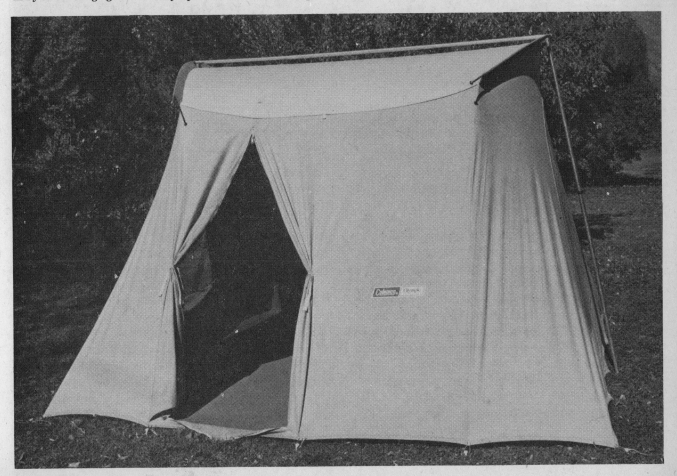

Eureka is well known for its unique Draw-Tite tents, which give great foul-weather protection. But Eureka also makes a complete line, from small pup tents to large family tents. This Mount Katahdin model is half the weight of a comparable Draw-Tite. The fly shown being attached is needed if it rains.

people who want to cook while camping in rainy country. A fold-down doorsill is essential for beach campers—easier to sweep out the sand.

We cannot prescribe the perfect tent for every camper, but we can describe some camping types and suggest tents which would be satisfactory for them.

Let's begin with a young couple, no kids or pets, small car, summer vacationers, no interest in overnight backpacking, and already owners of sleeping bags in which they slept when they owned a big station wagon. They could afford a $100 high-altitude tent, but they don't need it. They could afford weight but not too much bulk in the rolled-up package. Since it will be a long-term investment—they are confirmed overnight car-based campers and intend to use the tent for many years—an "economy" model might be a poor investment.

Our first choice from many good tents in this category would be the Coleman Compact III. The external frame is very easy to set up, no guys are needed, and it unfolds to a roomy 7 feet 3 inches by 7 feet, with 4-foot-6-inch ridge height. Rolled and bagged, it measures 30 by 10 inches, an easy fit in any automobile. Walls and roof are 6.4-ounces duck, flame-resistant, and the floor is nylon, double-coated with vinyl. Large screened windows, with rain shutters, provide ventilation and weather protection. The Compact III sells for $100, more or less—usually less.

This tent, and other similar models from reputable manufacturers, would also be a good choice for occasional canoe campers or as a satellite tent for the kids in conjunction with a motor home or other recreational vehicle. But only if one never intends to carry the tent in a pack, and only if a long-term investment is indicated.

Backpackers, climbers, long-portage canoe paddlers and cyclists, who treasure every ounce and cubic inch saved, are usually already informed and opinionated on the many tents available from Gerry, Holubar, Sierra Designs, North Face, Ski Hut, Recreation Co-Op, Alpsport, Eureka and other manufacturers. Rather than recommend any specific tent, we will briefly review the guidelines and mention one tent which is relatively unknown but worth seeking out.

Go-lighters usually figure 5 pounds as top tent weight, and they want the tent to roll up into a 6- by 18-inch package, including stakes and poles. Mountain and winter campers will sometimes accept 2 or 3 more pounds for the extra protection or live-in size they need. Walls are usually 1.9-ounce rip-stop nylon, flies even lighter at 1.6 ounce, but coated, and waterproof floors weigh 2 to 2½ ounces per square foot. These tents cost from $50 to $250 depending on size, weight (or lack of it), design and purpose. So-called mountain tents for two can be bought for less but should not be considered for any serious use.

The mystery tent I referred to is the Eclipse Tour Lite. Designed primarily for cyclists, it features a panoramic screened wall with awning/rain flap al-most as large as its 4- by 8-foot inside floor area, a 4-foot ridge, and a weight of less than 5 pounds with poles and stakes. It rolls to a compact 5 by 14 inches. Not the tent in which to sleep on Everest, but great for most summer and moderate-altitude use. Look for it at the better bicycle shops, or write Eclipse, Incorporated, P.O. Box 372, Ann Arbor, Michigan 48107.

Our next case is a family with two small children (too young for a separate tent), a big station wagon, or a sedan with a roof rack for camping equipment. Need a tent for weekend or all-week camping? Want living as well as sleeping space, a generous awning to cook or loaf under? That means a cabin, umbrella or modified wall tent, with stand-up headroom. Seven by nine feet would be a minimum floor area, and larger would be better. This is a summer cabin for families that prefer a tent or cannot afford a resort.

Unfortunately, this is the type of tent for which more people waste money on substandard products. Big tents need to be strong—they catch more wind and are beset by camp chair and table legs, scuffling

One of the long-life secrets of the Coleman Olympic may be its spring bar design.

children, and campground hounds. This is no place for backpack-weight synthetics. Yet many "family" tents at $70 to $150 are sold each year and self-destruct each summer. Better to pay $100 to $200 and have a tent which will last a generation, given reasonable care. Two suppliers that have proved their quality in family tents over the years are Eureka and Coleman. There are other good tents, but these are available nationwide, and both companies offer many models to fit a wide range of needs and budgets. An old favorite which offers modern engineering is the Coleman Olympic. It is easy to set up—two uprights, one crossbar and four spring-bar tension eave spreaders—yet it is one of the most windproof of the large tents. Sidewalls and roof are of 7-ounce material; floor is double-coated nylon. Cost $150 and up, depending on size.

Eureka, another pioneer in stress-pole no-guy design, offers several styles of family tents, including modified-wall, outside-pole umbrella and the unique cantilever Draw-Tite models. One of the newest, the 8- by 8-foot Great Western, features huge screened windows and a rain fly which attaches above the pole framework. The price is competitive with the Coleman Olympic.

We could go on giving examples, but by now you should have some ideas on how to begin choosing *your* best tent. A few loose ends need to be wrapped up, then you are on your own.

Awnings: Many modern tents have dispensed with awnings, for two very good reasons—they need guy ropes, and they catch wind, which can easily knock down or tear a tent. Many experienced campers have substituted separate flies—tarps, awnings or whatever you choose to call them—for outside shade or cooking areas.

Color: Tents used to be mostly green or tan or white. Some mountain tents were international orange, for rescue identification. Perhaps because orange nylon was readily available, or more likely because the discount houses could imply "mountain quality" on otherwise shoddy tents, everything from expedition models to family cabin tents is found in international distress orange. Think for a moment of what your favorite person will look like in the morning under orange-filtered light. Or consider the visual appeal of the already esthetically less-than-great camp chow in that same light. The better companies have stuck with white or light roofs to keep interior temperatures down and perceived colors realistic.

Another Coleman feature is the fold-down sill, which makes sweep-outs easy.

Lately there has been a lot of noise about flame-proofing and flame-resistant treatment. Some states require tents to be flame-treated. Early witches' brews to accomplish these aims tended to be smelly, stiff and heavy and in some cases affected fabric strengths and life, but these drawbacks are not found in the newest compounds. One fire scare will make the slight extra cost of a treated tent a bargain.

Even in treated tents, fire must be used with care. Don't cook inside unless you absolutely must, and be very careful with lanterns. Keep campfires away from tent walls and awnings, and don't smoke in your sleeping bag—it is probably not flame-resistant.

Now that you have been talked into spending twice what you intended for a tent, a few hints on tent care might be in order. You do want it to last long enough to justify the extra bucks. First, never store it wet. If you have to break camp in a monsoon, dry out the tent—unfolded—back home before you shelve it for the week or for the winter. Clean off any mud or grease before you take the tent down, and make sure all sand and stones are swept out. Good tents will seldom tear, even in high winds, but do repair any trouble spots before they become serious—this means a visual inspection before you strike the camp on Sunday night. Don't pack any tent, even the tough heavyweight, next to a leaky spare gas can or a sharp bumper jack. Finally, when you fold and roll the tent, brush out the dirt and pine cones as you go, and, of course, fold it floor-out, with all zippers closed. You may want to leave a vent or door closure slightly opened to let out trapped air when you fold and roll and then work toward that opening.

Coffeepot empty? Sleep on what we have discussed. And be sure your checkbook shows a good balance when you start shopping. There is no best tent for everybody and every use, but there is a best tent for you. Pay as much as you can afford, but no more than you need. Then give it hard use and good care, and your best tent will outlast your car, your sleeping bags and your charcoal grill. It may outlive all your camping gear except the cast-iron skillet and the gasoline lantern.

Outdoor Photography
by Sid Latham

The most difficult decision facing the outdoorsman photographer in the purchase of a new camera concerns weight. Price, of course, will enter into consideration, but with hefty packs, sleeping bags, provisions and perhaps a tent, heft and bulk can be a problem.

Let's consider what is required for the backpacker who wants to tote everything plus a means of recording a trip. The camera should be compact in size and tough enough to survive under fairly rough conditions. After he has learned the basics of how to take pictures, the photographer may also demand a camera that will allow him to change lenses, use filters, and attach a small electronic flash or even a cable release to trip the shutter gently.

There are some interesting small cameras available that are both lightweight and inexpensive. The most compact are those taking the popular 110-size film. A plethora of these pocket-sized wonders are on the market, ranging in price from $15 to well over $300. Minolta has a zoom SLR (single-lens reflex) that ranges from 25 to 50 millimeters, has automatic exposure control, takes a flash and weighs 11 ounces. Rollie, another top-quality 110, has a fast f2.8 lens. Remember, however, that the less you pay the less you get. In considering any 110 camera these are some guidelines to keep in mind: A fast shutter speed is essential to eliminate movement when taking pictures, and the less expensive and simpler cameras usually have only one speed for both daylight and flash exposure. The better cameras, and these run upward to $70, provide a relatively wide range of shutter speeds but have fairly slow lenses. Only when the buyer is willing to spend at least $100 will he find the combination of lens speed and sufficiently high shutter speeds needed to enable the equipment to handle most picture-taking situations.

There are many ecology-minded cameramen who don't mind trekking about with tons of equipment; many notable outdoor pictures by Weston were made with an 8 by 10 view camera on a bulky tripod. I won't deny that a larger negative will yield magnificent detail, but with modern film, correct exposure and precise processing, many smaller-sized negatives will deliver pictures that keep the cameraman happy. Many photographers refuse to go below 35-millimeter, and the new Minox 35EL could easily satisfy many campers. This isn't the chewing-gum-pack size Minox so popular in spy films, but one slightly larger. It takes

Camp scene improved with the use of two flashbulbs. The camera is on a tripod, one bulb set off to the left and the other inside the tent triggered by photo-eye.

a full-frame 35-millimeter negative and has a fairly fast f2.8 35mm wide-angle lens. The camera is an aperture-preferred auto-exposure camera, which means that the user sets the lens opening and the shutter does the rest. As to size, it has roughly the configuration of a pack of king-size cigarettes and fits comfortably in the pocket. The fact that it weighs only 7 ounces is much in its favor. The price is about $185.

Most aspiring photographers no sooner run a half-dozen rolls of film through their cameras before they start poring over equipment catalogs and dreaming of additional lenses. Unfortunately, neither 110's nor Minoxes will accept other lenses. For those who require more sophisticated equipment with a variety of lenses to handle any situation, the 35-millimeter camera is still the best. No one lugging a small 35-millimeter with a couple of lenses gets off easy either in weight or cost, but for the photographer who wants results this is the only way to go.

Of all the 35-millimeter cameras on today's market, the Olympus OM-1MD (motor drive) is perhaps the smallest and lightest. It offers a wide range of lenses that are tiny compared to some and are famed for their sharpness. An Olympus body costs about $185, and a choice of additional lenses can then be made.

There are three lenses that should be in everyone's pack: a wide-angle, a macro for closeups of trout flies, autumn leaves and flowers, and a telephoto. The most common use of a wide-angle is to permit pictures in situations where it's impossible to cut the sides of a tent or knock out cabin walls. Conversely, once the user has become experienced with a wide-angle, this lens can be better used for unusual vision or exaggerated foregrounds. How wide is wide? Modern wide-angles range from 15 millimeters through 35 millimeters. Care must be taken with the super-wides—15, 16, 18 or 20 millimeters—since they distort and distend, giving a falsified perspective. Used with care they will deliver unusual and dramatic pictures.

Barbary sheep in New Mexico driven across the rocks into camera range by a horseman. Motorized Olympus with Vivitar Series 1 Zoom. Ilford FP4 film.

Perhaps the most popular, used by many professionals as a normal lens, is the 35-millimeter wide-angle. It is wide enough to give sweeping vistas of mountains, a group of friends around the campfire and even a picture of a friend fighting a fish taken with both fisherman and photographer in the close confines of a canoe. Perhaps the shortest wide-angle that should be considered by the novice is the 24-millimeter, with the ultra wides regarded as special-purpose lenses.

There is a combination of two lenses in one which will save a bit of money and even some weight in your pack. The macro zooms give telephoto ranges and, with a twist of the lens, permit reasonably tight closeups. These are a fairly recent development in which the focal length is continuously variable across predetermined ranges. When first introduced, they ran from slightly above normal (70 to 205 millimeters); and now they are available from wide-angle (35 millimeters) to medium tele (85 millimeters) and even longer.

One advantage of any zoom to the backpacker is that one lens will give the range of several without crowding the pack with a lot of lenses. Offsetting this are two other factors; despite remarkable improvements in design and manufacture, few zooms match the quality of a single fixed-focus lens, and the zooms are still relatively heavy. However, many of these modern lenses are marvels of design ingenuity, deliver excellent enlargements and permit satisfactory projection of 35-millimeter color transparencies.

There is always a lot of pleasure in working with a zoom. Precise cropping of the picture is one great advantage, and a zoom will cut down some bulk in packing. The most interesting of them is the 70-210 Vivitar Series 1 Macro Zoom. While the name is a mouthful, this is a lens that gives a fairly good tele-range with the added advantage of moving in close to one-half life size. But what about the nature photographers who want to come in close to game? Let's clarify telephotos. They can be classed as medium long, 85 to 135 millimeters, 180 to 500, and some really Big Berthas, 1000 and up. The basic reason for a telephoto lens is to make a bigger image of a distant subject. The advantages of such long-range lenses in photographing sports, nature or dangerous action (wild game, for example) are obvious. The medium-long teles are favored for portraits by many photographers, since they give a more pleasing perspective.

As with all things photographic there are certain rules to bear in mind with telephotos. While the image is magnified, with subsequent increase in detail, the longer the focal length the greater the magnification but the shallower the depth of field. Many sportsmen have realized when spotting game through high-powered glasses or a 10-power telescope, both mirage and vibration are set up and even the user's heartbeat can be seen.

For the nature photographer a 200-millimeter lens should be the minimum, with perhaps more pleasing results obtained with a 300. Something longer might be nice to have but is not really necessary except for photographing Dall's sheep in Alaska.

Tele-extenders provide another way of reaching out—for example, a 135-millimeter lens plus a 2X extender becomes a 270. These are supplemental lenses that effectively double, or even triple, the focal

Hunters scouting game at the YO Ranch in Texas. Olympus camera with 24-millimeter wide angle lens and red filter. Ilford FP4 film.

The high country of Wyoming offers spectacular foreground vistas. Hasselblad camera and Tri-X film with 80-millimeter lens.

length of a given lens. There are, however, disadvantages about which the user should be cautioned. Tele-extenders will never deliver as sharp a picture as a lens of a given focal length, and they have a light loss of at least two stops in the lens. This isn't important in the bright altitudes of mountains, in snow or in brilliant beach scenes where the reflected light is very great, but in dim light in the woods tele-extenders won't satisfy the discriminating user. If the camera-

man appreciates that sharpness will suffer and effective apertures will be extremely small, the investment of about $30 may be worthwhile.

Film is something that few amateurs think about. Not so the professional, since there are black-and-white and color films suited for practically every photographic purpose. In my opinion the best black-and-white film is Ilford FP4, an English film of wonderful latitude with a comfortable speed rating of

A macro lens allows such closeups as this wood spider. Olympus camera with 50 macro and Ilford FP4 film.

Corsican ram pictured with a 500-millimeter mirror-reflex lens on Ilford FP4 film. The small doughnut effect is typical of this kind of lens.

Bone fishing at Cat Cay in the Bahamas. Olympus camera with 24-millimeter wide-angle lens, Ilford FP4 film and medium yellow filter.

125 ASA. It is a medium-fast film of full tonal range and should be considered for most outdoor shooting. Kodak's Tri-X is the fast film to use in dim light, deep in the woods or when it's raining or overcast. Tri-X will make pictures around the campfire possible and if the camera is braced will even permit pictures by candlelight.

Color films are popular, and transparency material for projection gives the best results. Kodachrome 64, Ektachrome X and, when the light is bad, High Speed Ektachrome with a rating of 160 ASA are best.

Filters are usually one camera accessory that often frightens photo fans. If we ignore all except those that will be a help we can eliminate hundreds of special filters that have nothing to do with outdoor photography. Let's consider filters for black-and-white film first. Most of us have photographed deep, fluffy clouds and then found when the pictures came back that the sky was clear. What happened? No filter is what happened. A deep yellow, deep red or even an orange would have given a dramatic effect to that picture that looked so great through the camera. Don't let

Two chums in a hurry. Olympus with 500-millimeter mirror lens and Ilford FP4 film.

filter factors scare you either. With a camera that meters through the lens, simply put the filter on and forget it. For color, a Skylight will help eliminate the blue haze and has no filter factor at all. Just place it over the lens and shoot. One plus is that a filter will protect expensive lenses from branches snapping back or rain drops falling. One filter that can be used with both types of film is the Polaroid. It will darken skies, emphasize clouds, eliminate many reflections and, in color, give an unbelievably rich saturation.

With all the weight a backpacker hauls about, taking a tripod may seem excessive, yet some sturdy method of anchoring a camera, especially with a long lens, is necessary. Many nature photographers allow at least 4 pounds for a solid tripod. If you don't want to carry one, C clamps that will fasten to a small tree or fence and bean bags on which to rest the lens are almost as good. Even a padded jacket atop a tree stump will give fairly solid support, and leaning against a tree or crouching on rocks will help to steady a camera. With a long lens a cable release is a great aid in tripping the shutter gently.

Packing fragile photographic equipment, particularly if your trip includes rock climbing, requires good protection for cameras and lenses. Sima Products recently introduced the Airshield Pouch. This is made of tough material that inflates with a few puffs of air and stores flat when not in use. The pouches come in three sizes to take almost any length of lens and are well worth the price of $0.95 to $5.95 to protect valuable lenses and cameras. There is even an 8 by 10 size that will hold a miniature tape recorder, light meters and all the other breakables that always seem to be present on an outdoor trip.

As for learning to take better pictures, the best advice is to expose film. Professionals constantly expend film, move about, change lenses and constantly seek that one fraction of a second that will give the picture they are looking for. In relation to the cost of any journey, overseas or over the hill, film is cheap and it must be exposed if a well-documented record is wanted. When enough pictures are taken and the junk ruthlessly edited out and tossed in the wastebasket, then, and only then, will there be progress toward taking better pictures of a once-in-a-lifetime trip.

Pick a Pack and Pack It

by Jim Bashline

During my army basic training days I was convinced that the standard G. I. pack had been designed by the enemy. It didn't fit anyone, jogged along uncomfortably with each step and soaked up water like a sponge. The military rucksack that was supposedly designed for the alpine troopers was a nearly equal abomination. That torture device featured a steel frame that weighed over 8 pounds, and the raw canvas straps converted shoulders into hamburger after a mile of hiking. In addition to that, it hung much too low on the back to allow the shoulders and hips a supporting advantage. As a result, on discharge day most of the soldiers I knew were convinced that they would never try backpacking for pleasure. A growing population with a need for rediscovering the outdoors has changed all that. Thank goodness, the backpacking equipment of today is far better.

Of course, some people, through the nature of their work or natural inclinations, have been backpacking for many years. Professional guides, surveyors, trappers and self-styled mountain men do it every day. They are not backpacking for pleasure; they do it because their livelihood depends on it. Drawing on their expertise, the new crop of backpacking manufacturers that has sprung up during the past fifteen years has put together a most amazing selection of lightweight gear. Some of the material available today would have astounded early explorers and casual campers. Rip-stop nylon, freeze-dried foods and dependable stoves that weigh ounces rather than pounds are space-age miracles that allow for extended outdoor treks without double hernias.

Next to comfortable, well-constructed hiking shoes, a pack is the most important item a backpacker must consider. Some will say the sleeping bag comes next but some hikers during warm months forego the bag altogether and rough it out on the ground. I'll take the bag, however, and for that reason, my pack preferences lean toward those that will accommodate a rolled-up bag.

Visiting a shop that caters to backpackers can be a frightening experience for the novice hiker. The plethora of goodies is both attractive and awesome. Making the right selection can spell the difference between a pleasant outing and a trip through an obstacle course. First off, the very best thing to do is to enlist the services of a friend or a friend of a friend who has done some serious walking. While some stores

The wide variety of packs available today makes selection difficult for the novice.
Try on as many as you can and walk around a bit.

employ knowledgeable salespeople who can advise without high pressuring, this is not generally the case. The experienced hiker knows in one minute whether the sales clerk knows the merchandise. The novice can't be sure, so rule number one is: make friends with an experienced backpacker.

Most manufacturers who intend to stay in the backpacking business make two or three frame sizes or market one that is adjustable for body size and configuration. Try as many different packs as possible. There is wide variation in frame design. The human figure is even more variable, but through sampling you'll find one that feels right. The best way to try a pack is out on the trail, but most dealers are not willing to give you one on a loan basis. They can't be blamed for that, but nothing prevents the shopper from trying on several in the store and walking up and down the aisles. You can even put something in the pack to suggest the heft of what you'll be carrying. You may feel foolish doing this, but after all it's you who will be out there sweating and climbing—not the salesperson. In stores that know their customers no one will laugh at you for sampling the goods. Be sure to wear the shoes you will be actually hiking in. The balance of a pack will change depending on the footgear worn. A small point but worth considering.

As with all outdoor gear, look at the workmanship carefully. Some very flimsy packs are on the market today, but you can spot them in a minute. The seams are poorly sewn and the fabric is paperthin. If the packframe is welded, check the joints for pinholes and sloppy alignment. If the frame is joined with plastic or metal tees, the assembly will be crooked and wobbly. The webbing and shoulder straps on cut-rate packs are narrow and ragged.

The nylon zippers found on many packs today are very popular. They won't freeze up in cold weather. I don't think they'll hold up as long as a good metal zipper, but they won't rust. On the other hand, a metal zipper won't either if it is given a shot of WD-40 once in a while. How the zipper is sewn to the material is more important than the zipper itself. With a haphazard alignment, the zipper won't work regardless of its quality.

The fewer screws, nuts and bolts that are used to hold a packframe together the longer it will last. Expect to pay at least $40 for a quality packframe, but price isn't always a good guideline. The material used for most packs these days is rip-stop nylon or another similar synthetic. It won't rot and can be treated to make it reasonably water resistant. Not waterproof, mind you, but water resistant—there is a whale of a difference. For complete waterproofing, use

A simple emergency kit for backpackers can be assembled for less than $2.

an ample poncho or tarpaulin that will cover both you and the pack in a storm. You may want to consider a pack that has one waterproof compartment. Several manufacturers make such a pack. It is lined with nonporous material, such as rubber or an acceptable synthetic. To line a pack completely with sheet rubber would add unnecessary weight, and that's what we're trying to avoid.

Without getting into brand names (and there are two dozen excellent packs on the market), it's safe to say that the most popular style of pack is one that offers a large center compartment, four or more side pouches with strap fasteners and a vacant spot on the bottom of the frame for sleeping bag or bedroll. There are minor variations on this theme, but this is the sort of pack you'll see most often. The most notable exception is the long rectangular bag that features four horizontal zippers dividing the pack into a quartet of more or less equal compartments. The bottom one of these is slightly larger, to contain a down or fiberfill sleeping bag.

Shoulder straps should be wide and comfortable with foam pads to ease the strain on the shoulders. A belly band is a useful addition, although some hikers don't like them. You'll have to be the judge of that, but I find them a great help on rough hilly terrain. The name "belly band" is not exactly right since the strap should ride just above the hip bones. For anatomical reasons, a belly band should ride lower on most female torsos than on a male's. These bands are padded so that your hips as well as your shoulders help support the weight of the pack.

There used to be an unwritten law that required all camping gear to be brown or olive-drab in color.

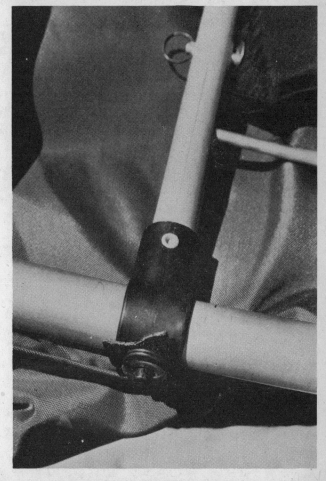

Construction techniques are varied too. Most types are acceptable but watch out for obvious imperfections.

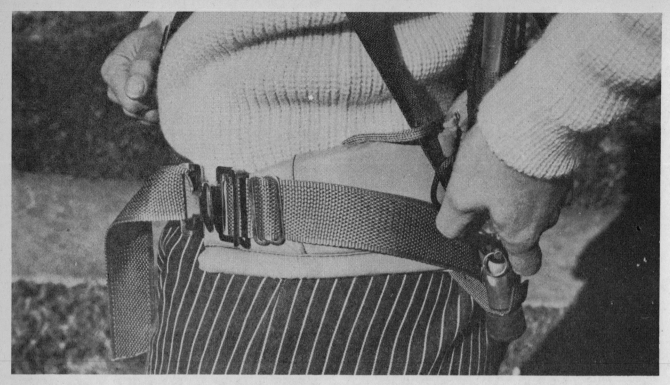

A belly band should ride just above the hips for all-day comfort.

Two different styles of belly bands. A wide one is better for long-distance traveling.

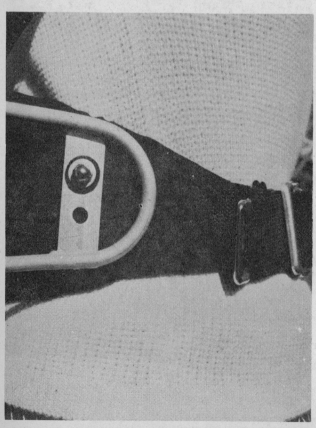

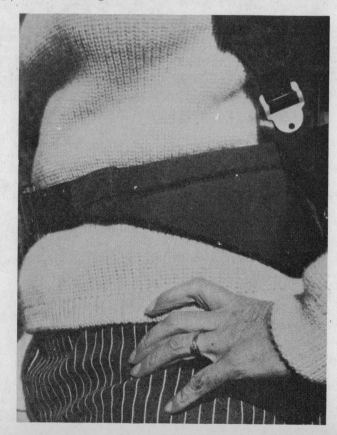

Happily this is not the case today. Camping equipment and particularly backpacks come in every imaginable shade from pale blue to hot orange, and that's good. Unless you are planning an assault on an enemy fort, it's an advantage to have a gaily colored pack. In case of an accident you'll be easier to find, and, besides, bright colors are spirit-lifting.

Now that you've decided on a pack, what should you put in it and how? I've seen a hundred lists of what to put in a pack and while a few items are universal, the selection becomes optional after tent, sleeping bag, extra socks and first-aid kit are mentioned. Not counting food and toiletries, my backpack always contains these things:

  Foam shorty pad for more comfortable sleeping
  First-aid kit
  Needle and thread (heavy duty nylon spool)
  Boy Scout mess kit
  Box of fish hooks and flies
  Pack fishing rod (tied on outside)
  Single burner propane or alcohol stove
  Down vest
  Extra shirt and pants
  Two extra pairs of socks

A belt knife and canteen can be carried on the hip, but I usually carry water in a wide-mouthed plastic jar in the pack. I don't like to have the canteen slapping my hip with each step.

What food to take along is a highly personal choice. But with the vast array of freeze-dried and powdered food available today, food for three days or even a week should not exceed 10 pounds.

In pounds versus bulk, the down sleeping bag is the lightest item you'll be carrying. It should be on the bottom of the packframe or stuffed in the lower compartment. Ideally, it should be available without going through and disturbing the entire pack contents. Going from the bottom of the pack up, lay in the extra clothing and the toiletries, then the food and finally the cooking gear and stove. The water bottle should be right on top. The side compartments ought to carry the extra socks, quick-energy rations like chocolate or jerky, extra film and of course maps and compass. The tent is usually tied on the top of the pack.

In general, the proper way to load a pack is to scale the weight gradually from the top to the bottom. The heaviest items should be near or above the level of your shoulders and the lightest stuff near your waist. When a pack begins to sag and bump your rump, fatigue sets in rapidly. Besides, there are really no muscles of consequence around most midsections. The larger back and shoulder muscles should carry the load and the weight should push down on them, not pull on them from the rear. The pack should be carried close to the body, but not so close that circulation is hampered. Tighten the shoulder straps to a snug position and do the same with the belly band. The pack that bounces and jounces with every step will wear the novice out in half an hour.

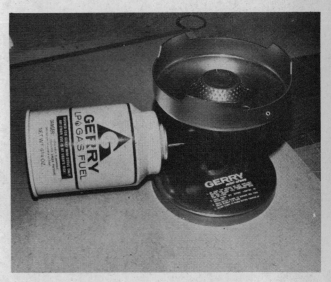

Single-burner propane stoves are ideal for lightweight backpackers, being easy to start and quick to heat. Be sure to carry the empty container out of the woods.

After five minutes of walking you'll quickly discover whether items need adjusting. If the stove or water can is rolling around or if the pack is heavily canted to one side, stop immediately and readjust. On the first day of the hike the temptation to keep on walking is great, but overcome it! Three minutes of making everything lie right will add to the trip's long-term pleasure.

While shoes are very important to the hiker, almost everyone has had experience in buying shoes. Either they fit or they don't. Packs are an entirely different matter. Few of us have much experience in carrying things on our back. Our ancestors did it, but modern living has created a bunch of poorly conditioned deltoid muscles. Don't try to lash on a new pack, fill it with a 60-pound load and take off for Mountain Misery. You ain't gonna make it! Forget about the pros lugging 70-pound packs up the side of K-2 and Canadian guides hauling 100 tons of moose meat on a tump line around their forehead. I can't do it on a three-day hike and neither can you. It takes years of hard hiking to develop the finely honed muscles required for such feats.

Carrying the backpack high on the shoulders will reduce fatigue. If it hangs too low, the back muscles will be pulled backward instead of supporting the weight in an upright position.

A well-packed pack.

An average pack for the novice backpacker should weigh no more than 35 pounds and 25 pounds would be better. That's for man or woman. This amount can be increased gradually with conditioning, but don't rush into it. If this year marks your first wilderness adventure, why not try carrying a light pack to and from the office everyday or wearing one while mowing the lawn or doing housework? Sure, the neighbors will think you've flipped your lid, but what of it? You'll be in far better shape when the time comes for the real thing.

The same holds for your hiking shoes. Buy a pair that fits well with a pair of woolen socks and wear them for at least a month before you hit the woods. Hiking shoes are built more ruggedly than those intended for street use and require a lot more break-in time. Mow the lawn in them. Wear them to market. Wear them anywhere, but wear them. It's the mark of a greenhorn to show up in the woods sporting a brand-new pair of shoes.

But in spite of my advice or the advice of others, the first-timer will invariably carry too many superfluous items on a hiking trip. Be as ruthless as you can. Get that pack weight down to 30 or 25 pounds if possible. And after you have a half-dozen trips under your belt, dump the entire pack contents out onto the kitchen floor. The items you didn't use at all (with the exception of the first-aid kit) should be tucked away— forever. Those that you used once should also be thrown away. The things that you used twice or more should be considered (but probably tossed away as well). Repack only the items you used at least once a day.

Warning: It will take at least 20 years of backpacking before you have the courage to do this. I still carry a strange little shaving mirror that sits on three folding legs. I don't need it, but I like it. I'll toss it away—next year.

Hiking scenes. Getting there is half if not most of the fun in backpacking. A little bit of an ordeal makes it more worth the effort.

Meals along the Trail
by Sheila Link

Backpackers seem to be sharply divided into two camps when it comes to meals along the trail.

The first, or "traditionalist," group prefers to eat meals as similar as possible to those they have at home. Their breakfasts run to orange juice, bacon and eggs or pancakes and sausages, with toast and coffee. Lunches generally begin with hot soup, progress to sandwiches and lemonade and finish with fruit and cookies. Dinners, though, are the main meal, and no effort is spared in packing and preparing. Steaks, either fresh or frozen, mashed potatoes, a green vegetable, followed by a dessert such as cherry cobbler, with coffee or tea—this is the sort of menu typical of the gourmet-type backpacker.

At the other extreme is the modern "go-light fanatic." Weighing every item on a postal scale before he packs it, this fellow has got weight reduction down to a science. And one of the best ways he has found to decrease pack weight is to modify his eating habits.

If you're willing to eat cold foods, it's unnecessary to carry either a stove or cooking pots. This represents a considerable saving in weight, but some people of the go-light persuasion go even further than simply eating cold foods. They make up highly nutritious food bars combining such ingredients as granola, diced fruits, honey, powdered milk, peanut butter and raw eggs. They eat one or more of these accompanied by a powdered drink mix for every meal.

Such a spartan menu doesn't have wide popular appeal, but it does offer several advantages. First, it curtails the need for elaborate meal planning and packing. Second, it reduces pack weight. Third, it eliminates meal preparation, saving time and energy. Fourth, there's no concern over having inclement weather interfere with meal preparation or dining. You may eat as you hike, as you watch a sunset or inside the warmth of your sleeping bag, with the happy knowledge that there will be no dishes to wash afterward.

Whether you opt for hearty, varied meals or a simple diet, there is much to be said for both positions. Traditionalists savor the sensual, social and psychological pleasures of "smoothing it," as opposed to roughing it. They probably enjoy the camping part of backpacking more than the hiking. Those who prefer lengthy or strenuous hiking will tend to join the "go-light" brigade and reserve their gustatory pleasures for their return to town.

The author preparing a camp meal.

Fortunately, it's not necessary to subscribe to either one of these extreme philosophies. One of the great attractions of backpacking is that there are almost no absolutes. The right way is your way—at least for you.

It is true, of course, that weight is a prime consideration in selecting the equipment and supplies you'll carry on your back. Unless you're either a big, muscular fellow in top condition or a masochist, you'll enjoy any hike far more with a light pack than with one that's noticeably heavy.

Happily, manufacturers of stoves, cooking gear and specialized foods have been working effectively to create quality lightweight items. By choosing carefully, we can enjoy tasty trail meals that are quite simple to prepare and offer a nutritious, varied and inexpensive diet.

Let's talk first about stoves. Since backpacking has become such an astonishingly popular activity, open fires are no longer acceptable in most areas. A tiny cookstove, therefore, is usually required.

The new stoves range in weight, style and price from a model called an Esbit, which is about the size of a pack of cigarettes, burns solid fuel tablets and costs $3.50, to an elaborate butane stove with its own built-in lighter. This one weights 28 ounces (with fuel) and costs $22.50. Between these two is an endless variety of miniature stoves which burn butane, solid fuel, alcohol or white gas. The choice is your own, but before you buy you should consider how, where and when you'll be using your backpacking stove. The little fuel-tablet stoves are great for boiling a cup of water for instant coffee or heating a can of soup. They're frustratingly inadequate for cooking anything more time-consuming or elaborate than bacon and eggs.

Butane-fueled stoves are a delight to use. They do not require priming or pumping, as do most alcohol and white-gas models. But butane is nearly worthless in cold weather because it won't vaporize, and in high altitudes, which require longer cooking times, the fuel in the little butane tanks is not sufficient for more than a couple of days.

In my opinion, the proper way to choose a stove is first to decide which fuel you prefer; then select a stove that uses that fuel.

In addition to a stove, you'll need cooking pots and tools. A nested aluminum kit is the best bet here. Some, like the Sigg, are of excellent design and quality. Light weight is important, but don't sacrifice sturdiness. You need a firm, moderately thick pan bottom if you are not to burn the food, and more than one hungry camper has lost a meal into the dirt or the fire when the handle of a cheap utensil bent or broke. Pots from home can be used, but they're usually quite bulky or have protruding handles that don't pack well.

Elaborate kitchen tools aren't necessary, but one gadget that is a real gem for camp cooking is a pair of tongs. You can use it to turn bacon or a steak, to lift or move pots and to serve food, to mention only a few of

Stoves for backpackers. *Back row:* **Svea 123-R, Primus Ranger; Alpin butane stove.** *Center row:* **tiny solid-fuel Esbit stove.** *Front row:* **Optimus 8-R; two D-Boone solid-fuel stoves; can of fuel tablets.**

its uses.

If you're going to hike in a wilderness area where there's lots of firewood available and ground fires are permitted, you may want to add an aluminum reflector oven to your kit. This nifty appliance will enable you to bake fresh breads or cakes and pies beside your campfire, adding zest to your meals and giving both your spirits and your ego a real boost.

Now for the food itself. If you want to go the simple, noncooking route, there are two ways. The first is to make up nutritious food bars, add a bunch of drink-mix packets, and let it go at that. Or, if you want more variety in your meals, here's a simple menu I've used for two-day hikes.

First-Day Lunch
crackers with cheese and salami
handful of sunflower seeds mixed with raisins and nuts
iced tea mix, hard candies

First-Day Dinner
half of a small cooked chicken, boned and wrapped in aluminum foil
tossed green salad with celery and carrot sticks, packed in covered plastic container
salad dressing packed in pharmacist's small plastic vial, to be added to greens when dinner is served
hard roll, buttered and wrapped in aluminum foil

Pots and pans for trail cooking. *Upper corners, left,* bottom, and, *right,* top of pot into which Coleman one-burner gasoline stove fits. *Top center:* small pot with wrap-around handle. *Center:* Sierra Club steel cup. *Right:* G.I. cup/pot. *Left:* Palco Cook Kit—pot, fry pan, handle, plastic cup. *Front center:* plastic plate; eating utensils. Note nylon sacks in which pots are packed to keep packsack clean.

hot tea or coffee
canned fruit or pudding, individual size

Second-Day Breakfast
cup of Tang orange drink
dried apricots and dates
buttered sweet roll
hot chocolate

Second-Day Lunch
Crunchy Granola bars (2)
tiny box of raisins
lemonade mix, hard candies

With this menu it's unnecessary to carry cooking pots. I heat water for my coffee, tea or cocoa in my Sierra Club steel cup, either over a tiny fire or on a little Esbit stove. If I have a fire I can warm the chicken and dinner roll near the coals, which is why they're foil-wrapped, but they can be eaten cold.

For an overnight hike, this is a tasty, well-balanced meal plan and the foods carried aren't heavy. Without refrigeration, however, fresh foods are practical only for such short trips. You can easily plan similar meals using the basic menu as a guide.

A selection of freeze-dried foods now available in sporting goods stores.

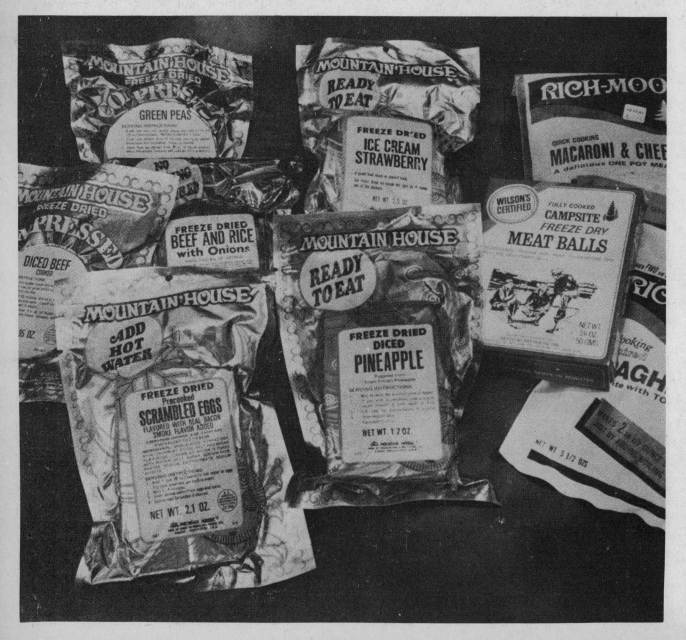

Supermarket shelves feature a wide variety of dehydrated and dry foods that are tasty, nourishing, inexpensive and very practical for backpacking.

You'll find an increasing variety of dehydrated foods on supermarket shelves and a wide choice of freeze-dried foods at better sporting goods stores. There's no satisfactory way to rate individual dishes. One person may rave about a certain brand of chicken stew, while another may find the same dish nearly inedible.

If cost is a consideration, shop the supermarkets; dehydrated foods are less expensive than freeze-dried items. Some canned goods are also worth considering, such as sardines, individual-sized cans of beans, puddings or fruit.

To select foods for a backpacking trip, read the labels carefully. Things to look for include cooking time required, amount of water needed and whether other ingredients are necessary. Some foods may be prepared right in their own packaging, which eliminates "pot walloping" and in some instances even dish washing.

A notable recent innovation is the *compressed* freeze-dried foods packaged by Mountain House, one of the top makers of trail foods. Items such as shrimp Creole, green peas, diced beef and chicken stew can be purchased in this form. According to the ads, the big advantage is reduced bulk. I can attest, however, that an even greater attraction is the excellent quality of these compressed foods. Some really are "as good as fresh."

Remember that freeze-dried and dehydrated foods must be reconstituted with water. If you expect water to be scarce along the trail, plan your menu accordingly.

The most practical, convenient way to carry your trail meals is to package everything needed for each meal in individual, labeled packets. For example, for your first trail breakfast, suppose the menu is powdered orange drink, dried apricots and raisins, oatmeal with powdered milk, and hot chocolate. Measure the required amount of powdered juice into a tiny plastic bottle such as a pill bottle. Put the apricots and raisins into a plastic sandwich bag. Use an individual packet (or two) of instant oatmeal. Put powdered milk and sugar, if desired, into another tiny plastic bottle. Use individual one-cup packets of hot chocolate. Place all these packages in a plastic bag, seal it and mark it "Breakfast #1."

Do the same with each meal, premeasuring such ingredients as sugar, instant coffee, butter (actually, margarine keeps fresher longer), salt and pepper, and bread.

When it's time for a meal you don't have to burrow through your pack looking for various items. Simply pull out the appropriate marked packet and you're ready to prepare a complete meal. The time spent at home preparing these meal packets is well worthwhile for the saving in time and frustration on the trail.

Because I prepackage all my trail meals in this way, I've become a scavenger, hoarding the tiny packets of salt and pepper, ketchup, mustard and sugar that are placed on airline trays and at fast-food chains. They are perfect for backpacking.

If you enjoy fussing over a meal even on the trail and have added a reflector oven to your outfit, pack some Bisquick, or a sourdough starter and flour, for some fresh-baked goodies in camp. Here's a good recipe for bannock, the traditional outdoorsman's bread.

The bannock's done, and the author removes it from her lightweight reflector oven.

CAMPER'S & BACKPACKER'S BIBLE

Bannock

1 cup Bisquick
  (or mix 1 cup flour, 1 teaspoon baking powder,
  ¼ teaspoon salt)
2 tablespoons oil

Add the oil and water to the Bisquick or flour mix. Form the dough into a ball, then flatten it to about a 1-inch-thick loaf. Place in a greased pan and bake slowly either in a reflector oven or a in a heavy pan tilted toward the fire. Bake until the crust is golden brown and the inside is dry. If possible, eat while hot.

If the go-light style appeals to you, here are a couple of recipes for nutritious food bars.

Homemade Fruit Pemmican Bars

1 pound dried dates
1 cup mixed nuts, chopped
4 ounces dried apricots
4 ounces pitted prunes
4 ounces raisins
4 ounces candied pineapple
4 tablespoons grated coconut

Chop the fruits, stir all ingredients together, then run the entire mixture through a meat grinder, using the coarse setting. Dust a cookie sheet liberally with confectioner's sugar and press the mixture onto it, smoothing with a spatula or similar tool to make a flat, solid, even "cake." Cut into bars, dust individually with powdered sugar, wrap in foil and set aside for a few weeks to dry. These will keep for a year without refrigeration and make excellent trail food.

Grain and Fruit Bars

2 cups whole wheat flour
½ cup wheat germ
½ cup powdered milk
1 teaspoon salt
1 cup soy flour (full fat)
1 cup chopped apricots
1 cup chopped dates
¼ cup dried brewer's yeast
4 large eggs
½ cup molasses
½ cup vegetable oil
1 teaspoon vanilla extract

Mix all ingredients thoroughly, then spread evenly on two 8-by 11-inch cookie sheets. Bake 2½ hours in a 225-degree oven. Turn oven heat off, but leave cakes in the oven until cool. Cut into bars, wrap individually in foil and store for trail use. Serve with powdered Gatorade or a powdered malted-milk mix for a surprisingly flavorsome and very nutritious meal.

Favorite Lunch or Snack Mix

Mix sunflower seeds, pumpkin seeds, raisins, chopped dried apricots and a variety of chopped or whole nuts in almost any ratio that pleases you. Carry in plastic sandwich bags. Eat with powdered lemonade mix, hot tea or any drink you prefer.

Backpacking is great fun, but remember that, like armies, hikers travel on their stomachs. Good trail meals are very important.

Public and Semi-Public Camping

by William M. Vogt

Years ago, two college buddies and I used to make annual pilgrimages from the Midwest to Oregon, where we would work during the summer. Camping along the way in national parks, municipal parks, state campgrounds and even a bandshell at the edge of a town in Idaho, we found that there also are a great many "semi-public" campgrounds operated by utilities, big land-owning commercial interests and a variety of local organizations.

That kind of traveling wasn't camping in the real sense; it was more like a series of one-night stands. Crowded campgrounds are now the rule, and it's no longer a simple matter of pulling off the road and setting up shelter.

Consider the following figures: Visitor days (in the national parks) have soared from 71 million in the late 1950's to a present annual rate of more than 200 million visitor days. The U.S. Forest Service says that more than twice as many campers use its campgrounds as did 15 years ago. The U.S. Army Corps of Engineers reports that over the past 20 years recreational use of its areas has increased seventeenfold.

Where does this leave the camper? It simply means that camping trips require more planning than they used to. Sometimes it's merely a matter of timing the trip so it takes place during off-peak months, weeks or days; it may mean using a less popular area as a base; or it could involve making advance reservations. It will almost certainly entail some letter writing and a small investment in a modest collection of booklets, brochures and maps, some of which are listed at the end of this article.

Gary Everhardt, director of the National Park Service, might as well have been speaking for all public agencies—state, local and private—when he said: "The continuing popularity of the parks makes advance-vacation planning more important than ever. The National Park Service welcomes every visitor, but those who come prepared will get a lot more out of their visit and avoid a lot of headaches, too."

National Parks. It is just as well to start with the national parks, where many of the headaches have been in recent years. The seriousness of the situation is reflected in cutbacks of such traditional services as guided nature walks, picnic areas, operating hours and trail and road maintenance. Despite this, the national parks continue to offer some of the finest camping experiences in the world.

Fees. Entrance fees to national parks are nominal, ranging from one to three dollars per private vehicle. If you're 62 or older, you can get a Golden Age Passport that admits you and your family past the gate. Once inside you will be charged an additional one to four dollars per night camping fee. (Golden Age Passport holders and their companions get a 50-percent discount at non-concessionaire operated facilities.)

Regulations. Although most individual campsites are available on a first-come first-served basis, in recent years some parks within the system have been experimenting with advance mail-in reservations. Check with the National Park Service or the headquarters of individual parks. Some parks require fire permits for primitive camping, and there are often permanent or temporary bans on open fires due to dry conditions. Thirty-nine National Park Service areas require permits for back-country camping, and more are expected to be added in the future. A number of areas, including Big Bend National Park in Texas Grand Canyon in Arizona and Grand Teton in Wyoming require permits for white-water float trips. Back-country and float-trip permits are free but are necessary to prevent campers from destroying the landscape by sheer weight of numbers.

National Forests and Grasslands. The U.S. Forest Service administers nearly 5000 campgrounds, ranging from concessionaire-operated sites with trailer hookups and all the trimmings to primitive campsites along back-country trails. Some campgrounds use a "pack it in—pack it out" policy whereby campers are

Isle Royal National Park in Minnesota is noted for its moose and other wildlife. It is accessible only by boat or float plane and offers truly outstanding back-country camping.

Shenandoah National Park (Virginia) offers backpacking as well as five developed campgrounds. Scenic overlooks along the way offer magnificent panorama of the oldest mountains in the U.S.

expected to carry out their own trash.

Fees. Fees at more highly developed areas range from one to four dollars per day for all occupants of one noncommercial vehicle. As with the national parks, the Golden Age Passport entitles campers over age 62 and their companions to a 50-percent discount.

Regulations. Most campsites are available on a first-come first-served basis, although some of the most frequently used campgrounds are beginning to require reservations. Permits are required for use of some back-country areas.

Unlike national parks, national forests are generally open to hunting. A proper license is required.

Corps of Engineers Areas. The U.S. Army Corps of Engineers manages more than 10 million acres of land and water across the country, and its campgrounds rank among the best. During the last couple of years, the Corps has implemented a shoreland management plan designed to offer more to visitors. Some of the Corps' water projects had become ringed with leased dock sites and other private developments that effectively excluded the general public. Under the new system, many of these sites are being phased out and the surrounding areas zoned for various uses, including camping.

Fees. The Corps has just begun charging fees to campers. During 1976, 521 family camping areas at 138 projects in 29 states initiated fees ranging from $1 to $3.50 per day, with an additional 50 cents for areas providing electrical hookups. At every recreational area where camping fees are charged, at least one free camping area is provided—usually less well developed than the fee areas. The Golden Age Passport applies here, too.

Other Public Areas. Other federal agencies offering recreational facilities include Bureau of Reclamation, Bureau of Land Management and U.S. Fish and Wildlife Service. Each of these agencies can send you descriptive material, a listing of their field offices and maps in some instances.

Don't overlook state and local campgrounds. Write to state fish and game or conservation agencies. Some states also have separate tourism departments that are part of a highway department or industrial development commission. Many states publish an official magazine—something on the order of *Outdoor Indiana, Virginia Wildlife* or the *New York Conservationist*. Back issues usually contain a wealth of information about public areas and campgrounds. Also, don't forget the state's chamber of commerce for information about land-owning industries that might have camping facilities open to the public.

Semi-Public Areas. As camping popularity increased, more and more people learned to avoid the crowds by turning to campgrounds of another sort—private ownership campgrounds that have many of the characteristics of publicly owned campgrounds. Such owners include utilities, wood-products concerns and other land-owning industries that maintain campgrounds as part of public-relations programs.

Many such campgrounds are available in conjunction with reservoirs and heavily forested areas that are equally as attractive as some of the government-run facilities. In the Southeast, for example, I visited a fine campground operated by the Philadelphia Electric Power Company. The area could accommodate 164 trailers and 54 tents; there were restrooms and hot showers, a dumping station and rowboat rentals on a 100-acre lake.

The camper should be aware, however, that on some of these areas—notably those owned by the wood-products industry—one must share the woods with a variety of other activities. Among the things one learns is that logging trucks take the outside curve on winding mountain roads. I once lost a side-view mirror from a four-wheel-drive vehicle in an encounter with a truckload of logs.

During dry periods when fire-hazard probability is high, an area might be closed to campers. It is advisable to check in before venturing onto such lands. If no one knows you are there and it becomes necessary to shut the woods down to travel, you might find yourself confronted by a locked gate, miles out in the middle of nowhere. I must plead guilty to this but it happened only once!

Other possible camping areas include county parks, municipal campgrounds and campgrounds run by church groups or civic organizations. These are some-

Backpackers in Olympic National Park. Park Service and other public agencies are leaning more and more toward encouraging use of fuel-fired campstoves rather than open fires.

times available to nonmembers for a moderate fee during periods of vacancy.

One cardinal rule is to *always* check with the owners of semi-public areas to learn regulations on reservations, open fires and closed sections, or more important, just to let them know you're there.

Getting Information. I usually begin planning a camping trip by studying a number of common service-station-variety roadmaps. Some of these go into considerable detail and may even include listings of public recreation areas. Next, most states have official highway maps available by mail from the highway department or over the counter at roadside visitors' centers. There is often more information on the back than on the map itself. Sometimes it's helpful to draw a 20-mile circle around one of the trip objectives to pinpoint potential campsites that are within easy driving distance of, say, a popular national park.

If you contact a federal-agency-run area start at the top rather than at the local office. It's just a matter of getting the big picture first. This way, it's easier to understand how a single national park, for example, fits into the broad general policies of the National Park Service. The parent agency can give you more addresses to help you narrow your search. From the National Park Service, you can learn of the individual park headquarters; from the U.S. Forest Service, regional offices; from the U.S. Army Corps of Engineers, district engineers; and so on.

Listed at the end of this article are some of the addresses and primary sources of information you will need. You can save some time by buying the publications at one of the regional government bookstores. A properly planned camping trip of any length begins months before the trip is actually taken. Incidentally, if you save these materials, you can avoid some of the preliminaries on your next trip. After a while, the planning becomes part of the game, much like a fisherman, hunter or gardener studying his catalogs and carefully mapping out his strategy for the coming season. Later, there are the rewards of having planned a trip that will be a cherished memory for years to come.

Address	Planning Aids	Address	Planning Aids
National Park Service Park Information 1013 Interior Building Washington, D.C. 20402	General information, addresses of headquarters of individual parks	Office of Information Bureau of Reclamation U.S. Department of the Interior Washington, D.C. 20402	General information about recreational opportunities on BUREC impoundments
Information Office U.S. Forest Service Department of Agriculture Washington, D.C. 20250	General information, addresses of regional offices	Public Information Office Bureau of Land Management U.S. Department of the Interior Washington, D.C. 20402	General information, addresses of district offices
Lakeside Recreation Areas Public Affairs Office Chief of Engineers U.S. Army Corps of Engineers Washington, D.C. 20314	General information, addresses of district engineers. Ask for the regional map that includes the state(s) you're interested in. The map includes written descriptions of all Corps projects, rules and regulations, and a chart showing recreational opportunities (the one for the Northeast, for example, lists 49 developed campgrounds and 36 primitive campgrounds)	Branch of Distribution U.S. Geological Survey 1C 402 National Center Reston, Virginia 22070	Standard source of topographic maps—has been trying out a new pocket-sized folding map of Mt. Rainier National Park, which may be ordered from the Survey's Denver office.
		U.S. Geological Survey P.O. Box 25286, Federal Center Denver, Colorado 80225	For maps west of Mississippi River

Check or money order must be enclosed with orders for the following publications. Specify title and stock number shown. Prices are subject to change.

U.S. Government
Printing Office
Washington, D.C. 20402

National Parks of the United States, a Map and Guide. GPO Stock Number 024-005-00546-3 (75¢)

Index of the National Park Service and Affiliated Areas. GPO Stock Number 024-005-00612-5 ($1.65)

Doorway to Adventure, Visit a Lesser Used Park. GPO Stock Number 024-005-00598-7 (70¢)

Camping in the National Park System. GPO Stock Number 024-005-00627-3 (85¢)

Winter Activities in the National Park System. GPO Stock Number 435-397-33 (50¢)

U.S. Government
Printing Office(Cont'd)

Back-Country Travel in the National Park System. GPO Stock Number 0-526-121 (70¢)

Search for Solitude. (Describes primitive and wilderness areas of the U.S. Forest Service—somewhat dated, but still useful.) GPO Stock Number 1970-371-415 (65¢)

Camping the National Forests, America's Playgrounds. GPO Stock Number 001-000-03452 (65¢)

National Forest Wilderness and Primitive Areas. GPO Stock Number 0101-00245 (20¢)

Backpacking in the National Forests. GPO Stock Number 0100-03312 (40¢)

Dinosaur National Monument (Colorado-Utah).

Setting Up a Camp Kitchen
by Sylvia Bashline

Back in 1907, Stewart Edward White in his book *Camp and Trail* allowed that "most people take into the woods too many utensils and of too heavy material. An ample outfit, judiciously selected, need take up little bulk or weight." The same holds true 70 years later. While we frequently use a car to lug our gear, overloading it is common and unnecessary.

The first ingredient for a successful camping trip is good preliminary planning. Before setting up a camp kitchen, construct a master list. This should be done a month or so before your first trip, while the whole family is stretched out on the living room floor poring over camping magazines, books, catalogs and road maps. Everyone will get a kick out of suggesting cooking equipment necessities and frivolities but the chief chef will have the final say on whether or not it goes on the list.

Naturally, every camping household will have different needs for the camping-kitchen list, depending on the number of family members and whether they camp in a tent, a camper or a plush motor home. In this article I'll concentrate on setting up a portable kitchen for a tent camper who cooks mainly on a two-burner propane stove, or a backpacker who uses a little single-burner stove.

Cooking over open fires is going out of style, especially in the populous East, for several reasons. Many campgrounds have a lack of firewood and if there is any to be bought, it is expensive. On heavily traveled hiking trails, it is esthetically offensive to keep tripping over the remains of "single meal" campfires, and on some stretches of the Appalachian Trail, a hiker passes by every 20 seconds in the summer months. Thank goodness they don't all feel the need to build a stone monument to their next meal but instead usually carry a one-burner stove.

No item, no matter how obvious, should be left out of the master list unless you want to be stuck five miles from nowhere without matches, or soap, or a knife. Start with the big basics like a camp stove and run the list all the way down to the can opener. Take several evenings to think about and add to it.

Here's a sample checklist to get you started:
Camp stove
Cooler
Dutch oven

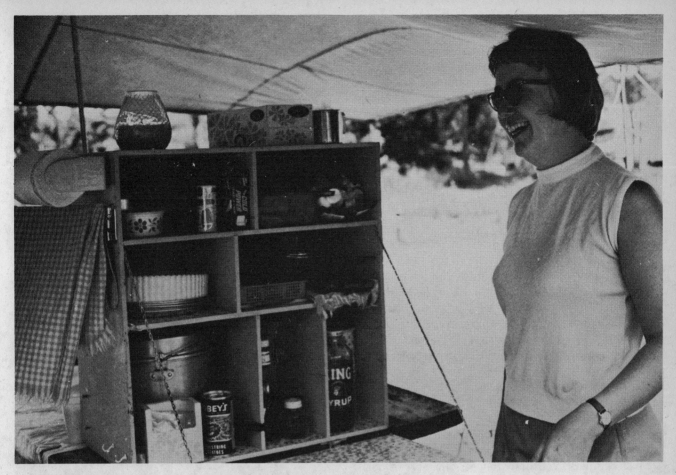

A well-designed camp kitchen. Notice the tarp over the whole area.

Grill
Asbestos gloves
Mixing bowls
Frying pan
Large kettle
Coffeepot
Knives
Measuring equipment
Potato peeler
Serving spoons
Spatula
Basic condiments
Dishcloth and towels
Eating silverware
Aluminum foil
Garbage bags
Matches
Newspapers
Napkins, plates and cups
Paper towels
Plastic bags
Scrub pads
Storage containers
Table cover
Can opener

Most camping experts believe in choosing the best-quality ice chest available. Durability is the biggest selling point of the high-priced models. Also, while using less ice, these usually will keep food cooler for a longer time than the cheap ones. The drain hole is very useful and in a pinch you can use the cooler for an extra seat. The polystyrene ones are handy but not durable and are difficult to keep clean. They are best used as an auxiliary cooler for soft drinks and the like.

I like horizonal chests better than vertical camp refrigerators, because cool air doesn't rise and you lose less of it when you open the door. Blocks of ice will last longer than ice cubes in all coolers. Many campers, on starting from home, freeze a couple of half-gallon waxed milk cartons of water or lemonade. These will cool the chest and you can drink the lemonade or water as it melts.

When packing the car for a camping trip arrange things so that you can get at the ice chest easily. This way you can take advantage of the excellent fresh produce that is often for sale along country roads in the summer. You can also fix lunches along the roadside with a minimum of effort when your cooler and portable kitchen supplies are easily reached.

At camp, try to concentrate your kitchen facilities under a canopy that ideally is connected with your tent or camper and also covers the picnic table. For the cook's peace of mind, a king-sized tarp is worth the investment to shield the kitchen site from wind, rain, assorted droppings from above and sometimes even the sun.

A folding metal frame to hold the camp stove at cooking level is well worth its cost. Place the stove (on its frame) near one end of the picnic table. Then the portable camp kitchen can be placed on the table, and your cooler and extra grub supply box can be stowed under the end of the table. Keeping everything at one end of the table within easy reach of the cook and the diners is easy on the chef and the clean-up crew. Wash dishes promptly after each meal and keep all food under cover to discourage insects and animals. The table cover should be wiped often and dishwater disposed of in a sewage system if possible. In a public campground, garbage should not be burned but placed in a plastic garbage bag for later disposal.

Most campers eventually devise some sort of portable kitchen box to hold cooking utensils and tableware and some of the food supply. Cooking is more organized when these are within easy reach. The boxes are often made of plywood and are compartmentalized to make it easier to find small items such as measuring spoons and condiments. Most have a drop-door with hinges and a chain to hold the door in place for extra work space. Several manufacturers sell these portable kitchens, but more satisfactory are those that are fashioned to fit your own individual needs. Quarter-inch plywood is heavy enough to be durable. A convenient size is 26 inches wide, 21 inches high and 12 inches deep. Anything much larger will be too cumbersome to lug around. Paint the box inside and out to protect it from the weather.

Some of the items that can be carried in the portable camp kitchen are salt, pepper, bread, toothpicks, matches, soap pads, detergent, coffee, tea, cereal, sugar, flour, crackers, aluminum foil, waxed paper, paper towels, napkins, cooking kit, cups, plates, silverware and a first-aid kit.

Little removable hooks on the side of the box are great for hanging dishcloths, towels, brushes, pot-holders and long-handled utensils. A paper-towel

Before your camping trip, transfer items from glass jars to plastic jars or bags.

holder can be fashioned out of a coat hanger for the other side of the box. Tupperware containers can be stacked in the kitchen for mixing bowls and to store leftovers.

Use a plywood box to tote heavy foodstuffs such as cans of beans, spaghetti sauce, breakfast juices and bulky utensils like a Dutch oven. Since the box is often on the ground, be sure the food it holds won't be ruined by dampness or inquisitive animals. To pack all these extras in the top-of-the-table kitchen box would make it too heavy.

Stick a small notebook and pencil in the portable camp kitchen to jot down items to be picked up on a shopping trip or a forgotten necessity for the next trip's master list. The latter might be a handy tool that a neighboring camper has come up with or just an old staple like thumbtacks to hold a garbage bag on the end of the picnic table.

Because facilities and utensils are limited, meals

Cooking kits that nest are useful if the kettle is large and the frying pan heavy enough to keep food from sticking.

should be simple and require a short cooking time or else you will spend far too much time at kitchen chores. Complicated recipes can be prepared outdoors but really shouldn't be attempted unless your sole purpose is to do that very thing.

Most camp cooking can usually be done with three utensils. One is a large kettle for stews, soups, spaghetti and even for dish washing. The second is a heavy frying pan, and the third is a pot for coffee, tea and cocoa, which can also double as a vegetable cooker or soup maker. New campers often try to make do with utensils borrowed from the household kitchen. Usually this is a mistake, since they are often not suitable for camp life and after a couple of camping trips are so dented, burned or blackened that they are no longer acceptable in the home kitchen. It's proba-

bly much cheaper in the long run to buy pans just for camp.

Cooking kits that nest are useful if the kettle is large and the frying pan heavy enough to keep food from sticking. Ordinarily you'll want a 12-inch frying pan to cook for four people. A 10-incher is a bit undersized for most camp menus, although it will do nicely for two or three people. Plastic compartmentalized plates should be part of the cooking kit, rather than aluminum ones which lose heat quickly. The same goes for cups. The only advantage a metal cup offers is that you can place it directly on the fire to heat your coffee water.

Drinking cups in camp can become a problem to the dishwasher. If you are trying to use plastic ones and cut down on throwaway garbage, they seem to be

The camp cooler should be the last item placed in the camper, so that lunches will be easier to prepare and you can add fresh produce along the route.

constantly dirty. In my camping kit, every member of our family has marked his or her cup with different-colored nail polish or paint, and they can be used over and over again with just a quick rinse when changing from Kool-Aid to milk.

Several aluminum pie pans are a permanent part of my portable kitchen. These make handy serving plates for sliced tomatoes, cold cuts and vegetables and sometimes substitute as a lid for the frying pan. Heavy-duty aluminum foil, in my opinion, is one of the absolute necessities. You can cook, bake, fry, steam, mix in and on it, and in a pinch you can shape a serving bowl out of it, besides the ordinary uses such as covering food. A couple of wooden spoons are always at hand in my kitchens, both at home and in the field. Everything seems to taste better when stirred with wood instead of metal. And you can't burn your lips as easily when you are testing the spaghetti sauce.

My favorite camping utensil is a 9-inch Dutch oven, the one with little legs, a rim on the cover and a bail handle. By arranging a bed of hot charcoal briquets under the oven and placing some on the lid, you can bake a pie, nut bread or biscuits, or cook a stew, roast a chicken and make scalloped potatoes. It's a kick to bake so easily in the open air.

To cut down on carrying a lot of kitchen gear, here are a few substitutions you can make. If you put your mind to it, you'll probably come up with a half-dozen more. You can use a can for a rolling pin. To save utensils, warm vegetables in their own cans. Use plastic bags for mixing foods; a clean wooden stick makes a good stirring implement. Be sure the wood is of a nonpoisonous species.

Since cooking substitutions may also be necessary when you are miles away from a market and minutes away from a meal, here are some equivalents:

1 cup butter	=	1 cup margarine
1 cup buttermilk	=	1 tablespoon lemon juice or vinegar and enough milk to make 1 cup liquid.
1 ounce chocolate	=	3 tablespoons cocoa plus 1 tablespoon butter
1 tablespoon flour	=	½ tablespoon cornstarch or 2 tablespoons quick tapioca.
1 cup milk	=	½ cup evaporated milk and ½ cup water
1 cup evaporated milk	=	1 cup double-strength powdered milk
1 cup white sugar	=	1 cup brown sugar
1 teaspoon baking powder	=	⅓ tsp. baking soda plus 1 teaspoon cream of tartar
1 cup honey	=	1¼ cup sugar plus ¼ cup liquid.

Here are some handy storage ideas:

To prevent salt from lumping, place a few grains of rice in the salt shaker. The rice will absorb the moisture.

Place a piece of lemon, orange or apple inside a plastic container of brown sugar to keep the sugar soft.

To keep cheese from molding, wrap it in cheesecloth that has been dipped in vinegar.

Place sugar, salt, pepper and powdered sugar in salt shakers with lids. Before traveling, place plastic wrap over the shaker under the lid and screw the lid on tightly. This will prevent spillage. In camp, remove the wrap. Be sure the shakers are labeled as to contents unless the contents can be seen through the material.

Store dried breadcrumbs in plastic bags to be used for meatloaves and casserole toppings. Cookie or cake crumbs can also be stored in bags for use as decorative goodies on puddings or Jell-O.

Blend the necessary quantities of muffin mix and biscuit mix (except for liquid and eggs) and place in plastic bags. Label well.

It's a cinch to bake in a Dutch oven. All it takes are a few hot charcoal briquets. In about 20 minutes a pan of hot cornbread will emerge from this Dutch oven.

Heavy aluminum foil is a necessity on any camping trip. Sil Strung has fashioned a large mixing bowl out of foil and is fixing a dinner of macaroni and cheese.

If bananas or avocados are green, storing them in a plastic bag will hasten ripening.

To store eggs, break them into a Tupperware plastic container. If the plastic jug has a spout, the eggs will come out of the spout one at a time. Use them within four days.

Place bread in a shoe box or rectangular plastic container to keep it from becoming smashed.

Place items from glass jars in plastic jars to prevent breakage during your travels. Put plastic jars in plastic bags for double security.

Buy butter or margarine in plastic cups for easier storage in the cooler—nothing is worse than watery butter when you're trying to build the Dagwood sandwich of all time.

Good pre-trip planning will make or break a camping trip and this is especially true when setting up a camp kitchen. If the cook can't relax, the rest of the family is also going to have a lousy time. Take plenty of time to set up your trip and you'll sail through your first venture like an old pro.

Camp kitchen scenes. These families are well prepared to enjoy their camping trip and not become slaves to the chores.

Kids as Kampers
by Lue Park

Camping with children is like having eggplant for dinner—either you thoroughly enjoy it and come back for more or you eye it with disdain, wondering how anyone could enjoy it.

The attitudes of families with growing children are just as sharply divided on the matter of camping. Some parents may like to camp but, because of the hassle, wouldn't consider doing so until the kids are older. Others continue camping as the children come along, including and adapting them, until they are a dedicated camping family.

Unfortunately, many of those parents who choose to wait until "the kids are old enough," find that when they are ready to go camping with the children, the kids would rather do something else. By the time children are considered old enough, they have passed through their formative years, and if they have grown up not camping, they are likely to have other ideas on how to spend their time.

In the early years it is the attitude of the parents, not of the kids, that holds the family back. Children do not need a lot of paraphernalia to be happy. All they need is to be comfortable, secure and well fed.

Even very young children can readily adapt, and parents will find that it really isn't too much trouble to go camping, even with infants, if they have planned ahead for all the necessities.

Forethought is the key to any successful camping trip, but it is particularly important if you are planning a trip with children.

The ages of the children will dictate what time of year you go, what type of camping you'll do, how far you'll travel and what you'll need to take along.

If you have preschoolers, you won't have to work around a school schedule. If the children are in school, you need to think in terms of school vacations. The main one is usually in the summer, but don't overlook the shorter vacations in spring and winter, since many parts of the country are at their best in those seasons.

It may be traditional to have Christmas at home with the family, but there's nothing that says you can't have a family Christmas in your tent or recreational vechicle on a warm desert. You just have to plan differently.

The type of camping you'll do will also depend on the family's budget, what you like to do, how long you

The Park family, camping with a small car and a tent trailer. Seated at table, from left, daughters Tracy and Kelly, standing, from left, Ed and Lue Park.

plan to stay and the time of year.

A tour trip isn't advisable with most youngsters under six. They don't care much about scenery, have a short attention span and get tired and restless with much travel. For this age group, a one-site camp will probably work out better.

Some families prefer to rough it and camp in a primitive area. Others like complete campsites, with running water, toilets and showers. Still others like the luxury campground such as United Safari, Ramada Camp Inns, Holiday Inn's Travel Parks, or KOA Kampgrounds.

Horse packing is a great way for a family to camp wilderness areas, especially if the children are too young for extensive backpacking. The horses do most of the work.

As the children become older and more capable of carrying loads, backpacking can be a good way to share wilderness adventures. For the boat-oriented family, a boat camping trip can combine many activities of interest—fishing, water skiing, cruising and swimming.

For any age, travel weariness is a problem, and the family that plans to travel too many miles per day is asking for trouble in the form of unhappy people. Pre-teens, especially, get the fidgets if they have to sit through hundreds of miles of sameness.

If a long trip is really necessary, some relief can be found by making frequent short stops. Let everyone out for a stretch and a bit of exercise. Toss a ball, throw a Frisbee or play tag. Teenagers can accept long trips if they are interested in the final destination. Not too many of us live near Yellowstone Park, so if you plan to camp at some such outstanding natural wonder, a long trip may be necessary. Again, breaking up the trip with frequent stops will help everyone.

Many hesitate to take infants camping because of the imagined problems of hauling all that extra gear for the baby. But an infant's needs are basic—he needs to be protected from bright sun, insects, wind and cold. You can check with your doctor on these problems, but usually common sense can be your guide.

ARTICLES

The Park crew on a canoe-camping trip in Minnesota with guide Clarence Sauve of Timber Bay Lodge, Babbitt, Minnesota. From left, Kelly and Tracy, son Jeff and author Lue Park.

If your baby is bottle-fed, you'll find the ease and convenience of the powdered formulas ideal for camping; but try them out ahead of time to make sure your child can tolerate the brand you choose. Disposable diapers are fine if you'll be in a place where you can dispose of them properly. Otherwise you'll need to plan to wash out a few diapers each day—a nuisance, granted, but not too difficult if you have the necessary equipment.

A baby isn't going to care where he sleeps as long as he is comfortable. Some parents take along a small collapsable playpen. It can do double duty as a bed at night and a safe play area during the day.

Hiking with a baby or toddler can be simplified by the use of one of the various kinds of baby carriers or packs. Little ones seem to enjoy the motion of the hiking parent and spend much of the time sleeping. A toddler enjoys viewing the scene from the height of his parent's back.

The pre-teen group is perhaps the easiest to travel with. Since most children are brought up in an urban society, the world of camping and the out-of-doors holds many mysteries for them. They enjoy exploring anywhere, whether it is in wilderness areas or at different selected campsites each night on a travel trip.

A bag of games and toys to keep youngsters busy in the car can be a real parent pacifier. Coloring sets, playing cards, picture books and crossword puzzles are all good selections. Games like checkers, chess or tick-tack-toe which have magnetized pieces are great for travel because the parts don't slide around. Twenty Questions and other word games can be enjoyed by the entire family while traveling, and kids usually delight in something in which everyone participates.

Older children might enjoy reading beforehand about the area that they are going to visit. Books or pamphlets on the plants, animals, geology or history of the area could interest them. Teenagers become bored most easily. They may enjoy camping but are reluctant to leave home because they don't want to leave their friends or miss something that may be going on there. You might consider spending a few days with just the family together, away from crowds, then another few days camping in an area where there are a number of other youngsters. Some of these are sure to be the same ages as your own. If it fits into your planning, you might take along a child's best friend, although with a large family you may have to rotate the children's turns to bring a special friend, if you want to keep peace.

Once you've decided when, where and how you are going to camp, you will need to plan well ahead of time what basic gear you need to take. Check over what you have and find out what you should buy to complete your list of needed equipment. If anything needs repairs, now is the time to make these. Discovering on a rainy night that the tent leaks is not what makes a camping trip great.

Even if you travel by some kind of recreational vehicle, it will add to everyone's comfort to include a

The author, right, has an attentive audience of two camping neighbor's kids as she fixes a campfire dinner.

Fishing is an activity most kids enjoy, and it provides something all family members can participate in. This is the author's son Jeff.

tent (or two, depending on the size of the family). This will give everyone more privacy, a place to change and sleep or just plain extra room for the kids and gear.

The kind of gear you take will of course depend on what kind of trip you take. If you are a beginning camping family, you might enjoy looking through the catalogs of firms that specialize in camping equipment and clothing. These will give you an idea of what you need and what kind of gear is best for your family and your type of camping.

Tent campers of course need a good tent, plus warm sleeping bags and pads, a good folding Coleman-type camp stove and an ice chest.

There are sleeping bags designed for children, but keep in mind that kids grow and you may be buying new sleeping bags every few years if you go that route. There is no reason why the kids can't start out in adult-size bags and grow into them. Just make sure the bags are warm and comfortable. Younger children may be more comfortable on cold nights if they also wear the bunny-type pajamas that will keep them warm if they wriggle out of the sleeping bag.

When buying sleeping bags, consider the differences between down bags and the new synthetics such as Dac II. Down bags are the ultimate in warmth for the weight and therefore are great for backpacking, but they will mat and lose their insulating qualities if they get wet. Dac II is less expensive and will probably serve you best if there is a danger of getting wet or for most car-camping situations. It dries quickly and is easy to care for. On an extended trip, if necessary, a Dac II bag can be brought to a laundromat for a quick wash and dry.

The same rules apply to clothing for kids on a camp trip as to those for adults. A camp trip which involves a lot of walking is not the time to break in new shoes or boots. Get boots well ahead of time so the wearer can break them in gradually. Sneakers have their place, but for much hiking, the kids need the support of well-made, sturdy boots with two pairs of socks—one lightweight, one wool to wear over the light pair. Even if you expect to be where the weather is warm, pack a warm jacket or sweater. It's easier not to wear it than to find that it is needed and not with you.

Old clothes in which children can play and feel free to get dirty are a must. It can spoil everyone's fun if the youngsters are expected to keep clean and be careful of their clothes. To the usual summer selection of T-shirts, jeans and shorts, add a long-sleeved shirt to protect arms from bugs and bushes. Cuffs on pants get in the way and collect dirt, but all clothes should have lots of pockets in which to carry things and put "treasures" that kids collect.

A clothing repair kit will aid in mending rips and sewing on buttons. Bright clothing will help you spot youngsters who tend to wander off. Sunglasses and hats will protect young eyes from glaring sun at high elevations.

Comfortable camp clothes should include some rain gear. Youngsters don't mind the rain and if they have proper gear, such as rain boots, jacket, pants and hat, there's no reason why they can't get out in the rain and enjoy themselves. Children are like nature themselves and they readily adapt when they are allowed to discover that days that are unpleasant to adults aren't necessarily unpleasant to them.

Another department of camping that needs a considerable amount of planning beforehand is the pantry. Camping is not the time to spring new and strange foods on the kids. For the sake of the camp cook, keep the meals simple, but make them delicious and nutritious. Small appetites at home can suddenly become large appetites on a camping trip, with the additional physical activity. Plan to have a lot of good-for-them snacks on hand and plenty of liquids. Items such as dried fruits, raisins, hard crackers, nuts and hard candies are good for munching along the trail when energy ebbs. Kids may like to have their own bags of such snacks each day to carry with them. Good snacks that can be made up ahead of time and frozen until ready to pack include hearty fruit-nut breads and cakes. A variety of cookies can be made or bought that will withstand being clutched in small hands or crammed into packs.

Camping is little different from home when it comes to bumps, scrapes and bruises. If you haven't already had a course in first aid, one would be helpful for at least one parent to take; if nothing else, it will help relieve the minds of anxious parents about taking little ones camping. By the time the children are grown and you've gone through all the "emergencies," you'll feel qualified to write your own first-aid book.

The hazards of camping are really few, and children are actually safer when camping than at home. Give them latitude and be reasonable about what they are permitted to do. When they wish to explore, they need rules about how far away they can stray and which spots may be dangerous. It is a good idea for the parents to take a tour with the kids on arriving at a campsite and then lay down the rules.

A whistle, worn on a cord around the neck, can be a good safety item. Tell each child that if he becomes lost, he is to stay in one place and blow the whistle. Keeping hatchets, knives and matches out of children's reach can assure parents and children that there won't be any accidents from bad cuts or fires.

Ed Park, right, shows Jeff and Kelly how to operate an outboard motor. Camping trips are good occasions for casual education.

Whether at home or camping, parents always need to stress that youngsters of any age must not eat any berries or plants that they are not completely familiar with.

Since a child's pace is different from that of an adult when hiking along a trail, there needs to be a compromise. It takes a bit of patience to give the children time to satisfy their interest in some trailside attraction yet not allow a lot of dawdling. Nature walks can be a good time to learn about many things—a time to talk of forest fires, wildlife, picking up trash, respect for trees and flowers, and consideration for others.

Children need to feel that they are a part of most family activities, and camping is an especially good time to get them involved. Even little ones can do their share by carrying wood for the campfire, pounding in tent stakes, blowing up air mattresses and so on.

Camping should provide a chance for each person to be alone for a time, as well as for family togetherness. Childhood memories are made from such things as quietly sitting alone watching a snail cross the trail, or picking wildflowers to take back to camp for Mom. When the family is gathered around the campfire at night, roasting marshmallows and telling stories, the togetherness is what the children will remember when they are adults.

Children seem to adapt quickly to nature, and with some advice and help along the way, they can develop a lifelong desire to "go camping" whenever possible.

Older children like Tracy can be taught map and compass work on camping trips.

Pets in Camp

by Dave Duffey

It may be hard for animal lovers to understand, but campers who tote the family pets along with their camping gear shouldn't be surprised if they get a more or less restrained welcome once the campsite operator sees a dog or cat.

And recreation seekers who decide to take the dog along to let it roam in the wide open spaces are courting disappointment if their base of operations is to be a well-managed campground. Some campgrounds, whether privately or publicly operated, ban dogs entirely. Most have rather stringent restrictions regarding the behavior and control of animals that are permitted on the grounds. Pet owners who camp may be unhappy with this situation. From their standpoint, however, it is likely to get worse and will certainly never improve until campers who travel with pets police themselves and control the behavior of their animals.

Most of the blame for a widespread reluctance to accept pets rests squarely on the heads of pet owners who are inconsiderate, blissfully ignorant or "don't give a damn—this is a free country" and so try the patience and offend the sensibilities of fellow campers by permitting their pets to commit noxious, annoying, disturbing and even destructive acts.

Pet fanciers sometimes claim that opposition to the presence of animals in camp is the fault of a few sour-ball animal haters. But even a person with a tolerant, even benevolent attitude regarding pets may become mightily disturbed when another camper's unleashed dog uses his tent for a latrine, his foot slips in pet excrement deposited on a trail's edge, an exuberant pup bowls over a frightened toddler or a cat picks its way across his food-laden picnic table. Campers who anticipated a night of blissful slumber under canvas are understandingly irritable after a night of unceasing yowls, yaps, yodels and barks from spoiled and lonely canines protesting confinement in strange surroundings.

Once the blame is properly assessed and accepted, perhaps conscientious campers who can't afford to board out pets during vacations or can't stand being separated from Duke or Tabby can take steps to assure a smile rather than a frown from campground supervisors and fellow campers when they arrive with a vehicle containing a friendly dog or a composed cat.

Consideration, control and acclimation or training can do a great deal toward alleviating the stresses and

When camping, this miniature schnauzer treats a travel crate as a home away from home.

strains an animal camper can inflict on human campers. Responsible campers accompanied by pets must expend thought and effort to assure that there will continue to be camping places that accept animals.

In addition to conforming to a basic rule that pets must be confined or leashed in inhabited areas, pet owners can adopt a simple and relatively inexpensive expedient that will go a long way toward solving many of the difficulties that camping with a pet entails. This is the purchase of animal travel crates as an essential item of camping equipment. Such crates are manufactured in an assortment of sizes, shapes and designs or can easily be constructed by a tool-handy man or woman.

A travel crate serves to confine an animal comfortably and restrict its activity while it is being transported to and from camp, thereby reducing the number of "pit stops" needed en route and the "constitutionals" that must be taken once camp is es-

tablished. But, more important, crates provide a "home away from home" in strange surroundings, whether the crated animal is left in the camper, brought into the tent or settled in the shade out of doors.

Once the animal is accustomed to a travel crate, this box represents security. In the crate, it is in familiar surroundings anywhere. An old piece of rug on the crate floor assures comfort and a night's sleep. During the day, if the animal is given two or three exercise periods, it will be content the rest of the time to lie in the crate and watch the parade of activity outside. Proper confinement and control is the secret of carefree and enjoyable camping with the family's pet. There are no comparable alternatives to utilizing a crate and training the pet to accept it.

Since cats usually present fewer problems and campers are more likely to take dogs, the following suggestions deal with canine camp followers.

If your dog is accustomed to being on a collar and

A good gun dog, like this pointer, is a vital accessory when hunters camp way back in. Twist and Dave Duffey.

chain at home, you may opt for staking it out next to your tent, camper or vehicle.

Naturally, a dog cannot be confined to a crate for the entire trip. It must be exercised and given some attention as well as being watered and fed. You may want to carry several gallons of "home brew" water along. In some dogs changes in water contribute to alimentary upsets. Meat and canned dog food contain less bulk than dry commercial food and will cut down the amount of waste and the number of times a dog "has to go." But whatever the food, it will have to evacuate a portion of the intake.

If your dog does relieve itself in an area where there is considerable pedestrian traffic or even off the beaten path, *clean up the mess.*

A lot of fun can be had by you and your dog if you walk it on a leash out of the inhabited area and then let it romp freely, chase chipmunks or whatever. Like a child, a dog must burn up some energy and will become restless and troublesome if it doesn't.

But don't turn it loose in the campground's "residential area" to get its exercise chasing people or cars, tangling with other dogs, or where it will disturb other campers. If it likes to swim, take it to a place on the lake or stream where other people aren't about, never to the beach and certainly not to a swimming pool. The camper who takes his pets along has the same responsibility to campground dwellers and custodians as he does to the other citizens and officials in his permanent place of residence.

Urban-oriented campers are often apprehensive about the safety of their pets in camp, fearing attacks by various wild animals. But on most developed campgrounds the chances of a dog tangling with an animal that will harm it, being struck by a poisonous snake, or stung by an insect, are no greater than the possibility that it will be attacked by a rabid squirrel in the park or bitten by a cornered rat in an alley.

Dogs confined to automobiles, like these Chesapeake Bay retrievers, should be provided with plenty of ventilation.

Again, confinement and control are factors. Most wild animals that stray into camp or are attracted by discarded foodstuffs are nocturnal by nature and, if not, are frightened off by all the daytime bustle. If a camp dog is where it should be, with its people while they enjoy an evening around a campfire and confined to his crate after they've bedded down, it won't become involved with raccoons raiding the garbage cans.

Because most camping is done in warm weather, the one constant hazard to dogs is heat stroke. The dog's crate must always be placed in a shaded, well-ventilated location. A dog should *never* be left in a motor vehicle or other closely confined area unless the windows are rolled all the way down, not just opened slightly. Again, a car crate permits leaving a dog in an opened-up car with no danger of its jumping out a window and running away. Fresh water should always be available to the dog; if this is sloppy or the weather is hot en route, give it ice cubes to lick.

Hiking, backpacking and wilderness camping are situations in which a dog fits naturally and is a companion to be freely enjoyed rather than a burden of responsibility. In these situations, however, some risks to a dog may be involved, particularly to an urban animal who hasn't encountered various natural hazards and learned from experience. And some dogs, rural or urban, never learn to leave well enough alone.

Wild creatures aren't likely to attack dogs, but many dogs can't refrain from challenging skunks and porcupines, and curiosity may prompt checking out a snake that means business. All dogs that go camping should be vaccinated against rabies, but other than that precautionary measure, in a situation far from a veterinarian or a motor vehicle to get to one, there's not a great deal that can be done to aid a dog that gets into serious trouble.

Mortality in dogs from poisonous snake bites runs about 50 percent and considerably less if the animal is quickly taken to a vet for treatment. A recommended procedure is to apply ice or a quick-freeze chemical to the area of the wound, keep the dog quiet and get professional treatment as quickly as possible. A cold stream might serve as a substitute for ice in localizing the venom as much as possible.

You have little choice except to stay put, keep the dog quiet and watch him suffer, or attempt to pack it out to obtain treatment and pray that, whatever you choose to do, it will be one of the lucky 50 percent. Give serious consideration to avoiding known snake country.

The discomfort a dog suffers when sprayed by a skunk is intense but temporary. Relieve some of it by dunking the dog in a lake or river. This will intensify the smell but will clear some of the fluid from the eyes and nose and wash it off the dog's coat. Since it is unlikely that you'll be packing a quantity of tomato juice or white vinegar—both fairly effective odor reducers—you and friend dog will have to learn to live with each other. Normal adjustment time is about 6 hours.

Porcupine quills are a far more serious matter. Get out as many as possible as quickly as possible. A small pair of pliers in your kit is worth its weight in gold. Smart dogs back off after getting just a few quills, and that is no big deal if the dog is docile and trusts you. I

Ensconced in a travel crate, dogs like this springer spaniel are content to watch the world go by.

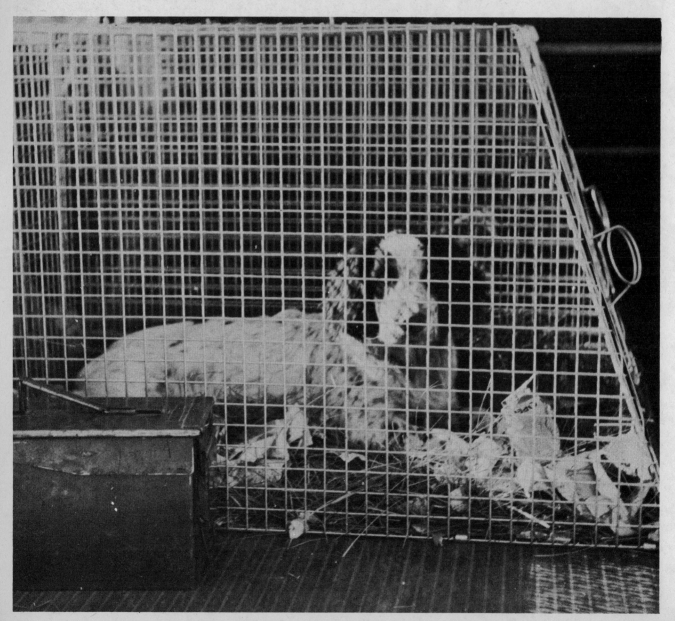

Well-behaved dogs and children are fun to take camping and cause no difficulties for other campers. Springer spaniel Satan's Pumpkin and Kevin Patrick Duffey, the author's grandson.

once had three dogs at one time with muzzles fringed with quills, but all were obedient and trusting and we resumed hunting 15 minutes later.

But a dog of a temperament that won't back off, who becomes more enraged the more quills it accumulates and repeatedly attacks a porky, will also be the toughest one to de-quill. It will have to be taken to a veterinarian to be anesthetized and treated.

In cases of mild quilling you may be able to pull out most of the quills with your fingers or with pliers. You may have to improvise a muzzle by putting a stick in the dog's mouth and then binding its jaws with a ripped-off shirttail or other piece of cloth. This will allow the removal of quills from the nose, muzzle, lips and part of the tongue. But if they're on the back of the tongue and in the throat, you will have to force the dog's mouth open as best you can and risk bites when you reach in and jerk.

I've heard all kinds of theories about pushing quills through, cutting them so they collapse, applying something to soften them, but nothing has ever worked for me except the heroic measure of jerking them out as fast as possible. A frantic dog will also break off some of the quills and the stubs that remain must be felt for and pulled.

If you are alone, get on the dog's back and hold it with your knees. If you have help, work facing the dog while the other person holds it. Cover the dog's eyes with one hand if you can. It hurts like hell when you pull a quill and if the dog sees your hand or the pliers approaching, it will anticipate pain, struggle more and may even snap. Get the worst of the quills out, then head for a vet. While the danger to the dog isn't as great as with snake bites, quills do move around, go deeper and deeper or eventually emerge, and there is some chance of delayed fatality or serious injury from undetected quills. Do remember pliers if you expect to be in quill-pig country.

An encounter with a bear is a remote possibility and of more concern to back-country travelers than it should be. Bear trouble is more likely in an established site in a national park where semi-tame animals abound, accustomed to humans and attracted by food and garbage. But it can be a frightening and even tragic experience. For that reason some hikers and campers consider taking a dog along for protection. This misguided thinking is based on mistaken ideas or ignorance of both domestic- and wild-animal behavior. If you do bump into a truculent bruin, the percentages indicate that the presence of a dog will be more of a liability than an asset.

If a dog is sensible, he won't mess with such an

Hundreds of thousands of hunting dogs are used outdoors and in backwoods camps annually with little risk of injury. Dhu, a Labrador retriever, and Michael Kevin Duffey, then aged 12, now father of Kevin.

intimidating foe. Yapping little mutts have been known to drive black bears up a tree, but blacks are unpredictable and grizzlies don't climb.

If your dog is aggressive, protective or just plain foolish, it may get too close to a bear. If the bear's first swipe misses or doesn't disable it, a dog may quickly lose its boldness and come kiting back to you for protection and solace—or to rev up shaken confidence before having another go at the bear. If the dog upsets the bear enough and returns to you with a quarter-ton of disgruntled destructiveness tight on its tail, you've got trouble.

In camp or on the trail, a sensible, well-trained dog is as much a pleasure as it is anywhere else. Fitted with dog-size panniers or packs, the larger breeds can even be useful in toting a few pounds of supplies or gear. For upland game and waterfowl hunters who camp out, dogs are invaluable.

But anyone venturing into the back country with a dog is well advised to get a good book on dog care and first aid. Don't just read it. Memorize it. Then you won't have to stand by helplessly if your dog suffers a mishap, and even if the accident should prove fatal, you'll know you did your best.

Again, control and training are important factors, even though a dog can be allowed virtual freedom in the wilderness. An obedient dog can be called and extricated from a potentially hazardous situation or stopped before something serious develops.

Hundreds of thousands of dogs hunt with their sportsmen owners for months out of every year in situations analogous to hiking and backpacking without suffering serious mishap. The out-of-doors is a natural place for dogs, and random risks attending having fun with a dog should be less cause for worry than the hazard of highway traffic. So the pleasures derived from sharing the countryside with a good dog more than outweigh a relatively rare incidence of risk.

In the civilized surroundings of supervised campgrounds it behooves those who take their dogs along to see that they are not nuisances but are acceptable to any normally tolerant fellow camper. Then those of us who take great pleasure in having our dogs share our tents and recreational vehicles, who train them properly and control their behavior, won't be penalized by an increase in PETS PROHIBITED signs.

Large dogs like this Great Dane are fun but pose transportation problems.

Camp Pests
by John W. Malo

Millions of Americans of all ages annually engage in outdoor recreation: camping, hiking, picnicking, canoeing and many, many other activities. As they take to the woods and waters, mountains and meadows, the purpose is primarily to have fun, to enjoy the outdoor break from workbench or desk is a blessed change from life's daily pattern.

Your participation does, however, often involve some unexpected encounters with small animals, flying and crawling insects, and other creatures who were there before you, but they can spoil your days afield only if you allow them to. Thanks to advances in chemistry, biology and outdoor know-how you can venture out with assurance that pests will not spoil your outing.

In trip planning, meeting insect and animal pests must be expected but fear should not lessen your ardor for outdoor activities. Considerations of danger should take a middle course between overconfidence that no animal will harm, and alarm at every insect, animal or sound.

Mosquitoes seem universal, but most pests are regional and must be considered individually. Some basic knowledge of how to avoid and treat pest problems—from mice to moose—will enhance the enjoyment of your adventuring. To enable you to focus on specific pests, they are listed alphabetically for quick reference. But, first, a general note on insect repellents.

Insect Repellents

As the peak of insect life is during the camping season, effective methods of dealing with these pests are most important for the enjoyment of the outdoor experience.

Deep Woods Off and 6-12 are easily applied and pleasant repellents. Off is available both as a cream that is rubbed into areas to be treated and spray from a pressurized can. The repellent's formula is endorsed by the U.S. Department of Agriculture. Follow instructions on all repellent containers to learn their effect on eyes, lips, certain fabrics and plastic-frame eyeglasses. For campers with skin sensitive to repellents, head nets that drape over broad-brimmed hats can be substituted.

Mosquitoes like the shelter of a tent and congregate there by the hundreds. Keep screens closed, and enter and leave quickly. Fifteen minutes before bedtime spray the tent with a bug bomb and close the flaps. The location of your campsite, picnic table or charcoal broiler represents another way in which you can combat insects: Choose a well-ventilated, high, dry site; a smudge fire drifting smoke over a camp or picnic site will deter flying insects. The ideal insect netting is bobbinet; its fine mesh screens out the smallest flying and crawling pests. Some protection against insects can be gained from long trousers and long-sleeved shirts, but neither should be tight-fitting, as insects can bite through the fabric.

Animal and Insect Pests

Antlered animals. Deer, moose and elk seldom infringe on camping areas, but occasionally one of them may get curious and come close enough to become entangled in a clothesline or tent rope. The hinterland moose at times will crash into a camp to investigate. This huge bovine-like animal is generally quite docile and rarely causes trouble. The size of this largest animal on the North American continent gives rise to fictitious ferocity, which of course is not typical, occuring mostly during the rutting or calf-raising season.

To avoid large animals and cut down on possible damage to equipment, select an open campsite, not hemmed in by a cliff, boulders, brush or clotheslines, and on an obvious travel route. A little noise helps to send animals lumbering away. Patience and caution are the watchwords, as it may take a while for an animal intruder to decide to end its visit.

Ants. Both small- and large-sized ants are found in the same species. The small ones can cause damage by getting into food rations. As a precaution, keep all food, especially sweets, in tightly covered cans—hung up on a line or rope between trees if the problem becomes serious.

The larger ants bite humans with their triangular teeth along the biting edges, working their jaws sidewise like a pair of shears. Before setting up camp, check your locale for ant hills and ant nests, also for the routes of travel used by ants. A clean campsite, without free-lunch scraps strewn about, will help keep ants at a minimum.

Bears. Black bears and grizzly bears have never heard of Smokey the Bear or Teddy Bear; they are wild animals that can be considered unpredictable and mean—a far cry from a Walt Disney animated cartoon. Bears can become bothersome at some locations. They are lazy—like you and me—instead of scrounging for food they readily gravitate to man's rations for an easy meal.

The black bear's behavior is prompted by a combination of inquisitiveness and hunger. The scent of such foods as bacon, cheese and fish drives the black bear to ripping, crushing and chewing food containers. It has capable claws and teeth, but it rarely attacks man, battling only when cornered and without an escape route or when protecting cubs.

The grizzly bear is an endangered species and not too common in camping areas. The grizzly is very intelligent and quickly learns to associate the smell of humans with free lunch. In times of great hunger their natural shyness turns to aggressiveness at the effortless food source of garbage dumps. Research dictates the following precautions when in the neighborhood of grizzlies: Never hike alone in bear country. Make your presence known to alert any bear in the area. Make noises by wearing bells, blowing a whistle, or loud talk. At the campsite, the clanging of pans, bright flashlight beams, poking up the fire or shouting will probably rout the grizzly. In face-to-face confrontations, remain calm. Do not move, speak in a soft, steady monotone and don't run. Remember, a grizzly can outrun a fast horse, so if possible, climb a tree if necessary. Never stand on a rise above a grizzly, as the uphill escape route is normal for them. Be alert when picking wild berries; bears, too, like to glean the fruit.

Because bears may not spook easily, other precautions include proper storage of aromatic foods, (underwater if necessary) and the use of a food cache, hanging it from the high branch of a tree too small to support the weight of a bear. Never, never take food into your sleeping bag with you. Bury garbage and wash dishes immediately after meals, and burn out all used tin cans. Alarms to alert campers can be improvised: lines stretched around the campsite with hanging pots or tin cans, stacking tinware on an inverted boat, canoe or loose board. A dog in camp in bear country can be a dangerous thing. Leave your pet at home, say many experts.

Chiggers. Pinpoint-sized chiggers have a king-sized bite; they burrow into the skin and cause irritation and itching. They seem to concentrate on the areas of a tight waistband or belt, blouse bottom and/or sock tops. The chigger is a grass dweller, therefore be careful when taking a rest stop, spreading out a picnic lunch or lying down. When hiking in grassy or prairie terrain, tuck pant legs into shoes or use high boots or leggings. For the prevention of chigger bites dust the body with sulfur powder or insect repellent beforehand. Once plagued, treat with ammonia, soda bicar-

The moose is quite docile and rarely causes trouble.

bonate paste or isopropyl alcohol.

Dogs. With the proliferation of pet dogs on crowded campgrounds, the odds increase that children may be bitten. Treat as a puncture wound: wash the injury thoroughly with soap and water to get rid of the saliva, apply antiseptic and cover with a sterile dressing. See a doctor at once.

However, the bite of a dog or any other animal infected with rabies is another matter, and if it is allowed to remain untreated, death can result. The animal must be captured and confined to determine whether or not it has rabies. All treatment beyond the simple first aid already explained must be administered by a physician—and quickly.

Mosquitoes. The mosquito is a widespread pest that irritates modern outdoorsmen, and in some species carry malaria and yellow fever, which scourged mankind for thousands of years. Not all mosquitoes bite human flesh and cause fever. We have learned to deal with their irritation; their bites, though annoying, become infected only when victims scratch the wounds.

The best defenses against mosquitoes are the application of commercial chemicals (see Insect Repellents) and the use of a pressurized bug bomb. Red apparel is considered to repel a mosquito and loose-fitting garments insulate against its proboscis. Vitamin B-1 tablets are recommended by some doctors for repelling various insects, although more research is needed before specific results can be confirmed.

Porcupines. In its search for salt, the porcupine can

inflict much damage to equipment. The perspiration that permeates canoe paddles, oars, gunwales, ax handles, hats, shoes, pack straps and other items is a source of salt, which the animal relishes. In porcupine country all gear and equipment should be put out of reach. The porkie has a short memory and even when it is stoned and driven away seems to forgive and returns again and again without a grudge.

The porkie does not shoot his quills, but arches its back and swishes its tail to drive quills deep into an intruder—man or animal. If you are stuck with quills, quickly yank them out with pliers before swelling sets in. Grasp the quill near the skin and with a slight turning motion jerk it out. First-aid treatment is that for a puncture wound. Pet dogs seem more often victimized than humans because of their habit of prowling in underbrush and thick cover. If quill wounds are severe see a doctor.

Raccoons. These animals, with their masked face markings and ringed tails, are a pleasure to watch as they come nosing about campsites and picnic grounds searching for food scraps. They are clever at opening boxes and bags and manage to untie pack straps and knots that would baffle a veteran escape artist. Though they are generally shy and take off when shooed, coons can become tough fighters when cornered, injured or molested by dogs.

Rodents (Mice, chipmunks and squirrels). The meadow mice and white-footed (deer) mice encountered by campers are much like the common house mouse. They feed upon almost any type of food that people eat. The meadow mouse favors the fields, the white-footed is found mostly in wooded areas. Mice, like other small rodents, extend their visits only when nuts, cereals, raisins or candy bars are available; without a freeloading incentive they soon leave. Tin containers and glass jars are mouse-proof, and traps can be used if the problem becomes serious.

The frisky chipmunks offer animated companionship, especially to children. If you are making an extended stay at one site, don't encourage them with too much kindness; they will gnaw through boxes and canvas bags, strew the contents and leave droppings.

Squirrels, like pikas in mountain states and voles and lemmings in northern forests, are certain to visit a campsite. Be careful about feeding them. They pose little physical danger, but they may be covered with lice, fleas or other parasites that carry dangerous diseases.

Never try to pet strange animals, as even a nip on the finger can be dangerous. Rabies virus is carried in the saliva of rodents and a skin puncture bite can transfer the germs to you, requiring a painful series of shots to save your life.

The grizzly bear is most dangerous when protecting cubs.

The threatened porcupine swishes its tail to drive quills into an intruder.

Scorpions. The scorpion, like the spider, serves to keep down the insect population, but a sting from its segmented tail is sharp and slightly venomous. However, only the aged, allergic or infirm camper is threatened with serious reaction to the scorpion's sting. You'll find scorpions in the folds of blankets and towels, in shoes and socks and even among your foodstuff. Check before donning apparel, preparing food or getting into sleeping bags at night. In scorpion country, turn your bags inside out and examine them carefully.

Skunks. The skunk's defensive spray is extremely irritating, causing temporary blindness to its enemies. The skunk reacts only when threatened, always giving a warning by arching its back, stamping its feet, aiming, then spraying. In fact, the skunk is a docile animal, completely harmless when not bothered. In the rare event of being sprayed in the eyes, wash immediately and repeatedly with clean water. Keep the eyes protected from light for several days. Mostly, though, only clothing and limbs are affected. The skin can be deodorized by washing with tomato juice, laundry bleach, vinegar, gasoline or ammonia. A diluted solution of vinegar is the most effective deodorant, according to Cornell University experts. Clothes should be washed repeatedly and hung in the sun for several weeks; if they are inexpensive, throw them away.

Snakes. Fatalities from poisonous snakes are practically nil; therefore the four commonest—rattler, copperhead, water moccasin and coral snake—need not threaten the plans of campers. Poisonous snakes do not stalk humans; the relatively few bites that occur annually stem largely from the surprise element, such as startling the snakes when climbing over rocks, through brush or over stone fences. Be careful where

The raccoon becomes a tough fighter when cornered, injured or molested by dogs.

you place hands and feet.

Once bitten, the victim should remain calm and lie down, to slow the circulation. Pioneer treatment remains valid today: apply a constriction band above the wound to keep the poison contained; make short and shallow knife or razor-blade incisions at the fang puncture marks to encourage bleeding; suck out the venom by mouth or suction rubber cup and keep repeating the suction; wash incisions with soap and water and keep the part moist with salt water; treat the victim for shock. Get to a physician as soon as possible.

Spiders. Danger from spiders is more psychological than physical. Spiders are beneficial in that insects compose most of their diet. Only the black widow and brown recluse spiders can harm, and neither is prevalent in rural places. The black widow's bite causes local swelling and redness; the pain is intense as it spreads over the body, and fever and copious perspiration occurs. Although the black widow's venom is highly toxic, very few people die from it. First call a doctor and meanwhile keep the patient quiet and warm. Should severe abdominal cramps develop, a hot tub will give relief.

Besides the black widow, the only American spider to be avoided is the brown recluse, found indoors as well as out. Its bite may cause an open wound that will not heal for several months.

Stinging insects. Hornets, wasps, bees, horseflies, deerflies and "no-see-ums" reach their greatest concentration during the camping months. Protection against them includes avoidance by selecting a proper campsite; effective screening with cheesecloth, bobbinet and head nets; repellents for temporary relief; and bug bombs which kill the pests.

Bee stings can be painful, poisonous and dangerous. Remove the stinger and gland with tweezers or forceps if it is imbedded. Baking soda paste or ammonia water provides relief. Calamine lotion is the standard pain-easing remedy for most painful stings and bites.

If you are allergic to the venom of stinging insects, the sting of a single such insect can be extremely dangerous and even fatal. According to statistics, there are more fatalities each year from the stings of hornets, wasps and bees than from the bites of poisonous snakes. Hornet or wasp venom is cumulative in many persons so that even if you have had no bad reaction from such stings in the past, the very next injection of the venom may tip the reaction into the violent or extremely serious type, requiring prompt medical attention. If you react to the bites of mosquitoes with raised red or white welts and pain, you should check with your physician as to what to do if you are stung by a wasp or hornet. There are several remedies and bee or hornet allergy kits that can be obtained by prescription which might save a vacation or even someone's life.

The rattlesnake is most likely to strike when startled or endangered.

Ticks. Some ticks are more a nuisance than a health hazard. However, in certain states and in Mexico, ticks are quite dangerous. They can carry Rocky Mountain spotted fever, which once claimed many lives; today, however, with prompt treatment and drugs the threat is minimal. The pajaroella tick of southern California bites but does not imbed itself in flesh, though its venom causes much discomfort. The most common ticks are the hard-shelled wood tick and the smaller soft-shelled one. They imbed their pincers in both humans and animals and gorge on body juices and blood. A newly imbedded tick can be removed by gentle pulling or by daubing with alcohol or gasoline. Also a heated knife blade, cigarette or burned match may induce the tick to back out. Precautionary measures and treatment include being alert to ticks crawling on the skin and checking the body after the day's activity. Cut a shallow incision in the bite and apply suction, then apply antiseptic for relief.

Although not usually serious, tick bites have been known to cause paralysis and coma when in a particular area of the body, as in the hair at the base of the skull. If you are in tick country and you or anyone in your party should experience numbness in any area or awkwardness in any movement look for a tick immediately. It might avert a tragedy.

One of the best defenses against any pest, animal or insect, is to know all you can about it. Where it might be found, what it is attracted to and what it shies away from (light, dampness, bright colors, wind, repellants, noise or fire). Visit your library or bookstore and invest in some of the excellent small paper-backed nature books that show pests in color. Among the best are the Golden Nature Guide entitled *Insect Pests,* and its companion book, *Spiders and Their Kin.* Both are excellent ammunition for your small war against campsite intruders.

Regardless of the inevitability of a few minor skirmishes with camp pests, don't let it prevent or spoil a camping or backpacking vacation. The chance of a serious encounter is almost microscopic.

Be Ready for Sudden Storms

by C. Herb Williams

Sudden storms can be miserable or even dangerous, but in most cases they can be reduced to the status of a nuisance or can even lead to some of our most enjoyable times in the outdoors.

The key to defusing storms, whether they're wind, rain, dust or snow, is in understanding them and being prepared. The preparation should be both physical and mental, and it's sometimes hard to tell which of the two is more important.

Mental preparation, which includes the ability to adapt to a bad situation, can be vital.

One couple, canoeing in the north country, was hit by a sudden storm which soaked their sleeping bags, foam mattresses and much of their clothing. They had neglected one of the basic rules in not having some way to keep their sleeping bags dry, even if the canoe tipped over. Heavy-gauge plastic bags take up almost no room and will do this. This is the type of bag that white-water kayak or canoe buffs carry, in which they pack a complete change of clothing in case of a spill.

Next time out, the couple had the plastic bags to protect their gear, but in the first instance, they were alone in the wilderness, their sleeping bags were soaked and in addition the rain kept on falling throughout the day and all night. They could have thrown up their hands in defeat and been completely miserable. It could have been worse because there's a thin line at times between discomfort and danger. Had the weather turned cold, they could have caught pneumonia. But they were resourceful. They zipped their sleeping bags together, folded a large piece of plastic they had along and inserted it into the sleeping bag like a big double sheet.

They crawled in between the folds of the plastic and slept warmly all night. They had to wear clothing for protection from the clammy feeling of the plastic and to absorb some of the condensation on the inside. The next day the sun came out, a brisk breeze sprang up and they were able to get everything dry.

Admittedly they were not as comfortable that first night as they would have been with dry bags, but, because they were able to improvise, they turned what could have been a disaster for their outing into a mere overnight nuisance.

Equally important was their attitude of facing up to a storm and overcoming hard luck instead of giving up.

This mental attitude cannot be overstressed. An

acquaintance who is in search and rescue work with the Air Force tells about a program of pulling pilots out of aircraft just before takeoff and then dropping them out in wild country over which they would have been flying. This is done on a random basis. On one occasion a pilot was stepping into his plane with only light street shoes, a light jacket and nothing in the way of survival gear. They dropped him off in the wilderness, just as he was dressed.

The rules were that he would have to stay in a certain area for two or three days, just as if he had ditched his plane in a remote area where he would need several days to walk out.

No sooner had they dropped him off than a storm blew in and cold rain began pouring down. It rained hard for two days. Other Air Force personnel were close by but they were there only in case it was evident that he was in serious trouble or was not going to survive.

At the end of three days, he had almost set up housekeeping in the woods. He had built a shelter, had a fire going and was dry. He was hungry and probably a little stiff from sleeping on the ground, but he had conquered the storm.

His mental attitude was right, and he also knew how to build a shelter, get out of the wind and protect himself from rain.

Most of us will never have to face as severe a test as that, but this pilot's experience shows that even without the equipment regular campers have, it's possible to take the worst that storms can do. With our good equipment, we should be able to tame most storms.

A crucial factor in riding out a storm is picking a good campsite to begin with.

Check where water will flow if it starts raining. Some of the most inviting-looking spots on level, smooth areas are the worst. They've been made level by water flowing from a rising stream or runoff from higher country. Every year some campers have their camps washed away because they camped on one of these flood plains or watersheds. Some of them even die in flash floods.

The dry washes of desert country are especially treacherous. You can be sitting in sunshine with no warning of trouble, while a thunderstorm miles away

A good camp for rain or wind. The tarp is securely fastened and covers both tent and table. The tent is ditched, and plastic covers the food and cooking equipment. Even the baby is safe.

starts a wall of water rushing down a wash, sweeping everything before it for many miles.

It takes only a minimum of looking around to be sure your spot is okay. Next, if there's any possibility of rain, a ditch should be dug all around your tent so that the water will run off and be carried away and not flow into or under the tent.

A tarpaulin can be priceless in rain or wind. Place it above the cooking area or set it up vertically for wind. For motor camping, it's best to carry your own poles. Get some round poles about 8 feet long and screw either eye bolts or open-end hooks into one end of each to hold guy ropes. These can be carried on a car-top rack where they're out of the way but easy to get to if you have to set up camp in a hurry.

Another potential storm danger is trees surround-ing your campsite. Be sure you're not setting up under what in loggers' language are dubbed "widow makers." A widow maker is a piece of a tree or a heavy branch that hangs up in surrounding trees and doesn't fall to the ground when the tree is cut. These heavy pieces can fall unexpectedly on an unfortunate logger, making a widow of his wife. This logger lore is something that campers should always keep in mind when pitching a tent, laying out a sleeping bag or backing into some spot with a travel trailer.

Some of the most beautiful forested areas have dead limbs and old snags that could blow down in a storm. High winds can even snap off standing timber and strew it around like jackstraws. The numbered and laid-out campsites in organized parks are usually free of such hazards, because the managers keep old snags

Wind turned this forest into a death trap overnight, knocking down the timber that is on the ground. The road made a natural wind tunnel. Note that trees away from the road were untouched.

Weyerhaeuser Company

This is a good launching area but a poor campground, for with high water the sand spit becomes river bottom.

and dead limbs cleaned up. Away from the organized camps, it's a different story, for there are natural widow makers in some of the most beautiful spots.

A final thing to check in setting up camp is the possibility of wind. Again, some of the most beautiful, picture-postcard types of campsites are not the best, for they are often on points of land jutting out into a large body of water or on a high point overlooking a valley.

If wind is a possibility, it's better to pick a more sheltered spot and then take in the picture-postcard view on foot and not from the door of your tent.

A tent collapsed around your head in the middle of the night is a frightening experience, to say nothing of the inconvenience. Possibly even worse is having wind uproot a tent and carry it like a deflated parachute for several hundred feet.

Anyone who camps out regularly is going to face wind at one time or another, and some of the best preparation is to know your tent well and be able to set it up properly. One of the most important things is to get the tent stakes securely into the ground.

Sometimes this means using rocks or logs to help make the stakes secure. Sand or soft ground makes for easy pounding of tent stakes but also easy pulling up by a wind.

If the various precautions mentioned here are followed, the battle is nearly won. The rest is in keeping an eye on tent ropes, stakes and rainfall during a storm to be sure everything is holding up well.

Storms can also strike while you're on your way to a camping spot, either in a recreational vehicle or on foot. It takes only one experience on a desert highway where commercial semi-truck and trailer rigs have been blown over to make a believer of a recreational-vehicle driver.

If the wind begins to pick up when you're passing through wind-prone country, slack off your speed. If the wind gets worse, pull off to the side of the road and wait out the blow. If at all possible, pick a spot where you can head into the wind, for a desert storm can overturn a recreational vehicle if it hits it broadside.

If you are on foot with a pack on your back, it's also a good idea to seek shelter and wait out the storm,

A dry wash makes a good highway, but the level spot that the truck is crossing can become a raging torrent from thunderstorms which spring up many miles away.

It pays to check out escape routes in case of high water. Another foot or so and this camper would have been marooned until the water dropped.

The high country can bring snow, but it doesn't bother these packers, who are heading into the Grand Canyon of Arizona for several days.

even if it means getting behind the schedule you have set up. For hiking, a poncho-type covering is worth many times its light weight. Get one that will cover your pack as well as yourself. This will keep you dry and also let excess body heat escape.

Waterproof jackets and pants have their place, but since they won't let a lot of perspiration escape, you can get soaking wet on the inside if you are working hard. Then when you stop or slow down, you can get chilled. The waterproof suits are great if you're not going to be exerting too much.

Wet clothing, from whatever cause, is one of the big contributors to hypothermia (loss of body heat), which kills a number of campers every year.

Some of the recently developed materials such as Fiberfill II are wonderful for cold, wet weather. Jim Whittaker, the first American to climb Mount Everest, put a Fiberfill II jacket in water until it was soaked, then put it on and hiked up a mountain in 30-degree weather and was warm. The jacket had somewhat the same effect as a diver's wet suit in preserving his body heat. This kind of clothing is designed for cold winter weather. For outdoor use in the other months, wool is hard to beat, for it also will keep one warm to a certain degree when it is wet. In addition, wool shirts can be used in the layer system, in which you have several different layers, including a wind-breaking shell to put on or take off as temperatures vary.

But despite the best plans or the best equipment, it's possible to get into a spot where you begin to suffer from hypothermia. The best preparation for this is mental, in your own living room, before starting out. Learn the symptoms of the onset of hypothermia and understand what happens. Then if you see them in yourself or a companion you can stop and seek shelter.

Hypothermia is caused by cold and aggravated by wetness, wind and exhaustion. It's the No. 1 killer of outdoor people and most cases occur in temperatures from 30 to 50 degrees, which are not normally considered cold.

Simply put, hypothermia begins when your body loses heat faster than it can produce it. The natural and right reaction to this is to exercise to speed up your blood flow. Your body itself can also make involuntary adjustments to keep a normal temperature in the vital organs. Both of these drain off reserve energy.

If the exposure continues until your energy reserves are gone, your body in effect starts shutting down the extremities. This includes your brain, and when cold reaches your brain, your judgment begins to decline. The frightening thing about this is that because of the very fact that you are losing judgment, you don't realize it. Next you begin to lose control of your hands and feet and can start stumbling. Finally comes stupor, collapse and death.

The time to prevent hypothermia is during the

That mottled, hazy sky could mean that a storm is building in the high country. The weather is warm at this moment, as seen by the fact that one hiker is in shirtsleeves. The pack on the standing hiker is a good one, with a tarp for shelter in case of heavy weather. You're on your own in a situation such as this.

Another good camp setup for rain. The baggage trailer is used as part of the anchoring system for the tarp which covers the table. Guy lines are taut and firmly anchored.

period of exposure and gradual exhaustion before the cold reaches your brain. If you know the early symptoms, you can recognize them in yourself or in a partner and do something about them. This means getting out of the wind, stopping, building a fire, fixing some warm food and even crawling into a sleeping bag.

Lightning is a final element of storms that can be handled if it is understood. If you are caught in a thunderstorm, remember that lightning strikes a conductor, which can be the tallest tree in an area, a peak, a ridge or even the pass between higher ridges. An open vehicle with a lot of metal, such as an open, off-road jeep, is a conductor. Ungrounded wires, such as fences, clotheslines, phone wire, guy wires and aerials, are also good lightning attracters.

There are two forms of lightning which can kill or injure. One is the giant spark we see which shoots down from a cloud to some object on earth. When lightning strikes it also spreads out and follows the lines of least resistance over the ground or down rocky peaks until its energy is spent. This is why animals are often killed at a distance from where the bolt actually struck. This is called "ground" lightning.

If you are caught on a lake or in water, get ashore as quickly as possible. In hills, get to a lower place. Stay away from wire fences or open spaces such as pastures or meadows where you might be the tallest thing around. Don't get under an isolated tree or the tallest tree in an area. A building is the safest place, but stay away from doorways, windows or telephones or electric stoves which could conduct current.

Houses aren't always available when you're camping, so if you are caught in the open, move anything metal away from yourself and then crouch down as low as possible to wait out the storm.

The chances of being hit by lightning are quite small to begin with. You can make the chances even less by heeding a few basic rules.

Many of these facts about storms, winds, rain and hypothermia are difficult for a novice to grasp at first, because we live in a controlled environment most of our lives. Our houses and work areas are kept at a constant temperature. We travel in cars, trucks, buses or planes with controlled temperatures. We even watch many sporting events from covered stadiums or on TV.

But one of the great joys of camping is in getting to know the weather again; to realize how cold it can get at night, even in the summer, or how hot it can get even in moderate climates or high in the mountains. This somehow takes you back to the basics of life and you feel a special kinship with nature that non-campers seldom get a chance to enjoy.

It has been said that there's some element of fear at the root of every substantial challenge. This is true of camping and the storms that at times come along.

Surviving the challenge of storms is one of the great satisfactions of life and is the reason that storms have led to some of the most memorable of camping experiences. Nor is overcome hardship the only thing remembered. Most campers will tell you that some of their happiest times have taken place in camp with the rain drumming on their tent or fly while they sat dry and comfortable with the light and warmth of a camp lantern to add cheer as they read a book, played cards or simply watched the storm pass over.

If you understand what to do to be ready for a storm, it may still be sudden, but it no longer need be frightening. Be ready for it, be calm and perhaps you too will even enjoy it.

On Your Own and Still Alive!

by Gene Kirkley

The loaded canoe was taking the downstream V's perfectly as the two occupants expertly guided their craft through the white water near the lower end of the chute. For scarcely more than an instant, their attention was drawn to two big deer that bounded along a narrow ledge above the rushing water. But those few seconds were time enough for the bow of the canoe to rise up on the sloping edge of a partially submerged boulder. The force of the water caught the stern, and in less time than it takes to tell it, the two found themselves in a survival situation.

The lone backpacker had wisely released his padded hip belt before attempting to follow the barely visible elk trail around the edge of the steep slope that led down to the mountain creek. The promise of trout for supper if he made it in time led him to chance the descent the "short way" to his campsite for the night. By the time he realized his foolishness, it was too late to turn back. As he inched his way down, a rock, loosened perhaps by the last passing elk, gave under his weight. Luckily, the small tree that stopped his fall held; removing his pack in his effort to regain the trail may have saved his life temporarily, but the sub-sequent loss of all his gear created a serious problem of survival.

These are only two examples of what can happen to a camper and backpacker to place him or her in a real survival situation. Actually, anything that causes a considerable deviation from the normal quite possibly could turn into a case of survival. Car trouble stranding a motorist in the desert, a power failure in suburban America, floods, earthquakes, tornadoes—these are only a few of the possibilities.

It's likely that most campers and backpackers would have an edge on the average citizen in being able to survive, but this article is written in the hope of adding a few percentage points to your chances of staying alive on your own.

Among the so-called experts on survival, there seems to be two basic philosophies. One group teaches skills and mind control necessary to survival in any conceivable situation. The other group, concerned with simple survival techniques, is more interested in the avoidance or prevention of circumstances that may lead to a need for survival.

And so you won't be guessing where I fit in, let me

A good knife, a compass, matches in a waterproof case and plastic bags in the storm kit just might save your life—if you have them with you.

state that I'm somewhere between the two. Had the two canoeists been more aware of what "could" happen, even the sudden sight of deer might not have deflected their attention and caused their trouble. Had the backpacker realized the seriousness of taking a chance, especially while alone, he might have chosen the long way down. At the same time, either party, on land or water, stands a chance of encountering unforeseen emergencies.

So, first of all, keep your wits about you. That can go a long way toward keeping you out of trouble. But in the event that trouble does happen, I hope you will remember enough of this to become a survivor—that is, to keep living one minute longer!

In order for life to continue, three elementary factors are "musts." It has been said that man can go for three minutes without air, for three days without water, and for three weeks without food. Maybe not comfortably, but still alive. But, if he can provide these three necessities, along with protection from heat or cold, he stands an excellent chance of holding on until he returns to normal conditions.

I won't go into the "air" bit, except to advise you to keep your head out of the sand and above water. But everyone should know simple artificial respiration in order to help another individual in need. Mountain climbers know the need for auxiliary oxygen supplies at high altitudes, but that, too, is a special subject that I'll not try to cover.

Water is something else. Our unfortunates in the first example may have been troubled with too much water, but often the camper and backpacker will be in country where water is in very short supply. Knowing how to get even a small amount could mean the difference between life and death. We'll get to that in a moment.

Have you ever been really hungry? I don't mean that feeling that comes just before lunch when you only had a cup of coffee for breakfast. I mean that feeling in your stomach that comes after the second or third day with no food. And except for a prolonged period without eating, the first two or three days are the worst. Just how important is food to the person trying to survive for one week, two weeks or even three weeks? Beyond that, nourishment must be provided in some form to keep the body functioning, but for the shorter periods, one must determine whether the plants, fish or animals procured for food return as much energy to the body as was expended in their procurement.

A shelter from the elements—sun, rain, snow or wind—can be comforting in more ways than one. The world, in wilderness or elsewhere, is a mighty big place in which to have to survive; a shelter can reduce it to a size with which you can cope.

The camper or backpacker who finds himself in a survival situation needs to do two things first of all: Build a fire, and then sit down and do a bit of thinking. No matter if the temperature is 110 degrees in the shade, you need the fire. The greatest danger that faces any individual under these circumstances is

A belt-type emergency kit kept separate from other gear can be mighty good insurance in a survival situation.

panic. Lost hunters have been known to throw away their guns and run until they fall from exhaustion. Others gripped by uncontrollable panic have even thrown away their clothing to run naked through snow and freezing temperatures. So build that fire; there's something about doing this that tends to calm the nerves and allow you to think. Then, even if you have to sit far back, do some thinking.

Will someone be looking for me, or must I get out on my own? If a search party can be expected, the lost person will probably be found sooner if he stays put and spends his time devising means of attracting attention to his position. However, if the individual is not injured, is able to travel, and is positive about his location and the direction to follow, slow and steady movement can be the right decision. Here again, the amount of emergency gear on hand may be a deciding factor. Confidence in one's ability to handle the situation can do much toward ensuring survival.

Before I go into each of the essentials for survival, let's think about something that has been the subject of much discussion since modern man began to venture into the wilderness. That is the emergency kit. These may vary from the complex to the very simple, but they share a common purpose: to add to your comfort and to help you survive.

The one that I carry in a zippered pouch that can be fastened to my belt would go a long way toward meeting my needs under survival conditions. It contains no less than four fire-starting methods, matches in a *waterproof* case, flint and steel with charred cloth and steel wool, a metal match, and a film container of carbide chips for extremely wet conditions. More about that when we discuss fire building. A hard plastic whistle for signaling and a special mirror complete with sighting hole will help me attract attention; other items are Band-Aids for minor cuts or blisters, water-purification tablets, compass, candle, insect repellent, nylon boot laces, a Swiss Army knife and a small flashlight. And while I don't always carry this on my belt, I do make certain that I have it along, and in a place separate from all other gear. An emergency kit inside a lost pack isn't going to do you much good.

An excellent personal survival kit can be assembled at home for just pennies. A pint can with the top cut out can hold the rest of the items and also serve for heating liquids. Seal it with a piece of plastic and several wraps of electrical tape. A piece of Christmas candle will help kindle a fire or heat water in the can. A small box of "strike anywhere" matches in a waterproof plastic bag. A plastic leaf bag, the 7-bushel size, with a hole cut in the lower end for the face makes

a good shelter from both wind and rain; a 30-gallon plastic garbage bag over the feet and legs serves to shelter the entire body; a few pieces of tape around the can for patching the bags or taping them together, plus eight or ten sugar cubes for instant energy, and you've got a kit to ensure your chances of survival. But only if you've got it with you! Add to it as you like.

Now, let's go back to those essentials for sustaining life. First of all, let's think about water. Your becoming thirsty tells you that your body needs water, and as the percentage of dehydration increases, so does the seriousness of the situation. The only way to prevent dehydration is through the intake of water in some form. By controlling sweating, the required amount can be reduced.

Your decision to stay put or move on is likely to be influenced by the availability of a usable water supply. If there is water in a spring, stream, lake or just a "seep" and you're not sure of its purity, it can be made safe for drinking by boiling for five minutes. Household bleach, four drops to the quart, will also purify it. Four to eight drops of iodine per quart works on these small quantities of water. Purification tablets are inexpensive and can be purchased at most sporting goods stores or drugstores.

The so-called desert still for procuring water by means of a sheet of plastic over a hole in the ground is fairly well known, but the vegetation-water still is fairly new. This is another use for the familiar plastic garbage bag, but be sure that the bag is not one that has been treated with chemicals to destroy fungus or bacteria. Simply described, this is the process: Fill a clean bag about three-fourths full of green non-poisonous vegetation, close the end and place the bag in the sun. The water produced tastes much like the material used, so choose something that isn't unpleasant to chew. I've used sweet gum or red gum leaves, and the water is quite good. Devise your own

A commercially available signal kit with flare gun and two kinds of smoke flares. Although this is too heavy for a backpacker, it could be a handy item to carry in the car, plane or boat.

Two fire saws made from bamboo along with the author's flint-and-steel fire-starting kit. The charred cloth or the natural tinder and steel wool (on the rock) work well with either the fire saws or the flint and steel.

If dry bamboo is available, a fire can be started much more easily than with the better-known bow-and-drill method.

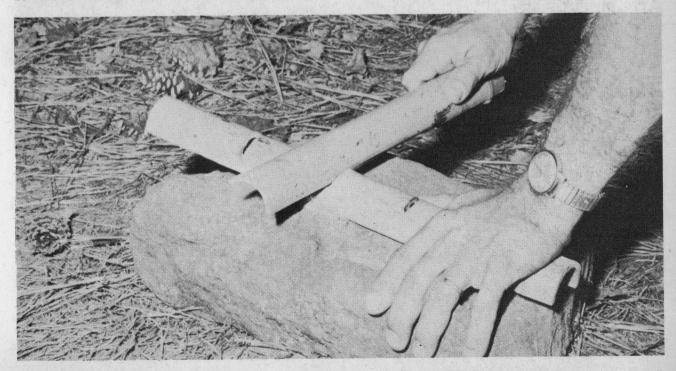

method of getting the most water out of the bag. I've been able simply to pour it out the mouth of the bag.

The person who is truly prepared for the unexpected will be familiar with as many ways as possible for securing water in his area. Moisture you must have, so learn all you can about how to find it.

If one could always count on having a plentiful supply of waterproof matches, there would be no need to worry about fire starting. But even if one is lucky enough to have any in a survival situation, chances are they won't last until the need for fire is over. Early outdoorsmen such as the famous Mountain Men carried flint and steel along with some charred cloth. They could kindle a fire as quickly as, or more quickly than you or I can with a match. With a bit of practice, it's still a good way to start a fire, especially if you have a small piece of fine steel wool for tinder. Steel wool, even if it has been wet, is excellent material for catching a spark and burning with a very hot flame long enough to ignite your other tinder. The new so-called metal match, when scraped with a knife blade, produces an abundance of sparks. A teaspoonful of carbide chips plus a little water produces a highly flammable gas that, when ignited with a spark, will burn long enough to start a good fire even under wet conditions.

All these are things that you have to bring with you. Let's hope you'll have at least one of them! But, if not, the Boy Scout bow-and-drill method of fire starting works if you have the proper wood and plenty of patience. There's also another way, called the fire saw, which I find easier. Take a piece of dry bamboo a foot or so long. Split it in half. On the round side of one piece, cut a notch barely through. Place your tinder under this notch and "saw" in the notch with the edge of the other half. The friction causes a glowing coal of fire to form in the notch and drop to the tinder below.

Take my advice and learn to build a fire as many ways as possible under all kinds of conditions. That skill could someday save your life.

Now what about shelter? Depending on where you are and the weather conditions, shelter of some kind could be one of the most important considerations in your fight for survival. Protection from rain, snow and wind is essential, but protection from the sun could be just as necessary for a person lost in the desert. Use what you have—a blanket, tarp, sheet of plastic, even the vehicle's upholstery if you are in a car—stranded, but some shelter is important! A brush lean-to, a snow cave or a rock shelter may be the answer under your survival conditions. A poncho, a space blanket or some other item in your gear can go a long way toward the construction of a comfortable shelter. And with a

A clean plastic garbage bag partially filled with green vegetation and placed in the sun will provide usable water in an emergency situation. The writer is shown here using sweet gum leaves; avoid using any poisonous plants.

An emergency shelter being built against a large boulder, using a poncho for the roof and natural materials available.

A simple, easy-to-build lean-to shelter using a space rescue blanket along with natural materials; leaves packed into a frame of sticks to close ends, browse for a bed, and rocks to reflect heat from a fire.

A deadfall trap that could help provide emergency food from small animals.

reflector fire in front, it can be mighty snug even in the coldest weather, especially if you've gathered a supply of firewood sufficient to last the night. Have twice what you think you'll need, and that should do it.

While many people may think that food is important, it is perhaps the least so under survival conditions. Food is necessary for the continued well-being of the individual, but, as I said earlier, we can do without it longer than we think with no lasting bad effects. If natural food, be it plant or animal, can be secured without expending more energy than the food itself will produce, fine. Otherwise, you might be better off in the long run to conserve your energy or expend it for something else.

There are many foods in nature for the person who has learned how to find and identify them. Almost any animal is edible, as are fish if you can catch them. And even though you may not derive a lot of energy from eating, the psychological effect of having found food on your own will be good, and quite possibly just the spark that keeps you going! Here again, as in learning ways to build a fire, the knowledge of even a few sources of wild food could be the edge you need to save your life.

If you have decided that you have to get out on your own, be extra careful to avoid injury or making your situation worse. Try to orient yourself and not use up precious energy traveling in circles. Downstream or downhill will usually lead you out.

Finally, there are two excellent rules that every camper and backpacker should follow: don't go out alone, and always let someone responsible know where you're going and how long you expect to be gone. If you do have trouble, it can be a mighty comfortable feeling to know that someone will be checking up if you don't return on time.

So try to anticipate and avoid trouble that could lead to a survival situation, and at the same time, be prepared both mentally and physically to meet the problem head on if it should happen to you. Then, if some day you should find yourself on your own, you would still be alive when your rescuers reached you, or would be able to make it out by yourself. You *can* survive—just keep living one minute longer!

Tips on Campfires, Woods and Axes
by Vin T. Sparano

In this age of camp stoves and cast-iron barbecues, it's refreshing to see people cooking over or huddled around a bright campfire. I'm not referring to a pile of miscellaneous lumber piled high and burning with a 6-foot flame. A good campfire is not big, but it burns bright and hot. It provides heat for cooking and warmth. It can toast marshmallows and it can also save your life.

It's easy to build the right campfire for your particular trip. If you're a hunter and you only want to brew a quick pot of coffee, you might try the Swedish Fire Lay. But on an overnight trip the Keyhole Fire is better. If it's windy, a Trench Fire or Indian Fireplace is best.

Let's start from the beginning and learn exactly how to build a campfire, how to select the right type and what firewoods burn best.

Before you build any fire, always clear an area about 10 feet in diameter. Make sure that there are no low-hanging tree limbs over the spot and that there is plenty of room within the circle for wood, pots and cooking supplies. Your fire will be in the center of this circle, so clear it of leaves, twigs and other debris that could ignite.

There are three basic ingredients in every good campfire:
(1) tinder—any small-sized wood or bark that burns quickly and easily
(2) kindling—small dry sticks (bigger than tinder) stacked loosely pyramid-shape or criss-crossed on top of the tinder.
(3) firewood—wood ranging from sticks a few inches in diameter to heavy logs. Obviously, firewood is not put on the fire until tinder and kindling are burning.

Tinder is easy to find. Aside from commercial fire starters, tinder includes paper, birch bark from dead trees, cedar bark and twigs. Rolled weeds and dead grass also work. The secret is getting tinder that will flare into flame almost instantly. A fuzz stick makes fine tinder; take a stick and shave splinters from it but leave shavings attached to the stick. This will burn as readily as any other tinder.

Kindling can be any small sticks stacked over the tinder. You should have no problem in finding plenty of kindling on the ground around camp. If you can't, break a few sticks off dead trees. Make sure the tree is dead. If a limb bends, it is probably alive and too green

The Hunter's Fire. Build the fire first, then roll the logs into place. This fire uses little fuel and takes little space.

The Swedish Fire Lay, a campfire that we don't see too often, is ideal for hunters and fishermen. It is made of three split logs about 12 inches long, propped up against one another tripod fashion. The fire is built at the base. The inside of the logs will eventually begin to burn, heat rises, and the top of the logs acts as a base for pots. It's an ideal fire for confined spaces.

For overnight trips, you'll need a bigger fire for cooking and the Keyhole Fire is excellent. As its name suggests, it is shaped like a keyhole. It is made completely with stones. The narrow section should run 2 or 3 feet long and narrow enough to support pots. This is an easy fire to keep going, since wood can be added to the fire in the circle and constantly kept burning and ready to be pushed under the pots when necessary.

If wood is scarce or you want to conserve what you have, build an Indian Fire, which is simply five or six medium-sized logs radiating outward from the center where the fire is built. As the wood burns, the logs are pushed toward the center, supplying more fuel. It's a good fire to use with dingle sticks or grates. (Dingle sticks are makeshift sticks that do a variety of jobs. They hold pots over a fire, make a rack for utensils or provide a place to hang a lantern or shirt.)

No need to build a big fire to brew a pot of coffee. I got this pot going over a Swedish Fire Lay. The fire is built under logs. This is a good design for confined places.

to be of any value for a campfire.

Always start small when building a fire. As soon as your tinder and kindling are burning, add wood no bigger in diameter than one inch. Once you have a bed of hot coals and the fire is not smoking a great deal, you can work up to bigger logs. Keep in mind that split wood burns more easily than whole logs.

The actual design of the campfire depends on several factors, such as the food to be cooked, the wind conditions, length of stay and so on.

If you want to cook only a quick trail lunch, there are two campfires that have been proved to work: the Hunter's Fire and the Swedish Fire Lay. For the Hunter's Fire, first build a small fire. When hot coals form, roll two logs to each side of the fire. Place the logs close enough together so that they can support pots. Eventually, the inside of the logs will also begin to burn. Remember to place the logs so that the wind will blow lengthwise between them. If this still doesn't supply enough draft, prop up the logs with small stones. The Hunter's Fire can also be made with rocks, but logs work better.

When wood is scarce, build this Indian Fire. Limbs radiate outward from fire and are pushed in as they burn. Note dingle stick and rocks. Pot height can be adjusted by moving the supporting rock.

The Indian Fireplace is another campfire that works fine on windy days. Dingle sticks hold pots over the fire. The hole is about 12 inches deep.

Wind can be a problem with campfires. There seems to be either too much or too little of it. There are ways to solve the problem, however. The Trench Fire, for example, is made in a rectangular hole in the ground about 12 inches deep. The fire in the hole will burn steadily, even in a high wind. Pots are placed on top of limbs or steel rods crossing the hole. The Indian Fireplace is similar to the Trench Fire, except that the hole is round and pots are held over it with dingle sticks and heavy stones.

Finally, there is the simple rock fireplace. This is built by placing flat rocks in the shape of a horseshoe. The rocks can either be placed close enough to support pots over a fire or a metal grate can be put across them. Another method is to use dingle sticks to get your pots over the fire.

Woods vary in how hot or fast they burn. Ash or maple makes good hot campfires, but willow doesn't. Oak and hickory are also good, but these hardwoods will quickly take the edge off an ax or a saw, which is something to remember if you're on an extended trip. If you want to avoid sparks and smoke, don't use pine, spruce, tamarack, basswood or chestnut.

The following chart lists the various woods according to the way they rank as campfire fuel:

Good	Fair	Poor
Ash	Beech	Willow
Hickory	Mulberry	Alder
Oak	Buckeye	Chestnut
Holly	Sycamore	Magnolia
Dogwood	Tamarack	Tulip
Apple	Pine	Catalpa
Birch	Cedar	White Elm
Maple	Juniper	Cherry
Locust	Spruce	
Mountain	Cottonwood	
mahogany	Fir	
	Aspen	

More important than building a campfire is learning how to put it out. When you break camp, douse the fire by sprinkling it with water. Don't pour the water; sprinkling is more effective. Stir up the embers and sprinkle again. Continue to do so until no more steam comes from the wood or ground.

Now that you know how and what kind of campfire to build, as well as something about the woods to use, let's discuss the subject of cutting firewood and the

A Keyhole Fire is best for overnight or extended camping trips. Once you have a good fire started in the circle, burning wood or hot coals are shoved under the pots.

Here I use a Trench Fire to prepare a lunch in a windy clearing. No matter how hard the breeze blows, the wood in this 12-inch hole will burn steadily.

all-important camp ax. Granted, there are times when a folding saw may be a better choice, but a camp ax will always be an essential tool for campers.

Skilled axmen claim that the most effective axhead should be designed to provide maximum wood-to-steel contact. The squarish Michigan axhead comes closest to this design concept and is preferable to the tomahawk head. The tomahawk has eye appeal and is the ax that novice campers will usually select in sporting goods stores, but it's a poor design when compared with the Michigan head. The Michigan is the ax to choose for most camp uses. Avoid the double-bit ax, unless you're a very experienced woodcutter.

A camp ax is essential gear on my trips, and I have very definite ideas about the designs and sizes I find easiest to use. I rank the common hand ax, which has a 12-inch handle and 1-pound head, as a second choice for most camp wood cutting. The ax I've found best is

Here are three common axhead styles. From left, double-bit, Michigan-type head, and tomahawk. The best style for campers is the Michigan. The double-bit is dangerous unless you're an experienced woodcutter and the tomahawk has too little steel-to-wood contact in the head.

My son Matt carving a fuzz stick, which makes an excellent fire starter. Shavings should be thin and left attached to the stick.

Dead saplings are cut away from a tree easily by bending them over and making a slanting, downward cut near the base.

CAMPER'S & BACKPACKER'S BIBLE

Your ax will be a lot safer if you keep the edge covered with a leather sheath or a makeshift case made from an inner tube and garden hose.

When trimming tree limbs, always cut toward the top of the tree and away from your body. Stand on the far side of the trunk.

When cutting kindling, hold the wood on a log or stump and cut at a 45-degree angle away from you.

the medium-sized or three-quarter ax, which has a 24- or 26-inch handle and a 2- to 2½-pound head. The medium-sized ax is a fine all-purpose ax that's light enough to carry but still heavy enough for most cutting. I've seen good axmen split logs as much as 12 inches across with this size of ax.

For cutting small wood, such as kindling, I hold a medium-sized ax about 10 inches from the head and swing it with one hand. Held this way, it's twice as effective as a hand ax because of its heavier head.

If you're looking for an ax for a permanent camp, you should choose a full-sized cabin ax. Weight is not a factor here, and a full-sized ax with a 36-inch handle and a 3½- to 4-pound head will make cutting easier. Once again, look for the Michigan-style head. It's a good choice, regardless of ax size.

You should also choose your ax handle carefully. Avoid fancy burls or knots in the wood, which may mean weak spots. Stay away from painted handles, since the paint can cover flaws. Look for handles with straight grains running the entire length. Handles are varnished for two reasons—eye appeal and protection of the wood against moisture—but bare wood affords a better grip. Your ax will feel better if you remove the varnish.

Before you cut any wood, there are a few safety factors to keep in mind. First, check the ax for a loose head or split handle. If the head continually comes loose, replace the handle. Temporarily, you can soak the handle in a stream or bucket of water. The wood will swell and tighten the head. A split handle can be taped and used in an emergency for light wood, but it can never be fully trusted. Replace it.

Check the edge. A dull ax is dangerous because it can bounce off wood and hit you. A sharp ax, however, digs into the wood. I sharpen my axes in two stages, using a Nicholson Black Diamond file first and then whetstone. After I anchor the axhead, I start with the metal file, drawing it from toe to heel (top to bottom) of the blade, about one inch from the edge. The reason for this is to cut off some of the metal from the blade so that the taper is uniform. Once you have a good taper, you can put a fine edge on the bit with a round whetstone. It's also wise to sandpaper any paint off the blade before starting, so that the paint won't clog your file.

The most common cutting job for campers is trimming limbs from fallen trees and cutting them into firewood length. This is easy and safe, if you follow certain rules. First, always trim toward the top of the tree, so that the limbs point away from your body. Keep the trunk between you and the limbs you're trimming. Stand on one side of the log, and trim the far side, then change positions. There's almost no chance of hitting your legs if there's a tree trunk between you and the blade. If this is not possible and you have to stand on the side that you're trimming, stand slightly forward of the limb and swing the ax so that the blade strikes the limb behind your legs.

To cut a limb into campfire lengths, hold it firmly against a stump or log and chop away from you at about a 45-degree angle. With the three-quarter ax, I have no trouble in cutting limbs up to one inch in diameter with a single blow.

In felling trees, the width of the initial cut or notch should be equal to the diameter of the tree. A 16-inch-wide tree, for example, needs at least a 16-inch-wide cut. Clear away all brush around the tree before starting. Saplings are taken out easily by bending them and making a slanting, downward cut near the base.

Here is some final advice on ax use:

(1) Never carry an ax over your shoulder. Hold it close to the head, blade pointed downward and at your side. If you trip, throw it away from you.

(2) Between cutting sessions, a single-bit ax blade can be buried in a log or placed flat on the ground with the blade under a log.

(3) Use a wooden chopping block. Never cut on rock or other hard surfaces.

(4) Never use the butt end of the axhead to drive anything heavier than a tent peg.

(5) A split handle is best removed by sawing it off below the head and driving the rest of it out backward with a steel bar. You can also burn it out if you bury the blade in wet earth to protect the heat-tempered edge.

(6) Logs can be split more easily if you aim for the cracks in the top end grain of a dry log. These cracks indicate weak sections in the grain.

New Breed of Blades

by Sid Latham

In the late 1960's, when the bench-made knife arrived on the sporting scene, every outdoorsman, day hiker and wilderness roamer had to own one of these very special blades. The fact that these knives, and the handful of experts crafting them, spoke eloquently of special steels, new handle materials and a particular shape for a special job made them all the more desirable. Soon there were knives for the skindiver, parachutist, fisherman, mountaineer, backpacker—in fact every kind except one to slash the strings of your tennis racquet when you missed a lob across the net. Actually, not much has been overlooked since George Herron, a top craftsman from Aiken, South Carolina, dreamed up a custom job for shucking oysters, and guaranteed to impress your guests the next time you have a backyard seafood bake.

Even among expert observers, the question arises, are all these knives necessary? The answer has to be "yes and no." No one knife or blade shape will do every task set for it and it's pretty difficult to skin a mouse and a moose with the same blade. Some of the highly specialized forms actually have a practical use, albeit for one particular purpose only. On the other hand, a backpacker who is concerned with weight and cost may be forgiven for wondering at the prices of some of this gleaming steel.

Make no mistake: a quality product costs money and a knife is no different from a sleeping bag, a rucksack or a mountain tent in this respect. There are degrees of value, and no hiker should be expected to pay $125 *per inch of blade* from a master knifesmith such as Bill Moran, and if he did, there would be a minimum wait of seven years for delivery. What causes these astronomical prices? Craftsmanship and the steel are the answers. Moran forges his blades and eventually comes up with a fine Damascus pattern that is unique. Moran's blades are crafted for collectors but they show how high a custom-crafted blade can run.

Steel is certainly the heart of the knife, but it is futile to say what steel is best. Every knife maker offers two or more different steels in his catalog. If the maker is a sportsman and uses his product in the field, he may eventually decide that one particular steel has an advantage over all others. Naturally, that is the steel he will use and brag about (which has to be taken

A wide range of knives for every outdoor purpose. *Left to right:* Schrade Loveless, $100; Mountain Friend Backpacker by Sid Birt, $100; The High Country by George Stone, $125; Gerber's Sportsman III, $32.50 and Sportsman II with drop-point blade, $23.50; Bob Ogg folder, custom-made, about $80; track folder distributed by Ithaca Guns, $67.50; small forward-lock folder by Ron Little, $125.

with a couple of grains of salt) and will insist that this particular steel will make the best knife ever.

What has resulted from all this enthusiasm for bench-made knives is the fact that the commercial cutlery firms have sat up and taken notice of the growing interest in all types of knives. Better steels and practical designs have become the hallmark of the latest offerings.

Schrade Cutlery is a good example. The company induced top knifeman Bob Loveless to design a sportsman's blade a couple of years ago. Loveless had

done the pioneering work with a new, exciting steel called 154-CM. This was a stainless steel developed for the high-temperature regions of the jet engines of 747 aircraft and its high chromium content coupled with 4 percent molybdenum made it an ideal knife steel from a metallurgical point of view. It had great strength, held an edge well and was rust-resistant.

The only problem with the mixture, from a technical point of view, is that it is extremely difficult to heat-treat, and Shrade unfortunately did not have the expertise to handle it. With all problems licked, however, the knife was introduced in late 1975 at almost double the predicted cost. Henry Baer, the head honcho of Schrade, had hoped to sell it for around $50, but was forced to double the price. Now, if you can find one, the cost will be about $100. Even so, expert knife users think it is a bargain considering that it is a knife by a master and crafted of his favorite steel.

Of course, everyone has a different opinion about the new interest in fine cutlery. Bob Loveless says: "It's simply the mediocrity of so many items on the market. Knife users want something of quality once again." To that end, cutlery firms have begun an upgrading of their products. Western Cutlery has improved its sportsman's line of Westmark knives and sells them in the $35 range. Others, such as Buck, Case and Gerber, have outdone themselves. Gerber, considered the top-of-the-line commercial outfit, has a brilliant designer, Al Mar, who spends much of his time visiting knife shows and talking to knife makers, and working at his designing board. Mar keeps a constant line of additions flowing into the Gerber catalog, and the fact he is a sportsman himself gives his opinion weight on command decisions for new knives.

Naturally a hiker's or backpacker's requirements are different from those of the big-game hunter or the

Survival knives. *Left to right:* Morseth; Randall; another Randall; Cooper; Loveless; Cooper with guthook for cutting parachute cords. Prices about $100.

fisherman. He may use knives for blazing a trail, opening tin cans, doing odd repairs or slicing rope. However, any knife can and should be regarded as a survival tool, and the blade must be long enough and sturdy enough to do some surprising jobs. Don't laugh—one day it may become necessary to lash a knife to a pole as a fish spear or a protective weapon. A hefty knife may be required to cut some stout limbs for an emergency crutch if someone takes a fall. A stout blade is not only necessary, but important. I've spent considerable time covering assignments in fairly backward areas of the Amazon Basin, Borneo and New Guinea, and while I never had to use a knife for defensive purposes, there were a few occasions when emergency calking of a dugout was necessary, and once I had to cut splints for a companion's broken wrist. So knives must do yeoman duty at the most unexpected times.

What knife to choose and what to pay can be very difficult problems for the novice knife buyer. An experienced hunter or a bird shooter will know from years in the field what is required in a knife. The amateur who has just taken up camping or backpacking will probably not be quite so knowledgeable. When backpacks, clothing, boots and everything else have been selected, knives are usually left till last and the choice may be an old pocket knife or a cheap sheath job with a scabbard more dangerous than safe.

Top to bottom: **Sturdy outdoor knives by Zack, Loveless and Rod Chappel; prices roughly $200 each.**

Track knife Trail Creek distributed by Ithaca Guns, an all- steel knife, about $69.

Three knives from Schrade Cutlery Corporation. *From top:* Drop-point Hunter, $15; wood-handled Backpacker, $10; Ellenville Lock-Blade, $7.95. These inexpensive knives will require better edges than the factory puts on but will do an excellent job in the field.

The custom makers, whose prices shot skyward for some years, have realized that the $50 knife shouldn't be forgotten. At the last knife show held in Dallas in the spring of 1976 hundreds of new makers offered some superb blades in the $50 range and some even for less. For the higher-priced offerings, the detailed workmanship, or fancy file work on the tang or blade will do nothing except make the knife look prettier and of course cost considerably more.

There are plenty of knives of various designs available in the stores, and if you can't find precisely what you're looking for, you haven't looked hard enough. Pricewise, there is some fine cutlery around for about $35, and the Gerber people craft excellent blades in a variety of lengths and shapes that should please the most exacting. The Gerber Presentation series, the company's top-quality hunting knives, begins with a 4-inch blade and runs up to a 5¼-inch heavy-duty knife. The average price is in the neighborhood of $50. However these knives are crafted of 440-C stainless steel and have solid Macassar ebony handles like the ones the custom boys use. Gerber's Armorhide line uses high-speed tool-steel blades, and the biggest of this series costs about $30 for a 5½-inch blade.

While experienced sportsmen believe that a 4-inch blade is sufficient for most chores, the camper, who may put his knife to more strenuous uses, will probably be happier with a slightly longer blade. Gerber recently introduced some fine large "folders." Many outdoorsmen admit to feeling uncomfortable with a long piece of steel swinging from their belts and prefer a sturdy "folder,"—as knives with folding blades are called. Two of the most practical are the Gerber folding Sportsman III and the Magnum Folding Hunter. Blades are 440-C steel with a Rockwell hardness of 57 to 59 and handles are Macassar ebony. The Sportsman III has the longer blade, 4½ inches, with the Magnum checking in at 3/4 inch less. These are big folders, and as they might be uncomfortable in a pocket all day long, both come with well-fitted belt pouches. They sell for about $35 and are excellent bargains. The better folders have blades that lock in the open position.

What of handle material for a knife? Well, for a very long time, stag—Sambar stag imported from India—was the choice of almost anyone crafting a knife. Not only is it exceptionally handsome but it is sturdy as well. However, politics entered knifedom; the Indian government placed an embargo on the exportation of stag and it is becoming difficult to obtain.

Ivory is a beautiful handle material but it was never practical on a working knife. It has a tendency to check and crack and won't stand the hard knocks that a sturdy working knife has to take. Choice ivory is expensive and difficult to obtain, and most knife makers, if they use it at all, charge higher prices for it.

Wood is still the preferred material and there is a wide selection of rare and exotic woods available. Oily tropical woods are excellent, and American woods such as walnut, maple, hickory and ash all make fine knife handles. Many years ago leather was popular, and when properly cut and placed on the tang and correctly treated, it made an excellent handle; all things being equal, it might last for many years. Many

Three custom-crafted knives. *Top:* a drop-point hunter by Horace Wiggins, 154-CM steel with seashell handle in epoxy; *center:* Bird & Fish knife by J.D. Clay with ivory Micarta handle, $65; *bottom:* a small drop-point hunter by George Herron, with osage-orange-wood handle, $50.

rare materials such as jade, mother-of-pearl or even petrified wood, are used, which will cost even more than the blade itself. Horace Wiggins, a superb craftsman from Mansfield, Louisiana, offers cactus and seashell for handles. With the exception of Wiggins' materials, the others mentioned are collector's items and of no practical use in the field. The best handle material is a man-made product called Micarta. Trademarked by Westinghouse, this is a phenolic compound that comes in a variety of colors and wood textures. The great advantage of this material is that it won't chip, crack, burn, warp, shrink or discolor. It makes the ideal knife handle and is the first choice of custom knife makers. Unfortunately, since it can't be molded or formed it is little used in commercial cutlery.

For a survival knife that can double as a practical field knife, there are few better than Randall's Model 18 Attack Survival knife, which comes with a saw edge atop the blade and a hollow handle for storing fish line, snare wire or medicines. This is not a lightweight knife, and the fact it costs nearly $100 will deter many campers from considering it.

A couple of knife makers besides Randall have paid special attention to the needs of the hiker and devised excellent knives that tip the scales at only a very few ounces.

Texan George Stone has devised a model called the High Country which comes with a cutout of metal on the ricasso to lighten the load. The blade is 4 inches long and has Micarta handle slabs. I've carried this knife in the swamps of Georgia and across a couple of mountains in Wyoming, and I admit I'm not aware of it riding on my belt. A new knife maker, Sid Birt of Bunker Hill, Idaho, devised a hiker's dream called the Mountain Friend Backpacker, which has metal cutouts in the tang and aluminum bolts holding the Micarta slabs. Birt says the knife weighs in at 4 ounces.

When talking about knives it's pretty difficult to overlook the bench-made knives. The makers seem to be able to supply any type of knife desired, though admittedly at fairly fancy prices. Judicious shopping will show the prospective buyer that not every custom craftsman wants his entire bank account for a practical piece of steel.

Some of the bench-made pocket folders in various blade lengths are bargains from Ron Little or Bob Ogg; both do sturdy folders for about $60 to $80.

All the American cutlery firms, plus the German, Italian and Japanese are offering excellent knives at about $15. Even Smith & Wesson, the gun firm, is now selling knives designed by Blackie Collins, although its prices will be near those charged for a bench-made knife.

For those who hesitate to spend top dollar, Schrade, Camillus and a few others craft some lower-priced cutlery that, if kept sharpened, will work well. Don't expect a cheap knife to take on any hard jobs, since its construction will not last more than a few years if it is constantly abused.

Remember that any knife should be used for its intended purpose. If it is a sportsman's knife, the blade should be used only for skinning game.

The proper edge on a skinning knife precludes twisting, chopping, hacking at tin cans and putting the edge to rough work, unless it has both a sturdy blade and a proper edge bevel. There are some knives with extra-sturdy and sharpened backs that will allow the user to hack branches and chop small pieces of wood, but these are fairly heavy and really not practical backpackers' knives.

After all this, let's try to describe the ideal knife for the hiker who travels in all climes. The steel should be either 440-C or 154-CM, both of which are reasonably rust-resistant. While both these steels are fairly difficult to sharpen, with proper treatment, they will hold an edge longer. Blade length should be about 5 inches, with a modest drop point rather than a big up-swept curve that is practical only for skinning game. The best choice of handle material is Micarta; the color is a matter of personal preference. Some knives come with a thong hole at the top of the handle, and this could be handy if the knife is being used in deep snow or around water.

Sheaths are important and are one aspect of knife making often ignored by the knife makers. A good sheath not only will keep the knife securely in place but will protect the wearer in a fall. Often the sheaths supplied by the cheap outfits are no better than cardboard. It's worth a couple of extra bucks to have a leather worker make a sturdy sheath. One fine knife maker who is also a top leather craftsman is Jack Barnett of Little, Colorado. Barnett is a true artist, and many knife makers have him make special sheaths if they require decorative tooling.

In caring for a knife, there are more don'ts than do's. Don't store your knife in a sheath; the sheath collects moisture and gives off fumes of tanning acids. The best advice on storing sporting cutlery is to keep it clean, rub a light coating of oil over the blade, and wrap it in wax paper. Leather requires little attention beyond a coating of Lexol every six months.

A good knife—and this means anything from a $15 store-bought job to a $200 custom-crafted jewel—doesn't demand too much attention. Keep it sharp, keep it clean and store it properly when not in use. With that treatment any knife will give years of faithful service.

Two quality handmade folders by George Herron. These cost about $200 each, are made of 154 CM steel and have handle slabs of African blackwood.

The Advantages of Buying Quality Equipment

by Thayne Smith

"You get what you pay for."

That phrase has been bandied about for many years, probably as long as man has found it necessary to barter for the items that make his everyday life more comfortable.

Is it always true? Not necessarily, especially when applied to camping.

Campers who have been making the outdoor scene for a number of years will tell you that there are certain brand names of merchandise—running from such items as knives and axes to tents and recreational vehicles—in which you can always put your trust. There are other brands—generally a little cheaper—which may or may not be dependable. In other words, some firms have a reputation for quality regardless of price, while others have a reputation for price only.

All this, generally, leads to frustration for the camping-equipment buyer, especially the guy or gal who is a "first timer" in the camping business. Regardless of the type of camper you hope to become, you will find literally thousands of items of camping supplies available.

In recreational vehicles, for example, there are seven types of units, ranging from tiny camping (tent) trailers at $500 or less to giant motor homes costing more than $50,000. Today, there are more than 400 recreational-vehicle manufacturers in the United States, many offering a full line of vehicles, others specializing in only one or two types.

A similar situation exists with most other camping items. The new camper or the "old pro" shopping for a new item can find equal opportunity for confusion whether he wants to buy a tent, sleeping bag, cooler, stove, jug, backpack frame and sack, knife, ax or even a compass—which he may need to find his way out of the maze of camping equipment offered in some giant stores.

In the appliance field, he may get involved in a decision on whether to purchase gasoline- or propane-powered stove, lantern, catalytic heater, and other products. In tents, sleeping bags, backpack sacks, knapsacks and other canvas items, he will find such terms as canvas weights, weaves, types of sewing, seams, reinforcement areas and others to confuse him.

What to do?

Basically, there are certain points of quality in every type of camping product which the would-be buyer should seek.

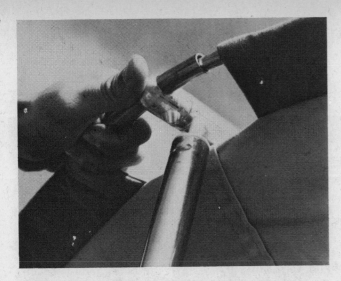

Strong, well-sewn grommets and heavy-duty aluminum poles with stout plastic tips are desirable qualities in selecting a tent.

For instance, take a good look at tents. You're a new camper, and you want something for your family of four (wife, two kids and self) that will serve you well but not deplete your entire savings.

First, seek a product that comes from an established manufacturer—one with a name for quality at a good price. There are many in the tent field. If in doubt, consult campers who are tenters or may be knowledgeable in the tent field.

Then be sure to look for a tent which is large enough for your family. Don't try to pack four people in a 4- by 6-foot mountain tent. Select something which will take four large sleeping bags, with extra room for tossing and turning and some space left over for storage of other items in the corners when it's raining.

There are many designs of tents available, and design can add to or detract from your comfort. If you like a cabin-type tent, remember that you can't stand up at the eaves (sides) if you're of average height, and that fact may have a bearing on the size of tent you really want.

Look for other features, such as waterproof flooring (some of the best tents have vinyl-coated floors, which are excellent for families with small children prone to spill things), and heavy-duty fabric. Vinyl flooring which extends a few inches up the sides of the tent furnishes extra waterproofing.

Check the tent seams to verify that strong, even stitching with heavy thread is provided, and make sure that stress points are reinforced. These areas include corners, ridges and roof peaks. Also look for storm flaps on all the doors and windows of the tent, large windows and doors (for best ventilation) with heavy-duty zippers and close-meshed screening (nylon is best) to keep insects out.

Before buying, you might investigate rental agencies in your area, and try out two or more brands and styles of tents before you finally decide. Consult with tent campers when you visit parks or campgrounds. They can provide a wealth of information and advice.

If you're in the market for sleeping bags, you'll need to consider many of the same factors that you look for in tent construction.

First, decide where you're going to use the sleeping bags. How cold is it likely to be? Will you be sleeping under the stars, in a tent or inside a vehicle? Will you be on the ground, a cot or an air mattress? How much wet weather can be expected, and how much rough handling in service and transportation will the bags be subjected to?

Keep in mind, first of all, that all sleeping bags are not alike, although they may appear to be. Nor will all of them keep you as warm and comfortable as you should be when camping. There are many differences in bags—in filling materials, durability and portability, size and shape, and price.

Most state laws require that sleeping bags carry "content identification tags" outside to tell you what the filling material is. Look at these closely. The type and amount of filling determine how warm and comfortable you'll be. The most widely used types of filling are down (goose and duck feathers, and sometimes chicken feathers), polyester-fiber fill such as DuPont's Dacron 88, acetate and waste, or reprocessed fibers. DuPont also has developed a lightweight fiber called Dacron II which is used by many sleeping bag makers as a substitute for down. It has many of the qualities of down, and is about 80 percent as warm as prime goose down (on a pound-to-pound basis).

Quality tents come with vinyl-coated floors, which extend a few inches up sidewalls to provide a waterproof floor area and simplify cleaning. A "must" for tenters with small children.

Reinforced corners—a second layer of canvas sewn in at stress points—are a mark of quality in tent construction. They also help prevent leakage.

the finest equipment. Department-store backpack offerings generally are not of the best quality, and even if they are, the salespersons in discount and department-store sporting goods shops generally are not experts on the needs of hikers and climbers.

There is great variety and room for much confusion in camping appliances and accessories, too.

In coolers and jugs, for example, two important factors are to be considered: outside construction and insulation material. Today's best coolers are constructed exclusively of plastic outer shells, liners and lids, or a combination of plastic and metal covers and plastic liners.

There are many good ones on the market. The best are not expensive when you consider their many uses and versatility. They have urethane foam-type insulation, metal or heavy-duty plastic handles and plastic drains. Most have trays, generally of plastic, for packing sandwiches, vegetables and fruits so that these do not have to be placed directly on ice.

Besides the filling material, check the lining (generally flannel or nylon), cover fabric (canvas or nylon) and zipper.

The lining is important. It should be heavy and durable as should the outside covering. A good-quality canvas is hard to beat. Nylon, of course, will wear like iron but is "slippery" on a tent floor or air mattress. Zippers should be the heavy-duty type. Seams on sleeping bags should be doubled, or lap-felled, so that the edges of the material are folded and sewn under, not exposed to jam zippers or tangle toes. The better sleeping bags have flaps sewn over zippers, too, so that the cold metal of the zipper doesn't strike you on the bare bottom when you roll over, or let in a lot of unwanted cold air!

The type of sewing on the bag itself may affect your comfort, too. Quilt-through construction is fine, as long as there is other covering along with it to prevent cold air from seeping into the bag at the seams. The double-wall type of construction is considered best for most sleeping bags.

As with tents and sleeping bags, there are many backpack frames and sacks on the market. A good, stoutly built frame is the first essential for comfortable backpacking. The sack must also be sturdy. Comfort is determined, first, by how the frame fits the body, and if it is easy to adjust as your load changes.

The best place to purchase a good backpack set is in a specialty store which outfits outdoorsmen for high adventure. It may cost a little more, but most specialty shops are owned and operated by professional climbers and hikers, who can give you a rundown on

Heavy-duty zippers, sewn in with strong nylon thread, are desirable in both tents and sleeping bags. Metal zippers are generally preferable to the nylon type.

The best coolers and jugs have walls at least an inch thick, filled with sandwich-type foam insulation to bond the walls together, giving the unit added strength.

In the very best coolers, the lids are also insulated. The discriminating buyer should always inquire if this is the case when he is looking at a product. Most cooler makers will provide you with tables of insulating quality upon request. Some provide this information in their catalogs.

Catalogs also can give the concerned buyer excellent leads to the quality of such items as stoves, catalytic heaters, and many types of lanterns—both gasoline and propane.

Before you make a purchase, determine the fuel-consumption rates and BTU inputs and outputs of the appliances. Why purchase Brand X stove, for instance, when Brand Y will give you much more heat and cooking power at less initial cost, with fuel savings tossed in? All makers of stoves, lanterns and catalytic heaters are required to reveal the operating statistics on their products, so don't be afraid to ask for them.

In addition, look for sturdiness in construction. Are stove grills, wind baffles and the stove box itself strong, with good welds, tight bolts and screws? Is the painting of good quality, and are hinges and handles chrome plated to protect against rusting?

Accessories are much like other products. If you need a quality knife, for instance, seek one made of stainless steel, which holds an edge. Brand names here are the best guide. There are many cheap foreign makes available, but most are not worth a good camper's glance.

The same is true of axes. A cast-iron ax, for instance, isn't going to last long. Good steel is needed, and a reputable hardware store with experienced clerks is the best place to find such an ax. Again, ask for brand names.

There are many, many advantages to the camper in purchasing quality equipment. Most important, it makes camping easier and more enjoyable and comfortable. Nothing can do more to spoil an otherwise

The best tents have rugged threshold areas on doors for serviceability and to prevent tearing from constant use. Thresholds should fold easily for sweeping out the tent and should be equipped with heavy-duty metal zippers for long wear.

fine outing than to have a stove malfunction in the midst of cooking a meal; a lantern act up when you're using it to tuck the kiddies into their sleeping bags for the night; a mild wind rip a big hole in the seam of a tent; or, heaven forbid, to awaken and find your joints aching and your body stiff because you have a sleeping bag that is far from adequate.

There are many ways to determine whether you're buying quality equipment for your outings. Some of the best are to shop at reliable stores; to seek out clerks who are campers and appear knowledgeable about the products they offer; to rent and use items before actual purchase if possible; and not to hesitate to ask questions.

Send queries to manufacturers about their products. Ask for comparisons with other brands of the same items. Most manufacturers know that they have competition and will be happy to stress the good points of their own products.

Most important, get advice from other campers, especially with those who have years of experience. Generally, you'll find them the friendliest folks around and they are not hard to locate. It's a safe bet that there is a campground near you; drive over and walk from site to site.

Most veteran campers are smart shoppers, and they are willing and ready to share their knowledge of products with you—whether the item is a vehicle, tent, stove, lantern or accessory, or the newest "can't live or camp without it" gadget on the market. These pros know that "you get what you pay for" is not always true. The smart ones get far more.

Ease of cleaning and rugged construction are shown in the tent threshold and doorway pictured here. The stake loop at right is sewn into the seam of the tent above the floorline to prevent tearing and give needed strength to stretch and hold the tent solidly.

Spacious and different, this Spanish-type tent boasts a side-door entrance (6 feet high), three-tone colors and seven large nylon-screened windows. Measuring 9 by 12 feet, it provides comfortable quarters for a family of five.

Selecting Quality Clothing

by Cam Sigler

Selecting quality clothing is as important in back-packing and hiking as selecting a quality frame for comfort, a pack for durability or a stove for dependability. The quality of your clothing will determine whether those days spent communing with nature are enjoyable or an exercise in frustration.

Outdoor garments are subjected to constant stress, strain and chafing. They are mistreated more than casual or dress clothing, therefore it is essential that they be constructed to withstand the abuse they receive. More important, the quality of your clothing can determine how well you will fare in an emergency situation. Therefore, you should select those garments which will perform best and on which you can depend.

Quality in outdoor clothing is determined by three primary factors: type and quality of material; quality of findings or hardware; quality and type of construction and sewing.

If the fabric is inferior, the overall quality is not good even if the sewing is excellent, and vice versa. If any factor is poor, the garment is unsatisfactory.

Fabrics

Fabrics fall into three basic categories, according to whether they are made from natural fibers, man-made fibers or blends of natural and man-made fibers.

The two natural fibers that you will be most concerned with are wool and cotton.

Wool. Wool is one of nature's most versatile fabrics. It is obtained from the fleece of sheep or lambs and sometimes from the hair of angora or cashmere goats or that of musk oxen. It is one of nature's best insulators against heat or cold.

In purchasing wool garments, you will encounter three classifications: virgin wool, reprocessed wool and reused wool. All wool garments, by law, must have the classification, or type of wool, on the content label.

Virgin wool, or new wool, is wool that has never been processed in any way before being manufactured into a finished product. It is the best quality wool.

Reprocessed wool is made from scraps of knitted,

A worsted wool has smooth surface.

woven or felted fabric that has never been used prior to being reduced to yarn a second time and then made into a finished product. Reprocessing breaks and shortens the fibers, but it can still be made into a good-quality garment.

Reused wool is exactly what the name implies: wool which has been reprocessed from used or worn products. It is the poorest quality and should be avoided if virgin or reprocessed fabric is available.

Two other terms you should be familiar with in connection with wool garments are worsteds and woolens.

Worsted wool garments are those which have a smooth, clear texture. Examples of worsteds are lightweight, smooth wool shirts. Worsteds are used extensively in tropical clothing and gabardines. The close knit and tight weaves make worsted extremely strong and durable with little bulk and minimum weight.

Woolens, on the other hand, are made from woolen yarns. They have a softer, more fuzzy appearance. The scratchy, fuzzy coats and shirts identified with lumberjacks and the outdoors are examples of woolens. Woolens have a looser weave, are very absorbent, and are desirable as outerwear.

Wool has many advantages as an outdoor fabric. It is air-conditioned. Its resilience maintains millions of air cells between fibers, giving it unique insulating properties. It is elastic, will stretch without being damaged and does not mat. Because of these qualities, it is warm in winter and cool in summer.

The natural absorbency of wool is one of its most important features, particularly to the hiker or backpacker who is constantly generating heat while walking or climbing. Wool absorbs as much as 30 percent of its own weight in moisture without feeling damp and 50 percent without becoming saturated. This prevents dampness from clinging to the body, thus keeping the skin dry and preventing chill. Wool is one of the best fabrics in the prevention of hypothermia (excess loss of body heat), a condition common to active climbers and backpackers.

In selecting garments, wool plays a significant part in the outdoors and should be considered as part of your wardrobe.

Cotton. Nature's other fiber of concern to the outdoorsman is cotton. It is a vegetable fiber obtained from the cotton plant. Since the prime fishing periods occur during spring, summer and early fall when the weather is warm, cotton and cotton-blend materials are often the uniform of the day.

There are two basic types of cotton fibers, long and short. Long fibers can be spun into fine, smooth and comparatively strong yarns. These long fibers are used extensively in lightweight tropical shirts, pants and tropical-weight jackets. One of the finest outdoor fabrics made is the Grenfell cloth of long-staple Egyptian cotton. However, because of high price and limited production, it is seldom found in today's market.

Woolen is looser weave, having rough, fuzzy texture.

The shorter fibers are used to produce coarser yarn for use in durable fabrics. These fabrics are not smooth and fine but tough and rugged. The popular cotton duck material is an example of short-fiber cotton. Coming in varying weights, it is one of the most popular materials for robust outdoor and work clothing.

There are different grades of duck material. The two encountered most frequently are single-ply duck and two-ply duck. The two-ply is made from two strands of yarn twisted together and woven into fabric. It is the more desirable material, being closely woven and tighter for greater strength. Distinguishing single-ply duck from two-ply is relatively simple. Single-ply is normally lighter in weight, loosely woven and impregnated with filler which gives body to the loose weave. After frequent cleanings, the body washes out, leaving a weak, loosely woven fabric. If you hold both fabrics up to a light, the one which passes more light through and has shaded areas is the single-ply. Two-ply is closely woven and passes comparatively little light through.

The major advantages of cotton are its absorbency, light weight and comfort. In warm weather it absorbs perspiration, keeping the skin cool and dry. The softness of 100 percent cotton makes it comfortable in lightweight pants and shirts, yet for a lightweight fabric it has strength. Cotton is also heat-resistant and holds its color well. Cotton is one of nature's finest natural fibers and should be near the top of the list for camping and backpacking clothing.

Nylons. Man-made fibers are of equal importance in outdoor garments and are being used more and more as new developments occur. The strongest man-made fiber in common use in garments is nylon.

Nylon was the first true synthetic fiber to be developed and is still the most popular because of its versatility. This is the backpacker's and climber's fabric. It is the most widely used fabric in the backpacking field. Its most important features are its amazing strength-to-weight relationship, so important when carrying the necessities of life on one's back. Nylon is used in protective clothing, woven into pack cloth to carry the essentials and even made into lightweight mountain homes.

It has enabled man to assault and conquer some of nature's most formidable mountains with a degree of safety and comfort unknown a decade ago.

The two most popular nylons for garments are nylon taffeta and rip-stop nylon. Both are tough, easily cleaned, dry quickly, hold their shape well and neither shrink nor stretch excessively. Nylon taffeta is a high-thread-count, plain-weave fabric. It is smooth

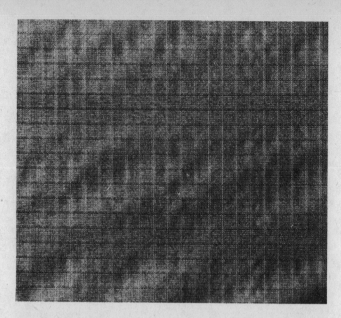

An example of rip-stop nylon. Notice the graphlike appearance of the cross threads. When punctured, the fabric will rip only to the closest heavy cross thread.

on both sides, usually with a sheen. It is made in weights from heavy to paper thin. Rip-stop nylon is woven so as to create slightly thicker threads on both sides of the fabric. These threads create small squares, making the fabric look like graph paper. The heavier threads stop tears. If the fabric is punctured the tear will stop ripping at the first strong thread it meets. Hence the term "rip-stop."

Both fabrics are used extensively in outdoor garments, the primary use being in insulated garments which must have bulk yet be light in weight.

Blends. Last but not least in the list of outdoor garment materials are the blends of natural and man-made fibers.

Synthetics blended with natural fibers have created a whole new line of fabrics. Blends can be created to serve specific purposes, taking advantage of the best qualities of both fibers.

Some of the more popular blends are of nylon and cotton. They give the absorbency of cotton with the strengthening qualities of nylon. The nylon-cotton blends wear well, dry quickly and hold their shape; they are easily cared for. Shirts, trousers and jackets can maintain their looks and shape after frequent wearings. This is important to the hiker who must at times wear the same clothing for many days.

The new polyester and cotton fabrics are popular today. The polyester contributes several properties such as wash-and-wear characteristics and resistance to abrasion and wrinkling. The cotton adds absorbency, heat resistance and softness.

Nylon is also being blended with wool to reduce cost and give strength to the fabric, again making use of the outstanding characteristics of both fibers.

There is a place in every camper's wardrobe for one or more of the fabrics mentioned. In selecting garments, be critical of the material. Analyze your use and determine which material or which mixture fills your needs best.

Findings

Next on your check list of a quality garment are the "findings" as they are called in the garment industry. Findings are such items as zippers, snaps, buttons, Velcro tape and other hardware used in the construction of a garment.

Check snaps by snapping and unsnapping them. If the tension is too tight, they can rip the fabric or be impossible to unsnap with one hand. If the tension is too loose, they will not provide security for valuables in pockets or for front closures. All snaps should be set through two layers of fabric, or backed by a second layer of material if used in single layer fabric.

Zippers can be inspected by trying them. Make sure

This is what can happen if snaps are set too tightly and not backed by double layer of fabric.

Snap is backed by extra fabric to prevent it from tearing single layer on garment.

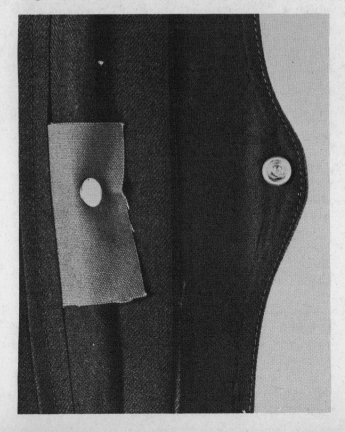

they set in the track properly. Zip and unzip them several times to be sure they operate properly. Zip them closed and tug on sides to be positive that teeth do not separate under tension.

Heavy outer garments need heavy-duty zippers, while lightweight garments and trousers should have medium- to light-weight brass or Delrin zippers.

Today you will find many garments, particularly jackets and fishing vests, with Velcro pocket closures. When checking these closures, stick and unstick them several times. Make sure they have a firm grip. If they are in the pocket of a fishing vest or shirt which you will often open with one hand, you don't want them too tight, so test them before you get on the stream. Good outdoor pants have a double security system on the front closures—combinations of hook and button, hook and snap, or snap and button.

Check buttons closely, making sure they are sewn well and will not pull off after only a few openings. Button and unbutton the garment, checking button size in relation to buttonholes. All of us have had shirts that wouldn't stay buttoned, and there are few things more annoying.

While inspecting findings there is another area that bears looking at. Some manufacturers save money by using inferior fabrics in hidden areas. In pants and parka pockets they use inexpensive pocket-lining materials. The hiker or backpacker never seems to have enough pockets for the essentials, much less for the choice little extras which may not be neccessities but

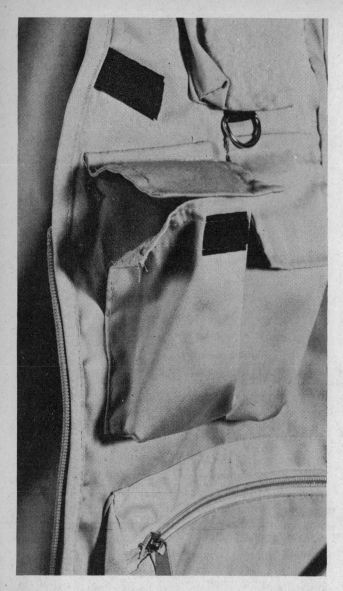

The pocket corner on this vest was neither bar-tacked nor back-tacked and ripped out on the first fishing trip.

make life on the trail more enjoyable. Therefore, it is essential that pockets be tough and dependable.

Pocket fabric should be a fine closely woven cotton, nylon or blend. If pockets are stiff or boardy, the fabric is loosely woven with filler added. After frequent use, it will tear through and you'll have to leave those cherished gadgets behind or get out the needle and thread.

Sewing and Construction

Now that you've looked at the fabric, buttons, snaps and so forth, let's make sure that all the pieces that go together to make up the garment will stay together.

On clothing which is constantly under stress, all pocket corners should be bar-tacked or back-tacked (sewn back on the same thread line before being tied off). This strengthens the corner stress points, preventing ripping and tearing of threads. It applies to all pockets whether on pants, shirts or jackets. Bar-tacks should also be used on the top and bottom of zippers and on all belt loops.

The strongest seam is the felled seam. This seam is used in heavy jackets and pants. It is very popular as a seat seam in pants because of its strength. The disadvantage of the felled seam is it cannot be let out to increase pants size.

The other common seam you will encounter is the serged seam. Serged seams are used on jackets, pants, shirts and most outdoor clothing. A serged seam is not as strong as a felled seam but will perform well if properly sewn.

If failure of a serged seam occurs, it is usually in the seat seam of pants which is under tension as you walk or climb. A weak serged seam can be identified by holding the pants on each side of the seam and pulling, as if you would pull it apart. If the seam separates and a large amount of light can be seen through the seam and around the threads, it is a weak seam.

Stitches most commonly used in outdoor clothing are the chain stitch and lock stitch.

Chain stitches are used often on serged seams. This stitch is also used on fabrics which stretch and give. The chain stitch is somewhat elastic and will give with the fabric. The drawback of a chain stitch is that once the thread, or chain link, is broken, the thread will continue to pull apart under stress.

A lock stitch is just what its name implies. Each stitch is locked in place. If the thread is cut, it pulls only to the next lock and will not pull apart. All quality garments of heavy fabric for fishermen, hunters or backpackers should use lock stitching. Most felled seams are sewn together with lock stitching. When you see two rows of thread on a serged seam, the chances are good that it's a double-needle lock stitch, which is excellent.

Identifying the difference between a lock stitch and chain stitch is simple. The lock stitch looks the same on both sides of a seam while the chain stitch has a single thread on the outside and multiple threads on the inside.

Just as quality in a pack means a little better temper in a frame, an extra grommet or stronger webbing, so quality in garments is the little extra bar-tacks or stitches which we often fail to notice even if they are present. These little extras often make the difference between a high-quality garment and a mediocre one.

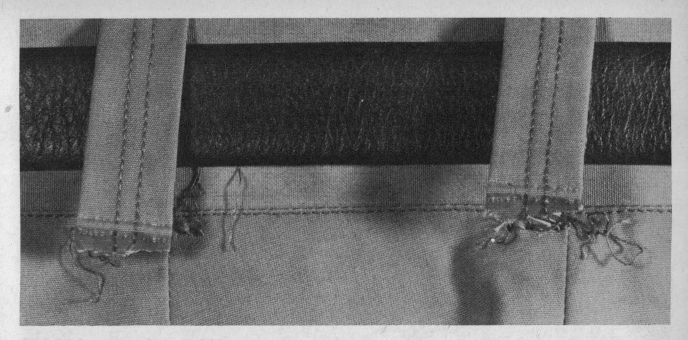

When belt loops are not bar-tacked this occurs.

A well-made belt loop, set into waist band on top and bar-tacked on the bottom.

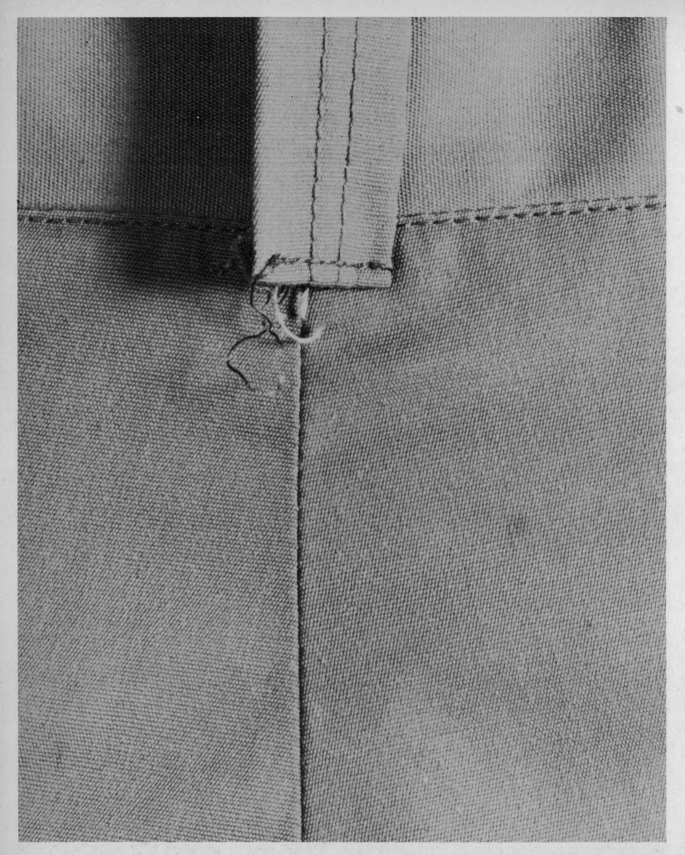

Serged seat seam.

Felled seat seam.

Insulated Clothing

In judging quality, insulated clothing is unique. Its quality is determined not only by fabric and construction but also by the quality of the insulation used to fill the garment. Fabric, findings and sewing in insulated clothing should meet the same criteria for quality as in uninsulated clothing.

The leading insulating material in quality garments is down, the soft underplumage of birds, primarily waterfowl, the best being prime goose down. The amount of insulation in a garment is determined by the maximum amount of dead air space created within the garment. Down produces more dead air space with less weight than any other material known.

Beware of regarding a garment as quality just because the label says it's down-filled. There are many different grades of down and the quality varies widely.

The quality of down is determined by its "filling power" (the measure of its ability to maintain a large volume with minimum weight or amount of filling material). For example, one jacket containing 6 ounces of prime goose down may have a greater insulative value than the same jacket containing 10 ounces of down. The 6 ounces, being of a higher grade, has greater fill power than the lesser grade, even though there are 4 more ounces of fill.

The price of down to a manufacturer depends on the grade. Generally, the price of a down garment will be directly related to the quality of down used. Good grades of down are the most expensive insulative materials used in clothing. Be suspicious of an inexpensive garment. The manufacturer has to make up the price difference by skimping on quality of insulation, fabric or construction.

When shopping for down-insulated garments, read the content label. The Federal Trade Commission establishes guidelines for the feather and down products industry. The commission stipulates the ways in which down can be mixed, named and labeled.

Ninety percent of any product labeled "goose down" or "duck down" must be from the species named. The label "waterfowl" can represent a combination of down from any type of waterfowl. The labels "waterfowl" or just "down" are found on inferior garments. In a quality garment, the manufacturer is proud to use the term "prime goose down," for this is recognized as quality. Also, beware of garments stating fill as 100 percent down, "all down" or "pure down." If the label states this, it must contain only down with no feather or down fiber, a portion of which down contains. One-hundred percent, or pure, down is prohibitive in cost. The writer does not know of any down wholesaler or manufacturer who uses 100 percent down.

In recent years there have been new innovations in synthetic filling agents for insulating garments. The standard for years has been Dacron 88, which is still widely used in inexpensive insulated garments. However, the Dacron is giving way to the superior synthetic materials such as Celanese's Polarguard and DuPont's new Fiber Fill II. The manufacturers of synthetics are constantly developing and improving their products. A made-up garment using the new synthetics is sometimes so close in appearance to a down garment that you must look at the label to tell the difference.

In making a choice between synthetic and down insulation, there are pros and cons on both sides. The synthetics are less costly than a quality down garment. They are a good choice for those who live in warm climates where insulated garments are used for only a short period of the year. Synthetics can stand rougher treatment than down and are easier to care for. When wet, they can be wrung out and will retain loft. They will, however, break down faster than down after repeated stuffings. They are a bit heavier than down garments and do not breathe (pass moisture and air away from the body) as well as down garments.

On the other hand, down garments are more expensive. Down does give more insulation against cold than any other fill. It retains its loft better than a synthetic after being compressed over a long period. Its major disadvantage is its extreme loss of insulative properties when wet. Down does breathe better than synthetics, hence its versatility and comfort within a wide range of temperatures.

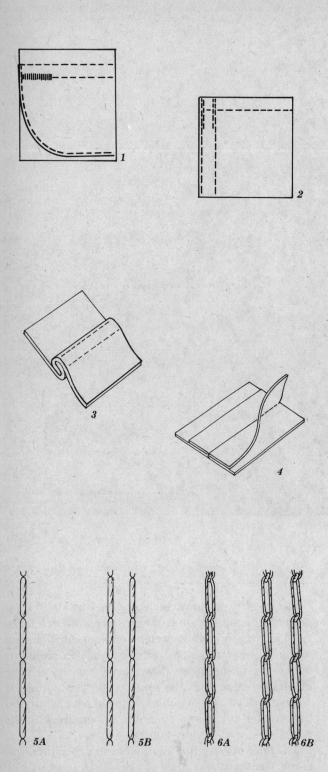

TAILORING TECHNIQUES

1. Top left: bar-tack; *2.* Top right: back-tack; *3.* Middle left: felled seam; *4.* Middle right: serged seam; *5A.* Lower left: single needle lock stitch; *5B.* Lower left: double needle lock stitch; *6A.* Lower right: single chain stitch; *6B.* Lower right: double chain stitch.

A high-quality insulated garment. Snaps through two layers of fabric; heavy duty Delrin zipper, Velcro pocket closures, pocket corners back-tacked, heavy nylon drawstrings, completely lock-stitched, even on quilting.

Making a choice between the two is a matter of when, where and how the garment will be used, and the state of your pocketbook.

How and Where to Buy

When purchasing outdoor garments, deal with establishments which have a reputation for quality. They are the ones which provide a guarantee against defects in material and workmanship—in effect, a guarantee of satisfaction.

A manufacturer of quality goods guarantees his product to the dealer, who in turn passes the guarantee on to the consumer. Buy brand names which are known as quality producers. These people didn't establish a national reputation for quality products by disappointing consumers.

Frequent those local dealers who have a reputation for quality and service. Check their guarantees; a good shop carries its own service guarantee over and above that of the manufacturer.

If it's specialty, high-quality items you are looking for, deal with the most reputable mail-order firms and outdoors outfitters, such as Eddie Bauer, L.L. Bean, The Orvis Company. They have been in business for many years and their success has been based on service. They provide quality products with a satisfaction or money-back guarantee. It is virtually impossible to lose money when dealing with such firms. They are concerned with your satisfaction. If you are not completely satisfied with their products, they will refund your money so that you may purchase elsewhere or replace a garment that was unsatisfactory.

PANTS

1. Double security closure; *2.* Zipper reinforced with bartack; *3.* High-count pocket lining; *4.* Bar-tacked belt loops; *5.* Pocket corners reinforced with bar tacks; *6.* Waistband cut on a bias using high-quality fabric.

PARKA

1. Fabric of high-count nylon taffeta or blend; *2.* All pocket corners bar-tacked or back-tacked; *3.* Heavy-duty, lightweight, two-way Delrin zipper; *4.* Storm flap over zipper, secured with Velcro closures; *5.* High-quality nylon drawstring in hood; *6.* Double-needle-stitched pockets for added strength; *7.* Raglan sleeve, serged for strength and comfort; *8.* Double constructed hood (two layers of fabric for added protection).

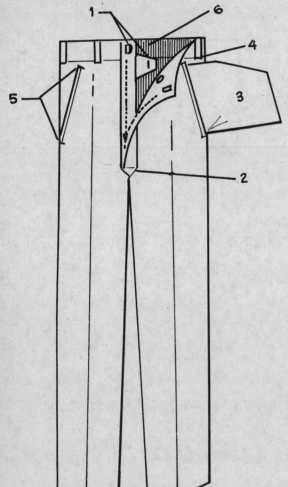

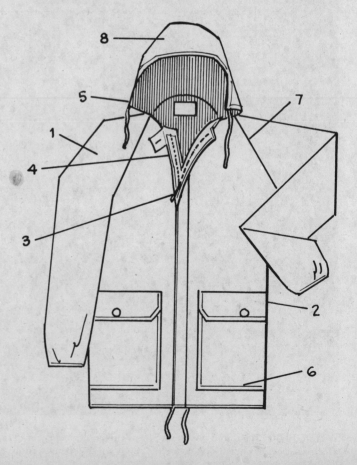

In many cases, the local sporting goods emporiums or specialty houses will be a bit higher in price than large chain stores. Although price may be better somewhere else, if the garment is not up to the job it was designed for, and it carries no guarantee, you are the loser.

Deal with reputable firms; the best price is not always the best deal.

HEAVY-DUTY JACKET

1. Felled side seam; *2.* Pocket corners reinforced with bar-tack or back-tack; *3.* High-quality fabric, closely woven; *4.* Set-in sleeve, serged or fell, with double-needle lock or chain stitch; *5.* Snaps through double layer or backed by extra layer of fabric; *6.* High-quality brass or nickel snaps; *7.* Heavy front placket for strength; *8.* Double fabric forms caps for greater weather protection.

OUTDOOR SHIRT

1. Nylon-lined collar, to prevent wear and chafing; *2.* Serged set-in sleeve; *3.* Front placket, adding strength and body to closure; *4.* Reinforced, properly sized button holes; *5.* Pocket corners back-tacked; *6.* Hem turned under and sewn to prevent excessive wear; *7.* Clean, strong serged seam for comfort and strength.

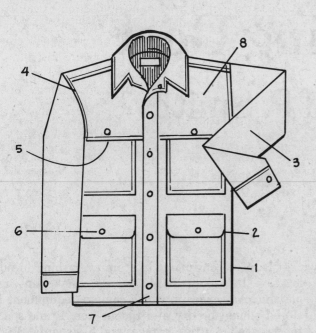

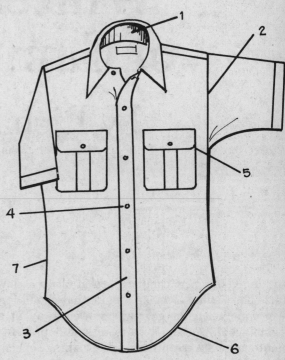

Winter Storage of Camping Gear

by Richard P. Smith

Nothing gets a new camping season off to a slower start than having to make repairs that should have been done when the gear was stowed away at the beginning of winter. Repair work and preventive maintenance are essential to proper storage of camping accessories and the first step toward starting off the next season's camping on the right foot.

Proper winter storage will prolong the life and usefulness of tents, sleeping bags, air mattresses or any other basic items. Furthermore, much time and energy will be saved if you know where all the gear is stashed and don't have to rack your brain to remember where you put it months before.

During the process of storage, you should make a complete list of equipment, noting the location of all items. Once complete, the list should be put where it won't be misplaced. A storage list is important for several reasons. First, it is a ready reference for finding any gear that is needed. Second, when you prepare for the next outing, it serves as a check list to make sure nothing essential is left behind. It also serves as a reminder of accessories that should be purchased for the coming season. Camping gear can often be purchased at bargain prices during the winter.

It is most convenient to store everything in one location, but space limitations may make this impossible. Any place in which camping equipment is stored should be dry and rodent-free. Prime spots for storage are attics, garages and basements. Basements are sometimes unsuitable because of dampness. Moisture encourages the development of mildew and mold on tents, sleeping bags and air mattresses. Mildew and mold weaken the material and leave a musty odor. Rafters in attics or garages are handy for storing tent poles. In fact, rafters can serve as the framework for a storage platform for all camping accessories. A number of boards long enough to lay across several rafters is all that is needed to complete the platform. The boards can be nailed in place if the platform is to be used permanently or simply laid in place if it is temporary.

Storage space can also be created under workbenches or tables by adding shelves between the floor and the top. Pieces of sturdy plywood cut to size work well as shelves. Heavy nails can be pounded halfway into wooden legs of benches for the plywood to rest on. Or blocks of wood can be attached to each leg at the desired height to support shelves. Unused shelves or space in closets can serve as storage sites. Other possibilities are empty trunks or boxes, cabinets or dressers, suitcases or coolers (for small items), and space under beds or couches. Although places to stash camping gear aren't limited to those mentioned, they are the most commonly used.

When you have decided on locations to store camping equipment, the gear must be readied. Tents should be cleaned, thoroughly dried and any tears repaired before storage. Tents can be set up in the backyard, laid out on the ground or hung on a line for cleaning and drying.

Dirt and mud on the tent walls (inside and out) and on the floor can be swept, brushed or vacuumed off. A hose is useful for rinsing off large areas of dirt and dried mud from the outside of a tent. Stains caused by pitch, sap, gum or bird droppings may require a stiff brush or a table knife for removal. An application of lighter fluid or turpentine is useful for removing sticky stains, but don't use these solvents if the fabric has been treated with wax, as the protective coating of wax will be dissolved along with the stain.

Rips and unstitched seams in tents can be repaired with an upholstery needle or an automatic awl and waxed thread. Damaged walls or roof should be resewn and also patched inside and out to add strength. Small tears can be fixed by covering them with electrician's tape, inside and out. Two pieces of tape perpendicular to each other, forming a cross, should be used to make such a repair. All repairs should be sprayed with a waterproofing compound after they are completed. Seams on nylon tents may need an application of sealant to prevent leakage and to plug pin or thread holes.

Tears in tent screens may either be patched or the torn edges sewn together. In most cases the latter method will be sufficient to keep insects out of a tent.

Handy kits are available commercially for replacing missing tent grommets; these include an anvil, punch and grommets of various sizes.

Tent zippers can be kept in good working order by rubbing them with beeswax or paraffin or spraying with a silicone lubricant. Slip-eze, a new spray lubricant designed for use on zippers, is manufactured by DuPont.

After tents are clean and repairs completed, the fabric should be allowed to dry thoroughly. This point can't be overemphasized. A wet or damp tent will mildew and the fibers will weaken during storage.

Erecting a tent to dry it is unnecessary. It can be hung on a line, draped over chairs, a porch rail, or a fence, or laid on a plastic or canvas tarpaulin. The tent should be turned occasionally to be sure all areas are adequately dried.

If a tent is set up for cleaning and repairs on a warm, sunny day, most of it will dry, although the bottom will need exposure to the sun before drying is complete. The drying process should be completed in a day. If the tent is not dry, take it indoors and finish the drying process the next day. Never leave a tent that is to be stored outside overnight; it will accumulate moisture from dew and condensation. If this should happen, allow another day for the tent to dry.

Once the tent is dry, wrinkles should be removed, and the tent then rolled up rather than folded. Creases and wrinkles that often occur in folded tents weaken the material and may result in future leaks or tears. Roll the tent as loosely as possible to prevent straining the material. Tents benefit by shaking out and rerolling a couple of times during winter storage when you check for mice.

Keep a list of what has been stored where so you can find any item quickly in an emergency.

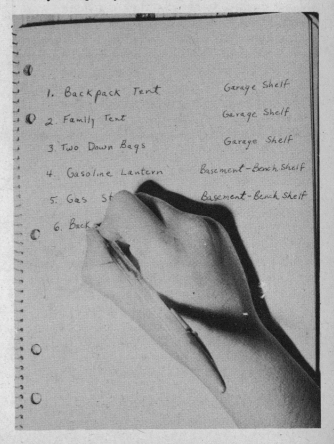

Plastic garbage bags are handy for storing rolled tents. The bags keep tents dustfree and dry and prevent insects from taking up residence. After the tent is inside the bag, squeeze out excess air and seal. Avoid storing heavy objects on top of tents; this will compress them and cause creases. Never put tents on a concrete floor for storage.

Tent poles, stakes and ropes should be cleaned and repaired before storage. Stakes that are dull should be cleaned and sharpened and bent poles or stakes straightened. Damaged ropes should be replaced. Poles for a single unit should be stored separately. They can be fastened together with tape or rope. If you own more than one tent, attach labels to designate which tent the poles go with; all sections of a frame for a single tent should be banded with tape of the same color. Stakes can be put in boxes or bags and also labeled. If tent ropes are removed they can be stored with the stakes. Never roll poles and stakes inside a tent for storage.

The procedure for readying sleeping bags for storage is similar to that for tents. Any rips or tears should be attended to. Most can be mended by sewing, either on a machine or by hand. Iron-on patches can be used satisfactorily on fabrics that are not sensitive to heat, but not on nylon.

Any filling that falls out of down sleeping bags from a rip or tear can be stuffed back in before the tear is mended. The blower on a vacuum cleaner works well to replace down. If additional filler is needed, it can be ordered from camping supply dealers, or perhaps from the manufacturer.

Sleeping bags can either be dry-cleaned or washed by hand or in a machine, depending upon the manufacturer's recommendation. Most synthetic fiber-filled bags can be handled by dry cleaners. Make sure that the laundry or cleaner knows how to handle the bag properly. Dry-cleaning solvents for down should never be chlorinated hydrocarbon fluids. Mild petroleum-based solvents are best. Be sure to ask what type of cleaning fluids a dry-cleaning establishment uses before leaving a down bag. Down sleeping bags can be washed by hand or machine, using soap, never detergents. Down bags can be hand-washed in a bathtub. Bags should be rinsed thoroughly to rid them of suds.

Drying down bags takes a long time. If a dryer is used it should be on the lowest heat setting. A number of cycles will be necessary to get the job done.

Tumbling in a dryer after washing improves the loft of down. After the bag is dry, the down can be

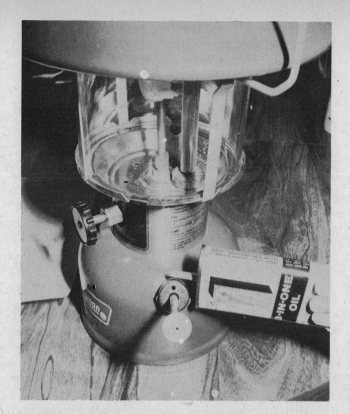

When storing gasoline lanterns, lubricate pump plunger and leather washer on pump shaft according to manufacturer's directions. Lightly oil control shaft.

If storage is to be for more than a few days, drain off gasoline fuel from lantern font to prevent gumming of generator.

redistributed by holding the bag at the end where the filling has accumulated and shaking it vigorously. Another method of redistributing down is to lay the bag on a clean, level surface, inside out, and beat it with a limber stick. Start at the point where most of the material has accumulated—most likely the bottom—and work up.

Don't hang a down sleeping bag over a clothesline. Lay it on a flat surface and turn it frequently. It may take several days to get the bag completely dry.

Some manufacturers of synthetic fiber-filled sleeping bags recommend machine washing in oversized washers. Detergents can usually be used to clean these types of bags, but be sure to read the instructions with each. When machine-washing a sleeping bag make sure the bag is evenly distributed around the drum to prevent the washer from vibrating.

Any sleeping bag that is dry-cleaned should be aired out thoroughly before storage and also before use. Some of the chemicals involved in the cleaning process are toxic and can cause sickness or death. Such harmful elements are dissipated when a bag is given adequate exposure outdoors.

Before storing a sleeping bag, the zipper can be rubbed with wax or sprayed with a lubricant to ensure proper functioning.

Ideally, sleeping bags should be stored in a relaxed condition, laid out flat. If sleeping bags are kept under tight compression for a prolonged period, the filling, natural or synthetic, tends to take a "set" and some of its warming qualities are lost. However, the space required to store a bag in a relaxed condition often makes this impractical. Rolling the bag loosely is the best alternative. Rolled bags can be placed in plastic bags to protect them from dust and dirt.

Air mattresses are best stored slightly inflated and in a relaxed condition, but, here again, they can be rolled loosely (not folded), with the air valve open. Mattresses should be put in a box, bag or other container for protection during storage. As with tents, don't put weighty objects on top of sleeping bags or mattresses.

Air valves on mattresses should be checked before storage. A damp cloth will remove any dirt from the threads. If the valve is brass, a light coating of oil will prevent corrosion and permit easy opening and closing.

If a mattress leaks, the puncture can be located by running water from a hose over the mattress while inflated, or the mattress can be immersed in

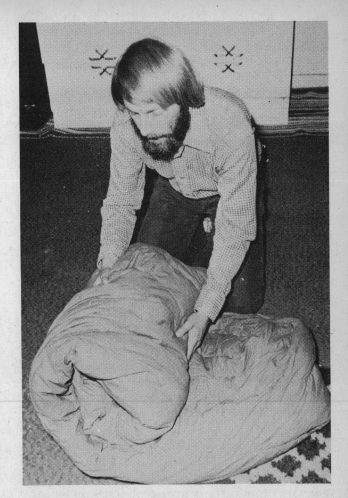

Sleeping bags should be rolled rather than folded and removed from storage occasionally and fluffed to maintain "loft" of down. Do not roll tightly.

water. Bubbles will show where air is escaping. Tire-patching kits are fine for repairing air mattresses. Be sure mattresses are dry before storing them.

Cots should be cleaned of any stains and weak or torn seams restitched. They should be covered with sheets or pieces of plastic for storing. Cots across rafters make a fine platform for storing other items.

Such appliances as lanterns and stoves also need attention before storing. Stoves get especially dirty during use, because grease splatters on them and bits of food and matchheads drop inside and on the burners. Be sure to clean them thoroughly. Spent matches and accumulated grime should also be removed from lanterns. The pump leather on lanterns and stoves should be oiled before the appliances are stored. There is a hole in the fixture surrounding the pump for the addition of lubricant. Damaged mantles on lanterns should be replaced. Mantles with holes in them are not safe to use. Before putting a new mantle in place, brush the air screen on the burner tube with an old toothbrush to make sure it is clean.

Prior to storing for any length of time, drain all fuel from stoves, lanterns and catalytic heaters. The best way to accomplish this is simply to use up the remaining fuel. If this isn't possible, the fuel can be saved in a tightly sealed, well-marked metal can or dumped into a hole in the ground and buried.

After dumping fuel out of the tanks, light the appliances to burn out any remaining in the generator or the tubes leading to it. If it is not burned out, the remaining fluid will form a residue inside, which may cause future problems.

Propane tanks can be removed from the units they power for storage, but smaller LP fuel containers should be left intact until empty. All camping fuels should be stored in a cool location away from any heat sources and out of direct sunlight.

If a kerosene- or gasoline-operated lantern is to be used in case of a power failure, it should be filled with fresh fuel periodically. Propane tanks can be left in place on units that serve as emergency standbys.

Stoves can be stowed away in their closed carrying cases with the fuel tank inside. Putting a stove inside a cardboard box, suitcase or plastic bag is a good way to protect it from dust and scratches.

When storing camp stoves, clean thoroughly to remove all grease and food odors that will attract mice. Dump fuel as with lantern and oil fuel pump.

Flashlights often come in handy year-round and can be left easily available. However, if you don't expect to use a flashlight for a month or more, it is wise to remove the batteries and clean the inside to prevent corrosion. All contact points can be cleaned with fine emery paper or a typewriter eraser or scraped with a pocketknife. If the batteries are good but the light burns dimly or not at all, a flashlight needs a new bulb, or the contacts cleaned. Check to see if the batteries are put in correctly.

Ice chests or coolers, jugs, thermos bottles, and canteens used for camping deserve a good cleaning. Chests can be washed with a damp cloth and a light application of baking soda. Jugs, thermos bottles and canteens should be rinsed with water. An application of baking soda will rid them of odors. The soda should be left in for about an hour and then rinsed out.

All these camping accessories should be air-dried with covers and lids off or open. Ice chests should be stored with the lid slightly open or with the drain cap removed and placed inside the chest. Incidentally, coolers are useful for storing small items of camping gear during the off season. Canteens, jugs and thermos bottles should be stored with the tops off.

Before putting a cooler away for the winter, the hinges and hasp should be lubricated. A sprinkling of talcum powder or cornstarch can also be applied

Hiking and camping boots should be carefully cleaned of all mud and stains before storage. Do not use grease on rubber bottoms or soles. Check for mice.

to the rubber seal around the top. This gives the seal longer life and prevents it from becoming sticky in hot weather. Small holes in plastic or Styrofoam chests can be patched with an application of clear nail polish. Plastic metal or solder can be used to repair metal coolers.

Chipped paint on ice chests can also be retouched. Any rust that has developed can be sanded off and the area covered with oil for protection.

Take care not to set coolers on rocks or any other sharp objects that may damage them. Also avoid putting objects that might puncture coolers on top of them or at the sides.

Cooking utensils should be given a thorough cleaning at home, then placed in bags, cloth or paper, or boxes for storage.

Packs that have been ripped should be repaired. Cloth-mending cement and patches of suitable material can be used on both canvas and nylon packs. Sewing the patch in place, in addition to the cement, reinforces the job and is usually necessary on large rips or tears. Bent packframes can usually be straightened. Be careful not to bend the aluminum too far or the metal will be further weakened and may break.

Light wire rings that hold pack pegs in place may be replaced with pieces of heavier wire. The light rings seldom hold up under continued use, especially where the pegs hold pack straps to the frame.

Make sure that any crumbs of food or food stains are removed from packs. If left, they may attract rodents, which can chew holes in the fabric. Packs, like other equipment, should be enclosed in plastic bags. Like coolers, packs can be used to store small camping accessories during the winter.

Camp axes and saws should be cleaned and sharpened for off-season storage. Lighter fluid, turpentine or nail-polish remover can be used to remove pitch. Steel wool will help get rid of rust. Heads and blades should be covered with a light coat of oil before storage to prevent rusting. Rough wooden handles can be smoothed with sandpaper. Rubbing linseed oil into the handle adds a nice finish. Damaged ax handles should be replaced rather than repaired. If the ax head is loose on the handle, pound in a wedge.

Don't forget about hiking boots. After a season of use they should be thoroughly cleaned. A stiff brush will usually get dirt out from cracks and crevices. Then give the boots a coat of polish and waterproofing. Shoe polish serves as a preservative on any leather items used in camping, such as sheaths for axes and knives.

Camping odds and ends—first-aid kits, binoculars, aluminum foil, clothesline, mirrors and compass, to name a few—can be conveniently stored in a backpack or a cooler if they are not needed during the winter. That way they will be handy when you are getting things together for the first camping trip of the year.

If you have a tent camper it can be readied for storage by draining the fuel from all fuel tanks and shutting off all gas lines. Water should also be drained from tanks and containers. Any dirt and grime on the inside of a camper can be washed off with soap and water; mud and dirt on the outside can be hosed off. Chipped paint should be touched up and chrome polished with automobile polish. Zippers can be treated the same way as those on regular tents and sleeping bags.

The wiring of all lights should be checked and any loose connections or short circuits repaired. Bare spots on wiring should be covered with tape. Additionally, all food and valuables should be removed from campers.

If possible, campers should be stored under cover, in a garage, barn or shed. Otherwise, cover camper with a good plastic tarpaulin and lash it down securely. If you live in a metropolitan area, be sure to check with local authorities about leaving a tent camper parked in a driveway for any length of time. This is illegal in some cities.

Setting campers up on blocks will take the weight off the wheels, which prevents the development of weak spots in tires and extends their life. An alternative is to move the camper periodically during the winter to distribute the weight evenly on tire treads.

It is a good idea to check all camping equipment at various intervals during the storage period. Tents, sleeping bags and air mattresses can be rerolled from the opposite end to prevent weak spots and keep the filling from taking a "set." If rodents have set up housekeeping in any of the gear, set traps to remove them.

Don't forget to keep your storage list up to date. If a piece of equipment is moved from its original location or lent out, be sure to note the new location on the list.

Proper winter storage of camping gear takes some time and thought, but the effort is well spent and will be appreciated when the camping bug hits you the next season. While friends and neighbors are completing repairs you made months earlier or are hunting for their equipment, you can be enjoying the trip you planned the previous fall.

How to Back a Trailer

by Katie McMullen

Campers of the early 1960's were familiar with a one-wheeled camping trailer. It attached to a car's rear bumper with two small hitches, and the one wheel swiveled around under the trailer body. It was an easy vehicle to park because it was merely an extension of the car's length. Anyone who could back up a car could back that trailer.

Two-wheeled trailers, on the other hand, often intimidate campers, as do those with dual axles. The thought of having to back camping and travel trailers into camping spaces surrounded by trees or other vehicles, or perhaps over bumpy campground roads at night, is enough to deter the timid from considering this type of camping.

But it shouldn't. Considering the number of recreational vehicles now being used in the U.S. and Canada, there is no reason for hesitation. If all those people could learn to do it, so can you.

A course has been developed by Dr. Bernard Loft at Indiana University called *Leisure-Time Living on Wheels*. It can be taken as a correspondence course with a certificate earned upon completion, or the manual used in the course can be purchased for home study. Write to the Independent Study Division, Indiana University, Owen Hall, Bloomington, Indiana 47401, for complete information.

The advantages of reading this course book thoroughly are that many aspects of trailer living are discussed. Purchasing, insurance, driving principles, handling a trailer and maintenance are covered. While a book cannot substitute experience, it can prepare you and give you the confidence that comes from knowledge of these subjects.

When it comes to backing a trailer or maneuvering it in any situation, competency is not restricted to either sex. Men and women can become equally proficient, and there is a decided advantage when more than one person in a family can handle trailering chores.

In preparing this article, I consulted several trailer owners, and most use similar techniques. Among the experts is Pat Stottler of Wichita, Kansas. She's a past president of the Kansas Camping Association, the state organization of NCHA, and is active in the Holiday Rambler Recreational Vehicle Club.

Pat began tailgate camping in the fifties with a

station wagon. She then progressed to a tent, later to a camping trailer, then to a 22-footer and eventually to her present 29-foot Holiday Rambler.

Pat thought the ideal job for her might be to travel around the country towing a trailer and giving demonstrations on handling it. She felt if more men could see a woman maneuvering a truck and trailer combination, they would have less hesitation in doing it themselves.

At Holiday Rambler rallies, there is always a trailer-backing competition. Participants drive their own tow vehicles, but hitch up to U-Haul trailers. The team of Pat Stottler and Jodie Law won a second, a third and three first places before they retired from the competition to help with judging.

In its early years, competition was divided into men's and women's events, and Pat once figured by timing that she and another woman would have finished second and fifth if they had been allowed to compete with the men. As a result, there is no longer any such division. Neither sex has a corner on proficient trailer handling.

Pat demonstrates her techniques as in the photos accompanying this article, and offers her tips for successful backing.

Use your mirrors. Practice backing your tow vehicle without the trailer, using the mirrors. On her pickup truck, Pat uses Junco West Coast mirrors, about 12 by 5 inches in size. When backing the camping trailer shown in the photos, she attaches extended mirrors to the front quarters of the car. Another practice method is to use a boat trailer, which gives good visibility.

Rely on your copilot. Stationing a second person behind the trailer as you back into position helps in judging distance. Using hand signals, he can indicate clearance from trees or picnic tables and guide you to the exact spot where hookups can be made most easily.

Allow plenty of clearance. Know the width of your vehicle and your trailer.

Only one person can give directions. Well-meaning camping neighbors often want to help a new arrival to get settled, but too many people shouting instructions at a driver confuses things. You have to ignore the crowd. Listen only to your copilot's directions, which should always be given in moderate tones.

Don't do anything fast. You may be following the correct procedure, but in spite of this the trailer may begin to jackknife. A sudden move could cause damage at that point, so all backing maneuvers should be done slowly. If necessary, pull out, straighten trailer and car, and start all over.

Armed with theory and keeping the diagrams of backing in mind, you are ready to practice. Look for

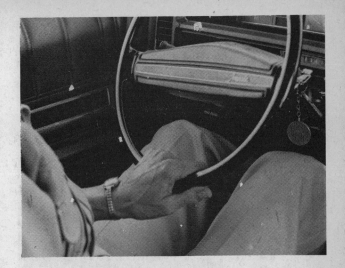

Beginning a left turn of the trailer, Pat's hand is at the bottom of the wheel. She gradually moves it clockwise using the palm of her hand. Once the trailer has started to the left, she will reverse her hand movement on the wheel to follow it.

Trailer has begun to turn left and move toward picnic shelter where hookup for electricity is mounted on post.

Pat is beginning to straighten car and trailer, but they will not be as close to the post as she wants them to be.

Now she is going to move the trailer to the right, so her car wheels are turned to the left.

This move brings her closer to the position she wants, next to the shelter. Now she must make sure the door clears the post.

Pat is moving her trailer back towards her copilot, who signals the distance with his hands. When he sees she has cleared the door of the trailer, he signals her to stop.

vacant supermarket or plant parking lots with marked-off spaces. These are ideal for practicing backing. You may have to go out on Sunday mornings to locate the ideal place to practice without gathering a crowd.

Take along some cardboard boxes or pylons to position during practice. If you hit them, you hurt nothing, but they give you targets to aim at while learning to use your mirrors and discovering how a trailer responds.

Now you are ready to back your trailer. It is easiest to back it to the left because of greater visibility. Car and trailer should be in a straight line. Place your hand at the bottom of the steering wheel, as shown in the photos. Begin turning your wheel clockwise, slowly, using the palm of your hand on the wheel. Turn the front wheels of your car to the right as if you were going to make a right-hand turn.

When your trailer has started to move in the intended direction to the left, slowly reverse the turn of the wheel so you will follow your trailer through the planned turn.

Once you have been successful in backing the trailer to the left, practice right-hand backing situations. After a while, the entire procedure will become almost routine.

Practice parallel parking along a curb, too. Pat practices parallel parking next to the curb in front of her home each time she comes out of the driveway. Don't pass up situations that give you an opportunity for practice.

When backing into a driveway, look for cars coming from either direction before you begin your maneuver. Make sure your driveway is clear of obstacles.

Having parked your trailer in a campsite, unhitch it from the tow vehicle and remove the mirrors. This makes it safer not only for others driving in the sometimes tight locations but also for pedestrians.

There are many accessories on the market that can assist you in backing situations. Visit a good RV dealer and ask about some of them. Some people like a mirror that mounts on the hitch for use when hitching the car to the trailer. Other trailerists add a jockeying hitch to the front bumper of their truck or tow vehicle and move the trailer into position by facing the trailer. This way they can look right down the right side of the trailer.

A relatively small trailer-backing device consists of a target that goes on the trailer, a sighting mirror on the inside rear-view mirror and a sighting dot on the rear window of a vehicle. When all three line up, your trailer is straight. Called the Bull's Eye Hitcher-Upper, it's available for $5 postpaid from P.O. Box 2612, Anaheim, California 92804.

Spot mirrors added at the bottom of side-view mirrors give added visibility along the side of a trailer. Keep your eyes peeled at campgrounds for devices other campers use to make trailer backing and parking easier for them. They'll be glad to explain them.

Then, despite all your skill, you may still encounter a campground situation that will completely defy your efforts. In that case, try to obtain another site or request assistance from the campground owner. There are some campgrounds which insist on parking your trailer for you. A few costly equipment replacements led them to establish such a rule.

Remember, don't let an imagined fear of backing a trailer cause you to decide trailering is not for you. After a little practice and a season of use, you'll wonder why you waited so long to try it.

Unhitching the trailer and removing mirrors are the last steps before setting up the trailer.

Put the "Good" in "Good Night"

by Gene Kirkley

The sun had already climbed above the treetops before the angry blue jay overhead succeeded in rousing me from a deep sleep. While he continued to insist that I had invaded his territory, I stretched, completely relaxed, in the comfort of my camp bed.

The day before had been one full of wonderful action; the hike up the mountain topped off with a couple of hours of fine fishing had left me tired and ready to call it a day. My camp was a simple one, and it didn't take long to eat supper and do the necessaries before climbing into bed. As I said good night to the world around me, I recalled other nights when there hadn't been much "good" to be found. I knew that this one would be different, though, and my sleeping so late had proved it.

Somewhere along the line, the idea evolved that campers have to rough it or else they're not really camping. 'Tain't so, friend! And if you're really interested in becoming an outdoorsman liberated from the bonds of permanent structures—that is, a camper—I know you'll want to put out the bit of effort that is needed to learn how to take off those rough edges.

You may have so conditioned yourself that you can literally run up mountains or paddle your own canoe for miles through white water or straddle a bronc for hours on the trail, but unless you are able to spend the night hours in comfort with the needed restful sleep, friend, you ain't a-gonna last for long.

Most of us these days spend our sleeping hours in air-conditioned or centrally heated rooms on over-sized beds with scientifically designed mattresses. Perhaps a mental block develops as a result; something tells us that it must be impossible to rest or get any sleep out there on the hard ground. Hopefully this book will encourage you to give it one more try so that you'll get rid of that block and join the millions of happy campers.

Actually, what makes for comfort, or what causes discomfort for the camper during the nighttime hours? Aside from shelter, which is discussed elsewhere, two basic things share the responsibility for putting the "good" in "good night" for the camper, regardless of the means by which he travels. They are temperature and bedding.

For the sake of convenience, let's think about temperature first. Hot or cold. I've spent many nights under both types of conditions, and it's a tossup as to which can be the most miserable. The camper who spends his outings at higher altitudes in the mountains may not have hot nights to complain about, but the one who does his camping in the lowlands in summertime has probably sweated his way through those long dark hours. That is, until he learned a few tricks to help him keep comfortably cool.

I learned the hard way never to pitch my tent where it would be in the late afternoon sun; the heat builds up inside like an oven and can stay that way long into the night. (That's fine for cold-weather camping, but a late afternoon sun can be somewhat hard to find in winter.) Try to pitch your camp in an open area that will allow any available breeze to reach you, and if that breeze comes over water, so much the better. I have on occasion hung towels dipped in water by my sleeping area for the cooling effect. While camping in dry, hot areas, a pan of water and a cloth with which to wipe arms, face and body can make you feel better and cooler in a hurry. I can recall several evenings when just fanning myself with a folded paper or even a tin plate did the trick of cooling me off so sleep would come.

It goes without saying that restraint in your personal activity during the time before going to bed will help a lot toward letting you "keep it cool."

Before we consider the other basic of bedding, just let me say that in hot-weather camping, I like to start out on top of the bed, but with provisions to crawl in as the night cools before morning. More on that later,

when we take up the subject of bedding with a wide temperature range of comfort.

A comfortable night in cold weather is dependent almost entirely on the bedding. Sure, a shelter that keeps you dry and out of the wind is essential, but in this article we're taking that for granted. Let's take a look at the camper's bed.

The old-time cowboy during round-up time carried a bedroll that provided comfort during almost any kind of weather: a heavy tarp wrapped around his quilts or blankets with his extra clothes also inside. But it was usually so heavy that a couple of them made a load for a packhorse or else the bedroll rode in the back of the chuckwagon.

Weight today is an important factor with the allowable being determined by the mode of travel. The camper going by pack train or boat can be happy with a heavier bedroll than the backpacker can manage. Not that the backpacker's bed won't be just as comfortable, for it surely can be. But it may be a bit more expensive!

I spent many nights camping as a youngster before I owned my first sleeping bag. My bedding consisted of two or more blankets folded together to form a bag and secured with large safety pins. Today, however, a sleeping bag acceptable for moderate-weather camping can be purchased for maybe less than the price of those same blankets, so let's confine our talk of bedding to what I think is the better way—a sleeping

Three typical sleeping bags ready for travel. *From left to right:* a Dacron II bag with 4 pounds of fill in a "stuff bag" instead of being rolled; a Dacron 88 bag with 4 pounds of fill; another Dacron 88 bag but with 5 pounds of fill and a wool blanket wrapped inside. The new Dacron II bag sleeps "warmer" than the heavy bag plus the blanket.

bag. Down through the years, bags have used for fill just about every kind of material imaginable. The old kapok-, cotton- or wool-filled bags of years ago are luckily things of the past. The acetate fibers are better than those but not as good as the polyester fiber-fill bags. Dacron 88 served well as fill for relatively light yet warm bags. The new Dacron II fill is the closest thing that I know of to natural down, which is the best insulation against cold that we have. The very soft breast feathers of a duck or goose hold air and retain all the body-generated heat. The main trouble with down is that it is expensive. Too, once a down bag or garment becomes wet, it is something of a problem to dry it out, especially in the field. Dacron II, on the other hand, costs less and is easier to care for. It is very resilient and almost as light in weight as the more expensive down.

The old saying, "You get what you pay for," is pretty much true when it comes to sleeping bags. If not 100-percent true, it is a good rule of thumb. Even if it causes you to have to skimp on something else, get the best bag you can afford. That good bag will have an outside cover that is strong and tear resistant, yet it will not be waterproof. I almost cringe with horror at the sight of some of the sleeping-bag ads that show a particular marvel lying directly on snow or spread out with its own little canopy to protect the sleeper from falling rain. Maybe the ad man expects the buyer to know better, and the ads are just supposed to look pretty.

It's like this: if the cover of the bag will not let it "breathe," moisture will condense on the inside, and the sleeper will have a miserably damp bed. If you've ever worn a really waterproof rain suit, you know what I mean. You'll be almost as wet with sweat as you would be if you didn't have on the suit in the rain!

The shape of the sleeping bag is up to the personal desires of the camper. Ranging from the rectangular to the true mummy, each has its own advantages and disadvantages. While the rectangular ones may be a bit heavier, the extra "moving around" space is worth it to those of us who shift positions during the night. If, as a backpacker, you feel that every ounce saved is worth the sacrifice, or you don't mind the confining feature of the mummy bag, that should be your choice. There are now some in-between bags that should be great for those who wish to save ounces but who must have a little more footroom than the mummy gives them. My wife and I recently used a pair of these that zip together to form a double bag. Although it was summertime, we were at an altitude of something over 9000 feet with the nighttime temperature taking a considerable drop. She's the cold-natured one of the family, and she declares she never got cold all night! If you're looking for something like this, be sure to get right and left models that will fit together.

Most of the older bags were lined with flannel that sure felt good when you crawled into it on a cold night. This type of liner is still available, but most of the newer bags are now lined with nylon or a similar material. At first thought, this would seem to be coldish, but on the whole I like it better. I really can't tell any difference in temperature, and since I do a

The Dacron II bag fluffs up readily even after being stored in the stuff bag. This type of bag offers the nearest thing to down in insulating quality and comfort.

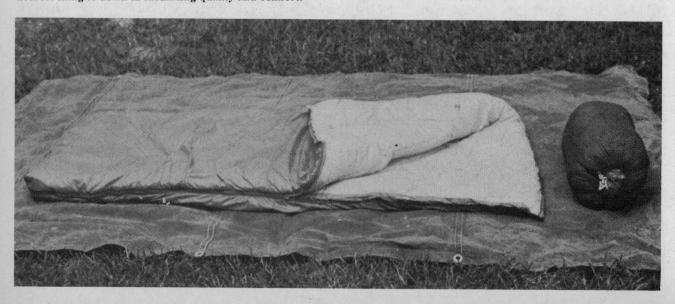

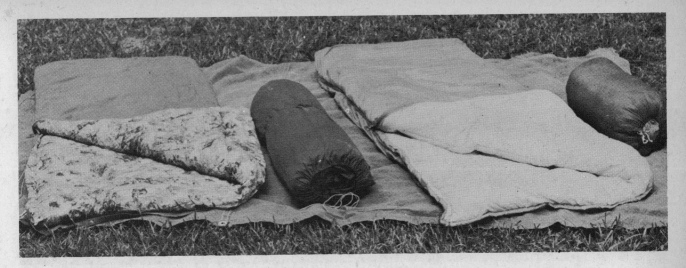

The Dacron 88 bag on the left is lined with cotton flannel, while the Dacron II bag on the right is lined with nylon. Personal preference is the best guide here.

good deal of turning during the night, I can do it without the bag tending to "twist" around me. The choice must be yours for your bag.

Before we take a look at some of the options you have in the way of camp mattresses, just this word about sleeping clothes or the lack of them. Somewhere or sometime during my impressionable youth, I read that in very cold weather, the only way to sleep warmly was in your birthday suit! So I tried it once and almost froze to death before I pulled on a suit of long johns. You may want to do a little experimenting yourself to find out what's best for you, but my favorite sleepwear when it's really cold is a suit of Dacron-insulated underwear. The covering makes for easy turning; the added insulation of the garments allows for the use of a lighter bag. The regular "thermal-knit" long johns also make good "pajamas" for me, but the regular home-style pajamas always seemed a bit out of place in camp.

Now for the mattress. Remember Ol' Toughie, who said only sissies would use such a thing? Nuts! Not only do you need softness and comfort, but the insulation from the cold ground is most important. Before the night is over, you'll lose a lot of body heat to the cold ground even in summer. Air mattresses that you inflate either with mouth and lung power or with a pump have been with us for a long time. When I bought my first one years ago, I thought I had found the ultimate for comfortable sleeping in camp. And they are good, but only so long as they don't leak down during the night to leave you stretched out on the hardest real estate in the county. My current one has a big patch on the edge covering a hole punched in it by baggage handlers for a major airline when I made

the mistake of packing it next to the outside of my duffle bag. (I later found the angular tear in the duffle bag that matched perfectly.) I didn't know about the leak until after I'd gone to bed the first night in camp, and, believe it or not, I patched that hole by flashlight and blew the mattress up again without getting out of my sleeping bag. It was too cold to crawl out, but the floor of that old trapper's cabin was too hard to sleep on without the mattress.

The weight of a good rubberized air mattress may be prohibitive for the person who counts the ounces; lightweight plastic ones won't survive very rough treatment. Even the lightest ones, only 48 inches long, can make a lot of difference in your sleeping comfort, as long as they hold air! In extremely cold weather, they tend to cause the sleeper to lose body heat as the shifting air in the tubes or compartments cools.

In recent years, the foam pad has become very popular with all kinds of campers, and while it isn't quite like the innerspring mattress you use at home, it can add a lot to your chances for a good night's sleep. I have one a full 6 feet long and covered in waterproof nylon that really does a fine job. I don't recommend it for the backpacker because of its bulk, but it does a good job of smoothing out the wrinkles underneath my bed. For backpacking, I have an Ensolite pad that's only 1/2 inch thick, 24 inches wide and 48 inches long. The weight is almost nothing, but the insulating quality of this material is unbelievable. You will be surprised at how much that thin pad will contribute to the comfort of your camp bed, provided you pick a fairly level and smooth piece of ground.

In addition to these different kinds of man-made mattresses, Mother Nature has provided much mate-

Three alternatives for padding and insulation under the sleeping bag. *Left to right:* a full-length foam pad in a nylon cover, a 48-inch Ensolite pad and a folded air mattress. The large foam pad is bulky but great for sleeping; the "shortie" is a favorite with backpackers; the air mattress, while it does make a soft bed, is heavy and blowing it up can be quite a job.

rial that can be used for your comfort. While the old-time camping manuals all went into great detail as to how to construct a "browse bed," I don't recommend it except in cases of emergency or in areas where the use of evergreen boughs will leave no significant mark on the environment. A bed that is almost as good and much easier to build can be made with leaves or straw or a material such as broom sedge. Before the days of the foam pad, I used to carry in my gear a mattress cover or tick. It didn't take long to gather enough leaves (dry ones) to fill it and, spread underneath the bed roll, it did a fine job of padding the rough spots and providing that required insulation from the ground. And it surely didn't take up much room in the pack!

Some campers seem to think they're too much trouble, but I like to use either sheets or a liner inside my sleeping bags. Not only do they provide an extra measure of comfort, but they are a great help in keeping the bag clean. And on hot nights a single thickness of sheet may be all the cover you need. If you don't use a commercial liner, it's easy to attach tie tabs to both the sheet and the inside of the bag. Double the sheet the long way and sew the tape to the folded edge of the sheet and to matching points inside the bag. The time required to do this is well spent, as the ties keep the sheet from bunching up in the bag.

If you use a pillow at home, by all means use one in camp. Not necessarily a foam or feather one, but some kind of head support—it can make the difference in whether or not your night is a good one. I've used just about everything you can think of for a pillow down

through the years I've camped: a small bag stuffed with leaves and grass, a rolled-up knapsack, a jacket wrapped around my shoes or boots, inflatable air pillows, and on and on. Lately I've come up with the best one of all! The stuff bags for our sleeping bags with a down jacket inside make a pillow equal to or better than the one at home.

For the camper who may still need some additional heating for comfortable sleep on those coldest nights, while an extension cord long enough to plug in a heating pad may not be available, there are commercial warmers that use either liquid fuel or solid-stick

A rolled and an open Ensolite pad (with yardstick to show length), a full-length foam pad and an inflated air mattress. Take your pick for your kind of camping.

For the extra comfort they provide: a down jacket inside the stuff bag makes an excellent pillow; a small inflatable pillow—this needs to be wrapped in a towel or shirt before it does much good; a light wool blanket for added warmth on very cold nights or for use while sleeping on top of bag when the weather is only cool; a sheet to help keep the bag clean and to use on hot nights.

fuel and do a good job of heating up your sleeping bag. A simple way of doing the same thing is to place a nonporous rock in the fire a while before bedtime. Let me emphasize that it should be nonporous; moisture can get inside one that is porous and cause quite an explosion when the rock is heated. I know; I've had it happen to me. I thought someone had dropped a stick of dynamite in my fire. After the rock gets hot, wrap it in a towel or something and place it in the foot of the bag before crawling in. You'll be as snug as a bug in a rug.

A final word of advice: never go to bed wearing damp clothing. It won't dry during the night, and you'll spend a miserable one. Dry socks can do a lot toward keeping your feet warm; wet ones mean cold feet all night. One of the best ways to insure warm feet is to wear a head covering. Your own doctor could explain that one to you, but, simply stated, it's like this: if your head is cold, less blood goes to your feet, and they'll get cold, too! A soft knit toque or navy "watch cap" is fine. Some say that as much as 40 percent of body heat can be lost if the head is uncovered.

Okay, friend, it's up to you! The great outdoors is waiting for you, but unless yours is truly a good night, you won't be able to enjoy it for long. A bit of knowledge plus a little effort on your part is all that's needed. Pleasant dreams and happy camps!

These campers, surprised in their teepee, did have a "good" night. The sleeper in the rectangular bag *(center)* obviously has much more moving room than the one to the right in the mummy-style bag.

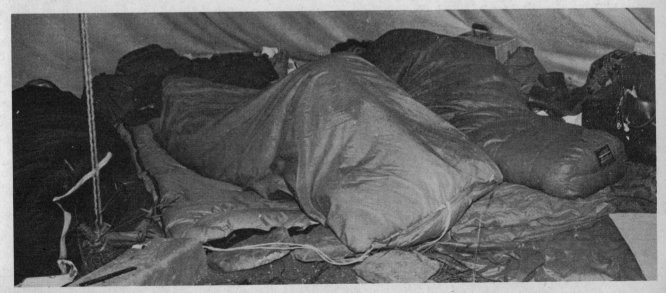

Keep Your Knife Sharp
by Sid Edmund

When I first became involved with knife makers and slowly learned about fine cutlery, I soon realized there was less knowledge about keeping knives in usable trim than about the metallurgical advantage of certain steels and other materials.

Knife buyers and other users of fine custom-crafted cutlery, and even users of lower-priced blades, are usually sophisticated about everything except keeping that piece of steel honed to a proper usable edge. Many people, when they think about sharpening a knife, think of their neighborhood butcher and try to emulate the way he uses a long hone steel. However, butcher knives are usually crafted of soft steels and the few swipes taken merely touch up the edges. Most sportsmen's knives, on the contrary, have very hard and durable edges, and the sharpening process is altogether different. There are some excellent hone steels for sportsmen made by Gerber and Schrade Cutlery which come in neat leather cases that form a handle for use. With hunting knives, however, these steels are used to establish a bevel or touch up an edge in the field. They will sharpen a knife well and are excellent for bringing out the edge after a half-hour's labor skinning a deer, but they should not be used as the primary instrument for placing a final edge on a knife.

Remember, the majority of knives delivered from a quality craftsman arrive already sharpened and some even with an edge that will shave the hair from your arm. But in spite of the myths of blades that will skin six moose, untold elephant and countless deer without ever touching a honing stone, and despite all claims to the contrary, any knife will require sharpening sometime during its lifetime.

When the sportsman lays some long green across a knife-maker's palm he may as well go the whole route and acquire first-rate sharpening gear at the same time. The finest stone is none too good to complement a fine knife and keep it in working trim.

A good whetstone is still the preferred method of putting an edge on a good knife and keeping it there. Whether you are sharpening a $200 custom job or a less expensive store-bought pocket folder, a top-quality bench stone is the one prime requisite for doing the job correctly. Although most knife makers seem to argue constantly about everything in knifedom, there

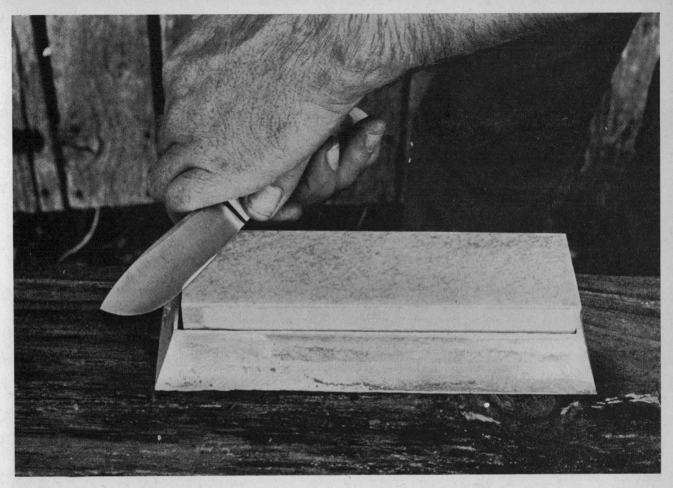

A soft Arkansas stone covered with honing oil is set in a stone cradle to hold it firmly. Grasp the handle in both hands and press down hard.

is general agreement on A.G. Russell's Arkansas Oilstones, and many knifesmiths offer them in their catalogs. The Russell stone is a carefully graded novaculite, a natural whetstone found in a small area of Arkansas and used by the majority of top knife makers. One of the reasons these stones have become so popular is that Russell is known to discard over 80 percent of the material quarried and cut, and to sell only the finest quality.

Remember that the care of a knife—that is, keeping it clean and in tip-top shape—is basically simple and actually requires less labor than cleaning a shotgun after a few rounds of skeet. The job requires only a few inexpensive bits and pieces of equipment and a fair amount of practice before you'll be able to put a professional edge on your knife.

When buying your first stone, a good rule of thumb is to obtain one an inch or so longer than the longest knife you intend to sharpen. The stone should last a lifetime, so the investment of a few extra dollars is worthwhile. Since you will be using two hands to guide the knife across the stone and to place pressure on it, a sharpening-stone cradle is an important accessory. The mount holds the stone firmly, and a C clamp fastens it to the workbench. The third and final item is a good-quality honing oil. Whetstones should never be used dry, and you should never use an oil that contains either molybdenum disulfide or graphite, for these will eventually clog the surface and glaze the stone. Russell's Sharpening & Honing Oil, Norton Bear Oil and Gerber's Honing Oil are recommended. The purpose of the oil is to float the tiny steel shavings above the surface of the stone and allow the blade to move across the top of the stone smoothly.

When you're ready to begin sharpening, always start with a clean knife. If you've just returned from a hunting trip, wash the blade in soap and water and dry it thoroughly. Otherwise you will grind fat, blood and dirt into the stone's surface and ruin it. With the blade clean, pour a liberal amount of oil onto the surface of the stone, making certain that every area is covered. Oil is cheap and it's better to use too much than too little. Even smear it about with your fingers. Then, holding the handle of the knife with both hands, place the blade to your right with the heel resting on the stone at a 20-degree angle. Bearing down hard, draw the blade across the stone in a slicing motion from heel to point so you end with the tip of the knife on the stone at the far left. As you near the curve toward the end of the blade, slightly change or lift the angle in order to maintain an even edge to the very tip. And remember to bear down hard. Andy Russell of Arkansas says: "Gentle swipes will do nothing but make you feel good. It's important to use as much pressure as possible, this cannot be overemphasized, and don't rock the blade as you draw it across the stone." After your first stroke, reverse the blade and repeat the same action from left to right. Do this, alternating sides, ten or fifteen times, then check the edge. The curve toward the tip may not be quite as sharp as the straight part of the blade. If this should happen,

repeat the action, paying close attention to those portions of the blade that don't quite suit you.

As Russell points out, "the angle you use is not quite as important as being able to hold and maintain the *same angle* stroke after stroke. Only practice will give this ability, and it's a good idea to work on some less expensive kitchen cutlery first. Not only will that save good field knives until you have learned these skills, but your wife will be pleased to have sharp kitchen knives for a change."

Like so many things in knife making, the angle of the edge is a matter of some small dispute, but you'll find most knife makers grind their edge bevel to roughly a 20-degree angle. If you are really fussy about this, take a small protractor and check the angle before you start. When the blade has been finished to your satisfaction, strop it across the palm of your hand or a piece of cardboard. This final touch smoothes any roughness down in line with the edge.

Probably the most important point in sharpening any knife is knowing when to stop. You don't make a

Continue slicing across the stone, pressing down hard. Note the roll of oil in front of the blade.

CAMPER'S & BACKPACKER'S BIBLE

knife sharper by honing to a finer edge, you only weaken the edge of the blade. All things being equal, the finer the edge the faster the blade will dull, and you soon reach the point of diminishing returns. Knifemakers and experienced hunters agree that a slightly coarse edge is to be preferred. By this we don't mean an edge that appears rough to the eye (although a microscope will reveal tiny sawteeth on the sharpest blade) but rather an edge that is the result of proper honing and stroping. Should you be among the many who insist upon shaving with their knives—a stunt that actually proves nothing—a few strokes across a Surgical Black Stone will do the trick nicely and let you shave the hair from your arm.

When the sharpening is completed, the stone should be cleaned. This is done by pouring more oil onto the surface and working it about with the fingers to let the steel filings removed by sharpening become loose and float to the surface. A few wipes with a rag and the stone is ready for the next time your knife requires attention. Should the stone become very dirty, take an old toothbrush and kerosene or a good household cleanser, give it a good scrubbing and set it aside to dry.

There are few rules of placing an edge on a knife. First, maintain the bevel ground onto the blade by the maker. Second, slice across the stone as though cutting a slice of cheese, taking an equal number of strokes in both directions. Finally, when a knife becomes dull sharpen it at once—a dull knife can be dangerous.

There are a number of other accessories that are excellent aids in keeping an edge on your knife. Among these are the Schrade and Gerber honing steels already mentioned and the Moon Stick produced by Case, a long, thin rod that is an excellent tool for a quick touch-up. The small pocket stones often seen riding on a knife sheath are fine for a quick touchup in the field but are much too short for proper honing.

Many sportsmen, and this includes experienced knifemen, find it difficult to maintain the proper angle when sharpening. For this purpose there are two

As you near the end of the stone, raise the tip slightly in order to sharpen the curve.

Sharpening aids. The black stone is the Surgical Black and the long white rod is a Case Moon Stick.

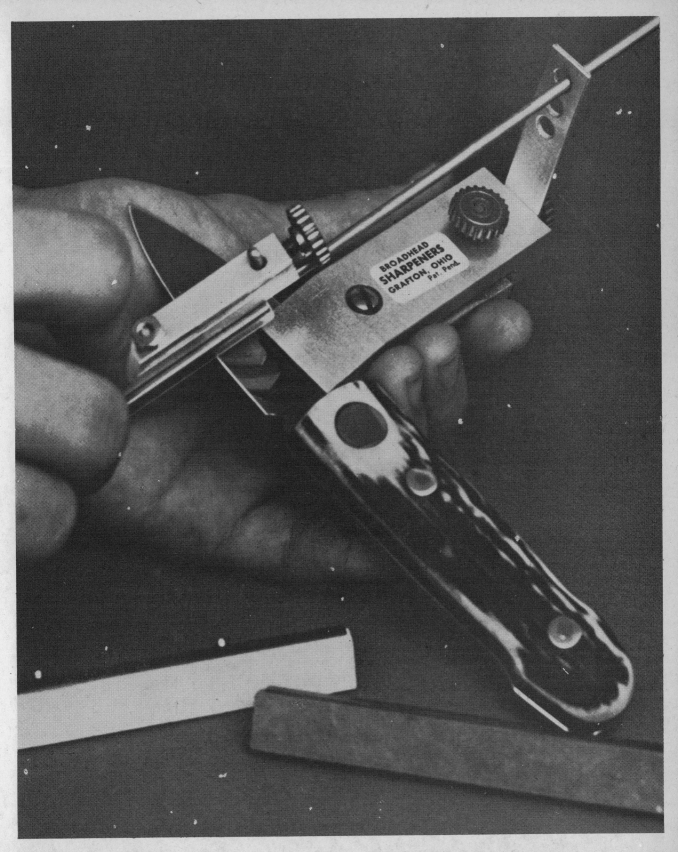

The Loray Sharpener in use. This is a new and innovative method of putting a razor edge to your knife.

excellent aids. The Buck Honemaster sells for about $5 and clamps onto the blade. It won't harm the steel since the insides of the two clamps are covered with Neoprene and the whole affair is tightened with a thumbscrew. The Razor Edge is a similar device except that an Allen wrench is used to tighten the clamp set-screws. With this one, cover the blade with tape, since the clamps have no protective liners and may harm or scratch the steel. John Juranitch sells the Razor Edge Sharpener for $11.95, the whole outfit comes in a zippered kit complete with stones.

Someone is always dreaming up a new and hopefully easier method of accomplishing the same thing. To that end Ray Longbrake, an inventive chap from Ohio, has devised the Loray Sharpener. This rig takes a different tack on sharpening; it uses a stationary clamp jig and separate hone stones. Admittedly, when it comes out of the box, it resembles a Rube Goldberg invention, but it works. Speed of sharpening is outstanding, and it doesn't take many swipes with the stone to begin laying on an excellent bevel. Should a favored knife have some chips along the edge, the Loray Sharpener will remove them in time. First begin with the coarse stone (100 grit) to obtain a burr, then progress to the medium stone (320 grit), and finally to the very fine stone (600 grit). Longbrake also supplies an excellent honing oil; use it in sufficient quantity. The Loray Sharpener is perhaps the most innovative device to come on the market in many years.

Generally speaking, you only need to use ordinary common sense when sharpening a knife. Remember that any good knife, whether it is a custom job that took ten months for delivery or a more modest store-bought blade, should be treated with reasonable respect and receive a modest amount of attention.

In spite of the advertising of some brash manufacturers, if you want to cut steel, get a bandsaw; a drill press will do a better job than any knife at punching holes in silver dollars. Use a knife for its intended purpose, take care of it, and you'll receive many years of faithful and useful service.

The Buck Honemaster shown on a Rod Chappel knife ready for use.

Classics

Some Companions for the Trail

THE GREAT OUTDOORS—and they are indeed great in every sense of the word—are remarkable in that they can be enjoyed as much in solitude as in the company of good companions. On the one hand, you have the opportunity to be alone with your thoughts, to gain new insights into old wisdom, and to partake of the bountifulness of nature as you choose. In the company of others, you are able to discover the mysterious alchemy that makes an amalgam of disparate individuals in the catalyzing world of nature.

Here and now we are concerned with recording some of the priceless wisdom of the world's greatest thinkers and writers who were also walkers and campers. How and where you approach this section of the CAMPER'S & BACKPACKER'S BIBLE will determine just how much you will be able to extract from it. No matter whether you stroll in the city, roam in the country, saunter, climb, hike, backpack or camp—here is an anthology selected from the works of some of the best companions you'll ever have along the trail.

In creating this anthology, we have made our own rules: Nothing would be included that is already too familiar or too accessible. Nothing that is merely inspirational; nothing sentimental; above all, nothing cynical; finally, nothing that would not be worth re-reading. We think we have succeeded, but the proof of the pudding is always in the eating.

The conventional anthology usually starts with the earliest works and comes forward in time. We have made ours a journey backwards through the years to demonstrate that nothing has really changed in our enjoyment of the outdoors. As the French proverb has it, the more things change, the more they remain the same.

Our journey begins with John Kieran's *A Spring Walk.* Widely known and respected for his daily sports column (the first signed column to appear in the prestigious *New York Times*) which began in 1927 and ran for many years, in 1938 he became an instant celebrity on "Information Please," a weekly radio quiz program. The range of Kieran's knowledge amazed listeners; he seemed to know everything about everything.

Books are perhaps the only companions possible for the solitary hiker. The selection entitled *Books* began life as a chapter in Stephen Graham's delightful volume *The Gentle Art of Tramping,* now out of print. Graham knew whereof he spoke, for he had tramped in the Caucasus mountains, in the Crimea, in the Urals, and once he even made a pilgrimage all the way to Jerusalem.

On the death in 1905 of Mr. William Sharp, a Scottish gentleman, biographer, novelist and poet, the world learned that it was he who had written about nature under the feminine nom de plume of Fiona Macleod. His *Where the Forest Murmurs* is a sensitive example of "her" work.

John Muir was born in Scotland and was brought to Wisconsin at an early age. By dint of great effort he managed to attend the state university at Madison, and an interest in nature he acquired there led to ambitious walking tours through neighboring states. He once walked from Indiana to the Gulf of Mexico; later in life he became a prime mover in the campaign to create Yosemite Park. In our excerpt he recounts his meeting there with the great essayist Ralph Waldo Emerson, "as serene as a sequoia."

Poet, essayist, novelist—and physician. That was Oliver Wendell Holmes. Exerting a strong influence over the practice of medicine in his time, literature was never more than an avocation for this energetic doctor. Holmes's major literary achievement lay in the essays he wrote for the *Atlantic Monthly,* a magazine he helped to name. The first of these were collected in a memorable volume entitled *The Autocrat of the Breakfast Table,* whence our selection comes.

Robert Louis Stevenson's background was prosperous middle class. Regrettably, he is regarded by many as "a children's writer," and his ability to create character, to write clean prose and to handle difficult material has been largely overlooked. His delightful *Travels with a Donkey* is a veritable gem of a book, blue-white and perfect. Our selection is from his informal essay *Virginibus Puerisque.*

As Mark Twain, Samuel L. Clemens achieved writing fame with his 1869 account of his travels in Europe and the Holy Land, *The Innocents Abroad,* which sold 40,000 copies in its first year. In the preface to it he said he intended to describe for the reader "how *he* would be likely to see Europe and the East if he looked at them with his own eyes instead of the eyes of those who traveled in those countries before him." In our excerpt, *The Ascent of the Rigi-Kulm,* taken from his 1880 sequel, *A Tramp Abroad,* he casts himself as an unaffected traveler from the Show-Me state of Missouri who intends to do things his way, even if it means taking three days to climb a modest-sized mountain.

Intended for a career in medicine, Francis Richard Stockton chose to become a wood engraver. Abandoning art for journalism, he is remembered primarily for a single short story, *The Lady or the Tiger,* which he wrote in 1884. Our selection is from *Rudder Grange,* a burlesque account of an expedition in a houseboat.

Henry David Thoreau's writing can be likened to a New England bed quilt pieced together with brilliant passages of variegated prose. His still-read classic, *Walden,* showed him at the top of his form; no one before or since has used such eloquence to plead for the simple life and to indict the twin evils of "busy-ness" and materialism. We reproduce an excerpt from his book *Excursions,* published posthumously in 1863, a year after Thoreau's death. (Only two of his books were published during his lifetime, *A Week on the Concord and Merrimac Rivers* in 1849 and *Walden* in 1854. Both were commercially unsuccessful.)

Bringing up the rear is our last walker, William Hazlitt. Because he found it difficult to express himself literarily, at twenty-one he turned to another form of expression, portrait painting. Only after he had painted a now-famous portrait of writer Charles Lamb did his interest in writing revive. Hazlitt suffered a nervous breakdown when his idol, Napoleon Bonaparte, was defeated at Waterloo (although he later wrote an impressive four-volume biography of his hero). When he died at the age of fifty-two, his last words were, "Well, I've had a happy life."

If one thing is evident in this gallery of walkers, it is that our group has included a large number of unconventional types, ideal companions along the trail. We hope you have enjoyed the pleasure of their company. Their like may not pass this way again.

—ROBERT F. SCOTT

A Spring Walk
by John Kieran

SIMPLE HONESTY COMPELS the warning that reading these words may possibly do you good and, therefore, you had better give some thought to the matter of dropping it right here. From this point you continue reading only at your own risk and peril.

Henry Thoreau, the American essayist and philosopher, once said: "If I knew for a certainty that a man was coming to my house with the conscious design of doing me good, I should run for my life." Quite right, too, but don't start running immediately because I herewith disclaim any conscious design of doing anybody any good.

I am merely setting down some reflections on a habit I have formed of walking at least two miles, if possible, every day. However, walking has been highly spoken of as a healthful exercise. In fact, many sedentary physicians prescribe it for patients, alleging that "a walk will do you good." Now, I view the matter in an entirely different light. I walk because I like to walk. I enjoy the exercise and I am entertained by what I see and hear along the way. It may be that the doctors are right in saying that "walking is good for you," but the only opinion I have to offer from a medical standpoint is that I have been taking daily walks for some thirty years and I conclude that, though habit-forming, the practice is not quickly fatal. If amiable mention of some of the enjoyments of walking stirs a reader to going for a walk which, as the weight of medical opinion has it, "will do him good," the blame lies on his own head and I wash my hands of it.

One thing about walking is that it costs practically nothing, which is an important item these days. It is also a highly respectable diversion—especially in the springtime—and often looked upon with admiration if the walker wears tweeds and carries a blackthorn stick, though that isn't the way I take to the road myself. Old clothes and a pair of field glasses with which to spy on birds are my equipment.

Walking is time-honored, hallowed by footprints famous in history. Plato expounded his philosophy while walking up and down an olive grove in an Athens park some 2,300 years ago. Peter the Hermit went on a walking tour of France and Germany in 1095 A.D. and stirred up the First Crusade, which eventually led to the others and a vast amount of long-distance walking.

There is no reason for boasting of walking as though it were a special talent or virtue possessed by an endowed few. Everybody who isn't bedridden walks to some extent every day. But to set out deliberately for a walk is another matter, and any discussion of it must include mention of relevant matters such as time, place, distance and weather conditions. Edward Payson Weston walked all the way across the United States. Dr. Livingstone walked across Africa. Admiral Peary finally reached the North Pole on foot, and Roald Amundsen arrived at the South Pole in similar plodding fashion which, I think, was going to extremes. I merely hope to get in my modest two miles or more a day, preferably over open and friendly country.

Often it takes me some hours because I so frequently stand around watching birds through my field glasses or stop to peer through a pocket magnifying glass at buds, leaves, flowers, seed pods, insects or other interesting items encountered en route. If it is good country, I never tire of going over the same ground and heartily concur in the opinion of the naturalist John Burroughs: "To learn something new, take the path today that you took yesterday."

There is a neighborhood swamp that I have been visiting since boyhood, and it still keeps turning up something new for me. There the skunk cabbages, brazenly poking their noses up through the snow and frozen ground in January, start the spring push. There the early birds from the South arrive in late February and the spring "peepers" sound off in March. It's in the swamp that the fresh greenery of the young year first catches the eye. Here is the home of the wood duck and the bittern, the spicebush and the marsh marigold, the speckled alder and the red maple.

Since I walk at all seasons, I encounter all sorts of weather, some of which I do not approve. I like walking in the spring rain when I am properly dressed for the occasion, but I never met a man, woman or beast who really enjoyed walking in a drenching downpour. Personally, I'm against high winds, too, by land or sea, especially at low temperatures when they cut like a knife. Tennyson moodily mentions "blasts that blow the poplar white" and such strong winds that "rooks are blown about the skies." Picturesque and poetical, to be sure, but Aeolus can put those winds back in the bag so far as I am concerned. Rain needn't bother a walker unless it is overdone, in which case it makes hard going. A curious thing that soon becomes apparent to one who is not easily balked of a daily walk is that, whether it is raining or blowing, the weather is never as bad outside as it looks through a living-room window.

I have good friends who share my liking for cross-country work and they double the enjoyment of a fine walk. But even if I start out alone, I meet many friends along the way. Eyebrows may be raised, or there may be some significant tapping of the forehead, when I mention some of these friends. One is a red-tailed hawk that I have come to know because it has several primary feathers permanently missing from its right wing.

Other friends are an assortment of painted turtles that sun themselves on a half-submerged log in my favorite swamp. Before we became well acquainted they would slide off into the water at my approach, but now that we know one another they acknowledge the friendship by remaining undisturbed as I go by. On several occasions, indeed, one or two have winked at me. Other firm friends are three tall tulip trees that stand on a roadside above a river, their great trunks looming up like Greek columns. Every time I meet these trees I feel the better for it.

Comfortable footwear is at the bottom of every enjoyable step along the road. If the shoe doesn't fit, no sensible walker would think of wearing it. Woolen socks are best. Dress optional, depending upon the weather. When in doubt, play it safe.

Take to the woods on windy days. It's quieter there. Keep your ears open. You can always hear more birds than you can see. Keep your eyes open. There are flowers in bloom through most months of the year, and trees are as interesting even in early spring as they are in summer. These are not sinister suggestions to stir up nonwalkers but merely my own rules of conduct. I have a few more. Take the sun over your shoulder for the best views. Avoid slippery footing as you would the plague, and don't sit on damp ground. Keep walking.

Books
by Stephen Graham

YOU NEED A BOOK, but you cannot carry Gibbon's *Decline and Fall* with you, even if you feel the need. The tramp's library is limited, for books are heavy. It is best to tramp with one book only. But it is a missed opportunity not to have one book. For you can gain an intimacy with a book and an author in that way, which it is difficult to obtain in a library or in the midst of the rush of the books of the season.

Each will have his choice though many will choose alike. The inexperienced may pop the latest yellow-back into the rucksack, not grasping that it will be read through in two lazy afternoons, and that then he will have no book to fall back upon. In the trenches in France a happy habit developed of leaving read books upon dry ledges in the dug-outs. One often came upon a treasure trove of the kind. But when tramping, you cannot leave books for others with much hope of their being found. And rarely does one find any stray literature unless it be some tract on the futility of sin.

It is better, therefore, to take with one a whole-time book. It is good to have a book that is full of meat, one with broad margins for scribblings and extra pages for thoughts, poems, thumb-nail sketches. After a long tramp it is nice to see a book which has been clothed with pencilings. It records in a way the spiritual life of the adventure, and will recall it to you when in later years you turn over the page again.

It is well to take a book that you do not quite understand, one that you have already nibbled at but have found difficult. I do not mean an abstruse work, but one you are just on the verge of understanding and making your own.

At different stages of development you will have different books. A boy just beginning to think could do worse than take *The Autocrat at the Breakfast Table*, or Thoreau's *Walden;* a little later comes *Erewhon* or *Eöthen*.

At eighteen *Sartor Resartus* or Carpenter's *Towards Democracy*, or Browning's "Paracelsus." A good deal depends on temperament as to whether a volume of Shelley or Keats will keep you company all the while. You read and reread a poem that you like until it begins to sing in your mind. It becomes your possession. There are marvelous passages lying hidden in a poem like "Paracelsus";

> *Ask the gier-eagle when she stoops at once*
> *Into the vast and unexplored abyss,*
> *What full-grown power informs her from the first*
> *Why she not marvels strenuously beating*
> *The silent, boundless regions of the sky!*

It is a poem of a man seeking life, seeking a way. It ought to move most young men who are on the threshold of life, unless they are dull or have been infected by cynicism. For my part, I look back loyally to the time when I was Paracelsus and could say his lines as from my own heart: " 'Tis time new hopes should animate the world," I whispered as I walked, and the new hopes were my hopes.

Much of "Paracelsus" should go into the true Tramp's Anthology, and with it, not contradicting it, Omar Khayyam and also O'Shaughnessy's

> *We are the music-makers,*
>   *And we are the dreamers of dreams*
> *Wandering by lone sea-breakers*
>   *And sitting by desolate streams*

and then certain delicious lines, untraced in origin, which Algernon Blackwood is fond of quoting:

> *Change is his mistress, Chance his counsellor*
>   *Love cannot hold him; Duty forge no chain*
> *The wide seas and the mountains call him*
>   *And grey dawns know his camp-fire in the rain.*

An ideal book to carry on a tramping expedition is undoubtedly an anthology of your own compiling, a notebook filled with your favorite verses.

Other books which I think of as the tramp grows in goodness and in grace are Ibsen's "Peer Gynt" or "Brand," preferably "Peer Gynt," there is much more in it. "Peer Gynt" is a very remarkable book; you can read it ten times and still fail to exhaust its poetry, its thought. It is a great book about life. It is moreover a true tramping book. Peer is a vagabond wandering about in the world, and it is never the world which is in question, but the state of his soul. "Brand" is not so much of a poem as the other, and is not so memorable. But it raises some of the eternal questions in a powerful way. If you are "sick of towns and men" "Brand" will rather indulge your mood, for it speaks Ibsen's impatience with the petty ways and lives of average men and women.

Socrates' *Dialogues* go well in the inner pocket, and so do Horace's *Odes,* if you are of a Horatian turn of mind and can read them. There are many, especially in Scotland, who like to take a Homer, and fancy themselves on the hills of Greece. For a classical scholar there are many books of profound and lasting interest; a Plotinus will last you a long while. For you have not merely to read it, but to resurrect a being who lived centuries ago in a different civilization. The human heart was the same, but almost everything else had a difference.

If the mind is just attracted to ancient philosophy, I know few books to compare with Pater's *Plato and Platonism,* for inner worth. I do not, however, think his *Marius* a good tramping book. Nature rebels against its cold chaste beauty. It needs, I think, a more artificial setting for its enjoyment.

Few novels are good tramping books. One gets through the story so quickly, and if there is no more than story there, the book is finished with. Still, there are a few knapsack companions worth having, such as *The Cloister and the Hearth, John Inglesant, Wilhelm Meister,* Dostoieffsky's *The Brothers Karamazoff.* All rather bulky, I am afraid, for ideas, though they keep other books thin, do swell the volume of a novel. A few ideas stated in conversation and baited with picturesque descriptions take three times the space they need in the essay. It is sometimes easier to understand them, but the expression is diffuse.

Plays, however, come near to being ideal. They take up little space. The dramatist has to censor his own work vigorously with a view to cutting down the excess of verbiage which his ideas naturally claim. He is forced into paradox and epigram. His work is full of hints and suggestions which are undeveloped. It is for you to develop them. As Ibsen said, "I ask the questions; it is for you to answer them."

A Shakespeare play is a delightful library. I nearly always take one. A drama like *Richard III* or *Othello* can be read over and over again. *As You Like It* and *A Midsummer Night's Dream* are the great open-air plays. You learn more about them with the birds and the stars to teach you than with the aid of the most genial producer or inspired professor. You make your camp in a natural theater among the trees, or in an arena among the rocks. There is an audience not altogether invisible. It waits, it has its programs, you have the book of the words and the brain full of moving figures. Sun and moon are working the limelight from the wings. Your camp fire is the footlights. Enter Man. Enter Hamlet. Enter Julius Cæsar, the gods, the ghosts. The tramp becomes an ancient type, a magician, a mystagogue—with a Shakespeare in his hand, in the midst of the worlds.

If modern drama rouses the fancy, you can take a Pirandello or a Shaw, and thresh it out—get a real opinion about it. It is worth while when you have to orientate your mind to certain writers of repute to make yourself intimate with at least one of their works.

I suppose some may prefer to read a book on the country through which they are tramping, and in that case a librarian's aid may be sought. There are now scores of volumes on almost every country in the world. It is as well to look over several of them before making a choice—many prove to be slaplash, ill-informed compositions.

Does one take accounts of travel in lands other than that one is tramping in? I imagine not. *Unknown Arabia* is out of place in a tramp through California. But a tramp's account of his own life is interesting reading anywhere, and one naturally thinks of W. H. Davies' autobiography in this connection. There are few tramp writers. But probably the best short story of Maxim Gorky's tells of his tramping life, and is called "The Fellow Traveller." Jack London's *Valley of the Moon* contains some tramping episodes. Jack London, Rudyard Kipling, Cunninghame Graham, Belloc, Chesterton, Carl Sandburg, Vachel Lindsay, are all delightful writers in the tramping mood and ask a place in the knapsack. Then there are Harry Franck's untiring pedestrian tours in Patagonia, China, and elsewhere, perhaps in too ponderous a form as yet for field use.

I once met a tramping publisher, *rara avis,* a very black swan; he began his life as a colporteur of the British and Foreign Bible Society and spent twenty years on the road, going from Bibles to leaflets, which he printed himself, and thence to booklets, thence to books and an office and a vast organization. He had a simple way of business. I handed him a manuscript; he opened a drawer and handed out a wad of notes, and the transaction was concluded without a word in writing. But I suppose that was unusual even in his business. There was a savor of tramp meeting tramp in the affair.

The Bible colporteur ought, at least, to know one book the better for his calling. When all is said, there is one book more worth taking then all the rest; poetry, philosophy, history, fantasy, treatise, novel and drama, you have all in one in the Bible, the inexhaustible book of books. You need not take it all, take the prophecies, the Psalms, the Gospels. It means much to tramp with one Gospel in the inner pocket of the coat.

—from *The Gentle Art of Tramping.* Copyright © 1926 by D. Appleton and Company. Reprinted by permission of Hawthorn Books, Inc.

Where the Forest Murmurs
by Fiona Macleod

IT IS WHEN THE TREES are leafless, or when the last withered leaves rustle in the wintry air, creeping along the bare boughs like tremulous mice, or fluttering from the branches like the tired and starving swallows left behind in the ebbing tides of migration, that the secret of the forest is most likely to be surprised. Mystery is always there. Silence and whispers, still glooms, sudden radiances, the passage of wind and idle airs, all these inhabit the forest at every season. But it is not in their amplitude that great woodlands reveal their secret life. In the first vernal weeks the wave of green creates a mist or shimmering veil of delicate beauty, through which the missel-thrush calls, and the loud screech of the jay is heard like a savage trumpet-cry. The woods then are full of a virginal beauty. There is intoxication in the light air. The cold azure among the beech-spaces or where the tall elms sway in the east wind, is, like the sea, exquisitely desirable, exquisitely unfamiliar, inhuman, of another world. Then follow the days when the violets creep through the mosses at the base of great oaks, when the dust of snow-bloom on the blackthorn gives way to the trailing dog-rose, when myriads of bees among the chestnut-blossoms fill the air with a continuous drowsy unrest, when the cushat calls from the heart of the fir, when beyond the green billowy roof of elm and hornbeam, of oak and beech, of sycamore and lime and tardy ash, the mysterious bells of the South fall through leagues of warm air, as the unseen cuckoo sails on the long tides of the wind. Then, in truth, is there magic in the woods. The forest is alive in its divine youth. Every bough is a vast plume of joy: on every branch a sunray falls, or a thrush sways in song, or the gauzy ephemeridae dance in rising and falling aerial cones. The wind moves with the feet of a fawn, with the wings of a dove, with the passing breath of the white owl at dusk. There is not a spot where is neither fragrance nor beauty nor life. From the tiniest arch of grass and twig the shrew-mouse will peep: above the shallowest rainpool the dragonfly will hang in miraculous suspense, like one of the faery javelins of Midir which in a moment could be withheld in mid-flight. The squirrel swings from branch to branch: the leveret shakes the dew from the shadowed grass: the rabbits flitter to and fro like brown beams of life: the robin, the chaffinch, the ousel, call though the warm green-glooms: on the bramble-spray and from the fern-garth the yellowhammer reiterates his gladsome song: in the cloudless blue fields of the sky the swifts weave a maze of shadow, the rooks rise and fall in giddy ascents and descents like black galleys surmounting measureless waves and sinking into incalculable gulfs.

Then the forest wearies of this interminable exuberance, this daily and nightly charm of exultant life. It desires another spell, the enchantment of silence, of dreams. One day the songs cease: the nests are cold. In the lush meadows the hare sleeps, the corncrake calls. By the brook the cattle stand, motionless, or with long tails rhythmically a-swing and ears a-twitch above the moist amber-violet dreamless eyes. The columnar trees are like phantom-smoke of secret invisible fires. In the green-glooms of the forest a sigh is heard. A troubled and furtive moan is audible in waste indiscoverable places. The thunder-time is come. Now in the woods may be seen and heard and felt that secret presence which in the spring months hid behind songs and blossoms, and later clothed itself in dense veils of green and all the magic of June. Something is now evident, that was not evident: somewhat is entered into the forest. The leaves know it: the bracken knows it: the secret is in every copse, in every thicket, is palpable in every glade, is abroad in every shadow-thridden avenue, is common to the spreading bough and the leaning branch. It is not a rumour; for that might be the wind stealthily lifting his long wings from glade to glade. It is not a whisper; for that might be the secret passage of unquiet airs, furtive heralds of the unloosening thunder. It is not a sigh; for that might be the breath of branch and bough, of fern-frond and grass, obvious in the great suspense. It is an enffable communication. It comes along the ways of silence; along the ways of sound: its light feet are on sun-rays and on shadows. Like dew, one knows not whether it is mysteriously gathered from below or secretly come from on high: simply it is there, above, around, beneath.

But the hush is dispelled at last. The long lances of the rain come slanting through the branches; they break, as against invisible barriers, and fall in a myriad pattering rush. The hoarse mutterings and sudden crashing roar of the thunder possess the whole forest. There are no more privacies, the secrecies are violated. From that moment the woods are renewed, and with the renewal the secret spirit that dwells within them withdraws, is not to be surprised, is inaudible, indefinitely recedes, is become remote, obscure, ineffable, incommunicable. And so, through veils of silence, and hot noons and husht warm midnights, the long weeks of July and August go by.

In the woods of September surely the forest-soul may be surprised, will be the thought of many. In that month the sweet incessant business of bird and beast lessens or is at an end. The woodpecker may still tap at the boles of gnarled oaks and chestnuts; the squirrel is more than ever mischievously gay; on frosty mornings, when the gossamer webs are woven across every bramble, and from frond to frond of the bronze-stained bracken, the redbreast tries and retries the poignant new song he has somehow learned since first he flaunted his bright canticles of March and April from the meadow-hedge or the sunned greenness of the beech-covert. But there is a general silence, a present suspense, while the lime yellows, and the birch takes on her pale gold, and oak and sycamore and ash slowly transmute their green multitudes into a new throng clad in russet or dull red or sunset-orange. The forest is full of loveliness: in her dusky ways faint azure mists gather. When the fawn leaps through the fern it is no longer soundlessly: there is a thin dry rustle, as of a dove brushing swiftly from its fastness in an ancient yew. One may pass from covert to covert, from glade to glade, and find the Secret just about to be revealed . . . somewhere beyond the group of birches, beside that oak it may be, just behind that isolated thorn. But it is never quite overtaken. It is as evasive as moonlight in the hollows of waves. When present, it is already gone. When approached, it has the unhasting but irretrieveable withdrawal of the shadow. In October this bewildering evasion is still more obvious, because the continual disclosure is more near and intimate. When, after autumns of rain and wind, or the sudden stealthy advent of nocturnal frosts, a multitude of leaves becomes sere and wan, and then the leaves strew every billow of wind like clots of driven foam or fall in still wavering flight like flakes of windless snow, then, it is surely then that the great surprise is imminent, that the secret and furtive whisper will become a voice. And yet there is something withheld. In November itself there are days, weeks even, when a rich autumn survives. The oaks and ashes will often keep their red and orange till after St. Luke's Peace; in sheltered parts of the forest even the plane, the sycamore, and the chestnut will flaunt their thin leopard-spotted yellow banners. I remember coming upon a Spanish chestnut in the centre of a group of all but leafless hornbeams. There seemed to be not a leaf missing from that splendid congregation of scarlet and amber and luminous saffron. A few

yards on and even the hardy beeches and oaks were denuded of all but a scattered and defeated company of brown or withered stragglers. Why should that single tree have kept its early October loveliness unchanged through those weeks of rain and wind and frosts of midnight and dawn? There was not one of its immediate company but was in desolate ruin, showing the bare nests high among the stark boughs. Through the whole forest the great unloosening had gone. Even the oaks in hollow places which had kept greenness like a continual wave suspended among dull masses of seaweed, had begun to yield to the vanishing call of the last voices of summer. Day by day their scattered tribes, then whole clans, broke up the tents of home and departed on the long mysterious exile. Yet this sentinel at the Gate of the North stood undaunted, splendid in warrior array. The same instinct that impels the soul from its outward home into the incalculable void moves the leaf with the imperious desire of the grey wind. But as, in human life, there are some who retain a splendid youth far into the failing regions of grey hair and broken years, so in the forest life there are trees which seem able to defy wind and rain and the consuming feet of frost.

The most subtle charm of the woods in November is in those blue spaces which lie at so brief a distance in every avenue of meeting boughs, under every enclosing branch. This azure mist which gathers like still faint smoke has the spell of silent waters, of moonlight, of the pale rose of serene dawns. It has a light that is its own, as unique as that unnameable flame which burns in the core of the rainbow. The earth breathes it; it is the breath of the fallen leaves, the moss, the tangled fern, the undergrowth, the trees; it is the breath also of the windless grey-blue sky that leans so low. Surely, also, it is the breath of that otherworld of which our songs and legends are so full. It has that mysteriousness, that spell, with which in imagination we endow the noon silences, the eves and dawns of faery twilights.

Still, the silence and the witchery of the forest solitudes in November are of the spell of autumn. The last enchantment of mid-winter is not yet come.

It is in "the dead months" that the forest permits the last disguises to fall away. The forest-soul is no longer an incommunicable mystery. It is abroad. It is a communicable dream. In that magnificent nakedness it knows its safety. For the first time it stands like a soul that has mastered all material things and is fearless in face of the immaterial things which are the only life of the spirit.

In these "dead months" of December and January the forest lives its own life. It is not asleep as the poets feign. Sleep has entered into the forest, has made the deep silence its habitation: but the forest itself is awake, mysterious, omnipresent, a creature seen at last in its naked majesty.

One says lightly, there is no green thing left. That, of course, is a mere phrase of relativity. There is always green fern somewhere, even in the garths of tangled yellow-brown bracken. There is always moss somewhere, hidden among the great serpentine roots of the beeches. The ilex will keep its dusty green through the harvest winter: the yew, the cypress, the holly, have no need of the continual invasion of the winds and rains and snows. On the ash and elm the wood-ivy will hang her spiked leaves. On many of the oaks the lovely dull green of the mistletoe will droop in graceful clusters, the cream-white berries glistening like innumerable pleiads of pearls. But these are lost in the immense uniformity of desolation. They are accidents, interludes. The wilderness knows them, as the grey wastes of tempestuous seas know a wave here and there that lifts a huge rampart of jade crowned with snow, or the long resiliency of gigantic billows which reveal smooth falling precipices of azure. The waste itself is one vast desolation, the more grey and terrible because in the mass invariable.

To go through those winter-aisles of the forest is to know an elation foreign to the melancholy of November or to the first fall of the leaf. It is not the elation of certain days in February, when the storm-cock tosses his song among the wild reefs of naked bough and branch. It is not the elation of March, when a blueness haunts the myriad unburst buds, and the throstle builds her nest and calls to the South. It is not the elation of April, when the virginal green is like exquisite music of life in miraculous suspense, nor the elation of May, when the wild rose moves in soft flame upon the thickets and the returned magic of the cuckoo is an intoxication, nor the elation of June, when the merle above the honeysuckle and the cushat in the green-glooms fill the hot noons with joy, and when the long fragrant twilights are thrilled with the passion of the night-jar. It has not this rapture nor that delight; but its elation is an ecstasy that is its own. It is then that one understands as one has never understood. It is then that one loves the mystery one has but fugitively divined. Where the forest murmurs there is music: ancient, everlasting. Go to the winter woods: listen there, look, watch, and "the dead months" will give you a subtler secret than any you have yet found in the forest. Then there is always one possible superb fortune. You may see the woods in snow. There is nothing in the world more beautiful than the forest clothed to its very hollows in snow. That is a loveliness to which surely none can be insensitive. It is the still ecstasy of Nature, wherein every spray, every blade of grass, every spire of reed, every intricacy of twig, is clad with radiance, and myriad form is renewed in continual change as though in the passionate delight of the white Artificer. It is beauty so great and complex that the imagination is stilled into an aching hush. There is the same trouble in the soul as before the starry hosts of a winter night.

—from *Where the Forest Murmurs* (1906)

Emerson at Yosemite

by John Muir

DURING MY FIRST YEARS in the Sierra I was ever calling on everybody within reach to admire the vast, billowy forests of conifers, but I found no one half warm enough until Emerson came. I had read his essays and felt sure that of all men he would best interpret the sayings of these noble mountains and trees. Nor was my faith weakened when I met him in Yosemite. He seemed as serene as a sequoia, his head in the empyrean; and forgetting his age, plans, duties, ties of every sort, I proposed a camping trip back in the heart of the mountains.

He seemed anxious to go, but considerately mentioned his party. I said: "Never mind. The mountains are calling; run away, and let plans and parties and dragging lowland duties all 'gang tap-sal-teerie.' We'll go up a cañon singing your own song, 'Good-by, proud world! I'm going home,' in divine earnest. Up there lies a new heaven and a new earth; let us go to the show." But alas, it was too late, too near the sundown of his life. The shadows were growing long, and he leaned on his friends. His party, full of indoor philosophy, failed to see the natural beauty and fullness of promise of my wild plan and laughed at it in good-natured ignorance, as if it were necessarily amusing to imagine that Boston people might be led to accept Sierra manifestations of God at the price of rough camping. Anyhow, they would have none of it and held Mr. Emerson to the hotels and trails.

After spending only five tourist days in Yosemite he was led away, but I saw him two days more; for I was kindly invited to go with the party as far as the Mariposa Big Trees. I told Mr. Emerson that I would gladly go to the sequoias with him, if he would camp in the grove. He consented heartily, and I felt sure that we would have at least one good wild memorable night round a sequoia campfire. Next day we rode through the magnificent forests of the Merced basin, and I kept calling his attention to the sugar pines, quoting his wood notes, "Come listen what the pine tree saith," and so forth, pointing out the noblest as kings and high priests, the most eloquent and commanding preachers of all the mountain forests, stretching forth their century-old arms in benediction over the congregations crowded about them. He gazed in devout admiration, saying but little, while his fine smile faded away.

Early in the afternoon, when we reached Clark's Station, I was surprised to see the party dismount. And when I asked if we were not going up into the grove to camp, they said: "No, it would never do to lie out in the night air. Mr. Emerson might take cold; and you know, Mr. Muir, that would be a dreadful thing." In vain I urged that only in homes and hotels were colds caught, that nobody ever was known to take cold camping in these woods, that there was not a single cough or sneeze in all the Sierra. Then I pictured the big climate-changing, inspiring fire I would make, praised the beauty and fragrance of sequoia flame, told how the great trees would stand about us transfigured in the purple light while the stars looked down between the great domes, ending by urging them to come on and make an immortal Emerson night of it. But the house habit was not to be overcome, nor the strange dread of pure night air, though it is only cooled day air with a little pure dew in it. So the carpet dust and unknowable reeks were preferred. And to think of this being a Boston choice! Sad commentary on culture and the glorious transcendentalism.

Accustomed to reach whatever place I started for, I was going up the mountain alone to camp and wait the coming of the party next day. But since Emerson was so soon to vanish, I concluded to stop with him. He hardly spoke a word all the evening, yet it was a great pleasure simply to be near him, warming in the light of his face as at a fire. In the morning we rode up the trail through a noble forest of pine and fir into the Mariposa Grove and stayed an hour or two, mostly in ordinary tourist fashion—looking at the biggest giants, measuring them with a tape line, riding through prostrate fire-bored trunks, and so forth, though Mr. Emerson was alone occasionally, sauntering about as if under a spell. As we walked through a fine group, he quoted, "There were giants in those days," recognizing the antiquity of the race. To commemorate his visit, Galen Clark, the guardian of the grove, selected the finest of the unnamed trees and requested him to give it a name. He named it Samoset, after the New England sachem, as the best that occurred to him.

The poor bit of measured time was soon spent, and while the saddles were being adjusted I again urged Emerson to stay. "You are yourself a sequoia," I said. "Stop and get acquainted with your big brethren." But he was past his prime and was now as a child in the hands of his affectionate but sadly civilized friends, who seemed as full of old-fashioned conformity as of bold intellectual independence. It was the afternoon of the day and the afternoon of his life, and his course was now westward down all the mountains into the sunset. The party mounted and rode away in wondrous contentment, apparently. I followed to the edge of the grove. Emerson lingered in the rear of the train, and when he reached the top of the ridge, after all the rest of the party were over and out of sight, he turned his horse, took off his hat, and waved me a last good-by.

I felt lonely, so sure had I been that Emerson of all men would be the quickest to see the mountains and sing them.

Gazing awhile on the spot where he vanished, I sauntered back into the heart of the grove, made a bed of sequoia plumes and ferns by the side of a stream, gathered a store of firewood, and then walked about until sundown. The birds, robins, thrushes, and warblers that had kept out of sight came about me, now that all was quiet, and made cheer. After sundown I built a great fire, and as usual had it all to myself. And though lonesome for the first time in these forests, I quickly took heart again—the trees had not gone to Boston, nor the birds; and as I sat by the fire, Emerson was still with me in spirit, though I never again saw him in the flesh. He sent books and wrote, cheering me on; advised me not to stay too long in solitude. Soon he hoped my guardian angel would intimate that my probation was at a close. Then I was to roll up my herbariums, sketches, and poems (though I never knew I had any poems), and come to his house; and when I tired of him and his humble surroundings, he would show me to better people.

But there remained many a forest to wander through, many a mountain and glacier to cross, before I was to see his Wachusett and Monadnock, Boston and Concord. It was seventeen years after our parting on the Wawona Ridge that I stood beside his grave under a pine tree on the hill above Sleepy Hollow. He had gone to higher Sierras, and, as I fancied, was again waving his hand in friendly recognition.

—from "The Forests of Yosemite Park," *Atlantic Monthly* (April, 1900)

The Pleasure of Walking
by Oliver Wendell Holmes

1.

YOU THINK YOU KNOW all about *walking,*—don't you, now? Well, how do you suppose your lower limbs are held to your body? They are sucked up by two cupping vessels, ("cotyloid"—cup-like—cavities,) and held here as long as you live, and longer. At any rate, you think you move them backward and forward at such a rate as your will determines, don't you? On the contrary, they swing just as any other pendulums swing, at a fixed rate, determined by their length. You can alter this by muscular power, as you can take hold of the pendulum of a clock and make it move faster or slower; but your ordinary gait is timed by the same mechanism as the movements of the solar system.

2.

I do not deny the attraction of walking. I have bored this ancient city through and through in my daily travels, until I know it as an old inhabitant of a Cheshire knows his cheese. Why, it was I who, in the course of these rambles, discovered that remarkable avenue called *Myrtle Street,* stretching in one long line from east of the Reservoir to a precipitous and rudely paved cliff which looks down on the grim abode of Science, and beyond it to the far hills; a promenade so delicious in its repose, so cheerfully varied with glimpses down the northern slope into busy Cambridge Street, with its iron river of the horse-railroad, and wheeled barges gliding backward and forward over it,—so delightfully closing at its western extremity in sunny courts and passages where I know peace, and beauty, and virtue, and serene old age must be perpetual tenants,—so alluring to all who desire to take their daily stroll, in the words of Dr. Watts,—

"Alike unknowing and unknown,"—

that nothing but a sense of duty would have prompted me to reveal the secret of its existence. I concede, therefore, that walking is an immeasurably fine invention, of which old age ought constantly to avail itself. . . .

3.

The pleasure of exercise is due first to a purely physical impression, and secondly to a sense of power in action. The first source of pleasure varies of course with our condition and the state of the surrounding circumstances; the second with the amount and kind of power, and the extent and kind of action. In all forms of active exercise there are three powers simultaneously in action,—the will, the muscles, and the intellect. Each of these predominates in different kinds of exercise. In walking, the will and muscles are so accustomed to work together and perform their task with so little expenditure of force, that the intellect is left comparatively free. The mental pleasure in walking, as such, is in the sense of power over all our moving machinery.

—from *The Autocrat of the Breakfast Table* (1887)

Walking Tours
by Robert Louis Stevenson

IT MUST NOT BE imagined that a walking tour, as some would have us fancy, is merely a better or worse way of seeing the country. There are many ways of seeing landscape quite as good; and none more vivid, in spite of canting dilettantes, than from a railway train. But landscape on a walking tour is quite accessory. He who is indeed of the brotherhood does not voyage in quest of the picturesque, but of certain jolly humours—of the hope and spirit with which the march begins at morning, and the peace and spiritual repletion of the evening's rest. He cannot tell whether he puts his knapsack on, or takes it off, with more delight. The excitement of the departure puts him in key for that of the arrival. Whatever he does is not only a reward in itself, but will be further rewarded in the sequel; and so pleasure leads on to pleasure in an endless chain. It is this that so few can understand; they will either be always lounging or always at five miles an hour; they do not play off the one against the other, prepare all day for the evening, and all evening for the next day. And, above all, it is here that your overwalker fails of comprehension. His heart rises against those who drink their curaçoa in liqueur glasses, when he himself can swill it in a brown john. He will not believe that the flavour is more delicate in the smaller dose. He will not believe that to walk this unconscionable distance is merely to stupefy and brutalise himself, and come to his inn, at night, with a sort of frost on his five wits, and a starless night of darkness in his spirit. Not for him the mild luminous evening of the temperate walker! He has nothing left of man but a physical need for bedtime and a double nightcap; and even his pipe, if he be a smoker, will be savourless and disenchanted. It is the fate of such an one to take twice as much trouble as is needed to obtain happiness, and miss the happiness in the end; he is the man of the proverb, in short, who goes farther and fares worse.

Now, to be properly enjoyed, a walking tour should be gone upon alone. If you go in a company, or even in pairs, it is no longer a walking tour in anything but name; it is something else, and more in the nature of a picnic. A walking tour should be gone upon alone, because freedom is of the essence; because you should be able to stop and go on, and follow this way or that, as the freak takes you; and because you must have your own pace, and neither trot alongside a champion walker, nor mince in time with a girl. And then you must be open to all impressions, and let your thoughts take colour from what you see. You should be as a pipe for any wind to play upon. "I cannot see the wit," says Hazlitt, "of walking and talking at the same time. When I am in the country I wish to vegetate like the country," which is the gist of all that can be said upon the matter. There should be no cackle of voices at your elbow, to jar on the meditative silence of the morning. And so long as a man is reasoning he cannot surrender himself to that fine intoxication that comes of much motion in the open air, that begins in a sort of a dazzle and sluggishness of the brain, and ends in a peace that passes comprehension.

During the first day or so of any tour there are moments of bitterness, when the traveler feels more than coldly towards his knapsack, when he is half in a mind to throw it bodily over the hedge, and, like Christian on a similar occasion, "give three leaps and go on singing." And yet it soon acquires a property of easiness. It becomes magnetic; the spirit of the journey enters into it. And no sooner have you passed the straps over your shoulder than the lees of sleep are cleared from you, you pull yourself together with a shake, and fall at once into your stride. And surely, of all possible moods, this, in which a man takes the road, is the best. Of course, if he *will* keep thinking of his anxieties, if he *will* open the merchant Abudah's chest and walk armin-arm with the hag—why, wherever he is, and whether he walk fast or slow, the chances are that he will not be happy. And so much the more shame to himself! There are perhaps thirty men setting forth at that same hour, and I would lay a large wager there is not another dull face among the thirty. It would be a fine thing to follow, in a coat of darkness, one after another of these wayfarers, some summer morning, for the first few miles upon the road. This one, who walks fast, with a keen look in his eyes, is all concentrated in his own mind; he is up at his loom, weaving and weaving, to set the landscape to words. This one peers about, as he goes, among the grasses; he waits by the canal to watch the dragon flies; he leans on the gate of the pasture, and cannot look enough upon the complacent kine. And here comes another, talking, laughing, and gesticulating to himself. His face changes from time to time, as indignation flashes from his eyes or anger clouds his forehead. He is composing articles, delivering orations, and conducting the most impassioned interviews, by the way. A little farther on, and it is as like as not he will begin to sing. And well for him, supposing him to be no great master in that art, if he stumble across no stolid peasant at a corner; for on such an occasion, I scarcely know which is the more troubled, or whether it is worse to suffer the confusion of your troubadour or the unfeigned alarm of your clown. A sedentary population, accustomed, besides, to the strange mechanical bearing of the common tramp, can in no wise explain to itself the gaiety of these passersby. I knew one man who was arrested as a runaway lunatic, because, although a full-grown person with a red beard, he skipped as he went like a child. And you would be astonished if I were to tell you all the grave and learned heads who have confessed to me that, when on walking tours, they sang—and sang very ill —and had a pair of red ears when, as described above, the inauspicious peasant plumped into their arms from round a corner. And here, lest you should think I am exaggerating, is Hazlitt's own confession, from his essay "On Going a Journey," which is so good that there should be a tax levied on all who have not read it:—

"Give me the clear blue sky over my head," says he, "and the green turf beneath my feet, a winding road before me, and a three hours' march to dinner—and then to thinking! It is hard if I cannot start some game on these lone heaths. I laugh, I run, I leap, I sing for joy."

Bravo! After that adventure of my friend with the policeman, you would not have cared, would you, to publish that in the first person? But we have no bravery nowadays, and, even in books, must all pretend to be as dull and foolish as our neighbours. It was not so with Hazlitt. And notice how learned he is (as, indeed, throughout the essay) in the theory of walking tours. He is none of your athletic men in purple stockings, who walk their fifty miles a day: three hours' march is his ideal. And then he must have a winding road, the epicure!

Yet there is one thing I object to in these words of his, one thing in the great master's practice that seems to me not wholly wise. I do not approve of that leaping and running. Both of these hurry the respiration; they both shake up the brain out of its glorious open-air confusion; and they both break the pace. Uneven walking is not so agreeable to the body, and it distracts and irritates the mind.

Whereas, when once you have fallen into an equable stride, it requires no conscious thought from you to keep it up, and yet it prevents you from thinking earnestly of anything else. Like knitting, like the work of a copying clerk, it gradually neutralises and sets to sleep the serious activity of the mind. We can think of this or that, lightly and laughingly, as a child thinks, or as we think in a morning doze; we can make puns or puzzle out acrostics, and trifle in a thousand ways with words and rhymes; but when it comes to honest work, when we come to gather ourselves together for an effort, we may sound the trumpet as loud and long as we please; the great barons of the mind will not rally to the standard, but sit, each one, at home, warming his hands over his own fire, and brooding on his own private thought!

In the course of a day's walk, you see, there is much variance in the mood. From the exhilaration of the start, to the happy phlegm of the arrival, the change is certainly great. As the day goes on, the traveler moves from the one extreme end towards the other. He becomes more and more incorporated with the material landscape, and the open-air drunkenness grows upon him with great strides, until he posts along the road, and sees everything about him, as in a cheerful dream. The first is certainly brighter, but the second stage is the more peaceful. A man does not make so many articles towards the end, nor does he laugh aloud; but the purely animal pleasures, the sense of physical well-being, the delight of every inhalation, of every time the muscles tighten down the thigh, console him for the absence of the others, and bring him to his destination still content.

Nor must I forget to say a word on bivouacs. You come to a milestone on a hill, or some place where deep ways meet under trees; and off goes the knapsack, and down you sit to smoke a pipe in the shade. You sink into yourself, and the birds come round and look at you; and your smoke dissipates upon the afternoon under the blue dome of heaven; and the sun lies warm upon your feet, and the cool air visits your neck and turns aside your open shirt. If you are not happy, you must have an evil conscience. You may dally as long as you like by the roadside. It is almost as if the millennium were arrived, when we shall throw our clocks and watches over the house-top, and remember time and seasons no more. Not to keep hours for a lifetime is, I was going to say, to live for ever. You have no idea, unless you have tried it, how endlessly long is a summer's day that you measure out only by hunger, and bring to an end only when you are drowsy. I know a village where there are hardly any clocks, where no one knows more of the days of the week than by a sort of instinct for the fête on Sundays, and where only one person can tell you the day of the month, and she is generally wrong; and if people were aware how slow Time journeyed in that village, and what armfuls of spare hours he gives, over and above the bargain, to its wise inhabitants, I believe there would be a stampede out of London, Liverpool, Paris, and a variety of large towns, where the clocks lose their heads, and shake the hours out each one faster than the other, as though they were all in a wager. And all these foolish pilgrims would each bring his own misery along with him, in a watchpocket! It is to be noticed there were no clocks and watches in the much-vaunted days before the flood. It follows, of course, there were no appointments, and punctuality was not yet thought upon. "Though ye take from a covetous man all his treasure," says Milton, "he has yet one jewel left; ye cannot deprive him of his covetousness." And so I would say of a modern man of business, you may do what you will for him, put him in Eden, give him the elixir of life—he has still a flaw at heart, he still has his business habits. Now, there is no time when business habits are more mitigated than on a walking tour. And so during these halts, as I say, you will feel almost free.

But it is at night, and after dinner, that the best hour comes. There are no such pipes to be smoked as those that follow a good day's march; the flavour of the tobacco is a thing to be remembered, it is so dry and aromatic, so full and so fine. If you wind up the evening with grog, you will own there was never such grog; at every sip a jocund tranquility spreads about your limbs, and sits easily in your heart. If you read a book—and you will never do so save by fits and starts—you find the language strangely racy and harmonious; words take a new meaning; single sentences possess the ear for half an hour together; and the writer endears himself to you, at every page, by the nicest coincidence of sentiment. It seems as if it were a book you had written yourself in a dream. To all we have read on such occasions we look back with special favour. "It was on the 10th of April, 1798," says Hazlitt, with amorous precision, "that I sat down to a volume of the new 'Heloise,' at the Inn at Llangollen, over a bottle of sherry and a cold chicken," I should wish to quote more, for though we are mighty fine fellows nowadays, we cannot write like Hazlitt. And, talking of that, a volume of Hazlitt's essays would be a capital pocket-book on such a journey; so would a volume of Heine's songs; and for "Tristram Shandy" I can pledge a fair experience.

If the evening be fine and warm, there is nothing better in life than to lounge before the inn door in the sunset, or lean over the parapet of the bridge, to watch the weeds and the quick fishes. It is then, if ever, that you taste Joviality to the full significance of that audacious word. Your muscles are so agreeably slack, you feel so clean and so strong and so idle, that whether you move or sit still, whatever you do is done with pride and a kingly sort of pleasure. You fall in talk with any one, wise or foolish, drunk or sober. And it seems as if a hot walk purged you, more than of anything else, of all narrowness and pride, and left curiosity to play its part freely, as in a child or a man of science. You lay aside all your own hobbies, to watch provincial humours develop themselves before you, now as a laughable farce, and now grave and beautiful like an old tale.

Or perhaps you are left to your own company for the night, and surly weather imprisons you by the fire. You may remember how Burns, numbering past pleasures, dwells upon the hours when he has been "happy thinking." It is a phrase that may well perplex a poor modern, girt about on every side by clocks and chimes, and haunted, even at night, by flaming dial-plates. For we are all so busy, and have so many far-off projects to realise, and castles in the fire to turn into solid habitable mansions on a gravel soil, that we can find no time for pleasure trips into the Land of Thought and among the Hills of Vanity. Changed times, indeed, when we must sit all night, beside the fire, with folded hands; and a changed world for most of us, when we find we can pass the hours without discontent, and be happy thinking. We are in such haste to be doing, to be writing, to be gathering gear, to make our voice audible a moment in the derisive silence of eternity, that we forget that one thing, of which these are but the parts—namely, to live. We fall in love, we drink hard, we run to and fro upon the earth like frightened sheep. And now you are to ask yourself if, when all is done, you would not have been better to sit by the fire at home, and be happy thinking. To sit still and contemplate,—to remember the faces of women without desire, to be pleased by the great deeds of men without envy, to be everything and everywhere in sympathy, and yet content to remain where and what you are—is not this to know both wisdom and virtue, and to dwell with happiness? After all, it is not they who carry flags, but they who look upon it from a private chamber, who have the fun of the procession. And once you are at that, you are in the very humour of all social heresy. It is no time for shuffling, or for big empty words. If you ask yourself what you mean by fame, riches, or learning, the answer is far to seek; and you go back into that kingdom of light imaginations, which seem so vain in the eyes of Philistines perspiring after wealth, and so momentous to those who are stricken with the disproportions of the world, and, in the face of the gigantic stars, cannot stop to split differences between two degrees of the infinitesimally small, such as a tobacco pipe or the Roman Empire, a million of money or a fiddlestick's end.

You lean from the window, your last pipe reeking whitely into the darkness, your body full of delicious pains, your mind enthroned in the seventh circle of content; when suddenly the mood changes, the weathercock goes about, and you ask yourself one question more: whether, for the interval, you have been the wisest philosopher or the most egregious of donkeys? Human experience is not yet able to reply; but at least you have had a fine moment, and looked down upon all the kingdoms of the earth. And whether it was wise or foolish, to-morrow's travel will carry you, body and mind, into some different parish of the infinite.

—from *Virginibus Puersique* (1881)

The Ascent of the Rigi-Kulm
by Mark Twain

THE RIGI-KULM is an imposing Alpine mass, 6,000 feet high, which stands by itself, and commands a mighty prospect of blue lakes, green valleys, and snowy mountains—a compact and magnificent picture three hundred miles in circumference. The ascent is made by rail, or horseback, or on foot, as one may prefer. I and my agent panoplied ourselves in walking costume, one bright morning, and started down the lake on the steamboat; we got ashore at the village of Waggis, three quarters of an hour distant from Lucerne. This village is at the foot of the mountain.

We were soon tramping leisurely up the leafy mule-path, and then the talk began to flow, as usual. It was twelve o'clock noon, and a breezy, cloudless day; the ascent was gradual, and the glimpses, from under the curtaining boughs, of blue water, and tiny sail-boats, and beetling cliffs, were as charming as glimpses of dreamland. All the circumstances were perfect—and the anticipations too, for we should soon be enjoying, for the first time, that wonderful spectacle, an Alpine sunrise—the object of our journey. There was (apparently) no real need to hurry, for the guide-book made the walking distance from Waggis to the summit only three hours and a quarter. I say "apparently," because the guide-book had already fooled us once—about the distance from Allerheiligen to Oppenau—and for aught I knew it might be getting ready to fool us again. We were only certain as to the altitudes—we calculated to find out for ourselves how many hours it is from the bottom to the top. The summit is 6,000 feet above the sea, but only 4,500 feet above the lake. When we had walked half an hour, we were fairly into the swing and humor of the undertaking, so we cleared for action; that is to say, we got a boy whom we met to carry our alpenstocks and satchels, and overcoats and things for us; that left us free for business.

I suppose we must have stopped oftener to stretch out on the grass in the shade and take a bit of a smoke than this boy was used to, for presently he asked if it had been our idea to hire him by the job, or by the year? We told him he could move along if he was in a hurry. He said he wasn't in such a very particular hurry, but he wanted to get to the top while he was young. We told him to clear out, then, and leave the things at the uppermost hotel and say we should be along presently. He said he would secure us a hotel if he could, but if they were all full he would ask them to build another one and hurry up and get the paint and plaster dry against we arrived. Still gently chaffing us he pushed ahead, up the trail, and soon disappeared. By six o'clock we were pretty high up in the air, and the view of lake and mountains had greatly grown in breadth and interest. We halted a while at a little public house, where we had bread and cheese and a quart or two of fresh milk, out on the porch, with the big panorama all before us—and then moved on again.

Ten minutes afterward we met a hot, red-faced man plunging down the mountain, with mighty strides, swinging his alpenstock ahead of him and taking a grip on the ground with its iron point to support these big strides. He stopped, fanned himself with his hat, swabbed the perspiration from his face and neck with a red handkerchief, panted a moment or two, and asked how far it was to Waggis. I said three hours. He looked surprised, and said—

"Why, it seems as if I could toss a biscuit into the lake from here, it's so close by. Is that an inn, there?"

I said it was.

"Well," said he, "I can't stand another three hours, I've had enough for today; I'll take a bed there."

I asked—

"Are we nearly to the top?"

"Nearly to the *top!* Why, bless your soul, you haven't really started, yet."

I said we would put up at the inn, too. So we turned back and ordered a hot supper, and had quite a jolly evening of it with this Englishman.

The German landlady gave us neat rooms and nice beds, and when I and my agent turned in, it was with the resolution to be up early and make the utmost of our first Alpine sunrise. But of course we were dead tired, and slept like policemen; so when we awoke in the morning and ran to the window it was already too late, because it was half-past eleven. It was a sharp disappointment. However, we ordered breakfast and told the landlady to call the Englishman, but she said he was already up and off at daybreak—and swearing mad about something or other. We could not find out what the matter was. He had asked the landlady the altitude of her place above the level of the lake, and she had told him fourteen hundred and ninety-five feet. That was all that was said; then he lost his temper. He said that between ———— fools and guide-books, a man could acquire ignorance enough in twenty-four hours in a country like this to last him for a year. Harris believed our boy had been loading him up with misinformation; and this was probably the case, for his epithet described that boy to a dot.

We got under way about the turn of noon, and pulled out for the summit again with a fresh and vigorous step. When we had gone about two hundred yards, and stopped to rest, I glanced to the left while I was lighting my pipe, and in the distance detected a long worm of black smoke crawling lazily up the steep mountain. Of course that was the locomotive. We propped ourselves on our elbows at once, to gaze, for we had never seen a mountain railway yet. Presently we could make out the train. It seemed incredible that that thing should creep straight up a sharp slant like the roof of a house—but there it was, and it was doing that very miracle.

In the course of a couple of hours we reached a fine breezy altitude where the little shepherd huts had big stones all over their roofs to hold them down to the earth when the great storms rage. The country was wild and rocky about here, but there were plenty of trees, plenty of moss, and grass.

Away off on the opposite shore of the lake we could see some villages, and now for the first time we could observe the real difference between their proportions and those of the giant mountains at whose feet they slept. When one is in one of those villages it seems spacious, and its houses seem high and not out of proportion to the mountain that overhangs them—but from our altitude, what a change! The mountains were bigger and grander than ever, as they stood there thinking their solemn thoughts with their heads in the drifting clouds, but the villages at their feet—when the painstaking eye could trace them up and find them— were so reduced, so almost invisible, and lay so flat against the ground, that the exactest simile I can devise is to compare them to ant-deposits of granulated dirt overshadowed by the huge bulk of a cathedral. The steamboats skimming along under the stupendous precipices were diminished by distance to the daintiest little toys, the sail-boats and row-boats to shallops proper for fairies that keep house in the cups of lilies and ride to court on the backs of bumble-bees.

Presently we came upon half a dozen sheep nibbling grass in the spray of a stream of clear water that sprang from a rock wall a hundred feet high, and all at once our ears were startled with a melodious "Lul . . . . . . l . . . . . . l . . . . . . lul-lul-*la*hee-o-o-o!" pealing joyously from a near but invisible source, and recognized that we were hearing for the first time the famous Alpine *jodel* in its own native wilds. And we recognized, also, that it was that sort of quaint commingling of baritone and falsetto which at home we call "Tyrolese warbling."

The jodeling (pronounced yodling—emphasis on the o), continued, and was very pleasant and inspirating to hear. Now the jodeler appeared—a shepherd boy of sixteen—and in our gladness and gratitude we gave him a franc to jodel some more. So he jodeled and we listened. We moved on presently, and he generously jodeled us out of sight. After about fifteen minutes we came across another shepherd boy who was jodeling, and gave him half a franc to keep it up. He also jodeled us out of sight. After that we found a jodeler every ten minutes; we gave the first one eight cents, the second one six cents, the third one four, the fourth one a penny, contributed nothing to Nos. 5, 6, and 7, and during the remainder of the day hired the rest of the jodelers, at a franc apiece, not to jodel any more. There is somewhat too much of this jodeling in the Alps.

About the middle of the afternoon we passed through a prodigious natural gateway, called the Felsenthor, formed by two enormous upright rocks, with a third lying across the top. There was a very attractive little hotel close by, but our energies were not conquered yet, so we went on.

Three hours afterward we came to the railway track. It was planted straight up the mountain with the slant of a ladder that leans against a house, and it seemed to us that a man would need good nerves who proposed to travel up it or down it either.

During the latter part of the afternoon we cooled our roasting interiors with ice-cold water from clear streams, the only really satisfying water we had tasted since we left home, for at the hotels on the continent they merely give you a tumbler of ice to soak your water in, and that only modifies its hotness, doesn't make it cold. Water can only be made cold enough for summer comfort by being prepared in a refrigerator or a closed ice-pitcher. Europeans say ice water impairs digestion. How do they know?—they never drink any.

At ten minutes past six we reached the Kaltbad station, where there is a spacious hotel with great verandahs which command a majestic expanse of lake and mountain scenery. We were pretty well fagged out now, but as we did not wish to miss the famous sunrise, we got through with our dinner as quickly as possible and hurried off to bed. It was unspeakably comfortable to stretch our weary limbs between the cool damp sheets. And how we did sleep!—for there is no opiate like Alpine pedestrianism.

In the morning we both awoke and leaped out of bed at the same instant and ran and stripped aside the window curtains; but we suffered a bitter disappointment again; it was already half-past three in the afternoon.

We dressed sullenly and in ill spirits, each accusing the other of over-sleeping. Harris said if we had brought the courier along, as we ought to have done, we should not have missed these sunrises. I said he knew very well that one of us would have had to sit up and wake the courier; and I added that we were having trouble enough to take care of ourselves, on this climb, without having to take care of a courier besides.

During breakfast our spirits came up a little, since we found by the guide-book that in the hotels on the summit the tourist is not left to trust to luck for his sunrise, but is roused betimes by a man who goes through the halls with a great Alpine horn, blowing blasts that would raise the dead. And there was another consoling thing: the guide-book said that up there on the summit the guests did not wait to dress much, but seized a red bed-blanket and sailed out arrayed like an Indian. This was good; this would be romantic; two hundred and fifty people grouped on the windy summit, with their hair flying and their red blankets flapping, in the solemn presence of the snowy ranges and the messenger splendors of the coming sun, would be a striking and memorable spectacle. So it was good luck not ill luck, that we had missed those other sunrises.

We were informed by the guide-book that we were now 3,228 feet above the level of the lake—therefore full two-thirds of our journey had been accomplished. We got away at a quarter past four, p.m.; a hundred yards above the hotel the railway divided; one track went straight up the steep hill, the other one turned square off to the right, with a very slight grade. We took the latter, and followed it more than a mile, turned a rocky corner and came in sight of a handsome new hotel. If we had gone on, we should have arrived at the summit, but Harris preferred to ask a lot of questions—as usual, of a man who didn't know anything—and he told us to go back and follow the other route. We did so. We could ill afford this loss of time.

We climbed, and climbed; and we kept on climbing; we reached about forty summits but there was always another one just ahead. It came on to rain, and it rained in dead earnest. We were soaked through, and it was bitter cold. Next a smoky fog of clouds covered the whole region densely, and we took to the railway ties to keep from getting lost. Sometimes we slopped along in a narrow path on the left hand side of the track, but by and by when the fog blew aside a little and we saw that we were treading the rampart of a precipice and that our left elbows were projecting over a perfectly boundless and bottomless vacancy, we gasped, and jumped for the ties again.

The night shut down, dark and drizzly and cold. About eight in the evening the fog lifted and showed us a well worn path which led up a very steep rise to the left. We took it and as soon as we had got far enough from the railway to render the finding it again an impossibility, the fog shut down on us once more.

We were in a bleak unsheltered place, now, and had to trudge right along, in order to keep warm, though we rather expected to go over a precipice sooner or later. About nine o'clock we made an important discovery—that we were not in any path. We groped around a while on our hands and knees, but could not find it; so we sat down in the mud and the wet scant grass to wait. We were terrified into this by being suddenly confronted with a vast body which showed itself vaguely for an instant and in the next instant was smothered in the fog again. It was really the hotel we were after, monstrously magnified by the fog, but we took it for the face of a precipice and decided not to try to claw up it.

We sat there an hour, with chattering teeth and quivering bodies, and quarreled over all sorts of trifles, but gave most of our attention to abusing each other for the stupidity of deserting the railway track. We sat with our backs to that precipice, because what little wind there was came from that quarter. At some time or other the fog thinned a little; we did not know when, for we were facing the empty universe and the thinness could not show; but at last Harris

happened to look around, and there stood a huge, dim, spectral hotel where the precipice had been. One could faintly discern the windows and chimneys, and a dull blur of lights. Our first emotion was deep unutterable gratitude, our next was a foolish rage, born of the suspicion that possibly the hotel had been visible three-quarters of an hour while we sat there in those cold puddles quarreling.

Yes, it was the Rigi-Kulm hotel—the one that occupies the extreme summit, and whose remote little sparkle of lights we had often seen glinting high aloft among the stars from our balcony away down yonder in Lucerne. The crusty portier and the crusty clerks gave us the surly reception which their kind deal in in prosperous times, but by mollifying them with an extra display of obsequiousness and servility we finally got them to show us to the room which our boy had engaged for us.

We got into some dry clothing, and while our supper was preparing we loafed forsakenly through a couple of vast cavernous drawing rooms, one of which had a stove in it. This stove was in a corner, and densely walled around with people. We could not get near the fire, so we moved at large in the arctic spaces, among a multitude of people who sat silent, smileless, forlorn and shivering—thinking what fools they were to come, perhaps. There were some Americans, and some Germans, but one could see that the great majority were English.

We lounged into an apartment where there was a great crowd, to see what was going on. It was a memento-magazine. The tourists were eagerly buying all sorts and styles of paper-cutters, marked "Souvenir of the Rigi," with handles made of the little curved horn of the ostensible chamois; there were all manner of wooden goblets and such things, similarly marked. I was going to buy a paper-cutter, but I believed I could remember the cold comfort of the Rigi-Kulm without it, so I smothered the impulse.

Supper warmed us, and we went immediately to bed—but first, as Mr. Baedeker requests all tourists to call his attention to any errors which they may find in his guide-books, I dropped him a line to inform him that when he said the foot-journey from Waggis to the summit was only three hours and a quarter, he missed it by just about three days. I had previously informed him of his mistake about the distance from Allerheiligen to Oppenau, and had also informed the Ordnance Department of the German government of the same error in the imperial maps. I will add, here, that I never got any answer to these letters, or any thanks from either of these sources; and what is still more discourteous, these corrections have not been made, either in the maps or the guide-books. But I will write again when I get time, for my letters may have miscarried.

We curled up in the clammy beds, and went to sleep without rocking. We were so sodden with fatigue that we never stirred nor turned over till the booming blasts of the Alpine horn aroused us. It may well be imagined that we did not lose any time. We snatched on a few odds and ends of clothing, cocooned ourselves in the proper red blankets, and plunged along the halls and out into the whistling wind bareheaded. We saw a tall wooden scaffolding on the very peak of the summit, a hundred yards away, and made for it. We rushed up the stairs to the top of this scaffolding, and stood there, above the vast outlying world, with hair flying and ruddy blankets waving and cracking in the fierce breeze.

"Fifteen minutes too late, at last!" said Harris, in a vexed voice. "The sun is clear above the horizon."

"No matter," I said, "it is a most magnificent spectacle, and we will see it do the rest of its rising, anyway."

In a moment we were deeply absorbed in the marvel before us, and dead to everything else. The great cloud-barred disk of the sun stood just above a limitless expanse of tossing white-caps—so to speak—a billowy chaos of massy mountain domes and peaks draped in imperishable snow, and flooded with an opaline glory of changing and dissolving splendors, whilst through rifts in a black cloud-bank above the sun, radiating lances of diamond dust shot to the zenith. The cloven valleys of the lower world swam in a tinted mist which veiled the ruggedness of their crags and ribs and ragged forests, and turned all the forbidding region into a soft and rich and sensuous paradise.

We could not speak. We could hardly breathe. We could only gaze in drunken ecstasy and drink it in. Presently Harris exclaimed—

"Why ――― nation, it's going *down*!"

Perfectly true. We had missed the *morning* horn-blow, and slept all day. This was stupefying. Harris said—

"Look here, the sun isn't the spectacle—it's us—stacked up here on top of this gallows, in these idiotic blankets, and two hundred and fifty well dressed men and women down here gawking up at us and not caring a straw whether the sun rises or sets, as long as they've got such a ridiculous spectacle as this to set down in their memorandum-books.

They seem to be laughing their ribs loose, and there's one girl there that seems to be going all to pieces. I never saw such a man as you before. I think you are the very last possibility in the way of an ass."

"What have *I* done?" I answered with heat.

"What have you done? You've got up at half past seven o'clock in the evening to see the sun rise, that's what you've done."

"And have you done any better, I'd like to know? I always used to get up with the lark, till I came under the petrifying influence of your turgid intellect."

"*You* used to get up with the lark—O, no doubt—you'll get up with the hangman one of these days. But you ought to be ashamed to be jawing here like this, in a red blanket, on a forty-foot scaffold on top of the Alps. And no end of people down here to boot; this isn't any place for an exhibition of temper."

And so the customary quarrel went on. When the sun was fairly down, we slipped back to the hotel, in the charitable gloaming, and went to bed again. We had encountered the horn-blower on the way, and he had tried to collect compensation, not only for announcing the sunset, which we did see, but for the sunrise, which we had totally missed; but we said no, we only took our solar rations on the "European plan"—pay for what you get.

—from *A Tramp Abroad* (1880)

We Camp Out
by Frank R. Stockton

MY WIFE AND I were both so fond of country life and country pursuits that month after month passed by at our little farm in a succession of delightful days. Time flew like a "limited express" train, and it was September before we knew it.

I had been working very hard at the office that summer, and was glad to think of my two weeks' vacation, which were to begin on the first Monday of the month. I had intended spending these two weeks in rural retirement at home, but an interview in the city with my family physician caused me to change my mind. I told him my plan.

"Now," said he, "if I were you, I'd do nothing of the kind. You have been working too hard; your face shows it. You need rest and change. Nothing will do you so much good as to camp out; that will be fifty times better than going to any summer resort. You can take your wife with you. I know she'll like it. I don't care where you go just so that it's a healthy spot. Get a good tent and an outfit, be off to the woods, and forget all about business and domestic matters for a few weeks."

This sounded splendid, and I propounded the plan to Euphemia that evening. She thought very well of it, and was sure we could do it. Pomona would not be afraid to remain in the house, under the protection of Lord Edward, and she could easily attend to the cow and the chickens. It would be a holiday for her too. Old John, the man who occasionally worked for us, would come up sometimes and see after things. With her customary dexterity Euphemia swept away every obstacle to the plan, and all was settled before we went to bed.

As my wife had presumed, Pomona made no objections to remaining in charge of the house. The scheme pleased her greatly. So far, so good. I called that day on a friend who was in the habit of camping out to talk to him about getting a tent and the necessary "traps" for a life in the woods. He proved perfectly competent to furnish advice and everything else. He offered to lend me all I needed. He had a complete outfit; had done with them for the year, and I was perfectly welcome. Here was rare luck. He gave me a tent, campstove, dishes, pots, gun, fishing-tackle, a big canvas coat with dozens of pockets riveted on it, a canvas hat, rods, reels, boots that came up to my hips, and about a wagonload of things in all. He was a real good fellow.

We laid in a stock of canned and condensed provisions, and I bought a book on camping out so as to be well posted on the subject. On the Saturday before the first Monday in September we would have been entirely ready to start had we decided on the place where we were to go.

We found it very difficult to make this decision. There were thousands of places where people went to camp out, but none of them seemed to be the place for us. Most of them were too far away. We figured up the cost of taking ourselves and our camp equipage to the Adirondacks, the lakes, the trout-streams of Maine, or any of those well-known resorts, and we found that we could not afford such trips, especially for a vacation of but fourteen days.

On Sunday afternoon we took a little walk. Our minds were still troubled about the spot toward which we ought to journey next day, and we needed the soothing influences of Nature. The country to the north and west of our little farm was very beautiful. About half a mile from the house a modest river ran; on each side of it were grass-covered fields and hills, and in some places there were extensive tracks of woodlands.

"Look here!" exclaimed Euphemia, stopping short in the little path that wound along by the river bank. "Do you see this river, those woods, those beautiful fields, with not a soul in them or anywhere near them; and those lovely blue mountains over there?"—as she spoke she waved her parasol in the direction of the objects indicated, and I could not mistake them. "Now what could we want better than this?" she continued. "Here we can fish, and do everything that we want to. I say, let us camp here on our own river. I can take you to the very spot for the tent. Come on!" And she was so excited about it that she fairly ran.

The spot she pointed out was one we had frequently

visited in our rural walks. It was a grassy peninsula, as I termed it, formed by a sudden turn of a creek which, a short distance below, flowed into the river. It was a very secluded spot. The place was approached through a pasture-field,—we had found it by mere accident,—and where the peninsula joined the field (we had to climb a fence just there), there was a cluster of chestnut and hickory trees, while down near the point stood a wide-spreading oak.

"Here, under this oak, is the place for the tent," said Euphemia, her face flushed, her eyes sparkling, and her dress a little torn by getting over the fence in a hurry. "What do we want with your Adirondacks and your Dismal Swamps? This is the spot for us!"

"Euphemia," said I, in as composed a tone as possible, although my whole frame was trembling with emotion, "Euphemia, I am glad I married you!"

Had it not been Sunday, we would have set up our tent that night.

Early the next morning, old John's fifteen-dollar horse drew from our house a wagon-load of camp-fixtures. There was some difficulty in getting the wagon over the field, and there were fences to be taken down to allow of its passage; but we overcame all obstacles, and reached the camp-ground without breaking so much as a teacup. Old John helped me pitch the tent, and as neither of us understood the matter very well, it took us some time. It was, indeed, nearly noon when old John left us, and it may have been possible that he delayed matters a little so as to be able to charge for a full half-day for himself and horse. Euphemia got into the wagon to ride back with him, that she might give some parting injunctions to Pomona.

"I'll have to stop a bit to put up the fences, ma'am," said old John, "or Mister Ball might make a fuss."

"Is this Mr. Ball's land?" I asked.

"Oh yes, sir, it's Mr. Ball's land."

"I wonder how he'll like our camping on it?" I said, thoughtfully.

"I'd 'a' thought, sir, you'd 'a' asked him that before you came," said old John, in a tone that seemed to indicate that he had his doubts about Mr. Ball.

"Oh, there'll be no trouble about that," cried Euphemia. "You can drive me past Mr. Ball's,—it's not much out of the way,—and I'll ask him."

"In that wagon?" said I. "Will you stop at Mr. Ball's door in that?"

"Certainly," said she, as she arranged herself on the board which served as a seat. "Now that our campaign has really commenced, we ought to begin to rough it, and should not be too proud to ride even in a—in a—"

She evidently couldn't think of any vehicle mean enough for her purpose.

"In a green-grocery cart," I suggested.

"Yes, or in a red one. Go ahead, John."

When Euphemia returned on foot, I had a fire in the camp-stove and the kettle was on.

"Well," said Euphemia, "Mr. Ball says it's all right, if we keep the fence up. He don't want his cows to get into the creek, and I'm sure we don't want 'em walking over us. He couldn't understand, though, why we wanted to live out here. I explained the whole thing to him very carefully, but it didn't seem to make much impression on him. I believe he thinks Pomona has something the matter with her, and that we have come to stay out here in the fresh air so as not to take it."

"What an extremely stupid man Mr. Ball must be!" I said.

The fire did not burn very well, and while I was at work at it, Euphemia spread a cloth upon the grass, and set forth bread and butter, cheese, sardines, potted ham, preserves, biscuits, and a lot of other things.

We did not wait for the kettle to boil, but concluded to do without tea or coffee, for this meal, and content ourselves with pure water. For some reason or other, however, the creek water did not seem to be very pure, and we did not like it a bit.

"After lunch," said I, "we will go and look for a spring; that will be a good way of exploring the country."

"If we can't find one," said Euphemia, "we shall have to go to the house for water, for I can never drink that stuff."

Soon after lunch we started out. We searched high and low, near and far, for a spring, but could not find one.

At length, by merest accident, we found ourselves in the vicinity of old John's little house. I knew he had a good well, and so we went in to get a drink, for our ham and biscuits had made us very thirsty.

We told old John, who was digging potatoes, and was also very much surprised to see us so soon, about our unexpected trouble in finding a spring.

"No," said he, very slowly, "there is no spring very near to you. Didn't you tell your gal to bring you water?"

"No," I replied; "we don't want her coming down to the camp. She is to attend to the house."

"Oh, very well," said John; "I will bring you water, morning and night,—good, fresh water,—from my well, for,—well, for ten cents a day."

"That will be nice," said Euphemia, "and cheap, too. And then it will be well to have John come every day; he can carry our letters."

"I don't expect to write any letters."

"Neither do I," said Euphemia; "but it will be pleasant to have some communication with the outer world."

So we engaged old John to bring us water twice a day. I was a little disappointed at this, for I thought that camping on the edge of a stream settled the matter of water. But we have many things to learn in this world.

Early in the afternoon I went out to catch some fish for supper. We agreed to dispense with dinner, and have breakfast, lunch, and a good solid supper.

For some time I had poor luck. There were either very few fish in the creek, or they were not hungry.

I had been fishing an hour or more when I saw Euphemia running toward me.

"What's the matter?" said I.

"Oh! nothing. I've just come to see how you were getting along. Haven't you been gone an awfully long time? And are those all the fish you've caught? What little bits of things they are! I thought people who camped out caught big fish and lots of them?"

"That depends a good deal upon where they go," said I.

"Yes, I suppose so," replied Euphemia; "but I should think a stream as big as this would have plenty of fish in it. However, if you can't catch any, you might go up to the road and watch for Mr. Mulligan. He sometimes comes along on Mondays."

"I'm not going to the road to watch for any fish-man," I replied, a little more testily than I should have spoken. "What sort of a camping out would that be? But we must not be talking here or I shall never get a bite. Those fish are a little soiled from jumping about in the dust. You might wash them off at that shallow place, while I go a little further on and try my luck."

I went a short distance up the creek, and threw my line into a dark, shadowy pool, under some alders, where there certainly should be fish. And, sure enough, in less than a minute I got a splendid bite,—not only a bite, but a pull. I knew that I had certainly hooked a big fish! The thing actually tugged at my line so that I was afraid the pole would break. I did not fear for the line, for that, I knew, was strong. I would have played the fish until he was tired, and I could pull him out without risk to the pole, but I did not know exactly how the process of "playing" was conducted. I was very much excited. Sometimes I gave a jerk and a pull, and then the fish would give a jerk and a pull.

Directly I heard some one running toward me, and then I heard Euphemia cry out:

"Give him the butt! Give him the butt!"

"Give him what?" I exclaimed, without having time even to look up at her.

"The butt! the butt!" she cried, almost breathlessly. "I know that's right! I read how Edward Everett Hale did it in the Adirondacks."

"No, it wasn't Hale at all," said I, as I jumped about the bank; "it was Mr. Murray."

"Well, it was one of those fishing ministers, and I know that it caught the fish."

"I know, I know. I read it, but I don't know how to do it."

"Perhaps you ought to punch him with it," said she.

"No! no!" I hurriedly replied, "I can't do anything like that. I'm going to try to just pull him out lengthwise. You take hold of the pole and go in-shore as far as you can and I'll try and get hold of the line."

Euphemia did as I bade her, and drew the line in so that I could reach it. As soon as I had a firm hold of it, I pulled in, regardless of consequences, and hauled ashore an enormous cat-fish.

"Hurrah!" I shouted, "here is a prize."

Euphemia dropped the pole, and ran to me.

"What a horrid beast!" she exclaimed. "Throw it in again."

"Not at all!" said I. "This is a splendid fish, if I can ever get him off the hook. Don't come near him! If he sticks that back-fin into you, it will poison you."

"Then I should think it would poison us to eat him," said she.

"No; it's only his fin."

"I've eaten cat-fish, but I never saw one like that," she said. "Look at its horrible mouth! And it has whiskers like a cat!"

"Oh! you never saw one with its head on," I said. "What I want to do is to get this hook out."

I had caught cat-fish before, but never one so large as this, and I was actually afraid to take hold of it, knowing, as I did, that you must be very careful how you clutch a fish of the kind. I finally concluded to carry it home as it was, and then I could decapitate it, and take out the hook at my leisure. So back to camp we went, Euphemia picking up the little fish as we passed, for she did not think it right to catch fish and not eat them. They made her hands smell, it is true, but she did not mind that when we were camping.

I prepared the big fish (and I had a desperate time getting the skin off), while my wife, who is one of the daintiest cooks in the world, made the fire in the stove, and got ready the rest of the supper. She fried the fish, because I told her that was the way cat-fish ought to be cooked, although she said that it seemed very strange to her to camp out for the sake of one's health, and then to eat fried food.

But that fish was splendid! The very smell of it made us hungry. Everything was good, and when supper was over and the dishes washed, I lighted my pipe and we sat down under a tree to enjoy the evening.

The sun had set behind the distant ridge; a delightful twilight was gently subduing every color of the scene; the night insects were beginning to hum and chirp, and a fire that I had made under a tree blazed up gayly, and threw little flakes of light into the shadows under the shrubbery.

—from *Rudder Grange* (1879)

A Winter Walk
by Henry David Thoreau

THE WIND HAS GENTLY murmured through the blinds, or puffed with feathery softness against the windows, and occasionally sighed like a summer zephyr lifting the leaves along, the livelong night. The meadow-mouse has slept in his snug gallery in the sod, the owl has sat in a hollow tree in the depth of the swamp, the rabbit, the squirrel, and the fox have all been housed. The watch-dog has lain quiet on the hearth, and the cattle have stood silent in their stalls. The earth itself has slept, as it were its first, not its last sleep, save when some street-sign or wood-house door has faintly creaked upon its hinge, cheering forlorn nature at her midnight work,—the only sound awake 'twixt Venus and Mars,—advertising us of a remote inward warmth, a divine cheer and fellowship, where gods are met together, but where it is very bleak for man to stand. But while the earth has slumbered, all the air has been alive with feathery flakes descending, as if some northern Ceres reigned, showering her silvery grain over all the fields.

We sleep, and at length awake to the still reality of a winter morning. The snow lies warm as cotton or down upon the window-sill; the broadened sash and frosted panes admit a dim and private light, which enhances the snug cheer within. The stillness of the morning is impressive. The floor creaks under our feet as we move toward the window to look abroad through some clear space over the fields. We see the roofs stand under their snow burden. From the eaves and fences hang stalactites of snow, and in the yard stand stalagmites covering some concealed core. The trees and shrubs rear white arms to the sky on every side; and where were walls and fences, we see fantastic forms stretching in frolic gambols across the dusky landscape, as if nature had strewn her fresh designs over the fields by night as models for man's art.

Silently we unlatch the door, letting the drift fall in, and step abroad to face the cutting air. Already the stars have lost some of their sparkle, and a dull, leaden mist skirts the horizon. A lurid brazen light in the east proclaims the approach of day, while the western landscape is dim and spectral still, and clothed in a sombre Tartarian light, like the shadowy realms. They are Infernal sounds only that you hear; the crowing of cocks, the barking of dogs, the chopping of wood, the lowing of kine, all seem to come from Pluto's barn-yard and beyond the Styx,—not for any melancholy they suggest, but their twilight bustle is too solemn and mysterious for earth. The recent tracks of the fox or otter, in the yard, remind us that each hour of the night is crowded with events, and the primeval nature is still working and making tracks in the snow. Opening the gate, we tread briskly along the lone country road, crunching the dry and crisped snow under our feet, or aroused by the sharp clear creak of the wood sled, just starting for the distant market, from the early farmer's door, where it has lain the summer long, dreaming amid the chips and stubble; while far through the drifts and powdered windows we see the farmer's early candle, like a paled star, emitting a lonely beam, as if some severe virtue were at its matins there. And one by one the smokes begin to ascend from the chimneys amid the trees and snows.

We head the sound of wood-chopping at the farmers' doors, far over the frozen earth, the baying of the house-dog, and the distant clarion of the cock,—though the thin and frosty air conveys only the finer particles of sound to our ears, with short and sweet vibrations, as the waves subside soonest on the purest and lightest liquids, in which gross substances sink to the bottom. They come clear and bell-like, and from a greater distance in the horizon, as if there were fewer impediments than in summer to make them faint and ragged. The ground is sonorous, like seasoned wood, and even the ordinary rural sounds are melodious, and the jingling of the ice on the trees is sweet and liquid. There is the least possible moisture in the atmosphere, all being dried up, or congealed, and it is of such extreme tenuity and elasticity that it becomes a source of delight. The withdrawn and tense sky seems groined like the aisles of a cathedral, and the polished air sparkles as if there were crystals of ice floating in it. . . .

The sun at length rises through the distant woods, as if with the faint clashing swinging sound of cymbals, melting the air with his beams, and with such rapid steps the morning travels, that already his rays are gilding the distant western mountains. Meanwhile we step hastily along through the powdery snow, warmed by an inward heat, enjoying an Indian summer still, in the increased glow of thought and feeling. Probably if our lives were more conformed to nature, we should not need to defend ourselves against her heats and colds, but find her our constant nurse and friend, as do plants and quadrupeds. If our bodies were fed with pure and simple elements, and not with a stimulating and heating diet, they would afford no more pasture for cold than a leafless twig, but thrive like the trees, which find even winter genial to their expansion.

The wonderful purity of nature at this season is a most pleasing fact. Every decayed stump and moss-grown stone and rail, and the dead leaves of autumn, are concealed by a clean napkin of snow. In the bare fields and tinkling woods, see what virtue survives. In the coldest and bleakest places, the warmest charities still maintain a foothold. A cold and searching wind drives away all contagion, and nothing can withstand it but what has a virtue in it, and accordingly, whatever we meet with in cold and bleak places, as the tops of mountains, we respect for a sort of sturdy innocence, a Puritan toughness. All things beside seem to be called in for shelter, and what stays out must be part of the original frame of the universe, and of such valor as God himself. It is invigorating to breathe the cleansed air. Its greater fineness and purity are visible to the eye, and we would fain stay out long and late, that the gales may sigh through us, too, as through the leafless trees, and fit us for the winter,—as if we hoped to borrow some pure and steadfast virtue, which will stead us in all seasons.

There is a slumbering subterranean fire in nature which never goes out, and which no cold can chill. It finally melts the great snow, and in January or July is only buried under a thicker or thinner covering. In the coldest day it flows somewhere, and the snow melts around every tree. This field of winter rye, which sprouted late in the fall, and now speedily dissolves the snow, is where the fire is very thinly covered. We feel warmed by it. In the winter, warmth stands for all virtue, and we resort in thought to a trickling rill, with its bare stones shining in the sun, and to warm springs in the woods, with so much eagerness as rabbits and robins. The steam which rises from swamps and pools is as dear and domestic as that of our own kettle. What fire could ever equal the sunshine of a winter's day, when the meadow mice come out by the wall-sides, and the chickadee lisps in the defiles of the wood? The warmth comes directly from the sun, and is not radi-

ated from the earth, as in summer; and when we feel his beams on our backs as we are treading some snowy dell, we are grateful as for a special kindness, and bless the sun which has followed us into that by-place.

This subterranean fire has its altar in each man's breast; for in the coldest day, and on the bleakest hill, the traveler cherishes a warmer fire within the folds of his cloak than is kindled on any hearth. A healthy man, indeed, is the complement of the seasons, and in winter, summer is in his heart. There is the south. Thither have all birds and insects migrated, and around the warm springs in his breast are gathered the robin and the lark.

At length, having reached the edge of the woods, and shut out the gadding town, we enter within their covert as we go under the roof of a cottage, and cross its threshold, all ceiled and banked up with snow. They are glad and warm still, and as genial and cheery in winter as in summer. As we stand in the midst of the pines in the flickering and checkered light which straggles but little way into their maze, we wonder if the towns have ever heard their simple story. It seems to us that no traveler has ever explored them, and notwithstanding the wonders which science is elsewhere revealing every day, who would not like to hear their annals? Our humble villages in the plain are their contribution. We borrow from the forest the boards which shelter and the sticks which warm us. How important is their evergreen to winter, that portion of the summer which does not fade, the permanent year, the unwithered grass. Thus simply, and with little expense of altitude, is the surface of the earth diversified. What would human life be without forests, those natural cities? From the tops of mountains they appear like smooth-shaven lawns, yet whither shall we walk but in this taller grass?

In this glade covered with bushes of a year's growth, see how the silvery dust lies on every seared leaf and twig, deposited in such infinite and luxurious forms as by their very variety atone for the absence of color. Observe the tiny tracks of mice around every stem, and the triangular tracks of the rabbit. A pure elastic heaven hangs over all, as if the impurities of the summer air, refined and shrunk by the chaste winter's cold, had been winnowed from the heavens upon the earth.

Nature confounds her summer distinctions at this season. The heavens seem to be nearer the earth. The elements are less reserved and distinct. Water turns to ice, rain to snow. The day is but a Scandinavian night. The winter is an arctic summer.

How much more living is the life that is in nature, the furred life which still survives the stinging nights, and, from amidst fields and woods covered with frost and snow, sees the sun rise. The gray squirrel and rabbit are brisk and playful in the remote glens, even on the morning of the cold Friday. Here is our Lapland and Labrador, and for our Esquimaux and Knisteneaux, Dog-ribbed Indians, Novazemnlaites, and Spitzbergeners, are there not the ice-cutter and wood-chopper, the fox, musk-rat, and mink?

Still, in the midst of the arctic day, we may trace the summer to its retreats, and sympathize with some contemporary life. Stretched over the brooks, in the midst of the frost-bound meadows, we may observe the submarine cottages of the caddice-worms, the larvae of the Plici-pennes; their small cylindrical cases built around them-selves, composed of flags, sticks, grass, and withered leaves, shells, and pebbles, in form and color like the wrecks which strew the bottom,—now drifting along over the pebbly bottom, now whirling in tiny eddies and dashing down steep falls, or sweeping rapidly along with the cur-rent, or else swaying to and fro at the end of some grass-blade or root. Anon they will leave their sunken habitations, and, crawling up the stems of plants, or to the surface, like gnats, as perfect insects henceforth, flutter over the surface of the water, or sacrifice their short lives in the flame of our candles at evening. Down yonder little glen the shrubs are drooping under their burden, and the red alderberries contrast with the white ground. Here are the marks of myriad feet which have already been abroad. The sun rises as proudly over such a glen as over the valley of the Seine or the Tiber, and it seems the residence of a pure and self-subsistent valor, such as they never witnessed; which never knew defeat or fear. Here reign the simplicity and purity of a primitive age, and a health and hope far remote from towns and cities. Standing quite alone, far in the forest, while the wind is shaking down snow from the trees, and leaving only the human tracks behind us, we find our reflection of a richer variety than the life of cities. The chickadee and nuthatch are more inspiring society than statesmen and philosophers, and we shall return to these last as to more vulgar com-panions. In this lonely glen, with its brook draining the slopes, its creased ice and crystals of all hues, where the spruces and hemlocks stand up on either side, and the rush and sere wild oats in the rivulet itself, our lives are more serene and worthy to contemplate. . . .

Now our path begins to ascend gradually to the top of this high hill, from whose precipitous south side we can look over the broad country of forest and field and river, to the distant snowy mountains. See yonder thin column of smoke curling up through the woods from some invisible farmhouse; the standard raised over some rural home-stead. There must be a warmer and more genial spot there below, as where we detect the vapor from a spring forming a cloud above the trees. What fine relations are established between the traveler who discovers this airy column from some eminence in the forest and him who sits below. Up goes the smoke so silently and naturally as the vapor exhales from the leaves, and as busy disposing itself in wreaths as the housewife on the hearth below. It is a hieroglyphic of man's life, and suggests more intimate and important things than the boiling of a pot. Where its fine column rises above the forest, like an ensign, some human life has planted itself,—and such is the beginning of Rome, the establishment of the arts, and the foundation of em-pires, whether on the prairies of America or the steppes of Asia.

And now we descend again, to the brink of this wood-land lake, which lies in a hollow of the hills, as if it were their expressed juice, and that of the leaves which are annually steeped in it. Without outlet or inlet to the eye, it has still its history, in the lapse of its waves, in the rounded pebbles on its shore, and in the pines which grow down to its brink. It has not been idle, though sedentary,

but, like Abu Musa, teaches that "sitting still at home is the heavenly way; the going out is the way of the world." Yet in its evaporation it travels as far as any. In summer it is the earth's liquid eye; a mirror in the breast of nature. The sins of the wood are washed out in it. See how the woods form an amphitheatre about it, and it is an arena for all the genialness of nature. All trees direct the trav-eler to its brink, all paths seek it out, birds fly to it, quadrupeds flee to it, and the very ground inclines toward it. It is nature's saloon, where she has sat down to her toilet. Consider her silent economy and tidiness; how the sun comes with his evaporation to sweep the dust from its surface each morning, and a fresh surface is constantly welling up; and annually, after whatever impurities have accumulated herein, its liquid transparency appears again in the spring. In summer a hushed music seems to sweep across its surface. But now a plain sheet of snow conceals it from our eyes, except where the wind has swept the ice bare, and the sere leaves are gliding from side to side, tacking and veering on their tiny voyages. Here is one just keeled up against a pebble on shore, a dry beech-leaf, rocking still, as if it would start again. A skillful engi-neer, methinks, might project its course since it fell from the parent stem. Here are all the elements for such a calculation. Its present position, the direction of the wind, the level of the pond, and how much more is given. In its scarred edges and veins is its log rolled up. . . .

But now, while we have loitered, the clouds have gath-ered again, and a few straggling snowflakes are beginning to descend. Faster and faster they fall, shutting out the distant objects from sight. The snow falls on every wood and field, and no crevice is forgotten; by the river and the pond, on the hill and in the valley. Quadrupeds are con-fined to their coverts and the birds sit upon their perches this peaceful hour. There is not so much sound as in fair weather, but silently and gradually every slope, and the gray walls and fences, and the polished ice, and the sere leaves, which were not buried before, are concealed, and the tracks of men and beasts are lost. With so little effort does nature reassert her rule and blot out the traces of men. Hear how Homer has described the same: "The snow-flakes fell thick and fast on a winter's day. The winds are lulled, and the snow falls incessant, covering the tops of the mountains, and the hills, and the plains where the lotus-tree grows, and the cultivated fields, and they are falling by the inlets and shores of the foaming sea, but are silently dissolved by the waves." The snow levels all things, and infolds them deeper in the bosom of nature, as, in the slow summer, vegetation creeps up to the entablature of the temple, and the turrets of the castle, and helps her to prevail over art.

The surly night-wind rustles through the wood, and warns us to retrace our steps, while the sun goes down behind the thickening storm, and birds seek their roosts, and cattle their stalls.

Though winter is represented in the almanac as an old man, facing the wind and sleet, and drawing his cloak about him, we rather think of him as a merry wood-chopper, and warm-blooded youth, as blithe as summer. The unexplored grandeur of the storm keeps up the spirits of the traveler. In winter we lead a more inward life. Our hearts are warm and cheery, like cottages under drifts, whose windows and doors are half concealed, but from whose chimneys the smoke cheerfully ascends. The imprisoning drifts increase the sense of comfort to sit over the hearth and see the sky through the chimney top, enjoying the quiet and serene life that may be had in a warm corner by the chimney side, or feeling our pulse by listening to the low of cattle in the street, or the sound of the flail in distant barns all the long afternoon. No doubt a skillful physician could determine our health by observing how these simple and natural sounds affected us. We enjoy now, not an oriental, but a boreal leisure, around warm stoves and fireplaces, and watch the shadow of motes in the sunbeams.

Sometimes our fate grows too homely and familiarly serious ever to be cruel. Consider how for three months the human destiny is wrapped in furs. The good Hebrew Revelation takes no cognizance of all this cheerful snow. Is there no religion for the temperate and frigid zones?

We know of no scripture which records the pure benignity of the gods on a New England winter night. Their praises have never been sung, only their wrath deprecated. The best scripture, after all, records but a meagre faith. Its saints live reserved and austere. Let a brave, devout man spend the year in the woods of Maine or Labrador, and see if the Hebrew Scriptures speak adequately to his condition and experience, from the setting in of winter to the breaking up of the ice.

Now commences the long winter evening around the farmer's hearth, when the thoughts of the indwellers travel far abroad, and men are by nature and necessity charitable and liberal to all creatures. Now is the happy resistance to cold, when the farmer reaps his reward, and thinks of his preparedness for winter, and, through the glittering panes, sees with equanimity "the mansion of the northern bear," for now the storm is over.

—from *Excursions* (1863)

On Going a Journey
by William Hazlitt

ONE OF THE PLEASANTEST things in the world is going a journey; but I like to go by myself. I can enjoy society in a room; but out of doors, nature is company enough for me. I am then never less alone than when alone.

"The fields his study, nature was his book."

I cannot see the wit of walking and talking at the same time. When I am in the country I wish to vegetate like the country. . . . I go out of town in order to forget the town and all that is in it. . . . I like more elbow-room and fewer incumbrances. I like solitude, when I give myself up to it, for the sake of solitude; nor do I ask for

"a friend in my retreat,
Whom I may whisper solitude is sweet."

The soul of a journey is liberty, perfect liberty, to think, feel, do, just as one pleases. We go a journey chiefly to be free of all impediments and of all inconveniences; to leave ourselves behind, much more to get rid of others. . . . For once let me have a truce with impertinence. Give me the clear blue sky over my head, and the green turf beneath my feet, a winding road before me, and a three hours' march to dinner—and then to thinking! It is hard if I cannot start some game on these lone heaths. I laugh, I run, I leap, I sing for joy. From the point of yonder rolling cloud I plunge into my past being, and revel there. . . . Then long-forgotten things, like "sunken wrack and sumless treasuries," burst upon my eager sight, and I begin to feel, think, and be myself again. Instead of an awkward silence, broken by attempts at wit or dull common-places, mine is that undisturbed silence of the heart which alone is perfect eloquence. No one likes puns, alliterations, antitheses, argument, and analysis better than I do; but I sometimes had rather be without them. . . . Is not this wild rose sweet without a comment? Does not this daisy leap to my heart set in its coat of emerald? Yet if I were to explain to you the circumstance that has so endeared it to me, you would only smile. Had I not better then keep it to myself, and let it serve me to brood over, from here to yonder craggy point, and from thence onward to the far-distant horizon? I should be but bad company all that way, and therefore prefer being alone. I have heard it said that you may, when the moody fit comes on, walk or ride on by yourself, and indulge your reveries. But this looks like a breach of manners, a neglect of others, and you are thinking all the time that you ought to rejoin your party. "Out upon such half-faced fellowship," say I. I like to be either entirely to myself, or entirely at the disposal of others; to talk or be silent, to walk or sit still, to be sociable or solitary. . . . "Let me have a companion of my way," says Sterne, "were it but to remark how the shadows lengthen as the sun declines." It is beautifully said; but, in my opinion, this continual comparing of notes interferes with the involuntary impression of things upon the mind, and hurts the sentiment. If you only hint what you feel in a kind of dumb show, it is insipid: If you have to explain it, it is making a toil of pleasure. You cannot read the book of nature without being perpetually put to the trouble of translating it for the benefit of others. I am for this synthetical method on a journey in preference to the analytical. I am content to lay in a stock of ideas then, and to examine and anatomise them afterwards. I want to see my vague notions float like the down of the thistle before the breeze, and not to have them entangled in the briars and thorns of controversy. For once, I like to have it all my own way; and this is impossible unless you are alone. . . . I have no objection to argue a point with any one for twenty miles of measured road, but not for pleasure. If you remark the scent of a bean-field crossing the road, perhaps your fellow-traveller has no smell. If you point to a distant object, perhaps he is short-sighted, and has to take out his glass to look at it. . . . Now I never quarrel with myself, and take all my own conclusions for granted till I find it necessary to defend them against objections. It is not merely that you may not be of accord on the objects and circumstances that present themselves before you—these may recall a number of objects, and lead to associations too delicate and refined to be possibly communicated to others. Yet these I love to cherish, and sometimes still fondly clutch them, when I can escape from the throng to do so. To give way to our feelings before company seems extravagance of affectation; and, on the other hand, to have to unravel this mystery of our being at every turn, and to make others take an equal interest in it (otherwise the end is not answered), is a task to which few are competent. We must "give it an understanding, but no tongue." My old friend Coleridge, however, could do both. He could go on in the most delightful explanatory way over hill and dale a summer's day, and convert a landscape into a didactic poem or a Pindaric ode. "He talked far above singing." If I could so clothe my ideas in sounding and flowing words, I might perhaps wish to have some one with me to admire the swelling theme; or I could be more content, were it possible for me still to hear his echoing voice in the woods of All-Foxden. They had "that fine madness in them which our first poets had"; and if they could have been caught by some rare instrument, would have breathed such strains as the following:—

> "Here be woods as green
> As any, air likewise as fresh and sweet
> As when smooth Zephyrus plays on the fleet
> Face of the curled streams, with flow'rs as many
> As the young spring gives, and as choice as any;
> Here be all new delights, cool streams and wells,
> Arbours o'ergrown with woodbine, caves and dells;
> Choose where tho wilt, whilst I sit by and sing,
> Or gather rushes to make many a ring
> For thy long fingers; tell thee tales of love,
> How the pale Phoebe, hunting in a grove,
> First saw the boy Endymion, from whose eyes
> She took eternal fire that never dies;
> How she convey'd him softly in a sleep,
> His temples bound with poppy, to the steep
> Head of old Latmos, where she stoops each night,
> Gilding the mountain with her brother's light,
> To kiss her sweetest."
>   —Fletcher's *Faithful Shepherdess.*

Had I words and images at command like these, I would attempt to wake the thoughts that lie slumbering on golden ridges in the evening clouds: but at the sight of nature my fancy, poor as it is, droops and closes up its leaves, like flowers at sunset. I can make nothing out on the spot:—I must have time to collect myself. . . .

I grant, there is one subject on which it is pleasant to talk on a journey; and that is, what one shall have for supper when we get to our inn at night. The open air improves this sort of conversation or friendly altercation, by setting a keener edge on appetite. . . . How fine it is to enter some old town, walled and turreted, just at approach of night-fall, or to come to some straggling village, with the lights streaming through the surrounding gloom; and then, after inquiring for the best entertainment that the place affords, to "take one's ease at one's inn"! These eventful moments in our lives' history are too precious, too full of solid, heart-felt happiness to be frittered and dribbled away in imperfect sympathy. I would have them all to myself, and drain them to the last drop: they will do to talk of or to write about afterwards. What a delicate speculation it is, after drinking whole goblets of tea—

"The cups that cheer, but not inebriate,"

and letting the fumes ascend into the brain, to sit considering what we shall have for supper—eggs and a rasher, a rabbit smothered in onions or an excellent veal-cutlet! . . . Then, in the intervals of pictured scenery and Shandean contemplation, to catch the preparation and the stir in the kitchen. . . . These hours are sacred to silence and to musing, to be treasured up in the memory, and to feed the source of smiling thoughts hereafter. . . . I associate nothing with my travelling companion but present objects and passing events. In his ignorance of me and my affairs, I in a manner forget myself. But a friend reminds one of other things, rips up old grievances, and destroys the abstraction of the scene. He comes in ungraciously between us and our imaginary character. . . . The *incognito* of an inn is one of its striking privileges—"lord of one's self, uncumber'd with a name." Oh! it is great to shake off the trammels of the world and of public opinion—to lose our importunate, tormenting, everlasting personal identity in the elements of nature, and become the creature of the moment, clear of all ties—to hold to the universe only by a dish of sweet-breads, and to owe nothing but the score of the evening—and no longer seeking for applause and meeting with contempt, to be known by no other title than *the Gentleman in the parlour!* . . . We baffle prejudice and disappoint conjecture; and from being so to others, begin to be objects of curiosity and wonder even to ourselves. . . . I have certainly spent some enviable hours at inns—sometimes when I have been left entirely to myself, and have tried to solve some metaphysical problem, as once at Witham-common, where I found out the proof that likeness is not a case of the association of ideas . . .—at other times I might mention luxuriating in books, with a peculiar interest in this way, as I remember sitting up half the night to read *Paul and Virginia,* which I picked up at an inn at Bridgewater, after being drenched in the rain all day. . . . It was on the tenth of April, 1798, that I sat down to a volume of the *New Eloise,* at the inn at Llangollen, over a bottle of sherry and a cold chicken. The letter I chose was that in which St. Preux describes his feelings as he first caught a glimpse from the heights of the Jura of the Pays de Vaud, which I had brought with me as a *bon bouche* to crown the evening with. It was my birthday, and I had for the first time come from a place in the neighbourhood to visit this delightful spot. The road to Llangollen turns off between Chirk and Wrexham; and on passing a certain point you come all at once upon the valley, which opens like an amphitheatre, broad, barren hills rising in majestic state on either side, with "green upland swells that echo to the bleat of flocks" below, and the river

Dee babbling over its stony bed in the midst of them. The valley at this time "glittered green with sunny showers," and a budding ash-tree dipped its tender branches in the chiding stream. How proud, how glad I was to walk along the high road that overlooks the delicious prospect, repeating the lines which I have just quoted from Mr. Coleridge's poems! But besides the prospect which opened beneath my feet, another also opened to my inward sight, a heavenly vision, on which were written, in letters large as Hope could make them, these four words, LIBERTY, GENIUS, LOVE, VIRTUE; which have since faded into the light of common day, or mock my idle gaze.

"The beautiful is vanished, and returns not."

Still I would return some time or other to this enchanted spot; but I would return to it alone. What other self could I find to share that influx of thoughts, of regret, and delight, the fragments of which I could hardly conjure up to myself, so much have they been broken and defaced. I could stand on some tall rock, and overlook the precipice of years that separates me from what I then was. I was at that time going shortly to visit the poet whom I have above named. Where is he now? Not only I myself have changed; the world which was then new to me, has become old and incorrigible. . . .

There is hardly anything that shows the short-sightedness or capriciousness of the imagination more than travelling does. With change of place we change our ideas; nay, our opinions and feelings. We can by an effort indeed transport ourselves to old and long-forgotten scenes, and then the picture of the mind revives again; but we forget those that we have just left. It seems that we can think but of one place at a time. The canvas of the fancy is but of a certain extent, and if we paint one set of objects upon it, they immediately efface every other. We cannot enlarge our conceptions, we only shift our point of view. The landscape bares its bosom to the enraptured eye, we take our fill of it, and seem as if we could form no other image of beauty or grandeur. We pass on, and think no more of it: the horizon that shuts it from our sight, also blots it from our memory like a dream. In travelling through a wild barren country I can form no idea of a woody and cultivated one. It appears to me that all the world must be barren, like what I see of it. In the country we forget the town, and in town we despise the country. . . . All that part of the map that we do not see before us is a blank. The world in our conceit of it is not much bigger than a nutshell. It is not one prospect expanded into another, county joined to county, kingdom to kingdom, lands to seas, making an image voluminous and vast;—the mind can form no larger idea of space than the eye can take in at a single glance. The rest is a name written in a map, a calculation of arithmetic. For instance, what is the true signification of that immense mass of territory and population known by the name of China to us? An inch of pasteboard on a wooden globe, of no more account than a China orange! Things near us are seen of the size of life: things at a distance are diminished to the size of the understanding. We measure the universe by ourselves, and even comprehend the texture of our being only piece-meal. In this way, however, we remember an infinity of things and places. The mind is like a mechanical instrument that plays a great variety of tunes, but it must play them in succession. One idea recalls another, but it at the same time excludes all others. In trying to renew old recollections, we cannot as it were unfold the whole web of our existence; we must pick out the single threads. So in coming to a place where we have formerly lived, and with which we have intimate associations, every one must have found that the feeling grows more vivid the nearer we approach the spot, from the mere anticipation of the actual impression: we remember circumstances, feelings, persons, faces, names that we had not thought of for years; but for the time all the rest of the world is forgotten! . . .

I have no objection to go to see ruins, aqueducts, pictures, in company with a friend or a party, but rather the contrary, for the former reason reversed. They are intelligible matters, and will bear talking about. The sentiment here is not tacit, but communicable and overt. Salisbury Plain is barren of criticism, but Stonehenge will bear a discussion antiquarian, picturesque, and philosophical. In setting out on a party of pleasure, the first consideration always is where we shall go to: in taking a solitary ramble, the question is what we shall meet with by the way. "The mind is its own place"; nor are we anxious to arrive at the end of our journey. I can myself do the honours indifferently well to works of art and curiosity. I once took a party to Oxford with no mean *éclat*—shewed them that seat of the Muses at a distance,

"With glistering spires and pinnacles adorn'd—"

descanted on the learned air that breathes from the grassy quadrangles and stone walls of halls and colleges—was at home in the Bodleian; and at Blenheim quite superseded the powdered Cicerone that attended us, and that pointed in vain with his wand to commonplace beauties in matchless pictures. As another exception to the above reasoning, I should not feel confident in venturing on a journey in a foreign country without a companion. I should want at intervals to hear the sound of my own language. There is an involuntary antipathy in the mind of an Englishman to foreign manners and notions that requires the assistance of social sympathy to carry it off. As the distance from home increases, this relief, which was at first a luxury, becomes a passion and an appetite. A person would almost feel stifled to find himself in the deserts of Arabia without friends and countrymen: there must be allowed to be something in the view of Athens or old Rome that claims the utterance of speech; and I own that the Pyramids are too mighty for any single contemplation. In such situations, so opposite to all one's ordinary train of ideas, one seems a species by one's-self, a limb torn off from society, unless one can meet with instant fellowship and support.— Yet I did not feel this want or craving very pressing once, when I first set my foot on the laughing shores of France. Calais was peopled with novelty and delight. The confused, busy murmur of the place was like oil and wine poured into my ears; nor did the mariners' hymn, which was sung from the top of an old crazy vessel in the harbour, as the sun went down, send an alien sound into my soul. I only breathed the air of general humanity. I walked over "the vine-covered hills and gay regions of France," erect and satisfied; for the image of man was not cast down and chained to the foot of arbitrary thrones: I was at no loss for language, for that of all the great schools of painting was open to me. The whole is vanished like a shade. Pictures, heroes, glory, freedom, all are fled: nothing remains but the Bourbons and the French people!—There is undoubtedly a sensation in travelling into foreign parts that is to be had nowhere else; but it is more pleasing at the time than lasting. It is too remote from our habitual associations to be a common topic of discourse or reference, and, like a dream of another state of existence, does not piece into our daily modes of life. It is an animated but a momentary hallucination. It demands an effort to exchange our actual for our ideal identity; and to feel the pulse of our old transports revive very keenly, we must "jump" all our present comforts and connexions. Our romantic and itinerant character is not to be domesticated. Dr. Johnson remarked how little foreign travel added to the facilities of conversation in those who had been abroad. In fact, the time we have spent there is both delightful, and in one sense instructive; but it appears to be cut out of our substantial, downright existence, and never to join kindly on to it. We are not the same, but another, and perhaps more enviable individual, all the time we are out of our own country. We are lost to ourselves, as well as our friends. So the poet somewhat quaintly sings,

"Out of my country and myself I go."

Those who wish to forget painful thoughts, do well to absent themselves for a while from the ties and objects that recall them; but we can be said only to fulfil our destiny in the place that gave us birth. I should on this account like well enough to spend the whole of my life in traveling abroad, if I could anywhere borrow another life to spend afterwards at home!

—from *New Monthly Magazine* (January, 1822)

Thoughts along the Way

Some Quotable Quotes from Great Thinkers on Hiking and Walking

Can two walk together, except they be agreed?

—AMOS III, 3

Every mountain means at least two valleys.

—ANONYMOUS

You can find plenty of people who know all the answers . . . it's the questions that confuse them.

—ANONYMOUS

It is a fact that not once in all my life have I gone out for a walk.

—MAX BEERBOHM

All walking is discovery. On foot we take the time to see things whole.

—HAL BORLAND

And as I turn me home,
My shadow walks before.

—ROBERT BRIDGES

There are no grotesques in nature.

—SIR THOMAS BROWNE

The year's at the spring
And day's at the morn;
Morning's at seven;
The hill-side's dew-pearled;
The lark's on the wing;
The snail's on the thorn;
God's in his heaven—
All's right with the world!

—ROBERT BROWNING

Early and provident fear is the mother of safety.

—EDMUND BURKE

The devil never yet asked his victims to take a walk with him.

—JOHN BURROUGHS

To find new things, take the path you took yesterday.

—JOHN BURROUGHS

"I'm sure nobody walks much faster than I do."
"He can't do that," said the King, "or else he'd have been here first." —LEWIS CARROLL

In every photographer, there is something of the stroller.

—HENRI CARTIER-BRESSON

I was especially fascinated by the notion of hurried journeys . . . A long journey, even with the most lofty purpose, may be a dull thing to read of if it is made at leisure; but a hundred yards may be a breathless business if only a few seconds are granted to complete it.

—JOHN BUCHAN

They came to the Delectable Mountains.

—JOHN BUNYAN

There is no other door to knowledge than the door nature opens; there is no truth except the truths we discover in nature.

—LUTHER BURBANK

Now bid me run, And I will strive with things impossible.

—JULIUS CAESAR

The road is always better than the Inn.

—CERVANTES

If there be any value in scaling the mountains, it is only that from them one can behold the plains.

—GILBERT KEITH CHESTERTON

A noise like of a hidden brook
In the leafy month of June,
That to the sleeping woods all night
Singeth a quiet tune.

—SAMUEL TAYLOR COLERIDGE

I nauseate walking.

—WILLIAM CONGREVE

O why do you walk through the fields in gloves,
Missing so much and so much?

—FRANCES CORNFORD

He likes the country, but in truth must own,

Most likes it when he studies it in town.

—WILLIAM COWPER

Now shall I walk
Or shall I ride?
"Ride," Pleasure said;
"Walk," Joy replied.

—W. H. DAVIES

We will go no more to the woods, the laurel-trees are cut.

—THEODORE DE BANVILLE

He trudg'd along unknowing what he sought,
And whistled as he went, for want of thought.

—JOHN DRYDEN

The Promised Land always lies on the other side of a wilderness.

—HAVELOCK ELLIS

Go out of the house to see the moon, and 'tis mere tinsel: it will not please as when its light shines upon your necessary journey.

—RALPH WALDO EMERSON

In the woods a man casts off his years, as the snake its slough.

—RALPH WALDO EMERSON

Society is always taken by surprise at any new example of common sense.

—RALPH WALDO EMERSON

The civilized man has built a coach, but he has lost the use of his feet.

—RALPH WALDO EMERSON

The sky is the daily bread of the eyes.

—RALPH WALDO EMERSON

Walking has the best value as gymnastics for the mind.

—RALPH WALDO EMERSON

What attracts my attention shall have it.

—RALPH WALDO EMERSON

Before supper walk a little; after supper do the same.

—ERASMUS

It is good to collect things; it is better to take walks.

—ANATOLE FRANCE

He that can travel well a-foot, keeps a good horse.

—BENJAMIN FRANKLIN

He that riseth late must trot all day.

—BENJAMIN FRANKLIN

Two roads diverged in a wood, and I—
I took the one less traveled by,
And that has made all the difference.

—ROBERT FROST

If an ass goes traveling, he'll not come home a horse.

—THOMAS FULLER

There is more to life than increasing its speed.

—GANDHI

I was never less alone than when by myself.

—EDWARD GIBBON

For more than six years I trod the pavement never stepping once upon mother earth—for the parks are but pavement disguised with a growth of grass.

—GEORGE GISSING

Everything has been thought of before, but the difficulty is to think of it again.

—JOHANN WOLFGANG GOETHE

Mountains are earth's undying monuments.

—NATHANIEL HAWTHORNE

The trees reflected in the river— they are unconscious of a spiritual world so near them. So are we.

—NATHANIEL HAWTHORNE

To linger silent among the healthful woods.

—HORACE

To a person uninstructed in natural history, his country or sea-side stroll is a walk through a gallery filled with wonderful works of art, nine-tenths of which

have their faces turned to the wall.

—THOMAS HUXLEY

Of all exercises walking is the best.

—THOMAS JEFFERSON

And the Lord said unto Satan, Whence comest thou? Then Satan answered the Lord, and said, From going to and fro in the earth, and from walking up and down in it.

—JOB I, 7

Walk while ye have the light, lest darkness come upon you.

—JOHN XII, 35

A visitor strolling through the noble woods of Ferney complimented Voltaire on the splendid growth of his trees. "Ay," he replied, "They have nothing else to do," and walked on without another word.

—SAMUEL JOHNSON

For what has made the sage or poet write
But the fair paradise of Nature's light?

—JOHN KEATS

He travels the fastest who travels alone.

—RUDYARD KIPLING

He went back through the Wet Wild Woods, waving his wild tail, and walking by his wild lone. But he never told anybody.

—RUDYARD KIPLING

When I am not walking, I am reading; I cannot sit and think, [but] books think for me.

—CHARLES LAMB

. . . the brisk exercise imparts elasticity to the muscles, fresh and healthy blood circulates through the brain, the mind works well, the eye is clear, the step is firm, and the day's exertion always makes the evening's repose thoroughly enjoyable.

—DR. DAVID LIVINGSTONE

Solitude is as needful to the imagination as society is wholesome for the character.

—JAMES RUSSELL LOWELL

For a small reward a man will hurry away on a long journey, while for eternal life many will hardly take a single step.

—THOMAS A. KEMPIS

We're tenting tonight on the old camp-ground,
Give us a song to cheer
Our weary hearts, a song of home
And friends we love so dear.

—WALTER KITTREDGE

Beware the pine-tree's withered branch!
Beware the awful avalanche!

—HENRY WADSWORTH LONGFELLOW

Is it not said: It is good walking when one hath his horse in his hand?

—JOHN LYLY

For love we Earth, then serve we all;
Her mystic secret then is ours;
We fall, or view our treasures fall,
Unclouded, as beholds her flowers
Earth, from a night of frosty wreck,
Enrobed in morning's mounted fire,
When lowly, with a broken neck,
The crocus lays her cheek to mine.

—GEORGE MEREDITH

In solitude
What happiness? Who can enjoy alone,
Or all enjoying, what contentment find?

—JOHN MILTON

We call that against nature which cometh against custom. But there is nothing, whatsoever it be, that is not according to nature.

—MICHEL EYQUEM DE MONTAIGNE

We can not fail in following
nature.
> —MICHEL EYQUEM
> DE MONTAIGNE

Now your true walker is mightily
"curious in the world," and he
goes upon his way zealous to
sate himself with a thousand
quaintnesses.
> —CHRISTOPHER MORLEY

You never know when an
adventure is going to happen.
> —CHRISTOPHER MORLEY

Who walks with beauty has no
need of fear;
The sun and moon and stars
keep pace with him;
Invisible hands restore the ruined
year,
And time, itself, grows beautifully
dim.
> —DAVID MORTON

The book of nature is that which
the physician must read; and to
do so he must walk over the
leaves.
> —PARACELSUS

I drew my bride, beneath the
moon,
Across my threshold; happy
hour!
But, ah, the walk that afternoon
We saw the water-flags in flower!
> —COVENTRY PATMORE

Nothing which we can imagine
about Nature is incredible.
> —PLINY THE ELDER

The mountaineer is . . . a lover
of freedom.
> —CHRISTINA ROSSETTI

Man is an animal, and his happiness depends on his physiology
more than he likes to think. . . .
Unhappy businessmen, I am
convinced, would increase their
happiness more by walking six
miles every day than by any
conceivable change of philosophy.
> —BERTRAND RUSSELL

Our mental make-up is suited to
a life of very severe physical
labor. I used, when I was younger,
to take my holidays walking. I
would cover 25 miles a day, and
when the evening came I had no
need of anything to keep me
from boredom, since the delight
of sitting amply sufficed. . . .
When crowds assemble in
Trafalgar Square to cheer to the
echo an announcement that the
government has decided to have
them killed, they would not do so
if they had all walked 25 miles
that day.
> —BERTRAND RUSSELL

What I know of the divine
sciences and Holy Scriptures,
I learnt in woods and fields. I
have had no other masters than
the beeches and the oaks.
> —ST. BERNARD OF CLAIRVAUX

I like to walk about amidst the
beautiful things that adorn the
world.
> —GEORGE SANTAYANA

The longing to be primitive is a
disease of culture.
> —GEORGE SANTAYANA

There is no cure for birth and
death save to enjoy the interval.
> —GEORGE SANTAYANA

Full many a glorious morning
have I seen,
Flatter the mountain tops with
sovereign eye,
Kissing with golden face the
meadows green,
Gilding pale streams with
heavenly alchemy.
> —WILLIAM SHAKESPEARE

Jog on, jog on, the footpath way,
And merrily hent the Stile-a;
A merry heart goes all the day,
Your sad tires in a mile-a.
> —WILLIAM SHAKESPEARE

One impulse from a vernal wood
May teach you more of man,
Of moral evil and of good,
Than all the sages can.
> —WILLIAM SHAKESPEARE

Solvency is entirely a matter of
temperament and not of income.
> —LOGAN PEARSALL SMITH

Man . . . walks up the stairs of
his concepts, [and] emerges
ahead of his accomplishments.
> —JOHN STEINBECK

Don't do anything. Just stand
there!
> —ADLAI STEVENSON

For my part, I travel not to go
anywhere, but to go.
> —ROBERT LOUIS STEVENSON

People love bypaths.
> —TAO TE CHING

The longest journey starts with
just one step.
> —TAO TE CHING

In the scheme of contemporary
reversal such pleasures as
walking—the time and the space
to walk in—these become the
new luxuries.
> —WALTER TELLER

To be a discoverer you must go
looking for something.
> —WALTER TELLER

He approaches the study of
mankind with great advantages
who is accustomed to the study
of nature.
> —HENRY DAVID THOREAU

I went to the woods because I
wished to live deliberately, to
front only the essential facts of
life, and see if I could not learn
what it had to teach, and not,
when I came to die, discover that
I had not lived.
> —HENRY DAVID THOREAU

If one advances confidently in
the direction of his dreams, and
endeavors to live the life which
he has imagined, he will meet
with a success unexpected in
common hours.
> —HENRY DAVID THOREAU

Take long walks in stormy
weather or through deep snow
in the fields and woods, if you
would keep your spirits up. Deal
with brute nature. Be cold and
hungry and weary.
> —HENRY DAVID THOREAU

The birds I heard today, which, fortunately, did not come within the scope of my science, sang as freshly as if it had been the first morning of creation.

    —HENRY DAVID THOREAU

The mass of men lead lives of quiet desperation. What is called resignation is confirmed desperation.

    —HENRY DAVID THOREAU

The swiftest traveler is he that goes afoot.

    —HENRY DAVID THOREAU

I have two doctors, my left leg and my right.

    —GEORGE M. TREVELYAN

We are all insane, anyway. Note the mountain climbers.

    —MARK TWAIN

The walking stick serves the purpose of an advertisement that the bearer's hands are employed otherwise than in useful effort, and it therefore has utility as an evidence of leisure.

    —THORSTEIN VEBLEN

*Afoot and light-hearted I take to the open road,
Healthy, free, the world before me,
The long brown path before me leading wherever I choose.
Henceforth I ask not good-fortune, I myself am good-fortune,
Henceforth I whimper no more, postpone no more, need nothing,
Done with indoor complaints, libraries, querulous criticisms,
Strong and content I travel the open road.*

    —WALT WHITMAN

*Conquering, holding, daring, venturing as we go the unknown ways,
Pioneers! O pioneers!*

    —WALT WHITMAN

It is always a silly thing to give advice, but to give good advice is absolutely fatal.

    —OSCAR WILDE

Today I have grown taller from walking with the trees.

    —KARLE WILSON

*One impulse from a vernal wood
May teach you more of man,
Of moral evil and of good.
Than all the sages can.*

    —WILLIAM WORDSWORTH

That inward eye which is the bliss of solitude.

    —WILLIAM WORDSWORTH

*The woods, my Friends, are round you roaring,
Rocking and roaring like a sea; . . .
Away we go—and what care we
For treasons, tumults and for wars?
We are as calm in our delight
As is the crescent-moon so bright
Among the scattered stars.*

    —WILLIAM WORDSWORTH

I will arise and go now.

    —WILLIAM BUTLER YEATS

Travel used to be a pleasure, now it has become an industry.

    —LIN YUTANG

Reference

Named Trails in the U.S. and Canada

U.S.—Interstate Trails

APPALACHIAN TRAIL

Mileage: 2000
Northern Terminus: Mount Katahdin, Maine
Southern Terminus: Springer Mountain, Georgia
Shelters: Over 230; 8-mile intervals
Markers: Trail blazed with white rectangular 2-inch by 6-inch painted markers; double white markers for turns.

States	Distances by Sections	
	Miles	Kilometers
Maine	277.8	447.1
New Hampshire/Vermont	282.9	455.3
Massachusetts/Connecticut	139.3	244.2
New York/New Jersey	158.7	255.4
Pennsylvania	141.7	228
Pennsylvania/Virginia	167	268.8
Shenandoah National Park	104.4	168
Virginia	344.4	554.3
Tennessee/North Carolina	270	434.5
North Carolina/Georgia	160.7	258.6

References

Appalachian Trail Club Headquarters
1718 N Street, N.W.
Washington, D.C. 20036
(202) 638-5306

Appalachian Trail Conference
P.O. Box 236
Harpers Ferry, West Virginia 25425
(304) 535-6331

BRANDYWINE TRAIL

Mileage: 37.5
Northern Terminus: Pottstown, Pennsylvania
Southern Terminus: Wilmington, Delaware
Markers: Trail blazed with white

States
Pennsylvania
Delaware

PACIFIC CREST NATIONAL SCENIC TRAIL

Mileage: 2400
Northern Terminus: Monument #78 at the Canadian Border
Southern Terminus: International Border at Mexico, 2.5 miles east of Tecate
Markers: Trail blazed with triangular emblem; pine tree in center encircled with "Pacific Crest Trail, National Scenic Trail."

States	Miles
Washington	514
Oregon	436
California	1454

References
U.S. Forest Service
California Region
Office of Information
630 Sansome Street
San Francisco, California 94111
(415) 556-0122

U.S. Forest Service
Pacific Northwest Region
P.O. Box 3623
Portland, Oregon 97208
(503) 221-2877

Pacific Crest Club
P.O. Box 1907
Santa Ana, California 92702
(No phone listing)

SUFFERN-MIDVALE TRAIL

Mileage: 12
Eastern Terminus: Railroad Station, Suffern
Western Terminus: Railroad Avenue, Midvale
Markers: Trail blazed with red signs.

States
New York
New Jersey

STERLING RIDGE TRAIL

Mileage: 8.4
Eastern Terminus: Route 210 (near Tuxedo Mountain)
Western Terminus: Hewitt
Markers: Trail blazed with blue on white signs.

States
New York
New Jersey

U.S.—Intrastate Trails

Explanation of symbols: (RT) round trip; (NS) not shown

ALASKA	Miles
White Mountains Trail	80

ARIZONA

Tonto Trail	(NS)
Kaibab Trail	(NS)
Rim Trail	4
Bright Angel Trail	(NS)
Rincon Spur Trail	(NS)
Hugh Norris Trail	4.8
Tanque Verde Ridge Trail	(NS)
Douglas Spring Trail	(NS)

ARKANSAS

Ozarks National Forest Region

Hurricane Creek Trail	7
Lost Valley (Clark Creek) Hike	3.5

Hot Springs National Park Area

Promenade Nature Trail	1
Dead Chief Trail	1.6
Gulpha Gorge Trail	(NS)
Goat Rock Trail	(NS)
Dogwood Trail	(NS)
Arlington Trail	(NS)
Sunset Trail	(NS)

Ouachita National Forest Region

Ouachita Trail	52
Caney Creek Trail	9
Pashubbe Hiking Trail	4
Rich Mountain Trail	2
Rattlesnake Ridge Trail	2
Horse Thief Springs Trail	4

Wild Horse Hiking Trail	2
Old Military Road Trail	3

CALIFORNIA

San Bernardino Region

Cable Canyon Trail	10
Pilot Rock Trail	(NS)
Crab Flats Trail	4
Holcomb Creek Trail	4
Green Valley Trail	4
Seven Pines Trail	(NS)
Wildhorse Creek Trail	6
Fish Creek Trail	5
Ponderosa Nature Trail	1
Falls Creek Trail	(NS)
Sky High Trail	17
Forsee Creek Ridge Trail	15
San Bernardino Peak Divide Trail	(NS)
Alger Creek Trail	6.5
Vivian Trail	14
Oak Glen Divide Trail	(NS)
Ford Canyon Trail	19
Morton Ridge Trail	(NS)
Wilson Creek Trail	(NS)
Little San Gorgonio Trail	(NS)
Wilshire Peak Trail	(NS)
Raywood Flat Trail	6

San Jacinto Mountain Region

Black Mountain Trail	7
Cinco Poses Trail	7
Webster Trail	(NS)
Fuller Ridge Trail	(NS)
Deer Springs Trail	(NS)

Devil's Slide Trail	(NS)
South Ridge Trail	(NS)
Scenic Trail	2.5
Sam Fink Trail	(NS)
Desert Divide Trail	(NS)
Ramona Trail	(NS)
Cahuilla Mountain Trail	(NS)
Palm Canyon Trail	14
Cactus Spring Trail	(NS)

San Gabriel Mountains Region

Gillette Mine Trail	(NS)
Big Tree Trail	(NS)
Dagger Flat Trail	7 (RT)
Stone Canyon Trail	8 (RT)
Vogel Flat Trail	14 (RT)
Arroyo Seco Trail	(NS)
Dark Canyon Trail	(NS)
Sam Merrill Trail	5 (RT)
Sunset Trail	(NS)
Colby Canyon Trail	6 (RT)
Idlehour Trail	5
Brown Mountain Loop	12
Sunset Ridge Loop	11
Mount Lowe Railway Loop Tour	12
Old Mt. Wilson Trail	7.5
Gabrielino National Recreation Trail	28 (RT)
Upper Winter Creek Trail	(NS)
East Trail	(NS)
Winter Creek Trail	(NS)
Rattlesnake Trail	4
Valley Forge Trail	3
Wolf Tree Nature Trail	(NS)
Mt. Hillyer Trail	.5

Twin Peaks Trail .5
Cooper Canyon Trail 2
Buckhart Trail 8
South Fork Trail 10 (RT)
Bear Creek Trail 2,5
Soldier Creek Trail 1 (RT)
Windy Gap Trail 2.5 (RT)
Baden-Powell Trail 4
Heaton Flat Trail 5
Blue Ridge Nature Trail 4 (RT)
Bear Flat Trail 1.5
Devils Backbone Trail (NS)
Ontario Peak Trail (NS)
Cucamonga Peak Trial (NS)
Silver Moccasin Trail 53

Desolation Wilderness Region

Twin Lakes Trail 1.4
Eagle Lake Trail (NS)
Willow Flat Trail (NS)

Salmon Trinity Alps Primitive Area Region

Jim Jam Ridge Trail (NS)
Rattlesnake Creek Trail (NS)

Coastal Redwoods Region

Coastal Trail (NS)
Redwood Circle Trail (NS)
Fern Canyon Trail (NS)

Yosemite Valley Region

Panorama Trail (NS)
Mist Trail (NS)
Buena Vista Trail (NS)
Mono Point Trail (NS)
Merced Lake Trail 2.7
Four Mile Trail 4
Yosemite Point Trail .3

Other Trails

Lava Crest Trail 339
Tahoe-Yosemite Trail 239
John Muir Trail 175
Sierra Crest Trail 137
Desert Crest Trail 406
California Riding and Hiking Trail (NS)
Sky Trail 1.2
Bear Valley Trail 4.4
Mt. Wittenberg Trail (NS)
Barney Lake Trail (NS)
High Sierra Trail (NS)
Sphinx Creek Trail (NS)

COLORADO

Rocky Mountain National Park

Emerald Lake Trail 2
Timber Creek Trail (NS)
Green Mountain Trail (NS)
North Inlet Trail (NS)
Fern Lake Trail (NS)
Flattop Mountain Trail (NS)

North Park Range

Wyoming Trail (NS)
Buffalo Ridge Trail (NS)
Ute Pass Trail (NS)
Main Fork Trail 2
Lone Pine Trail (NS)
Gilpin-Mica Basin Trail 7.5
Red Dirt Pass Trail (NS)
Fryingpan Trail 7
Big Creek Trail (NS)
Gilpin Lake—Gold Creek Circuit 9.5
Northern Peak Circuit 28

Other Trails

Vallecito Creek Trail 11.5
Doe Creek Trail (NS)
Rainbow Trail (NS)
Comanche Lake Trail (NS)
Eaglesmere Lake Trail (NS)
Tipperary Lake Trail (NS)
Lost Lake Trail (NS)
Gore Range Trail 10

Mesa Verde National Park

Spruce Canyon Trail 2.1
Pictograph Point Trail 2.3
Soda Canyon Overlook Trail (NS)
Knife Edge Trail 1.5

Gorge Range Region

Surprise Lake Circuit 10
Upper Cataract Lake Circuit 13
Mirror Lake Circuit 15

Flattops Region

Wall Lake—Parvin Lake Circuit 12
Trapper's Lake Circuit 4
Single Peak Circuit 20
White River Circuit 35

CONNECTICUT

Western Region

Mattatuck Trail 35
Quinnipiac Trail 21
Paugussett and Pomperaug Trails 9.7
River Trail .7
Pine Knob Loop Trail 2.5
Macedonia Brook State Park
Red Trail .3
Green Trail .5
Yellow Offshoot 1.1
Pine Hill Tree Trail 1.2
American Legion State Forest
Henry Buck Trail 1.5
Elliott Bronson Trail 1.5
Jesse Girard Trail 1.3
Charles Pack Trail 1.9
Robert Ross Trail 2
Sleeping Giant State Park
White Trail 2.8
Tower Path 1.6
Green Trail 2
Violet Trail 3.2
Yellow Trail 2.2
Orange Trail 2.4
Whitestone Cliffs Trail 3.7
Jericho Trail 3
Lone Pine Trail 3
Hancock Brook-Lion Head Trail 3 (RT)
Roy and Margot Larsen Wildlife Sanctuary
Naugatuck Trail 4.8

Central Region

Metacomet Trail 45
Shenipsit Trail 30
Charles Hubbard Memorial Trail 2.5
Cockaponset Trail 7.3
Mattabesett Trail 39

Eastern Region

Nipmuck Trail 21.5
Byram River Trail 5.3
James L. Goodwin State Forest
Airline Hiking Trail 3.66
Natchaug Trail 3
Pachaug State Forest
Castle Trail 1.5
Quinnebaug Trail (NS)
Nehantic Trail 14
Canonicus Trail 2.5
Narragansett Trail 20
Quinebaug Trail 9.7
Pachaug Trail 15

FLORIDA

The Florida Trail 700
Pinelands Trail (NS)
Mangrove Trail (NS)

GEORGIA

Chattahoochee National Forest Region

Tallulah (Rabun Bald) Ranger District
William Bartram Trail 8.5
Rabun Bald Trail 11

Big Ridge Trail 4
Brasstown Ranger District
Arkaguah Trail 5.5
Jack's Knob Trail 5.5
Chestatee (Cooper Creek) Ranger District
Yellow Mountain Trail 2.5
Mill Shoal Trail 4
Cohutta Ranger District
Jack's River Trail 11
Rough Ridge Trail 7.5
Tearbritches Trail 3.5
Chestnut Creek Trail 2
Conasauga River Trail 4.5

IDAHO

Sawtooth Mountains Region

Cave Trail 1
Rift Trail 4
Spangle Lakes—Queen's River Circuit 31
Spangle Lakes—Ardeth Lake—
Queen's River Circuit 36
Big Crater Loop 1.5

Priest Lake Region

Upper Lake Trail 3

ILLINOIS

Illinois and Michigan Canal Towpath 15
Waukegan-Kenosha Trail 18
Green Bay Trail 5.75
Illinois Prairie Path 40

INDIANA

Yellowwood Trail 20
Tulip Tree Trace 22
Muskhogen Trail 11

KENTUCKY

Daniel Boone National Forest Region

Pioneer Weapons Hunting Area
Carrington Rocks Trail 2.5
Cedar Cliffs Trail (NS)
Buck Branch Trail 1.5
Cave Run Trail 3
Crossover Trail 1
Hogpen Trail 2
Big Limestone Trail 6
Stanton District Area
Triple Arch Trek 14.4
Wildcat Trail 1.2
Rough Trail (NS)
Long Hunters Trek 13.1
Silvermine Arch Trail 1
Koomer Ridge Trail 8.5
Wittington Branch Trail 2
D. Boone Hut Trail (NS)
Pinch 'Em Tight Trail (NS)
London District and Cumberland Gap
National Park Area
Moonbow Trail 10
Ridge Trail 16
Dog Slaughter Trail 3
Sugar Run Trail 2.25
Lewis Hollow Trail 1.6
Woodson Gap Trail 2.25
Gibson Gap Trail 5
Chadwell Gap Trail 2.3
Ewing Trail 3.9
Wilderness Road Trail 14

MAINE

Mount Desert Island (Acadia National Park) Region

Hunters Beach Trail .25
Great Head Circuit 3.5
Cadillac Mountain Area
South Ridge Trail 3.5
West Face Trail 2.3
North Ridge Trail 1.8

Sargent Mountain Area

Giant Slide Trail	4.6
Sargent Mountain North Ridge Trail	1.2
Hadlock Brook Trail	2
Maple Spring Trail	2
Penobscot Mountain Trail	4
Jordan Cliffs Trail	2.9
Precipice Trail	8
Champlain Mountain Trail	4.1
Arcadia Mountain Trail	4
Flying Mountain Trail	1.8
Great Pond Trail	2.9
Western Trail	4.2
South Face Trail	3.6
Canada Cliff Trail	(NS)
Canada Ridge Trail	(NS)
Beech Mountain Trail	.6
Sargent Pond Trail	(NS)

Aroostook County Region

Round Mountain Trail	7.25
Horseshoe Mountain Trail	1.5
Priestly Mountain Trail	2

Piscataquis County Region

Moore's Pond Trail	4.8
Little Wilson Falls Trail	2.4
High Cut Hill Trail	0.9
Mount Kineo Trails	1–2
Squaw Mountain Trail	6.25
Gulf Hagas Trails	4

Baxter State Park (Mt. Katahdin Area) Region

Knife Edge Trail	1.1
Abol Trail	3.78

Oxford County Region

Grafton Notch State Park Area

Old Speck Link Trail	2.5
East Spur Trail	1
Eyebrow Trail	3.1
Cascade Brook Trail	1.6
Skyline Trail	3.5
Table Rock Trail	(NS)

Mahoosuc Mountain Range Area

Mahoosuc Trail	300
Goose Eye Trail	3
Carlo Col Trail	2.57
Notch Trail	2.8

Blueberry Mountain Area

White Cairn Trail	2.5
Stone House Trail	1.5

Franklin County Region

Saddleback Mountain Area

Saddleback Trail	2.5

Bigelow Range Area

Bigelow Range Trail	22.10
Firewarden's Trail	8.4

MARYLAND

Chesapeake and Ohio Region

Chesapeake and Ohio Canal Trail	184

Assateague Island Region

Assateague Island National Seashore Trail	29

Baltimore Metropolitan Region

Prettyboy Dam Circuit Hike	4.2
Mingo Forks Circuit Trail	3.8
Panther Branch Circuit Trail	4.2

MASSACHUSETTS

Cape Cod National Seashore Region

Province Lands Area

Beech Forest Trail	1

Pilgrim Heights Area

Pilgrim Spring Trail	.5
Small's Swamp Trail	.5

Marconi Station Area

Atlantic White Cedar Swamp Trail	1.25
Great Island Trail	8 (RT)

Nauset or Coast Guard Beach Section

Nauset Marsh Trail	1
Fort Hill or Red Maple Swamp Trail	.5
Buttonbush Trail	4

Barnstable County Agricultural Society Trails

Dopple Bottom Trail	67
Mashpee Pond Trail	40.1
Hathaway Ponds Trail	19
Cotuit Highlands Trail	59
Town Line Trail	16
Mystic Lake Trail	14
Race Lane Trail	12
Mill Pond Trail	2
Wequaquet Lake Trail	52.8

Miles Standish State Forest Region

Miles Standish State Forest Trail	2.1

Swansea Region

Margaret's Rock and Devil's Rock Trails	2

Ames Nowell State Park Region

Bridle Path	1.25
West Shore Trail	1

Blue Hills Reservation Region

Warner Trail	34

Plateau Region

Purgatory State Reservation Area

Purgatory Chasm Trail	.75
Memorial Trail	.3

Mount Wachusett Area

Jack Frost Trail	1.08
Mountain House Trail	1
Harrington Trail	1.5

Connecticut Valley Region

Metacomet-Monadnock Trail	300
Mount Grace Summit Loop	1.8
Round the Mountain Trail	(NS)
Snowshoe Trail	(NS)
Winchester Trail	.5
Northside Trail	2.5
Halfway Trail	2.75

Western Uplands Region

Elbow Trail	5.8 (RT)
Firetower Trail or Trail of the Ledges	2.5
Hopper Trail	(NS)
Money Brook Trail	(NS)
Indian Monument Trail	1.25

MICHIGAN

Isle Royale National Park Region

Rock Harbor Area

Albert Stoll, Jr. Memorial Trail	2.3
Rock Harbor Trail	10.5
Mt. Franklin Trail	2.2
Tobin Harbor Trail	3
Lookout Louise Trail	1
Daisy Farm Trail	2
Mount Ojibway Trail	1.7
Lake Richie Trail	2.3

Windigo Area

Huginnin Cove Loop Trail	7
Feldtmann Ridge Trail	14.3
Feldtmann Lake Trail	2.5
Greenstone Ridge Trail	45
Rock Harbor Trail	(NS)
Mount Franklin Trail	(NS)
Minong Ridge Trail	26

Trails running southwest–northwest

Indian Portage Trail	10.6
Siskiwit Falls Trail and Ishpeming Trail	7.4
Island Mine Trail	5
Lane Cove Trail	2.8
McCargoe Cove Trail	2.2

Porcupine Mountains Wilderness State Park Region

Lake Superior Trail	16
Pinkerton Trail	3
Little Carp River Trail	11
Cross Trail	5
Lost Lake Trail	4.5
Correction Line Trail	3
Lily Pond Trail	3
South Mirror Lake Trail	2.5
Big Carp River Trail	9
North Mirror Lake Trail	4
Government Peak Trail	8
Overlook Trail	3
Escarpment Trail	4
Union Springs Trail and Impoundment Trail	5.5
Presque Isle Trail	1

Hiawatha National Forest Region

Bay de Noc Grand Island Trail	25.8

Other Trails

Shore to Shore Trail	211

MINNESOTA

Superior National Forest Region

Crab Lake Trail	5
Cummings Lake Trail	5
Eagle Mountain Trail	9
La Croix Trail	8
Kekekabic Trail	38
Norway Trail	8
Sioux-Hustler Trail	27

Other Trails

Casey Jones Trail	12.5
Douglas Trail	15
Sakatah-Singing Hills Trail	42

MISSOURI

Clark National Forest Region

Berryman Trail	24
Big Piney Trail	17
Rock Pile Mountain Trail	5

Elephant Rocks State Park Area

Taum Sank Trail	28

Keith Spring Area

Trace Creek Trail	5

Mark Twain National Forest Region

Whites Creek Trail	20

MONTANA

Glacier National Park Region

Highline Trail	7.6

Bridger Wilderness Region

Upper Green River Lake Loop	4

Bob Marshall Wilderness Region

Danaher Basin–Pearl Basin Circuit	40
Chinese Wall–White River Circuit	65

NEVADA

Highway 50 Region

Crystal Basin Recreation Area

Hales Camp Trail	(NS)
South Fork Trail	10.2 (RT)
Grey Trail	(NS)
Parsley Bar Trail	(NS)

Desolation Wilderness Area

Bunker Lake Trail	1 (RT)
McKinstry Trail	(NS)
Loon Lake Trail	(NS)
Wentworth Jeep Trail	(NS)
Lyons Creek Trail	10 (RT)
Red Peak Trail	(NS)
Beauty Lake Trail	(NS)
Rockbound Pass Trail	(NS)
Twin Lakes Trail	(NS)
Smith Lake Trail	(NS)
Tyler Lake Trail	(NS)
Willow Flat Trail	(NS)
Highland Lake Trail	(NS)
4-Q Lakes Trail	24.8
Eagle Lake Trail	(NS)
Granite Lake Trail	2.4 (RT)
Ralston Trail	(NS)

Tahoe-Yosemite Trail	(NS)
General Creek Trail	9 (RT)
Clark Trail	(NS)
Tamarack Trail	7
Glen Alpine Trail	(NS)
Grass Lake Trail	(NS)
Floating Island Trail	9.2 (RT)
Hidden Lake Trail	(NS)

South Fork American and Upper Truckee
Rivers Area

Lovers Leap Trail	2.8 (RT)
Sayles Canyon Trail	(NS)
Bryan Meadow Trail	(NS)
Hawley Grade Trail	3.8 (RT)
Benwood Trail	(NS)
Dardanelles Lake Trail	8 (RT)
Big Meadow Trail	6.4 (RT)
Meiss Meadow Trail	(NS)
Willow Creek Trail	(NS)
Tucker Flat Trail	(NS)
Horsethief Canyon Trail	25

Interstate 80 Region

Placer County Big Tree Grove Area

Forest View Trail	(NS)
Big Trees Trail	(NS)

Granite Chief Area

Picayune Valley Trail	15.2 (RT)
Little Powderhorn Trail	5.6 (RT)
Big Powderhorn Trail	(NS)
Steamboat Trail	(NS)
Bear Pen Trail	2.9
Five Lakes Basin Trail	(NS)
Shanks Cove Trail	(NS)
Deer Park Trail	4.4 (RT)
Tinker Knob Trail	10.2 (RT)
Tevis Cup Trail	(NS)
Painted Rock Trail	15.6 (RT)

Grouse Ridge Recreation Area

Round Lake Trail	(NS)
Beyers Lake Trail	(NS)

Loch Leven Lakes Area

Loch Leven Lakes Trail	6.4 (RT)
Devils Peak Trail	(NS)
Salmon Lake Trail	(NS)
Cherry Point Trail	(NS)

Mt. Ross Area

Mt. Rose Trail	11.8 (RT)

Highway 49 Region

Malakoff Diggins Area

South Yuba Trail	12.2 (RT)
Humbug Trail	5.4 (RT)
Missouri Bar Trail	3.4 (RT)
Diggins Trail	(NS)
Blair Trail	2.4
Rim Trail	7 (RT)
Bedbug Smith Trail	2 (RT)

Ramshorn Area

Halls Ranch Trail	6 (RT)
Ramshorn Trail	5.2 (RT)

Wild Plum Area

Milton Creek Trail	(NS)
Haypress Creek Trail	8.2 (RT)
Hilda Trail	(NS)

North Yuba Area

Chapman Creek Trail	(NS)
Haskell Peak Trail	(NS)
Lunch Creek Trail	3.4 (RT)
Berry Creek Trail	6.6 (RT)
Deer Lake Trail	4 (RT)
Salmon Lake Trail	3.8 (RT)
Bear Lake Trail	(NS)
Ewell Lodge–Long Lake Trail	(NS)
Lily Lake Trail	1.4 (RT)
Gray Eagle Creek Trail	(NS)
Eureka Peak Trail	3 (RT)

Highway 70 Region

Feather Falls Scenic Area

Feather Falls Trail	10.6 (RT)

Bucks Lake Area

No Ear Bar Trail	2.6 (RT)
Oddie Bar Trail	(NS)
Hartman Bar Trail	9.2 (RT)
Gold Lake Trail	3.4 (RT)
California Riding and Hiking Trail	(NS)
Belden Trail	(NS)
Chips Creek Trail	9.4 (RT)
Ben Lomond Trail	(NS)
National Scenic Trail	(NS)

NEW HAMPSHIRE

Mount Cardigan Region

West Ridge Trail	1.3
Hurricane Gap Trail	.9
Clark Trail	3.5
Skyland Trail	4.4

White Mountains Region

Mount Moosilauke Area

Tunnel Brook Trail	6.5
Benton Trail	3.5
Carriage Road Trail	5
Gorge Brook Trail	2.7
Snapper Ski Trail	1.1

Franconia Range Area

Greenleaf Trail	3.25
Falling Waters Trail	2.8
Franconia Ridge Trail	5
Flume Slide Trail	3.45
Liberty Spring Trail	3.45
Garfield Trail	5
Garfield Ridge Trail	6.53

Pemigewasset Wilderness Area

Wilderness Trail	8.7
Carrigain Notch Trail	.5
Black Pond Trail	.83
Franconia Brook Trail	7.2
Bondcliff Trail	6

Mount Chocorua Area

Piper Trail	4.1
Brook Trail	4.2
Liberty Trail	4.5

Presidential Peaks Area

Gulfside Trail	6
Mount Clay Loop	(NS)
Valley Way Trail	3.47
Crawford Path	6.77
Ammonoosuc Ravine Trail	2.46
Tuckerman Ravine Trail	4.1

Carter-Moriah Range Area

Carter-Moriah Trail	13.9
Great Gulf Trail	7.76
Six Husbands Trail	2.2
Adams Slide Trail	1.26
Sphinx Trail	1
Mahoosuc Trail	27.24
Mahoosuc Notch Trail	2.75

Mount Sunapee State Park Area

South Province Ridge Trail	1
North Province Ridge Trail	1.12

NEW JERSEY

New Jersey Highlands Region

East of the Wyanokies Area

Allis Trail	2
High Mountain Brook Trail	(NS)
Hollow Trail	(NS)
Hewitt Trail	(NS)
Sterling Forest Trail	(NS)
Laurel Swamp Trail	(NS)

Wyanokie Plateau Area

Burnt Meadow Trail	.8
Horse Pond Mountain Trail	2
Carris Hill Trail	(NS)
Lower Trail	(NS)
Hewitt-Butler Trail	18
Stonetown Circular Trail	9.5
Kitchell Lake Trail	(NS)
West Brook Trail	(NS)
Wyanokie Circular Trail	8.7

Mine Trail	5.4
Macopin Trail	2.5
Otter Hole Trail	2
Torne Trail	1
Burnt Meadow Trail	(NS)
Lower Trail	1.7
Post Brook Trail	3
Stone Hunting House Trail	.5

South of Wyanokies Area

Towaco-Pompton Trail	8

Greenwood Lake Area

Bearfoot Ridge Trail	(NS)
Firehouse Trail	(NS)
State Line Trail	(NS)
Ernest Walter Trail	(NS)
Mountain Spring Trail	(NS)

Lake and Hills of Northern New Jersey Region

Jockey Hollow Area

Boy Scout Jockey Hollow Trail	17

Kittitinny Mountain Range Region

Stokes State Forest

Swenson Trail	4
Tinsley Trail	(NS)
Stony Brook Trail	(NS)
Tower Trail	(NS)

Upper Delaware Valley Region

Uhlerstown Circular	12
Stockton Circular	14

Pine Barrens of New Jersey Region

Batona Trail	30

NEW MEXICO

Winsor Trail	9
Crest Trail	(NS)

NEW YORK

Finger Lakes Region

Finger Lakes Trail	17

Catskills Region

Northern Area

Indian-Head Hunter Mountain Range Trail	23.19
Echo Lake Trail	2.8
Mink Hollow Trail	11.7
Becker Trail	2.4
Spruceton Trail	3.7
Shanty Hollow Trail	(NS)
Phoenicia Trail	2.15
Willow Trail	4.6
Diamond Notch Trail	4.5
Escarpment Trail	24
Blackhead Range Trail	4

Central Area

Phoenicia-East Branch Trail	9.85
Giant Ledge-Panther Mountain- Fox Hollow Trail	8.9
Wittenberg-Cornell Slide Trail	8.9
Hanley Corners Trail	3.55
Lost Clove Trail	3.05
Pine-Hill-Eagle Mountain- West Branch Trail	14.25
Seager-Big Indian Mountain Trail	4.1
Oliverea-Mapledale Trail	6.85
Trout Pond Trail	5.4
Campbell Mountain Trail	4.1
Little Spring Brook Trail	.6
Pelnor Hollow Trail	4
Mary Smith Trail	4.5
Neversink-Hardenburg	14.7
South Approach	2.75
North Approach	3.05
Long Pond Trail	3.9
Pakatakan-Dry Brook Ridge- Beaverkill Trail	14.1

Adirondacks Region

Northville Placid Trail	133

High Peaks Area

Elk Lake-Dix Trail	2.33
Avalanche Pass Trail	(NS)
Algonquin Mountain Trail	(NS)
Upper Works Trail	10.11
Van Hoevenberg Trail	7
Indian Pass Trail	7

Cranberry Lake Area

High Falls Truck Trail	1.5
Leary Trail	2.7
Plains Trail	4.7
Cat Mountain Trail	1.5
Dead Creek Flow Truck Trail	2.6
Buck Pond Trail	3
Five Ponds-Wolf Pond-Sand Lake Trail	2
Big Deer Pond Trail	2
Six Mile Creek Trail	2.05
Clear Pond Trail	4.2
Curtis Pond Trail	1.2
Darning Needle Pond Trail	2.4

Old Forge-Big Moose-Fulton Chain Area

Big Otter Lake Trail	8
Lost Creek Trail	5
East Pond Trail	3.8
Black Foot Pond Trail	1
Moose River Mountain Trail	.75
Scusa Access Trail	3.75
Woodhull Mountain Trail	8.5
Norridge Trail	6
Gull Lakes Trail	1
Russian Lake Trail	.75
Andes Creek Trail	.5
West Mountain Trail	2.5
Windfall Pond Trail	2
Bald Mountain Trail	1
Scenic Mountain Trail	4.5
Bubb Lake Trail	1
Safford Pond Trail	3.75
Snake Pond Trail	1

Blue Mountain Lake Area

Owls Head Mountain Trail	3.1
Sargent Ponds Trail	4.3
Tirrell Pond Trail	3.25
Wilson Pond Trail	2.9
Cascade Lake Trail	6.15
Peaked Hill Trail	2.25
Arnold Pond Trail	1.5
Severance Hill Trail	1.7
Gull Pond Trail	.75
Spectacle Pond Trail	1.6
Goose Pond Trail	.75
Pharaoh Mountain Firetower Trail	2.75
Short Swing Trail	9.7
Long Swing Trail	11
Treadway Mountain Trail	2
Bear Pond Trail	2.5
Lost Pond Trail	1.7
Berrymill Pond Trail	4.9
Pharaoh Lake Trail	2.3

Lake George Area

Tongue Mountain Range Trail	18
Black Mountain Firetower Trail	2.75
Prospect Mountain Trail	1.13

Palisades Region

Allison Trail	8.5
Little-Chism Trail	1.5

Bear Mountain-Harriman Parks Region

Anthony Wayne Trail	2.7
Blue Disc Trail	3.8
Breakneck Mountain Trail	1.6
Conklin's Crossing Trail	.65
Crown Ridge Trail	5
Deep Hollow Shelter Trail	.7
Diamond Mountain Trail	.4
Dunning Trail	3.4
Hillburn-Torne-Sebago Trail	4.7
Hurst Trail	.5
Kakiat Trail	7.2
Lichen Trail	.5
Long Mountain-Torne Trail	3.2
Major Welch Trail	3.3

Nurian Trail	3.3
Pine Meadow Trail	6.2
Popolopen Gorge Trail	4.3
Raccoon Brook Hills Trail	2.3
Ramapo-Dunderberg Trail	20.8
Red Cross Trail	7.6
Reeves Brook Trail	1
Seven Hills Trail	6.8
Skannatati Trail	4.8
Stony Brook Trail	1.6
Suffern-Bear Mountain Trail	24.3
Timp-Torne Trail	9.9
Tower Trail	.8
Triangle Trail	4.9
Tuxedo-Mt. Ivy Trail	10.3
Victory Trail	3
White Cross Trail	1.9
Long Path	25.5
Sherwood Path	1.9
Arden-Surebridge Trail	5

Storm King - Black Rock Forest Region

Stillman Trail	10.5
Sutherland Trail	(NS)
Scenic Trail	7.2
Sackett Mountain Trail	1.5
Ryerson Trail	(NS)
Huber Trail	(NS)
Arthur Trail	(NS)
Stropel Trail	(NS)
Compartment Trail	(NS)
Chatfield Trail	(NS)
Secor Trail	(NS)
Ledge Trail	(NS)
Black Rock Hollow Trail	(NS)
Reservoir Trail	(NS)
White Oak Trail	(NS)
Swamp Trail	(NS)
Hill of Pines Trail	(NS)

Schunemunk Mountain Region

Jessup Trail	(NS)
Western Ridge Trail	2.3
Barton Swamp Trail	1.6
Sweet Clover Trail	2.8
Forest Trail	2.3

Hudson Highlands East of the River Region

Mount Beacon–Breakneck Ridge–
Mt. Taurus Area

Three Notch Trail	8
Washburn Trail	2
Breakneck Ridge Trail	(NS)
Casino Trail	2.3

Taconics and Stissing Mountain Region

Race Brook Trail	1.7
Sunset Rock and Gray Birch Trails	4.75 (RT)
Alander Trail	(NS)
Bash Bish Falls	.8
Northrup Trail	1.3
Stissing Mountain Circular	1.7
Under Mountain Trail	2

Fahnestock State Park Region

Housatonic Range Trail	8

NORTH CAROLINA

Natahala National Forest Region

Cheoh District

Hooper Bald Trail	11.5
Laurel Top Trail	2.5
King Meadows Junction Trail	7.5
Big Snowbird Trail	6
Slickrock Creek Trail	8.25
Ike Branch Trail	2.75
Hangover Lead Trail	5.5
Nichols Cove Branch Trail	2
Big Fat Branch Trail	1.5
Deep Creek Trail	3
Naked Ground Trail	4.5
Haoe Trail	5.75

Stratton Bald Trail	8.5
Yellow Creek Mountain Trail	8

Tusquittee District

Snowbird Mountain Trail	6.5
Rim Trail	27
Big Stamp Trail	7

Wayah District

Trimont Trail	10.5
Holloway Branch Trail	1.5
Kimsey Creek Trail	3.7
Lower Trail Ridge Trail	3.5
Trail Ridge Trail	3.5
Park Gap Trail	4
Long Branch Trail	2.3
Hurricane Creek Trail	2
Big Indian Trail	3.7
Bearpen Gap Trail	2.7
Laurel Branch Trail	1.5
Appletree Trail	2
Laurel Creek Trail	2
Diamond Valley Trail	1
London Bald Trail	9
Nantahala Trail	6
Hickory Branch Trail	1.5
Junaluska Trail	4
Choga Trail	6
Tusquitee Loop Trail	8.5
Tusquitee Bald Trail	(NS)

Highlands District

Ellicotts Rock Trail	3.5

Pisgah National Forest Region

Pisgah District

Sorrell Creek Trail	2.5
Art Loeb Trail	32
Crawford Trail	2
Old Butt Knob Trail	3
Little East Fork Trail	5.8
Graveyard Fields	4.5
Big East Fork of Pigeon River Trail	4
Fork Mountain Trail	6
Bear Trail Ridge Trail	3
Haywood Gap Trail	5
Buckeye Gap Trail	4.5
Green Mountain Trail	7
Coon Hollow Trail	2
Courthouse Trail	2
Summey Cove Trail	2
Flat Laurel Trail	2.5
Big Bear Trap Trail	2.5
Farlow Gap Trail	5.3
Cove Creek Trail	4
Caney Bottom Trail	2
Butter Gap Trail	3
Cat Gap Trail	2.4
Horse Cove Trail	2
Kings Creek Trail	2
Looking Glass Rock Trail	5

Black Mountain & South Fork Mills River
Trail Networks

Sharpy Mountain Trail	7
Buckwheat Knob Trail	5
Soapstone Ridge Trail	1.3
Coon Tree Mountain Trail	2
Black Mountain Trail	4.5
Buckhorn Trail	2.7
Club Gap Trail	3
South Mills River Trail	11
Cantrell Creek Trail	2.2
Pounding Mill Trail	1.5
Mullinax Trail	1
Vineyard Gap Trail	3
Squirrel Gap Trail	7.9
Old Bradley Creek Gap Trail	4.2
Laurel Mountain Trail	8.4
Big Creek Trail	5
North Mills River Trail	2
Spencer Branch Trail	2.3
Trace Ridge Trail	3
Thompson Ridge Trail	2
Pilot Rock Trail	2

Toecane District

Mount Mitchell Trail 5.6
Maple Camp Bald Trail (NS)
Black Mountain Trail 6.5
Colberts Ridge Trail 3.7
Bald Knob Ridge Trail 2.8
Buncombe Horse Range Trail 8
Lost Cove Ridge Trail 3.1
Maple Camp Bald Trail 7
Big Butt Trail 7
Grandfather District
 Shortoff Mountain Trail 6
 Linville Gorge Trail 3.5
 Pine Gap Trail 2.5
 Bynum Bluff Trail .5
 Cabin Trail .5
 Babel Tower Trail 2.5
 Devils Hole Trail 1
 Sandy Flats Trail .5
 Spencer Ridge Trail 1.5
 Tablerock Trail 1
 Conley Cove Trail .7
 Pinch In Trail 1
French Broad District
 Pigeon River Trail 8

Great Smoky Mountains National Park Region

Abrams Falls Trail (NS)
Cucumber Gap Trail (NS)
Huskey Gap Trail (NS)
Alum Cave Trail (NS)
Boulevard Trails (NS)
Rainbow Springs Trail (NS)
Indian Creek Trail (NS)

OHIO

Shawnee State Forest Region

Shawnee Backpack Trail 20

Wayne National Forest Region

Vesuvius Trail 15

Other Trails

Buckeye Trail 760

OREGON

Rogue River Trail (NS)
Oregon Skyline Trail (NS)
Lostine River Trail 6
Santiam Lake Trail (NS)
Perdition Trail (NS)
Eagle Creek Trail (NS)
Horsetail Falls Trail 1
Timberline Trail 37
Tilly Jane Trail 1
Cooper Spur Trail (NS)
Gnarl Ridge Trail (NS)
Grizzly Park Trail (NS)
Triangulation Trail (NS)
St. Perpetua Trail 1.25
Riggin' Slinger Trail 1.4
Captain Cook Trail .6
Restless Waters Trail (NS)
Toketee Falls Trail (NS)
Cleetwood Trail (NS)
Lightening Springs Trail (NS)

PENNSYLVANIA

Allegheny National Forest Region

North Country Trail 78
Tanbark Trail 28
Minister Valley Trail 6
Twin Lakes Trail 6
Tracy Ridge Trail 4
Johnnycake Trail 2
Black Cherry Interpretive Trail 1.9

Western Region

Clark Run Trail 1.8
John P. Saylor Memorial Trail 11.3
Charleroi Interurban Trail 25
Warrior Trail 67

Baker Trail 140
Laurel Highlands Hiking Trail 75
Sandy Beaver Trail 23

Central Region

Black Forest Trail 42
Susquehannock Trail System 85
Darlington Trail 25
Donut Hole Trail System 32
Loyalsock Trail 57
Tuscarora Trail 92.5
Mid-State Trail 55
Forbes Road Historic Trail 29

Eastern Region

French Creek State Park
 Boone Trail (NS)
 Turtle Trail (NS)
 Raccoon Trail (NS)
 Lenape Trail (NS)
 Buzzard's Trail (NS)
 Fire Trail (NS)

Other Trails

Wilderness Trail 10
Delaware and Lehigh Canal Towpath Trail 60
Horse-Shoe Trail 124

RHODE ISLAND

Northwest Region

Walkabout Trail 8

Southwest Region

Breakheart Trail 14.3
Ben Utter Trail 4.3
Escoheag Trail 2
John B. Hudson Trail 1.6
Arcadia Trail 3.4
Tippecansett Trail 45.5

SOUTH CAROLINA

Sumter National Forest Region

Andrew Pickens Ranger District
 Foothills Trail 18
Kings Mountain State Park Area
 Gold Nugget Trail 1.5
Table Rock State Park Area
 Table Rock Trail 4
 Pinnacle Mountain Trail 4

TENNESSEE

Big Ridge State Park Region

Dark Hollow Trail 4
Indian Rock Trail 4
Indian Hollow Trail 2

Frozen Head State Park Region

Panther Branch Trail 2.5
North Mac Mountain Trail 3
Spicewood Trail 2.5
Boundary Trail 35

Pickett State Park Region

Hidden Passage Trail 8
Buff Trail 1
Rock Creek Trail 6
Hazard Cave Trail (NS)
Indian Rock House Trail (NS)
Ridge Trail 3
North Ridge Trail 7.5
Blue Beaver Trail 7.3
Piney River Trail 4
Twin Rocks Nature Trail 2
Laurel-Snow Pocket Wilderness Trail 8
Honey Creek Pocket Wilderness Trail 5
Virgin Falls Pocket Wilderness Trail 8

Cherokee National Forest Region

Tellico Ranger District
 Fodderstack Trail 11
 Mill Branch Trail 3.2
 Crowder Creek Trail 2.5

Pinestand Ridge Trail 5.1
North Fork of Citico Creek Trail 3.5
Brush Mountain Trail 6
South Fork of Citico Creek Trail 7.8
Grassy Branch Trail 4.5
Flats Mountain Trail 6.5
The Long Branch Trail 2.7
Hemlock Trail 3.5
McNabb Creek Trail 3.7
Laurel Branch Trail 3.1
Big Cove Branch Trail 3.2
Sugar Cove Trail 2.4
Bald River Trail 5.6
Cow Camp Trail 1
Henderson Mountain Trail 5.7
Brookshire Trail 3
Hiwassee District
 Chestnut Mountain Trail 3.5
 Unicoi Mountain Trail 6
 John Muir Trail 3
Ocoee Ranger District
 Lick Log Trail 8
 Big Frog Trail 6.5
 Big Creek Trail 6.4
 Wolf Ridge Trail 7
 Pace Ridge Trail 2
 Grassy Gap Trail 7
 Chestnut Mountain Trail 3
 Fork Ridge Trail 5
 Rough Creek Trail 6.5
 Low Gap Trail 1
 Caney Creek Trail 7.8
 Indian Flats Trail 5.6
 Rock Creek Trail 6.6
Nolichucky Ranger District
 Meadow Creek Mountain Trail 14.9
 Gum Springs Trail 2.6
 Big Jennings Creek Trail 5
 Stone Mountain Trail 4.3
Onaka Ranger District
 Laurel Fork Trail 6.1
 Leonard Branch Trail 2.8
 Patty Ridge Trail 5
Watauga Ranger District
 Pond Mountain Trail 7.9
 Holston Trail 12
 Josiah Creek Trail 3
 Flint Mill Trail 2.2
 Morrill Trail 2
 Iron Mountain Trail 20

UTAH

Highline Trail 6.5
Timpooneke Trail 9.1
Timpanogos Trail 8.3
White Canyon Trail 4
Fairyland Trail 8
Queens Garden Trail .8
Navajo Trail 1.5
Peek-a-boo Trail 3
Rainbow Point Trail (NS)
Rim Trail (NS)
East Rim Trail .6
Narrows Trail 15
West Rim Trail 13
Cuberant Lake Trail 2

VERMONT

Mount Equinox Trail 3 (RT)
Lye Brook Wilderness Trail 15.4 (RT)
Lye Brook Trail to waterfalls 4.6 (RT)
Keewaydin Trail 3.2 (RT)
Long Trail 5.5 (RT)
Leicester Hollow Trail 8 (RT)
Snake Mountain Trail 4 (RT)
Battell Trail 7.2 (RT)
Forest City Trail 7.5 (RT)
Mount Mansfield Area
 Bear Pond Trail 2.3 (RT)
 Hell Brook Trail 4 (RT)

Belvidere Mountain Area
Forester Trail ... 5.4 (RT)

VIRGINIA

Shenandoah National Park Region
Big Blue Trail	(NS)
Dickey Ridge Trail	9
White Oak Canyon Trail	5
Falls Trail	4.5

George Washington National Forest Region
Lee Ranger District
Massanutten Mountain Trail	23
Duncan Hollow Trail	8
Bear Wallow Trail	3
Massanutten Mountain North Trail	2

Pedlar District
Cold Springs Trail	4.5
St. Mary's River Trail	6
Stony Run Trail	3
Kennedy Ridge Trail	3.5

Dry River District
Slate Springs Mountain Trail	8
Slate Springs Trail	4
Big Hollow Trail	2
Mines Run Trail	3
Timber Ridge Trail	8
Sand Spring Mountain Trail	3
Grooms Ridge Trail	4
North River Trail	4
Dull Hunt Trail	8

Deerfield District
Shenandoah Mountain Trail	31
Jerkemtight Trail	4.5
Jerrys Run Trail	2.5
Ramseys Draft Trail	4.5
Dividing Ridge Trail	5
Walker Mountain Trail	8
North Mountain Trail	10
Elliott Knob Trail	4.5
Crawford Mountain Trail	6
Chimney Hollow Trail	3
Crawford Knob Trail	4

Jefferson National Forest Region
Mount Rogers District
Iron Mountain Trial	24
Little Laurel Creek Trail	3.5
Mount Rogers Trail	6.9
Iron Mountain Trail	10.5
Henley Hollow Trail	1.4
Horse Heaven Trail	3.1
Yellow Branch Trail	3.5

Blacksburg Ranger District
Potts Mountain Trail	7.5

New Castle Ranger District
Potts Mountain Trail	12
Potts Arm Trail	6
Price Broad Mountain Trail	10
Sulphur Ridge Trail	4.8
Lick Branch Trail	6.7
North Mountain Trail	13.2

Glenwood Ranger District
Wildcat Trail	4
Pine Mountain Trail	4.9
Cornelius Creek Trail	3.1
Piney Ridge Trail	3.5
Big Belfast Trail	3

WASHINGTON
Horseshoe Bend Trail	2
Elcelsior Ridge Trail	2
Skyline Divide Trail	2
Gargett Mine Trail	3
Lone Jack Mine Trail	1

Baker Lake Region
East Bank Trail	2
Baker River Trail	3

Diablo and Ross Dams Region
Thunder Arm Trail	1

Diablo Lake Trail ... (NS)

Darrington Region
Clear Creek Trail	1

Suiattle River Region
Buck Creek Trail	5
Green Mountain Trail	4.25
Downey Creek Trail	3
Sulphur Creek Trail	2
Suiattle River Trails	(NS)

Stevens Pass Region
Troublesome Creek Trail	1.5
Tonga Ridge Trail	1.5
Lake Susan Jane Trail	.75
Nason Ridge Trail	4.7

Icicle Creek Region
Icicle Creek Bridal Trail	2

Lake Wenatchee Region
South Shore Lake Trail	(NS)
Little Wenatchee Trail	1.5
Bluff View Trail	.25
Big Tree Loop Trail	.5
Mine View Trail	.25
Panther Creek Trail	1
Glacier Peak Wilderness Trails	2

Entiat River Region
Mad River Trail	(NS)
Stormy Mountain Trail	15

Lake Chelan Region
Lakeshore Trail	17.5

Stehekin River Region
Purple Creek Trail	8
Chelan Crest (Summit) Trail	36

North Cascades Region
Cascade Crest Trail	(NS)

Deception Pass State Park Region
Rosario Trail	(NS)
Cranberry Lake Trail	(NS)

Moran State Park Region
Mountain Lake Trail	3.6
Little Summit Lookout Trail	3.9
Cold Spring Trail	2
Twin Lake Trail	2.1
Around-the-Lake Trail	4 (RT)
South End Trail	(NS)

Hood Canal Region
Mount Ellinor Trail	2
Staircase Rapids Trail	3.5
Shady Lane Trail	.75
Dose Forks Trail	1.5

Olympics Region
North Area
Obstruction Point Trail	.75
Slab Camp Trail	1
Lake Creek Trail	2
Meadow Trail	4.6
High Ridge Loop Trail	1
Grand Lake Trail	2
Deer Park Trail	7.6
West Elwha Trail	2.6
Lake Mills Trail	1.9
Pyramid Peak Trail	3.5
Lover's Lane Trail	3.7

Northwest Area
Hall of Mosses Nature Trail	.75
Spruce Nature Trail	1.5

Southwest Area
Seven Beach Trails	12
Kalaloch Creek Trail	2
Queets River Loop Trail	3
Big Tree Grove Nature Trail	2
Enchanted Valley Trail	11

Other Trails
Lewis and Clark Trail	(NS)

WEST VIRGINIA

Dolly Sods Scenic Region
Blackbird Knob Trail	2
Red Creek Trail	6.5
Breathed Mountain Trail	2.5
Big Stonecoal Trail	4
Rocky Point Trail	2
Fisher Springs Trail	2
Little Stonecoal Trail	1.5
Cabin Mountain Trail	2.5
Dunkenbarger Run Trail	1.25
Rohrbaugh Plains Trail	3

Otter Creek Region
Otter Creek Trail	11
Yellow Creek Trail	3
McGowan Mountain Trail	2
Moore Run Trail	4
Turkey Run Trail	2
Green Mountain Trail	5
Big Spring Gap Trail	1
Shavers Mountain Trail	13

Cranberry Back Country Region
Trails Near the Middle Fork of Williams River
Little Fork Trail	3.5
County Line Trail	11.5
Turkey Mountain Trail	16
District Line Trail	3
Big Beechy Trail	4.5
North-South Trail	19.5

Trails in Cranberry River Area
Forks of Cranberry Trail	5.75
Kennison Mountain Trail	8.5
Cow Pasture Trail	7
Frosty Gap Trail	5.75
Pocahontas Trail	18

Spruce Knob–Seneca Rocks National Recreation Region
North Mountain Trail	23
Kimble Trail	11
Redman Trail	2
Landis Trail	(NS)
Spruce Mountain Trail	3.5
Lumberjack Trail	10
Seneca Creek Trail	11.5
The Allegheny Trail	8.5
Big Run of Gandy Trail	3
Swallow Rock Run Trail	2.5
Little Allegheny Trail	5
Horton-Horserack Trail	8

Greenbrier Region
Shavers Mountain Trail	16
Johns Camp Trail	1
Laurel Fork Trail	15.2
Camp Five Run Trail	1.5
Lynn Knob Trail	4.25
Beulah Trail	3.75
Middle Mountain Trail	1.5
McCray Run Trail	4.5
County Line Trail	5
Burner Mountain Trail	6
Chestnut Ridge Trail	5.5
Laurel Run Trail	2.5
Little Mountain Trail	5.2
McGee Run Trail	2.5

WISCONSIN
Ahnapee Trail	15
Sparta-Elroy Trail	32

Chequamegon National Forest Region
North Country Trail	60
Mt. Valhalla Trail	17
Flambeau Trail	60.5

Rock Island State Park Region
Rock Island State Park Trails	8

Park Falls Region
Tuscobia Trail	74

WYOMING

Yellowstone National Park Region

Lone Star Geyser Trail	7
De Lacy Creek Trail	3

Grand Teton National Park Region

Taggart Lake Trail	(NS)
Valley Trail	(NS)
Skyline Trail	(NS)

Granite Creek Trail	12
Death Canyon Shelf Trail	(NS)
Cascade Canyon Trail	(NS)
Paintbrush Canyon Trail	6.5

Bridger Wilderness Region

Highline Trail	(NS)
Porcupine Trail	(NS)
Twin Lakes Trail	(NS)

Other Trails

Swift Creek Trail	(NS)
Crystal Creek Trail	(NS)
West Tensleep Creek Trail	(NS)
Solitude Trail	7.5
Rock Creek Trail	(NS)
Shoshone Trail	14
Lonesome Lake Trail	32
Lizard Head Trail	(NS)
Bear's Ear Trail	(NS)

Canada—Intraprovincial Trails

ALBERTA — Miles

Banff National Park Region

Paradise Valley Circuit	11
Sundance Canyon Loop	1.3

Jasper National Park Region

Skyline Trail	27.4
Opal Hills Loop	5.1
Riley Lake Loop	5.7
Caledonia Loop Trip	20

Waterton Lakes National Park Region

Tamarack Trail	17.4
Carthew Trail	12.5
Lakeshore Trail	5
Crandell Mountain Circuit	12
"Mother Duck" Trail	14.5
North Fork Trail	5

BRITISH COLUMBIA

Kootenay National Park Region

Juniper Trail	2
Redstreak Trail	1.6

MANITOBA

Riding Mountain National Park Region

Ma-ee-gun Trail	.6
Ominnik Marsh Trail	1.2
Clear Lake Trail	15
Evergreen Trail	1
Loon's Island Trail	1.5
Arrowhead Trail	1.7
Brûlé Trail	2.6
Grey Owl Trail	10
Escarpment Trail	40
Muskrat Lake Trail	10
Kelwood Trail	3.2
Gorge Creek Trail	4
Burls and Bittersweet Trail	1.4
Packhorse Creek Trail	6
Moon Lake Trail	6
Cowan Lake Trail	5

NEW BRUNSWICK

Fundy Coast Region

Fundy Coast Walking Trail	25
Fundy Hiking Trail	40

Fundy National Park

Kinnie Brook Nature Trail	1
Big Dam Trail	5.5

Laverty Trail	5
Tracey Lake Trail	3
Caribou Plain Loop	2.5

NOVA SCOTIA

Cape Breton Island Region

Visge Bhan Falls Walking Trail	10
The Arcadian Trail	65

Cape Breton Highlands National Park

Jumping Brook Trail	7
Fishing Cove Trail	4
South Mountain to Lobster Lake Trail	4
Cap Rouge Circuit	2

Kejimkujik National Park

Mills Falls/Slapfoot Trails	7
Big Dam/Frozen Ocean Trail	6.5
Kejimkujik Circuit	33

ONTARIO

Bruce Trail	430
Ganaraska Trail	68
Highland Hiking Trail	17
Rideau Trail	200
Quinte-Hastings Recreational Trail	235

Unnamed Trails in the U.S. and Canada

U.S.—Intrastate Trails

ARKANSAS — Miles

Ozark National Forest Region

Richland Creek Campground to Twin Falls	3
Richland Creek Campground to Forest Road 1220	9
Whitaker Creek downstream	5
Arkansas Route 74 to Leatherwood Creek	2.75

Sylamore Forest Area

North Sylamore Creek to

Forest Road 1102	2.25
North Sylamore Creek to its headwaters	3

Hot Springs National Park Area

Gulpa Gorge Campground up

Indian Mountain	.5
Circle path around West Mountain	2.75

Ouachita National Forest Region

Rich Mountain Tower to Winding

Stair Mountain	22
Trail to Lover's Leap	(NS)
Trail around Cedar Lake	2

CALIFORNIA

San Bernardino Region

Cajon Pass to Cleghorn Mountain	8
Cleghorn Pass to Cajon Mountain Lookout	7
Cleghorn Fire Road to Sugarpine Springs, Sugarpine Mountain	8
Sawpit Canyon to Monument Peak	4
Bailey Canyon to Monument Peak	10
Rim of the World Highway to	

Marshall Peak	4
Arrowhead Springs to the Arrowhead, Arrowhead Peak	6
Saddle Flats to Pilot Rock	4
Toll Road Public Campground to the Pinnacles	6
North Shore Public Campground to Little Bear Creek	5
Deep Creek to Devil's Hole	3
Hook Creek to Deep Creek, Holcomb Creek, Tent Peg Trail Camp, Big Pine Flat	9
Coxey Meadow to Coxey Creek, Deep Creek	6
Hawes Ranch to Barrel Spring, Muddy Spring	6
Hawes Ranch to Shay Mountain	4
Hawes Ranch to Cox Creek, Holcomb Creek	6
Forest Road 3N12 to Delamar Mountain	2.5
Holcomb Valley Road to Bertha Peak	2
Double Mine (ruins) to Gold Mountain	4
Cactus Flat to Silver Peak (Blackhawk Mountain)	4

San Gabriel Mountain Region

Horse Trail Public Campground to

Liebre Mountain	6
Atmore Meadows to Gillette Mine, Bear Canyon	10
Bouquet Canyon to Big Oak Tree, Sierra Pelona	7
Gold Creek to Oak Spring,	

Fascination Spring	8
Big Tujunga via Trail Canyon to Tom Lucas Trail Camp, Big Cienaga	8
Big Tujunga via Stone Canyon Trail to Mt. Lukens	8
Angeles Crest Highway via Mt. Lukens Fire Road to Mt. Lukens	10
Altadena via Arroyo Seco to Oakwilde	9
Switzer Campground to Commodore Switzer Trail Camp, Bear Canyon, Bear Canyon Trail Camp	8
Millard Canyon to Dawn Mine	5
Millard Canyon to Millard Canyon Falls	1
Altadena to Rubio Canyon	1.5
Altadena to Henninger Flats	5
Eaton Saddle to Markham Saddle, Mt. Lowe	3
Eaton Saddle to Markham Saddle, San Gabriel Peak	3.5
Josephine Fire Road to Josephine Peak Lookout	6
Red Box to Strawberry Peak, Josephine Saddle, Colby Canyon	7
Red Box to Strawberry Spring, Strawberry Potrero	8
Sierra Madre via Little Santa Anita Canyon to Orchard Camp	9
Chantry Flat via Winter Creek to Mt. Wilson	(NS)
Duarte to Fish Canyon, Fish Cayon Falls	5
West Fork via Valley Forge Trail to Eaton Saddle, Mt. Wilson Road	(NS)
West Fork via Rattlesnake Trail to	

Upper Delaware Valley Region

Riegelsville to Easton	18 (RT)
Hike to Hexenkopf Rock	12
Delaware Palisades and Ringing Rocks	9
Uhlerstown to Upper Black Eddy	10
Ralph Stover State Park Hike	11
Hike to Devil's Tea Table	11
New Hope to Washington State Park and Bowman's Hill	9
Washington Crossing to Trenton	15 (RT)

The Pine Barrens of New Jersey

Hike around Lake Absegami in Bass River State Forest	15 (RT)
Lake Absegami to Martha	7
Oswego Lake in Penn State Forest to Bear Swamp	5 (RT)
Batsto to Atsion in Wharton State Forest	10
Hike around Pakim Pond in Lebanon State Forest	10

NEW YORK

Adirondacks Region

High Peaks Area

Route 9 to Summit of Giant	5
Ridge of Giant to bottom	6.75
Ridge of Giant to Keene	5.25
Trail up Mount Dix	6.7
Trail to Marcy from Elk Lake	10.96
Tahawus to Indian Pass	9 (RT)
Tahawus to Heart Lake	10.2
Tahawus to Heart Lake via Lake Colden	21 (RT)
Tahawus Ghost Town to Duck Hole	6.45

Moose River Recreation Area

Cedar River to Wakely Mountain	2.7
Interior Headquarters to Lost Pond	2
West Lake to South Lake	7.5
Pillsbury Lake to Cedar Lakes	2
West Lake to Brooktrout Lake	1.6
West Lake to Deep Lake	2.1
Horn Lake to Stink Lake	2.25
Western terminus of Primary Road to Red River	1

Lake George Area

Route 9N to Tongue Mountain	15.3
Shelving Rock Road to Pilot Knob	5.8
Erebus Mountain to Lake George	5.56
Fish Lake Pond to Lake George	3

Palisades Region

Fort Lee to Englewood Boat Basin	3
Englewood Boat Basin to Alpine Landing	5.5
Alpine to Forest View	2.5
Forest View to State Line	2
Fort Lee to Englewood Cliffs	2
Englewood Cliffs to Alpine	5.5
Alpine to Scout Camp	2.5

Scout Camp to State Line	2
State Line to Piermont	3
Piermont to Nyack	7.5
Nyack to Long Clove along the Ridge	6
Long Clove to Nyack by the Shore Path	6.5
Long Clove to Mt. Ivy	6.3

Shawangunk Mountains Region

Minnewaska Area

Wildmere House to Millbrook Mountain	4
Millbrook Mountain to Gertrude's Nose	1.8
Wildmere House to Lake Awosting	6
Ellenville to Lake Awosting	6
Lake Awosting to Sam's Point	4

Finger Lakes Region

Enfield Glen in Robert H. Treman State Park	3
Hike through Watkins Glen	3

Catskills Region

South Approach to Balsam Lake Mountain Observatory	2.75
North Approach to Balsam Lake Mountain Observatory	3.05
Woodland Creek to Winnisook Lodge	6
Winnisook Lodge to Wittenberg Mountain summit	3
Summit of Wittenberg Mountain to Woodland Valley	8.6
North of Slide Mountain—Giant Ledge and Panther Mountain	8

New York Central Former Rights-of-Way

Millwood Station to Croton Reservoir	3
Former Croton Lake Station to Lake Mahopac	10.5
Goldens Bridge to Lake Mahopac	7.2

SOUTH CAROLINA

Sumter National Forest Region

Kings Mountain State Park and Military Park Area	
York Lake to border of Park	5.5 (RT)
Lake Crawford to National Military Park	3
Corbin Mountain Area	
Base of mountain to lookout tower	2
Sassafras Mountain Area	
Fire tower to Hickory Nut Mountain	2

TENNESSEE

Cherokee National Forest Region

Tellico Ranger District	
Farr Gap to the Little Tennessee River	4
Forest Road 59 to Forest Road	3.4
Forest Road 126 to Sandy Gap	4.5
Ocoee Ranger District	

Sylco Recreation Area to Cookson Creek Road	6.5
Chilhowee Recreation Area to Tennessee Route 30	4
Thunder Rock Recreation Area to Forest Road 68	6.5
Nolichucky Ranger District	
Pigeon Valley Church to Forest Road 207	6.8
Unaka Ranger District	
Limestone Cove Recreation Area to Stamping Grounds Ridge	4.3
Watauga Ranger District	
U.S. 321 to Forest Road 39	3.5
Forest Road 87 to Holston Mountain	2.5

UTAH

Uinta Mountains

Christmas Meadows to Amethyst Lake	12
Christmas Meadows to Ryder Lake	19
Hayden Meadows to Blue Lake	11
Hayden Meadows to Jordan and Schuler Lakes	12
Mirror Lakes Campground to Bald Mountain	1.5
Mirror Lake Campground to Twin Lakes	(NS)

VIRGINIA

George Washington National Forest Region

Virginia Route 678 to Signal Knob	.5
Sherando Lake to Bald Mountain	4
Forest Road 249 to Hone Quarry Ridge	8
Chestnut Ridge to Little Bald Knob	7
Forest Road 95 to Tearjacket Knob	3.5

Jefferson National Forest Region

Forest Road 59 to Apple Orchard Falls	2.7
Forest Road 45 to Appalachian Trail	3
Virginia Route 782 to Appalachian Trail	3
Virginia Route 759 to Appalachian Trail	4.5

WISCONSIN

Chequamegon National Forest Region

Lake Three Campground to Brunsweiler River	3.8
Lake Three Campground to Marengo River	16.8
Beaver Lake Campground to Marengo River	10.8
Two Lakes Campground to Marengo River	28
Two Lakes Campground to Lake Owen Picnicgrounds	7
Forest Road 228 to Forest Road 392	12.8

Canada—Intraprovincial Trails

ALBERTA	Miles
Banff National Park Region	
Banff-Jasper Highway to Nigel Pass	4
Banff-Jasper Highway to Saskatchewan Glacier Viewpoint	1.5
Banff-Jasper Highway to Sunset Lookout	2.8
Banff-Jasper Highway to Sunset Pass	5.1
Banff-Jasper Highway to Pinto Lake	8.5
Banff-Jasper Highway to Glacier Lake Campsite	5.7
Banff-Jasper Highway to Sarbach Lookout	3.2
Waterfowl Lakes Campground to Chephren Lake	2.5
Waterfowl Lakes Campground to Cirque Lake	2.9
Crowfoot Glacier Viewpoint to Helen Lake	3.7

Crowfoot Glacier Viewpoint to Katherine Lake	5
Crowfoot Glacier Viewpoint to Dolomite Pass	5.5
Num-ti-jah Lodge to Bow Glacier Falls	2.7
Banff-Jasper Highway to Peyto Lake	.9
Banff-Jasper Highway to Hector Lake	1.3
Moraine Lake Picnic Area to Lower Consolation Lake	1.8
Moraine Lake to Eiffel Lake	3.5
Moraine Lake to Larch Valley	1.5
Moraine Lake to Sentinel Pass	3.6
Moraine Lake to Paradise Creek via Sentinel	10.4
Moraine Lake Road to Lake Annette	3.4
Lake Louise to Saddleback	2.3
Lake Louise to Plain-of-Six Glaciers Teahouse	3.3

Lake Louise to Plain-of-Six Glaciers Viewpoint	4.1
Lake Louise to Mirror Lake	1.6
Lake Louise to Lake Agnes	2.1
Lake Louise to Big Beehive	3.1
Temple Lodge to Boulder Pass	2.9
Temple Lodge to Skoki Lodge	6.5
Taylor Creek Picnic Area to Taylor Lake	3.9
Taylor Creek Picnic Area to O'Brien Lake	5.1
Boom Creek Picnic Area to Boom Lake	3.2
Eisenhower Warden Station to Tower Lake	4.8
Eisenhower Warden Station to Rockbound Lake	5.2
Johnston's Canyon Lodge to Lower Falls	.7
Johnston's Canyon Lodge to Upper Falls	1.7
Johnston's Canyon Lodge to Ink Pots	3.6
Eisenhower Picnic Area to Lower Twin Lake	4.5

1-A Highway to Eisenhower Lookout 2.3
Bourgeau Parking Lot to Healy Pass 5.7
Bourgeau Parking Lot to Egypt Lake 8.2
Bourgeau Parking Lot to Trans-Canada
via Whistling Valley 24.8
Trans-Canada Highway to Bourgeau Lake 4.6
Minnewanka Picnic Area to Aylmer
Lookout 6.9
Minnewanka Picnic Area to Aylmer Pass 8
Mount Norquay Parking Lot to
Elk Lake 8.4
Mount Norquay Parking Lot to
Cascade Amphitheatre 4.3
Trans-Canada Highway to Edith Pass 2.5
Mount Norquay to Trans-Canada via
Edith Pass 7.6
Spray Reservoir to Assiniboine Lodge via
Wonder Pass 12.4
Spray Reservoir to Assiniboine Lodge via
Assiniboine Pass 11
Sunshine Village to Assiniboine Lodge 16.9
Trans-Canada Highway to Cory Pass 4
Spray River to Mount Rundle Slope 3
Eisenhower Picnic Area to Smith Lake .9
Lake Minnewanka Road to C Level Cirque 2.4
Sundance Canyon to Bryant Creek via
Allenby Pass 28
Banff Townsite to Spray Reservoir 25
Spray Reservoir to Palliser Pass 15
Mount Norquay to Johnston Canyon
Lodge via Forty Mile Creek 24
Johnston Canyon Lodge to Baker Creek
via Pulsatilla Pass 22
Trans-Canada Highway to Lake
Minnewanka 9
Minnewanka Picnic Area to Devil's Gap 17
Baker Creek Cabins to Baker Lake 14
Mosquito Creek Campground to
Molar Pass 7
Trans-Canada Highway to Pipestone Pass 25
Pipestone Pass to Park Boundary 14
Dolomite Pass to Park Boundary 13
Banff-Jasper Highway to Howse Pass 17
Howse River to Forbes Brook
Headwaters 9
Banff-Jasper Highway to Castleguard
River 14
Alexandra River to Thompson Pass 8
East Boundary to Clearwater Pass 20
Clearwater River to North Boundary 8
Scotch Camp to Clearwater River 18
Minnewanka Road to East Boundary 45
Windy Warden Cabin to East Boundary 10
Scotch Camp to Red Deer Lakes 17
Cascade Fire Road to East Boundary via
Dormer Pass 22
Cascade Fire Road to Badger Pass 15
Cascade Fire Road to Sawback Lake 11
Panther River to Red Deer River 10

Jasper National Park Region

Maligne Lake to Bald Hills Lookout 3.2
Beaver Creek Picnic Area to
Jacques Lake 7.6
Edith Cavell Road to Tonquin Valley
Lodge 12
Cavell Chalet to Angel Glacier Viewpoint 2.0
Parking Area to Fryatt Creek Falls 12.2
Geraldine Fire Road to Lower
Geraldine Lake 1.1
Yellowhead Highway to Virl Lake 2.4
Yellowhead Highway to Dorothy Lake 2.4
Yellowhead Highway to Christine Lake 2.6
Banff-Jasper Highway to Lake Five 1.4
Banff-Jasper Highway to Wabasso Lake 1.7
Pyramid Lake to Palisade Lookout 6.7
Nature House to Kinney Lake 2.8
Nature House to Berg Lake 11
Jasper Warden Station to Caledonia Lake 2.6
Miette Hot Springs to Mystery Lake 8
Miette Hot Springs to Fiddle
River Headwaters 17

Celestine Fire Road to Vine
Creek Headwaters 6
Railway Line to Park Boundary 15
Celestine Lake Fire Road to
Twintree Lake 65
Snake Indian River to North Boundary via
Mowitch Creek 14
Snake Indian River to North Boundary via
Blue Creek 20
Robson Pass to North Boundry 27
Smoky River to Moose Pass 5
Smoky River to Carcajou Pass 4
Smoky River to Bess Pass 4
Yellowhead Pass to Centre Pass 13
Moab Lake to Athabaska Pass 27
Sunwapta Canyon to Fortress Lake 14
Camp Parker to Brazeau Lake via
Nigel Pass 20
Poboktan Creek Warden Cabin to Brazeau
Lake via Poboktan Pass 24
Poboktan Creek Warden Cabin to Maligne
Lake via Maligne Pass 30
Poboktan Creek to Brazeau River via
Jonas Pass 12
Brazeau Lake to Southesk River 26
Southesk River to Rocky River via
Southesk Pass 27
Cairn River to Rocky River Warden
Cabin via Southesk Lake 38
Jacques Lake to Rocky River Warden
Cabin 23

Waterton Lakes National Park Region

Snowshoe Fire Road to Goat Lake 1.5
Hell Roaring Boat Dock to Crypt Lake 5.4
Waterton Townsite Campground to
Bertha Lake 3.6
Camp INUSPI to Vimy Peak 7
Akamina Road to Crandel Lake .5
Information Centre to Bear's Hump .75
Akamina Road to Lineham Lakes 3.5
Akamina Highway to Lower Rowe Lake 2.5
Akamina Highway to Upper Rowe Lake 3.8
Red Rock Canyon Warden Station to
South Kootenay Pass 7
Snowshoe Cabin to Lost Lake 1.2
Snowshoe Cabin to Castle River Divide 1.9
Belly River Campground to International
Boundary 2.5

BRITISH COLUMBIA

**Glacier & Mount Revelstoke National
Parks Region**

Illecillewaet Campground to
Avalanche Crest 2.8
Illecillewaet Campground to
Perley Rock 3.5
Illecillewaet Campground to
Asulkan Valley Viewpoint 4
Illecillewaet Campground to
Marion Lake 1.6
Illecillewaet Campground to
Abbott Crest 4
Northlander Hotel to Balu Pass 3.4
Northlander Hotel to Trans-Canada via
Balu Pass 8.2
Trans-Canada Highway to Hermit Hut 1.7
Heather Lake to Millar Lake 3.7
Heather Lake to Eva Lake 4
Heather Lake to Upper Jade Lake 5.5
Illecillewaet Campground to
Glacier Crest 3.5
Illecillewaet Campground to
Illecillewaet Glacier Moraine 3
Trans-Canada Highway to Bald
Mountain Meadows 14.5
Trans-Canada Highway to Park Boundary 32
Silver Creek Bridge to Maunder Creek 4
Silver Creek Bridge to trail's end on West
Woolsey Creek 3.2
Trans-Canada Highway to Upper
Hamilton Creek 6.5

Kootenay National Park Region

Marbel Canyon Warden Station to
Tumbling Pass 9
Vermilion River to Floe Lake 6.3
Banff-Radium Highway to Kaufmann Lake 8.4
Banff-Radium Highway to Stanley Glacier
Meadows 2.6
Banff-Radium Highway to Park Boundary 5.2
Banff-Radium Highway to Cobb Lake 1.7
Vermilion Crossing to Honeymoon Pass 3.5
McLeod Meadows Picnic Area to Dog Lake 1.7
McKay Creek Campground to trail's end 3
Banff-Radium Highway to trail's end 3
Banff-Radium Highway to Nixon Lake .6
East Kootenay Fire Road to Pitts Pass 7
Banff-Radium Highway to Park Boundary 6
Vermilion Bridge to Park Boundary 5
Vermilion Crossing Picnic Area to
Upper Verendrye Valley 2.7
Banff-Radium Highway to Ball Pass 6
Marble Canyon Warden Station to
Ottertail Pass 9
Marble Canyon Warden Station to
Park Boundary via Ottertail 15
Ochre Creek to Goodsir Pass 7

Yoho National Park Region

Wapta Picnic Area to Sherbrooke Lake 1.9
Wapta Picnic Area to Paget Lookout 2.2
O'Hara Warden Cabin to Odaray Prospect 1.7
O'Hara Warden Cabin to Lake McArthur 2.2
O'Hara Warden Cabin to Lake Oesa 2
Opabin Plateau Circuit 3.2
Alpine Meadows to Linda Lake 2.5
Emerald Lake to Hamilton Lake 3.4
Field Warden Station to Burgess Pass 4.1
Field Warden Station to Emerald Lake via
Burgess Pass 8.5
Emerald Lake to Yoho Pass 3.9
Emerald Lake to Takakkaw via Yoho Pass 7.7
Yoho Pass-Burgess Pass Loop 11.9
Takakkaw Campground to Twin Falls 4.8
Twin Falls to Takakkaw Campground via
Highline 10.2
Wapta Falls Parking Area to Wapta Falls 1.5
Hoodoo Creek Campground to Hoodoos 1.9
Leanchoil Warden Station to Upper
Ice River 16
Trans-Canada Highway to Hunter Lookout 3.5
Ottertail Warden Station to McArthur
Creek 10
Ottertail Warden Station to Ottertail Pass 18
Ottertail River to Goodsir Pass 6
Lake O'Hara to Trans-Canada Highway via
McArthur Creek 17
Emerald Lake Circuit 3.3
Emerald Lake Parking Lot to
Emerald Basin 2.8
Emerald River Viewpoint to Amiskwi
Pass 20
1-A Highway to Ross Lake 1.8

NEW BRUNSWICK

Fundy National Park Region
Point Wolfe Road to Dickson Falls .75

NOVA SCOTIA

Western Region
Duncan's Cove to Ketch Harbor 3.5
Crystal Crescent Beach & Coote's Cove 3.25
Glen Margaret to Fourteen Mile House 9
Glen Margaret to Dover 6

Central Region
Porter's Lake to Goff's 9

Cape Breton Island Region
Sampson's Cove to Gros Nez (NS)

Kejimkujik National Park Region
Frozen Ocean to Peskawa Lake 15
Peskawa Lake to Mersey River 11

Sources for Topographic Maps

UNITED STATES

Public Inquiries Office
U.S. Geological Survey
108 Skyline Building
508 Second Avenue
Anchorage, Alaska 99501

Public Inquiries Office
U.S. Geological Survey
7638 Federal Building
300 North Los Angeles Street
Los Angeles, California 90012

Public Inquiries Office
U.S. Geological Survey
504 Custom House
555 Battery Street
San Francisco, California 94111

Public Inquiries Office
U.S. Geological Survey
1012 Federal Building
1961 Stout Street
Denver, Colorado 80202

Public Inquiries Office
U.S. Geological Survey
1028 General Services Building
19th and F Streets N.W.
Washington, D.C. 20244

Public Inquiries Office
U.S. Geological Survey
1C45 General Services Building
1100 Commerce Street
Dallas, Texas 75202

Public Inquiries Office
U.S. Geological Survey
8102 Federal Building
125 South State Street
Salt Lake City, Utah 84138

Public Inquiries Office
U.S. Geological Survey
1C402 National Center
Reston, Virginia 22092

Public Inquiries Office
U.S. Geological Survey
678 U.S. Court House
West 920 Riverside Avenue
Spokane, Washington 99201

CANADA

Publications and Air Photo Section
Institute of Sedimentary and
    Petroleum Geology
3303 33rd Street, N.W.
Calgary, Alberta T2L 2A7

Director, Technical Division
Department of Lands and Forests
Natural Resources Building
Edmonton, Alberta T5K 2E1

Director of Surveys and Mapping
Department of Lands, Forests and
    Water Resources
Parliament Building
Victoria, British Columbia V8B 1X5

Department of Renewable Resources
Survey Branch
1007 Century Street
Winnipeg, Manitoba R3H 0W4

Director of Crown Lands and
    Administration
Department of Mines and Energy
95 Bonaventure Avenue
St. John's, Newfoundland A1C 5T7

Ministry of Transportation and
    Communications
Record Services Section
Map Unit
Downsview, Ontario M3M 1J8

Canada Map Office
Department of Energy, Mines and
    Resources
615 Booth Street
Ottawa, Ontario K1A 0E9

Controller of Surveys
Lands and Surveys Branch
Department of Tourism and
    Renewable Resources
2340 Albert Street
Regina, Saskatchewan S4P 2V7

Ministry of Natural Resources
Map Office
6404 Whitney Block
Queen's Park
Toronto, Ontario M7A 1W4

Suggested Check List for Family Campers
Staying at Established Campgrounds

This does not include items of clothing which should be rough and ready items for hard outdoor wear, comfortable and suitable for weather and the type of activity planned. Check lists suitable for one person may appear ridiculous to another, so the reader might better merely use this list as a basis for one of his own tailored to his particular needs, his family's requirements and activities, and the type of camping he has planned to enjoy.

Tent, complete with all frames, poles, stakes and ground tarps. If more than one tent is used, each should be complete before leaving home.

Dining fly (open or screened) with all frames, poles, guys and stakes.

Camp stove (or stoves) with stand and fuel (propane, gasoline, alcohol or L/P).

Camp lantern/s using same fuel if possible as used by stoves.

Refrigerator large enough to hold sufficient ice for family needs plus food.

Sleeping bags for each member of party except small infant.

Air mattress, foam pad or cot for each member as preferred.

Air pump for inflating air mattresses. Also good to start stubborn campfire.

Folding table if none might be at tent site.

Folding chairs.

Cooking pots and pans, including large pail for carrying water, frying pan, bailed pots, and one pan big enough for dish washing or heating wash water.

Utensils, including knives, forks, spoons, serving spoons, spatulas, tongs, carving knife, long-handled fork (also used to make toast).

Plates, cups and bowls, plus staples and condiments to season food. Food up to tastes and requirements of individual campers.

Toaster for camp stove.

Lightweight tarpaulins to protect against sudden showers or night dampness.

Flashlights and spare batteries for each camper plus extra bulbs for searchlight types.

Ax or hatchet for kindling. A light ax is better than a small hatchet.

Small tool kit, including soft copper wire, small pliers with cutter, screwdriver to fit appliance screws, assorted nails and machine screws, rubber bands, small roll of 1″ paper masking tape. Also include a small flat file and whetstone for knives and ax.

Raingear for all party members plus rain boots for wet weather or wet grass.

Small shovel for latrine, garbage burial or excess water control.

25 feet of strong line or small rope for clothesline, lashing tarps and other uses.

Spring-clip clothespins for laundry on line, sealing packages, holding tarps, etc.

Short-handled broom and dustpan for tent housekeeping.

Small old rug for wiping feet before entering tent.

Small clip-on clothes hooks, mirror and trays for tent poles.

Waterproof matches, and/or lighter plus extra flints and fluid.

Bag of charcoal and small grill for special cooking.

Paper items, including towels, bags, toilet tissue, napkins, etc.

Washcloths, soap and towels, plus beach towels if swimming is included.

Bathing suits, trunks, beach shoes, etc.

Aluminum foil, plastic bags and covered bowls.

Cleaning pads and dish mop or dishcloths.

Sporting or hobby equipment, fishing tackle, cameras, bird identification guides, binoculars, etc.

Insect repellent, sunglasses and sun lotions.

First-aid kit plus personal medicines, and, if required, snake-bite kit and sting treatment.

Extra glasses or contact lenses or prescriptions for them.

Sewing kit plus extra buttons, shears, thimbles, stout thread, etc.

Personal toilet articles and personal needs.

Suggested Check List for Backpackers

A check list for backpackers can vary considerably, depending upon the length of the trail, weather conditions, altitudes and experience of the back-packer. Here is a basic list that can be used as a basis for your personal list tailored to your own trip, experience and preferences. Items of clothing are not included as they vary with weather, altitude, preferences and gender of the hiker. Just be sure they will be warm and protective enough for your planned hike, weather and altitude. Better to be too warm than too cold and you never can be too dry. Be especially sure your boots will be durable and comfortable for the trip. Never start with new or uncomfortable boots or those unsuitable for the terrain to be covered. Food has not been included as that too is a matter of personal preference, and is covered elsewhere in this CAMPER'S & BACK-PACKER'S BIBLE.

Shelter tent (selected for number in party or individual hiker) plus frame.

Sleeping bag for each member of party.

Foam pad or shorty air mattress for each hiker.

Packframe and pack selected and fitted to each hiker, as he prefers.

Raingear or poncho with hood, plus spare tarp for quick shelter.

Small stove and fuel and/or small grill for open fire cooking.

Repair kit for pack frame (pliers, spare parts, etc.) plus pack patching material.

Small camera and film and waterproof case or plastic bag.

Soft broad-brimmed hat, sun glasses and sun lotion.

Compass and trail maps of the area.

First-aid kit plus snake-bite kit.

Personal toilet articles, medicines and special personal items.

Binoculars.

Waterproof matches and/or lighter plus extra flints and liquid fuel.

Aluminum foil and plastic bags for cooking and storage.

Shaving equipment (a wind-up razor is excellent for the backpacker; no water, brush, soap or batteries required).

Soap and towels plus face cloth in waterproof plastic bag.

Toilet tissue, powder for chafing and Band-Aids for blisters.

Flashlight (three-battery model), spare batteries and bulb.

Belt hatchet or sheath knife, plus flat file and whetstone for sharpening.

Insect repellent and sting treatment if allergic to insects.

Sporting or hobby equipment such as fishing tackle, magnifying glass, mountaineering gear, rock hammer, etc.

Getting into a Heavy Load

Most backpackers have developed a method of putting on a pack. However, Camp Trails has a few recommendations which have proven to be easy and safe for both pack and packer.

Before following the suggestions outlined, start with a realistic weight, by loading the pack as if you were going on a hike.

1. Stand by the frame with the load side turned away. If you are righthanded, point your right foot toward the frame.
2. Stepping backward with the left foot and crouching slightly to slant the right thigh, drag or lift the frame to rest on the thigh.

3. Steadying the frame with the left hand, and holding the upper part of the right shoulder strap, put the right arm under the shoulder strap. Reach downward with the right hand to grasp the lower right corner of the frame. Twist the upper body to the right and pull the right shoulder strap in place.
4. Lifting the frame with your right hand, swing your right elbow back to slide the frame around on your back. While the frame is held high and far to the left, put the left arm through the shoulder strap and pull the strap into place.

5. Buckle the hipbelt in place and adjust the shoulder straps to hold the frame high on your back. Tighten the hipbelt to relieve the pressure on the shoulder straps.

To remove the pack reverse the procedure shown above. Just remember never let the loaded frame drop on one leg as damage may occur. With practice a loaded frame can be put on or taken off with ease and without injury or damage to packer or the frame.

—Courtesy of Camp Trails.

How to Remove Stains

ACID
Acid may change the color of the dye in a fabric so it should be removed at once. After rinsing thoroughly with cold water, sponge the spot with ammonia (one tablespoon per cup water) or baking soda (one tablespoon per cup water). Rinse well with water. Although white fabrics will not change color, acid will weaken the fiber so the same cleaning procedure applies.

The combination of the acid and the ammonia (or baking soda) combine to form a "salt." The combination causes the acid to become neutralized and will usually restore the original color. If the spot is not totally neutralized, however, discoloration may occur.

Materials that water-spot should be dampened and held over an open bottle of ammonia. If the color is affected by the ammonia, sponge the spot with white vinegar or acetic acid diluted with one part water; rinse thoroughly.

ALCOHOLIC BEVERAGES
First wipe up spilled drinks and sponge the spot with cool water. Then follow directions for nongreasy stains. Or sponge the spot with alcohol. Use one part alcohol to two parts water for treating acetates. If a stain remains, use a sodium perborate, chlorine bleach or hydrogen peroxide.

ANTIPERSPIRANT
Warm water and liquid detergent should remove this type of stain. If not, use a chlorine or sodium perborate bleach or hydrogen peroxide. If fabric becomes discolored, sponging with ammonia (diluted with an equal amount of water) may restore colors. Sponge or rinse with plain water. Do not iron an antiperspirant stain as the heat may destroy the fabric.

ASPHALT
See tar.

BANANA
See berry and fruit.

BEER
See alcoholic beverages.

BEET
See nongreasy stains.

BERRY AND FRUIT
See nongreasy stains. Or, for strong fabrics, pour boiling water on the stain. The method for this is to pour the water from a height of less than a yard onto the stain which is stretched.

Fruit and berry stains must be soaked in cool water immediately. Soap and water and ironing set the stain.

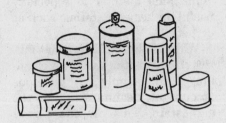

BLACK WALNUT
Boil washable fabrics in very soapy water if the stain is fresh. Use sodium perborate bleach or chlorine (very strong) on old stains. If the fabric is nonwashable, take it to a dry cleaner.

BLOOD
Blood stains should be soaked or rubbed in cold water until almost gone and then washed in warm water with a detergent. Add a few drops of ammonia to an old or stubborn stain.

For nonwashable fabrics sponge the stain with cold or lukewarm water. Hydrogen peroxide will usually remove any final traces. Sodium perborate or chlorine bleach may work also. Old stains set by heat can usually be removed with a warm solution of trisodium phosphate or Oakite.

To remove stains from a thick material such as carpeting, use an absorbent mixed to a paste with cold water. Spread the paste thickly on the stain, let it dry, then brush it off. Repeat this process until the stain disappears.

BLUEBERRY
See berry and fruit.

BUTTER
Butter stains will be removed

with ordinary laundering. For nonwashable fabrics, sponge with cleaning fluid. For delicate fabrics, try an absorbent. Dust it on and leave until the fat has been absorbed. Then brush it off. Repeat if necessary.

CANDLE WAX

Candle wax can be removed with the aid of an iron. First scrape away as much wax as possible taking care not to damage the fabric. Then place the stain between two pieces of white blotting paper and press with a warm iron. The paper will absorb the wax. Change the paper (paper towels or facial tissues) as the wax is absorbed. Any final traces can be removed with cleaning fluid.

Alcohol diluted with two parts of water will remove dye stains from colored wax. Rinse or sponge with water.

CANDY

Candy stains will usually be removed with ordinary laundering. For nonwashable fabrics, sponge the spots with plain warm water.

CARROT

See nongreasy stains.

CHERRY

See berry and fruit.

CHEWING GUM

There are two possible proce-

dures. The first being water, in the form of ice. Rub the ice on the gum spot, then scrape off the gum. This method is especially useful on heavy materials such as carpets.

Water is harmful to some fabrics. If this is the case, use cleaning fluid. Apply a generous amount of cleaning fluid to the gum stain. This procedure may be repeated if necessary. If a sugar stain remains, rub it lightly with water. This method is safe for all types of material.

CHILI SAUCE

See nongreasy stains.

CHLORINE

When used as a cleaning agent, chlorine bleach can have an adverse effect on some fabrics. Such fabrics have resin finishes which produce wash and wear qualities of wrinkle resistance, sheen and crispness. When chlorine bleach is applied to cottons, linens and rayons coated with this resin, the material becomes weakened and yellowed. The resin retains the bleach. The effect often does not appear until a hot iron is applied, which further weakens the fibers.

To counteract this mistake, rinse the fabric in water. Then soak it for a half hour in a half gallon of warm water mixed with 2 teaspoons of ordinary photographer's hypo (sodium thiosulfate).

Color remover may be used on fabrics that are colorfast or completely white.

CHOCOLATE

See combination stains.

COCOA

See nongreasy stains.

COFFEE AND TEA

For coffee or tea stains containing milk or cream see combination stains. When cream or milk is not included see nongreasy stains or use boiling water (only on strong fabrics). The method for this is to have the stain stretched over some sort of bowl. The water is then poured from a height of less than one yard. The fabric may then be laundered in the normal manner. Chemical bleach or sunlight can be used if the stain remains.

COMBINATION STAINS

With a combination of greasy and nongreasy stains, the nongreasy stain should be attended to first. Treat the spot with cool water and a detergent. Then rinse and let the material dry. Now sponge the stain with a cleaning fluid. Rinse the material and again let it dry. If there are any traces of the stain left, use a bleach.

COSMETICS

If the fabric is washable, pour detergent (liquid) onto the stain. Another method for washable fabrics is to rub detergent or soap into a dampened stain. Rinse the garment when the stain seems to be gone. The procedure may be repeated.

If the fabric isn't washable, cleaning fluid can be used. Rub the cleaning fluid into the stain until the stain is removed.

CRAYON

See cosmetics.

CREAM

Washable fabrics are to be rinsed with cool water. Afterwards, launder normally. Nonwashable fabrics are to be rubbed with cleaning fluid. Cool water is sponged on the stain after the cleaning fluid has evaporated.

CREAM SAUCE

Cream sauce is removed from washable fabrics with warm water and soap. Nonwashables should be first sponged with warm water, dried, then sponged with cleaning fluid.

CREAM SOUP

See cream sauce.

CURRANT

See berry and fruit.

CURRY

See turmeric.

DANDELION

See grass, flowers, foliage.

DEODORANT

See antiperspirant.

DYES

Dyes, when the stain is fresh, need to be soaked in detergent suds for a long time. If this doesn't work use chlorine bleach or color remover, depending on the strength of the fabric.

EGG

First, use a dull knife to scrape off as much as possible. The next step is to soak the spot with cold water. Hot water will set the stain. Washable fabrics may be laundered normally. Nonwashable fabrics may be sponged with cleaning fluid.

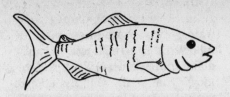

FISH SLIME

See nongreasy stains or make a solution of salt water. The ratio is a half cup of salt to two quarts of water. Soak or sponge the stain with the solution. First, rinse the salt water from the stain with water, then wash with soap and water.

FLYPAPER

Flypaper stains are removed using cleaning fluid.

GLUE

Plastic glue stains should be treated with either liquid detergent or vinegar. If the stain is fresh, the liquid detergent should be rubbed into the fabric. If the glue has hardened, soak the fabric in boiling vinegar (acetic acid may be used, also). Test the fabric first for reaction to such treatment. The fabric should be soaked until the glue has completely dissolved (sometimes longer than fifteen minutes). Rinse with plain water. See nongreasy stains for other glues and for mucilage but use hot water instead of cool.

GOOSEBERRY

See berry and fruit.

GRAPE

See berry and fruit.

GRASS, FLOWERS, FOLIAGE

Grass, flower or foliage stains can usually be removed from both washable and nonwashable fabrics by sponging with alcohol. Before treating stains on acetate, test the colors to make sure they will not be changed. Mild sodium perborate or chlorine bleach or hydrogen peroxide should take out any remaining marks.

GRAVY

Gravy stains should be soaked in cold water before laundering. Any remaining spots can be sponged off with cleaning fluid after the fabric is thoroughly dry. For nonwashable fabrics, sponge the spot with cool water, followed by cleaning fluid or an absorbent.

GREASE AND OIL

Oil and grease stains should be attended to immediately. Procedure for cleaning depends upon the material. With more delicate fabrics, use cleaning fluid or an absorbant. Apply absorbant to the stain and wait for it to develop a gummy consistency. Then rub it off and repeat as necessary.

For heavier fabrics, such as carpets, use a grainier absorbant like corn meal.

If the stain is from grime or metal filings, Vaseline should be applied and rubbed into the spot. Then cover the spot with a generous amount of cleaning fluid. For heavier stains such as axle grease or road oil, use the procedure for treatment of tar.

GREASY STAINS

If the material is washable, rub detergent into the stain, then wash. After laundering, if the stain still remains, use a grease solvent such as cleaning fluid. After applying the cleaning fluid with a sponge, let it dry. If the fabric has a special finish, it will often hold stains longer, requiring repeated applications of cleaning fluid.

Old stains or heat-set stains sometimes turn yellow and remain after a cleaning fluid treatment. Use a sodium perborate or chlorine bleach of hydrogen peroxide. If the material permits, the strong sodium perborate bleach is the best.

On nonwashable materials, apply cleaning fluid to the stain and repeat if necessary. Use bleach if yellow stains remain after treatment.

HACKBERRY
See berry and fruit.

HUCKLEBERRY
See berry and fruit.

ICE CREAM
See combination stains.

INK
Certain types of ink stains can be removed simply by washing; others need more involved treatment. Washing may, in fact, make the stain nearly impossible to remove. The material and ink should be tested. Make an ink mark on a similar fabric and wash. If ink is not removed from test material either amyl acetate or acetone should be used. If the fabric is acetate, Dynel, Arnel or Verel, sponge with pure amyl acetate. On other materials, sponge with acetone. Repeat as often as necessary.

Another method for removing ballpoint ink is to spray the spot with hair spray. Allow to dry thoroughly; then launder normally.

IODINE
If the fabric is not damaged by water, two procedures may be followed. For fresh stains only, plain water and sunlight will remove the stain. Simply sponge with water and dry in the sun (a warm radiator can be used also). The stain will disappear. For new and old stains sodium thiosulfate can be used. Make a solution with one tablespoon of sodium thiosulfate crystals and one pint of water. After the crystals have dissolved, apply the solution to the stain. Rinse with water. Test colored fabrics before using.

If the fabric may be damaged with water, use alcohol. Apply alcohol (dilute with water for use on acetate) continuously for several hours.

IRON RUST
Oxalic acid, lemon juice, ammonium bifluoride or cream of tartar can be used to remove rust stains from white fabrics that are washable. For colored fabrics, test each procedure first.

The ratio for cream of tartar solution is four teaspoons cream of tartar to one pint water. The solution should then be boiled. The fabric should be placed in the boiling solution until the stain is removed. Rinse with water.

One tablespoon of oxalic acid crystals should be added to a cup of water to form a solution. A few drops of this solution can be applied to the stain. Rinse with hot water immediately. The procedure may be repeated. On fabrics other than nylon, oxalic acid crystals can be applied directly to the stain. Again, rinse with hot water immediately. Be sure to rinse oxalic acid thoroughly from fabric because if it is not rinsed immediately and completely, it might destroy the fabric.

A tablespoon of ammonium bi-fluoride, which can be found in a drugstore, should be dissolved in a cup of water. Sponge the stain continuously until stain is removed (up to ten minutes). Rinse with water.

The procedure using lemon juice is, perhaps, the best method for removing iron rust stains because lemon juice can be used on virtually any fabric without the risk of damaging the cloth. Sponge the stain with water and then squeeze lemon directly on the stain. The next step is to hold the stain in the steam from a boiling kettle for a short time (three or four minutes should be enough). Rinse with water. Another procedure is to apply salt, first, and then lemon juice to the stain. Next, leave it in the sun until dry. Both procedures may be repeated.

The above procedures are for use on washable fabrics. It is just about impossible to remove iron rust stains from fabrics that must be dry-cleaned.

KETCHUP
See nongreasy stains.

LEATHER
Leather stains are difficult to remove. When there is friction between leather and another fabric, and that fabric contains tannin, a stain will be left on the leather. Wash the material if possible, otherwise apply a liquid detergent to the spot and rub. If the stain still remains, bleach the area with sodium perborate or hydrogen peroxide.

LIPSTICK
See cosmetics.

LIQUOR
See alcoholic beverages.

MAYONNAISE
See combination stains.

MEAT JUICE
See combination stains.

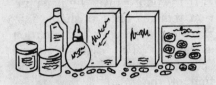

MEDICINE
Medicines of a gummy-type substance can be rubbed with cleaning fluid. If the fabric is washable, the next step would be to launder as usual. If the fabric isn't washable, rinse with the cleaning fluid.

Medicines dissolved in alcohol may be removed using alcohol. Certain fabrics, such as acetate, require diluted alcohol in the ratio of two parts water to one part alcohol.

Cough medicine, along with other medicines with sugar syrup as their bases, is removed with soap and water.

See instructions for iron rust for stains from medicines with iron. For medicines made of coloring matter, see instructions for dyes. Also see iodine, mercurochrome and silver nitrate.

MERCUROCHROME
Ammonia is used to remove mercurochrome stains from washable fabrics. The ratio is four tablespoons of ammonia to one quart of water. Soak the stain in the solution overnight.

Alcohol is used to remove these stains from nonwashable fabrics. The fabric (especially colored material) must be tested for reaction with alcohol. If the fabric survives the test, apply alcohol to the stain until the stain is removed. If the fabric is unable to survive alcohol, use liquid detergent and a very small amount of ammonia (no more than a drop). Apply this to the stain. This procedure may be repeated.

Mercurochrome stains are fairly easy to treat when the stain is fresh. It is much more difficult to treat when old.

MERTHIOLATE
See mercurochrome.

METALLIC STAINS
White vinegar, acetic acid or lemon juice will remove metallic stains. Sponge the stain with any of these acids and then with water. If this procedure results in color damage to the fabric, ammonia water (a mild solution) or baking soda mixed with water should restore the fabric to its original color. Never use bleach instead of the acids because it may result in permanent damage to the fabric.

MILDEW
Heavy mildew stains are almost impossible to remove since they can cause damage to the fabric itself. Washable fabrics with light mildew stains can be treated with soap and water. Sunlight should be used to dry the stain. If a trace remains, try a bleach. Take nonwashables to a dry cleaner.

It is important to brush surface growth off before washing. This must be done out of the house since the spores could spread onto something else.

MILK
See nongreasy stains.

MUCILAGE
See glue.

MUCUS
See fish slime.

MUD
The best procedure is to let the mud dry and then brush it off. If this doesn't remove the stain completely, see nongreasy stains.

MULBERRY
See berry and fruit.

MUSTARD
Mustard stains on nonwashable fabrics can be removed with alcohol. Sponge the stain with alcohol (dilute with water for use on acetate). Colored fabrics should be tested for reaction with alcohol first.

For washable fabrics or those with colors that cannot stand alcohol, rub liquid detergent into the dampened stain. If the stain remains, let washable fabrics soak overnight in a heated solution of detergent and water. A bleach (sodium perborate works well) can be used. Test fabric first.

NONGREASY STAINS
If the fabric is washable, sponge the stain with cool water as soon as possible. Immediate treatment with plain water will remove many stains. If necessary, soak stained article in cool water overnight. Afterwards, rub with liquid detergent. Rinse with water. If the stain remains, use a bleach. It is important to treat the stain immediately and before ironing since old stains and those that have been ironed are almost impossible to remove.

Cool water will also aid in the removing of nongreasy stains from nonwashable fabrics. Do not soak the stained article in water;

simply sponge. Liquid detergent can be rubbed into the stain. Rinse with water and alcohol (dilute with two parts water for acetate). Colored fabrics should be tested for reaction with alcohol. Use a bleach as a last resort.

PAINT

Stains of this nature can be removed when fresh, but are almost impossible to remove when old. If the material is washable, rub detergent into the spot, then wash. Often a solvent such as turpentine is also necessary. Sponge on the turpentine, then rub in the detergent. Soak the material overnight in hot water followed by a laundering. Repeat if necessary.

Directions on paint cans for thinning will give additional information for removing paint stains. Paints are produced with a mixture of solvents, and additions of these solvents thin the paint. Additions of these solvents also help to remove paint stains on fabrics. With turpentine paints, use turpentine as a solvent. For shellac, use alcohol. With aluminum paint, use trichloroethylene, except on Arnel or Kodel. With lacquers, use acetone, except on acetate, Arnel, Dynel or Verel. For such exceptions, use chemically pure amyl acetate. With water paints, a simple laundering should suffice. Treatment with the above solvents should preceed detergent treatments and laundering.

If the material is nonwashable, take a piece of cotton soaked with solvent and place it for a half hour directly onto the stain. Follow this with a small amount of detergent and rub. Remove detergent with alcohol if the dye in the material permits. Otherwise rinse with a small amount of water.

There are some effective commercial products on the market for removing paint.

PARAFFIN
See candle wax.

PEACH
See berry and fruit.

PEAR
See berry and fruit.

PENCIL
If an eraser is not effective on pencil-marked material, rub detergent into the area. If detergent does not suffice, preceed the detergent with ammonia. Repeat treatment if necessary.

Indelible pencil stains may be treated with a combination of alcohol and two parts of water. Then rub in detergent and wash. If the stain still remains, a bleach may be used, such as sodium perborate, chlorine or hydrogen peroxide.

PERFUME
See alcoholic beverages.

PERSPIRATION
Immediate treatment is required to remove perspiration stains. Warm water mixed with detergent should be sponged on the stain. If yellow stains appear after washing, use chlorine bleach or hydrogen peroxide.

If perspiration causes a change in the color of the fabric, ammonia, vinegar or cleaning fluid solution may sometimes help. New stains should be sponged with ammonia. If the stain is old, sponge with vinegar and rinse with water. Cleaning fluid mixed with water may also help.

If the odor caused by perspiration remains on a washable fabric after washing, a salt solution is helpful. The stained article should be placed in a salt solution of the ratio of four tablespoons salt to one quart water. The article should be allowed to soak for at least an hour.

Never iron an article until the perspiration stain is completely removed, as ironing will make the stain nearly impossible to remove.

PLASTIC
Stains are often left on fabrics when heat softens plastic hangers or buttons. Mothballs can cause the same effect. Amyl acetate or trichloroethylene soaked onto a cotton pad treats such stains. Sponge the area with the solvent, then leave the pad on the stain until the plastic loosens. This treatment can be repeated if necessary. Colored fabrics should be tested to make certain the dyes will not bleed.

PLUM
See berry and fruit.

RAISIN
See berry and fruit.

RASPBERRY
See berry and fruit.

RESINS
Solvents, such as cleaning fluid, turpentine or alcohol, are used to remove resinous stains. With acetate, dilute the alcohol with two parts of water. Apply the solvent with a sponge, rinse with cold water, then wash.

RUST
See iron rust.

SALAD DRESSING
See combination stains.

SAUCES
See combination stains.

SCORCH
If the fibers of the cloth have been damaged, it is impossible to restore the fabric to its original state. Scorched spots on wool are almost impossible to remove. Sandpaper (fine) or emery cloth can be used to brush the spot. This will, at least, make the stain less apparent.

For light scorch stains on washable fabrics, see nongreasy stains. Use hydrogen peroxide on light scorch stains on fabrics which aren't washable. Sponge the stain with peroxide (test on colored fabrics) and rinse with water.

SILVER NITRATE
Sponge the stain with cool water immediately. You may then launder the fabric normally. For stubborn stains, try iodine and sodium thiosulfate. Iodine (a few drops) may be applied. After a few minutes, sponge with diluted sodium thiosulfate (one teaspoon sodium thiosulfate to one cup water). Sponge with water.

SMOKE
See cosmetics.

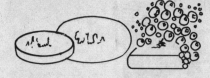

SOAP
Soap may cause a stain on poorly-rinsed-then-ironed fabrics. Removal of such stains is accomplished by simply rewashing thoroughly.

SOFT DRINKS
Stains caused by soft drinks can be removed by following the directions for nongreasy stains. The fresh stain should be immediately rinsed with cold water. They are more difficult to remove after they have dried, especially after ironing.

SOOT
See cosmetics.

STRAWBERRY
See berry and fruit.

SUGAR SYRUP
A stain caused by sugar syrup will be removed easily with laundering. For nonwashable material, soak the stain with warm water.

TAR
Certain solvents such as turpentine or cleaning fluid are used to remove tar stains. Scrape as much tar off as possible first. Then soak the stain in the solvent. Rinse with water or launder if possible. (See directions for removal of greasy stains.)

With tar stains on carpets be careful to rub tar off the area, rather than into the carpet. A light, upward brushing is a good method. This treatment will work for other tar related stains of road oil, axle grease, pitch or asphalt.

TEA
See coffee and tea.

TIN FOIL
See metallic stains.

TOBACCO
See grass, flowers, foliage.

TOMATO JUICE
See nongreasy stains.

TURMERIC
Certain foods contain a spice called turmeric, which leaves a bright yellow stain, especially on cottons. This spice is found in prepared mustard, curry powder and sometimes pickles.

If the material is washable, soak the cloth in ammonia or alcohol diluted with water. (Two parts of water to one part of alcohol is the suggested amount.) If the material is nonwashable, apply the mixture to the stained area only.

Follow the treatment, whether for washable or nonwashable fabrics, with a water rinse. A bleach may be needed on stubborn stains of this nature. Colored fabrics should be tested first to see if alcohol bleeds the dye. A good place to test colored material is on an inside seam.

UNKNOWN STAINS
See greasy stains, nongreasy stains or yellowing depending on appearance of stain.

URINE
See nongreasy stains unless the color of the fabric has been changed. If this is the case, ammonia, acetic acid or white vinegar must be used. If these don't work, use bleach (see medicine and yellowing).

VARNISH
See paint.

VASELINE
See greasy stains.

VEGETABLE
See nongreasy stains.

VINEGAR
See acid.

VOMIT
See fish slime.

WATER SPOTS
Water can cause a ring stain on certain fabrics such as taffeta,

moire, silk or rayon. These fabrics contain sizing or other finishing agents, which when mixed with water causes the ring. Sometimes these water rings can be removed with a brush or a rubbing between the hands. If this is not effective, steam the area by holding it over a boiling teapot or dampen the ring and rub outward from the center. The article should be ironed while it is damp.

WHITE SAUCE
See combination stains.

WINE
See alcoholic beverages.

YELLOWING
Storing of household linens and other clothing often causes yellow or brown stains. The brown stains are left by the iron particles in hard water which have turned to rust. Whether the stain is due to age or unknown causes, a bleach treatment works well. First wash the article (and this may be all that's needed). Then use a mild bleach such as sodium perborate or hydrogen peroxide. Follow this with an oxalic acid treatment as described for iron rust stains. Then use a strong bleach such as chlorine or sodium perborate. Finally, launder article thoroughly.

Brain Teasers for Car or Camp

HOW MANY OF THESE LICENSE PLATE MOTTOES DO YOU KNOW?

Alabama: Heart of Dixie
Alaska: North to the Future
Arizona: Grand Canyon State
Colorado: Centennial
Connecticut: Constitution State
Delaware: First State
Florida: Sunshine State
Hawaii: Aloha State
Idaho: Famous Potatoes
Illinois: Land of Lincoln
Indiana: Heritage State
Louisiana: Bayou State
Maine: Vacationland
Minnesota: 10,000 Lakes
Montana: Big Sky
New Hampshire: Live Free or Die
New Jersey: Garden State
New Mexico: Land of Enchantment
North Carolina: First in Freedom
North Dakota: Peace Garden State
Pennsylvania: Bicentennial State
Rhode Island: Ocean State
Vermont: See Vermont
West Virginia: Wild Wonderful
Wisconsin: America's Dairyland
American Samoa: Pago Pago Motu O Fiafiaga
Canal Zone: Funnel for World Commerce
Guam: Hafa Adai
Virgin Islands: American Paradise

Alberta: Wild Rose Country
British Columbia: Beautiful
Manitoba: Friendly
Nova Scotia: Canada's Ocean Playground
Ontario: Keep It Beautiful
Prince Edward Island: Seat Belts Save
Quebec: La Belle Province
Yukon: Home of the Klondike

HOW MANY OF THESE STATE NICKNAMES DO YOU KNOW?

Alabama: Cotton State
Alaska: Last Frontier, Land of Midnight Sun, Mainland State
Arizona: Grand Canyon State, Apache State
Arkansas: Land of Opportunity, Bear State
California: Golden State
Colorado: Centennial State, Silver State
Connecticut: Constitution State, Nutmeg State
Delaware: Diamond State, First State, Blue Hen State
Florida: Sunshine State, Everglade State
Georgia: Empire State of the South
Hawaii: Aloha State
Idaho: Gem State
Illinois: Prairie State
Indiana: The Hoosier (hoo-zher) State
Iowa: The Hawkeye State
Kansas: The Sunflower State, The Jayhawker State
Kentucky: Bluegrass State
Louisiana: Pelican State, Sportsman's Paradise
Maine: Pine Tree State
Maryland: Old Line State, Free State
Massachusetts: Bay State
Michigan: Wolverine State
Minnesota: Gopher State, North Star State
Mississippi: Magnolia State
Missouri: The Show Me State, Bullion State
Montana: The Treasure State, Big Sky Country
Nebraska: Cornhusker State
Nevada: Battle Born State, Silver State
New Hampshire: Granite State
New Jersey: Garden State
New Mexico: Land of Enchantment, Sunshine State
New York: Empire State
North Carolina: Tar Heel State, Old North State
North Dakota: Flickertail State, Sioux State
Ohio: Buckeye State
Oklahoma: Sooner State
Oregon: Beaver State, Sunset State
Pennsylvania: Keystone State
Rhode Island: Ocean State
South Carolina: Palmetto State
South Dakota: Coyote State, Sunshine State
Tennessee: Volunteer State
Texas: Lone-Star State
Utah: Beehive State, Mormon State
Vermont: Green Mountain State
Virginia: Old Dominion State
Washington: Evergreen State, Chinook State
West Virginia: Mountain State, Panhandle State
Wisconsin: Badger State
Wyoming: Cowboy State, Equality State

HOW MANY OF THESE STATE TREES DO YOU KNOW?

Alabama: Southern pine
Alaska: Sitka spruce

Arizona: Paloverde
Arkansas: Pine
California: Redwood
Colorado: Colorado blue spruce
Connecticut: White oak
Delaware: American holly
Florida: Sabal palm
Georgia: Live oak
Idaho: White pine
Illinois: Oak
Indiana: Tulip tree
Iowa: Oak
Kansas: Cottonwood
Kentucky: Tulip poplar
Louisiana: Cypress
Maine: Eastern white pine
Maryland: White oak
Massachusetts: American elm
Michigan: White pine
Minnesota: Norway pine
Mississippi: Magnolia
Missouri: Dogwood
Montana: Ponderosa pine
Nebraska: Cottonwood
Nevada: Single-leaf piñon
New Hampshire: White birch
New Jersey: Red oak
New Mexico: Piñon
New York: Sugar maple
North Carolina: Pine
North Dakota: American elm
Ohio: Ohio buckeye
Oklahoma: Redbud
Oregon: Douglas fir
Pennsylvania: Eastern hemlock
Rhode Island: Red maple
South Carolina: Palmetto
South Dakota: Black Hills spruce
Tennessee: Tulip poplar
Texas: Pecan
Utah: Blue spruce
Vermont: Sugar maple
Washington: Western hemlock
West Virginia: Sugar maple
Wisconsin: Sugar maple
Wyoming: Cottonwood

California: Golden poppy
Colorado: Rocky Mountain columbine
Connecticut: Mountain laurel
Delaware: Peach blossom
Florida: Orange blossom
Georgia: Cherokee rose
Hawaii: Hibiscus
Idaho: Syringa
Illinois: Wood violet
Indiana: Peony
Iowa: Wild rose
Kansas: Sunflower
Kentucky: Goldenrod
Louisiana: Magnolia
Maine: Pine cone and tassel
Maryland: Black-eyed Susan
Massachusetts: Mayflower
Michigan: Apple blossom
Minnesota: Showy ladyslipper
Mississippi: Magnolia
Missouri: Hawthorn
Montana: Bitterroot
Nebraska: Goldenrod
Nevada: Sagebrush
New Hampshire: Purple violet
New Jersey: Purple violet
New Mexico: Yucca
New York: Rose
North Carolina: American dogwood
North Dakota: Prairie rose
Ohio: Scarlet carnation
Oklahoma: Mistletoe
Oregon: Oregon grape
Pennsylvania: Mountain laurel
Rhode Island: Violet
South Carolina: Carolina yellow jassamine
South Dakota: Pasque
Tennessee: Iris
Texas: Bluebonnet
Utah: Sego lily
Vermont: Red clover
Virginia: American dogwood
Washington: Rhododendron
West Virginia: Rhododendron
Wisconsin: Violet
Wyoming: Indian paintbrush

HOW MANY OF THESE STATE FLOWERS DO YOU KNOW?

Alabama: Camellia
Alaska: Forget-me-not
Arizona: Saguaro (sah-WAH-ro) cactus blossom
Arkansas: Apple blossom

HOW MANY OF THESE STATE BIRDS DO YOU KNOW?

Alabama: Yellowhammer
Alaska: Willow Ptarmigan
Arizona: Cactus Wren
Arkansas: Mockingbird

California: California Valley Quail
Colorado: Lark Bunting
Connecticut: American Robin
Delaware: Blue Hen Chicken
Florida: Mockingbird
Georgia: Brown Thrasher
Hawaii: Nene
Idaho: Mountain Bluebird
Illinois: Cardinal
Indiana: Cardinal
Iowa: Eastern Goldfinch
Kansas: Meadowlark
Kentucky: Kentucky Cardinal
Louisiana: Brown Pelican
Maine: Chickadee
Maryland: Baltimore Oriole
Massachusetts: Chickadee
Michigan: Robin
Minnesota: Common Loon (Great Northern Diver)
Mississippi: Mockingbird
Missouri: Bluebird
Montana: Western Meadowlark
Nebraska: Western Meadowlark
Nevada: Mountain Bluebird
New Hampshire: Purple Finch
New Jersey: Eastern Goldfinch
New Mexico: Chaparral (Roadrunner)
New York: Bluebird
North Carolina: Cardinal
North Dakota: Western Meadowlark
Ohio: Cardinal
Oklahoma: Scissortailed Flycatcher
Oregon: Western Meadowlark
Pennsylvania: Ruffed Grouse
Rhode Island: Rhode Island Red
South Carolina: Carolina Wren
South Dakota: Chinese Ringneck Pheasant
Tennessee: Mockingbird
Texas: Mockingbird
Utah: Seagull
Vermont: Hermit Thrush
Virginia: Cardinal
Washington: Willow Goldfinch
West Virginia: Cardinal
Wisconsin: Robin
Wyoming: Meadowlark

HOW MANY OF THESE STATE MOTTOES DO YOU KNOW?

Alabama: We Dare Defend Our Rights
Alaska: North to the Future
Arizona: Ditat Deus (God Enriches)
Arkansas: Regnat Populus (The People Rule)
California: Eureka (I Have Found It)
Colorado: Nil Sine Numine (Nothing Without Providence)
Connecticut: Qui Transtulit Sustinet (He Who Transplanted, Still Sustains)
Delaware: Liberty and Independence
Florida: In God We Trust
Georgia: Wisdom, Justice and Moderation
Hawaii: Ua Mau Ke Ea O Ka Aina I Ka Pono (The Life of the Land Is Perpetuated by Righteousness)
Idaho: Esto Perpetua (It Is Forever)
Illinois: State Sovereignty—National Union
Indiana: The Crossroads of America
Iowa: Our Liberties We Prize and Our Rights We Will Maintain
Kansas: Ad Astra Per Aspera (To the Stars through Difficulties)
Kentucky: United We Stand, Divided We Fall
Louisiana: Union, Justice and Confidence
Maine: Dirigo (I Direct)
Maryland: Fatti Maschi, Parole Femine (Manly Deeds, Womanly Words), and Scuto Bonae Voluntatis Tuae Coronasti Nos (With Favor Wilt Thou Compass Us as With a Shield)
Massachusetts: Ense Petit Placidam Sub Libertate Quietem (By the Word We Seed Peace Only Under Liberty)
Michigan: If You Seek a Beautiful Peninsula, Look About You
Minnesota: L'Etoile du Nord (Star of the North)
Mississippi: Virtute et Armis (By Valor and Arms)
Missouri: Let the Welfare of the People Be the Supreme Law
Montana: Oro y Plata (Gold and Silver)
Nebraska: Equality Before the Law
Nevada: All for Our Country
New Hampshire: Live Free or Die
New Jersey: Liberty and Prosperity
New Mexico: Crescit Eundo (It Grows As It Goes)
New York: Excelsior (Ever Upward)
North Carolina: Esse Quam Videri (To Be Rather Than to Seem)
North Dakota: Liberty and Union, Now and Forever, One and Inseparable
Ohio: With God, All Things Are Possible
Oklahoma: Labor Omnia Vincit (Labor Conquers All)
Oregon: The Union
Pennsylvania: Virtue, Liberty and Independence
Rhode Island: Hope
South Carolina: Animis Opibusque Parati (Prepared in Mind and Resources)

South Dakota: Under God, the People Rule
Tennessee: Agriculture, Commerce
Texas: Friendship
Utah: Industry
Vermont: Freedom and Unity
Virginia: Sic Semper Tyrannis (Thus Always to Tyrants)
Washington: Al-ki (Bye and Bye)
West Virginia: Montani Semper Liberi (Mountaineers Are Always Free)
Wisconsin: Forward
Wyoming: Equal Rights

The Camper's & Backpacker's Bookshelf

BACKPACKING

Abel, Michael. **Backpacking Made Easy.** 2nd ed. (Illus.). 1975. 5.95; pap. 2.95. Naturegraph.

Angier, Bradford. **Home in Your Pack.** (Illus.). 1965. 4.50. Stackpole.

— — **Home in Your Pack: A Modern Handbook of Back Packing.** (Illus.). 1972. pap. 1.95. Macmillan.

Blankenship, Samuel. **A Backpacking Guide to the Southern Mountains.** 1975. pap. 1.95. Ballantine.

Blankenship, Samuel M. **A Backpacking Guide to the Southern Mountains.** rev. ed. 1974. pap. 1.95. Mockingbird Bks.

Bridge, Raymond. **America's Backpacking Book.** (Illus.). 1973. 14.95. Scribner.

Bunnelle, Hasse. **Food for Knapsackers And Other Trail Travelers.** 1971. pap. 3.95. Sierra.

Casewit, Curtis. **Hiking-Climbing Handbook.** (Illus.). 1969. 4.95. Hawthorn.

Cheney, Theodore. **Camping by Backpack & Canoe.** 1970. 7.95. Funk & W.

Colby, C. B., ed. **Camper's & Backpacker's Bible.** (Illus.). 1977. softbound. 7.95. Stoeger.

Consumer Complete Buying Guide to Camping & Backpacking. pap. 1.95. NAL.

Duncan S. Blackwell. **Backpacking, Tenting & Trailering, 1974.** 1974. 7.95; pap. 3.95. Rand.

Elman, Robert. **The Hiker's Bible.** (Illus.). 1973. pap. 2.50. Doubleday.

Fletcher, Colin. **New Complete Walker.** 1974. 10.00. Knopf.

Gibbs, Tony. **Backpacking.** (Illus.). 1975. 4.33. Watts.

Herz, Jerry. **The Compleat Backpacker.** 1973. pap. 1.50. Popular Lib.

Jansen, Charles. **Lightweight Backpacking.** 1974. pap. 1.50. Bantam.

Kelsey, Robert. **Walking in the Wild. The Complete Guide to Hiking & Backpacking.** (Illus.). 1974, 6.95; pap. 2.50. Funk & W.

Kemsley, William & Backpacker Editors. **Backpacking Equipment.** 1975. pap. 4.95. Macmillan.

Learn, C. R. **Backpacker's Digest.** pap. 6.95. Follett.

Look, Dennis A. **Joy of Backpacking. People's Guide to the Wilderness.** Harris Arthur S., Jr., ed. (Illus.). 1975. pap. 6.95. Jalmar Pr.

Lyttle, Richard B. **The Complete Beginner's Guide to Backpacking.** (Illus.). 1975. 5.95. Doubleday.

Manning, Harvey. **Backpacking, One Step at a Time.** 1973. pap. 2.95. Random.

Mendenhall, Ruth D. **Backpack Cookery.** (Illus.). 1974. 1.50. La Siesta.

— — **Backpack Techniques.** (Illus.). 1973. 1.00. La Siesta.

Merrill, Bill. **The Hiker's & Backpacker's Handbook.** (Illus.). 1972. pap. 2.95. Arc Bks.

Merrill, W. K. **Hiker's & Backpacker's Handbook.** (Illus.). 1971. 6.95. Winchester Pr.

Rethmel, Robert C. **Backpacking.** 5th ed. (Illus.). 1974. pap. 5.95. Burgess.

Riviere, Bill. **Backcountry Camping.** (Illus.). 1971. 6.95. Doubleday.

Ryback, Eric. **High Adventure of Eric Ryback.** (Illus.). 1971. 6.95. Chronicle Bks.

Ryback, Eric & Ryback, Tim. **The Ultimate Journey—Canada to Mexico Down the Continental Divide.** (Illus.). 1973. 7.95. Chronicle Bks.

Stout, James H. & Stout, Ann M. **Backpacking with Small Children.** (Illus.). 1975. 6.95. T Y Crowell.

Van Lear, Denise, ed. **The Best About Backpacking.** (Illus.). 1974. pap. 6.95. Sierra.

Winnett, Thomas. **Backpacking for Fun.** (Illus.). 1973. pap. 2.95. Wilderness.

CAMPSITES, FACILITIES, ETC.

Archibald, Fred, ed. **Good Camping in Florida, 1973.** (Illus.). 1973. pap. 1.95. Great Outdoors.

Boy Scouts of America. **Campsites & Facilities.** (Illus.). 1964. pap. 7.50. BSA.

California Campgrounds, & Trailer Parks, 1975. 1975. pap. 2.95. Rand.

Chase, Max & Chase, Linda. **Campground Guide for Tent & Trailer Tourists, 1975-76.** 13th ed. 1975. pap. 2.25. Campgrounds.

Cope, Robert & Cope, Claudette. **Canadian Camping & Caravaning.** (Illus.). 1975. pap. 4.95. Drake Pubs.

Crain, Jim & Milne, Terry. **Camping Around New England,** rev. ed. (Illus.). 1975. pap. 3.95. Random.

Fuller, Curtis G. **Woodall's Trailering Parks & Campgrounds, 1973.** 1974. pap. 6.95. Woodall.

Luce, William P. **Family Camping: A Self Instruction Guide to Camp Skills & Sites.** (Illus.). 1965. pap. 1.95. Macmillan.

Mallon, Roger & Mallon, Cathy. **Wilderness for Rent: Camping Around New York City.** (Illus.). 1971. pap. 2.95. Walker & Co.

Peterson, Ed., ed. **Midwest Campgrounds & Trailer Parks, 1975.** 1975. pap. 3.95. Rand.

— — **Northeast Campgrounds & Trailer Parks, 1975.** 1975. pap. 3.95. Rand.

— — **Southeast Campgrounds & Trailer Parks, 1975.** 1975. pap. 3.95.. Rand.

Publications International Ltd. **Consumer Guide Camping Equipment & Recreational Vehicle Report.** 1973. pap. 1.95. Doubleday.

Rand McNally. **Rand McNally 1975 Campground & Trailer Park Guide.** 1975. 6.95. Rand.

Rand McNally, ed. **European Campgrounds & Trailer Parks.** (Illus.). 1975. pap. 5.95. Rand.

Steinberg, Joseph L. **Camper's Favorite Campgrounds: The East Coast, from Maine to Florida.** (Illus.). 1974. pap. 7.95. Dial.

Tanquay, Peter. **Travel Adventure in Europe, with Tent, Van, or Motor Home.** (Illus.). 1970. 7.95. Trail-R.

Trailer Life's 1975 RV Campground & Services Directory. 1975. pap. 5.95. Hawthorn.

Triplett, Kenneth E. & Triplett, Mary R. **Free Camping in Florida.** 1973. pap. 3.30. Triplett Ents.

CAMPING

Angier, Bradford. **Skills for Taming the Wilds: A Handbook for Woodcraft Wisdom.** 1972. pap. 1.25. PB.

— — **Survival with Style.** (Illus.). 1972. 6.95. Stackpole.

Archibald, Fred, ed. **Good Camping in Florida 1973.** (Illus.). 1973. pap. 1.95. Great Outdoors.

Automobile Association Staff. **Guide to Camping & Caravanning Overseas: 1974.** (Illus.). 1974. pap. 3.95. Har-Row.

— — **Guide to Camping & Caravanning, 1975.** rev. ed. (Illus.). 1975. pap. 3.95. Har-Row.

Bale, Robert O. **What on Earth.** (Illus.). 1969. pap. 3.95. Am Camping.

Bauer, Erwin & Bauer, Peggy. **Camper's Digest.** 2nd ed. 1974. pap. 5.95. Follett.

Bearse, Ray. **The Canoe Camper's Handbook.** 1974. 7.95. Winchester Pr.

Belt, Forest H. **Easi-Guide to Camping Comfort.** (Illus.). 1974. pap. 3.50. Sams.

Berglund, Berndt. **Wilderness Survival.** 1972. 7.95. Scribner.

Boudreau, Eugene H. **Trails of the Sierra Madre.** 1973. pap. 3.75. Capra Pr.

Boy Scouts of America. **Camping.** (Illus.). 1966. pap. 0.55. BSA.

— — **Pioneering.** (Illus.). 1967. pap. 0.55. BSA.

Bridge, Raymond. **The Complete Snow Camper's Guide.** 1973. pap. 5.95. Scribner.

— — **Freewheeling: The Bicycle Camping Book.** 1974. 6.95; pap. 4.95. Stackpole.

Brown, Vinson. **Knowing the Outdoors in the Dark.** (Illus.). 1972. 7.95. Stackpole.

— — **Reading the Woods.** (Illus.). 1969. 7.95. Stackpole.

Cardwell, Paul, Jr. **America's Camping Book.** (Illus.). 1969. 10.00. Scribner.

Carpenter, Betty S. **Practical Family Campground Development & Operation.** (Illus.). 1971. pap. 4.50. Am Camping.

Cheney, Theodore. **Camping by Backpack & Canoe.** 1970. 7.95. Funk & W.

Cleaver, Nancy. **Camping & Family Fun Outdoors.** pap. 0.75. Univ Pub & Dist.

Colby, C. B., ed. **Camper's & Backpacker's Bible.** (Illus.). 1977. softbound. 7.95. Stoeger.

Colby, C. B. **First Camping Trip: How to Make It Easier & More Comfortable.** (Illus.). 1955. 3.99. Coward.

Complete Buying Guide to Camping & Backpacking. 1974. pap. 1.95. NAL.

Crain, Jim & Milne, Terry. **Camping Without Gasoline.** 1974. 4.95; pap. 1.65. Random.

Cunningham, Gerry & Hansson, Margaret. **Light Weight Camping Equipment & How to Make It.** rev. ed. (Illus.). 1976. 8.95; pap. 4.95. Scribner.

Dawson, Charlotte. **Recreational Vehicle Cookbook.** (Illus.). 1970. 3.95. Trail-R.

Dodd, E. **Mark Trail's Family Camping Tips.** 1971. pap. 1.00. Essandess.

Duncan, S. Blackwell. **Backpacking, Tenting, & Trailering, 1975.** (Illus.). 1975. pap. 4.95. Rand.

Engel, Lyle K. **The Complete Book of Motor Camping, 1973.** rev. ed. 1973. pap. 2.95. Arco.

Fabian, Leonard. **Family Book of Camping.** 1973. pap. 1.50. Stadia Sports Pub.

Filter Press Staff. **Camping Log Book for Trailer, Camper & Motor Home Uses.** (Illus.). 1974. 4.00; pap. 1.50. Filter.

Gabel, Peter S. **Camping Creates Community.** (Illus.). 1971. pap. 0.50. Am Camping.

Gibson, Walter B. **Key to Camplife.** pap. 1.00. Key Bks.

Gould, Heywood. **The Complete Book of Camping.** 1972. pap. 1.00. NAL.

Graves, Richard. **Bushcraft: A Serious Guide to Survival & Camping.** (Illus.). 1972. 10.00; pap. 3.95. Schocken.

Gray, Genevieve. **Casey's Camper.** 1973. 4.95; PLB 4.72. McGraw.

Grey, Hugh. **The Field & Stream Guide to Family Camping.** 1973. pap. 1.25. Popular Lib.

Guertner, Beryl. **Gregory's Outdoor Guide to Better Outdoor Living.** (Illus.). 6.50. (ABC). Soccer.

Hammet, Catherine T. **Your Own Book of Campcraft.** (Illus.). 1971. pap. 0.95. PB.

Hancock, Lyn. **There's a Seal in My Sleeping Bag.** (Illus.). 1972. 6.95. Knopf.

Harland, Arline P. & Harland, Edgar N. **Traveling with Tent & Trailer.** Bk. 52. (Illus.). 1973. pap. 3.95. Trail-R.

Henderson, Luis M. **Camper's Guide to Woodcraft & Outdoor Life.** Orig. Title: Outdoor Guide. 1972. pap. 3.00. Dover.

— — **Camper's Guide to Woodcraft & Outdoor Life.** (Illus.). 5.00. Peter Smith.

Homes & Camps in Forest Areas. 1974. pap. 2.00. Natl Fire Prot.

Hull, C. **Pickup Camper Manual.** (Illus.). 1974. pap. 4.95. Trail-R.

Hull, Clinton. **How to Select, Buy & Enjoy a Motor Home, Van, Camper, Tent-Top or Tent.** 1970. 4.95; pap. 4.95. Trail-R.

Jobson, John. **The Complete Book of Practical Camping.** (Illus.). 1977. softbound. 5.95. Stoeger.

Johnson, James R. **Advanced Camping Techniques.** (Illus.). 1967. 3.75; 3.44. McKay.
— — **Anyone Can Camp in Comfort.** 1964. 3.75. McKay.
Kenealy, James P. **Better Camping for Boys.** (Illus.). 1974. 4.95. Dodd.
Kephart, Horace. **Camping & Woodcraft.** (Illus.). 1948. 6.95. Macmillan.
Knap, Jerome. **The New Family Camping Handbook: A Complete Guide to Camping in North America.** (Illus.). 1975. 7.95. Pagurian.
Knobel, Bruno. **Camping-Out: 101 Ideas & Activities.** 1974. pap. 2.00. Wilshire.
Kreps, E. **Camp & Trail Methods.** (Illus.). pap. 2.00. Fur-Fish-Game.
Langer, Richard W. **The Joy of Camping: The Complete Four Seasons, Five Senses Practical Guide to Enjoying the Great Outdoors (Without Destroying It).** 1974. pap. 2.50. Penguin.
— — **The Joy of Camping: The Complete 4 Seasons, 5 Senses Guide to Enjoying the Great Outdoors (Without Destroying it),** 1973. 10.00. Sat Rev Pr.
Lowry, Thomas P., ed. **Camping Therapy, Its Use in Psychiatry & Rehabilitation.** 1974. 7.75. C C Thomas.
Luce, William P. **Family Camping: A Self Instruction Guide to Camp Skills & Sites.** (Illus.). 1965. pap. 1.95. Macmillan.
— — **Woodcraft & Camping.** (Illus.). 1974. pap. 4.00. Dover.
Mattson, Lloyd D. **Camping Guideposts.** (Illus.). 1972. pap. 1.95. Moody.
Merrill, W. K. **All About Camping.** (Illus.). 1970. pap. 3.95. Stackpole.
Miracle, Leonard. **Sportsman's Camping Guide.** 1965. pap. 4.50. Times Mirror Mag.
Miracle, Leonard & Decker, Maurice H. **Complete Book of Camping.** (Illus.). 1962. 6.95. Har-Row.
Morris, Dan & Morris, Inez. **Camping by Boat.** (Illus.). 1975. pap. 5.95. Bobbs.
— — **The Weekend Camper.** 1973. 5.95; pap. 3.95. Bobbs.
Nessmuk, pseud. **Woodcraft.** (Illus.). 1963. pap. 1.50. Dover.
Nordic World Editors. **Snow Camping.** 1974. pap. 2.50. World Pubns.
Nourse, Alan E. **The Outdoorsman's Medical Guide: Common Sense Advice & Essential Health Care for Campers, Hikers, & Backpackers.** (Illus.). 1974. pap. 3.95. Har-Row.
Ormond, Clyde. **Outdoorsman's Handbook.** 1975. pap. 1.95. Berkley Pub.
Paul, Aileen. **Kids Camping.** 1975. pap. 0.75. Archway.
— — **Kids Camping.** (Illus.). 1973. 4.95. Doubleday.
Petzoldt, Paul. **The Wilderness Handbook.** (Illus.). 1974. 7.95. Norton.
Power, John. **The Camper's Handbook.** 1974. pap. 2.95. Hippocrene Bks.
Riviere, Bill. **Backcountry Camping** (Illus.). 1971. 6.95; pap. 3.95. Doubleday.
— — **Camper's Bible.** rev. ed. (Illus.). 1970. pap. 2.50. Doubleday.
— — **Family Campers Bible.** 1975. pap. 2.50. Doubleday.
Robinson, John. **Camping & Climbing in Baja.** 3rd ed. (Illus.). 1972. 2.95. La Siesta.
Rossit, Edward A. **Snow Camping & Mountaineering.** (Illus.). 1970. 10.00; pap. 2.95. Funk & W.
Rowlands, John J. **Cache Lake Country.** (Illus.). 1959. 8.95. Norton.
Rutstrum, C. **The New Way of the Wilderness.** 1973. 4.95; pap. 2.95. Macmillan.
— — **North American Canoe Country.** 1965. 6.95. Macmillan.
RV. **Campground & Services Directory.** Date not set. pap. 5.95. Hawthorn.
Ryalls, Alan. **Modern Camping.** 1975. 7.95. David & Charles.
Ryalls, Alan & Marchant, Roger. **Better Camping.** (Illus.). 1974. 8.50. Soccer.

Saijo, Albert. **The Backpacker.** (Illus.). 1972. pap. 1.95. One Hund One Prods.
Schmidt, Ernest F. **Camping Safety.** (Illus.). 1971. pap. 0.50. Am Camping.
Schwartz, Alvin. **Going Camping: A Complete Guide for the Uncertain Beginner in Family Camping.** rev. ed. (Illus.). 1972. 5.95. Macmillan.
Sparano, Vin T. **The Complete Outdoors Encyclopedia.** (Illus.). 1973. 15.00. Har-Row.
Stebbins, Ray. **Cold-Weather Camping.** (Illus.). 1975. 10.00; pap. 4.95. Regnery.
Strung, Norman & Strung, Sil. **Camping in Comfort: A Guide to Modern Outdoor Vacations.** (Illus.). 1971. 7.50. Lippincott.
Tobey, Peter W., ed. **Two Wheel Travel— Motorcycle Camping & Touring.** (Illus.). 1972. pap. 3.00. Tobey Pub.
Tobey, Peter W. & Tucker, Tarvez, eds. **Two Wheel Travel—Bicycle Camping & Touring.** 2nd rev. ed. (Illus.). 1974. pap. 4.95. Tobey Pub.
Travel Camping the Four Seasons, 1973-1974. 1973. pap. 2.45. Woodall.
Trost, Lucille W. **Coping with Crib-Size Campers.** 1968. 2.75. Stackpole.
Tucker, Betty. **A Camper's Desert.** (Illus.). 1972. 1.00. La Siesta.
Van Matre, Steve. **Acclimatizing.** 1974. pap. 3.75. Am Camping.
Vic, J. V. **Camping & Caravaning.** (Illus.). pap. 3.50. Larousse.
Vinal, William G. **Nature Recreation.** (Illus.). 1940. pap. 2.75. Dover.
— — **Nature Recreation: Group Guidance for the Out-of-Doors.** 2nd ed. (Illus.). 5.00. Peter Smith.
Webb, Kenneth B. **Light from a Thousand Campfires.** (Illus.). 1960. pap. 3.95. Am Camping.
Welch, Mary S. **The Family Wilderness Handbook.** 1973. pap. 1.65. Ballantine.
Wells, G. S. **Modern ABC's of Family Camping.** (Illus.). 1967. 5.95. Stackpole.
Wells, George S. **Guide to Family Camping.** 1973. pap. 3.95. Stackpole.
Williams, P. F. **Camping Complete.** 1972. 10.00. Transatlantic.
Woodall Editors. **Woodall's Travel Camping the Four Seasons.** 1969. 1.95. S&S.
Zarchy, Harry. **Let's Go Camping: A Guide to Outdoor Living.** (Illus.). 1951. 5.69. Knopf.

CAMPING—OUTFITS, SUPPLIES, ETC.

Angier, Bradford. **Wilderness Gear You Can Make Yourself.** (Illus.). 1973. 6.95. Stackpole.
— — **Wilderness Gear You Can Make Yourself.** (Illus.). 1973. pap. 2.95. Macmillan.
Burch, Monte. **Outdoorsman's Fix-It Book.** (Illus.). 1974. 7.95; pap. 2.50. Har-Row.
Colby, C. B. **Today's Camping: New Equipment for Modern Campers.** (Illus.). 1973. 4.29. Coward.
Patty, Thomas F. & Shedenhelm, W. R. C., eds. **Complete Book of Camping & Backpacking.** (Illus.). 1973. pap. 2.95. Petersen Pub.
Publications International Ltd. **The Complete Buying Guide to Camping Equipment & Recreational Vehicles.** 1973. pap. 1.95. PB.
Sumner, Robert. **Make Your Own Camping Equipment.** (Illus.). 1976. pap. 6.95. Drake Pubs.

CAMPING—NORTH AMERICA

Caffey, David L. **Head for the High Country.** (Illus.). 1973. pap. 2.95. Abingdon.
Chaplin, Red. **Family Camping in New England.** (Illus.). 1973. pap. 3.95. Stone Wall Pr.

Crain, Jim & Milne, Terry. **Camping Around California.** 1975. pap. 5.95. Random.
— — **Camping Around the Appalachian Mountains.** 1975. pap. 3.95. Random.
— — **Camping Around Washington.** 1974. pap. 4.95. Random.
Dodd, Ed. **Mark Trail's Camping Tips.** (Illus.). 1969. pap. 1.00 Essandess.
James, Harry C. **Western Campfires.** (Illus.). 1973. 7.50. Northland.
Lowenkopf, Anne & Katz, Michael. **Camping with the Indians.** 1974. pap. 4.95. Sherbourne.
Rutstrum, Calvin. **Once Upon a Wilderness.** (Illus.). 1973. 6.95. Macmillan.
Trout, P. W. **Alaska by Pickup Camper.** (Illus.). 1972. pap. 3.95. Trail-R.

CANOES AND CANOEING

Angier, Bradford & Taylor, Zack. **Introduction to Canoeing.** (Illus). 1973. 6.95; pap. 3.95. Stackpole.
Appalachian Mountain Club. **N. E. Canoe Guide.** 1972. 7.75. Appalach. Mtn.
Arighi, L. Scott & Arighi, Margaret S. **Wildwater Touring.** (Illus.). 1974. 8.95. Macmillan.
Bearse, Ray. **The Canoe Camper's Handbook.** (Illus.). 1974. 7.95. Winchester Pr.
Bolz, J. Arnold. **Portage into the Past: By Canoe Along the Minnesota-Ontario Boundary Waters.** (Illus.). 1960. 6.50. U of Minn Pr.
Boy Scouts of America. **Canoeing.** (Illus.). 1968. pap. 0.55.BSA.
Byde, Alan. **Beginner's Guide to Canoeing.** 1973. 9.75. Transatlantic.
— — **Canoe Building in Glass-Reinforced Plastic.** (Illus.). 1974. 9.50. Transatlantic.
— — **Living Canoeing.** 2nd ed. (Illus.). 1974. 9.50. Transatlantic.
Carter, Randy. **Canoeing Whitewater.** 8th rev. ed. (Illus.). 1974. pap. 4.75. Appalachian Bks.
Cheney, Theodore. **Camping by Backpack & Canoe.** 1970. 7.95. Funk & W.
Colwell, Robert. **Introduction to the Water Trails in America.** (Illus.). 1973. 6.95; pap. 3.95. Stackpole.
Corbett, Roger & Matacia, Louis J. **An Illustrated Guide to Ten Beginner & Intermediate Canoe Trips.** 4th rev. ed. (Illus.). 1973. pap. 3.25. Matacia.
Davidson, James W. & Rugge, John. **The Complete Wilderness Paddler.** 1975. 10.00. Knopf.
Duncanson, Michael. **Canoe Trails of Southern Wisconsin.** 1974. pap. 4.95. Wisc T & T.
Durham, Bill. **Canoes & Kayaks of Western America.** 1974. pap. 7.50. Shorey.
Evans, G. Heberton, 3rd. **Canoeing Wilderness Waters.** (Illus.). 1975. 15.00. A S Barnes.
Evans, Jay & Anderson, Robert R. **Kayaking: The New Water Sport for Everyone.** (Illus.). 1975. 8.95; pap. 4.95. Greene.
Fillingham, Paul. **Complete Book of Canoeing & Kayaking.** (Illus.). 1974. 12.95. Drake Pubs.
Furrer, Werner. **Kayak & Canoe Trips in Washington.** (Illus.). 1971. pap. 2.00. Signpost Pubns.
Handel, C. W. **Canoe Camping: A Guide to Wilderness Travel.** 1953. 5.95. Ronald.
Handel, Carle W. **Canoeing.** (Illus.). 1956. 5.95. Ronald.
Harris, Thomas. **Down the Wild Rivers.** (Illus.). 1972. 4.95. Chronicle Bks.
Hazen, David. **The Stripper's Guide to Canoe-Building.** 2nd ed. 1974. pap. 6.95. Montana Bks.
Jaques, Florence P. **Canoe Country.** (Illus.). 1938. 5.00. U of Minn Pr.
Jenkinson, Michael. **Wild Rivers of North America.** (Illus.). 1973. 12.95. Dutton.
Kemmer, Rick. **A Guide to Paddle Adventure: How to Buy Canoes & Kayaks & Where to Travel.** 1975. 10.00; pap. 6.95. Vanguard.

Kenealy, James P. **Better Canoeing for Boys & Girls.** (Illus.). Date not set. 4.50. Dodd.

Knap, Jerome. **A Complete Guide to Canoeing in North America.** (Illus.). 1975. 8.95. Pagurian.

Lunt, Dudley C. **Woods & the Sea: Wilderness & Seacoast Adventures in the State of Maine.** (Illus.). 1965. 6.95. Knopf.

McNair, Robert E. **Basic River Canoeing.** 2nd ed. (Illus.). 1969. pap. 2.00. Am Camping.

McPhee, John. **The Survival of the Bark Canoe.** 1975. 7.95. FS&G.

Makens, James C. **Makens' Guide to U.S. Canoe Trails.** 1971. pap. 4.95. Le Voyageur.

Malo, John. **Malo's Complete Guide to Canoeing & Canoe-Camping.** 1970. pap. 1.95. Macmillan.

— — **Malo's Guide to Canoeing.** (Illus.). 1975. 8.95. Quadrangle.

Malo, John W. **Wilderness Canoeing.** (Illus.). 1971. 7.95; pap. 4.95. Macmillan.

Matacia & Cecil. **A Canoeing Log of the Shenandoah River.** (Illus.). pap. 6.95. Matacia.

Matacia, Louis J. & Corbett, Roger. **An Illustrated Guide to Ten White Water Canoe Trips.** (Illus.). 1972. pap. 3.25. Matacia.

Mead, Robert D. **The Canoer's Bible.** (Illus.). 1976. pap. 2.50. Doubleday.

Michaelson, Mike & Ray, Keith. **Canoeing.** (Illus.). 1975. 10.00; pap. 4.95. Regnery.

Nickerson, E. B. **Kayaks to the Arctic.** (Illus.). 1967. 4.95. Howell-North.

Perry, Ronald H. **Canoeing for Beginners.** 1967. pap. 2.50 Assn Pr.

Pursell, John. **Kayak Paddling Strokes: Techniques & Equipment.** 1974. Repr. of 1962 ed. pap. 1.50. Shorey.

Riviere, Bill. **Pole, Paddle, & Portage.** (Illus.). 1969. 6.95. Van Nos Reinhold.

— — **Pole, Paddle & Portage: A Complete Guide to Canoeing.** 1974. pap. 3.95. Little.

Robinson, William M. **Maryland-Pennsylvania Countryside Canoe Trails: Central Maryland Trips.** 1974. pap. 1.00. Appalachian Bks.

Ruck, Wolfgang E. **Canoeing & Kayaking.** (Illus.). 1974. 6.95. McGraw.

Rutstrum, Calvin. **North American Canoe Country.** 1965. 6.95. Macmillan.

Sandreuter, William O. **Whitewater Canoeing.** (Illus.). 1976. 8.95. Winchester Pr.

Sears, George W. **Adirondack Letters of George Washington Sears, Whose Pen Name Was Nessmuk.** Brenan, Dan, ed. (Illus.). 1962. 5.00. Syracuse U Pr.

Sevareid, Eric. **Canoeing with the Cree.** (Illus.). 1968. 4.75. Minn Hist.

Skilling, Brian, ed. **Canoeing Complete.** rev. ed. (Illus.). 1974. 12.50. Soccer.

Sutherland, C. **Modern Canoeing.** 5.75. Transatlantic.

Urban, John T., ed. **White Water Handbook for Canoe & Kayak.** 1972. pap. 2.00. Appalach Mtn.

Vaughan, Linda K. & Stratton, Richard H. **Canoeing & Sailing.** Lockhart, Aileene, ed. 1970. pap. 1.95. Wm C Brown.

COMPASS

Kjellstrom, Bjorn. **Be Expert with Map & Compass: The Orienteering Handbook.** 1972. pap. 3.95. Scribner.

Sipe, F. Henry. **Compass Land Surveying.** 1970. 5.00. McClain.

Slater, Leslie G. **Pocket Compass.** (Illus.). Date not set. pap. 1.00. Terry Pub.

FIRST AID

Aaron, James E., et al. **First Aid & Emergency Care: Prevention & Protection of Injuries.** (Illus.). 1972. pap. 4.95. Macmillan.

Abramson, Seth F. & Schultz, Dodi. **Home & Family Medical Emergencies.** 1973. 8.95. Creative Home Lib.

Acerrano, Anthony J. **The Outdoorsman's Emergency Manual.** (Illus.). 1976. 10.00. Winchester Pr.

American College of Surgeons Committee on Trauma. **Emergency Care of the Sick & Injured.** Kennedy, Robert H., ed. (Illus.). 1966. pap. 2.75. Saunders.

American National Red Cross. **Basic First Aid.** 4 vols. (Illus.). Set. pap. 2.95. slipcased. Doubleday.

— — **Standard First Aid & Personal Safety.** 1973. 3.50; pap. 1.95. Doubleday.

Angier, Bradford. **Being Your Own Wilderness Doctor.** 1975. pap. 4.95. Stackpole.

Annarino, Anthony A., et al. **Study Guide to First Aid, Safety & Family Health Emergencies.** 1967. 4.95. Burgess.

Arnold, Peter. **Check List for Emergencies.** (Illus.). 1974. pap. 1.95. Doubleday.

Arnold, Robert E. **What to Do About Bites & Stings of Venomous Animals.** 1973. 5.95. Macmillan.

Boy Scouts of America. **Emergency Preparedness.** (Illus.). 1972. pap. 0.55. BSA.

— — **Exploring Emergency Service.** (Illus.). 1971. pap. 1.20. BSA.

— — **First Aid.** (Illus.). 1972. pap. 0.55. BSA.

— — **First Aid Skill Book.** (Illus.). 1974. pap. 0.30. BSA.

Cole, Warren H. & Puestow, Charles B. **Emergency Care: Surgical & Medical.** 7th ed. 1972. 12.65. P-H.

Darvil, Fred T., Jr. **Mountaineering Medicine: A Wilderness Medical Guide.** 7th ed. 1975. pap. 1.00. Darvil Outdoor.

Dolan, Joseph P. & Holladay, Lloyd J. **First-Aid Management: Athletics, Physical Education, Recreation.** 1974. 8.95. Interstate.

Eastman, P. F. **Advanced First Aid Afloat.** 2nd ed. 1974. pap. 5.00. Cornell Maritime.

Edwards, William. **Home First Aid.** (Illus.). 1970. 6.95. Transatlantic.

Emergency Family First Aid Guide. 1.95. S&S.

Erven, Lawrence. **First Aid & Emergency Rescue.** Gruber, Harvey, ed. (Illus.). 1970. pap. 7.95. Glencoe.

Folson, Farnham. **Extrication & Casualty Handling Techniques.** (Illus.). 1975. pap. 10.00. Lippincott.

Gardner & Roylance. **New Advanced First-Aid.** (Illus.). 1969. 3.95. Butterworths.

Gardner, A. Ward & Roylance, Peter J. **New Essential First Aid.** 1971. 6.95. Little.

Hafen, Brent Q., et al, eds. **First Aid: Contemporary Practices & Principles.** 1972. pap. 3.95. Burgess.

Hartley, Joel. **First Aid Without Panic.** 1975. 8.95. pap. 4.95. Hart.

Henderson, John. **Emergency Medical Guide.** 3rd rev. ed. (Illus.). 1973. 11.00; pap. 3.95. McGraw.

Hendin, David. **Save Your Child's Life.** (Illus.). 1972. pap. 1.00. Enterprise Pubns.

Hudson, Ian & Thomas, Gordon. **What to Do Until the Doctor Comes.** 1969. 8.95. Mason Charter.

Kodet, E. Russel & Angier, Bradford. **Being Your Own Wilderness Doctor.** (Illus.). 1968. 4.95. Stackpole.

Lawson-Wood, D. & Lawson-Wood, J. **First Aid at Your Fingertips.** 1973. pap. 2.50. British Bk Ctr.

— — **First-Aid at Your Fingertips.** pap. 1.25. Weiser.

London, P. S. **A Practical Guide to the Care of the Injured.** (Illus.). 1967. 25.00. Longman.

Maltz, Stephen I. **First Aid & Safety for Everyone.** 1973. pap. 1.50. Wm C Brown.

Mitchell, Dick. **Mountaineering First Aid: A Guide to Accident Response & First Aid Care.** (Illus.). 1973. pap. 1.95. Mountaineers.

Nelson, Louise E. **Project-Readiness: A Guide to Family Emergency Preparedness.** (Illus.). 1975. 6.95. Horizon Utah.

Nourse, Alan E. **The Outdoorsman's Medical Guide: Common Sense Advice & Essential Health Care for Campers, Hikers & Backpackers.** (Illus.). 1974. pap. 3.95. Har-Row.

Pacy, Hans. **Road Accidents—Medical Aids.** (Illus.). 1972. Repr. 5.75. Longman.

Paine, Roger W., 3rd. **We Never Had Any Trouble Before: First Aid for Parents of Teenagers.** 1975. 7.95. Stein & Day.

Rothenberg, Robert E. **New American Medical Dictionary & Health Manual.** rev. ed. (Illus.). 1966. 6.95. Norton.

Vandenburg, Mary Lou. **Help! Emergencies That Could Happen to You, & How to Handle Them.** (Illus.). 1975. 3.95. Lerner Pubns.

Wilson, Judy. **Mother Nature's Homestead First Aid.** (Illus.). pap. 3.95. Oliver Pr.

Wurlitzer, Rudolph & Corry, Will. **The Family Book of First Aid.** (Illus.). 1970. pap. 1.25. Univ Pub & Dist.

FOREST RESERVES

Brockman, C. Frank & Merriam, Lawrence C., Jr. **Recreational Use of Wildlands.** 2nd ed. (Illus.). 1973. 13.95. McGraw.

Frome, Michael. **The National Forests of America.** (Illus.). 1968. 15.95. Country Beautiful.

Spring, Bob & Spring, Ira. **The Redwoods National Park.** (Illus.). 1975. pap. 2.95. Superior Pub.

Weiss, Raymond B. **A Scenic Guide to the Monongahela National Forest.** 1969. pap. 3.00. McClain.

HIKING

Bach, Orville. **Hiking the Yellowstone Backcountry.** (Illus.). 1973. pap. 4.95. Sierra.

Boy Scouts of America. **Hiking.** (Illus.). 1962. pap. 0.55. BSA.

Colby, C. B., ed. **Camper's & Backpacker's Bible.** (Illus.). 1977. softbound. 7.95. Stoeger.

Colwell, Robert. **Introduction to Foot Trails in America.** (Illus.). 1975. pap. B&N.

— — **Robert Colwell's Guide to Snow Trails.** 1973. 6.95; pap. 3.95. Stackpole.

Cooper, Ed & Gunning, Bob, photos by. **The Alpine Lakes.** (Illus.). 15.00 Mountaineers.

Dean, John. **Hiking the Inland Empire.** (Illus.). 1975. pap. 3.95. Signpost Pubns.

Doan, Daniel. **Fifty Hikes.** (Illus.). 1973. 8.95; pap. 5.95. NH Pub Co.

Elman, Robert. **The Hiker's Bible.** (Illus.). 1973. pap. 2.50. Doubleday.

Fawcett, Ken. **High Sierra Hiking Guide to Tower Peak.** Winnett, Thomas, ed. (Illus.). 1975. pap. 2.95. Wilderness.

Felzer, Ron. **High Sierra Hiking Guide to Devils Postpile.** (Illus.). 1971. pap. 1.95. Wilderness.

— — **High Sierra Hiking Guide to Hetch Hetchy.** Winnett, Thomas, ed. (Illus.). 1973. pap. 1.95. Wilderness.

— — **High Sierra Hiking Guide to Mineral King.** Winnett, Thomas, ed. (Illus.). 1972. pap. 1.95. Wilderness.

Fletcher, Colin. **New Complete Walker.** 1974. 10.00. Knopf.

Garvey, Edward B. **Appalachian Hiker.** (Illus.). 1971. pap. 4.50. Appalachian Bks.

Gibson, John. **Fifty Hikes in Maine.** (Illus.). 1976. pap. 5.95. NH Pub Co.

Goldmark, Pauline & Hopkins, Mary, compiled by. **The Gypsy Trail: An Anthology for Campers.** rev. ed. Repr. of 1914 ed. 14.75. Bks for Libs.

Grodin, Joseph R. **High Sierra Hiking Guide to Silver Lake.** (Illus.). 1976. pap. 3.95. Wilderness.

Harrison, C. William. **First Book of Hiking.** (Illus.). 1965. 3.90. Watts.

Hart, John. **Hiking the Bigfoot Country: Wildlands of Northern California & Southern Oregon.** (Illus.). 1975. pap. 7.95. Sierra.

Hiking. (Illus.). 1975. 3.50. T Y Crowell.

Hillaby, John. **Walk Through Britain.** (Illus.). 1969. 7.95. HM.

Hussong, Clara. **Nature Hikes.** (Illus.). 1973. 1.50. 3.95. Western Pub.

Hutchinson, M. **In a Wood.** 1960. 3.25. Intl Pubns Serv.

Jenkins, Jim & Robinson, John W. **High Sierra Hiking Guide to Kern Peak-Olancha.** Winnett, Thomas, ed. (Illus.). 1974. pap. 2.95. Wilderness.

Kelsey, Robert. **Walking in the Wild: The Complete Guide to Hiking & Backpacking.** 6.95. Funk & W.

Kelsey, Robert J. **Walking in the Wild.** (Illus.).1974. pap. 2.50. Funk & W.

Keyarts, Gene. **Forty Two More Short Walks in Connecticut.** Vol. 2. 1972. pap. 2.95. Pequot.

Lowe, Don & Lowe, Roberta. **One Hundred Southern California Hiking Trails.** (Illus.). 1972. pap. 5.95. Touchstone Pr Ore.

Merrill, Bill. **The Hiker's & Backpacker's Handbook.** (Illus.). 1972. pap. 2.95. Arc Bks.

Merrill, W. K. **Hikers & Backpackers Handbook.** (Illus.). 1971. 6.95. Winchester Pr.

Mitchell, Jim. **Hiking: A Curriculum Guide for Teaching Hiking.** rev. ed. 1974. pap. 2.50. Survival Ed. Assoc.

Monkhouse, Frank & Williams, Joe. **Climber & Fellwaker in Lakeland.** (Illus.). 1971. 9.95. David & Charles.

Nelson, Dick & Nelson, Sharon. **Fifty Hikes in Texas.** (Illus.). 1974. pap. 3.95. Tecolote Pr.

Pierce, Robert & Pierce, Margaret. **High Sierra Hiking Guide to Marion Peak.** Winnett, Thomas, ed. (Illus.). 1972. pap. 2.95. Wilderness.

— — **High Sierra Hiking Guide to Merced Peak.** Winnett, Thomas, ed. (Illus.). 1973. pap. 1.95. Wilderness.

Pyatt, Edward C. **A Climber in the West Country.** (Illus.). 1969. 5.95. David & Charles.

— — **Climbing & Walking in South East England.** (Illus.). 1970. 5.95. David & Charles.

Roberts, Harry N. **Movin' Out: Equipment & Techniques for Eastern Hikers.** (Illus.). 1975. pap. 3.95. Stone Wall Pr.

Robinson, John W. **High Sierra Hiking Guide to Mt. Goddard.** Winnett, Thomas, ed. (Illus.). 1973. pap. 1.95. Wilderness.

— — **High Sierra Hiking Guide to Mt. Pinchot.** Winnett, Thomas, ed. (Illus.). 1974. pap. 2.95. Wilderness.

— — **Trails of the Angeles.** Winnett, Thomas, ed. (Illus.). 1971. pap. 4.95. Wilderness.

Rudner, Ruth. **Wandering: A Walker's Guide to the Mountain Trails of Europe.** (Illus.). 1972. 8.95; pap. 3.95. Dial.

Sadlier, Paul & Sadlier, Ruth. **Fifty Hikes in Massachusetts.** (Illus.). 1975. pap. 5.95. NH Pub Co.

— — **Fifty Hikes in Vermont.** (Illus.). 1974. pap. 5.95. NH Pub Co.

Schaffer, Jeff. **The Tahoe Sierra.** Winnett, Thomas, ed. (Illus.). 1975. pap. 7.95. Wilderness.

Schwenke, Karl & Winnett, Thomas. **Sierra North.** 2nd ed. (Illus.). 1971. pap. 4.95. Wilderness.

Smith, Robert. **Hiking Maui: The Valley Isle.** 1975. pap. 2.95. Ritchie.

Sterling, E. M. **Trips & Trails, 1.** (Illus.). pap. 5.95. Mountaineers.

— — **Trips & Trails, 2.** pap. 5.95. Mountaineers.

Sullivan, Jerry & Daniel, Glenda. **Hiking Trails in the Midwest.** (Illus.). 1974. pap. 5.95. Greatlakes Liv.

— — **Hiking Trails in the Southern Mountains.** (Illus.). 1975. pap. 5.95. Greatlakes Liv.

Whitnah, Dorothy. **An Outdoor Guide to the San Francisco Bay Area.** Winnett, Thomas, ed. (Illus.). 1975. pap. 6.95. Wilderness.

Wilderness Press Editors. **High Sierra Hiking Guide to Yosemite.** rev. ed. Winnett, Thomas, ed. (Illus.). 1974. pap. 2.95. Wilderness.

Winnett, Thomas. **High Sierra Hiking Guide to Mono Craters.** (Illus.). 1975. pap. 3.95. Wilderness.

Winnett, Thomas & Roberts, Ed. **High Sierra Hiking Guide to Blackcap Mountain.** 2nd ed. (Illus.). 1975. pap. 2.95. Wilderness.

Winnett, Thomas, et al. **The Pacific Crest Trail: California.** (Illus.). 1973. pap. 4.95. Wilderness.

Wood, Robert L. **Trail Country.** 6.95. Mountaineers.

Wood, Robert S. **Pleasure Packing.** 1972. pap. 3.95. Condor Bks.

Woods, Bill & Woods, Erin. **Bicycling the Back Roads Around Puget Sound.** (Illus.). pap. 5.95. Mountaineers.

KNOTS AND SPLICES

Ashley, Clifford W. **Ashley Book of Knots.** (Illus.). 1944. 16.95. Doubleday.

Belash, C. A. **Braiding & Knotting.** 1974. pap. 1.50. Dover.

Belash, Constantine A. **Braiding & Knotting: Techniques & Projects.** (Illus.). 3.75. Peter Smith.

Blandford, Percy W. **Knots & Splices.** 1967. pap. 0.95. Arc Bks.

— — **Knots & Splices.** (Illus.). 1965. 4.50. Arco.

Burgess, Tom. **Knots, Ties & Splices: A Handbook for Seafarers, Travellers, & All Who Use Cordage; with Practical Notes on Wire & Wire Splicing, Anglers' Knots, Etc.** rev. ed. 1968. 2.50; pap. 1.95. Routledge & Kegan.

Day, Cyrus L. **Art of Knotting & Splicing.** 3rd rev. ed. (Illus.). 1970. 12.50. Naval Inst. Pr.

Gibson, Charles E. **Handbook of Knots & Splices: & Other Work with Hempen & Wire Rope.** (Illus.). 5.95. Emerson.

Gibson, Walter. **Fell's Official Guide to Knots.** 1961. pap. 2.95. Fell.

— — **Fell's Official Guide to Knots & How to Tie Them.** 1961. pap. 2.95. Magnet Bks.

Glass, Walter. **Key to Knots & Splices.** 2.00 Wehman.

— — **Key to Knots & Splices.** pap. 1.00. Key Bks.

Graumont, Raoul. **Handbook of Knots.** (Illus.). 1954. 3.50; pap. 2.50. Cornell Maritime.

Graumont, Raoul & Hensel, John. **Encyclopedia of Knots & Fancy Rope Work.** 4th ed. (Illus.). 1952. 15.00. Cornell Maritime.

— — **Splicing Wire & Fiber Rope.** (Illus.). 1970. pap. 3.50. Cornell Maritime.

Graumont, Raoul & Wenstrom, Elmer. **Fisherman's Knots & Nets.** (Illus.). 1948. 5.00. Cornell Maritime.

Hartzell, Warren & LaBarge, Lura. **Net-Making & Knotting.** (Illus.). 1974. 3.75. Sterling.

Knotting Crafts. (Illus.). 1975. 5.50. Intl. Pubns Serv.

Kreh, Lefty & Sosin, Mark. **Practical Fishing Knots.** (Illus.). 1975. softbound. 4.95. Crown/Stoeger.

Lewers, Dick. **Knots & Rigs: For Salt & Freshwater.** 1972. pap. 2.75. Reed.

Montgomery, Edward. **Useful Knots for Everyone.** (Illus.). 1973. 6.95; pap. 3.50. Scribner.

Porter Productions. **My Tie It Book.** (Illus.). 1975. 1.95. G&D.

Severn, Bill. **Rope Roundup: The Lore & Craft of Ropes & Roping.** (Illus.). 1960. 3.95. McKay.

Shaw, George R. **Knots: Useful & Ornamental.** 2nd ed. (Illus.). 1972. pap. 2.95. Macmillan.

Smith, Harvey G. **Arts of the Sailor.** (Illus.). 1968. pap. 1.75. Funk & W.

Smith, Harvey G. **Marlinspike Sailor.** rev. ed. (Illus.). 1969. 7.95. De Graff.

Snyder, Paul & Snyder, Arthur. **Knots & Lines.** (Illus.). 1970. 6.95. De Graff.

Svensson, Sam. **Handbook of Seaman's Rope Work.** (Illus.). 1972. 6.95. Dodd.

Wheelock, Walt. **Ropes, Knots & Slings for Climbers.** rev. ed. (Illus.). 1967. 1.00. La Siesta.

MAPS

Clausson, Martin P. & Friis, Herman R. **American & Foreign Maps Published by the U.S. Congress, 1789-1861.** (Illus.). 1975. pap. 30.00. Piedmont.

Dickinson, G. C. **Maps & Air Photographs.** 1969. 9.25. Crane-Russak Co.

Giachino, J. W. & Beukema, Henry J. **Drafting Technology.** 2nd ed. (Illus.). 1971. 8.50. Am Technical.

Greenhood, David. **Mapping.** rev. ed. 1964. 8.50; pap. 3.95. U of Chicago Pr.

Jennings, J. H. **Elementary Map Interpretation.** 1960. 1.75. Cambridge U Pr.

Kjellstrom, Bjorn. **Be Expert with Map & Compass: The Orienteering Handbook.** 1972. pap. 3.95. Scribner.

Riffel, Paul. **Reading Maps.** (Illus.). 1973. pap. 4.95. Hubbard Sci.

Speak, P. & Carter, A. H. **Map Reading & Interpretation.** 4th ed. (Illus.). 1974. pap. 3.50. Longman.

Tyner, Judith A. **The World of Maps & Mapping: A Creative Learning Aid.** Thrower, Norman J., ed. (Illus.). 1973. pap. 4.95. McGraw.

Van De Gohm, Richard. **Antique Maps for the Collector.** 1973. 7.95. Macmillan.

MAPS—CANADA

Canada Road Atlas, 1975. 1975. pap. 3.95. Rand.

Hare, Kenneth & Thomas, Morley. **Climate Canada.** 1974. 10.50. Wiley.

MOUNTAINEERING

Ahluwalia, H. P. **Higher Than Everest.** (Illus.). 1974. 6.00. Intl School Bk Serv.

Appalachian Mountain Club. **Maine Mountain Guide.** 1971. 6.50. Appalach Mtn.

Baker, Ernest A. **The British Highlands with Rope & Rucksack.** (Illus.). 1973. Repr. of 1933 ed. 11.50. British Bk Ctr.

Bauer, Erwin A. **Cross-Country Skiing and Snowshoeing.** (Illus.). 1976. softbound. 5.95. Stoeger.

Beery, Donald. **Call of the Mountains.** (Illus.). 1973. 7.00. McClain.

Blackshaw, Alan. **Mountaineering.** rev. ed. 1975. pap. 8.95. Penguin.

Bonington, Chris. **The Ultimate Challenge: The Hardest Way up the Highest Mountain in the World.** (Illus.). 1973. 12.50. Stein & Day.

Bonney, Orrin H. & Bonney, Lorraine G. **Field Book Wind River Range.** rev. ed. (Illus.). 1968. pap. 4.95. with supp. Bonney.

Boudreau, Eugene. **Trails of the Sierra Madre.** (Illus.). 1973. pap. 3.75. Scrimshaw.

Bridge, Raymond. **Climbing: A Guide to Mountaineering.** 1975. 12.50. Scribner.

Bunting, James. **Climbing.** Orig. Title: **Rock & Hill Climbing.** 1974. 2.95. T Y Crowell.

Casewit, Curtis. **Hiking-Climbing Handbook.** (Illus.). 1969. 4.95. Hawthorn.

Casewit, Curtis W. & Pownall, Richard. **Mountaineering Handbook: An Invitation to Climbing.** (Illus.). 1968. 7.25. Lippincott.

Clark, Ronald. **The Alps.** 1973. 15.95. Knopf.

Crew, Peter. **Dictionary of Mountaineering.** (Illus.). 1969. 5.95. Stackpole.
Darvil, Fred T., Jr. **Mountaineering Medicine: A Wilderness Medical Guide.** 7th ed. 1975. pap. 1.00. Darvil Outdoor.
Fedden, Robin. **The Enchanted Mountains: Quest in the Pyrenees.** 5.75. Transatlantic.
Haston, Dougal. **In High Places.** (Illus.). 1973. 5.95. Macmillan.
Hewitt, H. B., ed. **Peter Graham Mountain Guide: An Autobiography.** (Illus.). 1965. 12.95. Reed.
Higman, Harry W. & Larrison, Earl J. **Pilchuck, the Life of a Mountain.** 1949. pap. 10.00. Shorey.
Jacobson, Frederick L. **The Meek Mountaineer: A Climber's Armchair Companion.** (Illus.). 1974. 8.95. Liveright.
King, Clarence. **Mountaineering in the Sierra Nevada.** 1970. pap. 2.25. U of Nebr Pr.
Lewis, H. Warren. **You're Standing on My Fingers.** (Illus.). 1969. 5.95. Howell-North.
Lovelock, James. **Climbing.** 1975. 7.50. Hippocrene Bks.
Lyman, Tom & Riviere, Bill. **The Field Book of Mountaineering & Rock Climbing.** (Illus.). 1975. 8.95. Winchester Pr.
Meldrum, Kim & Royle, Brian. **Artificial Climbing Walls.** (Illus.). 1971. 5.75. Transatlantic.
Mendenhall, Ruth & Mendenhall, John. **Beginner's Guide to Rock & Mountain Climbing.** rev. ed. (Illus.). 1975. pap. 3.95. Stackpole.
— — **Introduction to Rock & Mountain Climbing.** (Illus.). 1969. 6.95. Stackpole.
Messner, Reinhold. **Seventh Grade.** 1974. 8.50. Oxford U Pr.
Moore, Terris. **Mt. McKinley: The Pioneer Climbs.** (Illus.). 1967. 6.95. U of Wash Pr.
Mountaineering: The Freedom of the Hills. 3rd ed. (Illus.). 9.95. Mountaineers.
Mummery, Albert F. **My Climbs in the Alps & Caucasus.** (Illus.). 1974. Repr. of 1896 ed. 15.00. Quarterman.
Oddo, G., intro. by. **Color Treasury of Mountain Climbing.** (Illus.). 1974. pap. 1.98. Crown.
Paulcke, Wilhelm & Dumler, Helmut. **Hazards in Mountaineering: How to Recognize & Avoid Them.** Bowman, E. Noel, tr. (Illus.). 1973. 9.95. Oxford U Pr.
Piggott, Margaret. **Discover Southeast Alaska: With Pack and Paddle.** (Illus.). 1975. pap. 7.95. Mountaineers.
Rebuffat, Gaston. **Between Heaven & Earth.** Brockett, E., tr. (Illus.). 1965. 15.00. Oxford U Pr.
— — **On Ice & Snow & Rock.** Evans, Patrick, tr. from Fr. (Illus.). 1971. 19.50. Oxford U Pr.
— — **Starlight & Storm: The Ascent of Six Great North Faces of the Alps.** 1968. 8.00. Oxford U Pr.
Robbins, Royal. **Basic Rockcraft.** (Illus.). 1970. 1.95. La Siesta.
Roper, Steve. **Climbers Guide to Yosemite Valley.** (Illus.). 1971. pap. 6.95. Sierra.
Rossit, Edward A. **Snow Camping & Mountaineering.** (Illus.). 1970. 10.00; pap. 2.95. Funk & W.
Rudner, Ruth. **Huts & Hikes in the Dolomites.** (Illus.). 1974. pap. 4.95. Sierra.
Ryback, Eric & Ryback, Tim. **The Ultimate Journey—Canada to Mexico Down the Continental Divide.** (Illus.). 1973. 7.95. Chronicle Bks.
Sayre, Woodrow W. **Four Against Everest.** (Illus.). 1971. pap. 0.95. Tower.
Scarr, Josephine. **Four Miles High.** (Illus.). 1966. 9.00. Intl Pubns Serv.
Scott, Doug. **Big Wall Climbing: Development, Techniques & Aids.** (Illus.). 1974. 12.50. Oxford U Pr.
Tabor, R. W. & Crowder, D. F. **Routes & Rocks in Mt. Challenger Quadrangle.** (Illus.). pap. 2.95. Mountaineers.
Ullman, James R. **Age of Mountaineering.** rev. ed. (Illus.). 1964. 8.95. Lippincott.

Unsworth, Walt. **The Encyclopedia of Mountaineering.** (Illus.). 1975. 12.95. St. Martin.
Wall, David. **Rondoy.** 1965. 7.50. Transatlantic.
Wheelock, Walt. **Ropes, Knots & Slings for Climbers.** rev. ed. (Illus.). 1967. 1.00. La Siesta.
Wheelock, Walt & Condon, T. **Climbing Mount Whitney.** rev. ed. (Illus.). 1974. 1.00. La Siesta.
White Mt. Guide. 1972. 9.00. Appalach Mtn.
Whymper, Edward. **Scrambles Amongst the Alps.** rev. ed. (Illus.). 14.50. Transatlantic.
Wilkerson, James A., ed. **Medicine for Mountaineering.** (Illus.). 7.50. Mountaineers.
Williams, Cicely. **Women on the Rope: The Feminine Share in Mountain Adventure.** (Illus.). 1974. 13.25. Intl Pubns Serv.
Wolford, Feaster. **Mountain Memories.** 1975. price not set. Macclain.

NATIONAL PARK SERVICE—UNITED STATES

Cameron, Jenks. **The National Park Service: Its History, Activities & Organization.** Repr. of 1922 ed. 15.00. AMS Pr.
Everhart, William C. **National Park Service.** (Illus.). 1972. 9.00. Praeger.
Sutton, Ann & Sutton, Myron. **Guarding the Treasured Lands: The Story of the National Park Service.** (Illus.). 1965. 3.75. Lippincott.
Swain, Donald C. **Wilderness Defender: Horace M. Albright & Conservation.** (Illus.). 1970. 10.75. U of Chicago Pr.
Tilden, Freeman. **Interpreting Our Heritage.** rev. ed. (Illus.). pap. 1.95. U of NC Pr.
— — **Intepreting Our Heritage.** (Illus.). 1967. pap. 2.75. AASLH.

NATIONAL PARKS AND RESERVES—UNITED STATES

Adams, Ansel & Newhall, Nancy. **This Is the American Earth.** (Illus.). 1960. 15.00. Sierra.
Allen, E. F. **Guide to the National Parks of America.** 34.95. Gordon Pr.
Barker, Ballard M. **Platt National Park.** 1975. 5.95. U of Okla Pr.
Blake, P. **God's Own Junkyard: The Planned Deterioration of America's Landscape.** 1964. pap. 2.95. HR&W.
Brockman, C. Frank & Merriam, Lawrence C., Jr. **Recreational Use of Wildlands.** 2nd ed. (Illus.). 1973. 13.95. McGraw.
Brooks, Maurice. **Life of the Mountains.** (Illus.). 1968. 5.50. McGraw.
Butcher, Devereux. **Exploring Our National Parks & Monuments.** 6th rev. ed. (Illus.). 1969. 8.95; pap. 4.95. HM.
Cameron, Jenks. **The National Park Service: Its History, Activities & Organization.** Repr. of 1922 ed. 15.00. AMS Pr.
Conservation Foundation. **Dominica: A Chance for a Choice.** (Illus.). 1970. pap. 2.00. Conservation Foun.
— — **National Parks for the Future.** 1974. pap. 3.50. Conservation Foun.
Country Beautiful Editors. **One Hundred One Wonders of America.** (Illus.). 1973. 25.00. Country Beautiful.
Darling, Frank F. & Eichhorn, Noel D. **Man & Nature in the National Parks: Reflections on Policy.** 2nd ed. (Illus.). 1969. pap. 1.50. Conservation Foun.
Dolezal, Robert J. **Exploring Redwood National Park.** (Illus.). pap. 5.95. Touchstone Pr Ore.
Eastman Kodak Company, ed. **Kodak Guide-America's National Parks.** pap. 1.50. Amphoto.
Everhart, William C. **National Park Service.** (Illus.). 1972. 9.00. Praeger.

Frome, Michael. **National Park Guide** (Illus.). 1975. 7.95; pap. 4.95. Rand.
Guggisberg, C. A. **Man & Wildlife.** (Illus.). 1970. 12.50. Arco.
Hampton, H. Duane. **How the U.S. Cavalry Saved Our National Parks.** (Illus.). 1971. 9.50. Ind U Pr.
Jackson, Earl. **Your National Park System in the Southwest, in Words & Color.** 2nd ed. (Illus.). 1967. pap. 2.50. SW Pks & Mnmts.
James, Harlean. **Romance of the National Parks.** (Illus.). 1972. Repr. of 1939 ed. 13.00. Arno.
Lindsay, Diana E. **Our Historic Desert.** (Illus.) 1973. 9.50. Copley Bks.
Matthews, William H., 3rd. **A Guide to the National Parks, Their Landscape—Geology, Vol. 1, Western Parks.** (Illus.). 1968. 10.95; pap. 5.95. Natural Hist.
Muir, John. **Our National Parks.** (Illus.). 1970. Repr. of 1901 ed. 11.50. AMS Pr.
— — **Our National Parks.** 1901. 7.95. Scholarly.
Peterson, Charles S. **Look to the Mountains.** 1975. 9.50. Brigham.
Rich, Pamela E. & Tussing, Arlon R. **The National Park System in Alaska: An Economic Impact Study.** 1972. pap. 5.00. U of Wash Pr.
— — **The National Park System in Alaska: An Economic Impact Study.** (Illus.). 1973. pap. 5.00. U Alaska Inst Res.
Rowe, Royle C. **Geology of Our Western National Parks & Monuments.** (Illus.). 1973. pap. 3.50. Binford.
Sunset Editors. **National Parks of the West.** rev. ed. 1970. 14.95. Lane.
Swain, Donald. **The National Parks.** 1969. 1.95. Am West.
Tilden, Freeman. **National Parks.** rev. ed. 1968. 15.00; pap. 4.95. Knopf.
Udall, Stewart. **The National Parks.** 1974. 3.95. Grossman.
Udall, Stewart L. **America's Natural Treasures.** (Illus.). 1971. 14.95. Rand.
— — **The National Parks of America.** rev. ed. Country Beautiful Editors, ed. (Illus.). 1972. 22.50. Country Beautiful.
United Nations List of National Parks & Equivalent Reserves, with Addendum, 1972. (Illus.). 1971-72. pap. 28.00. Bowker.
World Wildlife Fund. **World Wildlife Guide: A Complete Handbook Covering All the World's Outstanding National Parks, Reserves, & Sanctuaries.** Ross-Macdonald, Malcolm, ed. (Illus.). 1972. 8.95. Viking Pr.

NATURAL MONUMENTS

American Heritage Editors. **The American Heritage Book of Natural Wonders.** 1972. 16.50; deluxe ed. 19.00. McGraw.
Clark, Champ. **The Badlands.** 1975. 8.95. Time-Life.
Colby, C. B. **Wildlife in Our National Parks: Birds, Reptiles & Mammals.** (Illus.). 1965. 4.95. Coward.
Janus, Horst. **Nature As Architect.** (Illus.). 5.75. Ungar.

NATURE CONSERVATION

Arbib, Robert S., Jr. **The Lord's Woods.** 1971. 6.95. Norton.
Arneson, D. J. **Secret Places.** (Illus.). 1971. pap. 2.95. HR&W.
Baldwin, D. N. **The Quiet Revolution.** 1973. 9.95. Pruett.
Clark, John. **Rookery Bay: Ecological Constraints on Coastal Development.** (Illus.). 1975. pap. 4.00. Conservation Foun.
Conservation Foundation. **Dominica: A Chance for a Choice.** (Illus.). 1970. pap. 2.00 Conservation Foun.
Curry-Lindahl, Kai. **Conservation for Survival: An Ecological Strategy.** 1972. 7.95. Morrow.

Dennis, Eve. **Everyman's Nature Reserve: Ideas for Action.** (Illus.). 1973. 15.00. David & Charles.

Dorst, Jean. **Before Nature Dies.** 1971. pap. 3.95. Penguin.

Duffy, Eric. **Conservation of Nature.** (Illus.). 1970. 4.72. McGraw.

Ehrenfeld, David. **Conserving Life on Earth.** (Illus.). 1972. 10.00. Oxford U Pr.

Farvar, M. Taghi & Milton, John P., eds. **The Careless Technology: Ecology & International Development.** (Illus.). 25.00. Natural Hist.

Feiss, Carl, et al. **The Demographic, Political, & Administrative Setting.** 1973. pap. 1.00. Conservation Foun.

Frome, Michael. **Battle for the Wilderness.** 1974. 8.95. Praeger.

Gifford, John C. **On Preserving Tropical Florida.** (Illus.). 1972. 7.95. U of Miami Pr.

Gilliam, Harold. **Between the Devil & the Deep Blue Bay.** 1969. pap. 2.95. Chronicle Bks.

Gunter, A. Y. **The Big Thicket: A Challenge for Conservation.** 1972. 12.50. Jenkins.

Heald, Eric J. & Tabb, Durbin C. **Applicability of the Interceptor Waterway Concept to the Rookery Bay Area.** 1973. pap. 1.00. Conservation Foun.

Huth, Hans. **Nature & the American: Three Centuries of Changing Attitudes.** (Illus.). 1972. pap. 2.95. U of Nebr. Pr.

Krutilla, John V., ed. **Natural Environments: Studies in Theoretical & Applied Analysis.** 1973. 16.50. Johns Hopkins.

Line, Les, ed. **What We Save Now.** 1973. 10.00. HM.

Marine, Gene. **America the Raped.** (Illus.). 1969. 5.95. S&S.

Marx, Wesley. **The Pacific Shore.** (Illus.). 1974. 20.00. Dutton.

Myers, Phyllis. **Slow Start in Paradise.** 1974. pap. 1.00. Conservation Foun.

Nicholson, E. M. **Handbook to the Conservation Section of the International Biological Programme.** 1968. pap. 2.25. Lippincott.

Rookery Bay Area Project. 1974. pap. 2.50. Conservation Foun.

ORIENTATION

Disley, John. **Orienteering.** (Illus.). 1973. pap. 3.95. Stackpole.

Kjellstrom, Bjorn. **Be Expert with Map & Compass: The Orienteering Handbook.** 1972. pap. 3.95. Scribner.

Mooers, Robert L., Jr. **Finding Your Way in the Outdoors.** 1972. 6.95. Times Mirror Mag.

Ratliff, Donald E. **Map, Compass & Campfire.** (Illus.). 1970. pap. 1.50. Binford.

Rutstrum, Calvin. **Wilderness Route Finder.** 1967. 4.95. Macmillan.

OUTDOOR COOKERY

Ames, Mark & Ames, Roberta. **Barbecues.** new ed. 1973. pap. 0.95. Warner Bks.

Angier, Bradford. **Wilderness Cookery.** (Illus.). 1970. pap. 3.95. Stackpole.

Banks, James E. **Alferd Packer's Wilderness Cookbook.** (Illus.). 1969. 4.00; pap. 1.00. Filter.

Barker, Harriett. **The One Burner Gourmet.** (Illus.). 1975. pap. 4.95. Greatlakes Liv.

Butness, Marilyn A., ed. **Woodall's Campsite Cookbook.** 1971. pap. 2.95. S&S.

Bates, Joseph D., Jr. **Outdoor Cook's Bible.** (Illus.). 1964. pap. 2.50. Doubleday.

Beard, James A. **Fireside Cookbook.** (Illus.). 1969. 14.95. S&S.

Berglund, Berndt & Bolsby, Clare. **Wilderness Cooking.** 1973. 8.95. Scribner.

Brent, Carol D., ed. **Barbecue: The Fine Art of Charcoal, Gas & Hibachi Outdoor Cooking.** (Illus.). 1971. 4.95. Doubleday.

Bunnelle, Hasse. **Food for Knapsackers.** 1971. pap. 3.95. Sierra.

Bunnelle, Hasse & Sarvis, Shirley. **Cooking for Camp & Trail.** 1972. pap. 3.95. Sierra.

Carhart, Arthur H. **Outdoorsman's Cookbook.** rev. ed. 1962. pap. 0.95. Macmillan.

Crocker, Betty. **Betty Crocker's New Outdoor Cookbook.** (Illus.). 1967. 3.95; pap. 3.50. Western Pub.

Culinary Arts Institute Editorial Staff. **The Master Chef's Outdoor Grill Cookbook.** (Illus.). 1975. pap. 2.95. G&D.

Dawson, Charlotte. **Recreational Vehicle Cookbook.** (Illus.). 1970. 3.95. Trail-R.
— — **Trailerists Cookbook.** 2.95. Trail-R.

Dodd, Ed. **Mark Trail's Cooking Tips.** 1971. pap. 1.00. Essandess.

Douglas, Luther A. & Douglas, Conda E. **The Explorers Cookbook.** (Illus.). 1971. 14.95. Caxton.

Farmer, Charles J. & Farmer, Kathy, eds. **Campground Cooking.** 1974. pap. 6.95. Follett.

Fiske, Jean & Cross, Margaret. **Backpack Cookbook.** 1973. 7.95; pap. 3.00. Ten Speed Pr.

Fitzgerald. **Easy to Bar-B-Q Cook Book: A Guide to Better Barbecuing.** pap. 2.95. Pacifica.

Holm, Don. **Old-Fashioned Dutch Oven Cookbook.** 1969. pap. 3.95. Caxton.

Hughes, Stella. **Chuck Wagon Cookin'.** 1974. pap. 4.95. U of Ariz Pr.

Knap, Alyson. **The Outdoorsman's Guide to Edible Wild Plants of North America: An Illustrated Manual.** (Illus.). 1975. 8.95. Pagurian.

McElfresh, Beth. **Chuck Wagon Cookbook.** pap. 1.95. Swallow.

Macmillan, Diane D. **The Portable Feast.** (Illus.). 1973. 7.95; pap. 4.95. One Hund One Prods.

McMorris, Bill & McMorris, Jo. **The All Outdoors Cookbook.** (Illus.). 1974. 7.95. McKay.

Marshall, Mel. **Cooking Over Coals.** 1975. softbound. 5.95. Stoeger.
— — **The Family Cookout Cookbook.** 1973. pap. 0.95. Ace Bks.

Martin, George W. **The Complete Book of Outdoor Cooking.** (Illus.). 1975. 6.95. A S Barnes.

Mendenhall, Ruth D. **Backpack Cookery.** (Illus.). 1974. 1.50. La Siesta.

Messner, Yvonne. **Campfire Cooking.** (Illus.). 1973. pap. 1.95. Cook.

Morris, Dan & Morris, Inez. **Complete Outdoor Cookbook.** 1970. 8.95. Hawthorn.

Raup, Lucy G. **Camper's Cookbook.** 1967. pap. 3.75. C E Tuttle.

Riviere, William A. **Family Campers' Cookbook.** (Illus.). 1965. 4.95. HR&W.

Schubert, Ruth L. **The Camper's Cookbook.** 1974. pap. 3.50. Little.

Steindler, Geraldine. **Game Cookbook.** (Illus.). 1965. softbound. 4.95. Stoeger.

Stephens, Mae W. & Wells, G. S. **Coping with Camp Cooking.** 1968. 2.95. Stackpole.

Strom, Arlene. **Cooking on Wheels.** (Illus.). 1970. 4.95; pap. 2.95. Wheelwright.

Tarr, Yvonne Y. **The Complete Outdoor Cookbook.** (Illus.). 1973. 8.95. Quadrangle.

Thomas, Dian. **Roughing It Easy: A Unique Ideabook for Camping & Cooking.** (Illus.). 1974. 7.95; pap. 4.95. Brigham.

Tonn, Maryjane H., ed. **Ideals Outdoor Cook Book.** 1975. pap. 1.75. Ideals.

Woodall's Campsite Cookbook. pap. 2.95. Woodall.

OUTDOOR EDUCATION

American Alliance for Health, Physical Education, & Recreation. **Outdoor Education.** rev. ed. 1970. 1.50. AAHPER.

Crisp, Wynnlee. **Development & Use of the Outdoor Classroom: An Annotated Bibliography.** 1975. 6.00. Scarecrow.

Donaldson, George W. & Goering, Oswald. **Perspectives on Outdoor Education Readings.** 1972. pap. 4.95. Wm C Brown.

Garrison, Cecil. **Outdoor Education: Principles & Practice.** (Illus.). 1966. 9.50. C C Thomas.

Hammerman, Donald R. & Hammerman, William M. **Outdoor Education: A Book of Readings.** 2nd ed. 1973. pap. 7.95. Burgess.
— — **Teaching in the Outdoors.** 2nd ed. 1973. pap. 4.50. Burgess.

Milliken, Margaret, et al. **Field Study Manual for Outdoor Learning.** (Illus.). 1968. 3.95. Burgess.

Morris, Taylor. **The Walk of the Conscious Ants.** (Illus.). 1972. 6.95. Knopf.

Smith, Julian, et al. **Outdoor Education.** 2nd ed. (Illus.). 1972. 10.50. P-H.

Swan, Malcolm D., ed. **Tips & Tricks in Outdoor Education.** 1970. pap. 4.50. Interstate.

ROCK CLIMBING

Aleith, R. C. **Bergsteigen. Basic Rock Climbing.** (Illus.). 1975. 12.50; pap. 5.95. Scribner.

Harding, Warren J. **Downward Bound: A Counter Culture Guide to Rock Climbing.** (Illus.). 1975. 7.95; pap. 4.95. P-H.

Kloke, Dallas S. **Boulders & Cliffs: Climber's Guide to Lowland Rock in Skagit & Whatcom Counties.** (Illus.). 1971. pap. 2.50. Signpost Pubns.

Lyman, Tom & Riviere, Bill. **The Field Book of Mountaineering & Rock Climbing.** (Illus.). 1975. 8.95. Winchester Pr.

Mendenhall, Ruth & Mendenhall, John. **Beginner's Guide to Rock & Mountain Climbing.** rev. ed. (Illus.). 1975. pap. 3.95. Stackpole.
— — **Introduction to Rock & Mountain Climbing.** (Illus.). 1969. 6.95. Stackpole.

Rebuffat, Gaston. **On Ice & Snow & Rock.** Evans, Patrick, tr. from Fr. (Illus.). 1971. 19.50. Oxford U Pr.

Robinson, John. **Camping & Climbing in Baja.** 3rd ed. (Illus.). 1972. La Siesta.

Roper, Steve. **Climbers Guide to Yosemite Valley.** (Illus.). 1971. pap. 6.95. Sierra.

TRAILER CAMPS

Behrend, Herbert, ed. **Mobile Home Park Market Analysis & Economic Feasibility Study.** 1971. 5.50. Mobile Homes.

Behrend, Herbert, compiled by. **Mobile Home Park Plans & Specs: Preliminary Plans, General Specifications & Comparative Cost Outline,** 2 vols., Vol. 1. 1969. pap. 9.75. Mobile Homes.

Behrend, Herbert & Ghorbani, Daryoush, eds. **Mobile Home Park Plans & Specs: Complete Engineering Working Drawings, for Four Projects with Two Detailed Cost Breakdowns.** Vol. 2. 1970. pap. 16.00. Mobile Homes.

Hayes, Richard L. **Trailering America's Highways & Byways.** 2 vols. (Illus.). 1965. 3.95 ea. Vol. 1: The West; Vol. 2: The East. Trail-R.

Michelon, L. C. & Behrend, Herbert. **How to Build & Operate a Mobile Home Park.** 1970. 5.50. Mobile Homes.

Mobile Home Manufacturers Association, Consumer Education Division. **Bibliography: Mobile Home Industry.** 1973. pap. 0.75. Mobile Homes.

Mobile Home Parks. 1973. pap. 2.50. Natl Fire Prot.

Mobile Homes Manufacturers Association. **Environmental Health Guide for Mobile Home Communities.** 1971. pap. 2.25. Mobile Homes.

Mobile Homes Manufacturers Association, Land Development Division. **Mobile Home Site Planning Kit: Basic Information Concerning Park Development.** 1971. 10.00. Mobile Homes.

Newcomb, Robinson. **Mobile Homes: Analysis of Characteristics.** Pt. 1. (Illus.). 1972. pap. 15.00. Urban Land.

Nulsen, David. **All About Park for Mobile Homes & Recreation Vehicles.** 1973. 4.50. Trail-R.

— — **Manual for Purchasing a Mobile or Recreation Vehicle Park.** 1973. 25.00. Trail-R.

Nulsen, David R. & Nulsen, Robert. **Handbook for Developing Mobile Home & Recreation Vehicle Parks.** 1973. 29.95. Trail-R.

Nulsen, Robert H. **All About Parks for Mobile Homes & Trailers.** (Illus.). 2.75. Trail-R.

— — **Construction, Management, Investment Potential of Mobile Home & Recreational Vehicle Parks.** (Illus.). 1970. 10.95. Trail-R.

Rand McNally. **Rand McNally 1975 Campground & Trailer Park Guide.** 1975. 6.95. Rand.

Rouse, Art, ed. **Trailer Life's Recreational Vehicle Campground & Services Guide, 1974.** (Illus.). 1974. pap. 5.45. Chilton.

Simonds, Raymond L. **Handbook of Trailer Camping.** 4.95. Lee Pubns.

Sparer, Fred. **Complete Set Mobile Home Park Blue Prints & Specifications.** 24.95. Trail-R.

— — **How to Build Mobile Home Parks.** rev. ed. (Illus.). 1971. pap. 14.95. Trail-R.

— — **How to Build Recreational Vehicle Parks.** (Illus.). 1969. 12.95. Trail-R.

Wehrly, Max. **Mobile Homes: An Analysis of Communities.** Pt. 2. (Illus.). 1972. pap. 15.00. Urban Land.

Wilkinson, Tim. **Motor Caravanning.** (Illus.). 1968. 4.95. David & Charles.

Woodall's Trailering Parks & Campgrounds-1974. 1974. 6.95. S&S.

Woodall's Trailering Parks & Campgrounds-1974: Western States Edition. 1974. 2.95. S&S.

TRAILER CAMPS—DIRECTORIES

California Campgrounds, & Trailer Parks, 1975. 1975. pap. 2.95. Rand.

Chase, Max & Chase, Linda. **Campground Guide for Tent & Trailer Tourists, 1975-76.** 13th ed. 1975. pap. 2.25. Campgrounds.

Fuller, Curtis G. **Woodall's Mobile Home & Park Directory, 1974.** 1974. pap. 5.95. Woodall.

— — **Woodall's Trailering Parks & Campgrounds, 1973.** 1974. pap. 6.95. Woodall.

Peterson, Ed., ed. **Midwest Campgrounds & Trailer Parks, 1975.** 1975. pap. 3.95. Rand.

— — **Northeast Campgrounds & Trailer Parks, 1975.** 1975. pap. 3.95. Rand.

— — **Southeast Campgrounds & Trailer Parks, 1975.** 1975. pap. 3.95. Rand.

Woodall's Mobile Home & Park Directory-1974. 1974. 6.95. S&S.

TRAILS

Appalachian Mountain Club. **Massachusetts-Rhode Island Trail Guide.** 3rd ed. 1972. 7.75. Appalach Mtn.

Arizona Rock Trails. 1.95. Gembooks.

Bottcher, Betty & Davis, Mel. **Wasatch Trails.** (Illus.). 1973 pap. 1.50. Wasatch Pubs.

Chisholm, William V. **Chisholm's Trail Across Canada & the United States.** 6.95. Vantage.

Colwell, Robert. **Introduction to Foot Trails in America.** 1975. pap. 1.50. B&N.

— — **Introduction to Foot Trails in America.** 1972. pap. 3.95. Stackpole.

— — **Introduction to Water Trails of America.** (Illus.). 1973. 6.95; pap. 3.95. Stackpole.

Cushman, Dan. **Great North Trail: America's Route of the Ages.** Guthrie, A. B., Jr., ed. 1966. 7.95. McGraw.

Davis, Mel. **High Uinta Trails.** (Illus.). 1974. pap. 2.95. Wasatch Pubs.

Davis, Mel & Schimpf, Ann. **Cache Trails.** (Illus.). 1974. pap. 1.50. Wasatch Pubs.

Dicken, Samuel N. **Pioneer Trails of the Oregon Coast.** (Illus.). 1971. pap. 1.95. Oreg Hist Soc.

Gard, Wayne, et al. **Along the Early Trails of the Southwest.** (Illus.). 17.50; limited ed. 60.00. Jenkins.

Kenofer, L. **Rocky Mountain Trails.** rev. ed. 1970. pap. 4.50. Pruett.

Lowe, Don & Lowe, Roberta. **Eighty Northern Colorado Hiking Trails.** 1973. pap. 4.95. Touchstone Pr Ore.

— — **One Hundred Northern California Hiking Trails.** (Illus.). 1970. pap. 5.95. Touchstone Pr Ore.

Mitchell, Finis. **Wind River Trails.** Davis, Mel, ed. (Illus.). 1975. pap. 2.95. Wasatch Pubs.

New York-New Jersey Trail Conference & American Geographical Society. **The New York Walk Book.** (Illus.). 9.95; pap. 5.95. Natural Hist.

Price, Steven D. **Horseback Vacation Guide.** (Illus.). 1975. 7.95; pap. 4.95. Greene.

Pyatt, Edward C. **Coastal Paths of the South West.** (Illus.). 1971. 7.95. David & Charles.

Robinson, John W. **San Bernardino Mountain Trails.** 2nd ed. Winnett, Thomas, ed. (Illus.). 1975. pap. 5.95. Wilderness.

Spring, Ira L. & Manning, Harvey. **Wilderness Trails Northwest.** (Illus.). 1974. pap. 5.95. Touchstone Pr Ore.

Sullivan, Jerry & Daniel, Glenda. **Hiking Trails in the Midwest.** (Illus.). 1974. pap. 5.95. Greatlakes Liv.

Thomas, Bill. **Eastern Trips & Trails.** (Illus.). 1975. pap. 4.95. Stackpole.

— — **Mid-America Trips & Trails.** (Illus.). 1975. pap. 4.95. Stackpole.

Wentworth, E. N. **America's Sheep Trails: History, Personalities.** 1973. Repr. of 1948 ed. 49.00. Johnson Repr.

Westbrook, Anne & Westbrook, Perry. **Trail Horses & Trail Riding.** pap. 2.00. Wilshire.

Winnett, Thomas, ed. **High Sierra Hiking Guide to Mt. Abbot.** 1969. pap. 1.95. Wilderness.

WALKING

Browne, Waldo R., ed. **Joys of the Road.** Facs. ed. 1911. 8.75. Bks for Libs.

Cummings, George. **Walking for Road & Track.** (Illus.). 1957. 0.85. Assoc Bk.

Ducroquet, Robert, et al. **Walking & Limping: A Study of Normal & Pathological Walking.** (Illus.). 1968. 18.25. Lippincott.

Fuller, Raymond T. **Now That We Have to Walk: Exploring the Out-of-Doors.** facs. ed. Repr. of 1943 ed. 12.00. Bks for Libs.

Goode, Ruth & Sussman, Aaron. **The Magic of Walking.** 1969. pap. 2.95. S&S.

Johnson, Harry J. & Bass, Ralph. **Creative Walking for Physical Fitness.** (Illus.). 1970. pap. 1.00. G&D.

Krochmal, Arnold. **The Walker's Guide to Nature.** (Illus.). 1976. 7.95. Drake Pubs.

Pyatt, Edward C. **A Climber in the West Country.** (Illus.). 1969. 5.95. David & Charles.

— — **Climbing & Walking in South East England.** (Illus.). 1970. 5.95. David & Charles.

Takach, Mary J. **The Right Way to Walk for Health.** 1973. pap. 1.25. Univ Pub & Dist.

Trent, George, ed. **The Gentle Art of Walking: Selections from the New York Times.** 1971. 12.95. Arno.

Zochert, Donald. **Walking in America.** 1974. 10.00. Knopf.

WILDERNESS AREAS

Angier, Vena & Angier, Bradford. **At Home in the Woods: Living the Life of Thoreau Today.** (Illus.). 1971. pap. 1.50. Macmillan.

Baldwin, D. N. **The Quiet Revolution.** 1973. 9.95. Pruett.

Carrighar, Sally. **Home to the Wilderness: A Personal Journey.** 1974. pap. 1.95. Penguin.

Dasmann, Raymond F. **A Different Kind of Country.** 1970. 5.95; pap. 1.95. Macmillan.

— — **The Last Horizon.** 1971. pap. 2.95. Macmillan.

Frome, Michael. **Battle for the Wilderness.** 1974. 8.95. Praeger.

Gillette, Elizabeth, ed. **Action for Wilderness.** 1972. pap. 2.25. Sierra.

Hamper, Stanley R. **Wilderness Survival.** 1973. Repr. of 1963 ed. 1.29. Peddlers Wagon.

Jackson, Don. **Sagebrush Country.** (Illus.). 1975. 8.95. Time-Life.

Krutilla, John V., ed. **Natural Environments: Studies in Theoretical & Applied Analysis.** 1973. 16.50. Johns Hopkins.

La Monte, Francesca & Welch, Micaela. **Vanishing Wilderness.** 6.95. Liveright.

National Geographic Society, ed. **Wilderness U.S.A.** 3rd ed. (Illus.). 1975. 9.95. Natl Geog.

Plaisted, Ralph & Plaisted, Riki. **Wilderness Adventure: The Best Year of Our Lives.** (Illus.). 1975. 6.95. Dillon.

Rutstrum, Calvin. **The Wilderness Route Finder.** (Illus.). 1973. pap. 1.50. Macmillan.

Satterlund, Donald R. **Wildland Watershed Management.** 1972. 14.95. Ronald.

Spring, Ira L. & Manning, Harvey. **Wilderness Trails Northwest.** (Illus.). 1974. pap. 5.95. Touchstone Pr Ore.

Sutton, Ann & Sutton, Myron. **The Wild Places: A Photographic Celebration of Unspoiled America.** (Illus.). 1973. 27.50. Har-Row.

— — **Wilderness Areas of North America.** (Illus.). 1975. pap. 4.95. Funk & W.

— — **Wilderness Areas of North America.** (Illus.). 1974. 10.00. Funk & W.

Tanner, Ogden. **Urban Wilds.** (Illus.). 1975. 8.95. Time-Life.

Wood, Robert S. **Desolation Wilderness.** 2nd ed. (Illus.). 1975. pap. 3.95. Wilderness.

WILDERNESS SURVIVAL

Berglund, Berndt. **Wilderness Survival.** 1972. 7.95. Scribner.

Boy Scouts of America. **Wilderness Survival.** (Illus.). 1974. pap. 0.55. BSA.

Gearing, Catherine. **Field Guide to Wilderness Living.** 1973. pap. 3.95. Southern Pub.

Graves, Richard. **Bushcraft: A Serious Guide to Survival & Camping.** (Illus.). 1972. 10.00; pap. 3.95. Schocken.

Gregory, Mark, pseud. **Good Earth Almanac Survival Handbook.** (Illus.). 1973. pap. 1.95. Sheed.

How to Survive in the Wilderness. (Illus.). 1975. pap. 5.95. Drake Pubs.

Merrill, Bill. **The Survival Handbook.** 1974. pap. 1.95. Arc Bks.

Rutstrum, Calvin. **The Wilderness Life.** (Illus.). 1975. 7.95. Macmillan.

Szczelkun, Stefan A. **Survival Scrapbook 1: Shelter.** (Illus.). 1974. pap. 3.95. Schocken.

Welch, Mary S. **The Family Wilderness Handbook.** 1973. pap. 1.65. Ballantine.

WILDLIFE CONSERVATION

Allen, Durward L. **Our Wildlife Legacy.** rev. ed. (Illus.). 1962. 8.95; pap. 4.95. Funk & W.

Amory, Cleveland. **Man Kind? Our Incredible War on Wildlife.** 1974. 9.95. Har-Row.

Atwood, Margaret. **Animals in That Country.** 1969. pap. 1.95. Little.

Beazley, Mitchel. **The Atlas of World Wildlife.** (Illus.). 1973. 25.00. Rand.

Boy Scouts of America. **Fish & Wildlife Management.** (Illus.). 1972. pap. 0.55. BSA.

Brower, Kenneth. **With Their Islands Around Them.** (Illus.). 1974. 8.95. HR&W.

Burger, George V. **Practical Wildlife Management.** 1973. 10.00. Winchester Pr.

Caras, Roger, ed. **Vanishing Wildlife** (Illus.). 1971. 3.95. Barre.

Caras, Roger A. **Death As a Way of Life.** 1971. 5.95. Little.

— — **Last Chance on Earth: A Requiem for Wildlife.** (Illus.). 1972. pap. 2.95. Schocken.

Carson, Rachel. **Silent Spring.** 1973. pap. 1.25. Fawcett World.

— — **Silent Spring.** (Illus.). 1962. 7.95. HM.

Connery, Robert H. **Governmental Problems in Wild Life Conservation.** 1935. 15.00. AMS Pr.

Cornett, Jim. **Wildlife of the Southwest Deserts.** (Illus.). 1975. pap. 2.99. Nature Trails.

Craighead, John J. & Craighead, Frank C., Jr. **Hawks, Owls, & Wildlife.** (Illus.). 6.50. Peter Smith.

Curry-Lindahl, Kai. **Let Them Live: A Worldwide Survey of Animals Threatened With Extinction.** (Illus.). 1972. 9.95; pap. 3.95. Morrow.

Davids, Richard C. **How to Talk to Birds & Other Uncommon Ways of Enjoying Nature the Year Round.** (Illus.). 1972. 6.95. Knopf.

Diole, Philippe. **The Errant Ark: Man's Relationship with Animals.** 1974. 8.95. Putnam.

Douglas, William O. **A Wilderness Bill of Rights.** 1965. 7.50. Little.

Ehrenfeld, D. W. **Biological Conservation.** 1970. pap. 4.50. HR&W.

Farb, Peter. **Land & Wildlife of North America.** (Illus.). 1964. 9.32. Silver.

Fisher, James, et al. **Wildlife in Danger.** (Illus.). 1969. 12.95. Viking Pr.

Gabrielson, Ira N. **Wildlife Conservation.** 2nd ed. (Illus.). 1959. 5.95. Macmillan.

Grinnell, George B. & Sheldon. Charles, eds. **Hunting & Conservation.** 1970. Repr. of 1925 ed. 25.00. Arno.

Guggisberg, C. A. **Man & Wildlife.** (Illus.). 1970. 12.50. Arco.

Harrisson, Barbara. **Conservation of Nonhuman Primates in 1970.** 1971. 11.75. Phiebig.

Hayden, Sherman S. **International Protection of Wildlife.** 1970. Repr. of 1942 ed. 12.50. AMS Pr.

Hey, Douglas. **Wildlife Heritage of South Africa.** (Illus.). 1966. 14.25. Oxford U Pr.

Hickman, Mae & Guy, Maxine. **Care of the Wild Feathered & Furred: A Guide to Wildlife Handling & Care.** (Illus.). 1973. 7.95. pap. 3.95. Unity Pr.

— — **Wild Life Conservation in Theory & Practice.** 1972. Repr. of 1914 ed. 12.00. Arno.

Hornaday, William T. **Our Vanishing Wildlife: Its Extermination & Preservation.** 1970. Repr. of 1913 ed. 16.00. Arno.

Hovland, Carol & Hovland, David. **America's Endangered Wildlife.** 1972. pap. 0.95. Tower.

Hunter, Martin. **Canadian Wilds.** pap. 2.00. Fur-Fish-Game.

Hurrell, G. G. **Wildlife: Tame but Free.** 1969. 9.50. Transatlantic.

Inter-American Juridical Committee. **Convention on Nature Protection & Wild Life Preservation in the Western Hemisphere.** (Eng., Span., Port. & Fr.). 1940. pap. 1.00. OAS.

Laycock, George. **Autumn of the Eagle.** (Illus.). 1973. 6.95. Scribner.

Leopold, A. Starker & Darling, F. Fraser. **Wildlife in Alaska.** 1973. Repr. of 1953 ed. 10.25. Greenwood.

Leopold, Aldo. **Sand County Almanac.** 1970. pap. 1.50. Ballantine.

— — **Sand County Almanac: With Other Essays on Conservation from Round River.** (Illus.). 1966. 8.95. Oxford U Pr.

Levine, Stephen. **Planet Steward: Journal of Wildlife Sanctuary.** (Illus.). 1974. 9.95; pap. 4.95. Unity Pr.

McCoy, J. J. **Saving Our Wildlife.** (Illus.). 1970. 5.95. Macmillan.

Matthiessen, Peter. **Wildlife in America.** (Illus.). 1964. pap. 2.95. Viking Pr.

Moen, Aaron N. **Wildlife Ecology: An Analytical Approach.** (Illus.). 1973. 17.50. W H Freeman.

Niering, W. A. **Life of the Marsh.** 1967. 5.50. McGraw.

Perry, John. **World's a Zoo.** (Illus.). 1969. 6.95. Dodd.

Regenstein, Lewis. **The Politics of Extinction: The Shocking Story of the World's Endangered Wildlife.** (Illus.). 1975. 9.95. Macmillan.

Reiger, John F. **American Sportsmen & the Origins of Conservation.** (Illus.). 1975. 10.00. Winchester Pr.

Roosevelt, Theodore. **Theodore Roosevelt's America.** Wiley, Farida, ed. (Illus.). 1955. 7.50. Devin.

Saijo, Gompers. **North American Wildlife Coloring Album.** (Illus.). 1972. pap. 2.00. Troubador Pr.

Scheffer, Victor B. **A Voice for Wildlife.** 1974. 8.95. Scribner.

Stewart, Darryl. **Canadian Endangered Species.** 12.50. Vanguard.

Still, Henry. **Dirty Animal.** 1970. pap. 0.95. Tower.

Sutton, Ann & Sutton, Myron. **New Worlds For Wildlife.** (Illus.). 1970. 4.95. Rand.

Symposium of the British Ecological Society No. 11. **The Scientific Management of Animal & Plant Communities For Conservation.** Duffey, Eric & Watt, A. S., eds. (Illus.). 1972. 30.00. Lippincott.

Trefethen, James B. **An American Crusade for Wildlife.** (Illus.). 1975. 12.50. Winchester Pr.

Wildfire Control by Volunteer Fire Departments. 1973. pap. 2.00. Natl Fire Prot.

Wildlife Rescue. Date not set. price not set. Regnery.

Wood, Bentley. **Wildlife Ripoff—Texas Style: A Game Warden's Expose.** 1975. 7.50. Exposition.

Ziswiler, V. **Extinct & Vanishing Animals: A Biology of Extinction & Survival.** Bunnell, F. & Bunnell, Pr., trs. 1967. pap. 5.90. Springer-Verlag.

A Guide to the Guides

A selection of useful guidebooks to show you where to camp and backpack in the United States and Canada.

United States

American Heritage Editors. **American Heritage Guide: Natural Wonders of America.** 1972. 6.95. McGraw.

Baedeker, Karl, ed. **Baedeker's United States.** Orig. Title: The United States with an Excursion into Mexico. (Illus.). 1971. Repr. of 1893 ed. 8.95. Da Capo.

Baxter, Constance. **Greatest Mountain: Katahdin's Wilderness.** 15.00; pap. 6.50. Scrimshaw Calif.

Burgess, Samuel. **Jungmeister Junket: 50 States in a Biplane.** 8.50. Vantage.

Burroughs, Polly. **Exploring Martha's Vineyard.** pap. 2.95. Chatham Pr.

Colwell, Robert. **Introduction to the Water Trails in America.** (Illus.). 1973. 6.95; pap. 3.95. Stackpole.

Commager, Henry S. **Meet the U. S. A.** 6th ed. (Illus.). 1970. pap. 3.50. Inst Intl Educ.

Council on International Educational Exchange. **Where to Stay USA.** (Illus.). 1974. pap. 2.50. A Frommer.

--**Where to Stay, USA.** 1974. pap. 2.50. S&S.

Country Beautiful Editors, ed. **Four-Hundred Landmarks of America: Where to Go & What to See.** (Illus.). 1974. 25.00. Country Beautiful.

Ehrlich, Arnold. **The Beautiful Country: Maine to Hawaii.** 1970. 16.95. Viking Pr.

Eifert, Virginia S. **Of Men & Rivers: Adventures & Discoveries Along American Waterways.** (Illus.). 1966. 6.95. Dodd.

Federal Writers' Projects. **United States One: Maine to Florida.** 1938. Repr. 14.50. Somerset Pub.

Fisher, Allan C., Jr. **America's Inland Waterway.** (Illus.). 1973. 4.25. Natl Geog.

Fodor Guides to the United States, 1975. New England. 7.95; New York, New Jersey. 7.95; Mid-Atlantic. 7.95; The South. 7.95; Mid-West. 7.95; Southwest. 7.95; Rockies & Plains. 7.95; Far West. 7.95; Indian America. 10.95. McKay.

Ford, Norman D. **Travel Without Your Car.** 1975. pap. 3.50. Harian.

--**Off the Beaten Path.** rev & 14th ed. 1973. pap. 2.50. Harian.

Franke, David & Franke, Holly. **Safe Places.** (Illus.). 1972. 13.95. Arlington Hse.

--**Safe Places: East of the Mississippi.** (Illus.). 1973. pap. 1.95. Warner Bks.

--**Safe Places: West of the Mississippi.** (Illus.). 1973. pap. 1.95. Warner Bks.

Fuller, Curtis G. **Woodall's Trailering Parks & Campgrounds, 1973.** 1974. pap. 6.95. Woodall.

Haas, Ernst. **In America.** (Illus.). 1975. 42.50. Viking Pr.

Hart, John F., ed. **Regions of the United States.** 1972. pap. 5.95. Har-Row.

Harvard Student Agencies. **Let's Go: A Student Guide to the United States & Canada.** 1972. 3.95. Dutton.

Hunt, Charles B. **Natural Regions of the United States & Canada.** (Illus.). 1974. 14.95. W H Freeman.

Hunter, John F. **The Gay Insider U. S. A.** Hunter, John F., ed. 1972. pap. 3.95. Stonehill Pub Co.

Jeffers, Robinson & Lyon, Horace. **Jeffers Country.** 2nd ed. (Illus.). 8.50; pap. 5.00. Scrimshaw Calif.

Jenkins, Elmer, ed. **Guide to America.** 8.00. Pub Aff Pr.

Jordan, E. L. **Pictorial Travel Atlas of Scenic America: Bicentennial Edition.** rev. ed. 1973. 16.95. Hammond Inc.

Konikow, Robert B. **Discover Historic America.** (Illus.). 1974. 8.95; pap. 4.95. Rand.

Lanier, Alison. **Living in the USA.** 1973. 7.95. Scribner.

Lobeck, Armin K. **Airways of America.** 1970. Repr. of 1933 ed. 16.00. Kennikat.

McNair, Sylvia, ed. **Discover Historic America.** Rev. ed. (Illus.). 1975. pap. 4.95. Rand.

Marks-Highwater, J. **Fodor's Indian America.** 1975. (Illus.). 10.95. McKay.

Marquis, Arnold. **A Guide to America's Indians: Ceremonies, Reservations, & Museums.** (Illus.). 1974. 9.95; pap. 4.95. U of Okla Pr.

Mayer, S. L. & Steeh, J. A. **Director's Guide to the USA: A Trading & Traveling Companion for the Businessman.** (Illus.). 1972. 24.00. Beekman Pubs.

Morgan, James, ed. **Beauty of America.** (Illus.). 1971. 8.50. Hallmark.

Nagel Travel Guide to the U. S. A. French Language Edition. 1973. 29.00. Hippocrene Bks.

Nagel Travel Guide to the U. S. A. German Language Edition. 1973. 29.00. Hippocrene Bks.

Nagel Travel Guide to U. S. A. (Illus.). 1973. 29.00. Hippocrene Bks.

National Geographic Society, ed. **Vacationland U. S. A.** 1970. 9.95; deluxe ed. 18.90. Natl Geog.

Oglesby, Claire C. **Discover USA: the Bicentennial Travel Guide.** (Illus.). 1975. 8.95; deluxe ed. 15.00; pap. 5.95. Acropolis.

Rand McNally. **Rand McNally 1975 Campground & Trailer Park Guide (Nat'l Ed.).** 1975. 6.95. Rand.

Rouse, Art, ed. **Trailer Life's Recreational Vehicle Campground & Services Guide, 1974.** (Illus.). 1974. Pap. 5.45. Chilton.

Rowland, Howard S. & Rowland, Beatrice L. **The New York Times Guide to Adventure, Travel & Study, U.S.A.** rev. ed. Date not set. pap. 4.95. Quadrangle.

Schwartz, Alvin, et al. **America's Exciting Cities: A Travel Guide for Parents & Children.** (Illus.). 1966. 4.95. T Y Crowell.

Sprecher, Daniel, ed. **Guide to Annual Events in the United States: The United States East of the Mississippi River, Vol. 1.** pap. 4.95. Serina.

Thomas, Bill. **Tripping in America: Off the Beaten Track.** (Illus.). 1974. 7.95; pap. 3.95. Chilton.

Time-Life Editors. **The USA: A Visitor's Handbook.** 1973. pap. 1.65. Avon.

Udall, Stewart L. & Country Beautiful Editors. **National Parks of America.** (Illus.). 1966. 15.95. Putnam.

Udall, Stewart L. **Natural Wonders of America.** Orig. Title: America's Natural Treasures. (Illus.) 1971. 15.95. Country Beautiful.

U.S.A. Guide. Orig. Title: Pan Am's World —the USA. 5.95. Pan Am Pubns.

Warner Brothers' Records. **Book of the Road.** 1975. pap. 5.95. Ritchie.

Where to Stay: U.S.A. price not set. S & S.

Woodall Ed. **Woodall's Travel Camping the Four Seasons.** 1969. 1.95. S & S.

Woodall's Mobile Home & Park Directory—1974. 1974. 6.95. S & S.

Woodall's Trailering Parks & Campgrounds —1974. 1974. 6.95. S & S.

Woodall's Trailering Parks & Campgrounds —1974: Western States Ed. 1974. 2.95. S & S.

Southern States

Kosoy, Ted. **Kosoy's Budget Travel Guide to Florida & the South.** (Illus.). 1975. 7.95; pap. 2.95. St Martin.

Peterson, Ed, ed. **Southeast Campgrounds & Trailer Parks, 1975.** 1975. pap. 3.95. Rand.

Southeastern States. 1975. pap. 3.95. Rand.

Southwest

Armer, Laura A. **In Navajo Land.** (Illus.). 1962. 3.95. McKay.

Austin, Mary H. **Land of Journey's Ending.** (Illus.). 1969. Repr. of 1924 ed. 27.50. AMS Pr.

Bieber, Ralph P., ed. **Southern Trails to California in 1849.** (Illus.). 1974. Repr. of 1937 ed. 20.00. Porcupine Pr.

Browne, John R. **Adventures in the Apache Country: A Tour Through Arizona & Sonora, with Notes on the Silver Regions of Nevada.** (Illus.). 1973. Repr. of 1871 ed. 26.00. Arno.

Findley, Rowe. **Great American Deserts.** (Illus.). 1972. 4.25. Natl Geog.

Henderson, Randall. **On Desert Trails.** (Illus.). 1962. 7.50. Westernlore.

Kluckhohn, Clyde. **To the Foot of the Rainbow: Natural Bridge.** 1967. 7.00. Rio Grande.

Lesure, Thomas B. **All the Southwest.** 3rd rev. ed. 1974. pap. 3.50. Harian.

Nestler, Al. **Al Nestler's Southwest.** (Illus.). 1970. 12.50. Northland.

Seymour, Catryna T. **Enjoying the Southwest.** 1973. 7.95; pap. 3.50. Lippincott.

Southwest & South Central States. 1975. pap. 3.95. Rand.

Sunset Editors. **The Beautiful Southwest.** (Illus.). 1972. 12.95. Lane.

Wakeman, Norman H. **Southwest Desert Wonderland.** (Illus.). 1965. 3.25. Dodd.

Wheelock, Walt, ed. **Desert Peaks Guide One.** rev. ed. (Illus.). 1964. 1.00. La Siesta.

West

Athearn, Robert G. **Westward the Briton.** 1962. pap. 2.45. U of Nebr Pr.

Barnes, Demas. **From the Atlantic to the Pacific Overland.** (Illus.). 1973. Repr. of 1866 ed. 8.00. Arno.

California & the West Coast. 1975. pap. 3.95. Rand.

Federal Writers' Project. **Oregon Trail: The Missouri River to the Pacific Ocean.** (Illus.). 1971. Repr. of 1939 ed. 13.00. Somerset Pub.

Ferguson, Robert G. **Guidebook to Lost Western Treasure.** (Illus.). 1973. pap. 2.95. Ritchie.

Field, Matthew C., et al. **Prairie & Mountain Sketches.** Gregg, Kate L. & McDermott, John F., eds. (Illus.). 1957. 8.95. U of Okla Pr.

Hastings, Lansford W. **Emigrant's Guide to Oregon & California.** 2nd ed. 1969. 17.50. Da Capo.

Hollon, W. Eugene. **The Great American Desert Then & Now.** (Illus.). 1975. pap. 3.95. U of Nebr Pr.

Hughes, Harry & Dingler, Helen. **Picture Trails: Past to Present.** 1973. pap. 3.00. W a Linder.

Inman, H. & Cody, W. F. **Great Salt Lake Trail.** (Illus.). 1897. Repr. 10.00. Ross.

Jackson, Don. **Sagebrush Country.** (Illus.). 1975. 8.95. Time-Life.

James, Will. **Cow Country.** (Illus.). 1973. pap. 1.95. U of Nebr Pr.

Johnson, Overton. **Route Across the Rocky Mountains.** Winter, William H., ed. (Illus.). 1972. Repr. of 1932 ed. 10.00. Da Capo.

--**Route Across the Rocky Mountains, with a Description of Oregon & California.** 1966. Repr. of 1846 ed. 5.75. Univ Microfilms.

Langworthy, Franklin. **Scenery of the Plains, Mountains & Mines.** (Illus.). 1972. Repr. of 1932 ed. 12.50. Da Capo.

Ludlow, Fitz H. **Heart of the Continent.** (Illus.). 1971. Repr. 23.50. AMS Pr.

Meyer, Nancy. **Festivals of the West: Fairs, Fests & Other Entertainment.** (Illus.). 1975. pap. 4.50. Ritchie.

Moody, Ralph. **Old Trails West, Vol. 1.** 1973. pap. 1.25. Comstock Edns.

Muir, John. **Steep Trails.** Rade, William F., ed. (Illus.). 1970. 12.95. Berg.

Paden, Irene D. **Wake of the Prairie Schooner.** (Illus.). 1970. pap. 2.95. S Ill U Pr.

Parkman, Frances. **Oregon Trail.** Feltskog, E. N., ed. (Illus.). 1969. 22.00. U of Wis Pr.

Parkman, Francis. **Oregon Trail.** 1964. pap. 0.60. Airmont.

--**Oregon Trail.** pap. 0.75. NAL.

--**Oregon Trail.** (Illus.). 1931. 5.50. HR&W.

Peterson, Ed, ed. **Midwest Campgrounds & Trailer Parks, 1975.** 1975. pap. 3.95. Rand.

Ralph, Julian. **Our Great West.** facs. ed. 1893. 18.25. Bks for Libs.

Richardson, Albert D. **Beyond the Mississippi: From the Great River to the Great Ocean.** 1867. 31.50. Johnson Repr.

Ruth, Kent. **Touring the Old West.** (Illus.). 1971. 6.95. Greene.

Schwind, Dick. **West Coast River Touring: Rogue River Canyon & South.** (Illus.). pap. 5.95. Touchstone Pr Ore.

Society of American Travel Writers. **Exploring the Unspoiled West.** Vol. 1. (Illus.). 1974. pap. 2.95. Ritchie.

--**Exploring the Unspoiled West.** Vol. 2. (Illus.). 1974. pap. 2.95. Ritchie.

Sterling, E. M. **Western Trips & Trails.** 1974. pap. 3.95. Stackpole.

Sunset Editors. **Rivers of the West.** (Illus.). 1974. 12.95; deluxe ed. 16.50. Lane.

Twain, Mark. **Roughing It.** pap. 0.75. Airmont.

--**Roughing It.** Paul, Rodman W., ed. 1953. pap. 2.95. HR&W.

--**Roughing It.** (Illus.). Repr. of 1875 ed. 7.95. Har-Row.

--**Roughing It.** pap. 1.50. NAL.

Wagner, Geoffrey. **Canyons of the West: In Search of Another America.** (Illus.). Date not set. 12.50. A S Barnes.

Eastern States

Carter, Annette. **Exploring from the Chesapeak Bay to the Poconos.** rev. ed. (Illus.). 1975. 8.95; pap. 4.95. Lippincott.

Federal Writers' Project. **U. S. One, Maine to Florida.** 1938. 13.50. Scholarly.

Middle Atlantic States. 1975. pap. 3.95. Rand.

New England

Abbott, Katharine M. **Old Paths & Legends of the New England Border: Connecticut, Deerfield, Berkshire.** 1970. Repr. of 1907 ed. 13.50. Singing Tree.

--**Old Paths & Legends of New England: Saunterings Over Historic Roads with Glimpses of Picturesque Fields & Old Homesteads in Massachusetts, Rhode Island & New Hampshire.** Repr. of 1903 ed. 13.50. Gale.

Beach, Stewart. **New England in Color.** 4.95. Hastings.

Bryfonski, Dedria. **The New England Beach Book.** (Illus.). 1975. 6.95; pap. 3.95. Walker & Co.

Chapin, Suzy & Squier, Elizabeth. **The New Revised Guide to the Recommended Country Inns of New England.** (Illus.). 1974. pap. 3.95. Pequot.

Dollar-Wise Guide to New England: 1968. Essandess.

Duncan, Roger F. & Ware, John P. **A Cruising Guide to the New England Coast.** rev. ed. (Illus.). 1972. 15.00. Dodd.

Farny, Michael. **New England Over the Handlebars: A Cyclist's Guide.** 1975. pap. 4.95. Little.

Federal Writers' Projects. **Here's New England: A Guide to Vacationland.** 1939. Repr. 14.50. Somerset Pub.

Gabler, Ray. **The New England Whitewater River Guide.** (Illus.). 1975. pap. 5.95. Tobey Pub.

Glickman, Ann. **New England.** (Illus.). 1975. 30.00. Graphic Arts Ctr.

Hansen, Harry. **Longfellow's New England.** (Illus.). 1972. 7.95. Hastings.

Here's New England: A Guide to Vacationland. 1939. 14.50. Scholarly.

Kappel, Philip. **New England Gallery.** (Illus.). 1966. 20.00. Little.

Kingsbury, John M. **Rocky Shore.** (Illus.). 1970. 4.95. Chatham Pr.

Miser, A. & Pennypincher, A. **Factory Store Guide to All New England.** (Illus.). 1973. pap. 2.95. Pequot.

Northeastern States. 1975. pap. 3.95. Rand.

Peterson, Ed, ed. **Northeast Campgrounds & Trailer Parks, 1975.** 1975. pap. 3.95. Rand.

Proper, Ida S. **Mohegan, the Cradle of New England.** (Illus.). 8.00. NH Pub Co.

Sagendorph, Robb & Hale, Judson D., eds. **That New England.** (Illus.). 1966. 12.50; pap. 7.95. Yankee Inc.

Simpson, Norman T. **Country Inns & Back Roads.** 1975. pap. 3.95. Berkshire Traveller.

Thollander, Earl. **Back Roads of New England.** (Illus.). 1974. 10.95. Potter.

Tobey, Eric & Wolkenberg, Richard. **Northeast Bicycle Tours.** (Illus.). 1973. pap. 3.95. Tobey Pub.

Trent, Sophie. **My New England.** 1973. 4.00. William-F.

Waters, John F. **Exploring New England Shores: A Beachcomber's Handbook.** (Illus.). 1974. 7.95. Stone Wall Pr.

Wenkam, Robert. **New England.** (Illus.). 1974. 25.00. Rand.

Alabama

Adelman, Bob, ed. **Down Home.** 1974. pap. 5.95. Quadrangle.

Alabama: A Guide to the Deep South. 1941. 19.50. Scholarly.

Federal Writers' Project. **Alabama: A Guide to the Deep South.** 1941. Repr. 14.50. Somerset Pub.

Leeback, Neal G., ed. **Atlas of Alabama.** 1973. 8.75. U of Ala Pr.

Walker, Alyce B. & Hansen, Harry, eds. **Alabama: A Guide to the Deep South.** (Illus.). 1975. 12.95. Hastings.

Windham, Kathryn T. **Exploring Alabama.** 1974. 6.60. Strode.

Alaska

Alaska: A Guide to Alaska, Last American Frontier. 1939. 19.50. Somerset Pub.

Alaska Fishing Guide 1975-76. rev. ed. (Illus.). 1975. pap. 3.95: Alaska Northwest.

Alaska Travel Publications Editors. **Exploring Katmai National Monument & the Valley of Ten Thousand Smokes.** (Illus.). 1975. 7.50. Alaska Travel.

Anchorage-Fairbanks Visitors Guide: 1975. (Illus.). 1975. pap. 2.95. Alaska Northwest.

Balcom, Mary. **Ghost Towns of Alaska.** (Illus.). 1973. 2.95. Balcom.

--**Ketchikan: Alaska's Totemland.** (Illus.). 1973. 3.20. Balcom.

Barber, Olive. **Meet Me in Juneau.** (Illus.). 1960. 5.50. Binford.

Becker, Ethel A. **Treasury of Alaskana.** (Illus.). 1969. 12.95. Superior Pub.

Bridge, Raymond. **The Camper's Guide to Alaska, the Yukon, and Northern British Columbia.** 1975. 10.00; pap. 4.95. Scribner.

Brower, Charles D. **Fifty Years Below Zero.** (Illus.). 1942. 6.00. Dodd.

Brower, Kenneth. **Earth & the Great Weather: The Brooks Range.** 2nd ed. (Illus.). 1974. 10.98. Friends Earth.

Carey, Mary. **Alaska—Not for a Woman!** 1975. 12.50. Branden.

Carey, Niel. **Guide to the Queen Charlotte Islands.** (Illus.). 1975. pap. 2.95. Alaska Northwest.

Carrighar, Sally. **Moonlight at Midday.** (Illus.). 1958. 7.95. Knopf.

Coombs, Charles. **Bush Flying in Alaska.** (Illus.). 1961. 4.75. Morrow.

Cooper, Bryan. **Alaska: The Last Frontier.** (Illus.). 1973. 7.95. Morrow.

Fejes, Claire. **People of the Noatak.** (Illus.). 1966. 7.95. Knopf.

Friends of the Earth. **Earth & the Great Weather: The Brooks Range.** 1975. 27.50. Seabury.

Gordon, George B. **In the Alaskan Wilderness.** 1917. 25.75. AMS Pr.

Grinnell, Joseph. **Gold Hunting in Alaska.** facs. ed. (Illus.). 1901. pap. 4.00. Shorey.

Herndon, Booton. **Great Land: Alaska.** (Illus.). 1971. 6.95. Weybright.

Hilscher, Herb. **Alaska, USA.** 1959. 4.95. Little.

Johansen, Neil & Johansen, Elizabeth. **Exploring Alaska's Prince William Sound.** (Illus.). 1975. 7.50. Alaska Travel.

Johnson, Paul C. **Alaska.** (Illus.). 1974. pap. 2.75. Kodansha.

Keating, Bern. **The Inside Passage to Alaska.** 1976. 19.95. Doubleday.

Kohlstedt, E. D. **A Glimpse of Alaska.** Repr. of 1930 ed. pap. 1.00. Shorey.

MacDowell, L. D. **Trip to Wonderful Alaska.** facs. ed. 1906. pap. 2.00. Shorey.

Marshall, Robert. **Alaska Wilderness: Exploring the Central Brooks Range.** 2nd ed. Marshall, George, ed. & intro. by. (Illus.). 1970. 8.95; pap. 2.95. U of Cal Pr.

Miller, Mike & Wayburn, Peggy. **Alaska: The Great Land.** (Illus.). 1975. pap. 7.95. Sierra.

Miller, Orlando W. **The Frontier in Alaska & the Matahuska Colony.** (Illus.). 1975. 15.00. Yale U Pr.

The Milport. (Illus.). pap. 4.95. Alaska Northwest.

Morris, John J., ed. **Alaska.** (Illus.). 1972. 25.00. Graphic Arts Ctr.

Muir, John. **Travels in Alaska.** (Illus.). 1971. Repr. of 1915 ed. 9.50. AMS Pr.

--**Travels in Alaska.** 1915. Repr. 9.50. Scholarly.

Nienhauer, Helen. **Fifty-Five Ways to the Wilderness in Southcentral Alaska.** (Illus.). pap. 7.95. Mountaineers.

Olson, Sigurd F. **Runes of the North.** 1963. 6.95. Knopf.

Piggott, Margaret. **Discover Southeast Alaska: With Pack and Paddle.** 1975. pap. 7.95. Mountaineers.

Rowell, Rose. **Camper to Alaska.** (Illus.). 1975. 6.00. Exposition.

Satterfield, Archie. **Chilkoot Pass—Then & Now.** rev. ed. (Illus.). 1974. pap. 3.95. Alaska Northwest.

Satterfield, Archie & Jarman, L. **Alaska Bush Pilots in the Float Country.** (Illus.). 1969. 7.95. Superior Pub.

Saunders, Dan. **Alaska: Memoir of a Vanishing Frontier.** 1975. pap. 1.50. Avon.

Schwatka, Frederick. **A Summer in Alaska.** 1891. 29.50. AMS Pr.

Southeastern Alaska Visitor's Guide: 1975. (Illus.). 1975. pap. 1.95. Alaska Northwest.

Spring, N. **Alaska: The Complete Travel Book.** 1975. 8.95; pap. 4.95. Macmillan.

Spring, Norma. **Alaska, Travel Guide.** (Illus.). 1970. 6.95. Macmillan.

Sunset Editors. **Alaska.** rev. ed. (Illus.). 1966. pap. 2.95. Lane.

--**Alaska.** (Illus.). 1974. 12.95. Lane.

Thomas, Tay. **Only in Alaska.** 1969. 5.95. Doubleday.

Trout, P. W. **Alaska by Pickup Camper.** (Illus.). 1972. pap. 3.95. Trail-R.

Waugh, Hal & Keim, Charles J. **Fair Chase with Alaskan Guides.** (Illus.). 1972. pap. 3.95. Alaska Northwest.

Willoughby, Florance. **Alaskans All.** facs. ed. 1933. 12.75. Bks for Libs.

Arizona

Ahnert, Gerald T. **Retracing the Butterfield Trail in Arizona.** (Illus.). 9.75. Westernlore.

All About Arizona. 1968. 2.95. G&D.

Arizona Rock Trails. 1.95. Gembooks.

Bunker, Gerald. **Arizona's Northland Treks.** (Illus.). 1972. 1.00. La Siesta.

Cozzens, Samuel W. **Marvelous Country.** 1967. Repr. 10.00. Ross.

Cushing, Frank H. **Nation of the Willows.** 1965. 4.00. Northland.

Dedera, Don. **Arizona the Beautiful.** (Illus.). 1974. 18.95. Doubleday.

Dollar-Wise Guide to Arizona: 1968. Essandess.

Dutton, Davis & Tedi, Pilgren. **The Great Family Fun Guide to Arizona.** 1974. pap. 1.95. Comstock Edns.

Elmer, Carlos. **Arizona in Color.** 4.95. Hastings.

Evans, Douglas B. **Auto Tourguide to the Lake Mead National Recreation Area.** (Illus.). 1971. pap. 0.50. SW Pks & Mnmts.

Federal Writers' Project. **Arizona: The Grand Canyon State.** (Illus.). 1972. Repr. of 1940 ed. 24.50. Scholarly.

Lesure, Thomas B. **All About Arizona: The Healthful State.** rev. 10th ed. (Illus.). 1968. pap. 2.95. Harian.

Lowe, Charles H., Jr. **Arizona's Natural Environment: Landscapes & Habitats.** 1972. pap. 3.50. U of Ariz Pr.

Nelson, Dick & Nelson, Sharon. **Fifty Hikes in Arizona.** (Illus.). 1973. pap. 3.95. Teolote Pr.

Remington, Frederic. **On the Indian Reservations & Artist Wanderings Among the Cheyennes.** (Illus.). 1974. 4.00; pap. 1.50. Filter.

Sellers, William D. & Hill, Richard H., eds. **Arizona Climate.** rev. 2nd ed. 1974. 18.00. U of Ariz Pr.

Sunset Editors. **Arizona.** 4th ed. (Illus.). 1973. pap. 2.95. Lane.

Toll, David, ed. **Arizona.** (Illus.). 1971. 25.00. Graphic Arts Ctr.

Arkansas

Arkansas: A Guide to the State. 1941. 19.50. Somerset Pub.

DuVall, Leland, ed. **Arkansas: Colony & State.** 1974. pap. 4.25. Rose Pub.

Starr, Fred. **Climb the Highest Mountain.** 1964. 3.00. Chris Mass.

--**Of These Hills and Us.** 1958. 3.95. Chris Mass.

California

Austin, Mary. **The Land of Little Rain.** (Illus.). 1974. pap. 2.45. U of NM Pr.

Baugh, Ruth E. **Geographic Regions of California.** (Illus.). 1955. pap. 1.95. Pacific Bks.

Brenner, Clarence D. **Postmarks of Railway Post Offices & Route Agents in California.** (Illus.). 1975. pap. 2.50. J-B Pubs.

California: A Guide to the Golden State. 1939. 29.50. Somerset Pub.

California & the West Coast. 1975. pap. 3.95. Rand.

California Campgrounds & Trailer Parks, 1975. 1975. pap. 2.95. Rand.

California's Sea Frontier. pap. 1.95. Heritage Pr.

Camphouse, Marjorie. **Guidebook to the Missions of California.** (Illus.). 1974. pap. 2.95. Ritchie.

Clappe, Louise. **Shirley Letters.** (Illus.). 1970. pap. 2.95. Peregrine Smith.

Coy, Owen C. **California County Boundaries.** rev. ed. (Illus.). 1973. Repr. 15.00. Valley Calif.

Coyner, David H. **Lost Trappers: An Account of the Fur Trade.** 1969. Repr. of 1847 ed. 8.00. Rio Grande.

Dills, Elmer & One Hundred One Nights in California Editors, eds. **Best Restaurants of Los Angeles & Southern California.** (Illus.). 1975. pap. 2.95. One Hund One Prods.

Dollar-Wise Guide to California: 1968. Essandess.

Durrenberger, Robert. **California: The Last Frontier.** 1969. pap. 2.95. Van Nos Reinhold.

Dutton, Davis & Pilgreen, Tedi. **Where to Take Your Children in Northern California.** 1972. pap. 2.95. Ritchie.

--**Where to Take Your Children in Southern California.** (Illus.). 1971. pap. 2.95. Ritchie.

Federal Writers' Program, Florida. **Seeing Fernandina: A Guide to the City & Its Industries.** 1940. 7.00. AMS Pr.

Federal Writers' Project. **California: A Guide to the Golden State.** (Illus.). 1972. Repr. of 1939 ed. 29.50. Scholarly.

Ferlatte, William J. **A Flora of the Trinity Alps.** (Illus.). 1974. 10.95. U of Cal Pr.

Fletcher, Colin. **The Thousand-Mile Summer: In Desert & High Sierra.** (Illus.). 1964. 5.95. Howell-North.

Fradkin, Philip L. **California: The Golden Coast.** (Illus.). 1974. 14.95. Viking Pr.

Gagnon, Dennis. **Hiking the Santa Barbara Backcountry.** (Illus.). 1974. pap. 2.95. Ritchie.

The Gold Mines of California: Two Guidebooks. 1973. 11.00. Arno.

Hansen, Harry, ed. **California.** rev. ed. 1967. 9.95. Hastings.

Harris, Thomas. **Down the Wild Rivers.** (Illus.). 1972. 4.95. Chronicle Bks.

Hayden, Mike. **Guidebook to the Sacramento Delta Country.** 1973. pap. 2.95. Ritchie.

Jackson, Ruth. **Combing the Coast.** (Illus.). 1972. pap. 2.95. Chronicle Bks.

Johnson, Paul C. **California.** (Illus.). 1971. pap. 2.75. Kodansha.

Jones, Charles. **A Separate Place.** (Illus.). 1974. 14.95. Sierra.

Killeen, Jacqueline & One Hundred One Nights in California Editors, eds. **Best Restaurants of San Francisco & Northern California.** rev. ed. Orig. Title: One Hundred One Nights in California. (Illus.). 1975. pap. 2.95. One Hund One Prods.

Leadabrand, Russ. **Exploring California Byways No. 2: In & Around Los Angeles.** (Illus.). 1968. pap. 2.95. Ritchie.

--**Exploring California Byways No. 3: Desert Country.** (Illus.). 1969. pap. 2.95. Ritchie.

--**Exploring California Byways No. 4: Mountain Country.** (Illus.) 1970. pap. 2.95. Ritchie.

--**Exploring California Byways No. 5: Historic Sites of California.** 1971. pap. 2.95. Ritchie.

--**Exploring California Byways No. 6: The Owens Valley.** (Illus.). 1972. pap. 2.95. Ritchie.

--**Exploring California Byways No. 7: An Historical Sketchbook.** 1973. pap. 2.95. Ritchie.

--**Guidebook to Rural California.** (Illus.). 1972. pap. 2.95. Ritchie.

--**Guidebook to the San Jacinto Mountains.** Orig. Title: Guidebook to Sunset Ranges of Southern California. 1971. pap. 2.95. Ritchie.

Lewis, Leland. **Sea Guide: Southern California.** (Illus.). 25.00. Sea Pubns.

Lowe, Don & Lowe, Roberta. **One Hundred Southern California Hiking Trails.** (Illus.). 1972. pap. 5.95. Touchstone Pr Ore.

McChesney, Mary F. **Guidebook to the Spas of Northern California.** Date not set. pap. 2.95. Ritchie.

McDaniel, W. E. **The Red Coffee Can.** 1974. 5.00. Valley Calif.

McWilliams, Carey. **Southern California: An Island on the Land.** 1973. pap. 3.95. Peregrine Smith.

Makinson, Randell L. **A Guide to the Work of Greene & Greene.** (Illus.). 1974. pap. 4.95. Peregrine Smith.

Margolin, Malcolm. **East Bay Out.** (Illus.). 1974. pap. 2.95. Heyday Bks.

Marryat, Frank. **Mountains & Molehills.** (Illus.). 1975. Repr. of 1962 ed. 13.25. Greenwood.

Martin, Jim. **Guidebook to the Feather River Country.** (Illus.). 1972. pap. 2.95. Ritchie.

Meyer, Nancy. **Where to Take Your Guests in Southern California.** (Illus.). 1971. pap. 2.95. Ritchie.

Nordhoff, Charles. **California: for Health, Pleasure & Residence: A Book for Travellers & Settlers.** (Illus.). 1973. 8.95; pap. 3.95. Ten Speed Pr.

--**Northern California, Oregon & the Sandwich Islands.** (Illus.). 1974. 7.95; pap. 3.95. Ten Speed Pr.

Oakeshott, Gordon B. **California's Changing Landscapes.** (Illus.). 1971. 13.95; pap. 10.95 McGraw.

Olmsted, R. R., ed. **Scenes of Wonder & Curiosity.** (Illus.). 1962. 6.95. Howell-North.

Pomada, Elizabeth. **Places to Go with Children in Northern California.** (Illus.). 1973. pap. 2.95. Chronicle Bks.

Price, Raye. **Guidebook to the Canyonlands Country.** (Illus.). 1974. pap. 2.95. Ritchie.

Roberge, Earl, ed. **Napa Wine Country.** (Illus.). 1975. 35.00. Graphic Arts Ctr.

Rockwell, Mabel. **California's Sea Frontier.** 1964. pap. 2.25. McNally.

Ross, Thomas E. & Ross, Carol. **Great Bike Rides in Northern California.** 1973. pap. 2.95. Ritchie.

Satterfield, Archie & Kirk, Ruth, eds. **California Coast & Desert.** (Illus.). 1974. 25.00. Graphic Arts Ctr.

Shaw, William. **Golden Dreams & Waking Realities.** 1973. Repr. of 1851 ed. 15.00. Arno.

State Parks: California. rev. ed. 1972. 2.95. Lane.

Stock, Dennis. **California Trip.** (Illus.). 1970. 10.00; pap. 4.95. Grossman.

Sunset Editors. **Beautiful California.** rev. ed. (Illus.). 1969. 12.95. Lane.

--**Back Roads of California.** Thollander, Earl, ed. (Illus.). 1971. 10.95. Lane.

--**California State Parks.** 3rd rev. ed. (Illus.). 1974. pap. 2.95. Lane.

--**California Wine Country.** rev. ed. (Illus.). 1974. pap. 1.95. Lane.

--**Discovering the California Coast.** 1975. 14.95; deluxe ed. 18.50. Lane.

--**Gold Rush Country.** 4th rev. ed. (Illus.). 1972. pap. 2.95. Lane.

--**Northern California.** 4th ed. (Illus.). 1975. pap. 2.95. Lane.

--**Southern California.** rev. 4th ed. (Illus.). 1974. pap. 2.95. Lane.

--**Travel Guide to Northern California.** 4th ed. 1975. pap. 2.95. Lane.

Taylor, Bayard. **El Dorado: Adventures in the Path of Empire.** Two vols. in one. 12.00. Rio Grande.

Toll, David, ed. **California.** (Illus.). 1970. 25.00. Graphic Arts Ctr.

Trzyna, Thaddeus C. & Shank, William, eds. **The California Handbook: A Comprehensive Guide to Sources of Current Information & Action.** 3rd ed. (Illus.). 1975. pap. 15.00. Ctr Calif Public.

Walters, Robert E. **Cruising the California Delta.** (Illus.). 1975. 12.95. Haessner Pub.

Watkins, T. H. **California in Color.** 1970. 4.95. Hastings.

Welles, Annette. **The Los Angeles Guidebook.** 1971. pap. 4.95. Sherbourne.

Wieman, Harold. **Morro Bay Meanderings.** (Illus.). 1975. pap. 3.50. Padre Prods.

Wine Country: California. 1968. pap. 1.95. Lane.

Wood, Basil C. **The What, When & Where Guide to Southern California.** 1975. pap. 2.95. Doubleday.

Yeadon, David. **Exploring Small Towns: No. 1, Southern California.** 1973. pap. 2.95. Ritchie.

--**Exploring Small Towns: No. 1, Northern California.** (Illus.). 1974. pap. 2.95. Ritchie.

Colorado

Adams, Robert H. **White Churches of the Plains: Examples from Colorado.** (Illus.). 1970. 9.75. Colo Assoc.

Bueler, William M. **Roof of the Rockies: A History of Mountaineering in Colorado.** 1974. 9.95. Pruett.

Cardon & Hamby. **Colorful Colorado.** 1975. 6.00. Country Pr Co.

Casewit, Curtis W. **Colorado.** (Illus.). 1973. 10.95. Viking Pr.

--**Skiing Colorado: A Complete Guide to America's Number 1 Ski State.** 1975. pap. 3.95. Chatham Pr.

Coleman, James M. **Aesculapius on the Colorado.** 1971. 6.50. Encino Pr.

Colorado: A Guide to the Highest State. 1941. 24.50. Somerset Pub.

Ferrell, M. H. **The Silver San Juan.** (Illus.). 1973. 34.95. Pruett.

Fiester, M. **Blasted Beloved Breckenridge.** (Illus.). 1973. 19.95. Pruett.

Groat, William. **Colorado Adventures, Forty Trips in the Rockies.** 1974. pap. 3.50. Golden Bell.

Hansen, Harry & Federal Writers' Project, eds. **Colorado: A Guide to the Highest State.** rev. ed. 1970. 9.95. Hastings.

Hunt, Inez & Draper, Wanetta W. **Ghost Trails to Ghost Towns.** rev. ed. pap. 1.00. Swallow.

Kraemer, Elsa. **The West in Our Eyes.** (Illus.). 1972. 6.50. Kraemer.

Lamb, Margaret. **Colorado High Country.** (Illus.). pap. 1.75. Swallow.

Lanham, Urless. **The Enchanted Mesa: An Introduction to Its Natural History.** (Illus.). 1974. 8.95. Pruett.

LeRoy, L. W. & Finney, J. J. **Fading Shadows.** (Illus.). 1973. 12.50. Pruett.

Love, Frank. **Mining Camps & Ghost Towns Along the Lower Colorado.** 1974. 7.95. Westernlore.

Lowe, Don & Lowe, Roberta. **Eighty Northern Colorado Hiking Trails.** 1973. pap. 4.95. Touchstone Pr Ore.

Momaday, N. Scott. **Colorado.** (Illus.). 1973. 19.95. Rand.

Ormes, Robert M. **Guide to the Colorado Mountains.** rev. ed. 1970. 6.00. Swallow.

Parris, L. **Caves of Colorado.** (Illus.). 1973. 16.50. Pruett.

Shunk-Kender, photos by. **Christo: Valley Curtin, Rifle, Colorado, 1971-72.** 1973. 37.50. Abrams.

Talmadge, Marian & Gilmore, Iris. **Colorado Hi-Ways & By-Ways: A Comprehensive Guide to Picturesque Trails & Tours.** 1975. 4.95. Pruett.

Taylor, Robert G. **Colorado Road Log Atlas.** Vol. 1. Southwestern Colorado; Vol. 2. West Central Colorado; Vol. 3. Northwestern Colorado; Vol. 4. Northeastern Colorado; Vol. 5. Southeastern Colorado. (Illus.). 1975. Set. pap. 4.00; pap. 1.50. Filter.

Townshend, R. B. **Tenderfoot in Colorado.** (Illus.). 1968. 3.95. U of Okla Pr.

Wood, Myron & Wood, Nancy. **Colorado: Big Mountain Country.** rev. ed. (Illus.). 1972. 7.95. Doubleday.

Connecticut

Bixby, William. **The Connecticut Guide.** (Illus.). 1974. 10.00. Scribner.

Connecticut: A Guide to Its Roads, Lore & People. 1938. 24.50. Somerset Pub.

Keyarts, Eugene. **Short Walks in Connecticut.** Vol. 3. (Illus.). 1973. pap. 2.95. Pequot.

--**Short Walks in Connecticut.** Vol. 1. 3rd ed. (Illus.). 1973. pap. 2.95. Pequot.

Keyarts, Gene. **Forty-Two More Short Walks in Connecticut.** Vol. 2. 1972. pap. 2.95. Pequot.

Lapin, Nora & Cummings, Parke. **Fairfield County.** 1975. 7.95; pap. 4.95. Lawrence Hill.

Willard, Lawrence F. & Sizer, Alvin V. **Pictorial Connecticut.** 1962. 10.00. Coll & U Pr.

Delaware

Bodine, A. Aubrey. **Chesapeake Bay & Tidewater.** (Illus.). 1969. 19.95. Bodine.

Federal Writers' Project. **Delaware: A Guide to the First State.** Eekman, Jeanette, et al, eds. (Illus.). 1972. Repr. of 1938 ed. 24.50. Scholarly.

--**Delaware: A Guide to the First State.** 1938. Repr. 17.50. Somerset Pub.

Federal Writers' Project, Delaware. **New Castle on the Delaware: American Guide Ser.** 1936. 11.00. AMS Pr.

Quimby, Maureen O. **Eleutherian Mills.** (Illus.). 1973. pap. 1.95. Eleutherian Mills.

Florida

Allyn, Rube. **Water Wagon.** rev. ed. pap. 1.00. Great Outdoors.

Burt, Alvin. **Florida a Place in the Sun.** (Illus.). 1974. 14.95. Burda Pubns.

Carr, Harriett. **Canaveral, Cape of Storms & Wild Cane Fields.** 1974. pap. 2.50. Valkyrie Pr.

Cowles, Frank, Jr. **What to Look for in Florida & What to Look Out for.** rev. ed. 1974. pap. 1.95. Trend House.

Dunn, Bill & Wilkening, David. **Kidding Around: A Mom & Dad's Survival Guide to Metro Orlando.** 1973. pap. 1.00. Sentinel Star.

Dunn, Hampton. **Florida Sketches.** (Illus.). 1974. 6.95. E A Seemann.

--**Yesterday's Clearwater.** (Illus.). 1973. 8.95. E A Seemann.

Federal Writers' Project. **Florida: A Guide to the Southernmost State.** 11.95. Oxford U Pr.

Federal Writers' Project. Florida. **Seeing Fernandina: A Guide to the City & Its Industries.** 1940. 7.00. AMS Pr.

Federal Writers' Project, Florida. **Seeing St. Augustine.** 1937. 6.00. AMS Pr.

Florida: A Guide to the Southernmost State. 1939. 24.50. Somerset Pub.

Ford, Norman D. **Florida.** 16th rev. ed. (Illus.). 1960. pap. 3.00. Harian.

Gantz, Charlotte O. **A Naturalist in Southern Florida.** (Illus.). 1971. 7.95. U of Miami Pr.

Gilliland, Marion S. **The Material Culture of Marco Key, Florida.** 1975. 15.00. U Presses Fla.

Guide to Florida. rev. ed. 1973. pap. 3.95. Rand.

Hill, Jim & Hill, Miriam. **Fabulous Florida.** 2nd ed. (Illus.). pap. 3.95. Ambassador Pubns.

Holland, Claude V. **Tortugas Run.** 1973. 4.95; pap. 2.98. C V Holland.

Hudson, L. Frank & Prescott, Gordon R. **Lost Treasures of Florida's Gulf Coast.** (Illus.). 1973. pap. 1.95. Great Outdoors.

Jahoda, Gloria. **Other Florida.** 1967. pap. 2.95. Scribner.

Keating, Bern. **Florida.** (Illus.). 1972. 25.00. Rand.

Kosoy, Ted. **Kosoy's Budget Travel Guide to Florida & the South.** (Illus.). 1975. 7.95; pap. 2.95. St. Martin.

Lewis, Gordon. **Florida Fishing: Fresh & Salt Water.** (Illus.). 1957. pap. 1.75. Great Outdoors.

McMullen, Edwin W., Jr. **English Topographic Terms in Florida, 1563-1874.** 1953. pap. 5.50. U Presses Fla.

Marks, Henry & Riggs, Gene B. **Rivers of Florida.** (Illus.). 1974. pap. 4.95. Southern Pr.

Marth, Del. **Yesterday's Sarasota.** (Illus.). 1973. 8.95. E A Seemann.

O'Reilly, John. **Boater's Guide to the Upper Florida Keys: Jewfish Creek to Long Key.** (Illus.). 1970. 2.50. U of Miami Pr.

Powell, Richard, intro. by. **Florida: A Picture Tour.** (Illus.). 1972. 9.95. Scribner.

Rambler. **Guide to Florida, 1875.** Patrick, R. W., ed. (Illus.). 1964. 7.50. U Presses Fla.

Robin, C. C. **Voyage to Louisiana, 1803-1805.** 12.50. Pelican.

Russell, Franklin. **The Okefenokee Swamp.** (Illus.). 1973. 8.95. Time-Life.

Schofield, Arthur C. **Yesterday's Bradenton.** (Illus.). 1975. 7.95. E A Seemann.

Shoumatoff, Alex. **Florida Ramble.** (Illus.). 1974. 7.95. Har-Row.

Simmons, William H. **Notices of East Florida, with an Account of the Seminole Nation of Indians.** 1973. pap. 4.00. U Presses Fla.

Smiley, Nixon. **Florida: Land of Images.** (Illus.). 1972. 6.95. E A Seemann.

--**Yesterday's Florida.** (Illus.). 1974. 12.95. E A Seemann.

Steinmetz, Bob. **In the Land of Sunshine.** Smollon, Jim, ed. Orig. Title: Jayhawking Florida Traveler. (Illus.). 1972. pap. 1.00. Star Pub Fla.

Tolf, Robert W. **Guide to Florida Restaurants: Gold Coast Keys Edition.** (Illus.). 1974. pap. 1.95. Trend House.

--**Guide to Florida Restaurants: West Coast Central Edition.** (Illus.). 1974. pap. 1.95. Trend House.

--**How to Survive Your First Six Months in Florida; & Love Every Minute of It.** rev. ed. (Illus.). 1973. pap. 1.95. Trend House.

Triplett, Kenneth E. & Triplett, Mary R. **Free Camping in Florida.** 1973. pap. 3.30. Triplett Ents.

Writers Program, Florida. **Planning Your Vacation in Florida: Miami & Dade County, Including Miami Beach & Coral Gables.** 1941. Repr. 13.50. AMS Pr.

Georgia

Federal Writers Project, Georgia. **Augusta.** 1938. 12.50. AMS Pr.

Georgia: A Guide to Its Towns & Country-Side. 1940. 19.50. Somerset Pub.

Grady, James. **Architecture of Neel Reid in Georgia.** (Illus.). 1973. 29.75. U of Ga Pr.

Linley, John. **Architecture of Middle Georgia: The Oconee Area.** 1972. 17.50. U of Ga Pr.

Lovell, Caroline C. **Golden Isles of Georgia.** 1970. Repr. of 1932 ed. 10.00. Cherokee.

Russell, Franklin. **The Okefenokee Swamp.** (Illus.). 1973. 10.60. Silver.

Steed, Hal. **Georgia: Unfinished State.** 1971. Repr. 10.00. Cherokee.

Valentine, James & Hanie, Robert. **Guale: The Golden Coast of Georgia.** (Illus.). 1974. 29.50. Friends Earth.

Valentine, James & Earl, John, photos by. **Guale, the Golden Coast of Georgia.** (Illus.). 1975. 29.50. Seabury.

Hawaii

Barrow, Terence. **Incredible Hawaii.** (Illus.). 1974. pap. 2.50. C E Tuttle.

Clark, Sidney & Younger, Ronald. **All the Best in Hawaii.** (Illus.). 7.95. Dodd.

Fodor's Hawaii, 1976. 8.95. McKay.

Gellhorn, Eleanor C. **McKay's Guide to the Far East & Hawaii.** rev. ed. (Illus.). 1965. 6.95. McKay.

Glatzer, Hal. **Kamehameha County.** 1974. 2.50. Friendly World.

Grace, Jean M., ed. **Marine Atlas of Hawaii: Bays & Harbors.** 1974. 22.00. U Pr of Hawaii.

Hammel, Faye & Levey, Sylvan. **Hawaii on Ten Dollars a Day, 1971-72.** rev. ed. 1971. pap. 2.95. Essandess.

Hardiman, James W. & Cochard, Charles E., Jr. **Hammond Guide to Hawaii.** (Illus.). 1971. pap. 1.95. Hammond Inc.

Hawaii on Ten Dollars a Day: 1974-75 Edition. 1974. pap. 3.50. A Frommer.

Head, Timothy E. **Going Native in Hawaii: A Poor Man's Guide to Paradise.** (Illus.). pap. 2.75. C E Tuttle.

Hillman, Howard. **Hawaii at-a-Glance.** 1972. pap. 1.95. McKay.

Holiday Editors. **Travel Guide to Hawaii.** rev. ed. 1973. pap. 1.95. Random.

Inglott, Irene. **Tutu Grandma & Vic in Hawaii** (Illus.). 1970. pap. 1.50. Aquarius.

Kane, Robert S. **Hawaii A to Z.** 1975. 6.95; pap. 2.95. Doubleday.

Lawrence, Jodi. **Off the Beaten Track in Hawaii.** (Illus.). 1973. pap. 2.50. Nash Pub.

Noordhoff, Charles. **Northern California, Oregon & the Sandwich Islands** (Illus.). 1974. 7.95; pap. 3.95. Ten Speed Pr.

Paitson, Hupi & Paitson, Lloyd. **Maui: Notes from a Private Guidebook.** (Illus.). 1970. pap. 1.25. Aquarius.

Porteus, Stanley D. **Calabashes & Kings: An Introduction to Hawaii.** (Illus.). 1970. pap. 2.15. C E Tuttle.

Pratt, Helen G. **Hawaiians: An Island People.** (Illus.). 1963. 5.75. C E Tuttle.

Randall, John E. **The Underwater Guide to Hawaiian Reef Fishes.** (Illus.). 1975. 7.95. Harrowood Bks.

Siers, James. **Hawaii.** (Illus.). 1973. 10.95. Har-Row.

Sunset Editors. **Beautiful Hawaii.** (Illus.). 1972. 12.95. Lane.

--**Hawaii.** rev. ed. 1975. pap. 2.95. Lane.

TWA's **Budget Guide to Hawaii.** 1970. Essandess.

TWA's **Gateway Guide to Honolulu.** 1971. pap. 1.00. Essandess.

TWA's **Getaway Guide to Honolulu, 1973-74.** 1973. pap. 1.00. A Frommer.

Wallace, Robert. **Hawaii.** 1973. 8.95. Time-Life.

Wenkam, Robert. **Hawaii: Kauai, Oahu, Maui, Molokai, Lanai, & Hawaii.** (Illus.). 1972. 19.95. Rand.

--**Hawaii: The Big Island.** 1975. 25.00. Rand.

--**How to Photograph Hawaii.** (Illus.). 1973. 4.95. Rand.

--**Maui: The Last Hawaiian Place.** 2nd ed. Brower, Kenneth, ed. (Illus.). 1974. 10.98. Friends Earth.

Whitney, Henry M. **Hawaiian Guide Book for Travelers.** (Illus.). 1969. pap. 2.20. C E Tuttle.

Younger, Ronald. **All the Best in Hawaii.** (Illus.). 1972. 7.95. Dodd.

Idaho

Angelo, C. Aubrey. **Idaho: A Descriptive Tour.** 1971. Repr. 4.50. Ye Galleon.

Beatty, Robert O. **Idaho: A Pictorial Overview.** (Illus.). 1975. 35.00. Idaho First Natl Bank.

Federal Writers' Project. **Idaho: A Guide in Word & Picture.** 1937. Repr. 14.50. Somerset Pub.

--**Idaho: A Guide in Word & Picture.** 2nd ed. 1950. 10.95. Oxford U Pr.

Federal Writers' Project, Idaho. **Idaho Lore.** 1939. 14.00. AMS Pr.

Idaho: A Guide in Word & Picture. 1937. 14.50. Scholarly.

Illinois

Angle, Paul M. & McCree, Mary L., eds. **Prairie State: Impressions of Illinois, 1673-1967.** (Illus.). 1968. boxed 12.50. U of Chicago Pr.

Beck, Lewis Caleb. **A Gazetteer of the States of Illinois & Missouri: Containing a General View of Each State, a General View of Their Counties, & a Particular Description of Their Towns, Villages, Rivers, Etc.** (Illus.). 1975. Repr. of 1823 ed. 18.00. Gale.

Federal Writers' Project. **Illinois: A Descriptive & Historical Guide.** (Illus.). 1971. Repr. of 1947 ed. 34.00. Somerset Pub.

Federal Writers' Project, Illinois. **Galena Guide.** 1937. 6.50. AMS Pr.

Illinois: A Descriptive & Historical Guide. 1939. 29.50. Scholarly.

Koeper, Frederick. **Illinois Architecture from Territorial Times to the Present.** (Illus.). 1968. 11.00; pap. 3.25. U of Chicago Pr.

Wilson, Robert. **Young in Illinois.** 1975. pap. 5.00. December Pr.

Indiana

Alley, Jean & Alley, Hartley. **Southern Indiana.** (Illus.). 1965. 5.95; pap. 2.95. Ind U Pr.

Federal Writers' Project. **Indiana: A Guide to the Hoosier State.** 1941. Repr. 17.50. Somerset Pub.

Indiana: A Guide to the Hoosier State. 1941. 24.50. Scholarly.

Iowa

Federal Writers' Project. **Iowa: A Guide to the Hawkeye State.** 1938. Repr. 17.50. Somerset Pub.

Kirkpatrick, Inez. **Iowa Postal Routes.** 1975. pap. price not set. J-B Pubs.

Ramsey, Guy R. **Postmarked Iowa.** 1975. pap. price not set. J-B Pubs.

Kansas

Anderson, George L. **Kansas West.** (Illus.). Date not set. 8.95. Golden West.

Federal Writers' Project. **Kansas: A Guide to the Sunflower State.** 1939. Repr. 17.50. Somerset Pub.

Kansas: A Guide to the Sunflower State. 1939. 24.50. Scholarly.

Lyle, Wes & Fisher, James. **Kansas Impressions: Photographs & Words.** (Illus.). 1972. 5.95. U Pr of Kansas.

Muilenburg, Grace & Swineford, Ada. **Land of the Post Rock.** (Illus.). 1975. 13.50. U Pr of Kansas.

Patterson, Jerry G. **Kansas Travel Guide.** (Illus.). 1970. pap. 1.50. Campgrounds.

Kentucky

Coleman, J. Winston. **Historic Kentucky.** 1968. 9.95. Henry Clay.

Federal Writers' Project. **Kentucky: A Guide to the Bluegrass State.** 1939. Repr. 14.50. Somerset Pub.

Kentucky: A Guide to the Bluegrass State. 1939. 1950. Scholarly.

Louisiana

Douglas, Neil H. **Freshwater Fishes of Louisiana.** 1974. 12.95. Claitors.

Federal Writers' Project. **Louisiana: A Guide to the State.** 1941. Repr. 19.50. Somerset Pub.

Feibleman, Peter, **The Bayous.** (Illus.). 1973. 10.60. Silver.

Hansen, Harry & Federal Writers' Project, eds. **Louisiana: A State Guide.** rev. ed. 1971. 12.50. Hastings.

Hennick, Louis G. & Charlton, E. Harper. **Streetcars of Louisiana.** (Illus.). 1975. 19.95. Pelican.

Kniffen, Fred B. **Louisiana: Its Land & People.** (Illus.). 1968. 8.95. La State U Pr.

Morgan & Kerr. **Louisiana Scenes: The Lower Mississippi Valley.** 1962. 5.95. Claitors.

Morgan, Elemore & East, Charles. **Face of Louisiana.** (Illus.). 1969. 12.00. La State U Pr.

Overdyke, W. Darrell. **Louisiana Plantation Homes: Colonial & Ante Bellum.** (Illus.). 1965. 12.50. Architectural.

Maine

Appalachian Mountain Club. **Maine Mountain Guide.** 1971. 6.50. Appalach Mtn.

Attwood, Stanley B. **Length & Breadth of Maine.** 1973. pap. 3.50. Maine Studies.

Baxter, Constance. **Greatest Mountain: Katahdin's Wilderness.** 15.00; pap. 6.50. Scrimshaw Calif.

Bearse, Ray, ed. **Maine: A Guide to the Vacation State.** 2nd rev. ed. (Illus.). 1969. 7.95. HM.

Berchen, William. **Maine.** (Illus.). 1973. 10.95. HM.

Cameron, Jean W. **The Orchids of Maine.** 1951. pap. 1.00. Maine Studies.

Chadbourne, Ava H. **Cumberland County.** 1975. pap. 2.25. Wheelwright.

--**Knox County.** 1975. pap. 2.25. Wheelwright.

--**Maine Place Names & the Peopling of Its Towns: Washington County.** (Illus.). 1971. pap. 1.95. Wheelwright.

--**Maine Place Names & the Peopling of Its Towns: York County.** (Illus.). 1971. pap. 1.95. Wheelwright.

Cummings, O. R. **Trolleys to Augusta, Maine.** (Illus.). 1969. 4.00. De Vito.

Dibner, Martin. **Seacoast Maine: The People & Places.** (Illus.). 1973. 12.50. Doubleday.

Eckstrom, Fannie H. **Indian Place Names of the Maine Coast.** 1974. pap. 3.95. Maine Studies.

Federal Writers' Project. **Maine: A Guide Down East.** 1936. Repr. 14.50. Somerset Pub.

--**Maine: A Guide to the Vacation State.** 17.50. Somerset Pub.

Gibson, John. **Fifty Hikes in Maine.** (Illus.). 1976. pap. 5.95. NH Pub. Co.

Hunt, H. Draper, 3rd. **The Blaine House, Home of Maine's Governors.** (Illus.). 1974. 10.00; pap. 5.95. NH Pub Co.

Isaacson, Dorris A. **Maine: A Guide Down East.** 1970. 6.50. Courier-Gazette.

Isaacson, Dorris A., ed. **Maine: A Guide "Downeast."** 1971. 6.50. Greene.

Jennison, Keith. **Green Mountains & Rock Ribs.** (Illus.). pap. 3.50. Durrell.

--**Maine Idea.** (Illus.). pap. 3.50. Durrell.

--**Remember Maine.** (Illus.). 1967. pap. 3.50. Durrell.

Laverty, Dorothy B. **Millinocket: Magic City of the Maine Wilderness.** (Illus.). 1973. pap. 6.95. Wheelwright.

Leavitt, H. Walter. **Katahdin Skylines.** 1970. pap. 2.75. Maine Studies.

Lunt, Dudley C. **Woods & the Sea: Wilderness & Seacoast Adventures in the State of Maine.** (Illus.). 1965. 6.95. Knopf.

Maine: A Guide Down East. 1937. 19.50. Scholarly.

Merrill, Daphne W. **The Lakes of Maine: Facts & Legends.** 1973. 12.50. Courier-Gazette.

Nearing, Helen, intro. by. **The Good Life Album of Helen & Scott Nearing.** 1974. pap. 5.95. Dutton.

Perkins, James & Stevens, Jane. **Popham Beach Maine.** (Illus.). 1974. 14.95. Wheelwright.

Rich, Louise D. **The Coast of Maine.** (Illus.). 1975. 9.95; pap. 5.95. T Y Crowell.

--**Coast of Maine.** (Illus.). 1971. 8.95; pap. 3.95. T Y Crowell.

Rutherford, Phillip R. **Dictionary of Maine Place-Names.** 1971. 9.95. Wheelwright.

Simonoff, Elizabeth & Van Winkle, Edgar B. **Frenchman's Bay.** 1973. 9.95. Pequot.

State O'Maine Facts. 1974. 1.00. Courier-Gazette.

Teg, William. **Almuchicoitt.** 1950. 4.00. Chris Mass.

Wheelwright, Thea. **Along the Maine Coast.** (Illus.). 1975. pap. 4.95. Barre.

Writers Program, Maine. **Augusta-Hallowell on the Kennebec.** 1940. Repr. 10.00. AMS Pr.

--**Portland City Guide.** 1940. Repr. 20.00. AMS Pr.

Maryland

Bodine, A. Aubrey. **Chesapeake Bay & Tidewater.** (Illus.). 1969. 19.95. Bodine.

--**Face of Maryland.** (Illus.). 1970. 19.95. Bodine.

Cummings, J. W. **Vacation in Maryland.** (Illus.). 1975. 5.95. Vacation Pub.

Federal Writers' Project. **Maryland: A Guide to the Old Line State.** (Illus.). 1972. Repr. of 1940 ed. 24.50. Scholarly.

--Maryland: A Guide to the Old Line State. 1940. Repr. 17.50. Somerset Pub.

Footner, Hulbert. Maryland Main & the Eastern Shore. Repr. of 1942 ed. 8.00. Gale.

Morrison, Charles. The Western Boundary of Maryland. 1975. price not set. Macclain.

Massachusetts

Appalachian Mountain Club. Massachusetts-Rhode Island Trail Guide. 3rd ed. 1972. 7.75. Appalach Mtn.

Arrow Pub. Staff, ed. Arrow Street Guide of Lowell, Lawrence, Haverhill. 1974. 2.50. Arrow Pub.

Drake, Samuel A. Historic Mansions & Highways Around Boston. (Illus.). 1971. pap. 3.75. C E Tuttle.

Federal Writers' Project. Massachusetts: A Guide to Its Places & People. 1937. Repr. 19.50. Somerset Pub.

Glassman, Alfred, ed. Historic Bicentennial Information & Points of Interest in Eastern Massachusetts. 1975. 5.95. Herman Pub.

Harris, Stuart K., et al. Flora of Essex County, Massachusetts. Snyder, Dorothy E., ed. 1975. 12.50. Peabody Mus Salem.

Marshall, Anthony L. Truro, Cape Cod, As I Knew It. 6.95. Vantage.

Massachusetts: A Guide to Its Places & People. 1937. 29.50. Scholarly.

Rubin, Cynthia & Rubin, Jerome. Guide to Massachusetts Museums, Historic Houses & Points of Interest. 1972. pap. 1.95. Emporium Pubns.

Sadlier, Paul & Sadlier, Ruth. Fifty Hikes in Massachusetts. (Illus.). 1975. pap. 5.95. NH Pub. Co.

Safran, Rose, ed. Very Special Resorts. 1973. pap. 3.95. Berkshire Traveller.

Seventeen Seventy-Six Guides, Inc. The Seventeen Seventy-Six Guide for Massachusetts. (Illus.). 1975. pap. 3.95. Har-Row.

Universal Atlas of Metropolitan Boston & Eastern Massachusetts. 10th ed. 1974. pap. 4.50. Herman Pub.

Wood, William. Wood's New England Prospect. Colburn, Jeremiah, ed. 1966. 15.00. B Franklin.

Michigan

Andrews, Wayne. Architecture in Michigan: A Representative Photographic Survey. (Illus.). 1967. 7.95; pap. 3.95. Wayne St U Pr.

Federal Writers' Projects. Michigan: A Guide to the Wolverine State. (Illus.). 1972. Repr. of 1941 ed. 29.50. Scholarly.

Inglis, James G. Handbook for Travelers, Northern Michigan. (Illus.). 1973. pap. 3.75. Black Letter Pr.

Michigan: A Guide to the Wolverine State. 1941. 29.50. Somerset Pub.

Michigan Tourist Survey, 1957. 1958. pap. 2.00. Mich St U Busn.

Minnesota

Bolz, J. Arnold. Portage into the Past: By Canoe Along the Minnesota-Ontario Boundary Waters. (Illus.). 1960. 6.50. U of Minn Pr.

Eubank, Nancy. A Living Past: 15 Historic Places in Minnesota. 1973. pap. 1.75. Minn Hist.

Federal Writers' Project. Minnesota: A State Guide. 1938. Repr. 17.50. Somerset Pub.

Holmquist, June D. & Brookins, Jean A. Minnesota's Major Historic Sites: A Guide. rev. ed. (Illus.). 1972. 8.95; pap. 5.95. Minn Hist.

Holmquist, June D., et al. History Along the Highways: An Official Guide to Minnesota State Markers & Monuments. (Illus.). 1967. pap. 2.00. Minn Hist.

Jaques, Florence P. Canoe Country. (Illus.). 1938. 5.00. U of Minn Pr.

--Snowshoe Country. (Illus.). 1944. 5.50. U of Minn Pr.

Kennedy, Roger. Minnesota Houses: An Architectural & Historical View. 1968. 8.50. Dillon.

Minnesota: A State Guide. 1938. 24.50. Scholarly.

Moses, George, ed. Minnesota in Focus. (Illus.). 1974. 14.95. U of Minn Pr.

Poatgieter, A. Hermina & Dunn, James T., eds. Gopher Reader 2. (Illus.). 1975. 10.95. Minn Hist.

Singley, Grover. Tracing Minnesota's Old Government Roads. (Illus.). 1974. pap. 3.95. Minn Hist.

Writers' Program, Minnesota. The Bohemian Flats. 1941. Repr. 6.00. AMS Pr.

Mississippi

Crocker, Mary W. Historic Architecture in Mississippi. (Illus.). 1973. 12.50. U Pr of Miss.

Cross, Ralph D. & Wales, Robert W., eds. Atlas of Mississippi. 1974. 15.00. U Pr of Miss.

Federal Writers' Project. Mississippi: A Guide to the Magnolia State. (Illus.). 1972. Repr. of 1938 ed. 24.50. Scholarly.

--Mississippi: A Guide to the Magnolia State. 1938. Repr. 17.50. Somerset Pub.

Greenberg, Polly. Devil Has Slippery Shoes. 1969. 14.95. Macmillan.

Missouri

Basler, Lucille. A Tour of Old Ste. Genevieve. (Illus.). 1975. pap. 1.45. Patrice Pr.

Federal Writers' Project. Missouri: A Guide to the Show Me State. (Illus.). 1972. Repr. of 1941 ed. 29.50. Scholarly.

Missouri: A Guide to the 'Show Me' State. 1941. 29.50. Somerset Pub.

Montana

Federal Writers' Project. Montana: A State Guide Book. 1939. Repr. 14.50. Somerset Pub.

Miller, D. Ghost Towns of Montana. (Illus.). 1974. 17.50. Pruett.

Montana: A State Guide Book. 1939. 19.50. Scholarly.

Stuart, Granville. Montana As It Is. 1973. Repr. of 1865. ed. 9.00. Arno.

Wolf, James R. Guide to the Continental Divide Trail in Montana. (Illus.). 1975. price not set; pap. price not set. Mountain Pr.

Nebraska

Bartels, Michael M., et al. Railfans Guide to Nebraska. pap. 1.75. J-B Pubs.

Federal Writers' Project. Nebraska: A Guide to the Cornhusker State. 1939. Repr. 17.50. Somerset Pub.

Fitzpatrick, Lilian. Nebraska Place-Names. Fairclough, G. Thomas, ed. 1960. pap. 2.45. U of Nebr Pr.

Nebraska: A Guide to the Cornhusker State. 1939. 19.50. Scholarly.

Nicoll, Bruce H. & Keller, Ken R. Know Nebraska. rev. ed. 1961. 4.40; 1.00. Johnsen.

Nevada

Evans, Douglas B. Auto Tourguide to the Lake Mead National Recreation Area. (Illus.). 1971. pap. 0.50. SW Pks & Mnmts.

Federal Writers' Project. Nevada: A Guide to the Silver State. (Illus.). 1972. Repr. of 1940 ed. 14.50. Scholarly.

--Nevada: A Guide to the Silver State. 1940. Repr. 14.50. Somerset Pub.

Mitchell, Roger. Western Nevada Jeep Trails. (Illus.). 1973. 1.95. La Siesta.

Pilgreen, Tedi & Dutton, Davis. Where to Take Your Children in Nevada. (Illus.). 1973. pap. 2.95. Ritchie.

Truitt, Velma S. On the Hoof in Nevada. (Illus.). 1950. 24.50. Nevada Pubns.

New Hampshire

Federal Writers' Project. New Hampshire: A Guide to the Granite State. 1938. Repr. 17.50. Somerset Pub.

New Hampshire: A Guide to the Granite State. 1938. 24.50. Scholarly.

Teg, William. Almuchicoitt. 1950. 4.00. Chris Mass.

New Jersey

Bailey, Rosalie F. Pre-Revolutionary Dutch Houses & Families in Northern New Jersey & Southern New York. (Illus.). 1968. pap. 6.00. Dover.

Beck, Henry C. Roads of Home: Lanes & Legends of New Jersey. 1956. pap. 2.75. Rutgers U Pr.

Cawley, Margaret & Cawley, James. Exploring the Little Rivers of New Jersey. 3rd rev. ed. 1971. 6.00; pap. 2.95. Rutgers U Pr.

Cunningham, John T. This Is New Jersey. 2nd ed. 1968. 10.00. Rutgers U Pr.

Federal Writers' Project, Illinois. Princeton Guide. 1939. 5.00. AMS Pr.

Groff, Sibyl M. New Jersey's Historic Houses: A Guide to Homes Open to the Public. (Illus.). 1971. 6.95; pap. 1.95. A S Barnes.

Mole, Michaela M., ed. Away We Go: A Guidebook of Family Trips to Places of Interest in New Jersey, Nearby Pennsylvania & New York. rev. ed. 1971. pap. 2.95. Rutgers U Pr.

New Jersey: A Guide to Its Present & Past. 1939. 29.50. Scholarly.

Pepper, Adeline. Tours of Historic New Jersey. rev. ed. (Illus.). 1973. pap. 2.95. Rutgers U Pr.

Studley, Miriam V. Historic New Jersey Through Visitors' Eyes. 1964. 6.00. Rutgers U Pr.

New Mexico

Armstrong, Ruth. Enchanted Land: New Mexico. 1973. 10.00. C Horn.

Bunting, Bainbridge & Lazar, Arthur. Of Earth & Timbers Made: New Mexico Architecture. Orig. Title: Adobe & Timber. (Illus.). 1974. pap. 6.95. U of NM Pr.

Butcher, Russell D. New Mexico: Gift of the Earth. (Illus.). 1975. 16.95. Viking Pr.

Cozzens, Samuel W. Marvelous Country. 1967. Repr. 10.00. Ross.

Federal Writers' Project. New Mexico: A Guide to the Colorful State. (Illus.). 1972. Repr. of 1940 ed. 19.50. Scholarly.

--New Mexico: A Guide to the Colorful State. 1940 Repr. 17.50. Somerset Pub.

Fergusson, Erna. New Mexico. rev. ed. (Illus.). 1964. 7.95. Knopf.

Guide to New Mexico: W.P.A. Project. (Illus.). 1975. Repr. of 1940 ed. 15.00. Rio Grande.

Hillerman, Tony, ed. New Mexico. (Illus.). 1974. 25.00. Graphic Arts Ctr.

Looney, Ralph. Haunted Highways: The Ghost Towns of New Mexico. (Illus.). 1968. 12.95. Hastings.

Slater, John M. El Morro, Inscription Rock, New Mexico. (Illus.). 1961. 30.00. Dawsons.

Ungnade, Herbert E. Guide to the New Mexico Mountains. enl. & rev. 2nd ed. (Illus.). 1972. 7.50; pap. 3.45. U of NM Pr.

New York (State)

Bailey, Rosalie F. Pre-Revolutionary Dutch Houses & Families in Northern New Jersey & Southern New York. (Illus.). 1968. pap. 6.00. Dover.

Bennett, Ruth C. Grafton (N.Y.) Hills of Home. 3.95. Vantage.

Brown, Charles H. **Van Cortlandt Manor: A Guidebook.** (Illus.). pap. 0.50. Sleepy Hollow.

Conover, Jewel H. **Nineteenth-Century Houses in Western New York.** (Illus.). 1966. 10.00. State U NY Pr.

Cooper, William. **Guide in the Wilderness.** facs. ed. 1810. 7.50. Bks for Libs.

De Lisser, Richard L. **Picturesque Ulster.** (Illus.). 1969. pap. 10.50. Twines Catskill.

Dorst, Sally. **New York Food Book.** 1973. pap. 3.95. Workman Pub.

Federal Writers' Project. **New York: A Guide to the Empire State.** (Illus.). 1972. Repr. of 1940 ed. 29.50. Scholarly.

--**New York: Guide to the Empire State.** 1940. 11.95. Oxford U Pr.

--**New York State: A Guide to the Empire State.** 1940. Repr. 19.50. Somerset Pub.

Federal Writers' Project, New York. **Rochester & Monroe County.** 1937. 25.00. AMS Pr.

Giambarba, Paul. **Blue Water Views of Old New York.** (Illus.). pap. 3.95. Scrimshaw.

Hoeferlin, William. **Harriman Park Trail Guide.** 7th ed. (Illus.). 1974. pap. 1.50. Walking News.

Keller, Allan. **Sleepy Hollow Country.** (Illus.). Date not set. price not set. Sleepy Hollow.

Macia, Rafael. **The New York Bicycler.** 1972. pap. 2.50. S&S.

New York World. **The Conning Tower Book.** 35.00. Gordon Pr.

Philipsburg Manor: A Guidebook. (Illus.). pap. 0.75. Sleepy Hollow.

Reynolds, Helen W. **Dutch Houses in the Hudson Valley Before 1776.** (Illus.). 8.00. Peter Smith.

--**Dutch Houses in the Hudson Valley Before 1776.** (Illus.). 1965. pap. 5.00. Dover.

Thompson, John H., ed. **Geography of New York State.** (Illus.). 1966. 14.95. Syracuse U Pr.

Tobey, Eric & Wolkenberg, Richard. **Northeast Bicycle Tours.** (Illus.). 1973. pap. 3.95. Tobey Pub.

TWA's Getaway Guide to New York, 1973-74. 1973. pap. 1.00. A Frommer.

Van Der Donck, Adriaen. **Description of the New Netherlands.** O'Donnell, Thomas F., ed. 1968. 5.50. Syracuse U Pr.

Wade, Richard C., ed. **Regional Survey of New York & Its Environs.** 10 vols. (Illus.). 1974. 170.00. Arno.

Wilson, Edmund. **Upstate.** 1974. pap. 4.95. FS&G.

North Carolina

Federal Writers' Project. **North Carolina: A Guide to the Old North State.** 1939. Repr. 19.50. Somerset Pub.

--**North Carolina: A Guide to the Old North State.** (Illus.). 1972. Repr. of 1913. ed. 29.50. Scholarly.

North Dakota

Federal Writers' Project. **North Dakota: Guide to the Northern Prairie State.** 2nd ed. 1950. 10.95. Oxford U Pr.

North Dakota: A Guide to the Northern Prairie State. 1941. 14.50. Scholarly.

North Dakota: Guide to the Northern Prairie State. 1938. 14.50. Somerset Pub.

Roehrick, Kaye L., ed. **Brevet's North Dakota Historical Markers & Sites.** (Illus.). 1975. 7.95; pap. 3.95. Brevet Pr.

Ohio

Federal Writers' Project. **The Ohio Guide.** 1940. Repr. 19.50. Somerset Pub.

--**The Ohio Guide.** (Illus.). 1972. Repr. of 1940 ed. 29.50. Scholarly.

Frary, L. T. **Early Homes of Ohio.** (Illus.). 7.50. Peter Smith.

Perry, Dick & Goldflies, Bruce. **Ohio.** (Illus.). 1969. 5.95. Doubleday.

Oklahoma

Federal Writers' Project. **Oklahoma: A Guide to the Sooner State.** 1941. Repr. 17.50. Somerset Pub.

--**Oklahoma: A Guide to the Sooner State.** Debo, Angie & Oskison, John M., eds. (Illus.). 1972. Repr. of 1941 ed. 24.50. Scholarly.

Oregon

Atkeson, Ray. **Washington & Oregon in Color.** (Illus.). 1954. pap. 1.00. Binford.

Bleything, Dennis & Hawkins, Susan. **Getting off on 96 & Other Less Traveled Roads.** (Illus.). 1975; pap. 3.95. Touchstone Pr Ore.

Corning, Howard M. **Williamette Landings: Ghost Towns of the River.** rev. ed. 1973. 6.75; pap. 4.95. Oreg Hist Soc.

Farmer, Judith A. & Holmes, Kenneth L. **An Historical Atlas of Early Oregon.** 1973. 25.00. Geog Area Study.

Federal Writers' Project. **Oregon: End of the Trail.** 1941. Repr. 19.50. Somerset Pub.

Friedman, Ralph. **Oregon for the Curious.** (Illus.). 1972. pap. 3.95. Caxton.

Garren, John. **Oregon River Tours.** (Illus.). 1975. pap. 4.00. Binford.

Hastings, Lansford W. **Emigrant's Guide to Oregon & California.** 2nd ed. 1969. 17.50. Da Capo.

Hixon, Adrietta A. **On to Oregon.** 1971. Repr. 3.95; pap. 2.50. Ye Galleon.

Jackman, E. R. & Long, R. A. **The Oregon Desert.** (Illus.). 1964. 8.95. Caxton.

Jackman, E. R. & Scharff, John. **Steen's Mountain in Oregon's High Desert Country.** (Illus.). 1967. 30.00. Caxton.

Oregon: End of the Trail. 1940. 24.50. Scholarly.

Oregon Guide. (Illus.). 1975. 8.95; pap. 5.95. Binford.

Powell, Fred W., ed. **Hall J. Kelley on Oregon.** (Illus.). 1972. Repr. 15.00. Da Capo.

Satterfield, Archie. **Oregon Two.** (Illus.). 1974. 25.00. Graphic Arts Ctr.

Satterfield, Archie, ed. **The Oregon Coast.** (Illus.). 1972. 22.00. Graphic Arts Ctr.

Worcester, Thomas K. **A Portrait of Oregon.** (Illus.). 1973. 15.00. Touchstone Pr Ore.

Pennsylvania

Cawley, James & Cawley, Margaret. **Along the Old York Road.** 1965. 6.00; pap. 2.75. Rutgers U Pr.

Faris, John T. **Old Trails & Roads in Penn's Land.** (Illus.). 1969. Repr. of 1927 ed. 10.00. Friedman.

--**Old Trails & Roads in Penn's Land.** (Illus.). Repr. of 1927 ed. 10.00. Kennikat.

Federal Writers' Project. **Pennsylvania: A Guide to the Keystone State.** (Illus.). 1972. Repr. of 1940 ed. 29.50. Scholarly.

--**Pennsylvania: Guide to the Keystone State.** 1940. 10.95. Oxford U Pr.

Federal Writers' Project, Pennsylvania. **Erie: A Guide to the City & County.** 1938. 14.50. AMS Pr.

--**Northampton County Guide.** 1939. 12.50. AMS Pr.

Rhode Island

Appalachian Mountain Club. **Massachusetts-Rhode Island Trail Guide.** 3rd ed. 1972. 7.75. Appalach Mtn.

Federal Writers' Project. **Rhode Island: A Guide to the Smallest State.** 1937. Repr. 17.50. Somerset Pub.

--**Rhode Island: A Guide to the Smallest State.** (Illus.). 1972. Repr. of 1937 ed. 24.50. Scholarly.

Gemming, Klaus & Gemming, Elizabeth. **Block Island Summer.** (Illus.). 1972. 8.50. Chatham Pr.

Hitchcock, Henry-Russell. **Rhode Island Architecture.** 2nd ed. (Illus.). 1968. Repr. of 1939 ed. 17.50. Da Capo.

--**Rhode Island Architecture.** 1969. pap. 4.95. MIT Pr.

South Carolina

Bartram, W. **Travels Through North & South Carolina.** 35.00. Gordon Pr.

Federal Writers' Project. **South Carolina: A Guide to the Palmetto State.** 1941. Repr. 17.50. Somerset Pub.

--**South Carolina: A Guide to the Palmetto State.** (Illus.). 1972. Repr. of 1941 ed. 24.50. Scholarly.

--**South Carolina: Guide to the Palmetto State.** 1941. 10.95. Oxford U Pr.

Oliphant, S. C. **Mountains to the Sea.** 5.00. State Ptg.

Sloan, Eugene B. **Scenic South Carolina.** (Illus.). 1965. 8.50. State Ptg.

--**Scenic South Carolina.** 2nd rev. ed. (Illus.). 1971. 10.00. Lewis-Sloan.

Smith, Enoch. **Call of the Big Eastatoe.** 8.95. State Ptg.

Watson, Margaret. **Greenwood County Sketches: Old Roads & Early Families.** (Illus.). 1970. 12.50. Attic Pr.

Tennessee

Federal Writers' Project. **Tennessee: A Guide to the State.** 1939. Repr. 19.50. Somerset Pub.

--**Tennessee: A Guide to the State.** (Illus.). 1972. Repr. of 1939 ed. 24.50. Scholarly.

Texas

Dollar-Wise Guide to Texas. Essandess.

Federal Writers' Project. **Texas: A Guide to the Lone Star State.** 19.50. Somerset Pub.

--**Texas: A Guide to the Lone Star State.** (Illus.). 1972. Repr. of 1940 ed. 29.50. Scholarly.

Hansen, Harry & Federal Writers' Project, eds. **Texas: A Guide to the Lone Star State.** rev. ed. (Illus.). 1969. 9.95. Hastings.

Howard, Rex Z. **Texas Guidebook,** 5th ed. McCarty, F. M., ed. (Illus.). 1970. 5.95; pap. 2.95. Pelican.

Nelson, Dick & Nelson, Sharon. **Fifty Hikes in Texas.** (Illus.). 1974. pap. 3.95. Tecolote Pr.

Pratt, Kevin. **Thirty Bike Rides in the Austin Area.** 1973. 3.50. Jenkins.

Syers, W. E. **Off the Beaten Trail.** 7.00. Texian.

Texas Guidebook: Howard's Original. 5th ed. 4.95; pap. 2.95. F M McCarty.

Utah

Abbey, Edward. **Slick Rock: The Endangered Canyons of the Southwest.** (Illus.). 1974. pap. 4.95. Scribner.

--**Slickrock.** (Illus.). 1971. 27.50. Sierra.

Burton, Richard F. **City of the Saints.** Brodie, Fawn M., ed. (Illus.). 1963. 10.00. Knopf.

Federal Writers' Project. **Utah: A Guide to the State.** (Illus.). 1972. Repr. of 1941 ed. 24.50. Scholarly.

--**Utah: A State Guide.** 1941. Repr. 17.50. Somerset Pub.

Peterson, Charles S., et al. **Mormon Battalion Trail Guide.** (Illus.). 1972. 3.50. Utah St Hist Soc.

Piercy, Frederick. **Route from Liverpool to the Great Salt Lake Valley.** facs. ed. Brodie, Fawn M., ed. 1962. 10.00. Harvard U Pr.

Stegner, Wallace. **Mormon Country.** pap. 3.95. Hawthorn.

Vermont

Bassett, T. D., ed. **Outsiders Inside Vermont: Travelers' Tales of 358 Years.** (Illus.). 1967. 4.95. Greene.

Bearse, Ray, ed. **Vermont: A Guide to the Green Mountain State.** 3rd ed. (Illus.). 1968. 7.95. HM.

Beers, F. W. **Atlas of Windham County, Vermont.** 20.00. Greene.

Beers, F. W., et al. **Atlas of Addison County, Vermont.** (Illus.). 1970. Repr. 17.50. C E Tuttle.

--**Atlas of Chittenden County, Vermont.** (Illus.). 1970. Repr. 17.50. C E Tuttle.

--**Atlas of Washington County, Vermont.** (Illus.). 1970. Repr. 17.50. C E Tuttle.

Bundy, Robert E. **Just Visiting, & Other Vermont Sketches.** 1974. 3.75. Countryman.

Congden, Herbert W. **Old Vermont Houses, 1763-1850.** 1968. pap. 3.95. Bauhan.

Federal Writers' Project. **Vermont: A Guide to the Green Mountain State.** 1937. Repr. 14.50. Somerset Pub.

Grossinger, Richard, ed. **Vermont.** (Illus.). 1974. pap. 8.00. Io Pubns.

Hard, Margaret. **Footloose in Vermont.** (Illus.). 1969. 3.95; pap. 2.00. Vermont Bks.

Hill, Ralph N. **Vermont Album.** (Illus.). 1974. 12.50. Greene.

Jennison, Keith. **Vermont Is Where You Find It.** (Illus.). pap. 3.50. Durrell.

Kunin, Madeleine & Stout, Marilyn. **The Big Green Book: A Guide to Vermont.** (Illus.). 1975. 12.50. Barre.

Merkle & Vermont Historical Society. **This Is Vermont.** (Illus.). 1965. pap. 1.00. Carstens Pubns.

Perrin, Noel. **Vermont: In All Weathers.** (Illus.). 1973. 10.95. Viking Pr.

Sadlier, Paul & Sadlier, Ruth. **Fifty Hikes in Vermont.** (Illus.). 1974. pap. 5.95. NH Pub Co.

Virginia

Bodine, A. Aubrey. **Chesapeake Bay & Tidewater.** (Illus.). 1969. 19.95. Bodine.

--**Face of Virginia.** 2nd ed. (Illus.). 1971. 19.95. Bodine.

Federal Writers' Project. **Virginia: A Guide to the Old Dominion.** (Illus.). 1972. Repr. of 1940 ed. 29.50. Scholarly.

Harvill, A. M., Jr. **Spring Flora of Virginia.** (Illus.). 1970. 8.50. McClain.

Nutting, Wallace. **Virginia Beautiful.** 1974. pap. 4.95. EPM Pubns.

Virginia: A Guide to the Old Dominion. 1940. 29.50. Somerset Pub.

Writers Program, Virginia. **Jefferson's Albemarle: A Guide to Albemarle County & the City of Charlottesville, Virginia.** 1941. Repr. 9.50. AMS Pr.

Washington (State)

Atkeson, Ray. **Washington & Oregon in Color.** (Illus.). 1954. pap. 1.00. Binford.

Faber, Jim. **An Irreverent Guide to Washington State.** pap. 3.95. Doubleday.

Federal Writers' Project. **Washington: A Guide to the Evergreen State.** 1941. Repr. 19.50. Somerset Pub.

Furrer, Werner. **Kayak & Canoe Trips in Washington.** (Illus.). 1971. pap. 2.00. Signpost Pubns.

--**Water Trails of Washington.** 1973. pap. 2.50. Signpost Pubns.

Kirk, Ruth. **Washington State: National Parks, Historic Sites, Recreation Areas, & Natural Landmarks.** (Illus.). 1974. pap. 1.95. U of Wash Pr.

Kloke, Dallas S. **Boulders & Cliffs: Climber's Guide to Lowland Rock in Skagit & Whatcom Counties.** (Illus.). 1971. pap. 2.50. Signpost Pubns.

Marshall, Louise B. **High Trails: Guide to the Pacific Crest Trail in Washington.** 4th ed. (Illus.). 1973. pap. 4.95. Signpost Pubns.

Scofield, W. M. **Washington's Historical Markers.** (Illus.). 1967. pap. 1.95. Touchstone Pr Ore.

Sunset Editors. **Washington.** 3rd ed. (Illus.). 1973. pap. 2.95. Lane.

Washington Guide. (Illus.). 1975. 8.95; pap. 5.95. Binford.

Washington, D.C.

Babb, Laura L., ed. **The Washington Post Guide to Washington.** 1976. price not set; pap. price not set. McGraw.

Borreson, Mary Jo. **Washington D. C. Government City.** (Illus.). 1970. 4.72. McGraw.

Bright-Sagnier, Thierry. **An Insider's Guide to Washington at Night.** 1975. pap. 2.00. Washingtonian.

Colton, Amy. **Off the Beaten Track in Washington, D. C.** pap. 2.50. Nash Pub.

Coxe, Warren J., et al, eds. **A Guide to the Architecture of Washington, D. C.** 2nd ed. (Illus.). 1974. 7.95; pap. 5.95. McGraw.

Dollar-Wise Guide to Washington, D. C. 1968. Essandess.

Ein, Marion & Shabecoff, Alice. **The Whole Washington Handbook: Where to Go & What to Know.** 1975. pap. 3.95. Luce.

Federal Writers' Project. **Washington: City & Capital.** 1942. Repr. 17.50. Somerset Pub.

Friddell, Guy & Burda, Franz. **Washington the Open City.** 1974. 14.95. Burda Pubns.

Goode, James M. **The Outdoor Sculpture of Washington, D. C.** (Illus.). 1974. 15.00; pap. 4.95. Smithsonian.

Gurney, Gene. **Beautiful Washington.** (Illus.). 1969. 5.95. Crown.

Hagel, Keith & Robertson, Janet, eds. **Arrow Street Guide of Greater Washington, D. C.** 1973. 2.50. Arrow Pub.

Hannau, Hans W. **Washington, District of Columbia.** (Illus.). 1964. 2.95. French & Eur.

Hillman, H. **Washington, D. C. at a Glance.** 1972. pap. 1.95. McKay.

Love, Nancy. **Washington: The Official Bicentennial Guidebook.** (Illus.). 1975. pap. 3.00. Washingtonian.

Mann, Joan. **Washington.** (Illus.). 1973. pap. 2.75. Kodansha.

Sasek, Miroslav. **This Is Washington, D. C.** (Illus.). 1969. 4.95. Macmillan.

Shaw, Ray. **Washington for Children: An Unusual Guide for Families, Teachers, & Tourists.** 1975. 8.95; pap. 3.95. Scribner.

Truett, Randle B. **Washington Pocket Guide.** (Illus.). pap. 0.50. Hastings.

Truett, Randle B. & Federal Writers' Project, eds. **Washington, D.C. A Guide to the Nation's Capital.** rev. ed. (Illus.). 1968. 10.95. Hastings.

Turgeon, Charles F. & Richman, Phyllis C. **An Insider's Guide to Dining Out in Washington.** 1975. pap. 2.00. Washingtonian.

TWA's Getaway Guide to Washington, D. C., 1973-74. 1973. pap. 1.00. A Frommer.

Viorst, Judith & Viorst, Milton. **Washington, D.C. Underground Gourmet.** 1970. pap. 1.95. S&S.

Walker, John & Walker, Katharine. **The Walker Washington Guide.** rev. ed. Orig. Title: The Washington Guidebook. (Illus.). 1975. pap. 2.25. Guide Pr.

Washington D.C., A Guide to the Nation's Capital. 1941. 24.50. Scholarly.

Washington, D.C. on Ten Dollars a Day: 1974-75 Edition. 1974. pap. 3.50. A Frommer.

West Virginia

Beery, Donald. **Call of the Mountains.** (Illus.). 1973. 7.00. McClain.

Federal Writers' Project. **West Virginia: A Guide to the Mountain State.** (Illus.). 1972. Repr. of 1941 ed. 24.50. Scholarly.

Preble, Jack. **The Sinks of Gandy Creek.** (Illus.). 1969. 1.00. McClain.

West Virginia: A Guide to the Mountain State. 1941. 24.50. Somerset Pub.

Wisconsin

Brody, Polly. **Discovering Wisconsin.** (Illus.). 1973. 8.95. Wisconsin Hse.

Canoe Trails of Northeastern Wisconsin. 1972. pap. 5.00. Wisc T & T.

Derleth, August W. **Wisconsin Earth, a Sac Prairie Sampler.** 1971. Repr. of 1948 ed. 28.50. Greenwood.

Federal Writers' Project. **Wisconsin: A Guide to the Badger State.** (Illus.). 1972. Repr. 29.50. Scholarly.

--**Wisconsin: A State Guide.** 17.50. Somerset Pub.

Gard, Robert E. **This Is Wisconsin.** (Illus.). 1969. 7.95. Wisconsin Hse.

Gard, Robert E. & Bohrod, Aaron. **Wisconsin Sketches.** Lefebvre, Mark E., ed. (Illus.). 1973. 12.95. Wisconsin Hse.

Kouba, Theodore F. **Wisconsin's Amazing Woods—Then & Now.** (Illus.). 1973. 8.95. Wisconsin Hse.

Minnich, Jerry A. **A Wisconsin Garden Guide.** 1975. 13.95; pap. 5.95. Wisconsin Hse.

Palzer, Bob & Palzer, Jody. **Whitewater; Quietwater: A Guide to the Wild Rivers of Wisconsin, Upper Michigan, & NE Minnesota.** 2nd rev. ed. (Illus.). 1975. 12.95; pap. 7.95. Evergreen Paddleways.

Perrin, Richard W. E. **The Architecture of Wisconsin.** (Illus.). 1967. 7.50. State Hist Soc Wis.

Williams, Marjorie. **Bucks Camp Log.** 1974. 5.95. Wisconsin Sptmn.

Xan, Erna O. **Wisconsin My Home.** 1976. 12.50; pap. 4.25. U of Wis Pr.

Wyoming

Bonney, Orrin H. & Bonney, Lorraine. **Field Book.** Incl. Teton Range & Gros Ventre Range. rev., 2nd ed. (Illus.). 1974. pap. 4.95. Swallow.

--**Guide to Wyoming Mountains & Wilderness Areas.** rev. 3rd ed. (Illus.). 1975. 20.00. Swallow.

Federal Writers' Project. **Wyoming: A Guide to Its History, Highways & People.** 1941. Repr. 17.50. Somerset Pub.

--**Wyoming: Guide to Its History, Highways, & People.** 8.95. Oxford U Pr.

Wyoming: A Guide to Its History, Highways & People. 1941. 19.50. Scholarly.

CANADA

Alberta

Atlas of Alberta. 1970. 30.00. U of Toronto Pr.

British Columbia

Macaree, David. **One Hundred & Three Hikes in Southwestern British Columbia** (Illus.). pap. 5.95. Mountaineers.

Sierra Club of British Columbia. **The West Coast Trail & Nitinat Lakes.** 1974. pap. 3.95. David & Charles.

Western Living Magazine Editors, ed. **Backroads of British Columbia.** 1975. 10.95. David & Charles.

Newfoundland

Marin, Clive. **Fogo Island.** (Illus.). 1974. 4.95. Dorrance.

Nova Scotia

Barnard, M. **Nova Scotia.** Date not set. 8.95. McGraw.

Buckler, Ernest. **Nova Scotia: Window on the Sea.** (Illus.). 1973. 10.00. Potter.

Howe, Joseph. **Western & Eastern Rambles: Travel Sketches of Nova Scotia.** Parks, M. G., ed. (Illus.). 1973. 10.00; pap. 3.50. U of Toronto Pr.

Walden, Howard T., 2nd. **Anchorage Northeast.** (Illus.). 1971. 8.95. Morrow.

Ontario

Braithwaite, Max. **Max Braithwaite's Ontario.** (Illus.). 1975. 10.00. David & Charles.
Judd, W. W. **Vignettes of Nature in Southern Ontario.** 3.00. Carlton.
Ogburn, Charlton, Jr. **Continent in Our Hands.** (Illus.). 1971. 7.95. Morrow.

Prince Edward Island

Greenhill, B. J. **Westcountrymen in Prince Edward's Isle.** (Illus.). 1975. pap. 4.50. U of Toronto Pr.

Quebec (Province)

Grenier, Fernand, ed. **Quebec.** (Illus.). 1972. 10.00; pap. 5.00. U of Toronto Pr.
Pratson, Frederick J. **A Guide to Atlantic Canada.** (Illus.). 1973. pap. 3.95. Chatham Pr.

Saywell, John. **Quebec Seventy: A Documentary Narrative.** (Illus.). 1971. pap. 2.95. U of Toronto Pr.
Wilson, P. Roy. **The Beautiful Old Houses of Quebec.** (Illus.). 1975. 12.50. U of Toronto Pr.

Saskatchewan

Olson, Sigurd F. **Lonely Land.** (Illus.). 1961. 7.95. Knopf.

Magazines and Periodicals of Interest to the Camper and Backpacker

Adirondack (BM)
Established 1946
Circulation: 5000
Ivan Kusinitz, Editor
Adirondack Mountain Club, Inc.
172 Ridge Street
Glen Falls, New York 12801
(518) 793-7737

Adirondak Life (Q)
Established 1970
Circulation: 35,000
Lionel A. Atwill, Editor
Adirondak Life, Inc.
Willsboro, New York 12996
(518) 933-7808

All Outdoors Magazine (M)
Established 1947
Circulation: 150,000
Ralph Dice, Editor
Southwestern Association, Inc.
P.O. Box 700
Denison, Texas 75020
(214) 463-2440

American Alpine News (Q)
Established 1948
Circulation: 1500
Alan M. Rubin, Editor
American Alpine Club
113 East 90th Street
New York, New York 10038
(212) 722-1628

Appalachia (SA)
Established 1876
Circulation: 17,000
Phillip D. Levin, Editor
Appalachian Mountain Club
5 Joy Street
Boston, Massachusetts 02108
(617) 523-0636

Appalachian Trailway News (4 x yr.)
Established 1940
Circulation: 7000
P. H. Dunning, Editor
Appalachian Trail Conference
P.O. Box 236
Harpers Ferry, West Virginia 25425
(304) 535-6331

Backpacker (Q)
Established 1973
Circulation: 100,000
William Kemsley, Editor
Backpacker, Inc.
65 Adams Street
Bedford Hills, New York 10507
(914) 241-3240

Backpacking Journal (2 x yr.)
Established 1975
Circulation: 43,000
Andrew J. Carra, Editor
Davis Publications, Inc.
229 Park Avenue South
New York, New York 10003
(212) 673-1300

Better Camping (M)
Established 1960
Circulation: 80,000
Kirk Landers, Editor
Woodall Publishing Co.
500 Hyacinth Place
Highland Park, Illinois 60035
(312) 433-4550

Camper Coachman (M)
Established 1963
Circulation: 72,000
Bill Estes, Editor
Trailer Life Publishing Co.
23945 Craftman Road
Calabasas, California 91302
(213) 888-6000

Campground and RV Park Management
(8 x yr.)
Established 1970
Circulation: 14,000
Bob Behme, Editor
Rajo Publications, Inc.
Rt. 1, Box 877
Grass Valley, California 95945
(916) 273-3354

Camping (M, Jan.-June; BM, Sept.-Dec.)
Established 1926
Circulation: 11,000
Howard P. Galloway, Editor
Galloway Publications
5 Mountain Avenue
North Plainfield, New Jersey 07060
(201) 754-8662

Camping and Trailering Guide (M)
Established 1959
Circulation: 90,000
George S. Wells, Editor
Rajo Publications, Inc.
Rt. 1, Box 877
Grass Valley, California 95945
(916) 273-3354

Camping Industry (6 x yr.)
Established 1966
Circulation: 12,000
Clem Dippel, Editor
Fishing Tackle Trade News, Inc.
P.O. Box 70
Wilmette, Illinois 60091
(312) 256-0650

Camping Journal (8 x yr.)
Established 1962
Circulation: 273,000
Andrew J. Carra, Editor
Davis Publications
229 Park Avenue South
New York, New York 10003
(212) 673-1300

Camping Magazine (8 x yr.)
Established 1926
Circulation: 9000
Glenn T. Job, Editor
American Camping Association
Bradford Woods
Martinsville, Indiana 46151
(317) 342-8456

Canoe (BM)
Established 1973
Circulation: 30,000
Peter A. Sonderegger, Editor
Webb Co.
1999 Shepard Road
St. Paul, Minnesota 55116
(612) 647-7200

Caravanner (BM)
Established 1954
Circulation: 600,000
Frank Quattrocchi, Editor
Airstream
North Dixie Highway
Sidney, Ohio 45365
(513) 492-9175

Climbing (6 x yr.)
Established 1970
Circulation: 3000
Michael Kennedy, Editor
Mountaineering and Rockclimbing Magazine
P.O. Box E
Aspen, Colorado 81611
(303) 925-3414

Colorado (BM)
Established 1965
Circulation: 160,000
Jim Sample, Editor
Colorado Magazine, Inc.
7190 West 14th Avenue
Denver, Colorado 80215
(303) 238-0466

Colorado Outdoors (BM)
Established 1952
Circulation: 47,000
Charles Hjelte, Editor
Colorado Division of Wildlife
6060 Broadway
Denver, Colorado 80216
(303) 825-1192

Down River (M)
Established 1974
Circulation: 14,000
John R. Anderson, Editor
P. O. Box 366
Mountain View, California 94040
(415) 965-8777

Florida Sportsman (BM)
Established 1969
Circulation: 66,000
Karl Wickstrom, Editor
Wickstrom Publishers, Inc.
2701 South Bayshore Drive, Suite 501
Miami, Florida 33133
(305) 858-3546

Hoosier Outdoors (BM)
Established 1968
Circulation: 60,000
Thomas J. Glancy, Editor
Hoosier Publications, Inc.
209 South Calumet Road
Chesterton, Indiana 46304
(219) 926-2592

Hosteling (M)
Established 1972
Circulation: 22,000
Ralph Lusich, Editor
American Youth Hostels, Metropolitan
   New York Council
132 Spring Street
New York, New York 10012
(212) 431-7100

Illinois Parks and Recreation (BM)
Established 1970
Circulation: 4000
Kay F. Kastel, Editor
Illinois Park and Recreation Society
600 E. Algonquin Road
Des Plaines, Illinois 60016
(312) 297-6261

Journal of Christian Camping (6 x yr.)
Established 1969
Circulation: 5000
Samuel Johnson, Editor
Christian Camping International
P.O. Box H
White Bluff, Tennessee 37187
(815) 786-8453

Long Trail News (Q)
Established 1940
Circulation: 2000
Margaret M. Pons, Editor
Green Mountain Club
45 Part Street
Rutland, Vermont 05701
(802) 775-0495

Mariah (Q)
Established 1976
Circulation: 71,000
Lawrence J. Burke, Editor and Publisher
Mariah Publications Corporation
3401 W. Division Street
Chicago, Illinois 60651
(312) 342-7777

Mountain Safety Research Newsletter (2 x yr.)
Established 1969
Circulation: 27,000
Larry Penberthy, Editor
Mountain Safety Research
631 S. 96th Street
Seattle, Washington 98108
(206) 762-4244

Mountain Visitor (W)
Established 1964
Circulation: 10,000
William C. Postlewaite, Editor
Mountain Press
1 Ridge Road
Gatlinburg, Tennessee 37738
(615) 436-4175

Mountaineer (M)
Established 1907
Circulation: 6000
Paul Robisch, Editor
Mountaineers
P.O. Box 122
Seattle, Washington 98111
(206) 623-2314

Nebraskaland (M)
Established 1922
Circulation: 55,000
Lowell Johnson, Editor
Nebraska Game and Parks Commission
P.O. Box 30370
Lincoln, Nebraska 68503
(402) 464-0641

Northeast Outdoors (M)
Established 1968
Circulation: 20,000
John Florian, Editor
Northeast Outdoors, Inc.
95 North Main Street
Waterbury, Connecticut 06702
(203) 757-8731

Off Belay (BM)
Established 1972
Circulation: 8000
Ray Smutek, Editor and Publisher
12416 169 Avenue, S.E.
Renton, Washington 98055
(206) 226-2613

Outdoor Guide (M)
Established 1970
Circulation: 5000
Milton E. Wester, Editor
Frontier Press, Inc.
2718 Montana Avenue, No. 18
Billings, Montana 59101
(406) 248-3002

Outdoor Press (W)
Established 1966
Circulation: 24,000
Fred L. Peterson, Editor
Outdoor Press, Inc.
North 2012 Ruby Street
Spokane, Washington 99207
(509) 328-9392

Outdoor Recreation Action (Q)
Established 1966
Circulation: 17,000
George M. Kyle, Editor
Superintendent of Documents
Government Printing Office
Washington, D.C. 20402
(202) 783-3238

Ozark Graphic (M)
Established 1968
Circulation: 4000
Bill Royce, Editor
Bill Royce and Ken Lipps
P. O. Box 56
Doniphan, Missouri 63935
(314) 996-2340

Potomac Appalachian (M)
Established 1932
Circulation: 3000
Linda Volkert, Editor
Potomac Appalachian Trail Club
1718 North Street, N.W.
Washington, D.C. 20036
(202) 638-5306

Sierra Club Bulletin (10 x yr.)
Established 1892
Circulation: 150,000
Frances Gendin, Editor
Sierra Club
530 Bush Street
San F ancisco, California 94108
(415) 981-8634

Signpost (M)
Established 1966
Circulation: 4000
Louise B. Marshall, Editor and Publisher
16812 36th Avenue West
Lynnwood, Washington 98036
(206) 743-3947

Summit (M)
Established 1955
Circulation: 8000
J. M. Crenshaw, Editor
Summit Publishing Co.
44 Mill Creek Road
Big Bear Lake, California 92315
(714) 866-3682

Trail and Timberline (M)
Established 1918
Circulation: 4000
Kaye Bache, Editor
Colorado Mountain Club
2530 West Alameda Avenue
Denver, Colorado 80219
(303) 922-8315

Trail Walker (BM)
Established 1963
Circulation: 3000
Alfred Smallens, Editor
New York-New Jersey Trail Conference
Box 2250
New York, New York 10001
(212) 687-3000

Trails-A-Way (10 x yr.)
Established 1970
Circulation: 60,000
David Higbie, Editor
TAW Publishing Co.
9731 Riverside Drive
Greenville, Michigan 48838
(616) 754-7191

Up Rope (M)
Established 1941
Circulation: 250
Stevie Smith, Editor
Potomac Appalachian Trail Club
1718 N Street, N.W.
Washington, D.C. 20036
(202) 638-5306

Western Outdoor News (W)
Established 1954
Circulation: 80,000
Bill Rice, Editor
Western Outdoors Publications
3939 Birch Street
Newport Beach, California 92660
(714) 546-4370

Western Outdoors (M)
Established 1960
Circulation: 104,000
Burt Twilegar, Editor
Western Outdoors Publications
3939 Birch Street
Newport Beach, California 92660
(714) 546-4370

Wilderness Camping (BM)
Established 1971
Circulation: 70,000
Harry N. Roberts, Editor
Fitzgerald Communications, Inc.
1597 Union Street
Schenectady, New York 12309
(518) 373-2533

Canadian Periodicals

British Columbia Outdoors (BM)
Established 1945
Circulation: 26,000
A. G. Downs, Editor
Northwest Digest, Ltd.
P.O. Box 900, Station A
Surrey Center, British Columbia V3S 4P4
(604) 574-5211

Outdoor Canada (BM)
Established 1972
Circulation: 38,000
Sheila Kaighin, Editor
Outdoor Canada Magazine, Ltd.
Suite 300, 181 Eglinton Avenue, E
Toronto, Ontario M4P 1J9
(416) 487-1159

Pacific Hosteller (Q)
Established 1964
Circulation: 8000
Canadian Youth Hostels Association
  Pacific Region
1406 W. Broadway
Vancouver, British Columbia V6H 1H4
(604) 736-2674

Pathfinder (3 x yr.)
Established 1970
Circulation: 3000
Alfred Falk, Editor
Canadian Youth Hostels Association,
  Northwest Region
10922 88th Avenue
Edmonton, Alberta T6G 0Z1
(403) 439-3089

Recreation Canada (BM)
Established 1947
Circulation: 3000
Art C. Drysdale, Editor
Canadian Parks Recreation Association
333 River Road
Vanier City, Ontario K1L 8B9
(613) 746-0060

*Scope/Recreational Vehicle and
  Camping News (BM)*
Established 1968
Circulation: 25,000
Merton Publications, Ltd.
30 Key Hill Place
London, Ontario N6G 2G4
(519) 471-9109

*Explanation of Symbols: (M) Monthly; (BM) Bi-monthly; (SM) Semi-monthly; (W) Weekly; (Q) Quarterly

Federal, State and Provincial Agencies Concerned with Wildlife Protection and Exploitation

FEDERAL GOVERNMENT

Army Corps of Engineers
Department of Defense
Washington, D.C. 20314

Forest Service
Department of Agriculture
12th & Independence Avenues S.W.
Washington, D.C. 20250

National Oceanic and Atmospheric
Administration
Department of Commerce

National Ocean Survey C-44
Riverdale, Maryland 20840

National Park Service
Department of the Interior
Washington, D.C. 20240

STATE GOVERNMENTS

ALABAMA
Division of State Parks
Department of Conservation and
Natural Resources
64 North Union Street
Montgomery, Alabama 36104

ALASKA
Division of Parks
323 East 4th Avenue
Anchorage, Alaska 99501

ARIZONA
State Parks Board
State Capitol
1688 West Adams Street
Phoenix, Arizona 85007

ARKANSAS
Department of Parks and Tourism
149 State Capitol
Little Rock, Arkansas 72201

CALIFORNIA
Resources Agency
Department of Parks and Recreation
P.O. Box 2390
Sacramento, California 95811

COLORADO
Division of Parks and Outdoor
Recreation
1845 Sherman
Denver, Colorado 80203

CONNECTICUT
Parks and Recreation Unit
Department of Environmental
Protection
State Office Building
165 Capitol Avenue
Hartford, Connecticut 06115

DELAWARE
Division of Parks, Recreation and
Forestry
Department of Natural Resources and
Environmental Control
The Edward Tatnall Building
Legislative Avenue and William Penn
Street
Dover, Delaware 19901

FLORIDA
Department of Natural Resources
Crown Building Room 321
202 Blount Street
Tallahassee, Florida 32304

GEORGIA
Department of State Parks and
Historic Sites
270 Washington Street S.W.
Atlanta, Georgia 30334

IDAHO
Department of Parks and Recreation
Statehouse
Boise, Idaho 83720

ILLINOIS
Division of Parks and Memorials
Department of Conservation
605 State Office Building
Springfield, Illinois 62706

INDIANA
Division of Outdoor Recreation
Department of Natural Resources
612 State Office Building
Indianapolis, Indiana 46204

IOWA
State Conservation Commission
300 Fourth Street
Des Moines, Iowa 50319

KANSAS
Park and Resources Authority
801 Harrison Street
Topeka, Kansas 66612

KENTUCKY
Division of Travel
Department of Public Information
Capitol Annex
Frankfort, Kentucky 40601

LOUISIANA
State Parks and Recreation
Commission
P.O. Drawer 1111
Baton Rouge, Louisiana 70821

MAINE
Bureau of Parks and Recreation
Department of Parks and Recreation
State Office Building
Augusta, Maine 04333

MARYLAND
Department of Forest and Parks
Tawes State Office Building
Annapolis, Maryland 21404

MASSACHUSETTS
Division of Forests and Parks
Department of Environmental
Management
Leverett Saltonstall Building
100 Cambridge Street
Boston, Massachusetts 02202

MICHIGAN
Division of State Parks
Department of Natural Resources
Mason Building
Lansing, Michigan 48926

MINNESOTA
Division of Parks and Recreation
Department of Natural Resources
658 Cedar Street
St. Paul, Minnesota 55155

MISSISSIPPI
Park System
717 Robert E. Lee Building
Jackson, Mississippi 39201

MISSOURI
Division of Parks and Recreation
Department of Natural Resources
1204 Jefferson Street
Jefferson City, Missouri 65101

MONTANA
Division of Recreation and Parks
Department of Fish and Game
Helena, Montana 59601

NEBRASKA
Game and Parks Commission
2200 N. 33 Street
Lincoln, Nebraska 68503

NEVADA
State Park System
Department of Conservation and
Natural Resources
Nye Building, Room 221
201 South Fall Street
Carson City, Nevada 89710

NEW HAMPSHIRE
Parks Division
Department of Economic Development
and Resources
P.O. Box 856
Concord, New Hampshire 03301

NEW JERSEY
Bureau of Parks
P.O. Box 1420
Trenton, New Jersey 08625

Department of Conservation
Statehouse Annex
Trenton, New Jersey 08625

NEW MEXICO
State Park and Recreation
Commission
P.O. Box 1147
Santa Fe, New Mexico 87501

NEW YORK
Office of Parks and Recreation
Albany, New York 12223

NORTH CAROLINA
Division of State Parks
Department of Natural and Economic
Resources
P.O. Box 27687
Raleigh, North Carolina 27611

NORTH DAKOTA
Park Service
P.O. Box 139
Mandan, North Dakota 58554

OHIO
Division of Parks and Recreation
Department of Natural Resources
Fountain Square Building C
Columbus, Ohio 43224

OKLAHOMA
Industrial Development and
Park Department
500 Will Rogers Memorial Building
Oklahoma City, Oklahoma 73105

OREGON
Division of State Highways
State Parks and Recreation Branch
State Highway Building
Salem, Oregon 97310

PENNSYLVANIA
State Parks Bureau
Department of Environmental
Resources
2301 North Cameron Street
Harrisburg, Pennsylvania 17120

RHODE ISLAND
Division of Parks and Recreation

Department of Natural Resources
83 Park Street
Providence, Rhode Island 02903

SOUTH CAROLINA
Department of Parks, Recreation and
Tourism
1205 Pendleton Street
Columbia, South Carolina 29202

SOUTH DAKOTA
Department of Game, Fish and Parks
Sigurd Anderson Building
Pierre, South Dakota 57501

TENNESSEE
Division of State Parks
Department of Conservation
2611 West End Avenue
Nashville, Tennessee 37203

TEXAS
Department of Parks and Wildlife
John H. Reagan Building
Austin, Texas 78701

UTAH
Division of Parks and Recreation
Department of Natural Resources
1596 West North Temple
Salt Lake City, Utah 84116

VERMONT
Agency of Environmental
Conservation
Department of Forest and Parks
Montpelier, Vermont 05602

VIRGINIA
Division of State Parks
1201 State Office Building
Capitol Square
Richmond, Virginia 23219

WASHINGTON
State Parks and Recreation
Commission
P.O. Box 1128
Olympia, Washington 98504

WEST VIRGINIA
Parks and Recreation
Department of Natural Resources
1800 Washington Street
Charleston, West Virginia 25305

WISCONSIN
Division of Forestry, Wildlife and
Recreation
Department of Natural Resources
P.O. Box 450 M
Madison, Wisconsin 53701

WYOMING
Wyoming Recreation Commission
State Mail
Cheyenne, Wyoming 82002

CANADA

ALBERTA
Travel Alberta
10255-104 Street
Edmonton, Alberta T5J 1B1

BRITISH COLUMBIA
Department of Travel Industry
Parliament Building
Victoria, British Columbia V8V 1X4

MANITOBA
Tourist Branch
Department of Tourism, Recreation
and Cultural Affairs
200 Vaughan Street
Winnipeg, Manitoba R3C 1T5

NEW BRUNSWICK
Tourism New Brunswick
P.O. Box 1030
Fredericton, New Brunswick E3B 5C3

NEWFOUNDLAND, LABRADOR
Parks Division
Department of Tourism
P.O. Box 9340
St. Johns, Newfoundland A1A 2Y3

NORTHWEST TERRITORIES
Travelarctic
Yellowknife, Northwest Territories
X1A 2L9

NOVA SCOTIA
Department of Tourism
P.O. Box 130
Halifax, Nova Scotia B3J 2M7

ONTARIO
Ministry of Industry and Tourism
Queen's Park
Toronto, Ontario M7A 2E5

PRINCE EDWARD ISLAND
Tourism Information Division
P.O. Box 940
Charlottetown, Prince Edward Island
C1A 7M5

QUEBEC
Ministry of Tourism, Fish and Game
150 East Boulevard
Saint-Cyrille, Quebec G1R 4Y3

SASKATCHEWAN
Department of Tourism and
Renewable Resources
P.O. Box 7105
Regina, Saskatchewan S4P 3N2

YUKON TERRITORY
Department of Tourism, Conservation
and Information Services
P.O. Box 2703
Whitehorse, Yukon Y1A 2C6

Organizations and Associations of Interest to the Camper and Backpacker

ACRES, INC.
1802 Chapman Road   Phone: (219) 637-6264
Huntertown, Indiana 46748
Jane H. Dustin, Sec.
Founded: 1960
Members: 550
Dedicated to the preservation and acquisition of natural areas in northeastern Indiana. Purpose is to acquire and administer natural areas as living museums for educational and scientific purposes for public enjoyment. Has been successful in setting aside several representative samples of natural areas. Other land acquisitions are pending. Conducts guided field trips and lecture and film series. Maintains library. Publications: *Acres Quarterly.*

ADIRONDACK FORTY-SIXERS
c/o Mrs. G. Winifred Lamb   Phone: (518) 523-2080
One Valley Park
Lake Placid, New York 12946
G. Winifred Lamb, Pres.
Founded: 1948
Members: 1000
Persons who have climbed all 46 of the major peaks of the Adirondacks, a mountain area in northeast New York State. Major peaks are those 4000 feet or more in elevation, according to the Colvin Survey in the late 19th century. While many have trails marked by the state conservation department, 21 are officially trailless and about half of these are in remote areas requiring well-laid plans to complete the climbs. Publications: *Forty-Sixer Peaks, semiannual;* also has published booklet, *Climbed the Adirondack 46,* and book, *The Adirondack Forty-Sixers.* Convention/Meeting: semiannual—always Memorial Day weekend, Lake Placid, New York; and in the Fall, at various locations.

ADIRONDACK MOUNTAIN CLUB
172 Ridge Street   Phone. (518) 793-7737
Glens Falls, New York 12801
Grant Cole, Exec. Dir.
Founded: 1922
Members: 9000
Staff: 5
Local Groups: 24
Persons interested in the mountains, trails, camping, and forest conservation, especially in the Adirondack Mountain region of New York State. Conducts various recreational, conservation and educational activities. Maintains several miles of trails in the Adirondacks; operates two lodges. Annually sponsors winter mountaineering school and a rock climbing school. Promotes good conservation and forest management practices. Committees: Conservation; Lodge Operations; Maps and Guidebooks; Natural History; Outdoor Activities; Public Information and Education; Search and Rescue; Trails. Publications: *Adirondack,* bimonthly; also publishes guide to Adirondack trails, trees and rocks, canoe routes, and a map of the High Peak area of the Adirondacks. Convention/Meeting: annual—always November.

ADIRONDACK TRAIL IMPROVEMENT SOCIETY
St. Huberts, New York 12943   Phone: (518) 576-4411
Courtney G. Iglehart, Sec.
Founded: 1897
Members: 520
Staff: 10
Cuts and maintains trails on state and private property in Adirondacks; conducts education-recreational program for chil-

Adirondack Trail Improvement Society (Cont'd)
dren for two weeks prior to regular season, including High Peaks Camp for boys, ages 12-15; provides and maintains forest fire-fighting equipment; supports measures to preserve and protect the Adirondack region; cooperates with New York State Department of Environmental Conservation. Committees: Conservation. Publications: (1) *A.T.I.S. Trail Guide;* (2) *A.T.I.S. Trails on U.S. Topographical Maps of the Mt. Marcy Region.* Convention/Meeting: annual.

ALASKA CONSERVATION SOCIETY
P.O. Box 80192   Phone: (907) 452-2240
College, Alaska 99701
Katrina Stonorov, Exec. Sec.
Founded: 1960
Members: 1000
Staff: 1
Local Groups: 9
Individuals united to secure the wise use, protection and preservation of the scenic, scientific, recreational, wildlife and wilderness values of Alaska. Interests include land use planning, conservation, environmental matters, forestry, fishing, highway planning. Local chapters conduct educational programs. Maintains library. Publications: *Alaska Conservation Review,* quarterly.

ALBERTA FISH & GAME ASSOCIATION
8631 109th Street, Room 212   Phone: (403) 434-0655
Edmonton, Alberta T6G 1E8 Canada
Paul L. J. Morck, Sec.-Mgr.

ALPINE CLUB OF CANADA
P.O. Box 1026   Phone: (403) 762-3664
Banff, Alberta T0L 0C0 Canada
Evelyn S. Moorhouse, Mgr.
Founded: 1906
Members: 2200
Staff: 4
Sections: 12
Individuals interested in mountaineering. Objectives are: the encouragement, practice, and promotion of mountaineering and mountain crafts; the education of Canadians in appreciation of their mountain heritage; the exploration of alpine and glacial regions primarily in Canada; the preservation of the natural beauties of the mountains and of their fauna and flora; the promotion of mountain art and literature; the dissemination for scientific and educational purposes of knowledge concerning mountains and mountaineering through meetings, publications and a library; the exchange of information of educational or scientific value with other mountaineering clubs and organizations throughout the world. Conducts summer mountaineering and ski mountaineering camps. Builds and maintains huts and shelters for climbers. Conducts international climbing expeditions. Maintains library. Bestows awards. Committees: Camps; Climbing Standards; Clubhouse; Conservation; Editorial; Expeditions; Finance; Huts; Photographic; Ski Mountaineering. Publications: (1) *Gazette,* semiannual; (2) *Canadian Alpine Journal,* annual; (3) *Membership List,* biennial; also publishes climbers' guides and brochures. Affiliated with: Sports Federation of Canada; International Union of Alpine Associations. Convention/Meeting: annual—always August, Canmore, Alberta, Canada.

AMERICAN ASSOCIATION FOR CONSERVATION INFORMATION

c/o Ronald E. Shay   Phone: (503) 229-5425
Oregon Game Commission
Portland, Oregon 97208
Ronald E. Shay, Pres.
Founded: 1938
Members: 68

Professional society of officials of state and provincial conservation agencies formed primarily to share knowledge and experience to help member agencies do a better job. Sponsors annual awards program whereby winners in various categories of conservation education work are selected by a panel of judges. Committees: AACI TV Spot; Anti-Harvest Movement; Awards; Editor's Workshop; Postal Rate; Publicity and Action; Resolutions. Publications: (1) *Balance Wheel,* bimonthly; (2) *Yearbook.* Convention/Meeting: annual conference—always June; annual workshop—always February.

AMERICAN CANOE ASSOCIATION

4260 E. Evans Avenue   Phone: (303) 758-8257
Denver, Colorado 80222
Larry Zuk, Commodore
Founded: 1880
Members: 3900
Regional Groups: 11 (U.S. and Canada)
State Groups: 13

Governing body of canoe activity in North America. Dedicated to the sport of canoeing in all its facets and to the saving of streams and rivers. Sponsors races, cruises, encampments and training classes; provides information on canoeing matters; promotes safety and skill on the water; offers a book service. Committees: Canoe Poling; Long Distance (marathon and open canoe) Racing; Olympic (flatwater) Paddling; Rafting; Slalom and Wildwater Racing. Publications: *News Magazine,* 6/year; also publishes special articles. Convention/Meeting: annual—always November. Annual camp and meet are held during two weeks in August at ACA Sugar Island, Gananoque, Ontario, Canada.

AMERICAN COMMITTEE FOR INTERNATIONAL CONSERVATION

c/o The Wildlife Society   Phone: (202) 363-2435
3900 Wisconsin Avenue, N.W., Suite S-176
Washington, D.C. 20016
Fred G. Evenden, Sec.-Treas.
Founded: 1930
Members: 25

Associations interested in conservation and preservation of wildlife and other natural resources of the world. To stimulate, promote and finance research into status and ecology of threatened species; lend assistance to national and international organizations concerned with resources conservation, outside the U.S. Formerly: (1975) American Committee for International Wildlife Protection. Convention/Meeting: semiannual.

AMERICAN FORESTRY ASSOCIATION

1319 18th Street, N.W.   Phone: (202) 467-5810
Washington, D.C. 20036
William E. Towell, Exec. V. Pres.
Founded: 1875
Members: 78,000
Staff: 17

A citizen conservation organization working to advance the intelligent management and use of forests, soil, water, wildlife, and all other natural resources necessary for an environment of high quality. Seeks to promote an enlightened public apprecia-

American Forestry Association (Cont'd)

tion of natural resources and the part they play in the social, recreational, and economic life of the nation. Conducts Trail Riders of the Wilderness program of wilderness trips arranged for small groups of members. Presents annual distinguished service award and biennial Fernow Award. Sponsors a task force, Trees for People, which seeks to help meet national needs for forest products; enhance productivity of private, non-industrial forest resources; maximize benefits to private woodland owners; provide advice to forest owners; make legislative recommendations at the federal level. Publications: *American Forests Magazine,* monthly; also publishes books, reprints, and *The National Registry of Champion Big Trees and Famous Historical Trees.* Formed by merger of: American Forestry Congress (founded 1882) and American Forestry Association (an earlier organization). Convention/Meeting: annual.

AMERICAN GEOGRAPHICAL SOCIETY

Broadway at 156th Street   Phone: (212) 234-8100
New York, New York 10032
Dr. Robert B. McNee, Dir.
Founded: 1852
Members: 3000
Staff: 40

Professional geographers, educators, and others interested in all phases of geography. Devoted to research in geography and the dissemination of geographical knowledge. Produces maps, principally small and medium scale compilations of large areas, and thematic maps illustrating results of research. Engages in environmental research in urban and rural environments including detailed cartographic aspects. Sponsors lectures; presents awards and medals for outstanding research and contributions to geography and related fields. Maintains largest geographical library in the Western Hemisphere, including 225,000 books, 342,000 maps, 5270 atlases and many photographs covering all areas of geography and urban studies, regional science, cceanography, economics, demography, geology, soil science, and meteorology. Publications: (1) *Current Geographical Publications,* 10/year; (2) *Focus,* 10/year; (3) *Soviet Geography; Review and Translation,* 10/year; (4) *Geographical Review,* quarterly; (5) *Ubique* (newsletter), 3/year; also publishes many books, maps, and two serial atlases. Convention/Meeting: annual dinner—New York City.

AMERICAN GUIDES ASSOCIATION

P.O. Box B   Phone: (916) 662-6824
Woodland, California 95695
Loren L. Smith, Exec. Sec.
Founded: 1962
Members: 3000
Staff: 5
State Groups: 12

Professional guides who have trained and licensed under AGA supervision and those interested in wilderness travel for personal use or related professional occupations (Forest Service, Fish and Wildlife Service, Outward Bound, recreational service organizations). Purposes are: to train those with the highest qualifications for a life of service in wilderness outings; to improve the professional and ethical standards of those entering the profession of guiding; to maintain a school of guides and grant certificates to those who successfully complete the instructional and experience requirements. Offers backpack and survival guiding, cycle tour leadership. Conducts courses in paramedics, rock climbing, river guiding, etc. Maintains placement service and charitable program. Presents Silver Star Award for heroism. Maintains library. Publishes master schedule of chapter expeditions and area handbooks.

AMERICAN SCENIC AND HISTORIC PRESERVATION SOCIETY

15 Pine Street   Phone: (212) 344-3830
New York, New York 10005
Alexander Hamilton, Pres.
Founded: 1895
Members: 50
"To stimulate popular appreciation of scenic beauty and historic memorials of America."

AMERICAN SHORE AND BEACH PRESERVATION ASSOCIATION

10812 Admirals Way   Phone: (301) 299-5603
Potomac, Maryland 20854
Richard O. Eaton, Exec. Sec.-Treas.
Founded: 1926
Members: 1000
Staff: 1
Federal, state and local government agencies, private groups, and individuals interested in conservation, development and restoration of beaches and shore front of lakes and rivers. Publications: (1) *Newsletter,* monthly; (2) *Shore and Beach,* semiannual. Convention/meeting: annual.

AMERICAN WHITEWATER AFFILIATION

P.O. Box 321   Phone: no listing
Concord, New Hampshire 03301
Founded: 1954
Members: 3000
Affiliate Clubs: 90
Members and affiliates are interested in river travel by various means of paddlecraft. Promotes boating safety, technique, equipment, conservation programs. Publications: *American Whitewater,* quarterly. Affiliated with: American Camping Association; Sierra Club; and a number of other groups interested in paddlecraft.

AMERICAN YOUTH HOSTELS

National Campus   Phone: (703) 592-3271
Delaplane, Virginia 22025
Justin J. Cline, Act. Exec. Dir.
Founded: 1934
Members: 80,000
Staff: 25
Local Groups: 30
Sponsors inexpensive, educational and recreational outdoor travel opportunities, primarily by bicycle or on foot along scenic trails and by-ways. Maintains 130 overnight accommodations (hostels) in United States. Sponsors ski, canoe trips, etc., as well as foreign travel. Presents annual service awards, plus awards for cycling innovations and achievements. Publications: (1) *Hostel Guide and Handbook,* annual; (2) *High Road to Adventure,* annual. Affiliated with: International Youth Hostel Federation. Convention/Meeting: annual—always December.

AMERICA'S FUTURE TREES FOUNDATION

1200 Hanna Building   Phone: no listing
Cleveland, Ohio 44115
Administered by the National Wildlife Federation to finance a nationwide tree and wildlife habitat conservation program. Contributions provide for continuous tree plantings and for the maintenance and renewal of natural areas.

APPALACHIAN MOUNTAIN CLUB

5 Joy Street   Phone: (617) 523-0636
Boston, Massachusetts 02108
Thomas S. Deans, Exec. Dir.
Founded: 1876
Members: 23,000
Staff: 26
Regional Chapters: 8
To explore the mountains of New England and the adjacent regions for scientific and artistic purposes; to cultivate interest in geographical studies. Maintains 360 miles of trails, 20 shelters, and a 9-unit hut system open to public in White Mountains of New Hampshire. Works to conserve and protect the mountain country of New England. Conducts various public education workshops in hiking leadership and group safety. Offers public service program including recreation, conservation, backcountry facilities management, mountain search and rescue, recreation research, environmental education, and wilderness/urban social programs. Maintains one of the largest mountaineering libraries in the country and numerous map and photographic collections. Committees: Mountain Leadership and Safety. Publications: (1) *Appalachia Magazine,* 13/year; (2) *Bulletin,* monthly; (3) *Appalachia Journal,* semiannual; also publishes books, guides, and maps. Convention/Meeting: annual.

APPALACHIAN TRAIL CONFERENCE

P.O. Box 236   Phone: (304) 535-6331
Harpers Ferry, West Virginia 25425
Lester L. Holmes, Exec. Dir.
Founded: 1925
Members: 10,000
Local Groups: 70
Federation of trail and hiking clubs (70) and individuals (70,-000) interested in hiking. Manages the Appalachian Trail, a 2000 mile foot trail extending from Maine to Georgia along the crests of Appalachian ranges. Publications: *Appalachian Trailway News,* 4/year; also publishes trail guidebooks, maps, and other descriptive material for trail users. Convention/Meeting: biennial.

ASSOCIATION FOR ENVIRONMENTAL AND OUTDOOR EDUCATION

22901 106th W.   Phone: (209) 778-8902
Edmonds, Washington 98020
Cliff Nelson, Pres.
Founded: 1954
Members: 300
To provide environmental and outdoor education for school age children. Publications: (1) *Secretary's Newsletter,* 5/year; (2) *Newsletter,* 3/year. Formerly: (1969) Association for Outdoor Education. Convention/Meeting: annual.

ASSOCIATION FOR THE PROTECTION OF THE ADIRONDACKS

21 E. 40th Street, Rm. 704   Phone: (212) 532-4880
New York, New York 10016
Arthur M. Crocker, Pres.
Founded: 1901
Members: 600
A combined civic and conservation association of persons interested in conservation and protection of the Adirondack and Catskill Parks. Publications: (1) *Annual Report;* (2) *Membership List,* biennial; also publishes special subject reports. Convention/Meeting: annual—usually second Tuesday in April.

ASSOCIATION OF CONSERVATION ENGINEERS

c/o Ronald D. Hansen   Phone: (314) 751-4115
Missouri Dept. of Conservation
P.O. Box 180
Jefferson City, Missouri 65101
Ronald D. Hansen, Sec.-Treas.
Founded: 1961
Members: 140

Persons employed by or retired from any of the State agencies for the development of fish, wildlife, forestry, or recreational facilities, either in administrative, professional engineering, engineers-in-training, or general construction superintendents capacity. Encourages the educational, social, and economic interests of engineering practices which further the cause of fish, wildlife, and recreational developments. Gives Eugene Baker Conservation Engineering Award for the outstanding conservation engineering contribution. Publications: *Membership Directory*, annual. Convention/Meeting: annual.

BIG THICKET ASSOCIATION

P.O. Box 198   Phone: (713) 274-2971
Saratoga, Texas 77585
Howard Peacock, Pres.
Founded: 1964
Members: 900

Conservationists and others interested in preserving the wilderness area of southeast Texas known as the "Big Thicket." This unique natural region, comprising approximately 300,000 acres, contains a diversity of plant life found nowhere else in the United States. Native western plants such as cactus, yucca and mesquite share this area with live-oaks, magnolia, tupelo and others typical of the southwestern lowlands. Unusual, too, is the combination of tropical and temperate vegetation flourishing in the region. The unusual size of its trees, many of which are the world's largest examples of their species, also contributes to the distinctiveness of the area. The Thicket is one of the major resting places along the Gulf Coast for migratory birds; in addition, at least 300 species, many endangered, live there permanently. Big Thicket National Preserve of 84,550 acres was signed into law on October 11, 1974 and is comprised of 8 units, partly connected by stream corridors, scheduled for acquisition by 1980. The Association maintains a museum in Saratoga which attempts to interpret the area and which serves as an information center for visitors and researchers. Sponsors environmental education programs, seminars, and nature pilgrimages. An active program has been planned to acquire areas not included in the Preserve by donation or purchase. Maintains nature trail in Lance Rosier Memorial Park. Committees: Big Thicket National Advisory; Land Acquisition; Museum. Publications: (1) *Big Thicket Bulletin*, bimonthly; (2) *Museum Publications Series*, irregular; also publishes informational pamphlets, a bibliography and other material. Convention/Meeting: annual—always first Saturday in June, Saratoga, Texas.

BOY SCOUTS OF AMERICA

North Brunswick, New Jersey 08902   Phone: (201) 249-6000
Alden G. Barber, Chief Scout Exec.
Founded: 1910
Members: 5,803,885
Staff: 4609

Cubs (ages 8-10) 2,178,315; Scouts (ages 11-17) 1,678,003; Explorers (ages 15-20) 471,336. Total boy membership is 4,-327,654; adult leaders and volunteer workers, both men and women, total 1,476,231. "An educational program for the character development, citizenship training, and mental and physical fitness of boys." Has 63,067 packs, 70,568 troops, and 27,959 Explorer units. Conducts studies on problems and needs of youth and operation of BSA councils and districts; maintains

Boy Scouts of America (Cont'd)

BSA museum and library of 8000 volumes related to social studies, youth work, and history; compiles statistics. Publications: (1) *Boys' Life* (for boys), monthly; (2) *Exploring Magazine* (for Explorers), 6/year; (3) *Scouting Magazine* (for adults), 6/year; (4) *Annual Report to Congress;* also publishes Handbooks for Scouts, Cubs, and Explorers, merit badge pamphlets, and more than 2000 other BSA program items. Convention/Meeting: annual.

BOY SCOUTS OF CANADA

P.O. Box 5151   Phone: (613) 225-2770
Station F
Ottawa, Ontario K2C 3G7 Canada
J. P. Ross, Chief Exec.

BRUCE TRAIL ASSOCIATION

33 Hardale Crescent   Phone: (416) 762-0811
Hamilton, Ontario, L8T IX7 Canada
Ian C. Reid, Pres.
Founded: 1963
Members: 7500
Local Groups: 11

To maintain and develop the 430 mile footpath along the unique geological feature which goes for 430 miles through southern Ontario—the Niagara Escarpment. And to encourage the preservation of the natural environment of this and other areas of Ontario. Publications: *The Bruce Trail Guidebook; Bruce Trail News*, 4/year. Convention/Meeting: annual, always September.

BUREAU OF OUTDOOR RECREATION

Interior South   Phone: (202) 343-5721
18th & 19th Constitution
Washington, D.C. 20240
John Crutcher, Dir.

A division of the United States Department of Interior. Purpose is the development and coordination of effective programs of outdoor recreation. Activities are guided by the cabinet-level Federal Recreation Advisory Council.

CANADIAN CAMPING ASSOCIATION

102 Eglinton Avenue, E.   Phone: (416) 488-7345
Suite 203
Toronto, Ontario M4P 1E1 Canada

CANADIAN FAMILY CAMPING FEDERATION, INC.

P.O. Box 397   Phone: no listing
Rexdale, Ontario M9W 5L4 Canada
G. J. Hunt, Chm.
Founded: 1966
Members: 2000 families
Staff: 5

A federation of local camping clubs formed to permit Canadians to have a voice in the operation and use of Canada's natural resources. Publications: *Canadian Camper*, bimonthly.

CANADIAN INSTITUTE OF FORESTRY

P.O. Box 5000   Phone: (514) 457-9131
MacDonald College
Ste.-Anne de Bellevue
Montreal, Quebec H0A 1C0 Canada
Arthur G. Racey, Sec.-Mgr.
Members: 2250
Staff: 2-5

Formerly: Canadian Society of Forest Engineers. Annual Meetings: Fall.

CANADIAN NATURE FEDERATION

46 Elgin Street   Phone: (613) 238-6154
Ottawa, Ontario K1P 5K6 Canada
T. Mosquin, Exec. Dir.
A national non-profit organization for education and research in the conservation of wildlife, plants, soil, and water. Formerly Canadian Audubon Society.

CANADIAN PARKS/RECREATIONAL ASSOCIATION

333 River Road   Phone: (613) 746-7740
Vanier City, Ontario K1L 8B9 Canada
Dennis Neider, Exec. Dir.
Members: 2300
Staff: 2-5
A service, research and educational organization to stimulate and advance parks, recreation and leisure activities. Publication: *Recreation Canada*, bimonthly. Convention/Meeting: Annual.

CANADIAN YOUTH HOSTELS ASSOCIATION

333 River Road   Phone: (416) 746-0060
Vanier City, Ontario K1L 8B9 Canada
Dennis W. Lewis, Exec. Dir.
Founded: 1937
Members: 30,000
Staff: 16
Publications: *C.Y.H.A. Handbook*.

CITIZENS COMMITTEE ON NATURAL RESOURCES

1000 Vermont Avenue, N.W.   Phone: (202) 638-3396
Washington, D.C. 20005
John M. Burdick, Exec. Dir.
Founded: 1954
Staff: 2
Individuals interested in lobbying in behalf of conservation program dealing with government departments.

DESERT PROTECTIVE COUNCIL

P.O. Box 33   Phone: no listing
Banning, California 92220
Arthur B. Johnson, Exec. Dir.
Founded: 1954
Members: 700
Persons interested in safeguarding desert areas that are of unique scenic, scientific, historical, spiritual, and recreational value. Seeks to educate children and adults to a better understanding of the desert. Works to bring about establishment of wildlife sanctuaries for protection of indigenous plants and animals. The Desert Protective Council Education Foundation, a subdivision of the Council formed in 1960, handles educational activities and distributes reprints of desert and wildlife conservaton articles. Committees: Anza-Borrego; Off-Highway Vehicle; Power; State Lands; Wildlife. Publications: *El Paisano* (by Foundation), quarterly; also produces a publication each year on a special topic. Convention/Meeting: annual—always October.

EASTERN NATIONAL PARK AND MONUMENT ASSOCIATION

311 Walnut Street   Phone: no listing
Philadelphia, Pennsylvania 19106
Charles S. Marshall, Exec. Sec.
Promotes the historical, scientific, educational, and interpretive activities of the National Park Service through grants-in-aid for research; publication of historical literature; acquisition of museum collections and historic objects; development of park libraries; and acquisition of lands needed to preserve and protect important historical features adjacent to historical parks and monuments in the eastern United States.

FEDERATION OF OUTDOOR RECREATIONISTS

P.O. Box 68   Phone: (309) 734-3413
Monmouth, Illinois 61462
Robert N. L. Forman, Exec. Dir.
Founded: 1972
Recreational vehicle users organizations, trade associations, regional recreational vehicle and outdoor groups. Purpose is to conduct legal research and to fund test cases involving laws which are discriminatory against recreational vehicles and users, either by intent or enforcement. Conducts research and educational programs. Publishes monographs. Formerly: (1975) International Federation of Recreational Vehicle Users. Convention/Meeting: annual.

FEDERATION OF WESTERN OUTDOOR CLUBS

4534 ½ University Way, N.E.   Phone: (206) 632-6157
Seattle, Washington 98105
Hazel Wolf, Pres.
Founded: 1932
Members: 1341
Outdoor clubs (41) in western United States with combined membership of 48,000; associate members 1300. Promotes conservation of forests, wildlife, and natural features. Publications: *Western Outdoor Quarterly*. Convention/Meeting: annual—always Labor Day weekend.

FLORIDA TRAIL ASSOCIATION

P.O. Box 13708   Phone: (904) 378-8823
Gainesville, Florida 32604
Margaret Scruggs, Exec. Sec.
Founded: 1966
Members: 6000
Conservationists, hikers, and others interested in preservation of Florida wilderness and scenic areas. Maintains and develops the Florida Trail, which eventually will wind some 200 miles through public land and 500 miles through private land between the Everglades and Panama City; the trail will be divided into 26 sections, each about 25 miles long. Thirteen sections have been completed or are under construction. The association supports legislation which will assist the group in acquiring state right-of-way and help in maintaining the route. Holds seminars, workshops and "beginner weekends" for members to discuss and try out equipment and to instruct in its use. Sponsors hikes and canoe trips. Publications: *Newsletter,* quarterly; also maps of portion of trail on public land. Convention/Meeting: semiannual—May and November.

FRIENDS OF NATURE

Brooksville, Maine 04617   Phone: no listing
Martin R. Haase, Exec. Sec.
Founded: 1953
Conservationists "dedicated to maintaining the balance of nature for the mutual benefit of man and his plant and animal friends." Carries on educational work and maintains several nature sanctuaries. Convention/Meeting: annual.

FRIENDS OF THE EARTH

529 Commercial Street   Phone: (415) 391-4270
San Francisco, California 94111
David Brower, Pres.
Founded: 1969
International conservation organization which works to generate among people a new responsibility to the environment in which we live; to make the many important environmental issues that receive scant attention the subject of public debate; to select specific projects that offend the environment and hit these hard with every legal means possible. Publications: *Not Man Apart*, monthly.

FRIENDS OF THE WILDERNESS

3515 E. Fourth Street
Duluth, Minnesota 55804
William H. Magie, Exec. Sec.
Founded: 1949
Members: 17,364

Phone: (218) 722-6770

Persons interested in preservation of the Boundary Water Canoe Area of Minnesota, the wilderness canoe country of the Superior National Forest. Maintains library of 400 volumes pertaining to the area. Convention/Meeting: annual.

FUND FOR ADVANCEMENT OF CAMPING

19 S. La Salle Street, Room 1314
Chicago, Illinois 60603
Eleanor Eells, Dir.
Founded: 1965

Phone: (312) 332-0827

Serves as the Development Division of the American Camping Association. Seeks to increase the scope and effectiveness of camping for children and youth in America. Has funded pilot and innovative projects and research; provides camping scholarships. Sponsors Camping Unlimited, which conducts intergroup projects and activities. Conducts conferences and institutes. Publications: *Newsletter,* quarterly. Convention/Meeting: annual—with American Camping Association.

GIRL GUIDES OF CANADA

50 Merton Street
Toronto, Ontario M4S 1A3 Canada
Mrs. W. P. Gurd, Chief Commissioner

Phone: (416) 487-5281

GIRL SCOUTS OF THE U.S.A.

830 Third Avenue
New York, New York 10022
Dr. Cecily C. Selby, Exec. Dir.
Founded: 1912
Members: 3,291,000
Staff: 3000
Regional Groups: 6
Local Groups: 362

Phone: (212) 751-6900

Brownie Girl Scouts (ages 6, 7 and 8); Junior Girl Scouts (9-11); Cadette Girl Scouts (12-14); Senior Girl Scouts (14-17); adult volunteers and professional workers (both men and women interested in service to girls). Membership includes 2,755,000 girls and 536,000 adults. Purpose is "to inspire each girl to develop her own values and sense of worth as an individual and to provide opportunities for girls to experience, to discover, to share planned activities that meet their interests. These activities encourage personal development through a wide variety of projects in social action, environmental action, youth leadership, career exploration, coed groups, and community service." Program activities in the arts, home, out-of-doors and community projects are founded on the Girl Scout Promise and Law, service, troop management, citizenship, international friendship, and health and safety. Educational activities include conferences, leader training design, international friendship exchange program, research project on assessment of council effectiveness. Publications: (1) *American Girl,* monthly; (2) *Daisy,* 9/year; (3) *Girl Scout Leader,* 7/year. Convention/Meeting: triennial.

GOOD OUTDOOR MANNERS ASSOCIATION

12730 9th N.W.
Seattle, Washington 98177
Mrs. Karl Mehrer, Pres.
Founded: 1959
Members: 150

Phone: (206) 362-3271

Outdoor lovers, conservationists, resource management employees, housewives, doctors, lawyers, young people, outdoor

Good Outdoor Manners Association (Cont'd)

and conservation clubs, business firms, and other individuals and groups; represents approximately 50,000 persons through its 150 memberships. To prevent vandalism and thoughtless abuse of outdoor recreational resources through a public education program, using slide lectures, informational literature, quarterly newsletter, displays and demonstrations, and publicity in all possible media. Uses as its trademark "Howdy" the Good Outdoor Manners Raccoon. Makes occasional field studies of visitor use-and-abuse problems on recreation areas and recommends remedies; cooperates with public and private management interests and other organizations to coordinate and develop its campaign on a national level; sponsors facility repair and cleanup projects. Conducts annual national contest to locate and laud year's "Best Booster" of good outdoor manners and publicize costs, hazards and loss of privileges resulting from acts of "Worst Bust-er." Committees: Audio-Visual Aids Development; Awards; Book Shop; Display; Literature Development; Literature Mailing; Photography; Printing; Publicity; Speakers Bureau. Publications: (1) *Howdy's Happenings,* quarterly; (2) *Membership Roster,* irregular; also publishes educational materials and distributes teachers' kits. Formerly: (1960) Mountaineers' Good Outdoor Manners Committee. Convention/Meeting: annual.

HUTMEN'S ASSOCIATION

18 Pratt Street
Melrose, Massachusetts 02176
Charles F. Belcher, III, Sec.-Treas.
Founded: 1925
Members: 550

Phone: (617) 662-8688

Persons who have worked for the Appalachian Mountain Club in its hut system in the White Mountains (New Hampshire). The nine units of the hut system are open to the public for shelter and meals. Maintains a cabin in the White Mountains for Association members and holds semiannual reunions. Publications: *The Hutmen's Resuscitator,* 3/year. Convention/Meeting: annual—always December.

INTERCOLLEGIATE OUTING CLUB ASSOCIATION

c/o Joy Mara Sobolov
5424 Arlington Avenue
Bronx, New York 10471
Lou Levy, Exec. Sec.
Founded: 1932
Members: 30,000
Regional Group: 5

Phone: (212) 549-6354

Members or graduates from college outing clubs. To encourage safe enjoyment of the wilderness, while at the same time emphasizing the importance of preserving the wilderness in an unspoiled manner. Sponsors caving, canoeing, rock climbing, winter backpacking and other trips with experienced leaders providing guidance in safety, technique, and conservation. Publications: (1) *News,* monthly; (2) *Bulletin,* 4/year; (3) *Directory,* annual. Convention/Meeting: annual.

INTERNATIONAL ASSOCIATION OF GAME, FISH AND CONSERVATION COMMISSIONERS

1412 16th Street, N.W.
Washington, D.C. 20036
John S. Gottschalk, Exec. V. Pres.
Founded: 1902
Members: 384

Phone: (202) 232-1652

State and provincial game, fish and conservation departments (68) and officials (316). To educate the public to the economic importance of conserving natural resources and managing wildlife properly as a source of recreation and a food supply; to seek better conservation legislation, administration and enforcement. Presents annual Seth Gordon Award for distinguished service in wildlife conservation. Committees: Grizzly Bear;

International Association of Game, Fish and Conservation Commissioners (Cont'd)

Hunter Safety; Land Resources; Migratory Wildlife; Nongame Species; Predator Animal Policy; Rare and Endangered Species; Water Resources. Publications: (1) *Newsletter*, bimonthly; (2) *Proceedings*, annual. Formerly: (1917) National Association of Game Commissioners and Wardens. Convention/Meeting: annual—always second Monday in September.

INTERNATIONAL FEDERATION OF CAMPING AND CARAVANNING

Hirschmattstrasse 13
CH-6003 Lucerne, Switzerland
H. Pircher, Exec. Sec.
Founded: 1932
Members: 1.8 million
Staff: 4

Seeks to promote camping and caravanning activities; encourage the foundation of camping or caravanning groups; issue regulations; organize meetings and exhibitions; and provide full documentary and informational service about suitable camping sites and about the laws of each country relating to camping and caravanning. Commissions: Camping; Caravan; Rally; Technical; Youth. Convention/Meeting: annual International Rallye and General Assembly.

INTERNATIONAL ORIENTEERING FEDERATION

Tegnergatan 36 C
S-75227 Uppsala, Sweden
Inga Lowdin, Sec.-Gen.
Founded: 1961
Members: 23

Federation of national orienteering associations. Promotes the sport of orienteering, in which runners attempt in the shortest possible time to pass special check-points on a map (scale 1:2500 or 1:2000 are most common), by using the map and a compass to find these points in the terrain. Provides technical advice on foot and ski orienteering; issues maps and instruction courses; organizes international championships; compiles rules for competitions. Committees: Map; Public Relations; Ski Orienteering; Technical. Publications: (1) *Report*, annual; (2) *Rules and Standards*, irregular. Affiliated with: General Assembly of Sports International Federations. Convention/Meeting: biennial congress.

INTERNATIONAL UNION FOR CONSERVATION OF NATURE AND NATURAL RESOURCES

1110 Morges, Switzerland
Dr. Gerardo Budowski, Dir. Gen.
Founded: 1948
Members: 414

International federation of national governments (38) and national and international organizations (376) in 95 countries. Seeks to maintain and enhance the diversity of the biosphere by promoting rational management of the earth's resources; to halt the destruction of our natural environment; to promote the conservation of wild places and wild animals and plants in their natural environments. Continuously reviews and assesses world environmental problems, and promotes research relating to their solution. Maintains close working relations with the United Nations system; cooperates with Council of Europe, Organization of African Unity, Organization of American States, and other intergovernmental bodies; collaborates with International Council for Bird Preservation, International Council of Scientific Unions, and other non-governmental groups. Presents John Phillips Memorial Medal triennally for distinguished service in international conservation. Maintains library of 2500 volumes on nature conservation and wildlife management; IUCN Environmental Law Centre in Bonn, Federal Re-

International Union for Conservation of Nature and Natural Resources (Cont'd)

public of Germany. Commissions: Ecology; Education; Environmental Planning; Environmental Policy, Law and Administration; National Parks; Survival Service. Publications: (1) *Bulletin*, monthly; (2) *Yearbook;* (3) *New Series Publications*, irregular; (4) *Supplementary Papers*, irregular; also publishes occasional papers, environmental policy and law papers, monographs, and others. Affiliated with: World Wildlife Fund. Formerly: (1956) International Union for the Protection of Nature. Convention/Meeting: triennial general assembly/technical meeting.

INTERNATIONAL UNION OF ALPINE ASSOCIATIONS

29-31, Rue Des Delices
CH-1211 Geneva 11, Switzerland
Jean Juge, Pres.
Founded: 1932
Members: 44

National Alpine clubs and mountaineering federations. Is concerned with all questions related to mountaineering from an international viewpoint; coordinates research; facilitates exchange of information and documents; conducts expeditions; offers sherpas instruction. Seeks to standardize map and ski and footpath signs and to set up an international alarm center for mountaineering accidents. Committees: Awards; Methods of "Assurage"; Protection of the Mountain; Refugees; Security Materials; Ski-Alpinism; Youth. Publications: *Bulletin*, 5/year. Convention/Meeting: annual.

IOCALUM

c/o Alan Brooks   Phone: (303) 491-5571
Natural Resource Ecology Laboratory
Colorado State University
Ft. Colins, Colorado 80523
Alan Brooks, Exec. Officer
Founded: 1933
Members: 165

Alumni of undergraduate collegiate outing clubs (name, IOCAlum, stands for Intercollegiate Outing Club Alumni). To keep a roster of addresses and information on all alumni, announce outings of interest to members, and keep members informed about conservation issues directly affecting them. Maintains library. Sponsors "Super Trip" outing to an outstanding wilderness area. Publications: (1) *IOCAlum News*, 6/year; (2) *Directory*, annual; (3) *Products List*, annual. Affiliated with: Intercollegiate Outing Club Association. Convention/Meeting: annual—always May.

IOWA MOUNTAINEERS

P.O. Box 163   Phone: (319) 337-7163
Iowa City, Iowa 52240
John Ebert, Exec. Officer
Founded: 1940
Members: 532
Staff: 8
Regional Groups: 4

Objectives are: sponsorship of major summer mountain camps, foreign expeditions, rock climbing courses, weekend climbing outings, camping outings and half-day hikes; presentation of a series of "Adventure Film-Lectures" for community service; conservation and preservation of scenic wilderness areas, forests and streams. Conducts courses in rock climbing, mountaineering and cross country skiing and winter survival. Sponsors expeditions. Maintains library. Bestows awards for service or achievement. Committees: Film-Lecture; Outdoor Activities. Publications: (1) *News Bulletin*, bimonthly; (2) *Iowa Climber*, semiannual; also publishes brochures. Convention/Meeting: annual—always last Saturday in April, Iowa City, Iowa.

IZAAK WALTON LEAGUE OF AMERICA

1800 N. Kent Street, Suite 806   Phone: (703) 528-1818
Arlington, Virginia 22209
Jack Covenz, Exec. Dir.
Founded: 1922
Members: 52,000
Staff: 16
State Groups: 22
Local Groups: 600

Works to educate the public to conserve, maintain, protect and restore the soil, forest, water and other natural resources of the U.S.; promotes the enjoyment and wholesome utilization of those resources. Committees: Energy Resources; Environmental Education; Fish and Wildlife; Public Lands; Urban Environment; Water Quality; Water and Wetlands. Publications: (1) *Outdoor America,* monthly; (2) *National Directory,* annual; also publishes *E.P.—The New Conservation.* Absorbed: (1962) Friends of the Land. Convention/Meeting: annual—always July.

LEAGUE OF CONSERVATION VOTERS

324 C Street, S.E.   Phone: (202) 547-7200
Washington, D.C. 20003
Miss Marion Edey, Chm.
Founded: 1969
State Groups: 4

Not a membership organization; serves as the political arm of Friends of the Earth. "A nonpartisan campaign committee that supports those legislators who are working hardest to protect the environment; who have outstanding records in the preservation, restoration and rational use of the ecosphere." Selects outstanding candidates facing close races and raises money and manpower for their campaigns. Conducts research into the environmental voting records of members of Congress and publicizes the voting records on key environmental issues. Publications: (1) *How Your Congressman Voted on Critical Environmental Issues,* biennial; (2) *How Your Senator Voted on Critical Environmental Issues,* biennial.

LEAGUE TO SAVE LAKE TAHOE

695 North Lake   Phone: (916) 541-5388
Tahoe City, California 95730
Staff: 1

Membership comprised of individuals and organizations who give financial support to the League. Purpose is to "do all things and to perform all acts necessary to keep Lake Tahoe blue and to protect and preserve the natural beauty and grandeur of the Lake Tahoe area of California and Nevada; to promote and encourage the concept that all developments, improvements and man-made changes of any kind, which may be required to accommodate the proper and desirable growth of the area and provide the maximum recreational values, should place primary emphasis on preserving the natural beauty of the lake." Publications: *Newsletter,* quarterly. Convention/Meeting: annual.

MONTANA OUTFITTERS AND DUDE RANCHERS ASSOCIATION

P.O. Box 382   Phone: (406) 587-8232
Bozeman, Montana 59715
Alice Fryslie, Exec. Sec.
Founded: 1947
Members: 2761
Staff: 1

Outfitters and guides who operate wilderness trips in Montana for hunting, fishing and sightseeing parties using saddle and pack animals; operators of dude ranches. Sets standards of service to be provided by members; encourages preservation of back

Montana Outfitters and Dude Ranchers Association (Cont'd)
country and wise use of fish and game. Publications: *Montana Recreation Directory,* annual. Formerly: (1968) Montana Outfitters and Guides Association. Convention/Meeting: annual—always December.

THE MOUNTAINEERS

719 Pike Street   Phone: (206) 623-2314
Seattle, Washington 98101
Howard Stansbury, Bus. Man.
Founded: 1906
Members: 8000
Staff: 5
Regional Groups: 4

Persons over 14 years of age who are interested in exploring and studying the mountains, forests and water courses of the Northwest, in preserving the history and traditions of the region, and in encouraging protective legislation and other conservation activities. Conducts hiking, skiing, camping and mountain climbing expeditions; offers courses in safe mountain climbing. Owns five ski lodges and huts, and a rhododendron preserve of 170 acres near Bremerton, Washington, open to the public. Maintains library of 3000 volumes on mountaineering and related topics. Divisions: Conservation; Indoor; Outdoor; Property; Publications. Committees: Botany; Campcrafters; Climbing; Conservation Education; National Forests; National Parks; Outings; Photography; Players; Preserve Planning; Rhododendron; Safety; Ski Tours; State-County-Local Areas; Trail Trips; Viewfinders; and others. Publications: *The Mountaineer* (roster), annual; also publishes books and distributes conservation education materials. Affiliated with: Federation of Western Outdoor Clubs. Convention/Meeting: annual—always September, Seattle, Washington.

MOUNTAIN RESCUE ASSOCIATION

P.O. Box 67   Phone: no listing
Seattle, Washington 98111
Lynn K. Buchanan, Pres.
Founded: 1959
Members: 2500

Federation of 46 rescue units throughout the U.S. and Canada, with a total membership of 2500. Each unit must have at least 25 members, 5 of whom have had experience in climbing mountains over 10,000 feet and in carrying out approved rescue techniques. Promotes mountain safety education and acts as a central agency to coordinate the efforts and activities of member rescue units. Units exchange ideas and attempt to standardize, where possible, the equipment and techniques used. Has received grants from the American Alpine Club to standardize mountain rescue accident and search reports and to study and develop a portable rescue winch. Publications: *Newsletter,* quarterly; also publishes a directory, as part of semiannual convention minutes. Convention/Meeting: semiannual.

NATIONAL ASSOCIATION FOR ENVIRONMENTAL EDUCATION

5940 S. W. 73rd Street   Phone: (305) 666-3267
Miami, Florida 33143
Dr. Arden Pratt, Pres.
Founded: 1971
Members: 300
Staff: 2

Individuals associated with colleges, community colleges, public schools, environmental organizations, librarians from foreign countries; associate members include students in environmental studies and high school teachers and administrators. Objectives

National Association for Environmental Education (Cont'd)

are: to promote environmental education programs of the post-secondary level; to coordinate environmental education activities among such programs and educational institutions; to disseminate information about environmental education activities appropriate for such programs and institutions; to assist educational institutions in beginning or developing programs of this kind and to serve as a resource to them; to foster sharing of information about environmental education programs among institutions and individual members; to promote communication about environmental education; to promote the pooling of information, resources and activities in connection with such programs; to foster research and evaluation in connection with environmental education and other study and investigation of such programs. Has conducted a seminar to develop a curriculum in environmental education for secondary schools. Presents annual award to outstanding environmentalist or environmental educator, and annual Merit Award to deserving industry or individual. Publications: *Newsletter,* monthly; also publishes monographs, *Man and Environment* curriculum guide for secondary schools, and Higher Education Programs. Convention/Meeting: annual.

NATIONAL ASSOCIATION OF CONSERVATION DISTRICTS

1025 Vermont Avenue, N.W.   Phone: (202) 347-5995
Washington, D.C. 20005
Gordon K. Zimmerman, Exec. V. Pres.
Founded: 1947
Members: 3000
Staff: 16
Regional Groups: 7

Soil conservation districts, organized by the citizens of watersheds, counties or communities under provisions of state laws. To direct and coordinate through local, self-government efforts the conservations and development of soil, water and related natural resources; districts include over 90 percent of the nation's privately-owned land. Presents awards; maintains library of approximately 1500 volumes. Committees: District Operations; Education; Forestry; Great Plains; Legislation; Natural Environment; Public Lands; Research; Resource Planning and Development; Shore Erosion; Soil Stewardships; Water Resources; Youth. Publications: (1) *Tuesday Letter,* weekly; (2) *Directory,* annual; (3) *Proceedings of Annual Convention;* also publishes guides. Formerly: National Association of Soil Conservation Districts; (1970) National Association of Soil and Water Conservation Districts. Convention/Meeting: annual—always February.

NATIONAL ASSOCIATION OF COUNTY PARK AND RECREATIONAL OFFICIALS

1735 New York Avenue, N.W.   Phone: (202) 785-9577
Washington, D.C. 20006
Jayne S. Seeley, NACPRO Liaison
Founded: 1964
Members: 250
Staff: 1

Members are elected or appointed county government officials with parks and/or recreation advisory, administrative or policy-making authority. Stimulates interest in county park and recreation resources and works to obtain more effective use of public and privately owned land and water areas. Publishes brochure. Committees: Awards; Federal, State and Local Issues; NACPRO Liaison. Affiliated with: National Association of Counties. Convention/Meeting: annual conference.

NATIONAL ASSOCIATION OF STATE OUTDOOR RECREATION LIAISON OFFICERS

6425 S. Pennsylvania, Suite 11   Phone: (517) 393-9470
Lansing, Michigan 48910
John Greenslit, Exec. Dir.
Founded: 1967
Members: 55

One representative from each state and territory, to provide Congress with a consensus of the several states on legislative needs and in working with the Bureau of Outdoor Recreation. Under the Land and Water Conservation Fund Act, the Bureau of Outdoor Recreation provides funds to states for planning, acquiring and developing public outdoor recreational facilities; the states, in turn, make a portion of the grants available to local government for their projects.

NATIONAL ASSOCIATION OF STATE PARK DIRECTORS

c/o Division of Parks   Phone: (603) 271-3254
NH Dept. Of Resources & Economic Development
P.O. Box 856
Concord, New Hampshire 03301
George T. Hamilton, Sec.-Treas.
Founded: 1962
Members: 50

Directors of every state park system in the United States. Purposes are: to provide a common forum for the exchange of information regarding state park programs; to take collective positions on those issues which affect state park programs; to encourage the development of professional leadership in the administration of state park and recreation programs. Convention/Meeting: annual.

NATIONAL ASSOCIATION OF TRAILER OWNERS

1323 Main, P.O. Box 1418   Phone: (815) 958-1895
Sarasota, Florida 33578
Ward H. Patton, Jr., Pres.
Founded: 1956

Owners of travel trailers, campers and motor homes. Publications: (1) *Directory of Overnight and Vacation Parks;* (2) *Mobile Living Magazine.*

NATIONAL AND PROVINCIAL PARKS ASSOCIATION OF CANADA

47 Colborne Street, Suite 308   Phone: (416) 366-3494
Toronto, Ontario M5E 1E5 Canada
Robin W. Fraser, Pres.
Members: 2500
Staff: 5
Local chapters: 3
Publications: *Park News,* quarterly; *Parks for Tomorrow,* bimonthly.

NATIONAL AUDUBON SOCIETY

950 Third Avenue   Phone: (212) 832-3200
New York, New York 10022
Elvis J. Stahr, Pres.
Founded: 1905
Members: 340,000
Staff: 150
Local Groups: 320
Affiliated Groups: 275

Persons interested in conservation and restoration of natural resources, with emphasis on wildlife, wildlife habitats, soil, water and forests. Sponsors four Audubon workshops for teachers and youth leaders; nature lectures; wildlife tours. Supports a force of 18 wardens to patrol wildlife refuge areas and sanctuaries; produces films, posters and teaching materials for schools. Divisions: Educational Services; Lecture; Nature Centers; Research; Sanctuary; Service. Publications: (1) *Audubon Leader,* semimonthly; (2) *American Birds,* bimonthly; (3) *Audubon*

National Audubon Society (Cont'd)

Magazine, bimonthly; (4) *Nature Bulletins*, irregular. Formerly: (1935) National Association of Audubon Societies for the Protection of Wild Birds and Animals, Inc. Convention/Meeting: biennial.

NATIONAL CAMPERS AND HIKERS ASSOCIATION

7172 Transit Road   Phone: (716) 634-5433
Buffalo, New York 14221
Fran Opela, Office Mgr.
Founded: 1954
Members: 52,000 families
Local Groups: 2700
Family campers and hikers; others interested in outdoor activities and conservation. Through regional, state and field directors, assists in establishing local chapters where members meet to exchange information on routes, campsites, equipment, etc. National goals include recommendations to improve camping and hiking facilities; establishment of regional information centers to give campers reports on local roads, trails, campsites, game laws, etc.; exchange of camping and hiking equipment. Assists in teaching college short courses and YMCA courses in camping and outdoor recreation. Maintains national scholarship for NCHA members' children. Committees: Conservation; Education; Safety. Publications: *Tent and Trail Bulletin,* quarterly; also publishes *NCHA News,* 12 times a year in Camping Guide Magazine. Convention/Meeting: annual—always July.

NATIONAL CAMPGROUND OWNERS ASSOCIATION

P.O. Box 366   Phone: (415) 383-2959
Mill Valley, California 94941
Founded: 1967
Mary Matheson, Exec. Dir.
Members: 500
Staff: 1
State Groups: 38
Regular members are commercial campground owners and operators; associate members are manufacturers and suppliers of campground products and services. Promotes and protects the interests of the commercial campground industry with government officials and agencies, campers, the press, and the general public. Represents the campground industry in contact with RV manufacturers, RV dealers and other branches of the camping business. Works to develop better, more efficient, more profitable campground management and business methods.

NATIONAL CAMPING ASSOCIATION

353 W. 56th Street   Phone: no listing
New York, New York 10019
Katherine Morus, Exec. Sec.
Founded: 1947
Cooperative organization of camp owners and directors. Publications: *Directory of Camps and Schools,* annual. Convention/Meeting: biennial.

NATIONAL PARKS AND CONSERVATION ASSOCIATION

1701 18th Street, N.W.   Phone: (202) 265-2717
Washington, D.C. 20009
Anthony Wayne Smith, Pres.
Founded: 1919
Members: 45,000
Staff: 29
Private educational and scientific organization interested in the welfare and protection of national parks and in related fields of conservation, such as wilderness and wildlife preservation, ecological forestry and river basin management. Maintains a library for public use. Publications: *National Parks and Conservation Magazine: The Environmental Journal,* monthly: also publishes summaries of investigations into conservation-oriented social issues; *Preserving Wilderness in Our National Parks;*

National Parks and Conservation Assoc. (Cont'd)

Toward an Environmental Policy; Ecological Forestry Studies. Formerly: (1970) National Parks Association. Convention/Meeting: semiannual.

NATIONAL RECREATION AND PARK ASSOCIATION

1601 N. Kent Street   Phone: (703) 525-0606
Arlington, Virginia 22209
John Davis, Exec. Dir.
Founded: 1965
Members: 17,000
Staff: 85
Local Groups: 60
A public interest organization dedicated to improving the human environment through improved park, recreation and leisure opportunities. Its activities include: programs for the development and upgrading of professional and citizen leadership in the park, recreation and leisure field; dissemination of innovations and research; technical assistance to affiliated organizations, local communities and members; providing information on public policy; public education; and an extensive publications program. It has regional service centers in Atlanta, Chicago, Colorado Springs, Colorado, Hartford, Connecticut, and Sacramento, California. Maintains a library of 7000 volumes. Publications: (1) *Parks and Recreation Magazine,* monthly; (2) *Journal of Leisure Research,* quarterly; (3) *Therapeutic Recreation Journal,* quarterly; (4) *Guide to Books on Parks,* annual; also publishes books, pamphlets, management aids and newsletters. Formed by merger of: American Association of Zoological Parks and Aquariums; American Institute of Park Executives (founded 1898); American Recreation Society (founded 1938); National Conference of State Parks (founded 1921); National Recreation Association (founded 1906). Convention/Meeting: annual.

NATIONAL TRAILS COUNCIL

53 W. Jackson Boulevard   Phone: (312) 427-4256
Chicago, Illinois 60604
William S. Nemec, Acting Chm.
Founded: 1972
Members: 800
Staff: 2
Individuals and local and state trail organizations. Objectives are to: support the planning, promotion and execution of trail systems at the local, county, state, regional and national levels; establish guidelines for all varieties of trails; effect land use planning. Provides resources to planning agencies; services to trail organizations; reports to Federal agencies; resources for the promotion of responsible local projects. Conducts regional and national symposia. Maintains library. Publications: *Newsletter,* 4-5/year. Convention/Meeting: biennial symposium.

NATURAL AREA COUNCIL

145 52nd Street   Phone: (212) 421-0732
New York, New York 10022
Richard H. Pough, Pres.
Founded: 1957
Staff: 5
Persons concerned with the preservation of natural areas. Governed by 14-member board of leading conservationists.

NATURE CONSERVANCY

1800 N. Kent Street, Suite 800   Phone: (703) 524-3151
Arlington, Virginia 22209
Patrick F. Noonan, Pres.
Founded: 1917
Members: 25,000
Non-profit membership organization dedicated to the preservation of natural areas for present and future generations. Co-

Nature Conservancy (Cont'd)

operates with colleges, universities, public and private conservation organizations to acquire lands for scientific and educational purposes. Publications: *News,* quarterly. Formerly: (1946) Committee on Preservation of Natural Conditions, Ecological Society of America; (1950) Ecologists Union. Convention/Meeting: annual.

NEW ENGLAND TRAIL CONFERENCE

P.O. Box 145   Phone: (802) 875-3631
Weston, Vermont 05161
Anne Mausolff, Sec.
Founded: 1917
Local Groups: 46
A coalition of organizations with an interest in hiking, trail clearing and maintenance, and conservation; includes groups from six New England states and adjacent parts of New York state. Conference serves primarily as an information clearinghouse on hiking trails in New England. Maintains small library of current guidebooks and maps. Publications: *New England Trails,* annual; also publishes *Hiking Trails of New England* (map and bibliography), revised quinquennially. Convention/Meeting: annual.

NORTH AMERICAN FAMILY CAMPERS ASSOCIATION

P.O. Box 552   Phone: (617) 462-6455
Newburyport, Massachusetts 01950
Samuel R. Thoreson, Exec. Dir.
Founded: 1957
Members: 14,400
Staff: 5
State and Local Groups: 153
Families (13,155) interested in camping and the Association's programs; sustaining members (254) are manufacturers and dealers in camping equipment, campgrounds, and other services related to family campers. Mutual service organization that works to improve camping conditions; inform members about camping areas, equipment and techniques; promote good camping manners; and foster fellowship among family campers. Encourages and guides development of campgrounds; cooperates with conservation and legislative agencies for the good of camping. Sponsors major camping shows, clinics and workshops for the public; holds leadership conferences and seminars; sponsors annual Eastern Conference on Camping Areas for campground operators. Conducts good manners, conservation and anti-litter programs. Committees: Conservation; Leadership Training. Publications: (1) *News,* 25/year; (2) *Campfire Chatter,* bimonthly; (3) *NAFCAGram,* irregular; also publishes fact sheets and monographs on family camping. Formerly: (1959) New England Camping Association; (1967) New England Family Campers Association. Affiliated with: National Wildlife Federation. Convention/Meeting: regional camping convention held each May. State conventions held in September.

NORTHWEST GUIDES ASSOCIATION

6043 Thomas Avenue, S.   Phone: (612) 927-7564
Minneapolis, Minnesota 55410
C. B. Hanscom, Exec. Dir.
Members: 40
Sportsmen interested in the conservation and restoration of natural resources and wildlife. Engages in historical exploration, guiding in Wisconsin, Minnesota, and upper Michigan, big game hunting, and waterfowl and upland bird shooting. Sponsors women's auxiliary. Publications: *Newsletter;* also publishes bulletins. Convention/Meeting: annual—always March, Minneapolis, Minnesota.

OPEN ROAD "SEE AMERICA" CLUB

2601 Manhattan Beach Boulevard   Phone: (213) 772-2431
Manhattan Beach, California 90278
Carol Taylor, Exec. Dir.
Founded: 1966
Members: 14,200
Staff: 5
Local Groups: 75
Owners of Open Road recreational vehicles. Promotes and encourages social contact, recreation, travel pleasure and education of and between owners of these units (vechicles used for driving and camping). Supports legislation favorable to the recreation industry. Sponsors caravans and annual encampments. Publications: (1) *Along the Open Road,* monthly; (2) *Membership Directory,* annual. Formerly: (1973) Open Road Camper Clubs of America.

OUTDOOR EDUCATION ASSOCIATION

c/o Outdoor Laboratories   Phone: (618) 453-2121
Southern Illinois University Campus
Carbondale, Illinois 62901
Dr. Edward J. Ambry, Exec. Dir.
Founded: 1940
Members: 500
State Groups: 2
Independent Groups: 9
Persons interested in promotion of outdoor education, including school camping, and in extending the benefits to schools, colleges, and public and private agencies. Advocates living and learning in the out-of-doors as an integral part of school and organization programs; prepares advanced leaders at its national camp and conducts institutes and workshops for teachers, administrators, and leaders of church and youth serving agencies. Provides field services and consultant service in establishing outdoor education centers. Develops master plans for land use by schools, churches and private and agency camps. Maintains library on camping and outdoor education. Publications: (1) *Extending Education,* semiannual; (2) *Newsletter,* semiannual; also publishes a manual of trailer travel camping, and reports, booklets, reprints, plans, etc. dealing with various aspects of camping; disseminates films. Convention/Meeting: annual—always Carbondale, Illinois.

OUTDOOR ETHICS GUILD

P.O. Box 291   Phone: (703) 528-1082
Arlington, Virginia 22210
Bruce Bandurski, Pres.
Founded: 1967
Not a membership organization. Scientific/educational organization which exists for the purpose of promoting ethical behavior at the man/environ interface. It offers encouragement to individuals and organizations dealing squarely with pressing conservation issues by conveying praise. In response to invitations, presents treatises on ecomanagement in the U.S. and abroad. Has developed and sponsors two courses at the U.S. Department of Agriculture Graduate School. Has published a series of behavioral guidelines for scientists, hunters and fishermen, and tourists. Maintains limited clearinghouse service. Councils: Education. Convention/Meeting: annual.

OUTDOOR RECREATION INSTITUTE

5003 Wapakoneta   Phone: no listing
Washington, D.C. 20016
Dr. Radcliffe F. Robinson, Pres.
To advance outdoor recreational interests at all levels—family, local, state and national; to emphasize recreational objectives of natural resource conservation, through technical research and educational activities. Provides information service on recreational equipment; answers technical inquiries; gives talks to

Outdoor Recreation Institute (Cont'd)

groups on recreation, nutrition, foods, camping, etc.; conducts research in biology, pollution, recreational equipment and other topics. Divisions: Counsulting; Educational; Research. Publications: *Newsletter,* quarterly.

OUTDOOR WRITERS ASSOCIATION OF AMERICA

4141 West Bradley Road   Phone: (414) 354-9690
Milwaukee, Wisconsin 53209
Edwin W. Hanson, Exec. Dir.
Founded: 1927
Members: 1400
Staff: 3

Professional organization of newspaper, magazine, radio, television and motion picture writers and photographers (both staff and free-lance) and outdoor recreation and conservation. Presents annual awards; conducts surveys for educational and industrial organizations; compiles market data for writer members and offers liaison aid in writer assignments. Committees: Awards; Educational and Scholarship; Ethics; Youth Program. Publications: (1) *Outdoors Unlimited,* monthly; (2) *National Directory of Outdoor Writers,* annual; also publishes *Standard Check List of Common Names for Principal American Sport Fishes* and a youth education manual. Convention/Meeting: annual.

POTOMAC APPALACHIAN TRAIL CLUB

1718 N Street, N.W.   Phone: (202) 638-5306
Washington, D.C. 20036
Dr. Robert O. Wolf, Pres.
Founded: 1927
Members: 2500

Maintains 226 miles of Appalachian Trail in Pennsylvania, Maryland, West Virginia and Virginia, and about 232 miles of other foot trails. Is currently engaged in building the Virginia-West Virginia section of the 400-mile Big Blue-Tuscarora Trail (from Shenandoah National Park to the Susquehanna River north of Harrisburg, Pennsylvania). Builds and maintains locked cabins and open shelters for the use of the hiking public. Tests camping, backpacking and mountaineering equipment and advises on its suitability. Maintains a library which emphasizes wilderness camping, mountaineering, foot trails, backpacking, and natural and regional history of mid-Atlantic mountain area. Sections: Cross-Country Skiing; Mountaineering. Publications: *Potomac Appalachian,* 13/year; also publishes maps, guidebooks and pamphlets. Affiliated with: Appalachian Trail Conference. Convention/Meeting: annual—always January, Washington, D.C.

PRAIRIE CLUB

6 E. Monroe Street, Room 1507   Phone: (312) 236-3342
Chicago, Illinois 60603
Richard Spurgin, Pres.
Founded: 1908
Members: 900

Individuals united for: the promotion of outdoor recreation in the form of walks, outings, camping and canoeing; the establishment and maintenance of permanent and temporary camps; the encouragement of the love of nature; the dissemination of knowledge of the attractions of the country; the preservation of suitable areas in which outdoor recreation may be pursued. Maintains library. Committees: Annual Dinner; Camera; Canoe; Conservation; Deer Grove; Family Cottage; Farmhouse; Historical; Open Meeting; Publications; Saturday Walks Sunday Walks; Thanksgiving Dinner; Touring; Weekend Trips; Wilderness Outing. Publications: (1) *Bulletin,* 10/year; (2) *Directory,* biennial. Convention/Meeting: annual.

RACHEL CARSON TRUST FOR THE LIVING ENVIRONMENT

8940 Jones Mill Road   Phone: (301) 652-1877
Washington, D.C. 20015
Shirley A. Briggs, Exec. Dir.
Founded: 1965
Staff: 4

Not a membership organization. Governed by a Board of Directors and guided by a Board of Consulting Experts and a Board of Sponsors. To further the philosophy of Rachel Carson (scientist and author, 1907-1964) by developing through research and education an awareness of the problems of environmental contamination and to serve as a clearinghouse for ecological information. Is currently assembling a library of environmental science material, focusing on ways to deal with environmental contamination. Present emphasis is on chemical contamination.

RANGER RICK'S NATURE CLUB

1412 16th Street, N.W.   Phone: (202) 546-6234
Washington, D.C. 20036
Trudy D. Farrand, Editorial Dir.
Founded: 1967
Members: 550,000

Children's division of the National Wildlife Federation. Purpose is to teach young children to know and respect all things that grow and creatures that move so that all may act to conserve and wisely use the vital natural resources of the world. Publications: (1) *Ranger Rick for Class and Club,* 10/year; (2) *Ranger Rick's Nature Magazine,* 10/year; also publishes *Ranger Rick's Best Friends* (12 books each devoted to a different animal species).

RECREATION VEHICLE INDUSTRY ASSOCIATION

P.O. Box 204   Phone: (703) 968-7200
Chantilly, Virginia 22021
Douglas Tomas, Pres.
Founded: 1963
Members: 450
Staff: 20

Manufacturers (149) of travel trailers, camping (tent) trailers, truck mount campers and motor homes; suppliers (241) of accessories and equipment; associate members (20). "To promote the general welfare of the recreational vehicle industry, to unite all segments for effective influence on matters of public interest involving its betterment, and encourage the highest professional and ethical standards in business practices and general conduct." Conducts studies and research on monthly production, vehicle construction standards, recreational vehicle park development, and regulations governing use of recreational vehicles. Sponsors award program for best newspaper or magazine story, television or radio program, film, etc., in the field of recreation and use of recreational vehicles. Gives annual Man-of-the-Year Award to outstanding member of the industry, a National Service Award to an individual, corporation or organization outside of the recreational vehicle industry who has contributed in an outstanding way, and a National Legislative Award to an individual who has distinguished himself in legislative matters pertaining to the recreatonal vehicle industry. Sponsors annual scholarship program, offering educational courses in association management to qualified state and regional directors and their assistants. Publications: (1) *Reporter* (membership newsletter), monthly; (2) *Membership Directory,* 3/year; (3) *Buyer's Guide to Suppliers,* annual. Absorbed: (1968) Camping Trailer Manufacturers Association. Formerly: American Institute of Travel Trailer and Camper Manufacturers; (1975) Recreational Vehicle Institute. Convention/Meeting: annual Trade Exposition.

RECREATIONAL VEHICLE DEALERS OF AMERICA

711 Orchard Street   Phone: (312) 945-7770
Deerfield, Illinois 60015
Hilton C. Peaster, Exec. Dir.
Founded: 1968
Members: 1600
Staff: 6

Firms which have as their principal business the retail sale of recreational vehicles (commonly known as travel trailers, camping trailers, truck campers and motor homes) and who maintain a permanent business establishment open for business and service on what they sell for 12 months of the year. Objectives are: (1) information and liaison on government regulation of safety, trade, warranty and franchising; (2) improved dealer-manufacturer relations; (3) communications between dealers and between other state and local RV (recreational vehicle) associations; (4) education and training; (5) product, market and consumer research; (6) advertising, sales and service information; (7) professional RV dealership management information; (8) public relations and publicity between the RV dealers and the rest of the industry, the public and the government; (9) national retail RV statistics; (10) improved standards of service to the consumer; (11) local retail RV shows where needed for the benefit of local RV dealers; (12) improved availability and quality of campgrounds; (13) RV dealer seminars and regional service clinics. Has established RESCUE Plan (Refering Emergency Service for Consumers' Ultimate Enjoyment), a nationwide system for customers of member dealers which tells the customer where to get specialized service on his RV away from home. Committees: Consumer Service; Dealer-Manufacturer Relations; Education; Legislative; Liaison; Retail Show; Sales-Franchise. Publications: (1) *News,* monthly; (2) *Chapter Bulletins,* monthly; (3) *Membership Directory,* annual; (4) *Stolen RV Bulletin,* as needed. Absorbed: (1969) Recreational Dealer Association. Formerly: (1970) Recreational Vehicle Dealers Institute. Convention/Meeting: annual.

ROCKY MOUNTAIN RAMBLERS ASSOCIATION

1001 7 Avenue, S.W.   Phone: (403) 282-1330
Calgary, Alberta T2P 1A8 Canada
Patricia Donald, Sec.

SAVE OUR SHORES

P.O. Box 103   Phone: (617) 328-5510
North Quincy, Massachusetts 02171
Mrs. Nelson R. Saphir, Pres.
Founded: 1969
Members: 250,000

Sportsmen, women's clubs, cities and towns, professional people, commercial fishermen, businesses, school children. Seeks to promote the conservation, preservation and restoration of the waterways, foreshores and islands in Boston Harbor. Wishes to have the harbor a national recreation area and historic site. Conducts lectures. Has produced a file. Sponsors annual Harbor Clean-up. Publications: *News and Views of Boston Harbor* (newsletter). Formerly: (1972) Dorchester Bay-Boston Harbor and Islands Project. Convention/Meeting: semiannual.

SAVE-THE-REDWOODS LEAGUE

114 Sansome Street, Room 605   Phone: (415) 362-2352
San Francisco, California 94104
John B. Dewitt, Exec. Dir.
Founded: 1918
Members: 55,000
Staff: 10

Persons interested in preserving representative stands of Coast and Sierra Redwoods, as well as other trees, principally in California. Provides information on the Redwoods and the program

Save-the-Redwoods League (Cont'd)
to preserve them. Committees: Council Highway. Publications: (1) *Bulletin,* semiannual; (2) *Brochure,* annual; also publishes four educational pamphlets.

SAVE THE TALLGRASS PRAIRIE

4101 W. 54th Terrace   Phone: (913) 384-3197
Shawnee Mission, Kansas 66205
Charles D. Stough, Pres.
Founded: 1973
Members: 450

Seeks to unite all interests concerned with the movement to preserve and save portions of tallgrass prairies for scenic, recreational and wildlife preservation purposes. Promotes legislation for the creation of a Tallgrass Prairies National Park. Conducts educational programs and activities. Publications: *Newsletter,* quarterly. Convention/Meeting: annual.

SCENIC HUDSON PRESERVATION CONFERENCE

545 Madison Avenue, 13th Floor   Phone: (212) 755-3082
New York, New York 10022
Judith Melton, Exec. Sec.
Founded: 1963
Members: 21,000

Garden, civic, environmental, conservation and sportsmen groups (60); various towns, villages and municipalities; and individuals who espouse "a general concern for the natural resources of the Hudson River with particular emphasis on the preservation of the Hudson River Gorge and its attendant Highlands as an irreplaceable natural area of wilderness quality." Maintains speakers bureau. Publications: (1) *Newsletter,* quarterly; (2) *Bulletins,* irregular.

SEATTLE MOUNTAINEERS

P.O. Box 122   Phone: (206) 623-2314
Seattle, Washington 98111
James F. Henriot, Pres.
Founded: 1906
Members: 7000
Staff: 5

Persons interested in exploring and studying the mountains, forests and water courses of the Northwest; in preserving the history and tradition of the region; in encouraging protective legislation and other conservation activities. Conducts hiking expeditions; offers courses in safe mountaineering climbs. Maintains 3000 volume library on mountaineering, conservation, natural history and winter sports. Committees: Climbing; Conservation; Education; National Parks. Publications: (1) *The Mountaineer,* monthly (including special annual issue); (2) *The Mountaineer Roster,* annual; also publishes numerous books on mountaineering, trips and trails. Convention/Meeting: annual.

SIERRA CLUB

530 Bush Street   Phone: (415) 981-8634
San Francisco, California 94108
Michael McCloskey, Exec. Dir.
Founded: 1892
Members: 165,000
Staff: 125
Regional Groups: 200
Local Chapters: 50

All who feel the need to know more of nature, and know that this need is basic to man. "To protect and conserve the natural resources of the Sierra Nevada, the United States and the World; to undertake and publish scientific and educational studies concerning all aspects of man's environment and the natural ecosystems of the world; and to educate the people of the United States and the world to the need to preserve and restore the quality of that environment and the integrity of

Sierra Club (Cont'd)

those ecosystems." Works on urgent campaigns to save threatened areas, wildlife and resource; conducts annual environmental workshops for educators; schedules wilderness outings; presents awards; maintains library. Chapters and committees schedule talks, films, exhibits and conferences. Committees: Economics; Energy; Environmental Education; International Environment; Mountaineering; National Land Use; National Water Resources; Native American Issues; Outings; Population; Wilderness; Wildlife and Endangered Species. Departments: Conservation; Outings. Publications: (1) *National News Report,* weekly; (2) *Sierra Club Bulletin,* 10/year; (3) *Ascent, Sierra Club Mountaineering Journal,* annual; also publishes books and produces films, posters and exhibits. Affiliated with: United Nations (member with nongovernment organization status). Convention/Meeting: biennial Wilderness Conference; also holds quarterly board meetings.

SKYLINE TRAIL HIKERS OF THE CANADIAN ROCKIES

P.O. Box 5905 Station A   Phone: (403) 252-2804
Calgary, Alberta T2H 1Y4 Canada
K. Jamieson, Sec.
Founded: 1933
Members: 400

Independent, non-commercial group of mountain enthusiasts who promote hiking and sponsor four five-day hikes each summer in one of the national parks in the Canadian Rockies. Members are persons who have taken part in a hike sponsored by the Trail Hikers. Encourages construction of new hiking trails and maintenance and improvement of those already existing; preservation of National Parks, and interest in wild life. Publications: *Skyliner* (newsletter), 2-3/year. Affiliated with: Trail Riders of the Canadian Rockies. Convention/Meeting: biennial.

STUDENT CONSERVATION ASSOCIATION

Olympic View Drive   Phone: (206) 567-4798
Route 1, P.O. Box 573-A
Vashon, Washington 98070
Jack Dolstad, Exec. Dir.
Founded: 1964
Members: 1000
Staff: 5

Individuals, garden clubs, foundations and groups who support the Student Conservation Program. The program, conducted in cooperation with the National Park Service and U.S. Forest Service, enlists the voluntary services of high school, college and graduate students to aid in preserving the natural beauty of the national parks and forests while serving visitors. High School Wilderness Group participants build shelters, maintain trails and rehabilitate over-used areas. Older students assist the rangers and naturalists in various interpretive and management activities, such as giving nature talks, cataloging materials and trail patrol. Publications: (1) *SCP Newsletter,* semiannual; (2) *Evaluation Report,* annual. Convention/Meeting: annual—always May.

TRAIL RIDERS OF THE CANADIAN ROCKIES

P.O. Box 6742   Phone: (403) 243-5271
Postal Station D
Calgary, Alberta T2P 2E6 Canada
Founded: 1923

Recreational society providing access by horseback to remote areas of the Canadian Rockies; members are persons who have completed one ride under the auspices of the Trail Riders. Promotes construction of new trails in the Rockies, and maintenance and improvement of those already in use; encourages interest in wildlife. Publications: *Bulletin,* annual; also pub-

Trail Riders of the Canadian Rockies (Cont'd)

lishes brochures. Affiliated with: Skyline Trail Hikers of the Canadian Rockies. Convention/Meeting: annual.

TRAIL RIDERS OF THE WILDERNESS

American Forestry Association
1319 18th Street, N.W.   Phone: (202) 467-5810
Washington, D.C. 20036
Mary Ellen Walsh, Dir.
Founded: 1933
Staff: 1

Program of the American Forestry Association "to provide a simple and inexpensive means by which the American public can enjoy the wilderness areas of our country, and to provide knowledge about our forest resources and the need to conserve them." Spring, summer and early fall expeditions are conducted in the wilderness areas of 12 states and sometimes Alaska and Canada. Majority of rides are on horseback, but several are by canoe or hiking. Thousands of persons have taken part in the trail-riding vacations, which are open to anyone interested in exploration. Membership in American Forestry Association is required. Professional outfitters provide horses or canoes and all necessary equipment and crew. The U.S. Forest Service and National Park Service cooperate in organizing and conducting these trips and there are talks on forest policies and resource management at each national forest or park explored by Trail Riders. Publications: *Trail Riders of the Wilderness,* annual. Convention/Meeting: annual. Trail Riders in the New York City, Chicago, Illinois and Washington, D.C. areas have frequent reunions to discuss future trips and to exchange stories and pictures of past Trail Rides.

TRUSTEES FOR CONSERVATION

c/o Hilary Crawford, Jr.   Phone: (415) 362-2691
Mills Tower
220 Bush Street
San Francisco, California
Hilary Crawford, Jr., Pres.
Founded: 1954
Members: 75

To secure the support of the people and the government in the preservation of national parks and monuments, wildlife and wilderness areas through legislative activities. Convention/Meeting: annual—always December, San Francisco, California.

UPPER MISSISSIPPI RIVER CONSERVATION COMMITTEE

County Office Building   Phone: (301) 788-3991
1504 Third Avenue
Rock Island, Illinois 61201
C. W. Threinen, Chm.
Founded: 1943
Members: 70
State Groups: 9
Regional Groups: 8

Natural resources managers and biologists. Objectives are: to promote the preservation and wise utilization of the natural and recreational resources of the Upper Mississippi River; to formulate policies, plans and programs for conducting cooperative studies. Cooperative projects include creel census, commercial fishing statistics, waterfowl and wildlife censuses, hunter surveys, fish tagging, litter control, collection of boating and other recreational use data. Helps to define land management for public properties such as state parks, public hunting grounds, wildlife refuges, flood plain reserves and recreational lands. Functions as an advisory body on all technical aspects of fish, wildlife and recreation. Makes recommendations on conservation laws, programs and legislation to state and Federal governments. Maintains a continuing evaluation of the effects

Upper Mississippi River Conservation Committee (Cont'd)
of water control regulation and recreational resources. Technical Work Groups; Fish; Game; Law Enforcement; Pollution Publication; Recreation and Water Use. Gives annual Conservation Award for special achievement in preserving or protecting the Upper Mississippi River. Publications: (1) *News Letter,* quarterly; (2) *Proceedings,* annual; (3) *Membership Directory,* annual; also issues reports of special projects. Convention/Meeting: annual.

U.S. ORIENTEERING FEDERATION
P.O. Box 1081   Phone: (614) 594-6950
Athens, Ohio 45701
Dick Adams, Pres.
Founded: 1971
Members: 1000
Local Groups: 34
Individuals interested in the sport of orienteering (finding one's way in the out-of-doors using map and compass). Purposes are: to promote orienteering activities throughout the U.S.; to assist in establishing orienteering clubs; to establish and standardize the rules governing orienteering competition; to hold annual national championships; to provide incentives for performance and commendable achievement in orienteering; to approve all international orienteering events held in the U.S.; to select competitors to represent the U.S. in World Championships and other international competitions. Awards 6 U.S. Championship titles annually. Publications: (1) *Control Point* (newsletter), monthly; (2) *Orienteering—U.S.A.* (journal), quarterly. Convention/Meeting: annual.

WILDERNESS SOCIETY
1901 Pennsylvania Avenue, N.W.   (202) 293-2732
Washington, D.C. 20006
George Davis, Exec. Dir.
Founded: 1935
Members: 90,000
Staff: 35
Persons interested in preserving wilderness through educational programs, scientific studies and cooperation with local and state citizen organizations in resisting the destruction of wildland resources and wildlife. Conducts leadership training programs for citizen conservationists. Sponsors book award program for young people and a "A Way to the Wilderness" trip program. Publications: *Living Wilderness,* quarterly; also publishes *Wilderness Reports,* notices, and conservation alerts on critical conservation issues. Convention/Meeting: annual.

WILDERNESS WATCH
P.O. Box 3184   Phone: (414) 499-9131
Green Bay, Wisconsin 54303
Jerry Gandt, Pres.
Founded: 1969
State Groups: 5
Scientists, attorneys, artists, writers, other interested individuals. Advocates "sustained use of America's sylvan lands and waters." Focuses on land use policies at the Federal level and seeks to halt environmental depredation whenever and wherever it occurs. Conducts research and educational programs. Publications: *Watch It,* irregular; also publishes position papers. Convention/Meeting: annual.

Guide to Manufacturers and Suppliers

A & E Mobilaire
200 W. 146th Street
Gardena, California 90248

A & T Corp.
2260 Avenue A
Bethlehem, Pennsylvania 18001

Academy Broadway Corp.
5 Plant Avenue
Smithtown, New York 11787

Achilles K C I Corp.
4 Empire Boulevard
Moonachie, New Jersey 07074

Acme Products Co., Inc.
4347 Clary Boulevard
Kansas City, Missouri 64130

Adventure 16
10064 Bert Acosta
Santee, California 92701

Air Lift
2217 Roosevelt Avenue
Berkeley, California 94703

Airguide Instrument Co.
2210 Wabansia Avenue
Chicago, Illinois 60647

Aladdin Industries, Inc.
703 Murfreesboro Road
Nashville, Tennessee 37210

Aladdin Laboratories, Inc.
620 So. 8th Street
Minneapolis, Minnesota 55404

Alaska Sleeping Bag
13150 S.W. Dawson Way
Beaverton, Oregon 97005

Algoma Net Co.
310 Fourth Street
Algoma, Wisconsin 54201

Algonquin Distributors
8499 W. Riverside Drive
Niagara, New York 14304

All Aluminum Products, Inc.
Tulip & Westmoreland Streets
Philadelphia, Pennsylvania 19134

All American Emblem
P.O. Box 600
West New York, New Jersey 07093

All American Sports Co.
1507 Grande Vista Avenue
Los Angeles, California 90023

Allen Camper Mfg. Co., Inc.
RR #1, Box 16
Allen, Oklahoma 74825

Allen Sportswear, Bob
P.O. Box 477
Des Moines, Iowa 50302

Allied Griffin
2740 Auburn Boulevard
Sacramento, California 95821

Alp Sport
3235 Prairie Avenue
Boulder, Colorado 80302

Alpenlite
P.O. Box 851
Claremont, California 91711

Alpha Products
8999 W. Pleasant Valley Road
Cleveland, Ohio 44130

Alpine Aid
3839 Brockton Avenue
Riverside, California 92501

Alpine Crafts Co.
P.O. Box 2467
So. San Francisco, California 94080

Alpine Designs
6185 E. Arapahoe
Boulder, Colorado 80303

Alpine Hut
4725 30th Avenue North East
Seattle, Washington 98105

Alpine Mfg. Co., Inc.
10475 S.E. Division
Portland, Oregon 97266

Alpine Recreation
P.O. Box 54
Mount Vernon, New York 10552

Alvimar Mfg. Co.
1881 Park Avenue
Long Island City, New York 11101

Amalgamated Cordage Corp.
240 58th Street
Brooklyn, New York 11220

Ambassador Shoe Corp.
1 Sutton Road
Webster, Massachusetts 01570

Amerex Laboratories, Inc.
307 E. Nakoma
San Antonio, Texas 78216

American Cord & Webbing Co., Inc.
505 8th Avenue
New York, New York 10018

American Fiber-Lite
P.O. Box 67
Marion, Illinois 62959

American Footwear Corp.
1 Oak Hill
Fitchburg, Massachusetts 01420

American Formed Plastics Corp.
702 W. Beardsley Avenue
Elkhart, Indiana 46514

American Import Co. & TAICO Trading Corp.
1167 Mission Street
San Francisco, California 94103

American Safety Equipment Corp.
16055 Ventura Boulevard
Encino, California 91436

American Thermo-Ware Co.
16 Warren Street
New York, New York 10007

American Youth Marketing Corp.
60 Novner Drive
Cincinnatti, Ohio 45215

Ames
P.O. Box 1774
Parkersburg, West Virginia 26101

Ametek, Inc.
502 Indiana Avenue
Sheboygan, Wisconsin 53081

AMF Skamper
P.O. Box 338
Bristol, Indiana 46507

Andrews Products
Rt. 1, Box 4
Middlebury, Indiana 46540

Antelope Camping Equipment
21740 Granada Avenue
Cupertino, California 95014

Antietam Quilting Co.
Main Street
Fleetwood, Pennsylvania 19522

Antler
10 W. 33rd Street
New York, New York 10001

Anzen Products, Inc.
15314 E. Proctor Avenue
Industry, California 91745

Appleby Mfg. Co.
P.O. Box 591
Lebanon, Missouri 65536

Aquatic Plastic Co., Inc.
Industrial Park, Rt. 9
Brookfield, Massachusetts 01585

Arco
(see Enterprise Distribution, Inc.)

Arkansas Abrasives, Inc.
Sleepy Valley Road
Hot Springs, Arkansas 71901

Armac Enterprises, Inc.
1107 Broadway, Suite 1204-06
New York, New York 10010

Aroma Taste, Inc.
435 Toyama Street
Sunnyville, California 94086

Arrow Co., The
P.O. Box 186
Leesburg, Indiana 46508

Ashflash Corp.
151 Woodward Avenue
South Norwalk, Connecticut 06856

Aspen Alpine Equipment Ltd.
P.O. Box 4996
Aspen, Colorado 81611

Aspen Coach Corp.
2510 N. 47th Street
Boulder, Colorado 80301

Associated Campground Systems
3733 W. Warner Avenue
Santa Ana, California 92711

Astrup Co.
2937 W. 25th Streeet
Cleveland, Ohio 44113

Athalon Products
3333 E. 52nd Street
Denver, Colorado 80216

Atlantic-Pacific Mfg. Corp.
124 Atlantic Avenue
Brooklyn, New York 11201

Avco Corp.
10700 E. Independence
Tulsa, Oklahoma 74115

Ayr-Way Industries
RR #1
Wawaka, Indiana 46794

B & B Homes Corp.
Casper Air Terminal
1004 Bell Avenue
Casper, Wyoming 82601

Backpacker, Inc.
28 W. 44th Street
New York, New York 10036

Bamboo & Rattan Works, Inc.
901 Jefferson Street
Hoboken, New Jersey 07030

Bantam Travelware Corp.
Empire State Building, Suite 1210
New York, New York 10001

Barrows Enterprises, Inc.
1924 Washington Boulevard
Camanche, Iowa 52330

Basketville
Putney, Vermont 05346

Bata Shoe Co., Inc.
Belcamp, Maryland 21017

Bauer, Inc., Eddie
1737 Airport Way S.
Seattle, Washington 98134

Bausch & Lomb
1400 N. Goodman Street
Rochester, New York 14602

Bayfront Industries, Inc.
4225 Ponce De Leon Boulevard
Coral Gables, Florida 33146

Bead Chain Tackle Co.
110 Mountain Grove Street
Bridgeport, Connecticut 06605

Bean, Inc., L.L.
Freeport, Maine 04033

Bearcat Corp.
706 Logan Street
Goshen, Indiana 46526

Beck Outdoor Projects
P.O. Box 1038
Crescent City, California 95531

Beckel Canvas Products
P.O. Box 20491
Portland, Oregon 97220

Bee Plastics Corp.
2660 N. Clybourn Avenue
Chicago, Illinois 60614

Bell Industries
P.O. Box 2104
St. Paul, Minnesota 55109

Bell Mfg. Corp.
Highway 93 S.
Kalispell, Montana 59901

Bellweather
1161 Mission Street
San Francisco, California 94103

Bernard Food Industries, Inc.
222 S. 24th Street
San Jose, California 95103

BernzOmatic Corp.
740 Driving Park Avenue
Rochester, New York 14613

Bethany Fellowship, Inc.
6820 Auto Club Road
Minneapolis, Minnesota 55438

Big Game Products, Inc.
20551 Sunset
Detroit, Michigan 48234

Bike Athletic Products
20 Walnut Street
Wellesley Hills, Massachusetts 02181

Bishop's Ultimate Outdoor Equipment
6804 Millwood Road
Bethesda, Maryland 20034

Bison Camper, Inc.
S. Highway 65
Buffalo, Missouri 65622

Blacks
Box 4501, Station E.
Ottawa, Ontario
Canada

Blank Textiles, Inc.
366 5th Avenue
New York, New York 10001

Blanket Corp. of America
21st & Lippencott Street
Philadelphia, Pennsylvania 19132

Blazon Mobile Homes Corp.
102 W. Windsor Avenue
Elkhart, Indiana 46514

Bock Products, Inc.
1905 Hively Avenue
Elkhart, Indiana 46514

Bonair Boats, Inc.
15501 W. 109th Street
Lenexa, Kansas 66219

Bon-Aire Industries, Inc.
3240 Industry Drive
Signal Hill, California 90801

Boss Sports
221 W. 1st Street
Kewanee, Illinois 61443

Bowen Knife Co.
Rt. #3, Box 3245-A
Blackshear, Georgia 31516

Boyer Chemical Co.
1611 Church Street
Evanston, Illinois 60201

Boyle & Co., Inc., John
112 Duane Street
New York, New York 10007

Brand Industries, Inc.
1209 Virginia Avenue
Fairmont, West Virginia 26554

Brandt Sleepworks, A.
P.O. Box 889
Midlothian, Texas 76065

Brauer Brothers Mfg. Co.
817-19 N. 17th Street
St. Louis, Missouri 63106

Bright Star Industries, Inc.
600 Getty Avenue
Clifton, New Jersey 07015

Brohmann Knives Ltd.
88 Water Street
Pictou, Nova Scotia B0K 1H0
Canada

Browning
Rt. 1
Morgan, Utah 84050

Browning Arms Co. of Canada
5350 Ferrier Street
Montreal, Quebec H4P 1L9
Canada

Brunswick Corp.
P.O. Box 270
Tulsa, Oklahoma 74101

Buccaneer Mfg. Co., Inc.
35 York Street
Brooklyn, New York 11201

Buck Knives, Inc.
1717 No. Magnolia Ave.
El Cajon, California 92022

Buck Stop Lure Co.
3015 Grow Road
Stanton, Michigan 48888

Buckle & Blade, Inc.
150 Nassau Street
New York, New York 10038

Buicke & Sons, H.C.
90 Stark Street
Tonawanda, New York 14150

Burch Mfg. Co.
2055 Hubbell Avenue
Des Moines, Iowa 50317

Burgess Battery/Gould, Inc.
P.O. Box 3140
St. Paul, Minnesota 55165

Burke Co., J.E.
P.O. Box 549
Fond du Lac, Wisconsin 54935

Bushnell Optical Division
2828 E. Foothill Boulevard
Pasadena, California 91107

Butchart Nicholls
2 Germak Drive
Carteret, New Jersey 07008

Butwin Sportswear Co.
Finch Building, 6th Floor
St. Paul, Minnesota 55101

Byer Mfg. Co., The
Orono, Maine 04473

Byerly Trailer & Mfg. Co., Inc.
13988 Manchester Road
Manchester, Missouri 63011

Cabanarama Industries, Inc.
P.O. Box 945, Northwest Branch
Miami, Florida 33147

Cambria Spring Co.
3225 E. Washington Boulevard
Los Angeles, California 90023

Camel Mfg. Co.
329 S. Central Street
Knoxville, Tennessee 37902

Camillus Cutlery Co.
Main Street
Camillus, New York 13031

Camp and Trail Outfitters
112 Chambers Street
New York, New York 10007

Camp International
109 W. Washington
Jackson, Michigan 49204

Camp Kit Industries, Inc.
2440 Johnson Street
Elkhart, Indiana 46514

Camp Lite Products
2232 Lawrence Street
Denver, Colorado 80205

Camp 7, Inc.
802 S. Sherman
Longmont, Connecticut 80501

Camp-Site Mfg. of Texas, Inc.
1000 E. Lamesa Highway
Seminole, Texas 79360

Campbell Chain Co.
3990 E. Market Street
York, Pennsylvania 17403

Campco Ventures, Inc.
1891 Woolner Avenue
Fairfield, California 94533

Camp Trails
4111 W. Clarendon Avenue
Phoenix, Arizona 85019

Camp-ways
12915 S. Spring Street
Los Angeles, California 90061

Cannon Products, Inc.
2345 N.W. 8th Avenue
Faribault, Minnesota 55021

Cannondale Corp.
35 Pulaski Street
Stamford, Connecticut 06902

Canvas & Leather Bag Co., Inc.
37 W. Broad Street
Haverstraw, New York 10977

Canvas Specialty Co.
7344 E. Bandini Boulevard
Los Angeles, California 90022

Car Bak Camper Co.
1115 Twiggs Street
Tampa, Florida 33602

Cardinal Industries
7353 15th Street N.
St. Paul, Minnesota 55119

Caribou Campers, Inc.
Highway 97 S.
Brewster, Washington 98812

Car-Mic Enterprises, Inc.
Woodbine & McCalls Road
Delta, Pennsylvania 17314

Carr & Co., H. C.
6325 Colorado Street
Long Beach, California 90814

Carry Lite, Inc.
3000 W. Clarke Street
Milwaukee, Wisconsin 53210

Case & Sons Cutlery Co.
20 Russell Boulevard
Bradford, Pennsylvania 16701

Catamount Cap Manufacturers
Burgess Road
Bennington, Vermont 05201

Catawba Coach Co., Inc.
103 E. Henry Street
Belmont, North Carolina 28012

Cedar Crest Boot Co.
1415 Murfreesboro Pike
Nashville, Tennessee 37217

Celanese Fibres Marketing Co.
1211 Avenue of the Americas
New York, New York 10036

Centenary Mfg.
P.O. Box 39
Stirling, Ontario K0K 3E0
Canada

Central Sales Co.
3940 S. Memorial Drive
Tulsa, Oklahoma 74145

Central Specialties Co.
6030 Northwest Highway
Chicago, Illinois 60631

Century Chemical Products Co., Inc.
3380 W. Eleven Mile Road
Berkley, Minnesota 48072

Cerf Brothers Bag Co.
2827 S. Brentwood Boulevard
St. Louis, Missouri 63144

Challenger Mfg. Co.
118 Pearl Street
Mount Vernon, New York 10550

Champion Home Builders Co.
5573 E. North Street
Dryden, Michigan 48428

Champion Industries
35 E. Poplar Street
Philadelphia, Pennsylvania 19123

Champion Products, Inc.
4939 S. Austin Avenue
Chicago, Illinois 60638

Champion Sports Products
US Highway 9
Parlin, New Jersey 08859

Cheme Watt Corp.
511 W. Merrick Road
Valley Stream, New York 11580

Chesal Industries
3210 N. Pierce Street
Milwaukee, Wisconsin 53212

Cheshire Mfg. Co., Inc.
312 E. Johnson Avenue
Cheshire, Connecticut 06410

Chicago Tent & Textile
1900 W. 18th Street
Chicago, Illinois 60608

Chippewa Shoe Co.
925 1st Avenue
Chippewa Falls, Wisconsin 54729

Chromalloy Mfg.
713 Ottokee Street
Wauseon, Ohio 43567

Chuck Wagon Foods
Micro Drive
Woburn, Massachusetts 01801

Cinderella Recreational Products
11041 Mercantile
Stanton, California 90680

Clark Leather Products
348 Sycamore Street
W. Chicago, Illinois 60185

Clarks
P.O. Box 92, Belden Station
Norwalk, Connecticut 06852

Classic Caps, Inc.
28577 US #20 W.
Elkhart, Indiana 46514

Classic Mfg. Co.
US-12 & Klinger Lake Road
Sturgis, Michigan 49091

Clay Camper Co., Inc.
Rt. 4
Clay, West Virginia 25043

Clayborn Industries
County Road No. 3
Elkhart, Indiana 46514

Clayton Craft, Inc.
Acre Street
Guttenberg, Iowa 52052

Clear Creek
14631 Catalina Street
San Leandro, California 94577

Climb High, Inc.
227 Main Street
Burlington, Vermont 05401

Cline Industries, Inc.
P.O. Box 38
Rush Springs, Oklahoma 73082

Cloud Nine
(see M.H. Mfg. Corp.)

Clyomed
14 Farber Road
Princeton, New Jersey 08540

Coachmen Industries, Inc.
State Road 13 N.
Middlebury, Indiana 46540

Coghlan's
235 Garry Street
Winnipeg, Manitoba R3C 1H2
Canada

Cold River
234 Union Street
North Adams, Massachusetts 01247

Cole National Corp.
5777 Grant Avenue
Cleveland, Ohio 44105

Cole Outdoor Products of America, Inc.
801 P Street
Lincoln, Nebraska 68508

Coleman Co., Inc.
250 N. St. Francis
Wichita, Kansas 67201

Coles Co.
Space 8b6, Atlanta Merchandise Mart
Atlanta, Georgia 30303

Colorado Mountain Industries Corp.
1896 Reading Road
Cincinnati, Ohio 45215

Colorado Tent & Awning Co.
3333 E. 52 Avenue at Cook Street
Denver, Colorado 80216

Columbia Sportswear Co.
6600 N. Baltimore
Portland, Oregon 97203

Comfy
310 First Avenue S.
Seattle, Washington 98104

Compass Electronics
3700 24th Avenue
Forest Grove, Oregon 97116

Compass Instrument & Optical
104 E. 25th Street
New York, New York 10010

Complex American
441 Stuart Street
Boston, Massachusetts 02117

Computer Enterprises, Inc.
P.O. Box 503
Providence, Rhode Island 02901

Conestoga Mfg. Co.
N. Front Street
Woodburn, Oregon 97071

Conquest
(see World Famous Sales Co.)

Converse
55 Fordham Road
Wilmington, Massachusetts 01887

Coons Mfg., Inc.
2300 W. 4th Street
Oswego, Kansas 67356

Country Ways, Inc.
3500 Hwy. 101 S.
Minnetonka, Minnesota 55343

Covey Corp.
P.O. Box 1317
Houston, Texas 77001

Cox Trailers, Inc.
Box 338C
Grifton, North Carolina 28530

Cramer Products, Inc.
153 W. Warren
Gardner, Kansas 66030

Crazy Daisy Corp.
County Road 6
Elkhart, Indiana 46514

Creation Windows, Inc.
52629 Mobile Drive
Elkhart, Indiana 46514

Crowley Industries, Inc.
515 South Avenue E.
Crowley, Louisiana 70526

Crown Recreation, Inc.
184-10 Jamaica Avenue
Hollis, New York 11423

CSC Sales Co.
3347 N. Halstead
Chicago, Illinois 60657

Curley-Bates Co.
1130 Andover Park E.
Seattle, Washington 98188

Curtiss Campers, Inc.
Curtiss, Wisconsin 54422

Custom Hardtops
1768 Caspian Avenue
Long Beach, California 90810

Cutter Laboratories, Inc.
4th & Parker Streets
Berkeley, California 94710

D & R Industries, Inc.
7111 N. Capitol
Lincolnwood, Illinois 60645

D & R Sales, Inc.
P.O. Box 208
Oldsmar, Florida 33557

D & W Sales Engineers, Inc.
802 W. Beardsley Avenue
Elkhart, Indiana 46514

Dakon Corp.
1836 Gilford Avenue
New Hyde Park, New York 11040

Dakota Industries
P.O. Box 932
Sioux Falls, South Dakota 57101

Daley Foam Products, Inc.
61 McGrath Highway
Somerville, Massachusetts 02143

Dallas Cap and Emblem Mfg.
2924 Main Street
Dallas, Texas 75226

Dana Mfg. Corp.
115 Broadway
Port Ewen, New York 12466

Danielson Co.
755 N. Central
Kent, Washington 98031

Danner Shoe Mfg. Co.
7924 S.E. Stark Street
Portland, Oregon 97215

Dan's Trailer Supply, Inc.
255 Mountain Avenue
Berthoud, Colorado 80513

Dartmouth Outdoor Sports, Inc.
P.O. Box 960
Hanover, New Hampshire 03755

Davco
(see St. Bernice Mfg. Co.)

Davis Import & Export, D.L.
9916 Northridge Drive
Valley Station, Kentucky 40272

Dee Jay Mfg. Co.
515 Campbell Street
Rapid City, South Dakota 57701

Delong Sportswear
P.O. Box 189
Grinnell, Iowa 50112

Delta Industries, Inc.
305 Apple Street
Monroe, Louisiana 71201

Denver Tent Co.
1408 W. Colfax
Denver, Colorado 80204

Dexter Shoe Co.
31 St. James Avenue
Boston, Massachusetts 02116

Dickey Industries, Inc.
155 S. Superior Street
Toledo, Ohio 43602

Dillon Beck Mfg. Co.
1227 Central Avenue
Hillside, New Jersey 07205

Dinsmore Instrument Co.
1816 Remell Street
Flint, Michigan 48503

Divajex Industries
1513 E. St. Gertrude Place
Santa Ana, California 92705

Dog Supply House, Inc.
215 S. Washington
Greenfield, Ohio 45123

Dometic Sales, Inc.
P.O. Box 490
Elkhart, Indiana 46514

Donn-A-Camp Industries
Rt. 2
Merritt Island, Florida 32952

Donner Corp.
2110 Dana Avenue
Cincinnati, Ohio 45207

Dow Corning Corp.
Executive Consumer Products
Midland, Michigan 48640

DRI Lite Foods
11333 Atlantic Boulevard
Lynwood, California 90262

Duckster Sportswear, Inc.
481 Shelton Avenue
Hamden, Connecticut 06517

Dunham
Brattleboro, Vermont 05301

Duofold, Inc.
P.O. Drawer A
Mohawk, New York 13407

Duo-Therm
509 S. Poplar
LaGrange, Indiana 46761

DuPont de Nemours Co. Inc., E.I.
1007 Market Street
Wilmington, Delaware 19898

Dynalite Co.
215 S. Washington Street
Greenfield, Ohio 45123

Dynamic Fabricators, Inc.
111 Ohio Street
Monroeville, Indiana 46773

Dynaplastics
10314 E. Rush Street S.
El Monte, California 91733

Eagle Craft, Inc.
Markley Road
Plymouth, Indiana 46563

Eagle Enterprises, Inc.
55281 Jay Dee
Elkhart, Indiana 46514

Eagle Mfg. Co.
24th & Charles Streets
Wellsburg, West Virginia 26070

Eastern Canvas Products, Inc.
17 Locust Street
Haverhill, Massachusetts 01380

Eastern Freeze-Dry Corp.
(see Speedy Chef Food, Inc.)

Eastern Golf Co.
2537 Boston Road
Bronx, New York 10467

Eastern Mountain Sports, Inc.
1041 Commonwealth Avenue
Boston, Massachusetts 02215

Easton, Inc., James
7800 Haskell Avenue
Van Nuys, California 91406

Ebsco Industries, Inc.
Ebsco Building
Red Bank, New Jersey 07701

Eclipse, Inc.
P.O. Box 372
Ann Arbor, Michigan 48107

Edmont-Wilson
1300 Walnut Street
Coshocton, Ohio 43812

Eiger Mountain Sports
P.O. Box 306
Montrose, California 91020

El Rancho, Inc.
28564 Holiday Place
Elkhart, Indiana 46514

Elkhorn Leather Products Corp.
1842 Riverside Drive
Glendale, California 91201

Emblem Mfg. Co., Inc.
13915 S. Main Street
Los Angeles, California 90061

Emco Specialties
P.O. Box 853
Des Moines, Iowa 50304

Emergency Oxygen
5207 West Country Line Road
Milwaukee, Wisconsin 53223

Empire Footwear Co.
1100 E. Main Street
Endicott, New York 13760

Enterprise Distribution, Inc.
99 West Essex Street
Maywood, New Jersey 07607

Environmental Container System
P.O. Box 188
Grants Pass, Oregon 97526

Ero Industries, Inc.
1 S. Wacker Drive
Chicago, Illinois 60606

Estwing Mfg. Co.
2647 8th Street
Rockford, Illinois 61101

Eureka Tent, Inc.
625 Conklin Road
Binghamton, New York 13902

EZ Rider Camper Mfg.
503 Reservation Road
Marina, California 93933

EZ Sales and Mfg. Co.
1566 W. 134th Street
Gardena, California 90249

Eze-Lap Diamond Products
15164 Weststate Street
Westminster, California 92683

F & L Packing Corp.
681 Main Street, Building #62
Belleville, New Jersey 07109

Fabiano Shoe Co.
850 Summer Street
S. Boston, Massachusetts 02127

Fabrico Mfg. Corp.
1300 W. Exchange Avenue
Chicago, Illinois 60609

Fairfield Sporting Goods
1951 N. Fairfield Avenue
Chicago, Illinois 60647

Fame Mfg., Inc.
329 Mill Street
Saegertown, Pennsylvania 16433

Family Products, Inc.
P.O. Box 1600
Lowell, Massachusetts 01853

Famous Trails
5232 Lovelock Street
San Diego, California 92110

Faribo Woolen Mill Co.
P.O. Box 369
Faribault, Minnesota 55021

Faska Co.
1900 Canyon Close Road
Pasadena, California 91107

Fatsco
251 N. Fair Avenue
Benton Harbor, Michigan 49022

Fields Mfg. Co.
17307 E. Pine Street
Tulsa, Oklahoma 74138

Flaghouse, Inc.
18 W. 18th Street
New York, New York 10011

Flambeau Products Corp.
801 Lynn Avenue
Baraboo, Wisconsin 53913

Fly-Tiers Carry-All
46 Jane Street
New York, New York 10014

Folbot Corp.
Stark Industrial Park
Charleston, South Carolina 29405

Fonas Corp.
616 Beatty Road
Monroeville, Pennsylvania 15146

Forest City Products, Inc.
722 Bolivar Road
Cleveland, Ohio 44115

Forrest Mountaineering, Ltd.
1517 Platte Street
Denver, Colorado 80202

Four State Industries, Inc.
25745 Woodlawn
Elkhart, Indiana 46514

Frabill Mfg. Co.
2018 S. 1st Street
Milwaukee, Wisconsin 53207

Fredericks Rubber/Interstate
15 Shawmut Avenue
Hudson, Massachusetts 01749

Freeland Scope Stands, Inc.
3737 14th Avenue
Rock Island, Illinois 61201

Freeman Industries, Inc.
Tuckahoe, New York 10707

Freeze-Dry Foods, Ltd.
579 Speers Road
Oakville, Ontario L6K 2G4
Canada

Frostline Kits
452 Burbank Street
Broomfield, Colorado 80020

Fumol Corp.
49-65 Van Dam Street
Long Island City, New York 11101

Funk Brothers Hat & Cap Co.
1718 Washington Avenue
St. Louis, Missouri 63103

Fuqua Industries, Inc.
3800 First National Bank Tower
Atlanta, Georgia 30303

Gagne Associates, Inc.
1080 Chenango Street
Binghamton, New York 13901

Galaxie Corp.
P.O. Box 115
Elkhart, Indiana 46514

Game Winner Sportswear
515 Candler Building
Atlanta, Georgia, 30303

Garcia Corp.
329 Alfred Avenue
Teaneck, New Jersey 07666

Garco Mfg. Co.
2219 W. Grand Avenue
Chicago, Illinois 60612

Garelick Mfg. Co.
644 2nd Street
St. Paul Park, Minnesota 55071

Gem Top Mfg., Inc.
8811 S.E. Herbert Court
Clackamas, Oregon 97015

General Corp.
P.O. Box 8
Waukesha, Wisconsin 63186

General Foam Plastics Corp.
3321 Princess Anne Road
Norfolk, Virginia 23502

General Housewares Corp.
P.O. Box 4066
Terre Haute, Indiana 47804

General Licensing Corp.
16055 Ventura Boulevard
Encino, California 91316

General Playground Equipment, Inc.
1133 S. Courtland
Kokomo, Indiana 46901

General Recreation, Inc.
P.O. Box 25367
Albuquerque, New Mexico 87125

General Recreation Industries, Inc.
8700 N. Waukegan Road
Morton Grove, Illinois 60053

General Thermetics
11 Brookdale Place
Mount Vernon, New York 10550

General Trailer Mfg., Inc.
19000 W. 8 Mile Road
Southfield, Michigan 48075

Geneva Sales Co.
P.O. Box 551
Geneva, Illinois 60134

Gerber Legendary Blades
14200 S.W. 72nd Avenue
Portland, Oregon 97223

Gerico, Inc.
P.O. Box 998
Boulder, Colorado 80302

Gerry
5450 N. Valley Highway
Denver, Colorado 80216

Gibralter Industries
254 36th Street
Brooklyn, New York 11232

Gibson Mfg. Co.
2080 Commerce
Midland, Texas 79701

Girard Engineering Co.
24 Bater Road
Coldwater, Michigan 49036

Glacierware, Inc.
Route 145
Clinton, Connecticut 06413

Gladding Corp.
P.O. Box 586, Back Bay Annex
Boston, Massachusetts 02117

Gladding/Horrocks-Ibbotson
20-24 Whitesboro Street
Utica, New York 13502

Gladding Sleeping Bag
1224 W. Genessee Street
Syracuse, New York 13202

Gleason's Camper's Supply, Don
9 Pearl Street
Northampton, Massachusetts 01060

Gokey Co., The
21 W. 5th Street
St. Paul, Minnesota 55102

Gold Crown Campers Mfg., Inc.
Route 4
Atmore, Alabama 36502

Gold Star Camper Co.
11022 N. 21st Avenue
Phoenix, Arizona 85029

Goldberg Mfg. Co., Dave
600 W. Jackson Boulevard
Chicago, Illinois 60606

Goldberg, I.
902 Chestnut Street
Philadelphia, Pennsylvania 19107

Golden West Merchandiser
Kens Mountaineering-Wee Pak
Reno, Nevada 89502

Go-Lite Campers, Inc.
23rd & Somers
Fremont, Nebraska 68025

Goodwin Sporting Goods Co.
1333 Quebec Street N.
Kansas City, Missouri 64116

Go-Tag-A-Long Trailer Mfg.
240 High Street
Washingtonville, Ohio 44490

Gott Mfg. Co., Inc.
P.O. Box 652
Winfield, Kansas 67156

Gould, Inc.
931 Vandalia Street
St. Paul, Minnesota 55114

Granet Corp.
25 Loring Drive
Framingham, Massachusetts 01701

Grayline Housewares, Inc.
1616 Berkley Street
Elgin, Illinois 60120

Great Northern
4747 W. Peterson Avenue
Chicago, Illinois 60646

Great Pacific Iron Works
P.O. Box 150
Ventura, California 93001

Greb Shoes, Ltd
51 Ardelt Avenue
Kitchener, Ontario N2C 2E1
Canada

Greenway Campers Mfg. & Supply
1 Mile W. Bus 83
Pharr, Texas 78577

Greylock Mountain Industries, Corp.
234 Union Street
No. Adams, Massachusetts 01247

Griffolyn Co., Inc.
P.O. Box 33248
Houston, Texas 77033

Grizzly Mfg.
P.O. Box 1070
Hamilton, Montana 59840

Gudebrod Brothers Silk Co.
12 S. 12th Street
Philadelphia, Pennsylvania 19107

Gutmann Co., Inc.
900 S. Columbus Avenue
Mt. Vernon, New York 10550

H & H Surplus Center
305 W. Baltimore Street
Baltimore, Maryland 21223

Hall Mfg. Co., Inc., R.D.
9847 Glenoaks Boulevard
Sun Valley, California 91352

Halperin Company ,The
716 Columbus Avenue
Boston, Massachusetts 02120

Hampshire Mfg. Co.
Factory Street
Nashua, New Hampshire 03060

Hanover Glove Co., Inc.
2-10 Exchange Place
Hanover, Pennsylvania 17331

Harmony Ent., Inc.
704 Main Street N.
Harmony, Minnesota 55939

Hayden Trans-Cooler, Inc.
1531 Pomona Road
Corona, California 91720

Heila, Osmo O.
R.D. 1, Podunk Road
Trumansburg, New York 14886

Henckels Zwillingswerk, Inc.
1 Westchester Plaza
Elmsford, New York 10523

Henco Enterprises, Inc.
2241 Lake Street
Niles, Michigan 49120

Heritage Quilt, Inc.
212 5th Avenue
New York, New York 10010

Herman Shoe Co., Joseph
Millis, Massachusetts 02054

Herter's
Route 1
Waseca, Minnesota 56093

Hettrick Mfg. Co.
Taylorsville Road
Statesville, North Carolina 28677

Hi Lo Trailer Co.
100 Elm Street
Butler, Ohio 44822

Higgins-Delta Corp.
52652 Mobile Road
Elkhart, Indiana 46514

High & Light
139½ E. 16th Street
Costa Mesa, California 92627

Highland Outfitters
3579 University Avenue
Riverside, California 92502

Hillco, Inc.
123 S. Shoop Avenue
Wauseon, Ohio 43567

Himalayan Industries, Inc.
P.O. Box 5668
Pine Bluff, Arkansas 71601

Hine/Snowbridge
P.O. Box 1459
Boulder, Colorado 80302

Hinman Outfitters, Bob
1217 W. Glen
Peoria, Illinois 61614

Hirsch Display Fixtures, Inc.
Lake Cook & Pfingsten
Deerfield, Illinois 60015

Hirsch-Weis
5203 S.E. Johnson Creek Boulevard
Portland, Oregon 97206

Hiway Campers
8650 E. Main Street-US Rt. 40
Reynoldsburg, Ohio 43068

HJ Sports Accessories Corp.
35 Mileed Way
Avenel, New Jersey 07001

Hoffman and Associates, Robert
12540 Sanford Street
Los Angeles, California 90066

Hoffritz-Edwin, Inc., Jay
20 Cooper Square
New York, New York 10003

Holiday-Hut Mfg. Co., Inc.
Galt City Industrial Park
Milton, Florida 32570

Holloway Sportswear, Inc.
Drawer AB
Jackson Center, Ohio 45334

Hollowform, Inc.
6345 Variel Avenue
Woodland Hills, California 91324

Hol-Tite Product, Inc.
12 Dwight Place
Fairfield, New York 07006

Holubar
1975 30th Street
Boulder, Colorado 80302

Homelite
Riverdale Avenue Point
Chester, New York 10573

Honeywell, Inc.
5501 S. Broadway
Littleton, Colorado 80120

Hoosier Tarpaulin & Canvas Goods Co., Inc.
2825 East 56th Street
Indianapolis, Indiana 46220

Hop-Cap, Inc.
1730 W. Bike Street
Bremen, Indiana 46506

Hoyt Archery Co.
11510 Natural Bridge
Bridgeton, Missouri 63044

Hub Apparel, Inc.
47 Langley Road
Newton Center, Massachusetts 02159

Hull Mfg. Co.
P.O. Box 246
Warren, Ohio 44482

Hunter Outdoor Products, Inc.
234 Union Street
No. Adams, Massachusetts 01247

Hunters Equipment Mfg. Corp.
1220 S. Chadbourne
San Angelo, Texas 76901

Huntington Beach Trailer Supply
16242 Beach Boulevard
Huntington Beach, California 92647

Hycor, Inc.
North Woburn Industrial Park
Woburn, Massachusetts 01801

Ideal Products, Inc.
101 W. DuBois Avenue
DuBois, Pennsylvania 15801

Igloo Corp.
P.O. Box 19322
Houston, Texas 77024

Ikelite Mfg.
3301 N. Illinois Street
Indianapolis, Indiana 46208

Impecco Ltd.
P.O. Box 441
Teaneck, New Jersey 07666

Imperial American Co.
P.O. Box 878
Tyler, Texas 75701

Imperial Camper, Inc.
2512 N.E. 35th Street
Fort Worth, Texas 76111

Imperial Knife Co.
1776 Broadway
New York, New York 10019

Inca-One Corp.
9014 Lindblade Street
Culver City, California 90230

Indiana Trailer Supply
2600 S. Nappanee Street
Elkhart, Indiana 46514

Industrial Sales Co.
Patapsco & Barney Streets
Baltimore, Maryland 21230

Inland Marine
79 E. Jackson
Wilkes-Barre, Pennsylvania 18701

Innovar Industries
Highway 4 N.
Dunnell, Minnesota 56127

Insport, Inc.
1217 W. Glen
Peoria, Illinois 61614

Inst Awn, Inc.
2220 DuPont Drive
Anaheim, California 92806

Insul-Pak, Inc.
P.O. Box 175
Destin, Florida 32541

International Cap Corp.
55080 Phillips Street
Elkhart, Indiana 46514

International Products Trading, Inc.
380 Franklin Turnpike
Mahwah, New Jersey 07430

Intertherm, Inc.
3800 Park Avenue
St. Louis, Missouri 63110

IPCO
331 Lake Hazeltine Drive
Chaska, Minnesota 55318

Irving/Weather-Rite, Inc.
125 Enterprise Avenue
Secaucus, New Jersey 07094

Jack Frost Laboratories
3120 Industrial 33rd Street
Ft. Pierce, Florida 33450

Janoy, Inc.
2000 E. Center Circle Drive
Minneapolis, Minnesota 55441

JanSport
Paine Field Industrial Park
Everett, Washington 98204

Jayco, Inc.
P.O. Box 460
Middlebury, Indiana 46540

Jefferson, Ray
Main & Cotton Streets
Philadelphia, Pennsylvania 19127

Jet-Aer Corp.
100 Sixth Street
Paterson, New Jersey 07524

Jewel Yarn Co.
520 Broadway
New York, New York 10013

Jim's Mobile Supply
2700 Needmore Road
Dayton, Ohio 45414

Jo Lock Fabricators & Sportswear
1607 Dexter Avenue N.
Seattle, Washington 98109

Johnson & Johnson Athletic Division
George & Hamilton Streets
New Brunswick, New Jersey 08901

Johnson Camper Sales, Inc.
111 Ohio Street
Monroeville, Indiana 46773

Johnson Co., E.F.
299 Tenth Avenue S.W.
Waseca, Minnesota 56093

Johnson Co., Louis
P.O. Box 403
Highland Park, Illinois 60035

Jones Tent & Awning
2034 W. 11th Avenue
Vancouver, British Columbia V6J 2L9
Canada

K Enterprises
P.O. Box 2287
Menlo Park, California 94025

Kadas Kampers, Inc.
1724 Laskin Road
Virginia Beach, Virginia 23454

Kalmar Trading Corp.
901 Minnesota Street
San Francisco, California 94107

Kangaroo Products
815 Houser Way N.
Renton, Washington 98055

Kassnar Imports
P.O. Box 6097
Harrisburg, Pennsylvania 17112

Kaufman Footwear Ltd.
410 King Street W.
Kitchener, Ontario N2G 1C3
Canada

Kayot Marine Division
500 Kayot Boulevard
Mankato, Minnesota 56001

Kebek Industries, Inc.
601 Baxter Avenue
Knoxville, Tennessee 37921

Keezer Mfg. Co.
27 Chadwick Street
Plaistow, New Hampshire 03865

Keller Plastics, Inc.
18000 State Road 9
Miami, Florida 33162

Kel-Lite Industries, Inc.
P.O. Box K
Barstow, California 92311

Kelty Pack, Inc.
9281 Borden Avenue
Sun Valley, California 91352

Kemcraft Corp.
6221 14th Street W.
Bradenton, Florida 33507

Kenco Engineering
P.O. Box 88
Middlebury, Indiana 46540

Kendall Sports
20 Walnut Street
Wellesley Hill Massachusetts 02181

Kens Mountaineering/Wee Pak
155 N. Edison Way
Reno, Nevada 89502

Kent Sales & Mfg. Co.
449 Dodge Street
Kent, Ohio 44240

Kenway Campers, Inc.
6th & Railroad Streets
Esther, Missouri 63601

Kershaw Cutlery Co.
500 Ridgeway Road
Lake Oswego, Oregon 97034

Kiffe Products
184-10 Jamaica Avenue
Hollis, New York 11423

Kimberly Rose Co., Inc.
2211 N. Elston Avenue
Chicago, Illinois 60614

Kimco Electric Products, Inc.
2900 Peterson Avenue
Chicago, Illinois 60659

King Athletic Goods Corp.
2615 W. Hunting Park Avenue
Philadelphia, Pennsylvania 19129

King-Seeley Thermos Co.
Thermos Division
Norwich, Connecticut 06360

Kirkham's AAA Tent & Awning Co.
24 West 5th S.
Salt Lake City, Utah 84101

Kirn Kraft
107 W. Concord
Minneapolis, Kansas 67467

Klamerus & Co.
4557 W. 59th Street
Chicago, Illinois 60629

Klepper Corp., Hans
35 Union Square W.
New York, New York 10003

K-Mac & Co.
15404 Dooley Road
Addison, Texas 75001

Kodiak Mills, Inc.
P.O. Box 350
Osage, Iowa 50461

Kohler Co.
Kohler, Wisconsin 53044

Komito Bootmaker, Steve
351 Moraine Avenue
Estes Park, Colorado 80517

Kromer Cap Co., Inc.
759 North Milwaukee Street
Milwaukee, Wisconsin 53202

Krown Mfg. Co., Inc.
1165 Reynolds Road
Charlotte, Michigan 48813

KST Co.
Thermos Avenue
Norwich, Connecticut 06360

Kumbak Co.
808 Nicollet
Moberly, Missouri 65270

Kustom Fit Mfg. Co.
14108 S. Towne Avenue
Los Angeles, California 90061

Kwik-Kold, Inc.
P.O. Box 696
Moberly, Missouri 65270

Lamson & Goodnow Mfg. Co.
Shelburne Falls, Massachusetts 01370

Land & Sea International
720 Laurelwood Road
Santa Clara, California 95050

Larson Laboratories, Inc.
1320 Irwin Drive
Erie, Pennsylvania 16505

Lasco International
1382 W. 9th Street
Cleveland, Ohio 44113

Lauren Mfg. Co.
2228 Reiser Avenue S.E.
New Philadelphia, Ohio 44663

Lazy N Campers
Highway 121, RR 1
Warrensburg, Illinois 62573

Lea & Sachs, Inc.
350 N. Clark Street
Chicago, Illinois 60610

Leer Industries, Inc.
1750 McNaughton Street
Elkhart, Indiana 46514

Leigh Products Division
460 Main Street
Coopersville, Michigan 49404

Leisure Imports, Inc.
104 Arlington Avenue
St. James, New York 11780

Leisure Time Products, Inc.
P.O. Box 232
Nappanee, Indiana 46550

Leisureline Products
4 Allwood Avenue
Central Islip, New York 11722

Lewis & Clark Co., The
248 Farms Village Road
W. Simsbury, Connecticut 06092

Liberty Organization, Inc.
P.O. Box 306
Montrose, California 91020

Lifesaver Products, Inc.
15001 Calvert Street
Van Nuys, California 91401

'Lil' Colt Industries, Inc.
R.D. 2
Middleburg, Pennsylvania 17842

Lile Handmade Knives
Route 1
Russelville, Arizona 72801

Limmer and Sons, Peter
Intervale, New Hampshire 03845

Linabery Products, Inc.
490 Industrial Park Drive
Gladwin, Michigan 48624

Lindner Products Co.
P.O. Box 1703
Grand Rapids, Michigan 49501

Logan, Inc.
16952 Miliken Avenue
Irvine, California 92705

Longwood Equipment Co., Ltd.
132 Railside Road
Don Mills, Ontario M3A 1A3
Canada

Lord & Hodge, Inc.
22 Evergreen Avenue
Middletown, Connecticut 06457

Lowe Alpine Systems
1752 N. 55th
Boulder, Colorado 80301

L PS Research Labs, Inc.
2050 Cotner Avenue
Los Angeles, California 90025

Mac International
4850 W. Main Street
Skokie, Illinois 60076

Mad River Canoe, Inc.
P.O. Box 363
Waitsfield, Vermont 05673

Maggard Camper Sales
5624 Kearny Villa Road
San Diego, California 92123

Magneto Closures, Inc.
2900 Indiana Street
Baltimore, Maryland 21230

Maiden Campers
P.O. Box 92
Maiden, North Carolina 28650

Manitoba Tent & Awning Co.
1010 Logan Avenue
Winnipeg, Manitoba R3E 1P4
Canada

Mansfield Sanitary, Inc.
150 First Street
Perrysville, Ohio 44864

Maran Co.
Big Fork, Montana 59911

Marathon Rubber Products Co.
510 Sherman Street
Wausau, Wisconsin 54401

Margesson's
17 Adelaide Street E.
Toronto, Ontario M5C 1H4
Canada

Marine & Mobile Water Systems
6400 Marina Drive
Long Beach, California 90803

Mark Fore Vatco
109 Brookline Avenue
Boston, Massachusetts 02215

Markwell Arms Co.
2414 W. Devon Avenue
Chicago, Illinois 60645

Martin Archery, Inc.
Route 5
Walla Walla, Washington 99362

Martin Co., The
1150 W. 3rd Street
Cleveland, Ohio 44113

Martin Industries, Inc.
P.O. Box 730
Sheffield, Alabama 35660

Marv Enterprises, Inc.
7881 Hi-View Drive
N. Royalton, Ohio 44133

Mason Pacific, Inc.
2510 Daly Street
Los Angeles, California 90031

Master Lock Co.
2600 N. 32nd Street
Milwaukee, Wisconsin 53210

Maurice Sporting Goods
2701 W. Armitage Avenue
Chicago, Illinois 60647

Medalist/Universal
11525 Sorrento Valley Road
San Diego, California 92121

Medima
10 E. 40th Street
New York, New York 10016

Meerix Chemical Co.
2234 E. 75th Street
Chicago, Illinois 60649

Mehler-Zelte
99 W. Essex Street
Maywood, New Jersey 07607

Meier & Frank Merchandise Co.
5641 N. Washington Street
Denver, Colorado 80216

Merc-O-Tronic Instrument Corp.
215 Branch Street
Almont, Michigan 48003

Merit Watch Co., Inc.
630 Fifth Avenue
New York, New York 10020

Mermac Mfg. Inc.
P.O. Box 5268
Salem, Oregon 97304

Merri-Miller Mfg. Co.
110 Carlisle Street
Quincy, Ohio 43343

M. H. Mfg. Corp.
1107 Broadway
New York, New York 10010

Michaels of Oregon Co.
P.O. Box 13010
Portland, Oregon 97213

Michigan Wool Products Co.
1502 Milton Street
Benton Harbor, Michigan 49022

Midas
222 S. Riverside
Chicago, Illinois 60606

Midwest Outerwear, Inc.
603 N. Moore Road
Port Washington, Wisconsin 53074

Midwest Sales Co., Inc.
P.O. Box 360
Memphis, Tennessee 38101

Mid-Western Sport Togs
150 W. Franklin
Berlin, Wisconsin 54923

Milbolac, Inc.
Bethabra Station
Winston-Salem, North Carolina 27106

Minn-Apollo Corp.
90 N. Broadway Avenue
Des Plaines, Illinois 60016

Mirro Aluminum Company
P.O. Box 409
Manitowoc, Wisconsin 54220

Missoula RV Repair Center & Mfg. Co.
2605 Garfield
Missoula, Montana 59801

Mit-Shel Co.
640 S. Fifth
Quincy, Illinois 62301

Moby, Inc.
5132 Baur Avenue
Dayton, Ohio 45431

Mogal, Inc., Mitchell
440 Broadway
New York, New York 10013

Moline Corp.
P.O. Box 529
St. Charles, Illinois 60174

Monogram Industries, Inc.
4030 Freeman Boulevard
Redondo Beach, California 90278

Monroe Fabricators
3580 N. Elston Avenue
Chicago, Illinois 60618

Moor & Mountain
63 Park Street
Andover, Massachusetts 01810

Morris Frames, Inc.
P.O. Box 578
Dixon, California 95620

Morsan, Inc.
810 Route 17
Paramus, New Jersey 07652

Mountain Adventure Kits
P.O. Box 571
Whittier, California 90608

Mountain Equipment, Inc.
3208 E. Hamilton
Fresno, California 93702

Mountain House
(see Oregon Freeze Dry Foods, Inc.)

Mountain Paraphernalia
P.O. Box 4536
Modesto, California 95352

Mountain Products Corp.
123 S. Wenatchee Avenue
Wentachee, Washington 98801

Mountain Supply
808 R Street
Sacramento, California 95814

Mountaineering Equipage
2010 7th Street
Berkeley, California 94710

Muehleisen
1100 N. Johnson Avenue
El Cajon, California 92020

Multiaction Enterprises International
942 Van Auken Circle
Palo Alto, California 94303

Murphy Co., Inc., R.
Grotom-Harvard Road
Ayer, Massachusetts 01432

My Cap, Inc.
1730 Johnson
Elkhart, Indiana 46514

Namrok Industries, Inc.
Vernon Industrial Park
Vernon, Connecticut 06066

National Canvas Products Corp.
P.O. Box 955
Toledo, Ohio 43695

National Packaged Trail Foods
18607 St. Clair Avenue
Cleveland, Ohio 44110

Neeco Industries Ltd.
80 Galaxy Boulevard
Rexdale, Ontario M9W 4Y8
Canada

Neely Mfg. Co., Inc.
State Highway 2 W.
Corydon, Iowa 50060

Neese Idustries
P.O. Box 628
Gonzales, Louisiana 70737

Neil Co., F.J.
345 Hillside Avenue
Williston Park, New York 11596

Nelson Sales Co.
626 Broadway
Kansas City, Missouri 64105

Neonex International, Ltd.
17959 E. Valley Boulevard
City of Industry, California 91744

Newco, Inc.
148 S. Colony Street
Wallingford, Connecticut 06492

Newman Importing Co., Inc.
8461 Warner Drive
Culver City, California 90230

Nicholl Brothers, Inc.
1204 W. 27th Street
Kansas City, Missouri 64108

Nicolet Products
2927 East Avalon Drive
Phoenix, Arizona 85016

Nimrod, Inc.
500 Ford Boulevard
Hamilton, Ohio 45011

Norlund Co., O.A.
Water & Dorcas Streets
Lewistown, Pennsylvania 17044

Normark Corp.
1710 E. 78th Street
Minneapolis, Minnesota 55423

Norstar Ski Corp. Ltd.
37 Industrial Drive
Londonderry, New Hampshire 03053

North Face
1234 5th Street
Berkeley, California 94710

Northlander, Inc.
617 Water Street
Fitchburg, Massachusetts 01462

Northwood Campers
304 13th Street S.
Northwood, Iowa 50459

OLAM Outdoor Sports Products
P.O. Box 1616
Wilmington, North Carolina 28401

Oley Tooling, Inc.
Main Street
Oley, Pennsylvania 19547

OLM International Corp.
145 Sylvester Street S.
San Francisco, California 94080

Olsen Knife Co., Inc.
7-11 Joy Street
Howard, Michigan 49329

Olympic Style, Inc.
57941 Charlotte Avenue
Elkhart, Indiana 46514

Onan Corp.
1400 73rd Avenue N.E.
Minneapolis, Minnesota 55432

Optimus, Inc.
P.O. Box 307
La Mirada, California 90637

Oregon Freeze Dry Foods
770 W. 29th Avenue
Albany, Oregon 97321

Original Mink Oil, Inc.
10652 N.E. 112th
Portland, Oregon 97220

Orvis
Manchester, Vermont 05254

Outdoor Imports, Inc.
14621 Aetna Street
Van Nuys, California 91401

Outdoor Leisure Products, Inc.
P.O. Box 27424
Houston, Texas 77027

Outdoor Products
530 S. Main Street
Los Angeles, California 90013

Outdoor Sports Industries
518 17th
Denver, Colorado 80202

Outdoor Sports Mfg. Co.
P.O. Box 218
Forestville, Connecticut 06010

Outdoor Supply Co.
100 Merick Road
Rockville Center, New York 11570

Outdoor Venture Corp.
P.O. Box 337
Stearns, Kentucky 42647

Outers Laboratories, Inc.
Onalaska, Wisconsin 54650

Overlook Enterprises
3320 N. Federal Highway
Lighthouse Point, Florida 33064

Owatonna Campers, Inc.
RR 3
Owatonna, Minnesota 55060

P & C Mfg. Co.
1508 Highway 2 W.
Duluth, Minnesota 55810

P & S Camper Mfg. Co.
Highway 320 & Highway 77
Lott, Texas 76656

Pacific/Ascente
P.O. Box 2028
Fresno, California 93718

Pack In Products, Inc.
13277 Saticoy Street N.
Hollywood, California 91605

Pak Foam Products Co., Inc.
390 Pine Street
Pawtucket, Rhode Island 02862

Palco Products
Steel Street
Slatersville, Rhode Island 02876

Palmer Mfg. Inc.
P.O. Box 220
W. Newton, Pennsylvania 15089

Pantos Canvas Corp.
144 Moody Street
Waltham, Massachusetts 02154

Paradise Mfg. Co.
2840 E. 26th Street
Los Angeles, California 90023

Para-Gear Equipment Co.
5138 N. Broadway
Chicago, Illinois 60640

Pawtucket Foam Products
390 Pine Street
Pawtucket, Rhode Island 02862

Pennsylvania Sporting Goods Co.
1906 Jenkintown Road
Jenkintown, Pennsylvania 19046

Pet Chemicals, Inc.
P.O. Box 656
7781 N.W. 73rd Cour
Miami, Florida 33166

Peters Bag Corp.
Empire State Building, Suite 1210
New York, New York 10001

Petzoldt Wilderness Equipment, Paul
P.O. Box 78
Lander, Wyoming 82520

Phoenix Products, Inc.
US Highway 421
Tyner, Kentucky 40486

Pioneer Co.
106 W. 33rd
Boise, Idaho 83707

Plastilite Corp.
4909 N. 45th Street
Omaha, Nebraska 68112

Plastimayd Corp.
2204 S.E. 7th Avenue
Portland, Oregon 97214

Play-Mor Trailers, Inc.
Highway 63 S.
Westphalia, Missouri 65085

PLB International, Inc.
17 Newton Road
Plainview, New York 11803

Pleasure Homes Mfg. Co.
3020 N. Flora Road
Spokane, Washington 99216

Pleasure Mate Industries
Blue Star Highway
South Haven, Michigan 49090

Poloron Products, Inc.
165 Huguenot Street
New Rochelle, New York 10801

Ponderosa Campers
3516 LaGrande Boulevard
Sacramento, California 95823

Pony Coach, Inc.
P.O. Box 79027
Saginaw, Texas 76079

Porter Equipment Co.
9555 Irving Pard Road
Shiller Park, Illinois 60176

Portland Stove Foundry
57 Kennebec Street
Portland, Maine 04104

Powers & Co.
31st and Jefferson Streets
Philadelphia, Pennsylvania 19121

Precise Imports Corp.
3 Chestnut Street
Suffern, New York 10901

Premier Products
Rivervale Road & Prospect
River Vale, New Jersey 07675

Prepac, Inc.
188 W. 230th Street
Bronx, New York 10463

Priess Mfg. Co.
2029 Sheridan Avenue S.
Minneapolis, Minnesota 55404

Primus
1462 U.S. Route 20 Bypass
Cherry Valley, Illinois 61016

Progressive Dynamics, Inc.
507 Industry Road
Marshall, Michigan 49068

Promark
6640 W. Touhy Avenue
Chicago, Illinois 60648

Pueblo Tent & Awning Co., Inc.
106 W. First Street
Pueblo, Colorado 81003

Pure Water Associates
582 Pioneer Road
Waterloo, Iowa 50704

Q-Beam Corp.
4109 College Main
Bryan, Texas 77801

QP-Pants
3300 Atlantic Boulevard
Jacksonville, Florida 32207

Quabaug Rubber Co.
P.O. Box 155G
N. Brookfield, Massachusetts 01535

Quail Creek Industries, Inc.
511-515 Madison
Fredonia, Kansas 66736

Queen Cutlery Co.
P.O. Box 500
Franklinville, New York 14737

Quickick, Inc.
P.O. Box 4006
Baton Rouge, Louisiana 70821

Quoddy Moccasins
67 Minot Avenue
Auburn, Maine 04210

Raichle Molitor USA, Inc.
200 Saw Mill River Road
Hawthorne, New York 10532

Randall Made Knives
4857 S. Orange Blossom Terrace
Orlando, Florida 32802

Raven Industries, Inc.
205 E. 6th Street
Sioux Falls, South Dakota 57101

Ravenna Industries, Inc.
West Highway 2
Ravenna, Nebraska 68869

Ray-O-Vac
6414 Schroeder Road
Madison, Wisconsin 53711

Razorback Trailer Mfg., Inc.
2085 New Benton Highway
Little Rock, Arkansas 72209

Read & Emmerich, Inc.
110 W. 40th Street
New York, New York 10018

Rebal Camper, Inc.
RR 4
LaGrange, Indiana 46761

Rebel Mfg.
428 McKean Avenue
Donora, Pennsylvania 15033

Reco Recreation Equipment of Pennsylvania
P.O. Box 1722
York, Pennsylvania 17405

Recreational Equipment, Inc.
1525-11th Avenue
Seattle, Washington 98130

Recreational Products Marketing, Inc.
P.O. Box 7936
Waco, Texas 76710

Red Dale Coach
15 S. Bowen Street
Longmont, Colorado 80501

Red Head Brand Corp.
4949 Joseph Hardin Drive
Dallas, Texas 75236

Red Wing Shoe Co.
Red Wing, Minnesota 55066

Red-E-Kamp, Inc.
Mira Loma Space Center 811A
Mira Loma, California 91752

Redi-Enterprises
P.O. Box 3307
San Bernardino, California 92404

Reliance Products, Ltd.
1830 Dublin Avenue
Winnipeg, Manitoba R3H 0H3
Canada

Retco (see Rettinger Import Co.)

Rettinger Import Co.
70 Caven Point Avenue
Jersey City, New Jersey 07305

Reyco Reynes Products, Inc.
P.O. Box 1203
Sonoma, California 95476

Reynolds Precision Prod., Inc.
27 Pierce Avenue
W. Carrollton, Ohio 45449

Rich-Moor Corp.
P.O. Box 2728
Van Nuys, California 91404

Riggle Mfg. Co.
Route 1
Chilicothe, Montana 64601

Rigid Form, Inc.
121 S. Kallock
Richmond, Kansas 66080

Rigid Knives
9919 Prospect Avenue
Santa Fe, California 92071

Rivendell Mountain Works
P.O. Box 198
Victor, Idaho 83455

Rivers & Gilman Products, Inc.
Main Street
Hampden, Maine 04444

Robin & Sons, Inc., M.
555 Broadway
New York, New York 10003

Robin Hood Archery, Inc.
215 Glenridge Avenue
Montclair, New Jersey 07042

Rockford Textile Mills, Inc.
200 Mulberry Street
McMinnville, Tennessee 37110

Rockwood, Inc.
P.O. Box 299
Millersburg, Indiana 46543

Rod Lavers Action Insoles
26711 Nowestern Highway, Suite 519
Southfield, Minnesota 48076

Roloff Mfg. Corp.
400 Gertrude Street
Kaukauna, Wisconsin 54130

Rome Industries, Inc.
1703 W. Detweiller Drive
Peoria, Illinois 61614

Rosenthal Co.
220 E. 5th Street
St. Paul, Minnesota 55101

Rothenberg & Son, Inc.
2929 Atlantic Avenue
Brooklyn, New York 11207

Royal Red Ball
8530 Page Avenue
St. Louis, Missouri 63114

Ru-ko of Canda, Ltd.
Flagler Street
Miami, Florida 33101

RV, Group One
P.O. Box 7664
St. Paul, Minnesota 55119

Safariland Leather Products
1941 S. Walker Avenue
Monrovia, California 91016

Safesport Mfg. Co.
1810 Stout Street
Denver, Colorado 80202

Sai Sports Accessories, Inc.
8850 Monard Drive
Silver Spring, Maryland 20910

St. Bernice Mfg. Co.
600 W. Jackson Boulevard
Chicago, Illinois 60606

Sani-Craft Chemical Corp.
969 Magellan Drive
Sarasota, Florida 33580

Saranac Glove Co.
1263 Main Street
Green Bay, Wisconsin 54305

Saska Sports Industries
185 Valley Drive
Brisbane, California 94005

Saunier Co.
3216 5th Avenue
Pittsburgh, Pennsylvania 15213

Schlesingers for Tools, Inc.
1257 Utica Avenue
Brooklyn, New York 11203

Schoellkopf Products, Inc.
4949 Joseph Hardin Drive
Dallas, Texas 75236

Schrade Cutlery Corp.
30 Canal Street
Ellenville, New York 12428

Schreck Wholesale, Inc.
3110 N. Lincoln
Chicago, Illinois 60657

Schwarz Ski Imports, H. G.
3001 Red Hill Avenue
Costa Mesa, California 92626

Scotch Game Call Co., Inc.
60 Main Street
Oakfield, New York 14125

Scott Mfg.
3159 W. 68th Street
Cleveland, Ohio 44102

Scott Port-A-Fold, Inc.
701 Middle Street
Archbold, Ohio 43502

Seattle Tent & Fabric Products
900 North 137th
Seattle, Washington 98133

Seaway Importing Co.
7200 N. Oak Park Avenue
Niles, Illinois 60648

Sebring Forest Industries, Inc.
465 W. California Avenue
Sebring, Ohio 44672

Seidel & Son, Inc., Adolph
2323 Pratt Boulevard
Elk Grove Village, Illinois 60007

Sevylor USA, Inc.
6079 E. Slauson Avenue
Los Angeles, California 90040

Sewing Factory
13311 Beach Avenue
Marina Del Ray, California 90291

SGL Batteries Mfg. Co.
14650 Dequindre
Detroit, Michigan 48212

Shaw & Sons, M.G.
P.O. Box 31428
Los Angeles, California 90031

Shelton, Inc. of Bruce Mississippi
Route 2
Bruce, Mississippi 38915

Shepherd Products U.S., Inc.
203 Kerth Street
St. Joseph, Michigan 49085

Sherpa Design, Inc.
3109 Brookdale Road E.
Tacoma, Washington 98446

Sherwood Camping Trailers, A.
2000 Camfield Avenue
Los Angeles, California 90022

Shields RV Mfg., Inc.
1344 Norma Lane
Loveland, Ohio 45140

Shir, Inc., Benjamin
179 Lincoln Street
Boston, Massachusetts 02111

Sierra Designs
247 Fourth Street
Oakland, California 94607

Silton Bros., Inc.
3535 S. Broadway
Los Angeles, California 90007

Silva Co.
2466 N. State Road 39
La Porte, Indiana 46350

Silver-Top Mfg. Co., Inc.
Pulaski Highway
White Marsh, Maryland 21162

Simmons Gun Specialties
700 Rogers Road
Olathe, Kansas 66061

Sipes Co., Howe
249 E. Mallory Avenue
Memphis, Tennessee 38109

Ski Enterprises Sportech
100 Front Street
Keeseville, New York 12944

Ski Hut ,The
1615 University Avenue
Berkeley, California 94703

Slade's Hunting World, Glenn
3450 Gulf Freeway
Houston, Texas 77004

Slumberjack, Inc.
2103 Humboldt Street
Los Angeles, California 90031

Smilie Company,The
575 Howard Street
San Francisco, California 94105

Smith & Wesson
2100 Roosevelt Avenue
Springfield, Massachusetts 01101

Smith-Built Campers & Canopies, Inc.
14606 Pacific Avenue
Tacoma, Washington 98444

Smith-Worthington Saddlery
287 Homestead Avenue
Hartford, Connecticut 06112

Smoker Products, Inc.
649 Ft. Worth Avenue
Dallas, Texas 75208

Snow Lion Corp.
2611 8th Street
Berkeley, California 94710

Snowshoe Laboratories
P.O. Box 1022
Portland, Oregon 97207

Snowy Mt. Recreational Products
Airport Industrial Site
Lewistown, Montana 59457

Solari Sports Products
27992 Camino Capistrano
Laguna Beach, California 92677

Southern Trading Co.
P.O. Box 55326
Houston, Texas 77055

Southington Tool & Mfg. Co.
P.O. Box 595
Southington, Connecticut 06489

Southwest Quilt and Pad
P.O. Box 889
Midlothian, Texas 76065

Speaker Corp., J.W.
3059 North Weil Street
Milwaukee, Wisconsin 53212

Specialty Food Supply Co.
P.O. Box 391
Conneautville, Pennsylvania 16406

Speedy Chef Foods, Inc.
P.O. Box 1236
Lancaster, Pennsylvania 17604

Spenco Medical Corp.
6301 Imperial Drive
Waco, Texas 76710

Sport Chalet ,The
951 Foothill Boulevard
La Canada, California 91011

Sportana Industries, Inc.
116 Toledo Street
Farmingdale, New York 11735

Sportcaster Co., Inc.
Pioneer Square Station
Seattle, Washington 98104

Sportcraft Mfg.
4160 Foley
Waterford, Michigan 48095

Sportline
3300 W. Franklin Boulevard
Chicago, Illinois 60624

Sport-Obermeyer Ltd.
P.O. Box 130
Aspen, Colorado 81611

Sportowel & Sport Transfers
901 N. 27th Street
Milwaukee, Wisconsin 53208

Sports Equipment, Inc.
P.O. Box T
Mantua, Ohio 44255

Sports Leisure Products Co.
P.O. Box 5491
St. Louis, Missouri 63160

Sportshelf
P.O. Box 634
New Rochelle, New York 10802

Sportsmaster, Inc.
1355 Market Street
San Francisco, California 94103

Springbar
(see Kirkham's AAA Tent & Awning Co.)

Springer Company, Inc.
2101 W. Burbank Boulevard
Burbank, California 91506

Sprouter Mfg., Inc.
222 Sprouter Drive
Hearne, Texas 77859

Stag
(see Hirsch-Weis)

Star Line Trailer Co.
82 Torque Way
Baltimore, Maryland 21220

Starcraft Co.
2703 College Avenue
Goshen, Indiana 46526

Starter Sportswear
308 Morse Street
Hamden, Connecticut 06517

Stearns Mfg. Co.
P.O. Box 1498
St. Cloud, Minnesota 56301

Stebco Industries, Inc.
1020 W. 40th Street
Chicago, Illinois 60609

Stephenson's
23206 Hatteras Street
Woodland Hills, California 91364

Sterl Dri Corp.
P.O. Box 164
Saxonville, Massachusetts 01701

Stern Hats & Sportswear Corp.
197 Market Street
Lowell, Massachusetts 01852

Sterner Mfg. Co., Inc.
P.O. Box 242
Rancocas, New Hampshire 08073

Sterno, Inc.
300 Park Avenue
New York, New York 10022

Steury
310 Steury Avenue
Goshen, Indiana 46526

Stewarts Mfg.
6601 S. State Street
Salt Lake City, Utah 84107

Stith Mounts
P.O. Box 2427
San Antonio, Texas 78298

Stones Campers
RR 3
Arkansas City, Kansas 67005

Stor-a-Pack—Kamp Pack
(see Bernard Food Industries, Inc.)

Storm, Ltd., Peter
Smith Street
Norwalk, Connecticut 06851

Stow-A-Way Sports, Ind.
166 Cushing Highway (Route 3A)
Cohasset, Massachusetts 02025

Strawsine Mfg. Co.
502 S. Shiawassee
Coronna, Michigan 48817

Strohmeier Co., R.J.
P.O. Box 867
Castle Rock, Colorado 80104

Sturges Mfg. Co., Inc.
2030 Sunset Avenue
Utica, New York 13502

Subi-Sales Co.
5049 Crookshaut Road
Cincinnati, Ohio 45738

Sunline Coach Co., Inc.
RD 1, S. Muddy Creek Road
Denver, Pennsylvania 17517

Sunshine Cover & Tarp, Inc.
6863 Beck Avenue
N. Hollywood, California 91605

Sunshine International
1151 Belmont Avenue
Long Beach, California 90804

Supplier Services
1100 E. Hively Avenue
Elkhart, Indiana 46514

Survival Research Laboratories
17 Marland Road
Colorado Springs, Colorado 80906

Survival Systems, Inc.
1830 S. Baker Avenue
Ontario, California 91761

Swen Products
716 Vermilion Road
Duluth, Minnesota 55803

Swing-A-Way Mfg. Co.
4100 Beck Avenue
St. Louis, Missouri 63116

Swiss Colony
3023 Holiday Place
Elkhart, Indiana 46514

Swiss Ski Imports
559 Clay Street
San Francisco, California 94111

Tanfur
334 Broadway
Sheboygan Falls, Wisconsin 53085

Tarashinsky Merchandise Co.
256 Manhattan Avenue
Brooklyn, New York 11211

Taylor Instrument Co.
Arden, North Carolina 28704

Tejas Mfg. & Supply, Inc.
5025 College
Beaumont, Texas 77707

Tekonsha Engineering Co.
537 N. Church Street
Tekonsha, Michigan 49092

Telescope Folding Furniture Co., Inc.
Church Street
Granville, New York 12832

Tempco Quilters
414 First Avenue S.
Seattle, Washington 98104

10-X Mfg. Co.
P.O. Box 3408
Boulder, Colorado 80303

Terraqua, Inc.
1528 S. Centre Avenue
San Pedro, California 90731

Testworth Laboratories, Inc.
139 Commercial Road
Addison, Illinois 60101

Therm X Corp.
1280 Columbus Avenue
San Francisco, California 94133

Thermo-Chem Corp.
10516 E. Pine
Tulsa, Oklahoma 74116

Thetford Corp.
2300 Washtenaw
Ann Arbor, Michigan 48104

Thompson Co., Inc., E.A.
1333 Gough Street
San Francisco, California 94109

Thompson Service Co.
P.O. Box 657
Belleview, Florida 32620

Tho-Ro-Products, Inc.
335 Paterson Plank Road
Carlstadt, New Jersey 07072

Thoroughbred Kampers, Inc.
US 31 E.
Hardyville, Kentucky 42746

Timberland Footwear, Inc.
P.O. Box 370
Newmarket, New Hampshire 03857

Timberline Design, Ltd.
P.O. Box 183
Colorado Springs, Colorado 80901

Timely Products Corp.
210 Eliot Street
Fairfield, Connecticut 06611

Tip Top Toppers
1220 S.W. 12th Avenue
Pompano, Florida 33060

Todd Enterprises
530 Wellington Avenue
Cranston, Rhode Island 02910

Toledo Tent Co.
300 Fassett
Toledo, Ohio 43605

Toppertown, Inc.
1208 Clearlake Road
Cocoa, Florida 32922

Tote & Chair Products Co.
570 N. Franklin Street
Hanover, Pennsylvania 17331

Trail Tech
108-02 Otis Avenue
Corona, New York 11368

Trailblazer, Inc.
2971 South Madison
Wichita, Kansas 67216

Trailcraft, Inc.
P.O. Box 606
Concordia, Kansas 66901

Trailwise Mfg. Co.
2407 4th Street
Berkeley, California 94710

Trak, Inc.
Shawsheen Village Station
Andover, Massachusetts 01810

Transcanada Camping Supply, C.
1010 Logan Avenue
Winnipeg, Manitoba R3E 1P2
Canada

Transit Industries, Inc.
Airport Industrial Park
Pratt, Kansas 67124

Travel Equipment Corp.
64686 US 33
Goshen, Indiana 46526

Travelier Industries, Inc.
P.O. Box 9036
Greenville, South Carolina 29604

Trio Sporting Goods Mfg. Co.
1621-29 Carroll Avenue
Chicago, Illinois 60612

Trotwood Corp.
11 N. Broadway
Trotwood, Ohio 45426

Tru Trailer Mfg. Co.
RFD 2
Stonington, Connecticut 06378

True Temper Corp.
1623 Euclid Avenue
Cleveland, Ohio 44115

Tru-Nord
204 No. 9th Street
Brainerd, Minnesota 56401

Tuf-Wear
16th & Hickory
Sidney, Nebraska 69162

Turner Division Conrac Corp.
716 Oakland Road N.E.
Cedar Rapids, Iowa 52402

Tyrol Shoe Co., Ltd.
8535 Delmeade Road
Montreal, Quebec H4T 1M2
Canada

Udisco
2700 S. 900 W.
Salt Lake City, Utah 84119

Ultimate Experience
769 Cheham
Santa Barbara, California 93120

Unarco Industries/Unarco-Rohn
P.O. Box 2000
Peoria, Illinois 61601

Union Carbide
270 Park Avenue
New York, New York 10017

Union Mfg. Co.
290 Pratt Street
Meriden, Connecticut 06450

Union Mfg., Inc.
400 W. Allison
Chandler, Arizona 85224

Uniroyal, Inc.
1230 Avenue of the Americas
New York, New York 10020

United Cutlery & Hardware Products
108 E. 16th Street
New York, New York 10003

United Textile & Supply Co.
759-61 N. Spring Street
Los Angeles, California 90012

Universal Coach Co.
P.O. Box 612
Greensburg, Pennsylvania 15601

Universal Field Equipment
Mira Loma Space Center
Mira Loma, California 91752

Upland Enterprises, Inc.
426 Mt. Auburn Street
Cambridge, Massachusetts 02138

Upson Tools, Inc.
99 Ling Rd.
Rochester, New York 14612

US Sporting Goods, Inc.
P.O. Box 58321
Dallas, Texas 75207

Utica Duxbak Corp.
815 Noyes Street
Utica, New York 13502

Valor Corp. of Florida
5555 NW 36th Avenue
Miami, Florida 33142

Vanguard Industries, Inc.
M-86 West
Colon, Michigan 49040

Vasque
2460 South 3270 West
Salt Lake City, Utah 84125

Vaughan & Bushnell Mfg. Co.
P.O. Box 367
Hebron, Illinois 60034

Velsco, Inc.
180 Berry Street
Brooklyn, New York 11211

Venture IV Corp.
3215 Commercial Avenue
Northbrook, Illinois 60062

Vesely Co.
2101 N. Lapeer Road
Lapeer, Michigan 48446

Viking Recreation Vehicles
P.O. Box 488
Centreville, Michigan 49032

VSI Recreation Products
1410 E. Walnut Street
Fullerton, California 92631

Walker International
1901 W. Lafayette Boulevard
Detroit, Michigan 48216

Walker Mfg. Co.
206 Commercial Street
Emporia, Kansas 66801

Walker Shoe Co.
East Dixie Drive
Asheboro, North Carolina 27203

Walking News
P.O. Box 352
New York, New York 10013

Wallace Rainbow
31 & Jefferson Street
Philadelphia, Pennsylvania 19121

Walls Industries
P.O. Box 98
Cleburne, Texas 76031

Warnaco Group, The
5203 E. Johnson Creek Boulevard
Portland, Oregon 97206

Warp Bros.
1100 N. Cicero Avenue
Chicago, Illinois 60651

Water Pollution Control Systems, Inc.
6350 LBJ Freeway, Suite 122
Dallas, Texas 75240

Watrous & Co., Inc.
110 E. 23 Street
New York, New York 10010

Watt Campers
709 W. Old Route 422
Butler, Pennsylvania 16001

Wayne Mfg. Co., Inc.
Route 2, Monton Switch Road
Lafayette, Louisiana 70501

Weinbrenner Shoe Corp.
Polk Street
Merrill, Wisconsin 54452

Weiss Co., David S.
6404 S.W. Macadam Avenue
Portland, Oregon 97201

Wenzel Co.
1280 Research Boulevard
St. Louis, Missouri 63132

West Ridge Designs
305 NW 12th Avenue
Portland, Oregon 97209

West-Brook Camper Mfg., Inc.
15407 S. Broadway
Gardena, California 90248

Western Cutlery Co.
5311 Western Avenue
Boulder, Colorado 80302

Western Purifier Co.
4662 Lankershim Boulevard
N. Hollywood, California 91602

Western Trails, Inc.
61331 S. Highway 97
Bend, Oregon 97701

White Automotive Corp.
P.O. Box 1209
Colorado Springs, Colorado 80901

White Line Mfg.
P.O. Box 190
Bowden, Alberta T0M 0K0
Canada

Whiting Co., H.L.
230 W. Avenue 26
Los Angeles, California 90031

Wichita Canvas Supply, Inc.
2937 S. Kansas
Wichita, Kansas 67216

Wigwam Mills ,Inc.
3402 Crocker Avenue
Sheboygan, Wisconsin 53081

Wilderness Experience
9421 Winnetka Avenue
Chatsworth, California 91311

Willett Co., Inc., Tex
3964 W. Airline Highway
Waterloo, Iowa 50701

Wilson Travel Homes, Inc.
201 N. 3rd Street
Womelsdorf, Pennsylvania 19567

Windcutter Co.
1312 Maple
W. Des Moines, Iowa 50265

Winnebago Industries, Inc.
Junction Highways 9 & 69
Forest City, Iowa 50436

Wisconsin Aluminum Foundry
16th & Franklin Streets
Manitowoc, Wisconsin 54220

Wisconsin Mobile Homes, Inc.
4201 E. Washington Avenue
Madison, Wisconsin 53704

Wisconsin Shoe Co.
1039 S. 2nd Street
Milwaukee, Wisconsin 53204

Wiss & Sons Co., J.
400 W. Market Street
Newark, New Jersey 07107

Wolverine World Wide, Inc.
9341 Courtland Drive N.E.
Rockford, Michigan 49351

Wonder Corp. of America
24 Harborview Avenue
Stamford, Connecticut 06904

Wood Designs, Inc.
Port Trevorton, Pennsylvania 17864

Woods Bag & Canvas Co., Ltd.
90 River Street
Ogdensburg, New York 13669

Woodstream Corp.
Lititz, Pennsylvania 17543

Woolrich, Inc.
Woolrich, Pennsylvania 17779

World Famous Sales Co.
3580 N. Elston Avenue
Chicago, Illinois 60618

Wyoming Knife Corp.
115 Valley Drive
Casper, Wyoming 82601

Xantech Corp.
13038 Satkoy Street
N. Hollywood, California 91605

Yellowstone, Inc.
2400 Mishawaka Road
Elkhart, Indiana 46514

York Cutlery Co., Inc.
286-288 W. Market Street
York, Pennsylvania 17401

Yorkshire, Ltd.
Box 102
Harwinton, Connecticut 06790

Yorkville, Inc.
Ciro Road
N. Branford, Connecticut 06471

Yukon-Delta, Inc.
55241 Jay Dee Street
Elkhart, Indiana 46514

Zimmer Products, Inc.
Lower Maple Avenue
Elmira, New York 14901

ZZ Corp.
521 N. La Cienega, Suite 210
Los Angeles, California 90048

Specifications: Equipment

Boots

Manufacturer: L. L. Bean
Model No.: 3151C Maine Hunting
Height: 12″
Size: Men's, 3 to 14
Closure: Eyelets
Features: Water-resistant cowhide uppers; waterproof rubber bottoms; cushioned innersoles; split backstays.

Manufacturer: L. L. Bean
Model No.: 3175C Vibram Soled Hunting
Height: 9″
Size: 7 to 13
Closure: Eyelets
Features: Water-resistant leather uppers; waterproof rubber bottoms; Vibram lug outersoles and heels; scree collars.

Manufacturer: L. L. Bean
Model No.: 3192C Insulated Hunting
Height: 10″
Size: 3 to 14
Weight: 4 lbs. 2 oz.
Closure: Eyelets
Features: Water-resistant cowhide uppers; waterproof rubber bottoms; foam-lined bottoms; foam innersoles.

Manufacturer: L. L. Bean
Model No.: 3311C Maine Guide
Height: 6″
Size: Men's, 6½ to 13
Weight: 2 lbs. 12 oz.
Closure: Eyelets
Features: Oil-tanned uppers; arch-supporting steel shanks; heel counters; lug treads.

L. L. Bean Model No. 3329C

Manufacturer: L. L. Bean
Model No.: 3329C Katahdin
Height: 6″
Size: Men's, 7 to 13
Weight: 3 lbs.
Closure: Hooks, eyelets
Features: Weather resistant; padded and leather lined; arch-supporting steel shanks; Vibram lug outersoles and heels; scree collars.

Manufacturer: L. L. Bean
Model No.: 3332C Bass Climbing
Height: 6½″
Size: Men's, 7 to 13
Weight: 3 lbs.
Closure: Eyelets, hooks
Features: Water-repellent uppers; leather lined; arch-supporting steel shanks; Vibram Rocciabloc outersoles and heels; hinged heels.

Manufacturer: L. L. Bean
Model No.: 3335C Field Trial
Height: 8″

Size: Men's, 6½ to 13
Weight: 2 lbs. 6 oz.
Closure: Eyelets
Features: Oil-treated uppers; leather-lined vamp; arch-supporting soles; heel counters; crepe outersoles and heels.

L. L. Bean Model No. 3338C

Manufacturer: L. L. Bean
Model No.: 3338C Ruff Out Chukka
Size: Men's, 7 to 13
Weight: 3 lbs.
Closure: Eyelets
Features: Water-repellent uppers; arch-supporting steel shanks; padded insoles; Vibram Rocciabloc lug outersoles and heels; scree collars.

Manufacturer: L. L. Bean
Model No.: 3341C Hiking
Size: Men's, 6 to 13
Weight: 3 lbs.
Closure: Eyelets, hooks
Features: Oil-tanned uppers; arch-supporting steel shanks; leather innersoles; double-panelled lower half; Vibram Montagna lug outersoles and heels; scree collars; lace-to-toe.

Manufacturer: L. L. Bean
Model No.: 3376C Herman Survivors
Height: 9″
Size: Men's, 7 to 13
Weight: 4 lbs. 14 oz.
Closure: Hooks, eyelets
Features: Weather-resistant uppers; foam insulated and leather lined; arch-supporting steel shank; leather-wrapped, cushioned innersoles; Vibram Montagna Bloc outersoles and heels.

L. L. Bean Model No. 3376C

Manufacturer: L. L. Bean
Model No.: 3633C Camp
Height: 5½″
Size: Men's, 3 to 13
Features: Fleece lined; cowhide outersoles and rubber heels with counters; sheepskin innersoles.

Manufacturer: Browning
Model No.: 2740 Ridge Roamer II
Height: 6″
Size: Men's, 7 to 14
Closure: "D" rings, hooks
Features: Hand-oiled leather; leather-lined; cleated Vibram soles; steel shanks; padded tongues, ankles and collars.

Manufacturer: Browning
Model No.: 2940 Mountain Vibram
Height: 9″
Size: Men's, 7 to 14
Closure: "D" rings, hooks, eyelets
Features: Hand-oiled uppers; double-layered bottoms; cushioned leather innersoles; steel shanks; cleated Vibram outersoles; lace-to-toe; padded scree collars.

Manufacturer: Browning
Model No.: 3540 Men's Featherweight
Height: 9″
Size: Men's, 7 to 14
Closure: Eyelets
Features: Water repellent; leather lined; cushioned leather innersoles; steel shanks; crepe outersoles.

Manufacturer: Browning
Model No.: 4640 Chukka
Height: 4″
Size: Men's, 7 to 14
Closure: Eyelets
Features: Water repellent; leather lined; cushioned leather innersoles and ankle tops; steel shanks; crepe outersoles.

Manufacturer: Browning
Model No.: 7940 Waterproof
Height: 9″
Size: Men's, 7 to 14
Closure: "D" rings, hooks
Features: Waterproof; insulated and leather lined; cushioned innersoles; crepe lug outersoles.

Manufacturer: Danner
Model No: 775
Height: 8″
Size: Men's, 6 to 13
Weight: 4½ lbs.
Closure: Eyelets, hooks
Features: Oil-tanned uppers; Vibram Montagna lug; outersoles and heels; lace-to-toe.

Manufacturer: Danner
Model No.: 6490
Size: Men's, 5 to 14
Weight: 4¼ lbs.
Closure: "D" rings, hooks
Features: Waterproof uppers; leather lined; Montagna lug outersoles and heels.

Manufacturer: Danner
Model No.: 6920
Size: Men's, 5 to 13
Weight: 4½ lbs.
Closure: Eyelets, hooks
Features: Waterproof uppers; leather innersoles; steel shanks; logger counters; crepe outersoles and heels.

Manufacturer: Danner
Model No.: 6960
Size: Men's, 6 to 14
Weight: 5¼ lbs.
Closure: Eyelets, hooks
Features: Waterproof uppers; foam insulated; leather lined.

Danner Model No. 7204

Manufacturer: Danner
Model No.: 7204
Size: Men's, 7 to 13
Weight: 3 lbs.
Closure: Hooks
Features: Waterproof uppers; Vibram Depose Montagna Bloc outersoles and heels; scree collars.

Manufacturer: Danner
Model No.: 7269
Size: Men's, 6 to 14
Weight: 4½ lbs.
Closure: Eyelets, hooks
Features: Leather lined; Vibram Depose Montagna Bloc lug outersoles; lace-to-toe.

Manufacturer: Danner
Model No.: 7509
Size: Men's, 7 to 13
Weight: 6½ lbs.
Closure: "D" rings, hooks
Features: Hinged quarters; leather innersoles; tendon pads; Vibram Montagna Brevettata outersoles; scree collars.

Manufacturer: Dunham
Model No.: 6000
Size: Men's, 6 to 14
Closure: "D" rings, hook
Features: Leather lined; Security Montagna Vibram outersoles; scree collars; heel guards.

Manufacturer: Dunham
Model No.: 6005
Height: 8"
Size: Men's, 6 to 13
Closure: Tunnel and open hooks
Features: Leather lined; Security Roccia Vibram outersoles; heel guards.

Manufacturer: Dunham
Model No.: 6036
Size: Men's, 6 to 13
Closure: "D" rings, hooks
Features: Leather lined; forward-hinged uppers; Security Montagna Vibram outersoles; scree collars.

Manufacturer: Dunham
Model No.: 6042
Size: Men's, 6 to 13
Closure: Tunnel and open hooks
Features: Oiled, forward-hinged uppers; leather lined; Security Montagna Vibram outersoles; scree collars.

Manufacturer: Dunham
Model No.: 6075
Size: Men's, 6 to 13
Closure: Tunnel hooks
Features: Leather lined; Security Montagna Vibram outersoles; scree collars; heel guards.

Manufacturer: Dunham
Model No.: 7383 Mocc-Stomper
Height: 6"
Size: Men's, 6 to 13
Closure: Eyelets
Features: Lug outersoles.

Manufacturer: Dunham
Model No.: 7603
Height: 6"
Size: Men's, 6 to 13
Closure: Eyelets
Features: Waterproof; insulated and leather lined; cushioned innersoles.

Manufacturer: Dunham
Model No.: 7609 Duraflex
Height: 8"
Size: Men's, 6 to 13
Closure: Eyelets
Features: Waterproof; insulated and leather lined; cushioned innersoles.

Manufacturer: Fabiano
Model No.: 63 Lisa
Size: Men's, 4 to 15
Weight: 5 lbs.
Closure: Hooks, eyelets
Features: Oil-tanned uppers; leather lined; padded ankles; scree collars.

Fabiano Model No. 90

Manufacturer: Fabiano
Model No.: 90 Il Madre F.
Size: Men's, 4 to 15
Closure: Eyelets
Features: Scuff-resistant toe guards.

Manufacturer: Fabiano
Model No.: 179 Di-Di Forest Rangers Climbing
Height: 9"
Size: Men's, 4 to 14
Weight: 4 lbs.
Closure: Hooks, eyelets
Features: Oil-tanned uppers with hinged backs; insulated; cushioned innersoles; counters; box toe.

Fabiano Model No. 179

Fabiano Model No. 366

Manufacturer: Fabiano
Model No.: 366 A.E.F. Wax-Hide
Size: Men's, 4 to 15
Weight: 3½ lbs.
Closure: Hooks, "D" rings
Features: Oil-tanned uppers; waterproof bellows tongue; leather lined; padded ankles and scree collars; anti-stretch tapes.

Manufacturer: Fabiano
Model No.: 772 Mountain Master
Size: Men's, 4½ to 14
Weight: 6¾ lbs.
Closure: "D" rings, hooks
Features: Leather lined; steel shanks; hinged backs; scree collars.

Manufacturer: Herman
Model No.: 1-103 Waterproof Survivor
Height: 8"
Size: Men's, 6 to 14
Closure: Tunnel hooks, eyelets
Features: Waterproof; insulated and leather lined; cushioned innersoles; Vibram outersoles and heels.

SPECIFICATIONS: EQUIPMENT

Herman Model No. 7124

Manufacturer: Herman
Model No.: 4615 Hiker
Height: 6½"
Size: Men's, 6 to 14
Closure: "D" rings, hooks
Features: Leather lined; cushioned inner-soles; padded gussets; scree collars; Vibram outersoles and heels.

Manufacturer: Herman
Model No.: 7124 Craftsmen
Height: 8"
Size: Men's, 6 to 14
Closure: Eyelets
Features: Cushioned innersoles; crepe outer-soles and heels.

Manufacturer: Irving/Weather-Rite
Model No.: 2015
Size: 6 to 12
Closure: Ties
Features: Insulated; lined with fleece boa.

Manufacturer: Irving/Weather-Rite
Model No.: 2036
Size: 6 to 13
Closure: Zipper
Features: Nylon uppers.

Manufacturer: Irving/Weather-Rite
Model No.: 2038
Size: 5 to 10
Closure: Zipper
Features: Nylon uppers.

Manufacturer: Irving/Weather-Rite
Model No.: 4039
Size: 6 to 12
Closure: Zipper
Features: Insulated; cleated; cushioned soles.

Manufacturer: Kelty
Model: Down
Size: Men's, 4 to 13+
Weight: 9 oz.
Closure: Drawstring
Features: Down filled; insulated innersoles and outersoles.

Manufacturer: Komito
Model: Pivetta
Size: Men's, 4 to 13
Closure: Hooks, "D" rings
Features: Vibram Montagna outersoles; padded tongues.

Manufacturer: Komito
Model: Vercors
Size: Men's, 2 to 13
Closure: "D" rings, hooks
Features: Vibram Montagna outersoles; padded tongues.

Manufacturer: Margesson's
Model: Cascade (Raíchle)
Size: Men's, 7 to 13; women's 5 to 9½
Closure: "D" rings, hooks
Features: Leather lined; foam padded; steel shanks; Vibram Montagna outersoles; scree collars.

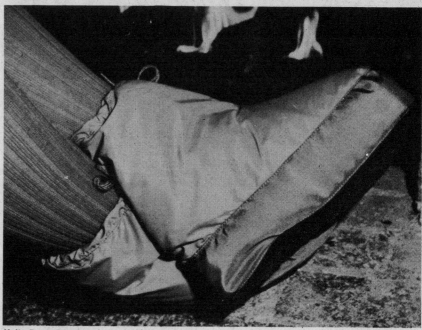

Kelty Down Boot

Manufacturer: Margesson's
Model: Cascade (Vasque)
Size: Men's, 6½ to 13; women's, 5 to 10
Closure: Hooks, eyelets
Features: Waxed uppers; cellulose innersoles; leather-lined quarter; steel shanks; Vibram lug outersoles and heels; scree collars.

Manufacturer: Margesson's
Model: Yosemite (Raíchle)
Size: Men's, 7 to 13; women's, 5 to 9½
Closure: Hooks, eyelets
Features: Greased uppers; leather lined; foam padded; leather innersoles; steel shanks; Vibram Montagna outersoles.

Manufacturer: Moor & Mountain
Model No.: 616 Light Mountain
Size: Men's, 4 to 14
Closure: Hooks, eyelets
Features: Oil-tanned uppers; leather lined; Roccia-Block lug outersoles and heels; steel shanks; padded scree collars.

Manufacturer: Moor & Mountain
Model No.: 617 Insulated
Height: 12"
Size: Men's, 6 to 14
Closure: Hooks
Features: Insulated; Vibram lug outersoles; steel-supported arches.

Manufacturer: Moor & Mountain
Model No.: 657 Trail
Size: Men's, 4 to 14
Closure: Hooks, eyelets
Features: Water-repellent uppers; lug outer-soles; toe caps.

Manufacturer: North Face
Model: Down Booties
Size: Men's, 4 to 13
Features: Down filled; ensolite soles; rip-stop tops; pack cloth bottoms.

Manufacturer: Retco
Model: Sno-Dri
Size: Men's, 7 to 13; boy's, 3 to 6; ladies', 5 to 10
Closure: Zipper
Features: Adjustable strap buckles; gripper soles and heels.

Manufacturer: Retco
Model: Snowblazer
Size: Men's, 7 to 13; boy's, 3 to 6; ladies', 5 to 10
Closure: Zipper, string
Features: Gripper soles; nylon and rubber bodies.

Manufacturer: Timberland
Model No.: 10061 Waterproof
Height: 6"
Size: Men's, 3½ to 13
Closure: Eyelets
Features: Waterproof; leather lined and in-sulated; cushioned leather innersoles; lug outersoles; scree collars.

Manufacturer: Timberland
Model No.: 10081 Waterproof
Height: 8"
Size: Men's, 3½ to 13
Closure: Eyelets
Features: Waterproof; leather lined and in-sulated; cushioned leather innersoles; lug outersoles.

Manufacturer: Timberland
Model No.: 15067 Waterproof
Height: 7"
Size: Men's, 7 to 13
Closure: "D" rings, hooks
Features: Waterproof; leather lined and in-sulated; cushioned leather innersoles; lug outersoles; scree collars; lace-to-toe.

Manufacturer: Timberland
Model No.: 35082 Outdoorsman
Height: 8"

Size: Men's, 7 to 13
Closure: Hooks, eyelet
Features: Leather lined; cushioned leather innersoles; padded collars.

Manufacturer: Timberland
Model No.: 40062 Hunter and Hiker
Height: 6″
Size: Men's, 4 to 13
Closure: "D" rings
Features: Leather lined; cushioned leather innersoles; lug outersoles; scree collars.

Vasque Model No. 6230

Manufacturer: Vasque
Model No.: 6230 Hiker II
Height: 6″
Size: Men's, 5 to 16
Closure: "D" rings, hooks
Features: Waxed uppers; leather-lined quarters; leather innersoles; steel shanks; Vibram Montagnabloc lug outersoles and heels; padded scree collars.

Manufacturer: Vasque
Model No.: 6240 Whitney II
Height: 6″
Size: Men's, 5 to 15
Closure: "D" rings, hooks
Features: Waxed uppers; leather-lined quarters; leather innersoles; steel shanks; Vibram Montagnabloc lug outersoles and heels; padded scree collars.

Vasque Model No. 6240

Vasque Model No. 7529

Manufacturer: Vasque
Model No.: 7529 Explorer
Height: 5″
Size: Men's, 6 to 14
Closure: Eyelets, hooks
Features: Waxed uppers; leather-lined quarters; cellulose innersoles; steel shanks; Vibram lug outersoles.

Manufacturer: Vasque
Model No.: 7535 Caribou
Size: Men's, 6 to 13
Closure: "D" rings, hooks
Features: Waxed uppers; cellulose innersoles; steel shanks; Vibram lug outersoles and heels.

Manufacturer: Wolverine
Model No.: 01001 Goodyear Welt
Height: 9″
Size: Men's, 6 to 13
Closure: Eyelets
Features: Water-resistant uppers; leather innersoles; steel shanks.

Manufacturer: Wolverine
Model No.: 01015 Cold Weather
Height: 9″
Size: Men's, 6 to 13
Closure: "D" rings, eyelets
Features: Water-resistant uppers; insulated; steel shanks; cushioned innersoles; Vibram outersoles and heels.

Manufacturer: Wolverine
Model No.: 02025 Wilderness
Size: Men's, 7 to 12
Closure: Hooks, eyelets
Features: Leather-lined; cushioned quarters; Vibram Security outersoles; padded gussets.

Manufacturer: Wolverine
Model No.: 03388
Height: 8″
Size: Men's, 6 to 13
Closure: Eyelets, hooks
Features: Water resistant; cushioned innersoles; Durables outersoles and heels; steel shanks.

Manufacturer: Wolverine
Model No.: 03392 Cold Weather
Height: 9″
Size: Men's, 7 to 13
Closure: Eyelets, hooks
Features: Leather lined and insulated; steel shanks; plio tuf Durables outersoles and heels; cushioned collars.

Manufacturer: Wolverine
Model No.: 03799
Height: 6″
Size: Men's, 6 to 14
Closure: Eyelets, hooks
Features: Water-resistant uppers; cushioned innersoles; steel shanks; Avon Perak outersoles and heels; drill vamp lined.

Clothing

Manufacturer: L. L. Bean
Model No.: 1349C
Type: Jacket
Size(s): S(36), M(38-40), L(42-44), XL(46-48)
Material: 85/15 wool-nylon
Weight: 2 lbs.
Color(s): Block plaid
No. of Pockets: 5
Closure: Zipper
Features: Cape over shoulders and chest.

L. L. Bean Model No. 1349C

Manufacturer: L. L. Bean
Model No.: 1398C
Type: Jacket
Size(s): S(34-36), M(38-40), L(42-44), XL(46-48), XXL(50-52)
Material: Rip-stop nylon outer shell; down filled
Weight: 20 oz.
Color(s): Dark blue, forest green
No. of Pockets: 2
Closure: Two-way zipper, snap storm flap
Features: Water repellent; drawstring at waist; down-filled collar.

Manufacturer: L. L. Bean
Model No.: 1412C Jac-shirt
Size(s): S, 37; M, 40; L, 43; XL, 46
Material: Rip-stop nylon outer shell; goose down filled
Weight: 18 oz.
Color(s): Navy, forest green, orange, beige
No. of Pockets: 2
Closure: Zipper
Features: Insulated collar.

Manufacturer: L. L. Bean
Model No.: 1415C
Type: Jacket
Size(s): S, 38; M, 41; L, 44; XL, 47; XXL, 50
Material: Nylon-cotton poplin; goose-down fill; nylon inner lining
Weight: 2 lbs. 10 oz.
Color(s): Tan, forest green, camouflage
No. of Pockets: 4
Closure: Zipper; button storm flap
Features: Drawstring waist; knit wrist bands.

Manufacturer: L. L. Bean
Model No.: 1439C
Type: Parka
Size(s): S, M, L, XL
Material: Polyester-cotton outer shell; poplin inner shell
Weight: 2 lbs.
Color(s): Olive reversible to white

No. of Pockets: 2
Closure: Zipper; drawstring
Features: Reversible; windproof; water repellent; elastic wrists.

Manufacturer: L. L. Bean
Model No.: 1641C
Type: Wilderness jac-shirt
Size(s): S, M, L, XL
Material: 85/15 virgin wool-nylon
Weight: 32 oz.
Color(s): Plaid
No. of Pockets: 4
Closure: Buttons
Features: Water resistant; shirt-style collar; button sleeves; side vents.

Manufacturer: Conquest
Model No.: 9001
Type: Vest
Size(s): XS, S, M, L, XL
Material: Down-proof rip-stop nylon, quilted to Polarguard
Color(s): Navy with tan lining
No. of Pockets: 2
Closure: Zipper
Features: All seams bound; machine washable and dryable.

Manufacturer: Conquest
Model No.: 9002
Type: Sweater
Size(s): XS, S, M, L, XL
Material: Down-proof rip-stop nylon, quilted to Polarguard
Color(s): Navy with tan lining
No. of Pockets: 2
Closure: Zipper
Features: Elastic wrist cuffs; all seams bound; machine washable and dryable.

L. L. Bean Model No. 1641C

Manufacturer: Conquest
Model No.: 9014
Type: Parka jacket
Size(s): XS, S, M, L, XL
Material: Down-proof rip-stop nylon, quilted to 2 layers of Polarguard
Color(s): Carbon brown with tan lining
No. of Pockets: 5
Closure: Zipper; snaps
Features: Drawcord waist; machine washable and dryable; elastic cuffs.

Manufacturer: Davco
Model No.: 234
Type: Jacket
Size(s): S, M, L, XL

Material: Water-repellent wool-blend outer shell insulated with Dacron polyester fiber fill; nylon quilted lining
Color(s): Red and black plaid
No. of Pockets: 5
Closure: Buttons
Features: Neoprene game pocket.

Manufacturer: Davco
Model No.: 267
Type: Jacket
Size(s): S, M, L, XL
Material: Wool blend
Color(s): Red and black plaid
No. of Pockets: 2
Closure: Buttons
Features: Rounded tails.

Manufacturer: Davco
Model No.: 484
Type: Jacket
Size(s): S, M, L, XL
Material: Nylon shell; Dacron insulation; acetate lining
Color(s): Gold, red, green, black
No. of Pockets: 2
Closure: Zipper
Features: Knit collar and wristlet.

Manufacturer: Davco
Model No.: 801
Type: Pants
Size(s): S, M, L, XL
Material: Cotton outer; acrylic insulation; acetate lining
Color(s): Red
No. of Pockets: 4
Closure: Zipper
Features: Knit anklets.

Manufacturer: Davco
Model No.: 900 Hunting Coat
Size(s): S, M, L, XL
Material: Cotton outer shell; acrylic insulation; acetate lining
Color(s): Red
No. of Pockets: 2
Closure: Zipper
Features: Knit wristlets.

Manufacturer: Davco
Model No.: 1208
Type: Vest
Size(s): S, M, L, XL
Color(s): Orange
No. of Pockets: 2
Closure: Zipper front
Features: Knit collar.

Manufacturer: Davco
Model No.: 1220
Type: Coverall
Size(s): Men's: S, M, L, XL; men's talls: M, L, XL, XXL, XXXL; ladies', teens': S, M, L; tots': S, M
Material: 200 Denier-coated oxford nylon
Color(s): Assorted
No. of Pockets: 4
Closure: Zippers; snaps
Features: Waterproof; wind tight; detachable hood.

Manufacturer: Davco
Model No.: 6310
Type: Coverall
Size(s): Men's, ladies', teens': S, M, L, XL; tots': S, M
Material: Denier oxford outer shell; bonded DuPont Dacron 88 polyester insulation; nylon taffeta lining
Color(s): Orange, navy, black, red
No. of Pockets: 4
Closure: Zipper; snaps
Features: Water resistant; detachable hood; knit collar and wristlets.

Manufacturer: Davco
Model No.: 6992

Type: Snorkel jacket
Size(s): Men's S(36-38), M(40-42), L(44-46), XL (48-50); teens' (ladies'): S(10-12), M(14-16), L(18-20)
Material: Nylon outer shell; bonded DuPont Dacron polyester insulation; nylon taffeta lining
Color(s): Loden green or navy blue with orange lining
No. of Pockets: 3
Closure: Zippers; buttons
Features: Fur-trimmed hood; hood adjustment strap.

Manufacturer: Davco
Model No.: 9020
Type: Ski jacket
Size(s): Men's: S, M, L, XL; ladies': S, M, L
Material: Water repellent nylon outer shell; 5.2 oz. PolySlim insulation
Color(s): Navy blue, royal blue
No. of Pockets: 3
Closure: Zipper
Features: Hood; inside storm cuffs.

Manufacturer: Gerry
Model No.: C100
Type: Jacket
Size(s): S(34-36), M(38-40), L(42-44), XL(46-48)
Material: 60/40 cotton-nylon
Color(s): Dune brown, forest green, navy blue, blaze orange
No. of Pockets: 5
Closure: Zipper
Features: Hood; water resistant.

Manufacture: Gerry
Model No.: C214
Type: Parka
Size(s): XS, S, M, L, XL
Material: Polyurethane-coated nylon
Weight: 11 oz.
Color(s): Moss green, blue
Features: Hood; waterproof; rainproof net opening in back; drawstring waist.

Manufacturer: Holubar
Model No.: 103051C
Type: Parka
Size(s): Women's: XXS(6-8), XS(8-10), S(12-14), M(16-18); men's: S(34-36), M(38-40), L(42-44), XL(46-48)
Material: 65/35 polyester-cotton outer shell, goose down filled
Weight: 2 lbs.
Color(s): Denin blue
No. of Pockets: 2
Closure: Zipper
Features: Elastic cuffs; hemline drawstring; stand-up down-filled collar.

Manufacturer: Holubar
Model No.: 103093C
Type: Parka
Size(s): Women's: XS(8-10), S(12-14), M(16-18); men's: S(34-36), M(38-40), L(42-44), XL(46-48)
Material: 65/35 polyester-cotton outer shell; down filled
Weight: 2 lbs. 12 oz.
Color(s): Forest green, navy, tan
No. of Pockets: 3

Closure: Zipper; down-insulated snap flap
Features: Inside waist drawstring; down-insulated collar, snaps for optional hood; knit-cuffed sleeves.

Manufacturer: Holubar
Model No.: 103127C
Type: Parka
Size(s): Women's: XS(8-10), S(12-14), M(16-18); men's: S(34-36), M(38-40), L(42-44), XL(46-48)
Material: Rip-stop nylon, goose down filled
Weight: 2 lbs. 14 oz.
Color(s): Navy, orange
No. of Pockets: 5
Closure: Two-way zipper; down insulated snap flap
Features: Two separate down layers; water repellent; inner stretch nylon cuffs; two drawstring system at waist and bottom hem; down-filled collar.

Manufacturer: Holubar
Model No.: 103234C
Type: Down pants
Size(s): M(28-31), L(32-35)
Material: Rip-stop nylon outer shell, goose down filled
Weight: 1 lb. 10 oz.
Color(s): Navy, orange
No. of Pockets: 2
Closure: Zippered legs with down-insulated snap flap
Features: Elastic waist with drawstring; suspender loops; elastic ankle bands.

Kelty Windstoppers

Manufacturer: Holubar
Model No.: 205005C
Type: Parka
Size(s): Women's: XS(8-10), S(12-14), M(16-18); men's: S(34-36), M(38-40), L(42-44), XL(46-48)
Material: Polyester-cotton outer shell
Weight: 1 lb. 5 oz.
Color(s): Navy, forest green, orange
No. of Pockets: 5
Closure: Two-way zipper; wind flap
Features: Hood with drawstring; drawstring waist; Velcro wrist bands.

Manufacturer: Kelty
Model: Pullover Windstopper
Type: Jacket
Size(s): One size fits all
Material: 2.5 oz. nylon taffeta
Color(s): Blue, gold
No. of Pockets: 2
Features: Hood.

Manufacturer: Kelty
Model: Wind Pants
Size(s): S(28-30, 30″), M(32-34, 32″), L(34-38, 34″)
Material: 2.5 oz. nylon taffeta
Color(s): Blue, gold
Closure: Leg zippers
Features: Lap folded seams; elastic waist and cuffs.

Manufacturer: Kelty
Model: Windstopper
Type: Jacket
Size(s): One size fits all
Material: 2.5 oz. nylon taffeta
Color(s): Blue, gold
No. of Pockets: 2
Closure: Concealed nylon zipper
Features: Drawstring hood, waist and bottom; adjustable cuffs.

Manufacturer: North Face
Model: Down Vest
Size(s): XXS, XS, S, M, L, XL
Material: 65/35 polyester-cotton
Weight: 22 oz. (average)
Color(s): Navy, burnt orange
Closure: Snaps, zipper
Features: Hip elastic-tensioned fit; high down-stuffed collar.

North Face Serow Parka

North Face Down Vest

Manufacturer: North Face
Model: Serow Parka
Type: Jacket
Size(s): XS, S, M, L, XL
Material: 60/40 cloth shell; goose down insulation
Weight: 2 lbs. 10 oz. (average)
Color(s): Navy, tan
No. of Pockets: 6
Closure: Snaps, zipper
Features: Velcro-closed cuffs; waist drawcord.

Manufacturer: North Face
Model: Sierra Parka
Size(s): XXS, XS, S, M, L, XL
Material: 65/35 polyester-cotton
Weight: 25 oz. (average)
Color(s): Navy
No. of Pockets: 2
Closure: Snaps, zipper
Features: Elastic cuffs; hip drawcord.

Manufacturer: North Face
Model: Mountain Parka
Size(s): XS, S, M, L, XL
Material: 60/40 outer shell; taffeta liner
Weight: 30 oz. (average)
Color(s): Steel blue, forest green
No. Pockets: 7
Closure: Snaps; zipper; Velcro
Features: Hood.

Manufacturer: Sierra Designs
Model: Down Shirt
Size(s): Men's: S(34-36), M(37-39), L(40-42), XL (42-44),; women's: S(32-33), M(34-35), L(36-37)
Material: Nylsilk outer; rip-stop nylon inner; goose down filled
Weight: 14 oz.
Color(s): Blue, chestnut (beige inner standard)
No. of Pockets: 2
Closure: Snaps
Features: Insulated cuffs with snaps; 4″ insulated collar.

Manufacturer: Sierra Designs
Model: Goose Down Vest
Size(s): XS(30-32), S(34-36), M(38-40), L(42-44), XL(46-48)
Material: Supernyl quilted with goose down
Weight: 12 oz.
Color(s): Navy, green, cranberry
No. of Pockets: 2
Closure: Snaps
Features: Drawcord at waist; stuffsack; high goose down collar.

Manufacturer: Sierra Designs
Model: Mountain Parka
Size(s): XS(30-32), S(34-36), M(38-40), L(42-44), XL(46-48)
Material: 60/40 cotton-nylon outer shell, nylon inner shell

North Face Sierra Parka

Weight: 1 lb. 12 oz.
Color(s): Navy, green, orange
No. of Pockets: 7
Closure: Zipper; snap flap
Features: Hood with drawstring; water repellent.

Sierra Designs Whitney Parka

Sierra Designs Goose Down Vest

Manufacturer: Sierra Designs
Model: Whitney Parka
Size(s): XS (30-32), S (34-36), M (38-40), L (42-44), XL (44-46)
Material: Supernyl quilted with goose down
Weight: 1 lb.
Color(s): Navy, green, cranberry
No. of Pockets: 3
Closure: Zipper; down-filled snap flap
Features: Drawcord at waist; stuffsack; high down-filled collar

Manufacturer: Sierra Designs
Model: Wilderness Wool Jacket
Size(s): S, M, L, XL
Material: 85/15 wool-nylon
Weight: 21 lbs.
Color(s): Red/green, green/beige
No. of Pockets: 4
Closure: Buttons

Manufacturer: Stag
Model No.: 40006
Type: Woodsmen jacket
Size(s): S, M, L, XL, XXL
Material: Wool
Color(s): Plaid
No. of Pockets: 6
Closure: Buttons
Features: Double layer of fabric over shoulders.

Manufacturer: Stag
Model No.: 41038
Type: Jacket
Size(s): S, M, L, XL
Material: Polyester-cotton outer shell; Dacron Fiberfill II filling; nylon lining
Color(s): Navy, green
No. of Pockets: 5
Closure: Two-way zipper; snap storm flap
Features: Fiberfill II hood.

Manufacturer: Stag
Model No.: 41040
Type: Jacket
Size(s): S, M, L, XL
Material: 60/40 Dacron-nylon outer shell; nylon lining
Color(s): Navy, suede, green
No. of Pockets: 2
Closure: Two-way zipper; snap storm flap
Features: Water repellent; hidden wind cuffs.

Compasses/Altimeters/Pedometers

Manufacturer: Academy
Model No.: 316 Lidded
Type: Compass
Material: Metal
Features: Jeweled needle pinion; luminous dial and needle, needle button lock; hinged lid.

Manufacturer: Academy
Model No.: 342 Lensatic
Type: Compass
Material: Plastic
Features: Floating luminous dial jeweled pivot; luminous directional line; hinged lid.

Manufacturer: Gokey
Model No.: 1-3422 Pedo
Type: Pedometer
Features: Measures distances up to 25 miles.

Manufacturer: Gokey
Model No.: 1-3426 Silva Huntsman
Type: Compass
Features: Liquid filled; sun dial; protractor base; anti-static; waterproof.

Manufacturer: Gokey
Model No.: 1-3427 Silva Ranger
Type: Compass
Features: Waterproof; liquid filled; sapphire jewel bearing; luminous points; scale markings; protractor base plate; anti-static.

Manufacturer: Moor & Mountain
Model No.: 510 Digital
Type: Pedometer
Features: Reads up to 99.9 miles.

Manufacturer: Moor & Mountain
Model No.: 533 Voyager
Type: Compass
Features: Liquid filled; sapphire bearing; luminous; ruler and map scales.

Manufacturer: Moor & Mountain
Model No.: 539 Pocket Backpacker's
Type: Altimeter
Features: Measures to 15,000'; outside bezel to calibrate from benchmarks; barometric pressure adjusting screw; leather case.

Manufacturer: Precise
Model No.: 23207 Pathfinder
Type: Compass
Material: Chrome
Features: Luminescent letters; directional arrow; lid.

Manufacturer: Precise
Model No.: 23212 Lensatic Pathfinder
Type: Compass
Material: Plastic
Features: Luminous points and dial.

Manufacturer: Precise
Model No.: 24202 Compass King
Type: Compass
Material: Metal
Features: Luminous dial; needle and arrow; jeweled bearing; movable direction-of-travel arrow; lid.

Manufacturer: Precise
Model No.: 24219 Compass King
Type: Compass
Material: Brass
Features: Liquid-filled; pin on.

Manufacturer: Precise
Model No.: 24248 Suunto SP-68 Standard
Type: Compass
Features: Luminous points; rotating onyx needle bearing in a liquid-filled, waterproof, direct-reading capsule; scales and rules.

Precise Model No. 24219

Manufacturer: Precise
Model No.: 24256 Suunto M-311 Field Marshall
Type: Compass
Material: Aluminum
Features: Direct-reading capsule body with scale and rule; leather sleeve strap.

Manufacturer: Precise
Model No.: 24265 Suunto KB-14/360R
Type: Compass
Material: Non-corrosive alloy
Features: Floating dial with magnet in hermetically sealed, liquid-filled capsule; sighting lens with slit aperature and cross hair; case.

Manufacturer: Precise
Model No.: 24271 Lensatic Bearing
Type: Compass
Features: Fixed focus lens system; direct and reciprocal azimuth dial; leather case.

Manufacturer: Precise
Model No.: 25232 Compedo
Type: Compass/Pedometer
Features: Measures up to 25 miles; magnetic compass.

Manufacturer: Precise
Model No.: 25235 K & R
Type: Pedometer
Material: Cycolac
Features: Measures up to 25 miles.

Manufacturer: Precise
Model No.: 26202
Type: Map measure and compass

Manufacturer: Recreational Equipment
Model No.: B46-130 Gischard
Type: Altimeter
Material: Plastic
Features: Calibrated to 16,000'; temperature compensated; carrying case; wall mounting bracket.

Manufacturer: Recreational Equipment
Model No.: B46-508 Safari Compass 16
Type: Compass
Features: Liquid filled; jewel bearing; sighting mirror with luminous points; protractor base plate with rule; anti-static; waterproof.

Manufacturer: Recreational Equipment
Model No.: B46-514 Explorer III
Type: Compass
Material: Plastic
Features: Waterproof; liquid filled; jewel bearing; protractor base plate with rules; anti-static.

Manufacturer: Recreational Equipment
Model No.: B46-524 Scout
Type: Compass
Material: Plastic
Features: Liquid filled; luminous needle; jewel bearing; base plate with rules.

Manufacturer: Silva
Model No.: Explorer 1—type 1
Type: Compass
Material: Metal
Features: Waterproof; liquid filled; luminous points; sapphire jewel bearing; protractor base plate with interchangeable scales; magnifying glass; anti-static.

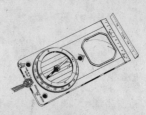

Silva Explorer 1—type 1

Manufacturer: Silva
Model No.: Prospector—type 25
Type: Compass
Features: Waterproof; liquid filled; luminous points; declination adjustment; anti-static; closes into box.

Manufacturer: Silva
Model No.: Wrist—type 4W
Type: Compass
Features: Waterproof; liquid filled; sapphire jewel bearing; luminous points; anti-static capsule interchangeable with 4S/22 base plate.

Manufacturer: Silva
Model No.: 29
Type: Pedometer
Features: Digital display; measures up to 99.9 miles.

Manufacturer: Silva
Model No.: 1040
Type: Altimeter/Barometer
Features: Scaled to 15,000'; aneroid barometer; mountable.

Manufacturer: Ski Hut
Model No.: J203 Thommens
Type: Altimeter
Features: Reads up to 21,000'; temperature compensated; barometric scale; leather case.

Manufacturer: Ski Hut
Model No.: J315
Type: Compass
Material: Plastic
Features: Liquid filled; meridian lines; loop.

Cooksets/Utensils/Grills

Manufacturer: Camp-ways
Model No.: 121
Type: Mess
Material: Aluminum
Weight: 12 oz.
Features: 5-piece set including pots and cup.

Manufacturer: Camp-ways
Model No.: 127T
Type: Nesting Billies
Material: Aluminum, Teflon coated (frypans)
Weight: 28 oz.
Features: 8-piece set.

Manufacturer: Camp-ways
Model No.: 130
Type: Cook set
Material: Aluminum, polyethylene
Weight: 3 lbs. 2 oz.
Serves: 4
Features: Includes pots, coffeepot, plates and cups.

Manufacturer: Camp-ways
Model No.: 131
Type: Cook set
Material: Aluminum, polyethylene
Weight: 5 lbs. 3 oz.
Serves: 6
Features: Includes pots, coffeepot, plates and cups.

Manufacturer: Camp-ways
Model No.: 135
Type: Cook set
Material: Aluminum
Weight: 14 oz.
Serves: 2
Features: Includes pots, plates and cups.

Manufacturer: Camp-ways
Model No.: 158
Type: Pot with bail handle
Size: 9½" diameter, 6" deep
Weight: 22 oz.
Capacity: 4 qt.

Manufacturer: Central Specialties
Model No.: KC-33
Type: Kitchen caddy
Material: Vinyl
Serves: 6
Features: 33 pieces; includes utensils and accessories.

Manufacturer: Coghlan's
Model No.: 7625 BP
Type: Cup
Material: Stainless steel
Features: Stay-cool rim.

Manufacturer: Coghlan's
Model No.: 702
Type: G.I. pocket can opener
Material: Nickel-plated steel
Features: Includes 2.

Manufacturer: Margesson's
Model No.: 407
Type: Cook kit
Size: 16, 18 and 20 cm. pots
Features: 4-piece set.

Manufacturer: Mirro
Model No.: M-4352
Type: Cook kit
Material: Aluminum, polyethylene, polypropylene
Color(s): White

Serves: 4
Features: 12 pieces.

Manufacturer: Mirro
Model No.: M-4355
Type: Cook kit
Material: Aluminum, thermo plastic, Teflon II coated frypans
Color(s): Red
Serves: 6
Features: 20 pieces.

Manufacturer: Mirro
Model No.: M-4362
Type: Cook kit
Material: Aluminum
Serves: 1
Features: Includes pan, kettle, dish and cup.

Manufacturer: Mirro
Model No.: M-4384
Type: Coffeepot
Capacity: 6 cups

Manufacturer: Mirro
Model No.: M-4742
Type: Campfire grid
Sizes: 12½" x 6½"
Material: Steel
Features: Fold-away legs.

Manufacturer: Mirro
Model No.: C-5560
Type: Coffeepot
Capacity: 20 cup

Manufacturer: Mirro
Model No.: M-3475-53
Type: Clamp handle
Material: Aluminum

Camp-ways Model No. 121

Camp-ways Model No. 127T

Coghlan's Model No. 702

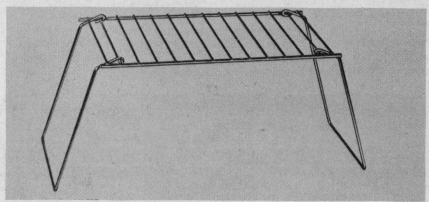

Mirro Model No. M-4742

Coghlan's Model No. 7625 BP

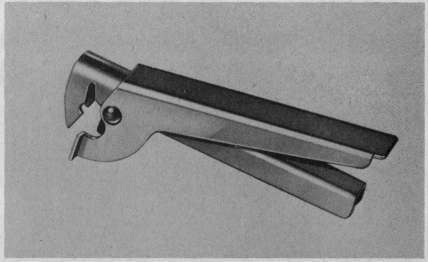

Mirro Model No. M-3475-53

Mirro Model No. S-2206-53

Mirro Model No. M-4384

Mirro Model No. C-5560

Camp-ways Model No. 135

Manufacturer: Mirro
Model No.: S-2206-53
Type: Collapsible cup
Material: Aluminum
Capacity: 4½ oz.

Manufacturer: Palco
Model No.: 313
Type: Grid
Size: Grid, 13″ x 9½″; rod, 15″ high
Features: Adjusts up and down.

Manufacturer: Palco
Model No.: 314

Type: Grid
Size: 16″ x 9″
Features: Folding legs.

Manufacturer: Recreational Equipment
Model No.: B28-330
Type: Grid
Size: 5″ x 15″
Material: Stainless steel
Weight: 2¾ oz.
Features: Nylon carrying case.

Manufacturer: Scott
Model No.: 1045

Type: Dutch oven
Size: 10″
Material: Aluminum
Weight: 4 lbs.
Features: Rustproof.

Manufacturer: Scott
Model No.: 1048
Type: Dutch oven
Size: 12″
Material: Aluminum
Weight: 7 lbs.
Features: Rustproof; includes legs.

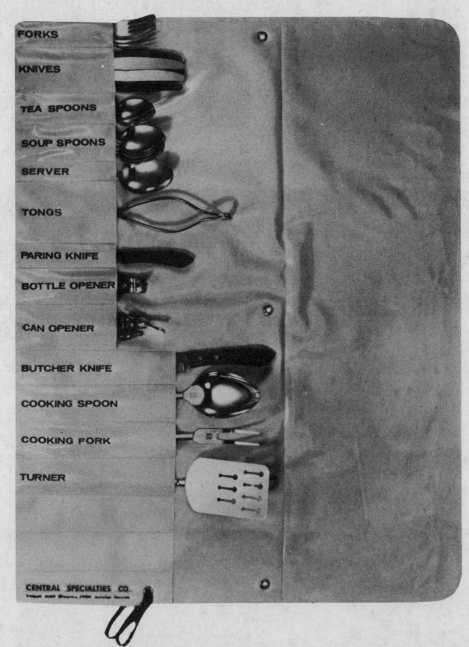

Central Specialties Model No. KC-33

Cots

Manufacturer: Byer
Model No.: 25A
Dimensions: 25" x 76" x 15½"
Frame Material: Hardwood
Weight: 15 lbs.
Color: Green
Features: Slip-on cover; 3 metal reinforced legs.

Manufacturer: Byer
Model No.: 25BX
Dimensions: 25" x 76" x 15½"
Frame Material: Hardwood
Weight: 14 lbs.
Color: White
Features: Slip-on cover; metal reinforced center legs.

Manufacturer: Camp-ways
Model No.: 630
Color: Blue
Features: 4 square legs.

Manufacturer: Colorado Tent & Awning
Model No.: 2D
Dimensions: 25" x 76"
Frame Material: Wood
Weight: 14¼ lbs.
Features: 3 metal reinforced legs.

Manufacturer: Colorado Tent & Awning
Model No.: 4W
Dimensions: 25" x 72"
Frame Material: Wood
Weight: 13¼ lbs.
Color: White
Features: Metal reinforced center legs.

Manufacturer: Colorado Tent & Awning
Model No.: 10
Dimensions: 52" x 22"
Frame Material: Wood
Weight: 10 lbs.
Color: White, olive drab
Features: Child size.

Manufacturer: Imperial American
Model No.: 1111C
Dimensions: 72" x 26"
Features: Adjustable headrest.

Manufacturer: Imperial American
Model No.: 2101C
Dimensions: 76" x 26"
Features: Double decker.

Manufacturer: Imperial American
Model No.: 2500C
Dimensions: 7½" high
Features: 3 U-shaped legs.

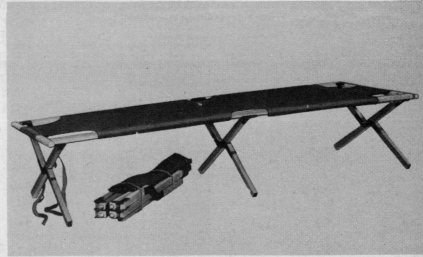

Byer Model No. 25A

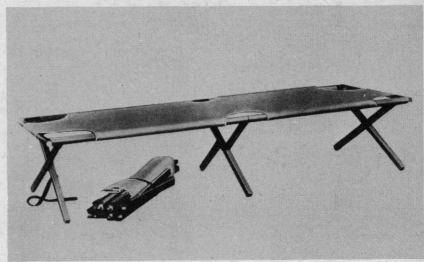

Byer Model No. 25BX

First Aid/Survival

Manufacturer: Alpine Aid
Model: Hiker
Type: First Aid
Dimensions: 3¾" x 3¼" x 1"
Weight: 4 oz.
Contents: Band-Aids; aspirin; salt tablets; moleskin; razor blade; needle; first-aid card; ointment.

Manufacturer: Alpine Aid
Model: Expedition
Type: First Aid
Dimensions: 7" x 5" x 3"
Weight: 21 oz.
Contents: Aspirin; salt tablets; needle; ammonia inhalants; bandages; insect repellent towelettes; antibiotic ointment; razor blade; survival manual.

Manufacturer: Camp-ways
Model No.: 176
Type: Signal mirror
Dimensions: 3" x 4"
Weight: 1 oz.
Features: Lightweight; unbreakable.

Manufacturer: Camp-ways
Model No.: 181
Type: Mirror
Dimensions: 4½" x 5½"
Weight: 7 oz.
Features: Lightweight; unbreakable.

Manufacturer: Coghlan's
Model No.: 7620
Type: Water disinfectant
Contents: 50 tablets
Features: One tablet will disinfect approximately one quart of water.

Manufacturer: Coghlan's
Model No.: 7735
Type: Whistle
Features: Nickel-plated brass; lanyard included.

Manufacturer: Cutter
Model: Pocket Pack
Type: First Aid
Dimensions: 2⅞" x 4¼" x ½"
Weight: 1½ oz.
Color: Tan
Contents: First-aid guide; adhesive bandages; wound wipe; Anacin tablets; alcohol prep and gauze pads; knuckle bandage
Features: 24 items; 6 clear, double pockets.

Cutter: Pocket Pack

Manufacturer: Cutter
Model: Travel Pack
Type: First Aid
Color: Tan
Contents: First-aid instructions; gauze; eye, adhesive, antiseptic and alcohol pads; adhesive bandages and strips; ammonia inhalants; scissors; Anacin; knuckle bands
Features: 50 items.

Cutter Travel Pack

Manufacturer: Cutter
Type: Snake bite kit
Color: Grey
Features: 3 suction cups.

Cutter Snake Bite Kit

Manufacturer: Cutter
Type: Insect repellent cream
Features: Unbreakable flask; flip-tip dispenser.

Manufacturer: Cutter
Type: Insect repellent spray
Weight: 7 oz. or 14 oz.

Manufacturer: Forest City
Model No.: 2154 Camping Kit
Type: First Aid
Color: Assorted
Contents: First-aid booklet; cream; gauze bandage and pads; antiseptic towelettes; sterile cotton; plastic strips; adhesive tape; Bayer aspirin; compass; scissors; mirror; candle; fuel; salt tablets; box matches
Features: Reusable plastic container.

Cutter Insect Repellent Cream

Cutter Insect Repellent Spray

Manufacturer: Forest City
Model No.: 2810 Ouch Kit
Type: First Aid
Color: Assorted
Contents: First-aid book; cream; adhesive bandages and strips; antiseptic towelettes; gauze pads
Features: Contoured, reusable plastic container.

Manufacturer: Forest City
Model No.: 2815 Bike & Hike Kit
Type: First Aid
Features: Salt tablets; mirror; matches; reflector tape; reusable plastic container.

Manufacturer: Margesson's
Model: McKirdy's Repalfly
Type: Insect repellent cream

Manufacturer: Margesson's
Model: Tro-Pell
Type: Insect repellent liquid
Features: Effective against mosquitoes, black flies.

Manufacturer: Margesson's
Model: Piz Buin
Type: Sun cream

Manufacturer: Margesson's
Type: Drinking water tablets

Manufacturer: Nicolet
Model: Mini Kit
Type: Survival
Dimension: 5″ x 6″
Weight: 4 oz.
Contents: Compass; waterproof matches; candles; razor blade; fish line; hooks; sinkers; adhesive bandages; antiseptic; strip tape; gauze pads; burn ointment; safety pins; Hershey non-melt tropical chocolate bars; Pillsbury space food sticks; fuel tablets; whistle; aluminum foil; survival instructions
Features: Waterproof, resealable, plastic bag.

Manufacturer: Nicolet
Model: Klondike Kit
Type: Survival
Dimensions: 4″ x 6″ x 7″
Weight: 2¼ lbs.
Color: Green
Contents: 2-man plastic tube tent with nylon cord; Hershey chocolate drink mix envelopes and tropical chocolate bars; dehydrated beef and dehydrated vegetable soup packets; Pillsbury space food sticks; gum; salt packets; aluminum foil; adhesive bandages and pads; aspirin; antacid, water purification and fuel tablets; tape; antiseptic; insect repellent; burn ointment; safety pins; razor blade; fish hooks, line; sinkers; candles; waterproof matches; compass; magnifying glass; whistle; steel wool; survival manual
Features: Belt-attached duck container.

Manufacturer: Nicolet
Model: Yukon Kit
Type: Survival
Dimensions: 4″ x 6″ x 4″
Weight: 1½ lbs.
Color: Green
Contents: Space rescue blanket
Features: Belt-attached canvas container.

Manufacturer: Nicolet
Model: Survivor I
Type: Survival
Weight: 2¾ lbs.
Color: Green
Contents: Survival manual; 1-man plastic tube tent with nylon cord; high energy and dehydrated food; cups; aluminum foil; first-aid kit, including insect repellent and water purification tablets; fire starter kit, including fuel tablets; waterproof matches; candle and steel wool; whistle; mirror; signals; fishing pack; space rescue blanket; compass; cablesaw; snare wire; razor blade; tissue; etc.
Features: Over 80 items; belt-attached duck container with inner plastic bag.

Manufacturer: Nicolet
Model: Survivor II. Same as Model Survivor I except:
Dimensions: 4″ x 6″ x 9″
Weight: 3¼ lbs.
Color: Orange
Contents: 2-man tent; knife; 2 space blankets
Features: Over 90 items; belt-attached duck container with inner plastic bag and box.

Manufacturer: Nicolet
Model: Survivor IV
Type: Survival
Weight: 15 lbs.
Color: Blue
Contents: Survival manual; 2-man tube tents; cable saw; hacksaw blade; knife; mirror; compass; space rescue blankets; paper and poly-film blankets; metal match; nylon mosquito netting; snare wire; whistles; razor blades; safety pins; tissue; paper note tablet; pencil; candles; fuel; malt and water purification tablets; steel wool; waterproof matches; plastic bags; gauze; bandages; tape; burn ointment; antiseptic; aspirin; antacid pills; insect repellent; ammonia inhalants; soap; pemmican; soup;

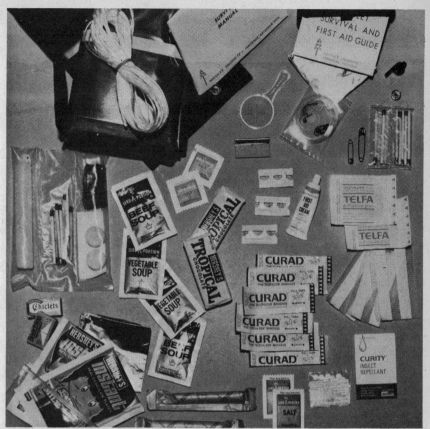

Nicolet Klondike Kit

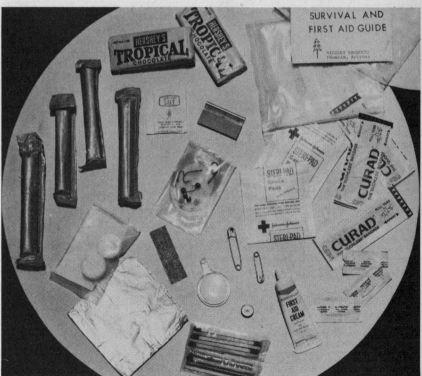

Nicolet Mini Kit

space food sticks; non-melt chocolate bars; chocolate and orange drink mix; salt; trail cookies; cherry drops; coffee; tea; sugar; spoons; aluminum foil cups; etc.

Features: Vinyl-coated duck container; contents sealed within waterproof plastic bags.

Manufacturer: Survival Research Laboratories
Model: Individual Survival Pack
Dimensions: 6″ x 5″ x 9″
Weight: 4 lbs. 5 oz.
Color: International yellow
Contents: Survival manual; meat pemmican and chocolate bars; cooking foil; food and water bags; water purification tablets; matches; all-weather fire-starters; flint; steel; tinder; candle; compass; knife; saw; nylon cord; shelter poncho; rescue blanket; anti-glare goggles; insect repellent stick; anti-exposure sun stick; aspirin; soap bar; toilet tissue; compress; gauze and adhesive bandages; adhesive tape; burn and boric acid ointment; ammonia inhalants; antiseptic swabs; small-game snare wire; fish line; hooks; sinkers; razor blade; whistle; mirror; day/night signal flare; ground to air emergency signal code; etc.

Features: Waterproof, belt-attached container.

Manufacturer: Survival Research Laboratories
Model: Trail Kit
Type: Survival
Dimensions: 5½″ x 3½″ x 1″
Weight: 8 oz.
Contents: Chocolate bars; cooking foil; matches; all-weather fire starters; compass; insect repellent; soap tissues; ammonia inhalant; antiseptic swabs; adhesive bandages; small-game snare wire; fish line and hooks; sinkers; razor blade; whistle; ground to air emergency signal code; survival instructions

Features: Waterproof, resealable pouch.

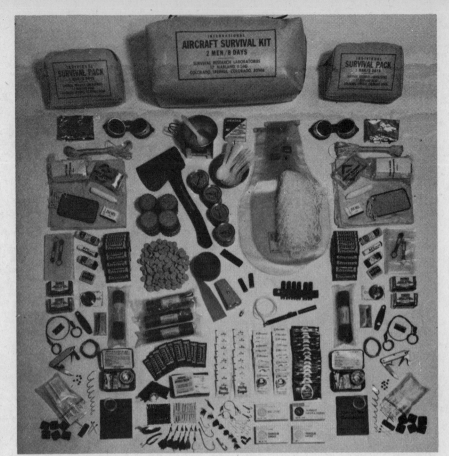

Survival Research Laboratories Individual Survival Pack

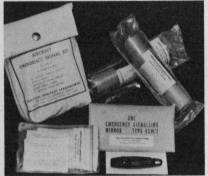

Survival Research Laboratories Aircraft Emergency Signal Kit

Manufacturer: Survival Research Laboratories
Model: Personal First Aid and Survival Kit
Dimensions: 3¾″ x 3¼″ x 2½″
Weight: 15 oz.
Contents: First-aid card; scissors; tweezers; triangular, gauze and adhesive bandages; gauze pads; adhesive tape; burn and eye ointment; tincture of Merthiolate; ammonia inhalants; ACP counterpain tablets; sodium chloride tablets; sea sickness and water purification tablets; Q tabs

Features: Waterproof, adhesive-lined container.

Manufacturer: Survival Research Laboratories
Model: 1 to 5 Passenger FAA Approved Kit
Type: First Aid
Contents: Adhesive and triangular bandages; Merthiolate swabs; ammonia inhalants; bandage compresses; burn and eye ointment

Features: Dust- and moisture-proof metal container.

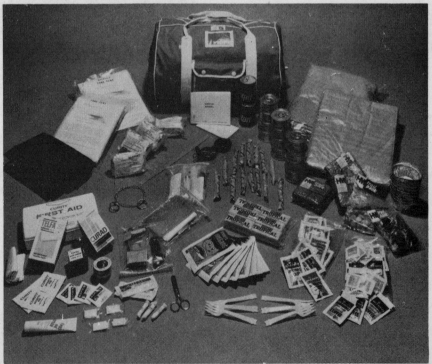

Nicolet Survivor IV

Manufacturer: Survival Research Laboratories
Model: Aircraft Emergency Signal Kit
Dimensions: 2″ x 5″ x 7″
Weight: 1 lb.
Contents: 50 matches; whistle; mirror; 2 day/night signal flares; ground to air emergency signal code
Features: Watertight case.

Manufacturer: Survival Research Laboratories
Model: ACR-4F Rescue Lite
Weight: 10½ oz.
Features: Waterproof; flashing strobe light.

Manufacturer: Survival Research Laboratories
Model: Combination Day and Night Signal
Features: Orange smoke; red flare beacon; sealed in plastic bag.

Manufacturer: Survival Research Laboratories
Model: Survival-7 Aerial Signal Flare Kit
Contents: Launcher; 7 aerial signal flare cartridges

Manufacturer: Survival Research Laboratories
Model: Chemical Seawater Desalting Kit
Features: Provides 7 pints of drinking water.

Manufacturer: Survival Research Laboratories
Type: Water purification tablets
Contents: 100 tablets
Features: Each tablet purifies 1 pint of water.

Manufacturer: Survival Research Laboratories
Model: Firepak
Contents: 20 matches; all-weather fire starters
Features: Waterproof, resealable pouch.

Manufacturer: Survival Research Laboratories
Model No.: 170 Match Roll
Dimensions: 3½″ x 3″ x 1¾″
Weight: 5½ oz.
Contents: 170 wood matches; striking strip
Features: Matches wrapped in paraffin-dipped muslin; resealable vinyl pouch.

Manufacturer: Survival Research Laboratories
Model: Rescue Blanket
Dimensions: 56″ x 84″
Weight: 1¾ oz.
Color: Orange with silver on reverse side
Features: Windproof and waterproof; reflects back 90% of body heat.

Manufacturer: Survival Systems
Model No.: KS-1, KS-2, KS-3
Type: Survival
Color: Red
Contents: Signals (smoke, flares, panel, mirror); first aid; cooking gear; food/energy supplements; fire starting fuel; shelter

Manufacturer: Survival Systems
Model No.: KSE-1
Type: Signal
Dimensions: 6″ x 8″ x 2″
Weight: Under 1 lb.
Color: Red
Contents: 3 skyblazers; flashlight; whistle; fire starter; panel; mirror; smoke

Manufacturer: Survival Systems
Model No.: SSK-1
Type: Signal
Dimenions: 3″ x 5″ x 2″
Weight: 5 oz.
Color: Red
Contents: Ten-mile mirror; red smoke; fire starter kit; 2 aerial flares
Features: Belt attachment.

Survival Research Laboratories Trail Kit

Survival Reseach Laboratories Firepak

Food

Manufacturer: Chuck Wagon
Model No.: B2—Eggs & Hash Browns
Type: Dehydrated
Items: Eggs, potatoes, biscuits, tea, sugar
Features: Guaranteed for 12 months; available in 2, 4 or 6 serving packets.

Manufacturer: Chuck Wagon
Model No.: B5—Ranch Style
Type: Dehydrated
Items: Oatmeal, eggs, cocoa, milk for cereal
Features: Guaranteed for 12 months; available in 2, 4 or 6 serving packets.

Manufacturer: Chuck Wagon
Model No.: L1—Bowl of Chili
Type: Dehydrated
Items: Beans, crackers, vanilla pudding, fruit drink
Features: Guaranteed for 12 months; available in 2, 4 or 6 serving packets.

Manufacturer: Chuck Wagon
Model No.: L2—Mac Cheese
Type: Dehydrated
Items: Beef bouillon, macaroni and cheese, chocolate pudding, cookies, tea, sugar
Features: Guaranteed for 12 months; available in 2, 4 or 6 serving packets.

Manufacturer: Chuck Wagon
Model No.: S4—Italian Spaghetti
Type: Dehydrated
Items: Chicken broth, spaghetti with tomato sauce, fruit, biscuits, fruit drink, cocoa
Features: Guaranteed for 12 months; available in 2, 4 or 6 serving packets.

Manufacturer: Chuck Wagon
Model No.: S5—Chicken Good 'N Hearty
Type: Dehydrated
Items: Chicken, carrots, biscuits, gel dessert, tea, sugar
Features: Guaranteed for 12 months; available in 2, 4 or 6 serving packets.

Manufacturer: Chuck Wagon
Model No.: CB #1
Type: Dehydrated
Items: Cheese spread, biscuits, cocoa, plastic knives
Features: Guaranteed for 12 months; 20 servings.

Manufacturer: Chuck Wagon
Model No.: M-9
Type: Dehydrated
Items: Bouillon, vegetable and rice dinner, biscuits, cocoa
Features: 4 servings.

Manufacturer: Chuck Wagon
Model: Mixed Fruit
Type: Dehydrated
Weight: 1 oz. (per serving)
Features: No sugar added; available in 2, 4 or 6 serving packets.

Manufacturer: Chuck Wagon
Model: Golden Corn
Type: Freeze dried
Weight: ½ oz. (per serving)
Features: Available in 2, 4 or 6 serving packets; 15-minute cooking time.

Manufacturer: Chuck Wagon
Model: Chicken Stew
Type: Dehydrated
Weight: 3⅛ oz. (per serving)
Features: 15- to 20-minute cooking time; available in 2, 4 or 6 serving packets.

Manufacturer: Chuck Wagon
Model: Compressed Cereal Bar
Weight: 1½ oz. (per serving)
Features: 2 servings.

Manufacturer: Mountain House
Model No.: 426 Green Beans
Type: Freeze dried compressed
Weight: 1.6 oz.
Features: Approximate reconstituted servings per pouch: five 4-oz. servings.

Manufacturer: Mountain House
Model No.: 435 Beef Flavored Rice
Type: Freeze dried compressed
Weight: 5 oz.
Features: Approximate reconstituted servings per pouch: two 10-oz. servings.

Manufacturer: Mountain House
Model No.: 602 Beef and Rice w/Onions
Type: Freeze dried
Weight: 4.80 oz.
Features: Approximate unit serving reconstituted: two 8-oz. servings.

Manufacturer: Mountain House
Model No.: 610 Shrimp Creole
Type: Freeze dried
Weight: 3.80 oz.
Features: Approximate unit serving reconstituted: two 8-oz. servings.

Manufacturer: Mountain House
Model No.: 616 Pork Chops (Raw)
Type: Freeze dried
Weight: 2.40 oz.
Features: Approximate unit serving reconstituted: 4 chops.

Manufacturer: Mountain House
Model No.: 624 Chocolate Ice Cream
Weight: 2.50 oz.

Manufacturer: Mountain House
Model No.: 625 Green Peas
Type: Freeze dried
Weight: 1.80 oz.
Features: Approximate unit serving reconstituted: serves 3-4.

Manufacturer: Mountain House
Model No.: 639 Peaches
Type: Freeze dried
Weight: 1 oz.
Features: Approximate unit serving reconstituted: serves 2.

Manufacturer: Mountain House
Model No.: 641 Cheese Omelette
Type: Freeze dried
Weight: 2.40 oz.
Features: Approximate unit serving reconstituted: serves 2.

Manufacturer: Mountain House
Model No.: 648 Granola and Raisins w/Milk
Type: Freeze dried
Weight: 4 oz.
Features: Approximate unit serving reconstituted: two 4-oz. servings.

Manufacturer: Mountain House
Model No.: 654 Chicken Salad
Type: Freeze dried
Weight: 2.75 oz.
Features: Approximate unit serving reconstituted: 4 sandwiches.

Manufacturer: Mountain House
Model No.: 662 Breakfast No. 3
Type: Freeze dried
Weight: 1 lb. 2.9 oz.
Items: Orange beverage, eggs, hash browns, cooking oil, cocoa
Features: 4 servings.

Manufacturer: Mountain House
Model No.: 676 Dinner No. 3
Type: Freeze dried
Weight: 3 oz.
Items: Chicken noodle soup, vegetable-beef stew, orange drink, chocolate pudding
Features: 4 servings.

Manufacturer: Mountain House
Model No.: 850 Orange Drink
Type: Freeze dried
Weight: 3.50 oz.
Features: Approximate unit serving reconstituted: serves 4.

Manufacturer: Mountain House
Model No.: 860 Beef Noodle Soup
Type: Freeze dried
Weight: 1.50 oz.
Features: Approximate unit serving reconstituted: serves 4.

Manufacturer: Mountain House
Model No.: 870 Instant Butterscotch Pudding
Type: Freeze dried
Weight: 5 oz.
Features: Approximate unit serving reconstituted: serves 4.

Manufacturer: National Packaged Trail Foods
Model: French Toast
Weight: 3 oz. (2 servings)
Features: Available in 2, 4 or 6 serving packets.

Manufacturer: National Packaged Trail Foods
Model: Grape Spred-Itt
Weight: 1½ oz. (2 servings)
Features: Available in 2, 4 or 6 serving packets.

Manufacturer: National Packaged Trail Foods
Model: Macaroni 'N Cheese
Weight: 6 oz. (2 servings)
Features: Available in 2 or 4 serving packets.

Manufacturer: National Packaged Trail Foods
Model: Chicken a la King
Weight: 4 oz. (2 servings)
Features: Available in 2, 4 or 6 serving packets.

Manufacturer: National Packaged Trail Foods
Model: Potatoes au Gratin
Weight: 3 oz. (2 servings)
Features: Available in 2, 4 or 6 serving packets.

Manufacturer: National Packaged Trail Foods
Model: Peas 'N Carrots
Weight: 1½ oz. (2 servings)
Features: Available in 2, 4 or 6 serving packets.

Manufacturer: National Packaged Trail Foods
Model: Ginger Bread
Weight: 4 oz. (2 servings)
Features: Available in 2, 4 or 6 serving packets.

Manufacturer: National Packaged Trail Foods
Model: Sweet Milk Cocoa
Weight: 4 oz. (2 servings)
Features: Available in 2, 4 or 6 serving packets.

Manufacturer: National Packaged Trail Foods
Model: Cherry Cobler
Weight: 6 oz. (2 servings)
Features: Available in 2, 4 or 6 serving packets.

Manufacturer: Rich-Moor
Model No.: 00111 Blueberry Pancakes
Weight: 11¼ oz.
Features: Makes twelve 5″ pancakes.

Manufacturer: Rich-Moor
Model No.: 00404 Chicken Rice Dinner
Weight: 10¾ oz.
Features: Four 9½-oz. servings.

Manufacturer: Rich-Moor
Model No.: 00505 Beef Stroganoff
Weight: 12¾ oz.
Features: Four 12-oz. servings.

Manufacturer: Rich-Moor
Model No.: 00604 Hamburgers
Weight: 2 oz.
Features: Two 2-oz. servings.

Manufacturer: Rich-Moor
Model No.: 00803 Hash Brown Potatoes
Weight: 6½ oz.
Features: Four 4-oz. servings.

Manufacturer: Rich-Moor
Model No.: 00906 Swiss Cheese with Imitation
  Bacon
Weight: 4¼ oz.
Features: Four 2-oz. servings.

Manufacturer: Rich-Moor
Model No.: 01018 Neapolitan Ice Cream
Weight: 2⅛ oz.
Features: Four ⅔-oz. servings.

Manufacturer: Rich-Moor
Model No.: 01505 Pineapple Cheese Cake
Weight: 11 oz.
Features: Four 5½-oz. servings.

Manufacturer: Rich-Moor
Model No.: 01704 Breakfast #4
Items: Applesauce, scrambled eggs and ham,
  hash browns, cocoa, cooking oil
Features: 4 servings.

Manufacturer: Rich-Moor
Model No.: 1706 Quick Breakfast #6
Items: Apple chips, natural nuggets/milk,
  trail brunch, cocoa
Features: 4 servings.

Manufacturer: Rich-Moor
Model No.: 01804 Lunch #4
Items: Apple slices, cheddar cheese, crisp
  toast, orange Gatorade
Features: 4 servings.

Manufacturer: Rich-Moor
Model No.: 01806 Quick Trail Lunch #6
Items: Beef jerky, trail cookies, tropical choc-
  olate bars, quick energy bars
Features: 4 servings.

Manufacturer: Rich-Moor
Model No.: 02001 Dinner #1
Items: Chicken rice soup, chili mac with
  beef, chocolate pudding, fruit punch
Features: 4 servings.

Manufacturer: Rich-Moor
Model No.: 02003 Dinner #3
Items: Tomato noodle soup, vegetable stew/
  beef, dumplings, butterscotch pudding, or-
  ange drink
Features: 4 servings.

Manufacturer: Rich-Moor
Model No.: 02007 Quick Trail Dinner #7
Items: Beef soup, lasagna with meatballs,
  lemon pie, grape drink
Features: 4 servings.

Manufacturer: Rich-Moor
Model No.: 11160 Granola Grabber
Weight: 2 oz.
Features: One 2-oz. serving.

Manufacturer: Rich-Moor
Model No.: 20111 Cheese Romanoff with Ham
Weight: 5¾ oz.
Features: Two 10½-oz. servings.

Manufacturer: Rich-Moor
Model No.: 20112 Turkey Supreme
Weight: 5¾ oz.
Features: Two 10½-oz. servings.

Manufacturer: Rich-Moor
Model No.: 20500 Natural Nuggets Cereal
Weight: 5½ oz.
Features: Two 2¾-oz. servings.

Manufacturer: Rich-Moor
Model No.: 20551 Orange Gatorade
Weight: 1¾ oz.
Features: Four 8-oz. servings.

Manufacturer: Rich-Moor
Model No.: 20702 Trail Snack #2
Items: Beef roll (2), gorp, trail brunch (2),
  cotlets (2)
Features: 2 servings.

Manufacturer: Rich-Moor
Model No.: 20802 Dinner #2
Items: Chicken stew, corn, butterscotch pud-
  ding, lemon-lime drink
Features: 2 servings.

Manufacturer: Rich-Moor
Model No.: 42110 Beef & Pizza Bar
Weight: 2 oz.

Manufacturer: Rich-Moor
Model No.: 42113 Chili Bar
Weight: 2 oz.

Manufacturer: Stor-a-Pack—Kamp Pack
Model: De Luxe Cornbread Mix
Weight: 8½ oz.
Features: 4 to 6 large servings.

Manufacturer: Stor-a-Pack—Kamp Pack
Model: Western Omelette w/Peppers, Onions
Weight: 4 oz.
Features: 4 to 6 large servings.

Manufacturer: Stor-a-Pack—Kamp Pack
Model: Potato Soup Supreme
Weight: 5½ oz.
Features: 4 to 6 large servings.

Rich-Moor

Manufacturer: Stor-a-Pack—Kamp Pack
Model: Instant Peanut Butter Mix
Weight: 5 oz.
Features: 4 to 6 large servings.

Manufacturer: Stor-a-Pack—Kamp Pack
Model: Oregon Sweet Garden Peas
Weight: 3 oz.
Features: 4 to 6 large servings.

Rich-Moor Model No. 20111

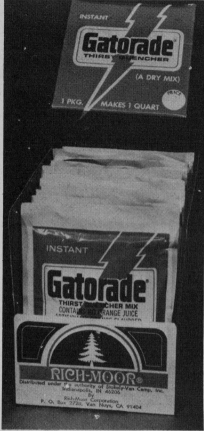

Rich-Moor Model No. 20551

Manufacturer: Stor-a-Pack—Kamp Pack
Model: Strawberry Flavored Milk Shake
Weight: 7 oz.
Features: 4 to 6 large servings.

Manufacturer: Stor-a-Pack—Kamp Pack
Model: Chocolate 5 Star Drink-A-Meal
Weight: 9 oz.
Features: 4 to 6 large servings.

Manufacturer: Stor-a-Pack—Kamp Pack
Model: Beef Chop Suey
Weight: 7¼ oz.
Features: 4 to 6 large servings.

Manufacturer: Stor-a-Pack—Kamp Pack
Model: Chicken Imperial
Weight: 8 oz.
Features: 4 to 6 large servings.

Kits

Manufacturer: Frostline
Model No.: C10
Type: Jacket
Size: Men's: S, M, L, XL; ladies': M, L, XL
Material: Rip-stop nylon with nylon taffeta interlining with rip-stop nylon lining
Weight: 2 lbs. 2 oz.
Color(s): Assorted
Insulation: Northern goose down
Features: 2-way front zipper.

Frostline Model No. C10

Manufacturer: Frostline
Model No.: C15
Type: Hood
Size: S to M, L to XL
Material: Taffeta, rip-stop or mountain cloth
Color(s): Assorted
Insulation: Polarguard
Features: Self-sealing closure and drawstring; available with down insulation.

Manufacturer: Frostline
Model No.: C18
Type: Booties
Size: XS, S, M, L, XL
Material: Rip-stop nylon
Weight: 5 oz.
Color(s): Medium blue, forest green
Insulation: Northern goose down

Manufacturer: Frostline
Model No.: C19
Type: Overboots
Size: XS, S, M, L, XL
Material: Nylon; Ensolite insole and back of heel; waterproof naugahyde sole
Weight: 9 oz.
Color(s): Sage green, medium blue
Features: Drawstring top; tie cord at ankle.

Manufacturer: Frostline
Model No.: C23
Type: Parka
Size: Men's: XS, S, M, L, XL; ladies': S, M, L, XL

Material: Nylon taffeta
Weight: 1 lb. 15 oz.
Color(s): Assorted
Insulation: Northern goose down
Features: 2-way zipper; drawstring bottom.

Manufacturer: Frostline
Model No.: C28
Type: Jacket
Size: Men's: XS, S, M, L, XL; ladies': S, M, L, XL
Material: Nylon taffeta
Weight: 1 lb. 8 oz.
Color(s): Assorted
Insulation: Northern goose down
Features: 2-way zipper; bottom drawstring.

Manufacturer: Frostline
Model No.: C30
Type: Mitts
Size: S, M, L, XL
Material: Taffeta
Weight: 9 oz.
Color(s): Assorted
Insulation: Down with goose down gauntlet
Features: Stretch-knit nylon cuff; double mitten inner and outer shell.

Manufacturer: Frostline
Model No.: C36
Type: Pants
Size: S, M, L, XL
Material: Taffeta
Weight: 1 lb. 4 oz.
Color(s): Assorted
Insulation: Northern goose down
Features: Carrying case; separating leg zippers; washable or dry cleanable.

Manufacturer: Frostline
Model No.: C39
Type: Parka
Size: Men's: XS, S, M, L, XL; ladies': S, M, L, XL
Material: Mountain cloth with lighter polyester/cotton lining
Color(s): Assorted with tan lining
Features: Water repellent; machine washable; zipper with self-sealing strips on flap; hand pockets behind cargo pockets.

Manufacturer: Frostline
Model No.: C41
Type: Jacket
Size: Men's: XS, S, M, L, XL; ladies': S, M, L, XL
Material: Nylon taffeta or denim blue chambray cloth with rip-stop nylon lining
Weight: 1 lb. 5 oz.
Color(s): Assorted
Insulation: Polarguard
Features: Zipper with snap-down flap; stand-up collar for extra protection.

Manufacturer: Frostline
Model No.: C42
Type: Vest
Size: Men's: XS, S, M, L, XL; ladies': S, M, L, XL
Material: Rip-stop nylon or chambray cloth
Weight: 11 oz.
Color(s): Red, kelly green, denim blue; with navy lining
Insulation: Polarguard
Features: Yoke material included; snaps and snap setting tool included; stuff sack available.

Manufacturer: Frostline
Model No.: C65
Type: Shirt
Size: Men's: XS, S, M, L, XL; ladies': S, M, L, XL
Material: Rip-stop nylon or denim blue chambray cloth with rip-stop nylon lining
Weight: 13 oz.

Color(s): Denim blue, kelly green, denim with navy lining
Insulation: Down
Features: Snaps; straight or curved shirttail; washable or dry cleanable.

Manufacturer: Frostline
Model No.: C66
Type: Vest
Size: Men's: S, M, L, XL; ladies': M, L, XL
Material: Rip-stop nylon or denim blue chambray cloth
Weight: 10.5 oz.
Color(s): Assorted
Insulation: Northern goose down
Features: One-way zipper; stuff sack available.

Frostline Model No. C66

Manufacturer: Frostline
Model No.: PO4
Type: Pack
Size: 20½″ x 16″ x 8″
Material: Urethane-coated nylon pack cloth
Weight: 1 lb. 11 oz.
Color(s): International orange, sage green
Features: Fits adult frame up to 16″ wide; side pockets; 2-way zippers.

Manufacturer: Frostline
Model No.: PO7 Hatch-back Sack
Type: Pack
Size: 22″ x 16″ x 9″
Material: Urethane-coated nylon pack cloth
Weight: 1 lb. 12 oz.
Color(s): International orange, sage green
Features: Zippers with waterproof flaps; entire front opens; self-adhering cinch straps; fits any adult frame up to 16″ wide.

Manufacturer: Frostline
Model No.: S6 Cougar
Type: Sleeping bag
Size: Regular, large
Material: Rip-stop nylon; nylon taffeta baffles
Weight: Standard: 5 lbs. 10 oz., 6 lbs. 1 oz.; winter: 5 lbs. 15 oz., 6 lbs. 8 oz.
Color(s): Navy, medium blue, forest green; with gold lining
Insulation: Northern goose down, polyether

pad
Features: Built-in, full-length pad; zipper; standard and winter models.

Manufacturer: Frostline
Model No.: S7 Loafer
Type: Sleeping bag
Size: Standard, winter
Material: Rip-stop nylon
Weight: Standard: 5 lbs. 2 oz.; large: 5 lbs. 7 oz.
Color(s): Medium blue with gold lining
Insulation: Down
Features: 2 zippers with down-filled flap; square foot.

Manufacturer: Frostline
Model No.: S9 Cirrus
Type: Sleeping bag
Size: Regular, large
Material: Rip-stop nylon
Weight: Regular: 3 lbs. 8 oz.; large: 3 lbs. 15 oz.
Color(s): Navy, medium blue, forest green; with gold lining
Insulation: Polarguard
Features: Zipper with insulated flap.

Manufacturer: Frostline
Model No.: T10H Kodiak
Type: Tent
Size: Total length: 10′ 6″; floor size: 7′ 6″ x 4′ 6″; height (highest point): 45″
Material: Rip-stop nylon
Weight: 6 lbs. 6 oz.
Color(s): Moss green, medium blue, bright yellow
Features: Nylon zippers; tent poles pre-assembled with elastic cord; waterproof; steep walls; wide top; floorless vestibule.

Manufacturer: Frostline
Model No.: T12H Sun-lite
Type: Tent
Size: Total length: 9′; floor size: 7′ 1″ x 4′ 3″; height (highest point): 42″
Material: Rip-stop nylon; Urethane-coated nylon
Weight: 5 lbs. 14 oz.
Color(s): Moss green, medium blue, bright yellow
Features: 2-way zippers; A-frame; overhang.

Manufacturer: Frostline
Model No.: W10
Type: Poncho
Size: Medium (57″ x 76″), large (63″ x 85″)
Material: Urethane-coated nylon
Weight: Medium: 16 oz.; large: 20 oz.
Color(s): Assorted
Features: Grommets; snaps; drawstring hood; extension kit available for pack poncho; waterproof.

Manufacturer: Frostline
Model No.: W12
Type: Chaps
Material: Urethane-coated nylon
Weight: 4½ oz.
Color(s): Assorted
Features: Individual pant legs; self-cut length; waterproof.

Manufacturer: Holubar
Model No.: 200014B Polarbag
Type: Sleeping bag
Size: Inside lengths: 5′ 10″, 6′ 6″
Material: Rip-stop nylon
Weight: 4 lbs. 9 oz., 5 lbs. 1 oz.
Color(s): Royal blue
Insulation: Northern goose down
Features: Y.K.K. Delrin zipper; drawstring for hood and shoulder; stuff sack; rated to −20°F.

Manufacturer: Holubar
Model No.: 200030C Teton
Type: Sleeping bag
Size: Lengths: 6′ 0″, 6′ 6″
Material: Rip-stop nylon

Frostline Model No. T10H

Holubar Model No. 200030C

Weight: 42 oz., 48 oz.
Color(s): Blue
Insulation: Goose down
Features: Flame retardant; Y.K.K. Delrin zipper with full length draft tube; shoulder and hood drawstrings; stuff sack included; rated to −15°F.

Manufacturer: Holubar
Model No.: 202044B Chinook
Type: Sleeping bag
Size: Inside lengths: 5′ 10″, 6′ 6″
Material: Rip-stop nylon
Weight: 4 lbs. 6 oz.; 4 lbs. 13 oz.
Color(s): Navy blue
Insulation: Northern goose down
Features: 2-way Y.K.K. Delrin zipper; rated to 0°F; locking drawstring.

Manufacturer: Holubar
Model No.: 202010B
Type: Sleeping-bag liner
Size: 5′ 10″, 6′ 6″
Material: Rip-stop nylon
Weight: 9 oz.
Features: Attaches with Velcro tabs and ties; washable and dryable; fits kit bags only.

Manufacturer: Holubar
Model No.: 203067C Sequoia
Type: Jacket
Size: Men's: S, M, L, XL; women's: XXS, XS, S, M
Material: Supernyl
Weight: 1 lb. 10 oz.
Color(s): Forest green, navy
Insulation: Down
Features: Y.K.K. Delrin zipper; elastic cuffs; hemline drawstring.

Manufacturer: Holubar
Model No.: 203083C Kinnikinic (in kit form)
Type: Sweater
Size: Men's: S, M, L, XL; women's: XS, S, M
Material: Rip-stop nylon
Weight: 14 oz.
Color(s): Navy, forest green
Insulation: Down
Features: Knit cuffs and collar; patch pockets; snap front closure with overflap.

Manufacturer: Holubar
Model No.: 203109C Aleutian
Type: Vest
Size: Men's: S, M, L, XL; women's: XS, S, M

Material: Rip-stop nylon
Weight: 12 oz.
Color(s): Forest green, navy
Insulation: Down
Features: Y.K.K. Delrin zipper; nylon knit collar; drawstring bottom; slash front pockets.

Manufacturer: Holubar
Model No.: 203117C Vagabond
Type: Vest
Size: Men's: S, M, L, XL; women's: XS, S, M
Material: Supernyl
Weight: 12 oz.
Color(s): Copper, navy, forest green
Insulation: Northern goose down
Features: Slash pockets; stand-up collar; water repellent; bottom hemline drawstring; snap front closure.

Manufacturer: Holubar
Model No.: 203133C
Type: Boots
Size: XS, S, M, L, XL
Material: Supernyl with expedition felt insoles; Ranchero soles
Weight: 10 oz.
Color(s): Gold, navy
Insulation: Down
Features: Elastic band in back; Velcro closure at top.

Manufacturer: Holubar
Model No.: 203141C
Type: Mittens
Size: Men's: S, M, L, XL; women's: XS, S, M
Material: Supernyl with goatskin palms
Weight: 5 oz.
Color(s): Navy or black
Insulation: Down
Features: Waterproof; nylon loop fastenings.

Manufacturer: Holubar
Model No.: 205005C Boulder Mountain
Type: Parka
Size: Men's: S, M, L, XL; women's: XS, S, M
Material: Storm cloth with supernyl lining
Weight: 1 lb. 5 oz.
Color(s): Navy, forest green, orange
Features: Y.K.K. Delrin zippers; drawstring; Velcro closures.

Manufacturer: Holubar
Model No.: 20502A Leggins
Type: Gaiters
Size: 17″ (height)
Material: Polyester, cotton stormcloth (double layer)
Weight: 12 oz.
Color(s): Navy, orange
Features: Water repellent; Y.K.K. Delrin zippers; storm flaps with Velcro closures; elastic at ankle and bottom; drawstring closure top.

Frostline Model No. P07

Holubar Model No. 208090A

Holubar Model No. 203133C

SPECIFICATIONS: EQUIPMENT

Manufacturer: Holubar
Model No.: 206003C Backpack
Type: Poncho
Size: Front hemline: medium (39″), large (43″); extended rear hemline: medium (74″), large (78″); width: medium (60″), large (68″)
Material: Nylport
Weight: Medium, 22 oz.; large, 24 oz.
Color(s): Orange, avocado
Features: Off-center hood.

Manufacturer: Holubar
Model No.: 207027 Nomad
Type: Tent
Size: Front peak: 5′ 6″; rear peak: 28″; floor length: 10′ 5″; width (maximum): 72″; roll size: 10″ x 2″
Material: Rip-stop nylon, nylport
Weight: 10 lbs. 4 oz.
Color(s): Blue canopy, avocado floor, forest green rainfly
Features: Zipper on overhang; Y.K.K. Ziplon coil zippers on side vents; reinforced stake-out points for 14 included stakes.

Manufacturer: Holubar
Model No.: 207043 Super Tube
Type: Tent
Size: Flat size: 9′ x 10′
Material: Nylport
Weight: 2 lbs. 10 oz.
Color(s): Avocado
Features: Flame retardant; mosquito nets; drawstring closures; nylon tape tabs for guyline pull outs; no poles needed.

Manufacturer: Holubar
Model No.: 208066A Trucker
Type: Pack
Size: Main compartment: 12″ x 15″ x 6″; outside pocket: 9″ x 8½″ x 3″
Material: Cordura nylon
Weight: 12 oz.
Color(s): Assorted

Features: Waterproof; nylon web straps; accessory strap medallions on bottom; Y.K.K. Coilon zippers.

Manufacturer: Holubar
Model No.: 208090A Travelite
Type: Pack
Size: 18″ x 14″ x 8″
Material: 11.5 oz. Cordura nylon
Weight: 22 oz.
Color(s): Assorted
Features: Urethane coating; perimeter Y.K.K. coil zipper.

Manufacturer: Moor & Mountain
Model No.: 950 Altra
Type: Parka
Size: XS, S, M, L
Material: Rip-stop nylon
Weight: 2.30 lbs.
Color(s): Navy, green
Insulation: Down
Feature: Hip length; raglan sleeves; double (polyester-insulated) outside and inside stash pocket; waist drawstring; 2-way Talon coil zipper; Velcro patch draft flap.

Manufacturer: Moor & Mountain
Model No.: 951 Altra
Type: Hood
Material: Rip-stop nylon
Weight: .50 lb.
Color(s): Navy, green

Manufacturer: Moor & Mountain
Model No.: 952 Altra
Type: Parka
Size: XS, S, M, L
Material: 65/35 Dacron cotton
Weight: 2.50 lbs.
Color(s): Navy, rust
Insulation: Down
Features: Hip length; raglan sleeves; double (polyester-insulated) outside and inside stash pocket; waist drawstring; 2-way Talon coil zipper; Velcro patch draft flap.

Manufacturer: Moor & Mountain
Model No.: 953 Altra
Type: Hood
Material: 65/35 Dacron cotton
Weight: .40 lbs.
Color(s): Navy, rust

Manufacturer: Moor & Mountain
Model No.: 955 Mountain Altra
Type: Parka and hood
Size: XS, S, M, L, XL
Material: 65/35 Dacron cotton polyester cotton lining
Weight: 3.00 lbs.
Color(s): Navy, green, rust
Features: Breathable; semi water repellent; machine washable; double hand-warmer pockets plus cargo pockets; inside stash pocket; drawstring; 2-way Talon coil zipper with Velcro draft flap; adjustable sleeve closures.

Manufacturer: Moor & Mountain
Model No.: 956 Altra
Type: Vest
Size: XS, S, M, L, XL
Material: Rip-stop nylon
Weight: 1.40 lbs.
Color(s): Navy, red
Insulation: Down
Features: Velcro patch closure; double hand-warmer (polyester-insulated) pockets; down-filled collar.

Manufacturer: Moor & Mountain
Model No.: 957 Altra
Type: Vest
Size: XS, S, M, L, XL
Material: 65/35 Dacron cotton
Weight: 1.75 lbs.
Color(s): Navy, green
Insulation: Down
Features: Velcro patch closure; double hand-warmer pockets; down-filled collar.

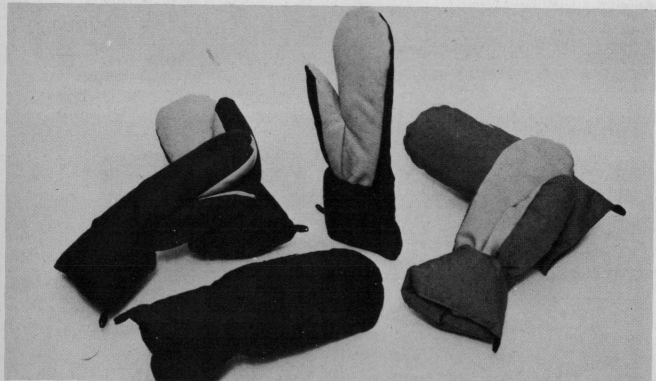

Holubar Model No. 203141C

Knives

Manufacturer: Browning
Model No.: 2518
Type: Folding
Length of Blade(s): 1⅝″, 1½″, 2½″
Handle Material: Rosewood
Weight: 1.6 oz.
Features: Brass frame; 440 cc stainless steel; medium 3-blade packet.

Manufacturer: Browning
Model No.: 2718 F0 Outdoorsman
Type: Folding
Length of Blade(s): 1¾″, 3¼″
Handle Material: Celluloid
Weight: 4.75 oz.
Features: 10 tools in 1 including: scissors, saw blade, screwdriver.

Manufacturer: Browning
Model No.: 2718 F2 Fish and Bird
Type: Folding
Length of Blade(s): 2″, 2¾″
Handle Material: Black sandalwood
Sheath Material: Grain leather
Weight: 3.75 oz.
Features: 440 cc steel blades.

Manufacturer: Browning
Model No.: 3018 F2 Hunting
Type: Folding, 2 blades
Length of Blade(s): 3″
Handle Material: Black sandalwood
Sheath Material: Grain leather
Weight: 6.5 oz.
Features: 440 cc steel blades.

Manufacturer: Browning
Model No.: 3318 F2 Trapper
Type: Folding, 2-blade packet
Length of Blade(s): 3¼″
Handle Material: Rosewood
Weight: 4 oz.

Manufacturer: Browning
Model No.: 4018 F Multipurpose Hunter I
Type: Folding
Length of Blade(s): 4″
Handle Material: Tropical hardwood
Sheath Material: Grain leather
Weight: 7.5 oz.
Features: Positive lock to prevent folding in use; 440 cc steel blades.

Manufacturer: Browning
Model No.: 5518
Type: Straight
Length of Blade(s): 5½″
Handle Material: Tropical hardwood
Sheath Material: Grain leather
Weight: 9.1 oz.
Features: 440 cc steel blade.

Manufacturer: Browning
Model No.: 6018 Fillet
Type: Straight
Length of Blade(s): 6″
Handle Material: Cork
Sheath Material: Grain leather
Weight: 1.75 oz.

Manufacturer: Buck
Model No.: 105 Pathfinder
Type: Straight
Length of Blade(s): 5″
Handle Material: Ebony
Sheath Material: Saddle leather

Manufacturer: Buck
Model No.: 107 Scout
Type: Straight
Length of Blade(s): 4″
Handle Material: Buckarta
Sheath Material: Saddle leather
Features: Skinning sweep blade.

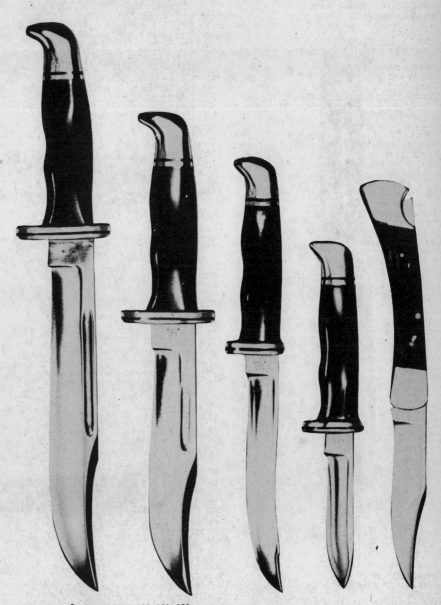

Buck Model Nos. 105; 110; 116; 119; 120

Manufacturer: Buck
Model No.: 110 Hunter
Type: Folding
Handle Material: Golden-grain Macassar ebony
Sheath Material: Saddle leather
Features: Positive lock in open position; brass bolsters and liner forged in one piece; 4⅞″ overall.

Manufacturer: Buck
Model No.: 116 Caper
Type: Straight
Length of Blade(s): 3¼″
Handle Material: Ebony
Sheath Material: Saddle leather

Manufacturer: Buck
Model No.: 119 Special
Type: Straight
Length of Blade(s): 6″
Handle Material: Ebony
Sheath Material: Saddle leather
Features: Bowie styled; blood groove; heavy all-around knife work.

Manufacturer: Buck
Model No.: 120 General
Type: Straight
Length of Blade(s): 7½″
Handle Material: Ebony
Sheath Material: Saddle leather
Features: Heavy, Bowie styled.

Manufacturer: Buck
Model No.: 124 Frontiersman
Type: Straight
Length of Blade(s): 7″
Handle Material: Buckarta Slab
Sheath Material: Saddle leather
Features: Heavy-duty uses.

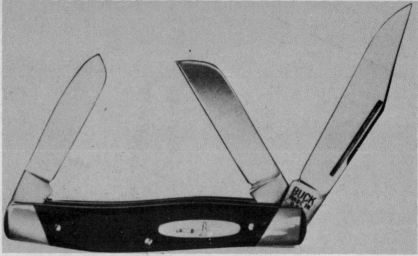

Buck Model No. 307

Buck Model No. 124

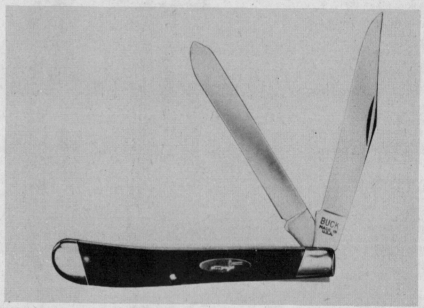

Buck Model No. 311

Manufacturer: Buck
Model No.: 307 Wrangler Pocket
Type: Folding
Handle Material: Ebony
Features: Stainless steel pivot pins; 4¼″ closed.

Manufacturer: Buck
Model No.: 311 Yachtsman pocket
Type: Folding
Handle Material: Ebony
Features: Stainless steel pivot pins; 4⅜″ closed.

Manufacturer: Buck
Model No.: 313 Muskrat
Type: Folding
Handle Material: Ebony
Features: Rustproof, unbreakable pivot pins; 3⅞″ closed.

Manufacturer: Buck
Model No.: 317 Trailblazer

Type: Folding
Handle Material: Ebony
Sheath Material: Saddle leather
Features: Rustproof, unbreakable pivot pin; 5¼″ closed.

Manufacturer: Compass (Panther)
Model No.: 533 Angler
Type: Folding
Handle Material: Ebony hardwood
Features: 5″ closed; blade with fish scaler and hook remover.

Manufacturer: Compass (Panther)
Model No.: 580 Folding Hunter
Type: Folding
Handle Material: Ebony hardwood
Features: 4¾″ closed; leather pouch.

Manufacturer: Compass (Panther)
Model No.: 560 Folding Hunter
Type: Folding
Handle Material: Ebony hardwood

Features: Saw blade to cut through bone, twigs and brush.

Manufacturer: Compass (Panther)
Model: Backpacker
Type: Folding
Features: 3½″ closed.

Manufacturer: Compass (Panther)
Model: Champion (Victorinox)
Type: Folding
Features: 3½″ closed.

Manufacturer: Compass (Panther)
Model: Craftsman (Victorinox)
Type: Folding
Features: 3½″ closed.

Manufacturer: Compass (Panther)
Model: Pioneer (Victorinox)
Type: Folding
Handle Material: Ribbed Alox
Features: ½″ closed.

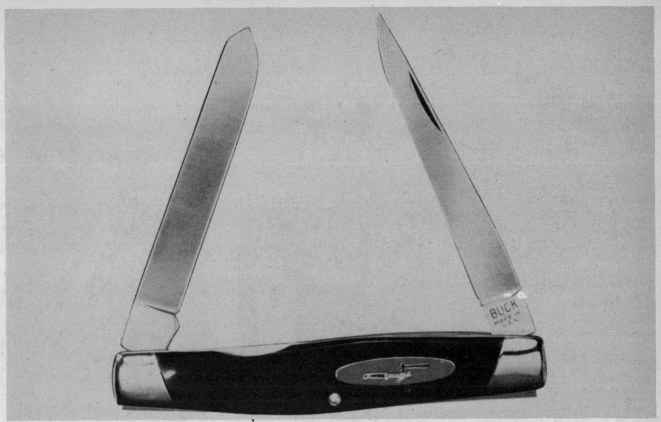

Buck Model No. 313

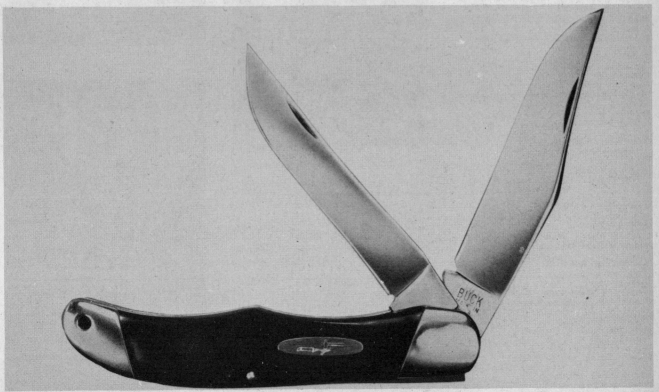

Buck Model No. 317

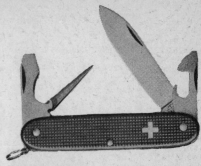

Compass Champion

Compass Craftsman

Compass Pioneer

Manufacturer: Gerber
Model No.: A-400 Drop Point
Type: Hunting
Length of Blade(s): 4″
Handle Material: Armorhide
Features: Leather belt scabbard; handle hole for a lanyard.

Manufacturer: Gerber
Model No.: FsII and IId Sportsman
Type: Folding
Length of Blade(s): 3½″
Handle Material: Steel, brass, hardwood inlays
Features: Built-in blade lock and safety pause.

Manufacturer: Gerber
Model No.: FsIII Sportsman III
Type: Folding
Length of Blade(s): 4½″
Handle Material: Steel, brass, hardwood inlays
Features: Grain leather belt scabbard.

Manufacturer: Gerber
Model: MFH Magnum Hunter
Type: Folding
Lenth of Blade(s): 3¼″
Handle Material: Steel, brass, hardwood inlays
Features: Belt scabbard included.

Manufacturer: Gerber
Model No.: 1K-3 Handyman
Type: Folding
Length of Blade(s): 3″, 2¾″
Handle Material: Steel, brass, Macassar ebony inlays
Features: Rustproof; wire stripping and screwdriver blade; all purpose.

Manufacturer: Gerber
Model No.: 400 S
Type: Straight
Length of Blade(s): 4″
Handle Material: Macassar ebony
Features: Double-wedge ground blade.

Manufacturer: Gerber
Model No.: 425 S
Type: Straight
Length of Blade(s): 4¼″
Handle Material: Macassar ebony

Manufacturer: Gerber
Model No.: 450 S
Type: Straight
Length of Blade(s): 4½″
Handle Material: Macassar ebony

Manufacturer: Gerber
Model No.: 475 S
Type: Straight
Length of Blade(s): 4¾″
Handle Material: Macassar ebony

Manufacturer: Gerber
Model No.: 525 S
Type: Straight

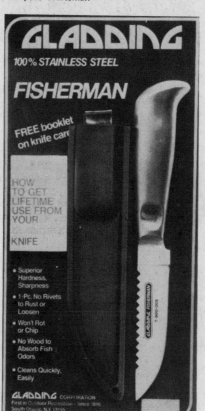

Gladding Fisherman

Length of Blade(s): 5¼″
Handle Material: Macassar ebony

Manufacturer: Gladding
Model: Angler
Type: Folding
Features: Stay-open folding lock; serrated scaler back edge; 420 stainless steel.

Manufacturer: Gladding
Model: Fillet
Type: Straight
Handle Material: Stainless steel
Features: Fishing; filleting; "self-bailing" sheath; finger groove.

Manufacturer: Gladding
Model: Fisherman
Type: Straight
Length of Blade(s): 4⅞″
Handle Material: Stainless steel

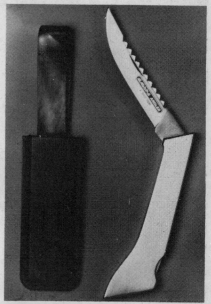

Gladding Angler

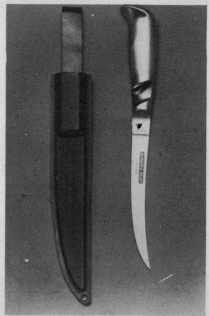

Gladding Fillet

Manufacturer: Palco
Model No.: 977 Backpackers
Type: Folding

Manufacturer: Precise
Model No.: 10325 Buffalo Skinner
Type: Straight
Length of Blade(s): 5½"
Handle Material: Staglite, brass
Features: Stainless vanadium steel.

Manufacturer: Precise
Model No.: 10623 Large Skinner
Type: Straight
Length of Blade(s): 4½"
Handle Material: Brass bolsters, grained wood
Sheath Material: Cowhide

Manufacturer: Precise
Model No.: 10831 DS1
Type: Straight
Length of Blade(s): 4¼"
Handle Material: Brass finger guard, butt cap, gunstock
Sheath Material: Brass riveted, grain leather
Features: Broad blade; skinning; 54° to 57° Rockwell.

Manufacturer: Precise
Model No.: 11839 DS9
Type: Folding
Handle Material: Brass finger guard, butt cap, gunstock
Sheath Material: Brass riveted, grain leather
Features: 3" closed.

Manufacturer: Precise
Model No.: 16524 Classic Hunter
Type: Straight
Length of Blade(s): 5½"
Features: Serrated edge; "Wear Ever" sheath with bonded sharpening stone.

Manufacturer: Precise
Model No.: 16536 Large Traditional Hunter
Type: Straight
Length of Blade(s): 5"
Handle Material: Pressed and polished leather
Sheath Material: Grain leather
Features: Swedish blue steel.

Palco Model No. 977

Manufacturer: Precise
Model No.: 16711 Backpacker
Type: Folding
Features: 7 blades.

Manufacturer: Precise
Model No.: 16931 Scout
Type: Folding
Features: 6 blades; lanyard chain.

Manufacturer: Precise
Model No.: 16934 Master Fisherman
Type: Folding
Features: 10 blades plus lanyard chain.

Manufacturer: Valor
Model No.: 4000090 Wilderness
Type: Folding
Handle Material: Handrubbed rosewood
Features: Locking blade; 5½" closed.

Manufacturer: Valor
Model No.: 4000424 Wildcat

Type: Straight
Length of Blade(s): 4½"
Handle Material: Pakka wood, steel
Features: Rustproof.

Manufacturer: Valor
Model No.: 4000429 Bowie Hunting
Type: Straight
Length of Blade(s): 6"
Handle Material: Stag
Features: Rustproof.

Manufacturer: Valor
Model No.: 4000507
Type: Folding
Handle Material: Pakka
Features: 5" closed; locking blade.

Manufacturer: Valor
Model No.: 4017004
Type: Straight
Length of Blade(s): 4"
Handle Material: Pakka wood
Features: Bowie style.

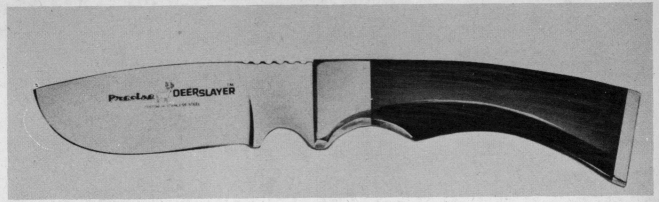

Precise Model No. 10831 DS1

Lanterns

Manufacturer: Ashflash
Model No.: 1022
Type: Gasoline
Features: Double mantle; waterproof ventilator; inner-coated fuel storage area.

Ashflash Model No. 1022

Manufacturer: Ashflash
Model No.: 1045
Type: Propane
Cylinder Weight: 14.1 oz. or 16 oz. disposable
Features: Double mantle; propane cylinder included.

Manufacturer: Ashflash
Model No.: 1056
Type: Fluorescent
Fluorescent Tube: 6 watt, 9″
Duration: 6000 hrs.
Features: Concealed handle; fluorescent tube included; 6-volt batteries not included.

Manufacturer: Ashflash
Model No.: 1092
Type: Fluorescent
Fluorescent Tube: 6 watt, 9″
Dimensions: 11″ x 5½″ x 3″
Duration: 6000 hrs.
Features: Carry handle; fluorescent tube and 18-foot adapter cord included; battery not included.

Manufacturer: Ashflash
Model No.: 7826
Type: Battery
Battery: 6 volt
Dimensions: 12″ x 8″ x 3″
Features: Dimmer switch; steel ring for hanging; battery included.

Ashflash Model No. 1045

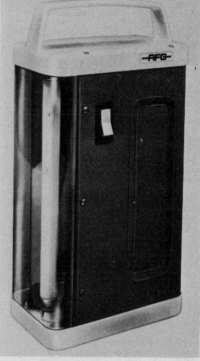

Ashflash Model No. 1092

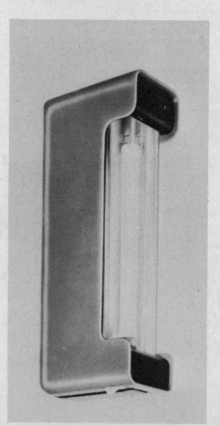

Ashflash Model No. 1056

Ashflash Model No. 7826

Manufacturer: Ashflash
Model No.: 7830
Type: Battery
Battery: 6 volt, twin terminal
Features: Unbreakable lens guard; adjustable head and blinker arm; separate switches; battery included.

Ashflash Model No. 7830

Manufacturer: Ashflash
Model No.: 7858
Type: Fluorescent
Fluorescent Tube: 6 watt, 9″
Duration: 6000 hrs.
Features: Concealed handle; fluorescent tube; 18-foot adapter cord and two 6-volt batteries included.

Manufacturer: Ashflash
Model No.: 7886
Type: Battery
Battery: 6 volt
Features: Unbreakable case; lens guard; battery included.

Manufacturer: BernzOmatic
Model No.: TX006
Type: Propane
Cylinder Weight: 14.1 oz. or 16 oz. disposable
Duration: 5 to 7 hrs.
Features: Double mantle; 16 oz. cylinder included; light equivalent to a 200-watt bulb.

BernzOmatic Model No. TX006

Manufacturer: BernzOmatic
Model No.: TX007
Type: Propane
Cylinder Weight: 14.1 oz. or 16 oz. disposable
Duration: 10 to 14 hrs.
Features: Single mantle; 16 oz. cylinder included; light equivalent to a 100-watt bulb.

BernzOmatic Model No. TX007

Manufacturer: BernzOmatic
Model No.: TX750
Type: Propane
Cylinder Weight: 14.1 oz. disposable
Duration: 10 to 14 hrs.
Features: Single mantle; dual beam; 14.1 oz. cylinder included; light equivalent to a 100-watt bulb.

BernzOmatic Model No. TX750

Manufacturer: Coleman
Model No.: 201700
Type: Kerosene
Dimensions: 11⅝″ x 5⅛″
Duration: 9 hrs.
Features: Single mantle.

Manufacturer: Coleman
Model No.: 275710
Type: Coleman Fuel
Dimensions: 13½″ x 8½″
Duration: 8 hrs.
Features: Double mantle; frosted globe.

Manufacturer: Coleman
Model No.: 220 J195
Type: Coleman Fuel
Dimensions: 13⅞″ x 6″
Duration: 8 hrs.
Features: Double mantle.

Manufacturer: Coleman
Model No.: 5114 A700
Type: Propane
Cylinder Weight: 14.1 oz. or 16.4 oz. disposable
Dimensions: 18⅜″ x 7¾″
Duration: 7 to 20 hrs.
Features: Double mantle; hooks up to bulk tank.

Manufacturer: Coleman
Model No.: 5350 B710
Type: Electric or battery
Battery: 6 volt
Dimensions: 13¼″ x 8⅞″ x 4¾″
Features: Rechargeable.

Manufacturer: Moor & Mountain
Model No.: 502
Type: Candle
Dimensions: 4″ x 7″ x 5″
Weight: ½ lb.
Duration: Up to 6 hrs.
Features: Folds flat to ¾″ x 5″; dripless; smokeless.

Manufacturer: Moor & Mountain
Model No.: 520
Type: Candle
Dimensions: 5″ x 2″
Weight: ⅖ lb.

Manufacturer: Primus
Model No.: 2173
Type: Propane
Cylinder Weight: 16.4 oz. disposable
Duration: 10 to 15 hrs.
Features: Cylinder included.

Manufacturer: Primus
Model No.: 2176
Type: Propane
Cylinder Weight: 14.1 oz. or 16.4 oz. disposable
Duration: 15 hrs.
Features: Single mantle; 16.4 oz. cylinder included; polyurethene footstand.

Manufacturer: Primus
Model No.: 2186
Type: Propane
Cylinder Weight: 14.1 oz. or 16.4 oz. disposable
Duration: 6 hrs.
Features: Double mantle; 16.4 oz. cylinder included; polyurethene footstand.

Manufacturer: Ray-O-Vac
Model No.: LM 85M 663
Type: Battery
Features: Includes battery.

Manufacturer: Ray-O-Vac
Model No.: 180 SM 1997
Type: Fluorescent
Features: Includes 2 batteries.

Manufacturer: Ray-O-Vac
Model No.: 360 SM 3330

Type: Fluorescent
Features: Includes 4 batteries.

Manufacturer: Trailblazer
Model No.: PL1490
Type: Propane
Cylinder Weight: 16.4 oz.
Features: Single mantle; includes cylinder.

Manufacturer: Trailblazer
Model No.: PL3000
Type: Propane
Cylinder Weight: 14.1 oz.
Features: Double mantle; includes cylinder.

Manufacturer: Wonder
Model No.: Bleuet C200
Type: Butane
Weight: 15 oz.
Features: Single mantle; folds up; frosted globe.

Manufacturer: Wonder
Model: Comfort
Type: Butane
Weight: 20 oz.
Features: Single mantle; frosted globe.

Manufacturer: Wonder
Model: Galaxy
Type: Battery
Battery: 3 D cells
Features: Plastic; batteries included.

Manufacturer: Wonder
Model No.: Lumoqaz C200
Type: Butane
Weight: 25 oz.
Features: Single mantle; fully vented hood.

Coleman Model No. 275710

Mattresses

Manufacturer: Colorado Tent & Awning
Model No.: AM-200
Type: Air
Dimensions: 28″ x 72″
Material: Vinyl-laminated woven fabric
Weight: 3 lbs.
Features: "I" beam construction; ideal pressure button.

Manufacturer: Colorado Tent & Awning
Model No.: AM-290
Type: Air
Dimensions: 30″ x 74″
Material: Vinyl-laminated woven fabric
Weight: 4½ lbs.
Features: Floating tuft construction; ideal pressure button.

Manufacturer: Colorado Tent & Awning
Model No.: BP-121 Shortie
Type: Air
Dimensions: 23″ x 50″
Material: Vinyl-laminated woven fabric
Weight: 2 lbs.
Features: "I" beam construction; drain for fast deflation; ideal pressure button.

Manufacturer: Colorado Tent & Awning
Model No.: BP-350
Type: Air
Dimensions: 26½″ x 72″
Material: Vinyl-laminated woven fabric
Weight: 2¾ lbs.
Features: Floating tuft construction; ideal pressure button.

Manufacturer: Converse
Model No.: 3895
Type: Air
Dimensions: 30″ x 72″
Material: Rubber-coated nylon
Weight: 5 lbs. 4 oz.
Features: Box type; waffle construction.

Manufacturer: Converse
Model No.: 3896
Type: Air
Dimensions: 30″ x 77″
Material: Rubber-coated nylon
Weight: 5 lbs. 9 oz.
Features: 5 tubes with pillow; "I" beam construction.

Manufacturer: Converse
Model No.: 3898
Type: Air
Dimensions: 30″ x 72″
Material: Rubber-coated nylon
Weight: 4 lbs. 12 oz.
Features: 5 tubes; "I" beam construction.

Manufacturer: Hampshire
Model No.: 010-0 Comfort King
Type: Air
Dimensions: 30″ x 72″
Material: Rubberized cloth
Features: Waffle-type tufting; gusseted side panel construction.

Manufacturer: Hampshire
Model No.: 011-8 La Siesta. Same as Model No. 010-0 Comfort King
Dimensions: 30″ x 76″
Features: Built-in pillow; plaid surface.

Manufacturer: Hampshire
Model No.: 103-7 Back-Pak Mat
Type: Air
Dimensions: 30″ x 72″
Material: Vinyl

Manufacturer: Hampshire
Model No.: 203-5 Station Wagon
Type: Air
Dimensions: 60″ x 72″
Material: Vinyl
Features: Two No. 103-7 mats with five grom-

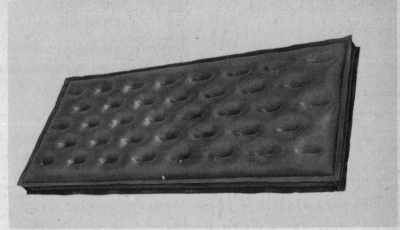

Hampshire Model No. 010-0

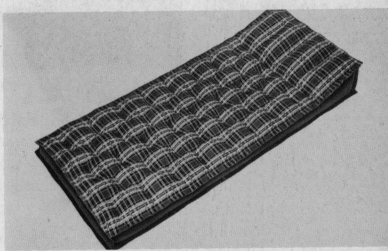

Hampshire Model No. 011-8

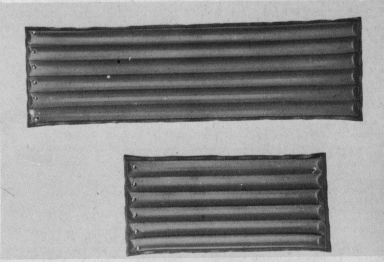

Hampshire Model No. 719-4   Hampshire Model No. 720-3

mets to snap them together along the sides.

Manufacturer: Hampshire
Model No.: 205-8 Deluxe Camper's Mat
Type: Air
Dimensions: 39″ x 74″
Material: Cotton fabric
Features: Pinked non-raveling edges.

Manufacturer: Hampshire
Model No.: 226-4 Wagoneer
Type: Air
Dimensions: 51″ x 74″
Material: Cloth
Features: Station-wagon mat; 7 tubes; inner coating; full size—no snaps or grommets.

Manufacturer: Hampshire
Model No.: 702-4 Nylo-Rest Camping Mattress
Type: Air
Dimensions: 34″ x 72″
Material: Nylon cloth
Features: Co-polymer inner coating.

Manufacturer: Hampshire
Model No.: 719-4
Type: Air
Dimensions: 28″ x 72″
Material: Coated nylon
Inflation System: Mouth
Features: 6 air chambers with individual valves; drawstring stuff sack; repair kit.

Manufacturer: Hampshire
Model No.: 720-3
Type: Air
Dimensions: 28″ x 44″
Material: Coated nylon
Inflation System: Mouth
Features: 6 air chambers with individual valves; drawstring stuff sack; repair kit.

Manufacturer: Kelty
Model: Air Mattress
Type: Air
Dimensions: 22″ x 46″
Material: 11 mil vinyl plastic
Weight: 10 oz.
Features: Patch kit; individual tube inflation; outer tubes larger for cradle effect.

Manufacturer: Kelty
Model: Air Pillow
Type: Air
Dimensions: 11″ x 16″
Material: 11 mil vinyl
Weight: 4½ oz.
Features: Used alone or snapped to matching air mattress.

Manufacturer: Kelty
Model: Nylon Covered Foam Pad
Type: Polyurethane pad
Dimensions: 1½″ x 20″ x 40″
Material: 2.7 oz. nylon taffeta cover
Weight: 23 oz.
Features: Oval-shaped pouch serves as stuff bag or pillow with extra clothes; removable cover for cleaning; top is uncoated for breathability.

Manufacturer: Kelty
Model: Vinyl Covered Foam Pad
Type: Polyurethane pad
Dimensions: 1½″ x 20″ x 40″
Material: 7 mil vinyl plastic cover
Features: Breather valves; dust and rainproof sealed seams.

Manufacturer: North Face
Model: Foam Pads
Type: Foam
Dimensions: Regular: 20″ x 36″; large: 20″ x 50″
Material: Cotton top with waterproof coated bottom
Weight: Regular: 17 oz.; large: 23 oz.
Features: Tie strings sewn in; roll to 5″ diameter.

Manufacturer: North Face
Model: Ensolite
Type: Closed cell vinyl foam
Dimensions: Regular: 42″; large: 56″
Material: Vinyl
Weight: Regular: 14 oz.; large: 18 oz.

Manufacturer: Ski Hut
Model No.: NE1 Full, NE0 Half Ensolite sheets
Type: Unicellular
Dimensions: Full: 42″ x 56″; Half: 21″ x 56″
Material: Ensolite
Features: Assorted thicknesses and weights.

Manufacturer: Ski Hut
Model No.: S39/B, S10/BL Airlift Mattresses
Type: Air
Dimensions: S39/B: 20″ x 42″; S10/BL: 22″ x 72″
Material: Rip-stop nylon taffeta shell poly-vinyl air tubes
Weight: S39/B: 20 oz.; S10/BL: 40 oz.
Features: Nylon zipper closure; individual tube inflation; punctured tubes replaceable (one spare included); stuff sack.

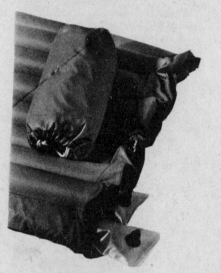

Ski Hut Model No. S39/B

Manufacturer: Ski Hut
Model No.: S121 Sleeping Pad
Type: Unicellular
Dimensions: ⅜″ x 19″ x 42″
Material: Ensolite
Weight: 14 oz.
Features: Rolled size: 5″ x 19″; doesn't soak up water like foam rubber.

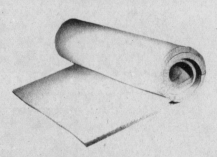

Ski Hut Model No. S121

Manufacturer: Ski Hut
Model No.: S122 Slimline Pad
Type: Foam
Dimensions: 2″ x 21″ x 38″

Material: Waterproof Nylport nylon cover
Weight: 29 oz.
Features: Rolls into own hood; rolled size: 9″ x 6″ x 20″.

Ski Hut Model No. S122

Manufacturer: Ski Hut
Model No.: S123/3, S123/6
Type: Convoluted foam mat
Dimensions: S123/3: 2″ x 21″ x 38″; S123/6: 2″ x 21″ x 76″
Material: Polyurethane
Weight: S123/3: 16 oz.; S123/6: 32 oz.

Ski Hut Model No. S123/3

Manufacturer: Ski Hut
Model No.: S125 Ever-Rest Pad
Type: Closed cell
Dimensions: 22″ x 44″
Material: Polyurethane foam
Weight: 13 oz.
Features: Molded configuration creates air pockets; rolled size: 5″ x 22″.

Ski Hut Model No. S125

Manufacturer: Ski Hut
Model No.: S340 Air Cushion (Stebco)
Type: Air
Dimensions: 15″ x 18″
Material: Nylon
Weight: 5 oz.

Manufacturer: Ski Hut
Model No.: S345 Good Companion Air Bed (Thomas Black)
Type: Air
Dimensions: 22″ x 45″
Material: Rubberized cotton canvas
Weight: 30 oz.
Features: 4 longitudinal tubes; separate inflating pillow.

Packs

Manufacturer: Academy
Model No.: 615
Type: Knapsack
No. Pockets: 1
Closures: Strap
Color(s): Green
Weight: 1 lb.
Volume Capacity: 942.5 cu. in.
Features: Duck harness.

Manufacturer: Academy
Model No.: 3733 Bonanza
Type: Pack and frame
No. Pockets: 7
Closures: Drawstrings, zippers
Color(s): Blaze orange
Weight: 4¼ lbs.
Volume Capacity: 4508 cu. in.
Features: Anodized aluminum frame.

Manufacturer: Academy
Model No.: 5732 Andes
Type: Pack and frame
No. Pockets: 6
Closures: Straps, metal and nylon zippers
Color(s): Red
Weight: 5 lbs.
Volume Capacity: 6615 cu. in.
Features: Anodized frame; 3-section main compartment; nylon padded waist strap.

Manufacturer: Academy
Model No.: 6624 Rucksack
Type: Pack and frame
No. Pockets: 3
Closures: Straps, zipper
Color(s): Green
Weight: 3¼ lbs.
Volume Capacity: 2783 cu. in.
Features: Aluminum frame.

Manufacturer: Academy
Model No.: 6645 Apache
Type: Soft
No. Pockets: 2
Closures: Nylon zippers
Color(s): Marsh brown
Weight: 2 lbs.
Features: Front-loading divided main compartment; full-width bottom compartment; leather strap tabs for accessories.

Manufacturer: Academy
Model No.: 6735 Dakota
Type: Pack and frame
No. Pockets: 3
Closures: Nylon zippers
Color(s): Marsh brown
Weight: 4⅙ lbs.
Volume Capacity: 4158 cu. in.
Features: Anodized frame; leather strap tabs for accessories; nylon ax loop; rear map pocket.

Manufacturer: Alpine Designs
Model No.: 447 Summit
Type: Soft
No. Pockets: 1
Closures: Zippers
Color(s): Camel, navy, red
Weight: 1 lb. 8 oz.
Volume Capacity: 1150 cu. in.
Features: Adjustable, padded, reinforced shoulder harness; ice-ax carrier; 3 accessory strap holders; leather bottom.

Manufacturer: Alpine Designs
Model No.: 448 Eiger II
Type: Soft
No. Pockets: 3
Closures: Drawstrings, clamps, zippers
Color(s): Camel, navy, red
Weight: 2 lbs. 9 oz.
Volume Capacity: 2100 cu. in.
Features: Adjustable, padded, reinforced shoulder harness; map pocket; 9 accessory strap holders, including 2 for skis.

Alpine Designs Model No. 447

Alpine Designs Model No. 448

Alpine Designs Model No. 450

Manufacturer: Alpine Designs
Model No.: 450 Prospector
Type: Pack and frame
No. Pockets: 5
Closures: Drawstrings, clamps, zippers
Color(s): Camel, navy, red
Weight: 4 lbs. 6 oz.
Volume Capacity: 3500 cu. in.
Features: Plastic frame; collapsible hold-open bar; 4 "D" rings; ice-ax carrier; corner slits in shelf between main compartments.

Manufacturer: Antelope
Model No.: 3280 Convertible
Type: Pack and frame
No. Pockets: 4
Closures: Delrin zippers
Weight: 4 lbs. 10 oz.
Volume Capacity: 3450 cu. in.
Features: Two 30" x 1" straps for accessories; ice-ax loop; 3 accessory strap holders.

Manufacturer: Browning
Model No.: 3161647 Mackenzie
Type: Pack and frame
No. Pockets: 6
Closures: Drawstrings, zippers
Color(s): Brook blue
Volume Capacity: 3360 cu. in.
Features: Adjustable aluminum frame; corner openings; "D" rings; leather patches.

Manufacturer: Browning
Model No.: 4361527 Beltpacker
Type: Belt pack
Closures: Zipper, snaps
Color(s): Brook blue
Features: 2 expandable compartments; 2 leather patches.

Manufacturer: Camp Trails
Model No.: 472 Trekker
Type: Soft pack
No. Pockets: 2
Closures: Drawstrings, coil zippers
Color(s): Orange, blue, green, brown
Weight: 1 lb. 2 oz.
Volume Capacity: 1865 cu. in.
Features: Extendable top; leather patches.

Manufacturer: Camp Trails
Model No.: 473 Scrambler
Type: Pack and frame
No. Pockets: 3
Closures: Drawstrings, coil zippers
Color(s): Blue, brown
Weight: 2 lbs. 5 oz.
Volume Capacity: 2777 cu. in.
Features: Converts from rucksack to soft pack; extendable top; leather patches.

Manufacturer: Camp Trails
Model No.: 600 Gemini
Type: Pack and frame
No. Pockets: 3
Closures: Toggle lock, zippers
Color(s): Denim blue, bark brown
Weight: M, 3 lbs. 3 oz.; L, 3 lbs. 6 oz.
Volume Capacity: 2677 cu. in.
Features: Converts from backpack to internal rucksack; aluminum frame; leather patches; cinch straps.

Manufacturer: Camp Trails
Model No.: 603 Adjustable II
Type: Pack and frame
No. Pockets: 5
Closures: Drawstrings, coil zippers, Velcro
Color(s): Orange, blue, green
Weight: M, 3 lbs. 11 oz.; L, 3 lbs. 12 oz.
Volume Capacity: M, 2780 cu. in.; L, 3050 cu. in.
Features: Adjustable aluminum frame; adjustable, padded shoulder strap and hipbelt; spreader bar; map pocket.

Camp Trails Model No. 473

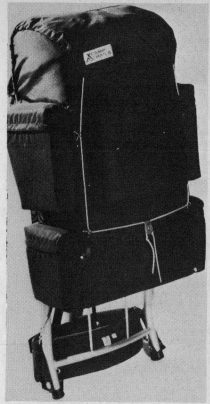

Camp Trails Model No. 605

Camp Trails Model No. 603

Features: 2 front-loading compartments; aluminum frame; spreader bar; cinch straps.

Manufacturer: Camp Trails
Model No.: 605 Astral
Type: Pack and frame
No. Pockets: 6
Closures: Drawstrings, Delrin zippers, Velcro
Color(s): Orange, blue, green, bark brown
Weight: M, 4 lbs. 6 oz.; L, 4 lbs. 8 oz.
Volume Capacity: M, 4150 cu. in.;
    L, 4330 cu. in.
Features: Aluminum frame; extendable top; adjustable, padded shoulder strap and hip-belt; leather patches; map pocket.

Manufacturer: Camp Trails
Model No.: 606 Centuri
Type: Pack and frame
No. Pockets: 5
Closures: Drawstrings, Delrin zippers
Color(s): Denim blue, bark brown
Weight: M, 4 lbs. 2 oz.; L, 4 lbs. 4 oz.
Volume Capacity: M, 3860 cu. in.;
    L, 4345 cu. in.
Features: Aluminum frame; extendable top; spreader bar; leather patches; Velcro accessory holder.

Manufacturer: Camp Trails
Model No.: 608 Corona
Type: Pack and frame
No. Pockets: 3
Closures: Drawstrings, coil zippers, Velcro
Color(s): Orange, green
Weight: 2 lbs. 13 oz.
Volume Capacity: 1885 cu. in.
Features: Adjustable aluminum frame; adjustable, padded shoulder straps and hip-belt; map pocket.

Manufacturer: Camp-ways
Model No.: 410 Wolverine
Type: Pack and frame
No. Pockets: 3
Closures: Drawstrings, zippers

Manufacturer: Camp Trails
Model No.: 604 New Horizon (M, L)
Type: Pack and frame
No. Pockets: 5
Closures: Drawstring, toggle lock, coil zippers
Color(s): Orange, blue, green, bark brown
Weight: M, 3 lbs. 12 oz.; L, 3 lbs. 15 oz.
Volume Capacity: 3325 cu. in.

Camp Trails Model No. 606

Camp Trails Model No. 608

Color(s): Rust, royal blue, forest green
Weight: 2 lbs. 13 oz.
Volume Capacity: 1987 cu. in.
Features: Aluminum frame; padded hipbelt;
 spreader bar; leather patches; lashing
 strap; map pocket.

Manufacturer: Camp-ways
Model No.: 430 Strider
Type: Pack and frame
No. Pockets: 5
Closures: Drawstrings, zippers
Color(s): Rust, royal blue, forest green
Weight: 48 oz.
Volume Capacity: 2776 cu. in.
Features: Aluminum frame; padded shoulder
 harness; spreader bar; leather patches;
 map pocket.

Manufacturer: Camp-ways
Model No.: 435D Tradewind Deluxe
Type: Pack and frame
No. Pockets: 6
Closures: Drawstrings, zippers
Color(s): Rust, royal blue, forest green
Weight: 4 lbs. 6 oz.
Volume Capacity: 3130 cu. in.
Features: Aluminum frame; spreader bar;
 leather patches; lashing straps; map pocket.

Manufacturer: Camp-ways
Model No.: 445 Sundowner
Type: Pack and frame
No. Pockets: 5
Closures: Drawstrings, zippers
Color(s): Rust, royal blue, forest green
Weight: 4 lbs. 6 oz.
Volume Capacity: 2776 cu. in.
Features: Aluminum frame; spreader bar;
 leather patches; lashing straps; map
 pockets.

Manufacturer: Camp-ways
Model No.: 780 Eiger Mountain
Type: Soft
Closures: Zippers
Color(s): Brown, forest green
Weight: 2 lbs.
Volume Capacity: 2950 cu. in.
Features: Padded hipbelt; crampon patches;
 ax loop.

Camp-ways Model No. 410

Camp-ways Model No. 430

Camp-ways Model No. 445

SPECIFICATIONS: EQUIPMENT

Camp-ways Model No. 435D

Manufacturer: Coleman
Model No.: 750
Type: Pack
No. Pockets: 4
Closures: Drawstrings, nylon zippers
Color(s): Red
Weight: 23½ oz.
Volume Capacity: 1949 cu. in.
Features: Pass-throughs in compartment divider.

Manufacturer: Coleman
Model No.: Peak 1
Type: Frame
Weight: 33 oz.
Features: Flexible, slotted, plastic frame; lash points; lash tabs on shoulder straps and hipbelt; extension bar.

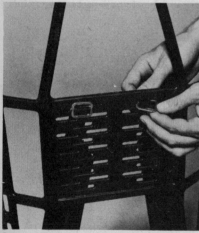

Coleman Peak 1

Manufacturer: Coleman
Model No.: 770 Peak 1
Type: Pack
No. Pockets: 5
Closures: Drawstrings, nylon zippers
Color(s): Rust
Weight: 38 oz.
Volume Capacity: 2350 cu. in.
Features: Detachable fanny pack; pass-throughs in compartment divider; map pocket; ax loop; 4 patches.

Manufacturer: Colorado Tent & Awning
Model: Summit

Type: Pack and frame
No. Pockets: 4
Closures: Zippers
Color(s): Columbian blue
Weight: 4 lbs.
Volume Capacity: 2156 cu. in.
Features: Aluminum alloy frame.

Manufacturer: Colorado Tent & Awning
Model: Hitchhiker
Type: Touring pack
No. Pockets: 1
Closures: Drawstring, zipper
Color(s): Bright orange, blue
Weight: 2 lbs.

Manufacturer: Colorado Tent & Awning
Model: Frontier
Type: Pack sack
Closures: Straps
Weight: 36 lbs.
Volume Capacity: 4680 cu. in.
Features: 3 straps for accessories.

Manufacturer: Colorado Tent & Awning
Model: SBB Suedeback
Type: Boot bag
No. Pockets: 1
Closures: Zippers
Color(s): Green, blue, yellow, orange
Weight: 3 lbs.
Volume Capacity: 2080 cu. in.
Features: Shoulder strap included.

Manufacturer: Colorado Tent & Awning
Model: RBR Minuteman
Type: Boot bag
No. Pockets: 1
Closures: Zippers
Color(s): Green-blue, gold-orange, red-white-blue
Weight: 2½ lbs.
Volume Capacity: 2080 cu. in.
Features: Optional shoulder strap.

Manufacturer: Colorado Tent & Awning
Model No.: 1 Arcticreel
Type: Creel
Closures: Snap
Weight: 13 oz.
Volume Capacity: 540 cu. in.
Features: Removable lining; fish measuring scale.

Manufacturer: Colorado Tent & Awning
Model No.: 20 Arcticreel
Type: Creel
No. Pockets: 1
Closures: Zipper
Weight: 1 lb.
Volume Capacity: 560 cu. in.
Features: Tackle pocket; removable lining; fish measuring scale.

Coleman Model No. 770

Manufacturer: Gokey
Model No.: 1-1136
Type: Bicycle touring
Weight: 3 lbs.
Volume Capacity: 2200 cu. in.
Features: Adjustable; side stiffeners; lash points.

Gokey Model No. 1-1136

Manufacturer: Himalayan
Model No.: 1 Daytripper
Type: Soft pack
No. Pockets: 1
Closures: Drawstring, zipper
Color(s): Blue
Weight: 9 oz.
Volume Capacity: 1156 cu. in.
Features: Converts to pouch with belt loops; webbing for sleeping-bag attachment.

Manufacturer: Himalayan
Model No.: 6 Beginner Combination
Type: Pack and frame
No. Pockets: 3
Closures: Drawstrings, buckles
Color(s): Blue
Weight: 2 lbs.
Volume Capacity: 1640 cu. in.
Features: Aluminum alloy frame; accessory tab; map pocket.

Manufacturer: Himalayan
Model No.: 8 Easy Rider
Type: Pack and frame
No. Pockets: 5
Closures: Straps, Velcro
Color(s): Blue
Weight: 2 lbs. 10 oz.
Volume Capacity: 2210 cu. in.
Features: Aluminum alloy frame; adjustable shoulder straps; map pocket.

Manufacturer: Himalayan
Model No.: 8B/11F Easy Rider Deluxe. Same as Model No. 8 Easy Rider except:
Weight: 3 lbs. 2 oz.
Features: Padded hipbelt.

Manufacturer: Himalayan
Model No.: 10 Professional
Type: Pack and frame
No. Pockets: 3
Weight: 2 lbs. 14 oz.
Volume Capacity: 2558 cu. in.
Features: Aluminum alloy frame; adjustable shoulder straps; adjustable padded hipbelt; map pocket.

Manufacturer: Himalayan
Model No.: 21 Mini
Type: Child's soft
Closures: Drawstring
Color(s): Red
Weight: 6 oz.
Volume Capacity: 748 cu. in.

Manufacturer: Himalayan
Model No.: 22
Type: Handlebar
Closures: Nylon zipper
Color(s): Blue
Weight: 2 oz.
Features: Straps on handlebar, crossbar or behind seat.

Manufacturer: Himalayan
Model No.: 24 Deluxe
Type: Bike, motorcycle
Closures: Nylon zipper, Velcro
Color(s): Blue
Weight: 10 oz.
Features: Masonite backing; use on handlebar, crossbar or luggage carrier.

Manufacturer: Himalayan
Model No.: 28 All-Purpose
Type: Bike, motorcycle
Closures: Straps
Color(s): Red
Weight: 4 oz.
Volume Capacity: 284 cu. in.
Features: Use on handlebar, crossbar or behind seat.

Manufacturer: Himalayan
Model No.: 29
Type: Bicycle touring pannier
Closures: Nylon zippers
Color(s): Blue
Weight: 3 lbs. 12 oz.
Features: Masonite backing; lashing tabs.

Manufacturer: Himalayan
Model No.: 60 Luggage Cycle
No. Pockets: 1
Closures: Zippers
Color(s): Red
Weight: 1 lb. 12 oz.
Features: Fits on sissy bar or luggage rack; use as backpack; lashing straps.

Manufacturer: Himalayan
Model No.: 210 Nuptse
Type: Pack and frame
No. Pockets: 2
Closures: Drawstring
Color(s): Blue
Weight: 2 lbs.
Volume Capacity: 1854 cu. in.
Features: Detachable main bag; anodized aluminum alloy frame; tunnels behind pockets; 4 leather strap tabs.

Manufacturer: Himalayan
Model No. 240 Kuli
Type: Pack and frame
No. Pockets: 5
Closures: Straps, zippers
Color(s): Blue
Weight: 4 lbs. 8 oz.
Volume Capacity: 3516 cu. in.
Features: Anodized aluminum alloy frame; 8 leather strap tabs; duffel/stuff bag.

Manufacturer: Himalayan
Model No.: 250 Khumbu
No. Pockets: 3
Closures: Straps, zippers
Color(s): Blue
Weight: 4 lbs. 4 oz.
Volume Capacity: 2827 cu. in.
Features: Detachable main bag; anodized aluminum alloy frame; tunnels behind pockets; 3 leather strap tabs; duffel/stuff bag.

Manufacturer: Holubar
Model No.: 108035A Royal
Type: Soft
No. Pockets: 2
Closures: Drawstring with V-slide, Delrin zippers
Color(s): Navy, orange
Weight: 3 lbs.

Features: 2 internal aluminum stays; top lid compartment; 2 accessory strap holders; leather ski guards.

Manufacturer: Holubar
Model No.: 108043A
Type: Belt pack
Closures: Nylon zipper
Color(s): Navy, orange
Weight: 8 oz.
Volume Capacity: 390 cu. in.
Features: 2 attachment rings.

Manufacturer: Holubar
Model No.: 750135B Colorado
Type: Pack and frame
No. Pockets: 6
Closures: Drawstrings, zippers, locking slider
Color(s): Forest green
Weight: M, 3 lbs. 14 oz.; L, 4 lbs. 3 oz.; XL, 4 lbs. 5 oz.
Volume Capacity: M, 2972 cu. in.; L, XL, 3472 cu. in.
Features: Zip-out packbag divider; aluminum alloy hold-open frame; map pocket.

Manufacturer: Holubar
Model No.: 756049A
Type: Touring pannier
No. Pockets: 6
Color(s): Red, navy
Weight: 2 lbs. 6 oz.
Volume Capacity: 2000 cu. in.
Features: Spring suspension system; aluminum stiffeners; luggage handle.

Manufacturer: Holubar
Model No.: 756056A
Type: Standard touring handlebar
No. Pockets: 3
Closures: Zipper, snap
Color(s): Red, navy
Weight: 1 lb. 4 oz.
Volume Capacity: 680 cu. in.
Features: Spring suspension system; aluminum bottom stiffeners; shoulder strap; map pocket.

Manufacturer: Holubar
Model No.: 756064A
Type: Light touring pannier
No. Pockets: 2
Closures: Coil zippers
Color(s): Red, navy
Weight: 1 lb. 14 oz.
Volume Capacity: 1100 cu. in.
Features: Spring suspension system; aluminum stiffeners; luggage handle.

Manufacturer: Kelty
Model No.: D4 Mountaineer
Type: Pack and frame
No. Pockets: 4
Closures: Drawstrings, metal zippers
Color(s): Olive green
Weight: S, 54 oz.; M, 56 oz.; L, 60 oz.; XL, 62 oz.

Kelty Model No. D4

Volume Capacity: S, 1686 cu. in.; M, 1874 cu. in.; L, 2388 cu. in.
Features: Aluminum alloy hold-open frame.

Manufacturer: Kelty
Model: Serac
Type: Pack and frame
No. Pockets: 5
Closures: Drawstrings, metal and polyester zippers
Color(s): Red, olive green
Weight: M, 80 oz.; L, 82 oz.; XL, 86 oz.
Volume Capacity: M, 3443 cu. in.; L, 4171 cu. in.; XL, 4449 cu. in.
Features: Adjustable frame; accessory strap holders; ice-ax loop.

Kelty Serac

Kelty Belt Pocket

Manufacturer: Kelty
Model: Haul Pack
Closures: Strap
Color(s): Bright blue
Weight: 2 lbs. 9 oz.
Volume Capacity: 1550 cu. in.
Features: Ice-ax loop; accessory strap holders.

Kelty Haul Pack

Manufacturer: Kelty
Model: Rucksack
No. Pockets: 3
Closures: Drawstrings, zippers
Color(s): Bright blue
Weight: 2 lbs. 14 oz.
Volume Capacity: 2800 cu. in.
Features: Expandable main compartment; ski slots.

Kelty Rucksack

Kelty Cargo Bag

Manufacturer: Kelty
Model: Sleeping Bag Pack
Closures: Nylon zipper
Color(s): Red, blue
Weight: 5½ oz.

Manufacturer: Kelty
Model: Cargo Bag
No. Pockets: 1
Closures: Polyester zippers
Color(s): Royal Blue
Features: Available with shoulder strap.

Manufacturer: Kelty
Model: Belt Pocket
Closures: Zipper
Color(s): Burnt orange
Weight: 3 oz.
Volume Capacity: 87 cu. in.

Manufacturer: Medalist/Universal
Model: Conestoga
Type: Soft
No. Pockets: 3
Closures: Drawstrings, zippers
Color(s): Navy, eli blue, forest green
Weight: M, 2 lbs. 5 oz.; L, 2 lbs. 6 oz.
Volume Capacity: M, 3507 cu. in.; L, 4490 cu.. in.
Features: Adjustable padded shoulder straps; accessory patches.

Manufacturer: Medalist/Universal
Model: Dimension Six
Type: Pack and frame
No. Pockets: 4
Closures: Drawstrings, nylon zippers
Color(s): Tan, blue, forest green
Weight: 4 lbs. 10 oz.
Volume Capacity: 4100 cu. in.

Features: Adjustable aluminum frame; adjustable padded shoulder straps and hipbelt.

Manufacturer: Medalist/Universal
Model: Loadmaster
Type: Pack and frame
No. Pockets: 5
Closures: Nylon zippers
Color(s): Tan, blue, forest green
Weight: M, 4 lbs. 5 oz.; L, 4 lbs. 14 oz; XL, 5 lbs.
Volume Capacity: M, 3580 cu. in.; L, XL, 4100 cu. in.
Features: Aluminum frame; hold open; ax strap; accessory patches; map pocket.

Manufacturer: Medalist/Universal
Model: Loadmaster Expedition Standard
Type: Pack and frame
No. Pockets: 9
Closures: Drawstrings, nylon zippers
Color(s): Wine, coppertone, navy
Weight: M, 4 lbs. 11 oz.; L, 5 lbs. 3 oz.
Volume Capacity: M, 3333 cu. in.; L, 4050 cu. in.
Features: Aluminum frame; lashing patches; ice-ax carrier and crampon patch.

Manufacturer: Medalist/Universal
Model: Nomad
Type: Pack and frame
No. Pockets: 4
Closures: Drawstrings, nylon zippers
Color(s): Red, orange, forest green, eli blue
Weight: S, 3 lbs. 8 oz.; M, 3 lbs. 9 oz.; L, 3 lbs. 12 oz.; XL, 3 lbs. 13 oz.
Volume Capacity: S, M, 2534 cu. in.; L, XL, 3078 cu. in.
Features: Aluminum frame; adjustable padded shoulder straps and hipbelt.

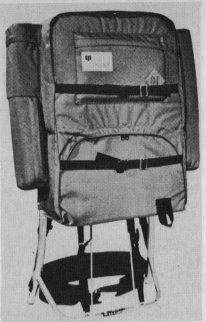

Medalist/Universal Loadmaster

Manufacturer: Medalist/Universay
Model: Nordic Mark II Deluxe
Type: Soft
Closures: Drawstrings, straps, nylon zippers
Color(s): Tan, blue, forest green
Weight: 1 lb. 12 oz.
Volume Capacity: 2002 cu. in.
Features: Leather bottom; ski slots; ice-ax loop; accessory patches; "D" ring.

Manufacturer: Medalist/Universal
Model: Trailmaster Standard
Type: Pack and frame
No. Pockets: 6
Closures: Drawstrings, nylon zippers
Color(s): Wine, coppertone, navy
Weight: S, 3 lbs. 15 oz.; M, 4 lbs.; L, 4 lbs. 3 oz.; XL, 4 lbs. 4 oz.
Volume Capacity: S, M, 2762 cu. in.; L, XL, 3298 cu. in.
Features: Aluminum frame; hold open; ax strap; accessory patches.

Manufacturer: Moor & Mountain
Model No.: 250 Standard
Type: Handlebar
No. Pockets: 1
Closures: Zipper
Weight: .94 lb.
Features: Metal frame and shock cord suspension; removable foam liner; map case.

Manufacturer: Moor & Mountain
Model No.: 251 Professional
Type: Handlebar
No. Pockets: 8
Closures: Zippers
Weight: 1.25 lbs.
Features: Metal frame and shock cord suspension; shoulder strap; foam liner; map case.

Manufacturer: Moor & Mountain
Model No.: 252
Type: Seat
Closures: Zipper
Weight: .28 lb.
Features: Nylon webbing reinforced pack.

Manufacturer: Moor & Mountain
Model No.: 256 Standard
Type: Pannier
Closures: Zippers

Weight: 1.42 lbs.
Volume Capacity: 1610 cu. in.
Features: Rear panel stiffener; carrying handle.

Manufacturer: North Face
Model: Pack & Frame
No. Pockets: 5
Closures: Zippers
Color(s): Navy, forest green, flaming orange
Weight: S, 4 lbs. 2 oz.; M, 4 lbs. 4 oz.; L, 4 lbs. 7 oz.; XL, 4 lbs. 8 oz.
Volume Capacity: S, M, 3348 cu in.; L, XL, 3892 cu. in.
Features: Aluminum alloy frame; adjustable padded shoulder straps and hipbelt; hold open; "D" rings.

Manufacturer: North Face
Model: Cannondale Saddle
Closures: Coil zippers
Color(s): Bright blue, canary yellow
Weight: 4 oz.
Volume Capacity: 264 cu. in.
Features: Carrying strap; plastic latches.

Manufacturer: North Face
Model: Guide Pack
Type: Rucksack
No. Pockets: 4
Closures: Straps, zippers
Color(s): Navy, orange, forest green
Volume Capacity: 2382 cu. in.
Features: Padded shoulder straps; map pocket; patches; haul loop.

Manufacturer: North Face
Model No.: BP22 Cannondale
Type: Bicycle rack
Closures: Zippers
Color(s): Bright blue, canary yellow
Weight: 29 oz.
Volume Capacity: 1200 cu. in.
Features: Aluminum frame; carrying strap.

Manufacturer: North Face
Model No.: BP24 Cannondale Handlebar
Type: Bicycle
No. Pockets: 1
Color(s): Blue, canary yellow
Weight: 12 oz.
Volume Capacity: 495 cu. in.
Features: Aluminum frame; map pocket; anti-sway cord; reflector; carrying strap.

Manufacturer: Pak Foam
Model No.: TP-1 Trek Pak
Type: Bicycle pannier
Closures: Delrin Zippers
Weight: 48 oz.
Volume Capacity: 3000 cu. in.
Features: Converts to internal frame backpack; stiffeners; 2 map pockets.

Manufacturer: Pak Foam
Model No.: FP-2
Type: Fanny
Closures: Nylon zippers
Weight: 6 oz.
Features: Side zippers.

Manufacturer: Recreational Equipment
Model No.: B02-065 Cruiser
Type: Pack and frame
No. Pockets: 5
Closures: Drawstrings, zippers
Color(s): Lobster red, blue, sage green
Weight: 4 lbs.
Volume Capacity: 2436 cu. in.
Features: Aluminum frame; extra top crossbar; pass-through opening between compartments.

Manufacturer: Recreational Equipment
Model No.: B02-137 Basic Cruiser
Type: Pack and frame
No. Pockets: 3
Closures: Zippers
Color(s): Light blue
Weight: 3⅛ lbs.
Volume Capacity: 1784 cu. in.

Pak-Foam Model No. TP-1

Features: Aluminum frame; adjustable padded shoulder straps.

Manufacturer: Recreational Equipment
Model No.: B02-200 Super-Pak
Type: Pack and frame
No. Pockets: 5
Closures: Drawstrings, zippers
Color(s): Royal blue
Weight: 4¼ lbs.
Features: Aluminum alloy frame; ice-ax carrier; patches.

Manufacturer: Recreational Equipment
Model No.: B02-250 Scout (Jansport)
Type: Pack and frame
No. Pockets: 3
Closures: Nylon zippers
Color(s): Red
Weight: 2⅝ lbs.
Volume Capacity: 1657 cu. in.
Features: Top and bottom extension bar frame.

Manufacturer: Recreational Equipment
Model No. B02-310 Cascade 2 (Jansport)
Type: Pack and frame
No. Pockets: 2
Closures: Nylon zippers
Color(s): Red, blue
Weight: 3⅞ lbs.
Volume Capacity: 2572 cu. in.
Features: Anodized aluminum frame; 5 accessory strap holders; ice-ax loop.

Manufacturer: Recreational Equipment
Model No.: B02-405 Corsair Junior
Type: Pack and frame
No. Pockets: 2
Closures: Drawstrings, nylon zippers
Color(s): Orange
Weight: 2 lbs.
Volume Capacity: 1225 cu. in.
Features: Aluminum frame; adjustable padded shoulder straps.

Manufacturer: Recreational Equipment
Model No.: B02-407 Astral Horizon
Type: Pack and frame
No. Pockets: 5
Closures: Drawstrings, zippers
Color(s): Blue
Features: Aluminum alloy frame; adjustable padded shoulder straps and hipbelt.

Manufacturer: Recreational Equipment
Model No.: B04-202 Millet 521 (Sacs Millet)
Type: Rucksack

No. Pockets: 2
Closures: Drawstrings, strap
Color(s): Red, blue, yellow
Weight: 1 lb.
Volume Capacity: 1437 cu. in.
Features: Ice-ax carrier; crampon attachments; hauling loop.

Manufacturer: Recreational Equipment
Model No.: B04-208 Millet 545 (Sacs Millet)
Type: Rucksack
No. Pockets: 1
Closures: Strap, zippers
Color(s): Blue
Weight: 2⅜ lbs.
Volume Capacity: 1575 cu. in.
Features: Padded frame; steel brace at waist; ice ax; crampon and ski straps; hauling loop.

Manufacturer: Recreational Equipment
Model No.: B04-212 Millet 165 (Sacs Millet)
Type: Rucksack
No. Pockets: 1
Closures: Straps
Color(s): Blue, grey
Weight: 3¾ lbs.
Volume Capacity: 2856 cu. in.
Features: Steel braced and padded frame back; ice-ax and crampon carrier; ski straps; hauling loop; map pocket.

Manufacturer: Recreational Equipment
Model No.: B04-226 Millet 586 (Sacs Millet)
Type: Rucksack
No. Pockets: 4
Closures: Straps, zippers
Color(s): Blue
Weight: 2⅝ lbs.
Volume Capacity: 1575 cu. in.
Features: Padded frame; steel-braced backband; map pocket.

Manufacturer: Recreational Equipment
Model No.: B04-505 Summit II
Type: Rucksack
Closures: Nylon zippers
Color(s): Blue, lobster red
Weight: 1⅛ lbs.
Features: Haul loop; ice-ax holder.

Manufacturer: Recreational Equipment
Model No.: B04-930 Kletter
Type: Rucksack
Closures: Straps, zippers
Color(s): Green
Weight: 2 lbs.
Volume Capacity: 1463 cu. in.
Features: Padded back; 11 patches; hauling loop.

Manufacturer: Rivendell
Model: Jensen
Type: Soft
Closures: Nylon zippers
Color(s): Silver-grey
Weight: 2½ lbs.
Volume Capacity: S, 3037 cu. in.; M, 3105 cu. in.; L, 3173 cu. in.; XL, 3241 cu. in.
Features: Vertical center partition; 4 accessory straps; patches.

Manufacturer: Ski Hut
Model No.: R172 Trailwise 72
Type: Pack and frame
No. Pockets: 5
Closures: Drawstrings, zippers
Color(s): Blue, brown, orange
Weight: 64 oz.
Volume Capacity: L, 5423 cu. in.
Features: Aluminum alloy frame; adjustable padded shoulder straps and hipbelt; hold open; hauling strap.

Manufacturer: Ski Hut
Model No.: R173 Trailwise 73
Type: Pack and frame
No. Pockets: 3
Closures: Drawstrings, zippers
Color(s): Blue, brown, orange
Volume Capacity: 2924 cu. in.

Features: Aluminum alloy frame; adjustable padded shoulder straps and hipbelt; 2 patches; 2 accessory straps.

Manufacturer: Ski Hut
Model No.: R174 Trailwise 74
Type: Pack and frame
No. Pockets: 3
Closures: Drawstrings, zippers
Color(s): Blue, brown, orange
Volume Capacity: L, 2924 cu. in.
Features: Aluminum alloy frame; adjustable padded shoulder straps and hipbelt; 2 patches; 2 accessory straps.

Manufacturer: Springbar
Model No.: 1830 Dimension 6 (Universal)
Type: Pack and frame
Color(s): Tan, blue, forest green
Features: Adjustable aluminum frame; adjustable padded shoulder straps; padded hipbelt.

Manufacturer: Springbar
Model No.: 1860 Roadrunner
Type: Pack and frame
No. Pockets: 2
Closures: Drawstrings, nylon zippers
Color(s): Blue, orange
Features: Aluminum alloy frame; spreader bar; fishing rod pouch.

Manufacturer: Springbar
Model No.: 2010 Chamoix (W.E.)
Type: Soft
Closures: Drawstring
Features: Padded shoulder straps and hipbelt; patches.

Manufacturer: Springbar
Model No.: 2060 Junior
Type: Soft day

Closures: Drawstrings
Color(s): Navy, green, red, orange

Manufacturer: Springbar
Model No.: 2130 Nordic (Universal)
Type: Soft
No. Pockets: 2
Closures: Straps
Color(s): Blue, green, tan
Features: Ski slots behind pockets; padded shoulder straps and hipbelt.

Manufacturer: Stag
Model: Sourdough
Type: Pack and frame
No. Pockets: 4
Closures: Drawstrings, nylon zippers, Velcro
Color(s): Navy blue, red
Volume Capacity: 2988 cu. in.
Features: Hold open; map pocket; frame not included.

Manufacturer: Stag
Model No.: 5+5
Type: Pack and frame
No. Pockets: 5
Closures: Drawstrings, nylon zippers
Color(s): Navy blue
Volume Capacity: 5724 cu. in.
Features: Map and pole pockets; patches; frame not included.

Manufacturer: Stag
Model No.: 33522
Type: Soft
No. Pockets: 2
Closures: Straps, nylon zippers
Color(s): Royal blue
Volume Capacity: 2520 cu. in.
Features: 2 aluminum rod frames; padded back; 8 lashing points; tote handle.

Recreational Equipment Model No. B02-200

Recreational Equipment Model No. B04-930

Raingear

Kelty Poncho Shelter Half

Manufacturer: Academy
Model No.: 103
Type: 2-piece rainsuit
Size(s): S, M, L, XL
Color(s): Orange
Material: Vinyl
Features: Detachable hood; front zippers; drawstring waist.

Manufacturer: Academy
Model No.: 338
Type: Parka jacket
Size(s): XXS, XS, S, M, L, XL
Color(s): Yellow
Material: Cloth outer shell, rubber inner
Features: Front zipper; drawstring hood.

Manufacturer: Academy
Model No.: 1921
Type: Poncho
Size(s): 50" x 80"
Color(s): Reverses from olive to yellow
Material: Reverses from fabric to rubber
Features: Drawstring hood.

Manufacturer: Academy
Model No.: 6608
Type: 2-piece rainsuit
Size(s): S, M, L, XL
Color(s): Rust
Material: Textile
Features: Drawstring hood; 3 pockets; front zippers.

Manufacturer: Academy
Model No.: 7902
Type: Parka rainsuit
Size(s): S, M, L, XL
Color(s): Reverses from olive to red
Material: Reverses from textile to rubber
Features: Drawstring hood; 2 pockets; bib overall with elastic suspenders.

Manufacturer: L. L. Bean
Model No.: 1573C
Type: Parka
Size(s): XS, S, M, L
Weight: 19 oz.
Color(s): Forest green
Material: Nylon
Features: Drawstring hood; front zipper; 2 pockets.

Manufacturer: L. L. Bean
Model No.: 1574C. Same as Model No. 1573C except:
Size(s): XL

Manufacturer: L. L. Bean
Model: Yellow Rain Suit
Type: Jacket and pants
Size(s): S, M, L, XL
Color(s): Yellow
Material: Vinyl-coated cotton
Features: Elastic waist; 2 pockets; visored hood.

Manufacturer: Converse
Model No.: 3213
Type: Parka jacket
Size(s): S, M, L, XL
Weight: 0.9 lb.
Color(s): Green
Material: Nylon
Features: Full zipper; 2 pockets; fold-away drawstring hood.

Manufacturer: Converse
Model No.: 3215
Type: Trousers
Size(s): S, M, L, XL
Weight: 0.8 lb.
Color(s): Green
Material: Nylon
Features: Elasticized waist.

Manufacturer: Converse
Model No.: 3216
Type: Pullover shirt
Size(s): S, M, L, XL
Weight: 1.7 lbs.
Color(s): Green
Material: Urethane-coated nylon
Features: Fold-away drawstring hood; elasticized cuffs.

Manufacturer: Davco
Model No.: 8900
Type: 2-piece rainsuit
Size(s): S, M, L, XL, XXL
Color(s): Green, orange, yellow
Material: Nylon
Features: Front zipper; elastic waist; 3 pockets; attached hood.

Manufacturer: Davco
Model No.: 8904
Type: Parka
Size(s): S, M, L, XL, XXL
Color(s): Green, orange, yellow
Material: Nylon
Features: Front zipper; 3 pockets; attached hood.

Manufacturer: Irving/Weather-Rite
Model No.: 1690
Type: Poncho
Size(s): 52" x 80"
Color(s): Red, yellow, orange, olive drab, clear
Material: Heavy-gauge vinyl
Features: Snap closures.

Manufacturer: Irving/Weather-Rite
Model No.: 5281
Type: Poncho
Size(s): 50" x 80"
Color(s): Reverses from olive drab to yellow
Material: Reverses from nylon to rubber
Features: Snap-button closures; attached hood with adjustable drawstrings.

Manufacturer: Kelty
Model: Poncho Shelter Half
Size(s): 52" x 108"
Weight: 14 oz.
Color(s): Green, red, blue
Material: Nylon

Manufacturer: Kelty
Model: Rain Chaps
Size(s): M, L

Weight: 4 oz.
Color(s): Green, red, blue
Material: Nylon
Features: Belt ties.

Manufacturer: Moor & Mountain
Model No.: 637
Type: Pack poncho
Size(s): 52″ x 108″
Weight: .87 lb.
Color(s): Green, blue, red
Material: Coated nylon
Features: Cut to fit over pack; snaps for adjustable length; reversible snaps for combining 2 ponchos; tent stake loops.

Manufacturer: Moor & Mountain
Model: 638
Type: Rain chaps
Size(s): M, 27″ to 31″; L, 31″ or longer
Weight: 1.5 lbs.
Material: Coated nylon
Features: Tie on side to belt.

Manufacturer: Recreational Equipment
Model No.: C16-225
Type: Rain parka
Size(s): Men's: S, M, L, XL; women's: S, M, L
Weight: ¾ lb.
Color(s): Navy, red, green
Material: Coated nylon
Features: Drawstring hood with bill; inner drawstring; 3 snap-down pockets; 2-way zipper; elastic cuffs with snap closures.

Manufacturer: Recreational Equipment
Model No.: C35-080
Type: Parka
Size(s): M, L
Weight: ⅞ lb.
Color(s): Red
Material: Nylon
Features: Full-length pullover; front pocket; zippered side openings; drawstring hood.

Manufacturer: Recreational Equipment
Model No.: C35-100
Type: Rainsuit
Size(s): S, M, L, XL
Weight: 3.5 lbs.
Color(s): Yellow
Material: Vinyl-coated cotton
Features: Welded seams; drawstring hood; snap front with flap; 3 pockets; elastic-waist pants; snap cuffs.

Manufacturer: Recreational Equipment
Model No.: C35-170
Type: Rain pants

Size(s): XS, S, M, L (in regular or long)
Weight: ⅜ lb.
Color(s): Navy
Material: Coated nylon
Features: Wide legs; drawstring waist; snap closure at ankles.

Manufacturer: Retco
Model No.: 6100
Type: Rainsuit
Size(s): S, M, L, XL
Color(s): Forest green, navy blue, yellow, blaze orange, black
Material: Nylon with rubber backing

Manufacturer: Retco
Model No.: 8100
Type: Parka
Size(s): S, M, L, XL
Color(s): Olive drab
Material: Rubber
Features: Front zipper; 2 pockets; attached hood.

Recreational Equipment Model No. C16-225

Recreational Equipment Model No. C35-080

Refrigerators/Ice Chests

Manufacturer: Coleman
Model No.: 5253A Snow-Lite Cooler
Dimensions: 18½″ x 11″ x 13¼″
Material: Welded steel, plastic liner
Capacity: 7 gal.
Features: Bail hamper handles; positive lock; removable lid; deep, dry storage tray.

Manufacturer: Coleman
Model No.: 5254C Snow-Lite Low Boy Cooler
Dimensions: 22½″ x 13½″ x 12½″
Material: Welded steel, plastic liner
Capacity: 10½ gal.
Features: Recessed handles with bottle openers; deep, dry storage tray; leak-proof drain.

Manufacturer: Coleman
Model No.: 5256C Snow-Lite Colossal Cooler
Dimensions: 28″ x 15¼″ x 15⅞″
Material: Welded steel, plastic liner
Capacity: 20 gal.
Features: 25-lb. size block-ice tub; food tray; gallon water bottle; tub can be used for dry storage; lid used for tray.

Manufacturer: Coleman
Model No.: 5257 Snow-Lite Three Way Cooler
Dimensions: 26½″ x 15¾″ x 17½″
Material: Welded steel, plastic liner
Capacity: 17 gal.
Features: Urethane insulation; 3-way convertibility (left or right handed, or on its back); cold-water-tap dispenser; 4 trays with 8 shelf ledges.

Manufacturer: Coleman
Model No.: 5280A Poly-Lite Cooler
Dimensions: 22½″ x 13½″ x 12¼″
Material: Polyethylene, plastic liner
Capacity: 8½ gal.
Features: Hamper handles for one-hand carry; deep, dry storage tray.

Manufacturer: Coleman
Model No.: 5286 Poly-Lite Cooler
Dimensions: 25¾″ x 13¾″ x 15″
Material: Polyethylene, plastic liner
Capacity: 12 gal.
Features: Slide-up handles; food tray; built-in snap latch; hinged lid.

Manufacturer: Coleman
Model No.: 5287 Poly-Lite Cooler
Dimensions: 29½″ x 15¼″ x 15″
Material: Polyethylene, plastic liner
Capacity: 14 gal.
Features: Sliding lid brace locks lid open; insulated hinged lid can be used as seat; deep, dry storage.

Manufacturer: Coleman
Model No.: 5289 Poly-Lite Super Cooler
Dimensions: 34¼″ x 15¼″ x 16½″
Material: Polyethylene, plastic liner
Capacity: 19 gal.
Features: Ice tub with top for block ice or dry storage; food tray; sliding-lid brace locks lid open.

Manufacturer: Igloo
Model: 25-Quart Ice Chest
Material: Plastic
Features: Hinged friction-lock lid; removable food tray.

Manufacturer: Igloo
Model: 48-Quart Ice Chest
Material: Plastic
Features: Snap-lock lid; removable food tray; waffle designed seat-top lid supports 300 lbs.; polyurethane seat cushion with Velcro straps available.

Coleman Model No. 5257

LEFT OR RIGHT-HAND DOOR   HORIZONTAL

Manufacturer: Igloo
Model: 68-Quart Igloo
Material: Plastic with odor-resistant ABS plastic lining
Features: Swing-up handles with tie-down loops; snap-lock seat-top lid; removable food tray; polyurethane seat cushion with Velcro straps available.

Manufacturer: Igloo
Model: 86-Quart Ice Chest
Material: Plastic
Features: Two different sized food trays; cutting board doubles as a food tray top; plastic 1 gallon jug; polyurethane seat cushion with Velcro straps available.

Manufacturer: Igloo
Model: Sturdy Jug
Material: Polyethylene
Capacity: 3 or 6 gal.
Features: Contoured tops; side handles; 6″ detachable plastic spout.

Manufacturer: Igloo
Model: 3-Gallon Cooler
Material: Plastic
Capacity: 3 gal.
Features: Sure-grip handle; wide-mouth lid.

Manufacturer: King-Seeley Thermos
Model No.: 7719 Cooler
Dimensions: 13″ x 18¼″ x 13½″
Material: Urethane
Capacity: 37 qts.
Features: Removable food tray; drain.

Manufacturer: King-Seeley Thermos
Model No.: 7721 Cooler
Dimensions: 13½″ x 22″ x 14″
Material: Aluminum
Capacity: 45 qts.
Features: Rustproof base; urethane insulation; safety latch; tray; drain; bottle opener; chest divider available.

Manufacturer: King-Seeley Thermos
Model No.: 7729 Cooler
Dimensions: 10½″ x 19½″ x 11½″
Material: Enameled steel case
Capacity: 24 qts.
Features: Top carrying handle; expanded bead insulation.

Manufacturer: King-Seeley Thermos
Model No.: 7730 Cooler
Dimensions: 14½″ x 29″ x 14½″
Material: Urethane
Capacity: 72 qts.
Features: Removable food tray; drain.

King-Seeley Thermos Model No. 7719

King-Seeley Thermos Model No. 7793

Manufacturer: King-Seeley Thermos
Model No.: 7732 Cooler
Dimensions: 14½″ x 29″ x 14½″
Material: Urethane
Capacity: 72 qts.
Features: Removable food tray; drain.

Manufacturer: King-Seeley Thermos
Model No.: 7745 Cooler
Dimensions: 14½″ x 25″ x 14½″
Material: Urethane
Capacity: 55 qts.
Features: Removable lid; rustproof.

Manufacturer: King-Seeley Thermos
Model No.: 7747 "Super 100" Cooler
Dimensions: 17⅛″ x 35½″ x 16¾″
Capacity: 100 qts.
Features: Rustproof construction; 1½ gallon water jug/ice separator; food tray with cutting-board cover; food/ice compartment with cover tray.

Manufacturer: King-Seeley Thermos
Model No.: 7751 Cooler
Dimensions: 13½″ x 22″ x 14″
Material: Enameled steel
Capacity: 45 qts.
Features: Rustproof base; urethane insulation; hinged lid; safety latch; tray; drain; chest divider available.

Manufacturer: King-Seeley Thermos
Model No.: 7756 Cooler
Dimensions: 13½″ x 28″ x 14″
Material: Enameled steel
Capacity: 58 qts.
Features: Rustproof base; urethane insulation; hinged lid; safety latch; tray; drain; chest divider available.

King-Seeley Thermos Model No. 7730

Manufacturer: King-Seeley Thermos
Model No.: 7758 Cooler
Dimensions: 13½″ x 28″ x 13″
Material: Enameled steel case
Capacity: 57 qts.
Features: Safety latch; urethane insulated; "Atherlite" liner lid.

Manufacturer: King-Seeley Thermos
Model No.: 7784/18 Spout Jug
Material: Urethane
Capacity: 1 gal.
Features: Rustproof.

Manufacturer: King-Seeley Thermos
Model No.: 7792 Faucet Jug
Material: Urethane
Capacity: 2 gal.
Features: Rustproof; fast-flow faucet.

Manufacturer: King-Seeley Thermos
Model No.: 7793 Faucet Jug
Material: Urethane
Capacity: 3 gal.
Features: Fast-flow faucet; molded handle; rustproof.

Sleeping Bags

Manufacturer: Browning
Model No.: 4060 Wind River
Type: Mummy
Shell: 1.9 oz. rip-stop nylon
Lining: 1.9 oz. rip-stop nylon
Carry Weight: Regular, 3 lbs. 9 oz.; large, 4 lbs. 10 oz.; expedition, 5 lbs. 4 oz.
Color(s): Regular, large: brook blue; expedition: crater lake blue
Insulation: Northern goose down
Closure: 2-way self-repairing zipper with Velcro lock
Features: Minimum temperature rating; regular and large, —10°F; expedition, —20°F.

Manufacturer: Browning
Model No.: 4160 Eldorado
Type: Full rectangular
Shell: 1.9 oz. rip-stop nylon
Lining: 1.9 oz. rip-stop nylon
Carry Weight: Regular, 4 lbs. 7 oz.; expedition, 5 lbs. 4 oz.
Color(s): Crater lake blue
Insulation: Northern goose down
Closure: 2-way self-repairing zipper with Velcro lock
Features: Minimum temperature rating: regular, 0°F; expedition, —10°F.

Manufacturer: Browning
Model No.: 4360 Shenandoah
Type: Full rectangular
Shell: 1.9 oz. rip-stop nylon
Lining: 1.9 oz. rip-stop nylon
Carry Weight: 6 lbs. 10 oz.
Color(s): Frost line green
Insulation: Dacron 88
Closure: 2-way zipper with Velcro lock
Features: Minimum temperature rating, 15°F.

Manufacturer: Cloud Nine
Model No.: 155 D2 Hiker
Type: Mummy
Shell: 70 Denier nypol
Lining: 70 Denier nypol
Color(s): Navy blue
Insulation: Dacron 88
Closure: Self-repairing nylon zipper
Features: Fully weather stripped; washable.

Manufacturer: Cloud Nine
Model No.: 5712 Everest
Type: Mummy
Shell: Rip-stop nylon
Lining: Taffeta nylon
Color(s): Blue
Insulation: Dacron II
Closure: Self-repairing nylon zipper
Features: Fully weather stripped; tie strings for rolling and storage; washable.

Cloud Nine Model No. 5712

Manufacturer: Cloud Nine
Model No.: 8080 High Sierra
Type: Adult
Shell: Rip-stop nylon

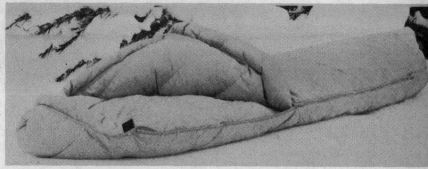

Browning Model No. 4060

Browning Model No. 4160

Lining: Rip-stop nylon
Color(s): Blue
Insulation: Dacron II
Closure: Nylon zipper
Features: Tie strings for rolling and storage; washable.

Cloud Nine Model No. 8080

Manufacturer: Cold River
Model No.: 7231-1 Polar Bear
Shell: 70 Denier rip-stop nylon
Lining: 70 Denier rip-stop nylon
Color(s): Blue with green lining
Insulation: Dacron Fiberfill II
Comfort Range: 20° to 55°F
Closure: Nylon zipper

Manufacturer: Cold River
Model No.: 7231-2 Glacier
Shell: 70 Denier rip-stop nylon
Lining: 70 Denier rip-stop nylon
Color(s): Blue with green lining
Insulation: Dacron Fiberfill II

Comfort Range: 20° to 55°F
Closure: Nylon zipper

Manufacturer: Cold River
Model No.: 7237 Firebird
Shell: 70 Denier downproof rip-stop nylon
Lining: 70 Denier downproof rip-stop nylon
Color(s): Red
Insulation: Dacron Fiberfill II
Comfort Range: 15° to 50°F
Closure: Nylon zipper
Features: Non-sewn outer shell.

Manufacturer: Cold River
Model No.: 7499 Arctic Cloud
Shell: 70 Denier downproof rip-stop nylon
Lining: 70 Denier downproof rip-stop nylon
Color(s): Navy blue
Insulation: Duck down
Comfort Range: 15° to 60°F
Closure: #10 two-way Delrin zipper.

Manufacturer: Cold River
Model No.: 7535 Sherpa
Shell: 70 Denier rip-stop nylon
Lining: 70 Denier rip-stop nylon
Color(s): Green
Insulation: Fortrel Polarguard fiberfill
Comfort Range: 15° to 50°F
Features: Diagonal overlap construction;
Closure: #5 Delrin zipper drawstring top with fix lock.

Manufacturer: Coleman
Model No.: 8122-704
Shell: Cotton sheeting
Lining: Flannel
Color(s): Green with red and black checkered lining
Insulation: Acryfil fiber
Closure: Aluminum zipper
Features: Tie tapes.

Manufacturer: Coleman
Model No.: 8122-760
Shell: Cotton sheeting
Lining: Cotton percale
Color(s): Gold with print lining
Insulation: Acryfil fiber
Closure: Aluminum zipper
Features: Tie tapes; washable.

Manufacturer: Coleman
Model No.: 8124-632
Shell: Cotton sheeting
Lining: Flannel
Color(s): Blue print with solid blue lining
Insulation: Insul 200 polyester fiber
Closure: Aluminum zipper

Manufacturer: Coleman
Model No.: 8125-600
Type: Mummy
Shell: Rip-stop nylon
Lining: Rip-stop nylon
Insulation: Dacron II
Color(s): Navy blue with light blue lining
Closure: 2-way polyester zipper
Features: Stuff sack.

Manufacturer: Coleman
Model No.: 8125-675
Shell: Rip-stop nylon
Lining: Rip-stop nylon
Color(s): Red with yellow lining
Insulation: Dacron II
Closure: 2-way polyester zipper
Features: Stuff sack.

Manufacturer: Coleman
Model No.: 8164-606
Shell: Cotton sheeting
Lining: Flannel
Color(s): Red and blue print with blue lining
Insulation: Dacron 88
Closure: Aluminum zipper
Features: Tie tapes; washable.

Manufacturer: Coleman
Model No.: 8164-711
Shell: Poplin
Lining: Flannel
Color(s): Brown with white and brown print lining
Insulation: Dacron 88
Closure: Aluminum zipper
Features: Tie tapes; washable.

Manufacturer: Coleman
Model No.: 8167-890
Shell: Cotton duck
Lining: Flannel
Color(s): Green with red plaid lining
Insulation: Dacron 88
Closure: Aluminum zipper
Features: Full-width carrying flap with handles.

Manufacturer: Coleman
Model No.: 8553-559
Type: Taper
Shell: Rip-stop nylon
Lining: Rip-stop nylon
Carry Weight: 5 lbs.
Color(s): Walnut brown with gold lining
Insulation: Dacron II
Closure: 2-way zipper
Features: Drawstring with cord lock; nylon stuff sack.

Manufacturer: Coleman
Model No.: 8553-702
Type: Mummy
Shell: Rip-stop nylon
Lining: Rip-stop nylon
Carry Weight: 6 lbs. 4 oz.
Color(s): Gator green with beige lining
Insulation: Dacron II
Closure: 2-way zipper
Features: Drawstring and cordlock top; nylon stuff sack.

Manufacturer: Comfy
Model No.: 105 Himalaya
Shell: 1.8 oz. rip-stop nylon

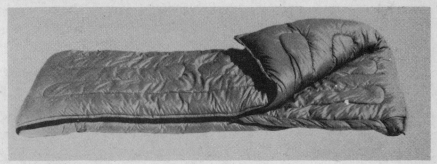

Comfy Model No. 105

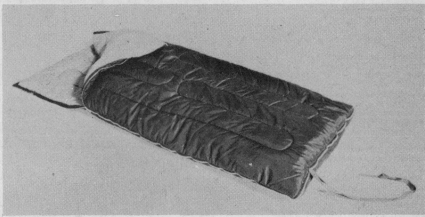

Comfy Model No. 201

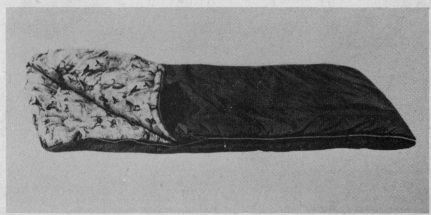

Comfy Model No. 314

Comfy Model No. 343

Lining: 1.8 oz. rip-stop nylon
Carry Weight: 5⅛ lbs.
Color(s): Columbia blue
Insulation: Northern goose down
Closure: Nylon zipper
Features: Drawstring hood with clamp; comfort indicator, −20°F.

Manufacturer: Comfy
Model No.: 132 Cliff Trail
Shell: 1.8 oz. rip-stop nylon
Lining: 1.8 oz. rip-stop nylon
Carry Weight: 3⅞ lbs.
Color(s): Plum
Insulation: Northern goose down
Closure: Nylon zipper
Features: Drawstring hood with slamp; comfort indicator, −5°F.

Manufacturer: Comfy
Model No.: 149 Grizzly
Shell: 1.8 oz. rip-stop nylon
Lining: 1.8 oz. rip-stop nylon
Carry Weight: 4½ lbs.
Color(s): Whiskey/brown
Insulation: Northern goose down and Polarguard combination
Closure: Nylon zipper
Features: Drawstring hood with clamp; comfort indicator, 0°F.

Manufacturer: Comfy
Model No.: 159 Wayfarer
Shell: 1.8 oz. rip-stop nylon
Lining: 1.8 oz. rip-stop nylon
Carry Weight: 5 lbs.
Color(s): Scarlet/navy
Insulation: Down and Polarguard
Closure: Nylon zipper
Features: Comfort indicator, −5°F.

Manufacturer: Comfy
Model No.: 161 Trail Hiker
Shell: 1.8 oz. rip-stop nylon
Lining: 1.8 oz. rip-stop nylon
Carry Weight: 3¼ lbs.
Color(s): Scarlet
Insulation: Northern down
Closure: Nylon zipper
Features: Comfort indicator, 10°F.

Manufacturer: Comfy
Model No.: 201 Adirondack
Shell: 1.8 oz. rip-stop nylon
Lining: 1.8 oz. rip-stop nylon
Carry Weight: 3⅝ lbs.
Color(s): Burgundy
Insulation: DuPont Fiberfill II
Closure: Nylon zipper
Features: Drawstring hood with clamp; comfort indicator, 10°F; machine dryable.

Manufacturer: Comfy
Model No.: 204 Cordillera
Shell: 1.8 oz. rip-stop nylon
Lining: 1.8 oz. rip-stop nylon
Carry Weight: 4¾ lbs.
Color(s): Whiskey
Insulation: DuPont Fiberfill II
Closure: Nylon zipper
Features: Drawstring hood with clamp; comfort indicator, 10°F; machine dryable.

Manufacturer: Comfy
Model No.: 314 Sunset
Shell: DuPont nylon
Lining: DuPont nylon
Carry Weight: 5½ lbs.
Color(s): Navy with Columbia blue lining
Insulation: DuPont Dacron 88
Closure: Nylon zipper
Features: Quilted through construction; comfort indicator, 20°F.

Manufacturer: Comfy
Model No.: 343 Valley Forge
Shell: 8 oz. cotton duck
Lining: Flannel
Carry Weight: 8¼ lbs.
Color(s): Green with print lining
Insulation: DuPont Dacron 88

Closure: Aluminum zipper
Features: Comfort indicator, 15°F.

Manufacturer: Gladding
Model: Patched Jean
Shell: Cotton denim
Lining: Tricot
Color(s): Blue patchwork print with red lining
Insulation: Polyester
Closure: Aluminum zipper

Manufacturer: Gladding
Model No.: 1776 Stars and Stripes
Shell: 70 Denier nylon
Lining: Cotton flannel
Color(s): Red, white and blue striped; red and blue stars on white lining
Insulation: Polyester fiberfill
Closure: Aluminum zipper

Gladding Model No. 1776

Gladding Model No. 7521

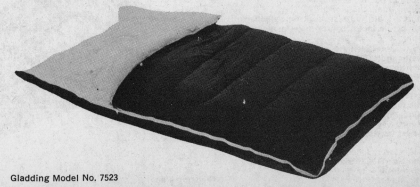

Gladding Model No. 7523

Manufacturer: Gladding
Model No.: 7521 Warrior
Shell: Nylon
Lining: Tricot
Color(s): Assorted
Insulation: Polyester
Closure: Aluminum zipper

Manufacturer: Gladding
Model No.: 7523 Chieftain
Shell: Nylon
Lining: Tricot
Color(s): Assorted
Insulation: Polyester
Closure: Aluminum zipper

Manufacturer: Gladding
Model No.: 7524 Medicine Man
Shell: Nylon

SPECIFICATIONS: EQUIPMENT

Lining: Nylon
Color(s): Blue with color-coordinated lining
Insulation: Polyester
Closure: Aluminum zipper

Manufacturer: Gladding
Model No.: 7526 Tomahawk
Shell: 70 Denier
Lining: 70 Denier
Color(s): Navy blue
Insulation: Polyester Fiberfill
Closure: Aluminum zipper

Manufacturer: Gladding
Model No.: 7571 Hiker
Shell: Rip-stop nylon
Lining: Rip-stop nylon
Color(s): Blue
Insulation: Dacron Fiberfill II
Closure: Zipper
Features: Nylon carrying bag with drawstring included; blind-finish zipper.

Manufacturer: Gladding
Model No.: 7572 Mountaineer
Type: Rectangular
Shell: Rip-stop nylon
Lining: Rip-stop nylon
Color(s): Blue with forest green lining
Insulation: Dacron Fiberfill II
Closure: Zipper
Features: Blind-finish zipper.

Manufacturer: Gladding
Model No.: 7575 Northwoodsman
Type: Mummy
Shell: Rip-stop nylon
Lining: Rip-stop nylon
Color(s): Blue
Insulation: Dacron Fiberfill II
Closure: Nylon zipper
Features: Drawstring top; quiltless construction; carrying sack.

Manufacturer: Great Northern
Model No.: 3014-6 Jupiter
Shell: Rip-stop nylon
Lining: Brushed tricot
Color(s): Brown with coordinated lining
Insulation: Poly-luxe
Closure: Aluminum zipper
Features: Weather-stripped zipper; tie tapes; approximate temperature rating, 30°F.

Manufacturer: Great Northern
Model No.: 4024-6 Cougar
Shell: Drill
Lining: Flannel
Color(s): Gold with coordinated scenic print lining
Insulation: Dacron 88
Closure: Aluminum zipper
Features: Weather-stripped zipper; tie tapes; approximate temperature rating, 20°F.

Manufacturer: Great Northern
Model No.: 4084-4 Adventurer
Shell: 8 oz. duck
Lining: Flannel
Color(s): Brown with coordinated scenic print lining
Insulation: Dacron 88
Closure: Aluminum zipper
Features: 2 air mattress pockets; detachable canopy; tie tapes; approximate temperature rating, 20°F.

Manufacturer: Great Northern
Model No.: 6033-4 Mt. Everest
Shell: Rip-stop nylon
Lining: Rip-stop nylon
Color(s): Electric blue
Insulation: Polarguard
Closure: Nylon coil zipper
Features: Tapered barrel hood; cord lock drawstring top; Velcro tab enclosure.

Manufacturer: Jones Tent & Awning
Model No.: P 7021 Black Tusk
Type: Barrel
Shell: Rip-stop nylon

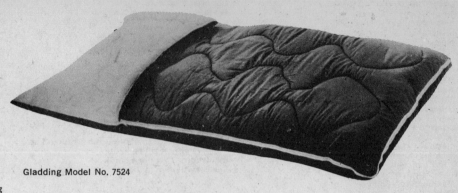

Gladding Model No. 7524

Gladding Model No. 7526

Gladding Model No. 7571

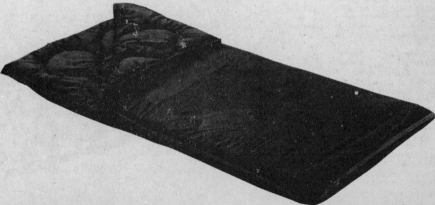

Gladding Model No. 7572

Jones Model No. P 7028

Lining: Rip-stop nylon
Carry Weight: 4 lbs. 4 oz. (with 2 lbs. down)
Color(s): Dark green
Insulation: Goose down
Closure: Zipper
Features: Stuff bag; tie strap; detachable flan-
nelette lining optional.

Manufacturer: Jones Tent & Awning
Model No.: P 7028 Mount Logan
Type: Mummy
Shell: Rip-stop nylon
Lining: Rip-stop nylon
Carry Weight: 5 lbs. 13 oz.
Color(s): Bright orange
Insulation: Goose down
Closure: Zipper
Features: Coke bottle shape.

Manufacturer: Jones Tent & Awning
Model No.: P 7031 Diamond
Type: Barrel
Shell: Rip-stop nylon
Lining: Rip-stop nylon
Carry Weight: 5 lbs. 8 oz. (with 2½ lbs. down)
Color(s): Royal
Insulation: Goose down
Closure: Zipper
Features: Detachable down hood.

Manufacturer: Jones Tent & Awning
Model No.: P 7033 Banff
Type: Mummy
Shell: Rip-stop nylon
Lining: Rip-stop nylon
Carry Weight: 3 lbs. 14 oz. (with 2 lbs. down)
Color(s): J.C. Royal
Insulation: Goose down
Closure: Nylon zipper
Features: Draw-tite down hood.

Manufacturer: Jones Tent & Awning
Model No.: P 7041 Combo-Pak
Type: Mummy
Shell: 1.9 oz. rip-stop nylon
Lining: 1.9 oz. rip-stop nylon
Carry Weight: 5 lbs. 8 oz.

Insulation: Goose down and Dacron Fiberfill II
Closure: Delrin zipper
Features: Waterproof stuff bag.

Manufacturer: Jones Tent & Awning
Model No.: P 7043 Jasper
Type: Tapered
Shell: Rip-stop nylon
Lining: Rip-stop nylon
Carry Weight: 4 lbs. 2 oz. (with 2 lbs. down)
Color(s): Sailing blue
Insulation: Goose down
Closure: Nylon zipper

Manufacturer: Jones Tent & Awning
Model No.: P 7053 Cariboo
Type: Mummy
Shell: Rip-stop nylon
Lining: Rip-stop nylon
Carry Weight: 3 lbs. 6 oz. (with 2 lbs. down)
Insulation: Down
Closure: Nylon zipper

Manufacturer: Jones Tent & Awning
Model No.: P 7054 Chilcotin
Type: Tapered
Shell: Rip-stop nylon
Lining: Rip-stop nylon
Carry Weight: 3 lbs. 8 oz. (with 2 lbs. down)
Color(s): Assorted
Insulation: Down
Closure: Nylon zipper

Manufacturer: North Face
Model: Littlefoot
Type: Mummy
Shell: Rip-stop nylon
Lining: Rip-stop nylon
Carry Weight: 2 lbs. 13 oz.
Color(s): Royal blue, tan
Insulation: DuPont Dacron Fiberfill II
Closure: Delrin zipper
Features: Temperature range to 20°F; fire re-
tardant; non-locking sliders for quick exit;
child size.

Manufacturer: North Face
Model: Bigfoot
Type: Mummy
Shell: Rip-stop nylon
Lining: Rip-stop nylon
Carry Weight: Regular, 4 lbs. 4 oz.; large, 4
lbs. 10 oz.
Color(s): Royal blue, tan
Insulation: Fiberfill II
Closure: YKK Ziplon coil zipper
Features: Temperature range to 20°F.

Manufacturer: North Face
Model: Chamois
Type: Mummy
Shell: Rip-stop nylon
Lining: Rip-stop nylon
Carry Weight: Regular, 3 lbs. 12 oz.; large, 4
lbs. 1 oz.
Color(s): Cruise navy
Insulation: Goose down
Closure: Optilon coil zipper
Features: Temperature range to −5°F.

Manufacturer: North Face
Model No.: Chrysalis
Type: Semi-rectangular
Shell: Rip-stop nylon
Lining: Rip-stop nylon
Carry Weight: 2 lbs. 1 oz.
Color(s): Royal blue
Insulation: Goose down
Closure: Optilon coil zipper
Features: Temperature range to 30°F;
intended for summer use.

Manufacturer: North Face
Model: Ibex
Type: Mummy
Shell: Rip-stop nylon
Lining: Rip-stop nylon
Carry Weight: Regular, 4 lbs. 3 oz.; large, 4
lbs. 8 oz.
Color(s): Cruise navy, chianti, forest green
Insulation: Goose down
Closure: Optilon coil zipper
Features: Temperature range to −15°F.

North Face Chrysalis

Carry Weight: 111⅓ oz.
Color(s): Blue
Insulation: Grey goose down
Closure: YKK nylon Delrin zippers
Features: Independent drawcord closures; Velcro fastening of section between hoods; minimum temperature, 10°F.

Manufacturer: Ski Hut
Model No.: Ultralight SU/1
Type: Mummy
Shell: 1.9 oz. rip-stop nylon
Carry Weight: 50 oz.
Color(s): Midnight blue, burgundy
Insulation: Goose and duck down blend
Closure: 2-way nylon zipper
Features: Waterproof stuff sack included.

Manufacturer: Slumberjack
Model No.: Pinnacle-90
Type: Adult
Shell: Rip-stop nylon
Lining: Rip-stop nylon
Total Weight: 3 lbs. 15 oz., 4 lbs. 7 oz., 4 lbs. 15 oz.
Insulation: Goose down
Comfort Range: —5° to 60°F, —15° to 50°F, —25° to 40°F
Closure: 2-way zipper, Velcro at collar
Features: Oval raised foot area; drawstring hood with anti-freeze locking device.

Manufacturer: Slumberjack
Model: Safari
Type: Mummy
Shell: Rip-stop nylon
Lining: Rip-stop nylon
Total Weight: 3 lbs. 3 oz.
Insulation: Goose down
Comfort Range: 0° to 60° F

Manufacturer: North Face
Model: North Face Bag
Type: Mummy
Shell: Rip-stop nylon
Lining: Rip-stop nylon
Carry Weight: Regular, 5 lbs. 4 oz.; large, 5 lbs. 8 oz.
Color(s): Acapulco gold
Insulation: Goose down
Closure: Optilon coil zipper
Features: Temperature range to —30°F; double draft flaps.

Manufacturer: Ski Hut
Model: Trailwise Slimline 3 SS/3
Type: Mummy
Shell: Tenaya nylon
Carry Weight: 47½ oz.
Color(s): Blue, orange
Insulation: White goose down
Closure: Nylon zipper
Features: Water repellent; minimum temperature, 0°F.

Slumberjack Pinnacle-90

Manufacturer: Ski Hut
Model: Trailwise Chevron 3 SC/3
Type: Mummy
Shell: Tenaya nylon
Carry Weight: 68 oz.
Color(s): Blue, orange
Insulation: White goose
Closure: YKK 2-way nylon zipper
Features: Water-repellent; self-forming drawcord hood; minimum temperature, —20°F.

Manufacturer: Ski Hut
Model No.: Trailwise Norrland 2 SN/2
Type: Mummy
Shell: Tenaya nylon
Carry Weight: 57½ oz.
Color(s): Blue or orange
Insulation: White goose down
Closure: YKK nylon zipper
Features: Self-forming drawcord hood; minimum temperature, 5° F.

Manufacturer: Ski Hut
Model: Trailwise Double Mummy SD
Type: Mummy
Shell: Tenaya nylon

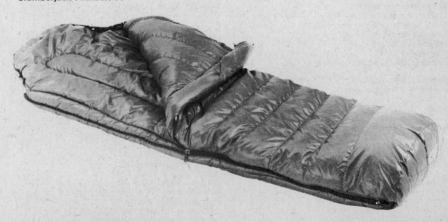
Slumberjack Sundown II

Closure: Zipper
Features: Nylon drawstring hood with anti-locking device.

Manufacturer: Slumberjack
Model No.: Sundown II
Type: Adult
Shell: Rip-stop nylon
Lining: Rip-stop nylon
Total Weight: 5 lbs. 8 oz.
Insulation: Dacron II, goose down
Comfort Range: —10° to 45°F
Closure: 2-way coil zipper, Velcro at collar
Features: Center baffle for separation of down and fiberfill; nylon drawstring at hood.

Manufacturer: Slumberjack
Model No.: Alta II
Type: Tapered
Shell: Rip-stop nylon
Lining: Rip-stop nylon
Carry Weight: 7 lbs. 2 oz.
Insulation: Dacron II
Comfort Range: —10° to 45°F
Closure: 2-way zipper
Features: Raised foot area; convertible hood with nylon drawstring.

Manufacturer: Slumberjack
Model: Bluebird
Type: Rectangular
Shell: Rip-stop nylon
Lining: Rip-stop nylon
Total Weight: 4 lbs. 8 oz.
Insulation: Dacron II
Comfort Range: 25° to 65°F
Closure: 2-way zipper

Manufacturer: Stag
Model No.: 260 4 Seasons 4-in-1 Bag
Shell: Outer, duck; inner, poplin
Lining: Flannel
Carry Weight: 13¾ lbs.
Insulation: Hi Loft Thermo-Fluf Polyester
Comfort Range: 10° to 55°F
Closure: Zippers
Features: Inner and outer bags zip together.

Manufacturer: Stag
Model No.: 4735
Shell: Cotton
Lining: Tricot flannel
Carry Weight: 9 lbs.
Insulation: Hi Loft Thermo-Fluf
Comfort Range: 35° to 55°F
Closure: Zipper
Features: Designed for wagons, campers and trailers; snap-down top; washable.

Manufacturer: Stag
Model No.: 8507
Shell: Nylon
Lining: Nylon
Carry Weight: 4 lbs. 12 oz.
Color(s): Royal blue
Insulation: Dacron II
Comfort Range: 10° to 55°F
Closure: 2-way Delrin zipper
Features: Washable; double-layer construction.

Manufacturer: Stag
Model No.: 8509
Shell: Nylon
Lining: Cotton

Carry Weight: 7 lbs.
Color(s): Brown
Insulation: Dacron II
Comfort Range: 10° to 40°F
Closure: 2-way Delrin zipper
Features: Double-layer construction.

Manufacturer: Stag
Model No.: 9514 Cascade
Type: Mummy
Shell: Rip-stop nylon
Lining: Rip-stop nylon
Carry Weight: 3 lbs. 14 oz.
Color(s): Blue
Insulation: Dacron Fiberfill II
Comfort Range: 10° to 40°F
Closure: YKK 2-way zipper
Features: Drawcord hood; Velcro tab.

Manufacturer: Stag
Model No.: 9520 Adirondack
Type: Tapered
Shell: Rip-stop nylon
Lining: Nylon taffeta
Carry Weight: 4 lbs. 8 oz.
Color(s): Maroon
Insulation: Dacron Fiberfill II
Comfort Range: 10° to 40°F
Closure: YKK 2-way zipper
Features: Drawcord shoulder.

Manufacturer: Stag
Model No.: 9528 Cascade
Type: Mummy
Shell: Rip-stop nylon
Lining: Rip-stop nylon
Carry Weight: 6 lbs. 2 oz.
Color(s): Blue
Insulation: Dacron Fiberfill II
Comfort Range: —15° to 15°F
Closure: YKK 2-way zipper
Features: Drawcord hood; Velcro tab; X-long.

Manufacturer: Stag
Model No.: 9530 Cascade
Type: Tapered
Shell: Rip-stop nylon
Lining: Rip-stop nylon
Carry Weight: 4 lbs. 4 oz.
Color(s): Blue
Insulation: Dacron Fiberfill II
Comfort Range: 10° to 40°F
Closure: YKK 2-way zipper
Features: Insulated weatherflap; drawcord shoulder.

Manufacturer: Stag
Model No.: 9552 Pacific Crest
Type: Tapered
Shell: Rip-stop nylon
Lining: Rip-stop nylon
Carry Weight: 5 lbs.
Color(s): Juniper green
Insulation: Polarguard
Comfort Range: 10° to 40°F
Closure: YKK 2-way zipper
Features: Velcro tab; drawcord shoulder.

Manufacturer: Stag
Model No.: 9814 Blue Ridge
Type: Mummy
Shell: Rip-stop nylon
Lining: Nylon taffeta
Carry Weight: 12 lbs. 8 oz.
Color(s): Green
Insulation: Dacron Fiberfill II
Comfort Range: 10° to 40°F
Closure: YKK 1-way zipper
Features: Drawcord hood.

Manufacturer: Stag
Model No.: 10516 Explorer
Shell: Poplin
Lining: Cotton
Carry Weight: 12 lbs. 8 oz.
Insulation: Goose down
Comfort Range: —15° to 40°F
Closure: 2-way Delrin zipper
Features: Outside storm flap; head flap; air mattress pockets; duffel bag.

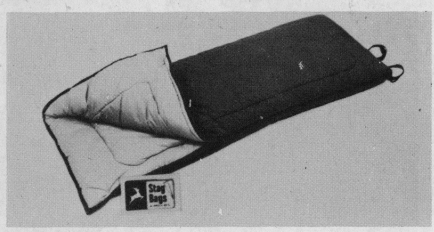

Stag Model No. 8507

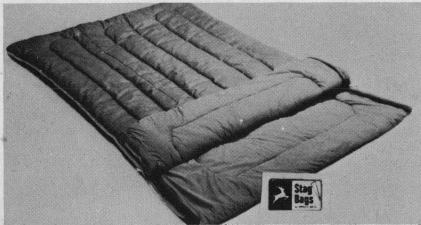

Stag Model No. 4735

Stag Model No. 9520

Manufacturer: Stag
Model No.: 10520 Yukon
Type: Mummy
Shell: Rip-stop nylon
Lining: Rip-stop nylon
Carry Weight: 3 lbs. 8 oz.
Color(s): Blue
Insulation: Northern goose down
Comfort Range: 10° to 40°F
Closure: YKK 2-way zipper
Features: Drawcord hood; Velcro tab on zipper; draft tube.

Stag Model No. 9530

Manufacturer: Stag
Model No.: 10524 Yukon
Type: Mummy
Shell: Rip-stop nylon
Lining: Rip-stop nylon
Carry Weight: 5 lbs. 8 oz.
Color(s): Blue
Insulation: Northern goose down
Comfort Range: —15° to 15°F
Closure: YKK 2-way zipper
Features: Drawcord hood; Velcro tab on zipper; draft tube.

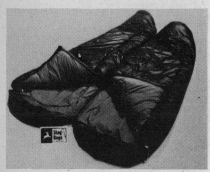

Stag Model No. 10520

Manufacturer: Stag
Model No.: 10525
Type: Tapered
Shell: Rip-stop nylon
Lining: Rip-stop nylon
Carry Weight: 3 lbs. 8 oz.
Color(s): Blue
Insulation: Northern goose down
Comfort Range: 10° to 40°F
Closure: YKK 2-way zipper
Features: Drawcord shoulder; draft tube.

Stag Model No. 8509

Stag Model No. 9514

Manufacturer: Stag
Model No.: 10527 Alpine
Type: Tapered
Shell: Nylon taffeta
Lining: Nylon taffeta
Carry Weight: 4 lbs. 12 oz.
Color(s): Brown
Insulation: Duck down
Comfort Range: 10° to 40°F
Closure: YKK 2-way zipper

Stag Model No. 10525

Stoves/Heaters

Manufacturer: Ashflash
Model No.: 1052
Type: Heater
Fuel type: Propane
BTU's: 4000
Features: Propane tank not included; automatic adjustment to altitude extremes; nickel-plated safety grill.

Manufacturer: Ashflash
Model No.: 1061
Type: Stove
Dimensions: 7½" (diagonal)
No. of Burners: 1
Fuel type: Propane
BTU's: 64,000
Features: Single valve control.

Manufacturer: Ashflash
Model No.: 1065. Same as Model No. 1061 except:
Tank Weight: 16.4 oz.
Fuel type: Propane
Features: Includes tank.

Manufacturer: Ashflash
Model No.: 1085
Type: Stove
Dimensions: 18½" x 12" x 13½"
No. of Burners: 2
Fuel type: Propane
BTU's: 13,000
Features: Canister not included; pressure regulator.

Ashflash Model No. 1085

Manufacturer: L. L. Bean
Model No.: 2548C Parlor
Type: Stove
Dimensions: 31.3" x 25.5" x 22.5"
Fuel type: Wood
Features: Fuel loaded by side or front; front partially screened for fireplace.

Manufacturer: L. L. Bean
Model No.: 5297C Kangaroo Kitchen
Type: Stove
Dimensions: 5" x 14" x 16"
Weight (total): 12 lbs.
Cylinder Weight: 14 oz.
No. of Burners: 1
Fuel type: Propane
Features: Aluminum griddle; pressurized cooking; washes dishes by using oven as heated dish pan and cover; fuel cylinder not included.

Manufacturer: L. L. Bean
Model No.: 5322C Mini Butane

Type: Stove
Dimensions: 24 cu. in. (1½" deep x 4½") when closed
Weight (total): 7.8 oz. (without cartridge)
Cartridge Weight: 10 oz. with 6½ oz. fuel
No. of Burners: 1
Fuel type: Butane
BTU's: 5000
Features: 3-hour cooking time; includes cartridge.

Manufacturer: L. L. Bean
Model No.: 5325C Hiker
Type: Stove
Dimensions: 5" x 3¾"
Weight (total): 18 oz.
No. of Burners: 1
Fuel type: White gasoline or Coleman fuel
Features: ¾-hour cooking time; self-cleaning; detachable cup.

Manufacturer: BernzOmatic
Model No.: HT-5000
Type: Heater
Weight (total): 6 lbs.
Cylinder Weight: 14.1 oz. or 16 oz.
Fuel type: Propane
BTU's: 1000 to 5000 per hour
Features: 16 oz. disposable cylinder included; tip-proof cylinder stand.

BernzOmatic Model No. ST810A

BernzOmatic Model No. HT-5000

Manufacturer: BernzOmatic
Model No.: HT10,000
Type: Heater
BTU's: 10,000
Features: 5-foot hose assembly and standard POL fitting for bulk tank operation; automatic ignition—no matches required; constant heat output down to −25°F.

Manufacturer: BernzOmatic
Model No.: ST810A
Type: Stove
Dimensions: 14" x 20" x 3½"
No. of Burners: 2
Fuel type: Propane
BTU's: 10,500 each burner
Features: Burners independently controlled; cylinders not included.

Manufacturer: BernzOmatic
Model No.: ST820
Type: Stove
Dimensions: 14" x 20" x 3½"
No. of Burners: 2
Fuel type: Propane
BTU's: 10,500
Features: 2 independently controlled regulated burners; automatic lighting; drip pan; 5" hose assembly; propane fuel not included.

Manufacturer: BernzOmatic
Model No.: TX550L
Type: Stove
Dimensions: 11¼" x 11¼" x 4¼"
Cylinder Weight: 14.1 oz. (disposable)
No. of Burners: 1
Fuel type: Propane
Features: Non-regulated; cylinder included.

Manufacturer: BernzOmatic
Model No.: TX850L
Type: Stove
Dimensions: 20¾" x 14½" x 4¼"
No. of Burners: 2
Fuel type: Propane
Features: Non-regulated; use with disposable cylinders.

BernzOmatic Model No. TX550L

Manufacturer: BernzOmatic
Model No.: TX850WC
Type: Stove
Dimensions: 20¾" x 14½" x 4⅛"
No. of Burners: 2
Fuel type: Propane
Features: Cylinder not included.

BernzOmatic Model No. TX850WC

Manufacturer: BernzOmatic
Model No.: TX950
Type: Catalytic heater
Cylinder Weight: 14.1 oz.
Fuel type: Propane
BTU's: 1000 to 7000 per hour
Features: Includes cylinder; regular valve; steel case; storage for spare propane cylinder.

BernzOmatic Model No. TX950

Manufacturer: Coleman
Model No.: 576
Type: Stove
Dimensions: Maximum width, 4⅝"; maximum height, 6½"

Weight (total): 2 lbs. 10 oz.
Canister Weight: 10 oz.
No. of Burners: 1
Fuel type: Coleman fuel or white gas
BTU's: 8500
Features: X-shaped windshield.

Manufacturer: Coleman
Model No.: 425E499 Economy
Type: Stove
Dimensions: 18" x 11½" x 4⅞"
No. of Burners: 2
BTU's: 18,700
Features: 2-hour burning time; adjustable flame.

Manufacturer: Coleman
Model No.: 426D499 Deluxe
Type: Stove
Dimensions: 28½" x 13¾" x 6¼"
No. of Burners: 3
BTU's: 25,800
Features: Adjustable flame; Band-A-Blu burners; all burners on high; 2-hour burning time.

Manufacturer: Coleman
Model No.: 502-700 Sportster
Type: Stove
Dimensions: Diameter, 5½"
Weight (total): Less than 3 lbs.
No. of Burners: 1
Features: Combination cook kit/carrying case.

Coleman Model No. 502-700

Manufacturer: Coleman
Model No.: 512A708 Chill Chaser
Type: Catalytic heater
Dimensions: Height, 10½"; diameter, 8½"
BTU's: 3500
Features: Platinum catalyst.

Manufacturer: Coleman
Model No.: 515A708 Winter Cat
Type: Catalytic heater
Dimensions: Height, 11¾"; diameter, 11¾"
BTU's: 5000 to 8000
Features: Platinum catalyst; Dial-Temp adjusts the warmth.

Manufacturer: Coleman
Model No.: 5400A700 Standard
Type: Stove
Dimensions: Folded, 20½" x 12" x 4"
Canister Weight: 14.1 oz. or 16.4 oz.
No. of Burners: 2
Fuel type: Propane
BTU's: 10,000 each burner
Features: Can use bulk tank.

Manufacturer: Coleman
Model No.: 5410A700 Deluxe

Type: Stove
Dimensions: Folded, 20½" x 12" x 4"
Canister Weight: 14.1 oz. or 16.4 oz.
No. of Burners: 2
Fuel type: Propane
BTU's: 10,000 each burner
Features: Can use bulk tank; bottle not included.

Manufacturer: Coleman
Model No.: 5418A700
Type: Stove
Dimensions: 7¼" x 7¼" x 12"
Canister Weight: 16.4 oz.
No. of Burners: 1
Fuel type: Propane
BTU's: 8000
Features: Regulator valve for flame adjustment; bottle is third support leg.

Manufacturer: Coleman
Model No.: 5418-708
Type: Stove
Dimensions: Opened, 14" x 12" x 10"; closed, 11" x 7" x ½"
Canister Weight: 16.4 oz.
No. of Burners: 1
Fuel type: Propane
BTU's: Adjustable up to 8000
Features: 2½- to 6-hour cooking time; 2 folding legs; fuel supply is third leg.

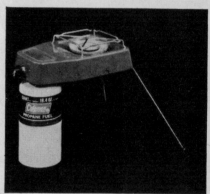

Coleman Model No. 5418-708

Manufacturer: Coleman
Model No.: 5445A700
Type: Heater
Dimensions: 16⅛" x 8⅝" x 8"
Canister Weight: 14.1 oz. or 16.4 oz. disposable bottles
Fuel type: Propane
BTU's: 2000 to 5000
Features: Safety shut-off valve; can use bulk tank.

Manufacturer: Coleman
Model No.: 5480-708
Type: Catalytic heater
Canister Weight: 14.1 oz. or 16.4 oz.
Fuel type: Propane
BTU's: 4000 to 10,000
Features: Shut-off valve; fully adjustable; operated on disposable bottles or refillable tank; chrome grill.

Manufacturer: Colorado Tent & Awning
Model: Noble Cook
Type: Stove
Dimensions: 19½" x 24½" x 26½"
Weight (total): 100 lbs.
No. of Burners: 4
Features: 6" stove pipe not included.

Manufacturer: Colorado Tent & Awning
Model: Regular Sheep Herder
Type: Stove
Dimensions: 19½" x 13½" x 10"
Weight (total): 22 lbs.
Fuel type: Wood

Features: Set of telescope stove pipes included.

Manufacturer: Colorado Tent & Awning
Model: Oregon Style Sheep Herder. Same as Model Regular Sheep Herder except:
Dimensions: 27½" x 13½" x 10"
Weight (total): 24 lbs.
Features: Firebox door opens on end.

Manufacturer: Margesson's
Model: Browning Stove or Gerry Mini MK II
Type: Stove
Fuel type: LP gas
Features: Compact; fuel not included.

Manufacturer: Margesson's
Model: MSR
Type: Stove
No. of Burners: 1
Fuel type: Gasoline
Features: Includes pump; built-in flint; starter; wind screen.

Manufacturer: Margesson's
Model No.: Optimus 111B
Type: Stove
Fuel type: White non-leaded gas

Features: Fixed pump on fuel type; effective at higher altitudes; made of steel.

Manufacturer: Margesson's
Model No.: Optimus 8R. Same as Model No. Optimus 111B except:
Features: Light; compact; does not include pump.

Manufacturer: Margesson's
Model No.: Optimus 99. Same as Model No. 111B except:
Features: Aluminum; separate cover doubles as small pot; pot gripper; wind screen.

Manufacturer: North Face
Model: Bleuet
Type: Stove
Weight (total): 1 lb. 9 oz.
Fuel type: Butane
Features: Fuel cartridge not included; 2¼- to 4-hour cooking time.

Manufacturer: North Face
Model No.: Svea 123
Type: Stove
Weight (total): 1 lb.
Fuel type: White gas

Features: Includes tank; 1¼-hours cooking time.

Manufacturer: Precise
Model No.: 53480 Phoebus 725
Type: Stove
Weight (total): 2 lbs. 1 oz.
Fuel type: Gasoline
Features: Wind guard.

Manufacturer: Precise
Model No.: 53481 Phoebus 625
Type: Stove
Weight (total): 2 lbs. 14 oz.
Fuel type: Gasoline
Features: Includes steel pump and tank; wind guard and metal box.

Manufacturer: Primus
Model No.: 2228 Pioneer
Type: Infrared radiation heater
Fuel type: Butane
BTU's: Between 500 and 2000
Features: Valve controlled heat; cartridge lasts 7 hours.

Manufacturer: Primus
Model No.: 2255 Ranger
Type: Stove
Dimensions: 12½" x 3" x 3"

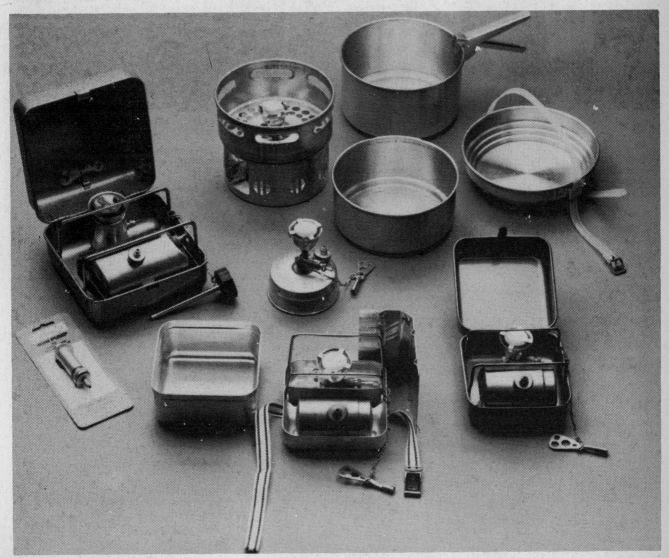

Margesson's Model No. 111B

Canister Weight: 13 oz.
Fuel type: Butane
BTU's: 4800
Features: 4-hour cooking time per cylinder; cartridge not included.

Primus Model No. 2228

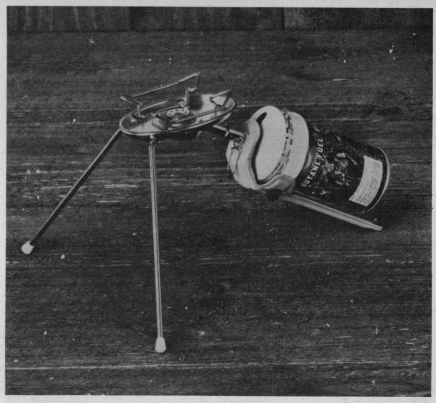

Primus Model No. 2255

Manufacturer: Primus
Model No.: 2312 Uni-Flow Four
Type: Heater
Dimensions: 10¾″ x 8½″ x 10″
Weight (total): 4 lbs. 2 oz.
Fuel type: Propane
BTU's: 3000
Features: Low silhouette.

Manufacturer: Primus
Model No.: 2319 Uni-Flow Five
Type: Heater
Dimensions: 17¾″ x 8½″ x 10″
Weight (total): 6 lbs.
Fuel type: Propane
BTU's: 5000
Features: Heat adjustable.

Manufacturer: Primus
Model No.: 2328
Type: Infra-Red heater
Dimensions: 9.5″ x 7.3″
Weight (total): 1.1 lbs.
Fuel type: Propane
BTU's: 3000
Features: Uses disposable cylinders or can be converted to larger refillable bottles with an adapter; cylinder not included.

Manufacturer: Primus
Model No.: 2329
Type: Infra-Red heater
Dimensions: 13.5″ x 12.6″ x 6.1″
Weight (total): 5 lbs.
Fuel type: Propane
BTU's: 8800
Features: Safety shut-off valve shuts off gas flow if flames go out; uses disposable cylinders or can be converted to larger refillable bottles with an adapter.

Manufacturer: Primus
Model No.: 2361 Grasshopper
Type: Stove

Weight (total): 2½ lbs.
Cylinder Weight: 14 oz.
No. of Burners: 1
Fuel type: Propane
BTU's: 4800
Features: 8- to 10-hour cooking time; cylinder included.

Manufacturer: Primus
Model No.: 2384 Gour-Mate
Type: Stove
Dimensions: 21″ x 11½″ x 4″
Weight (total): 2 lbs.
No. of Burners: 2
Fuel type: Propane
BTU's: 10,000
Features: Porcelanized sealed cooktop; wind shield; safety valve automatically shuts gas off.

Manufacturer: Primus
Model No.: 2385 Ultima
Type: Stove
Dimensions: 21″ x 11½″ x 4″
Weight (total): 12¾ lbs.
No. of Burners: 3
Fuel type: Propane
BTU's: 2 burners, 10,000; 1 burner, 6400
Features: Removable nickel-plated steel grid; operates from disposable or refillable cylinders; 3′ hose assembly with medium pressure regulator for disposable cylinders or safety post; maximizes efficiency at all altitudes and weather conditions.

Manufacturer: Primus
Model No.: 2391 Camper
Type: Stove
Dimensions: 22″ x 14″ x 4″
Weight (total): 8 lbs. 12 oz.
No. of Burners: 2
Fuel type: Propane
BTU's: 6400

Features: 6-hour cooking time; windshield; holds 2 cylinders; cylinders not included.

Manufacturer: Primus
Model No.: 2393 Streamliner
Type: Stove
Dimensions: 19″ x 11″ x 3⅞″
Weight (total): 8 lbs.
No. of Burners: 2
Fuel type: Propane
BTU's: 6400
Features: 6-hour cooking time; cylinders not included.

Manufacturer: Primus
Model No.: Duo-Flow Six
Type: Heater
Dimensions: 14¾″ x 7¾″ x 13″
Weight (total): 12 lbs. 2 oz.
Fuel type: Propane
BTU's: 6500
Features: Stores three 14.1 oz. disposable cylinders; dual direction of heat flow.

Manufacturer: Recreational Equipment
Model No.: B25-350 Gaz S200
Type: Stove
Weight (total): ⅞ lb. (without fuel)
No. of Burners: 1
Fuel type: Butane
Features: Not recommended for extreme cold; cartridge not included.

Manufacturer: Speaker
Model No.: 1118
Type: Stove
Dimensions: 3″ x 4″ x ¾″
Weight (total): 3½ oz.
No. of Burners: 1
Fuel type: Tablets
Features: Fuel tablets included.

Manufacturer: Springbar
Model No.: 3060 Sierra
Type: Stove
Dimensions: Diameter, 4½"
Weight (total): 7.9 oz. (without fuel)
No. of Burners: 1
Fuel type: LP gas
Features: Burns about 3 hours.

Manufacturer: Springbar
Model No.: 3630 Yukon
Type: Stove
Dimensions: 25" x 11" x 9"
Fuel type: Coal, wood, charcoal, gasoline, kerosene, diesel oil or heating oil
BTU's: 60,000
Features: Includes spark arrestor, stove pipe, fittings and burning unit for liquid fuel.

Manufacturer: Springbar
Model No.: 3640. Same as Model No. 3641 except:
Dimensions: 28" x 13½" x 10¼"

Manufacturer: Springbar
Model No.: 3641
Type: Stove
Dimensions: 19¾" x 13½" x 10¼"
Fuel type: Wood
Features: Heating or cooking uses; stove pipe; hinged doors on fire box and baker box.

Manufacturer: Trailblazer
Model No.: 2100 Topper
Type: Stove
Weight (total): Less than 3½ lbs.
Canister Weight: 16.4 oz.
Fuel type: Propane
BTU's: 6400
Features: Wind deflection ring and pan support; adjustable control valve.

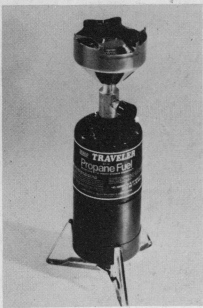
Trailblazer Model No. 2100

Manufacturer: Trailblazer
Model No.: 2150 Pot-lucker
Type: Stove
Canister Weight: 6¼ oz.
No. of Burners: 1
Fuel type: Butane
BTU's: 6200
Features: Pan support/wind deflector; 2 cooking pans included.

Manufacturer: Trailblazer
Model No.: 4000

Type: Infrared catalytic heater
Canister Weight: 14.1 oz. or 16.4 oz.
Fuel type: Propane
Features: Operates at peak efficiency regardless of temperature or altitude; control valve.

Manufacturer: Trailblazer
Model No.: 5000
Type: Catalytic heater
Canister Weight: 14.1 oz. (inside storage for 2)
Fuel type: Propane
Features: Chromed-steel grill; steel case.

Trailblazer Model No. 5000

Manufacturer: Trailblazer
Model No.: 7200 Deluxe
Type: Stove
Dimensions: Folded, 20" x 11" x 3¼"
No. of Burners: 2
Fuel type: Propane
BTU's: 10,000 each
Features: Grill and drip pan; comfort-styled handle.

Wonder Globetrotter

Manufacturer: Trailblazer
Model No.: 7300 Standard
Type: Stove
No. of Burners: 2
Fuel type: Propane
BTU's: 10,000 each
Features: Adjustable; folding wind screens; removable grill; disposable cylinders or adapted to bulk tank.

Manufacturer: Wonder
Model No.: Baby 200
Type: Heater
BTU's: 2500
Features: Parabolic heat shield; safety wire grill; tip-proof base; adjustable heat output; battery igniter.

Manufacturer: Wonder
Model: Dinner Set
Type: Stove
Weight (total): 32 oz.
No. of Burners: 1
Features: Multi-purpose; indoors or out; excellent for larger utensils.

Manufacturer: Wonder
Model: Globetrotter
Type: Stove
Weight (total): 12 oz. (includes cartridge)
No. of Burners: 1
Fuel type: Butane
Features: Compact; 1-hour cooking time; 2 cooking pans with removable handles.

Manufacturer: Wonder
Model: Instaflam
Type: Stove
Weight (total): 21 oz. (includes fuel)
No. of Burners: 1
Features: Piezo-electric ignition.

Trailblazer Model No. 7200

Tents/Tarps

Manufacturer: Academy
Model No.: 170
Type: Wall
Base Size: 7′ x 9′
Height (highest point): 6½′
Material: Nylon
Weight: 54 lbs.
Color(s): Olive drab
Frame: Aluminum
Features: 3-zippered entrance; screened windows on all sides; flame retardant.

Manufacturer: Academy
Model No.: 193
Type: Mountain
Base Size: 5′ x 7′
Height (highest point): 3½′
Material: Nylon
Weight: 20 lbs.
Color(s): Blue/orange
Frame: Aluminum
Sleeping Capacity: 2
Features: 3-zippered, screened entrance; screened windows on all sides; front overhang; flame retardant.

Manufacturer: Academy
Model No.: 202
Type: Dome
Base Size: 5′ x 7′
Height (highest point): 3½′
Material: Nylon
Weight: 26 lbs.
Floor: Nylon
Frame: Aluminum
Features: 3-zippered entrance; nylon mesh windows on all sides; window flaps.

Manufacturer: Browning
Model No.: 1160 Sawtooth II
Type: Backpacker
Base Size: 5′ x 7′
Height (highest point): 40″
Material: Nylon
Weight: 5 lbs.
Color(s): Brook blue
Floor: Nylon
Frame: Aluminum
Sleeping Capacity: 2
Features: Taffeta rain fly; flame retardant; screened doors and windows.

Camp Trails Model No. 722

Manufacturer: Browning
Model No.: 1260 Sawtooth III
Type: Backpacker
Base Size: 6′ x 8′
Height (highest point): 50″
Material: Nylon
Weight: 6 lbs. 12 oz.
Color(s): Brook blue
Floor: Nylon
Frame: Aluminum
Sleeping Capacity: 3
Features: Taffeta rain fly; flame retardant; screened doors and windows.

Manufacturer: Camp Trails
Model No.: 722 Manzanita

Base Size: 7′ x 4′ 8″
Height (highest point): 3′ 6″
Material: Nylon
Weight: 4 lbs. 10 oz.
Color(s): Bark brown, ivory
Floor: Nylon tub design
Frame: Aluminum
Sleeping Capacity: 2
Features: Fly; 2-zipper closure; screened rear window; fire retardant.

Manufacturer: Camp Trails
Model No.: 723 Chinquapin
Base Size: 7′ x 4′ 8″
Height (highest point): 3′ 6″
Material: Nylon
Weight: 5 lbs. 2 oz.
Color(s): Bark brown, ivory
Floor: Nylon bathtub
Frame: Aluminum
Sleeping Capacity: 2
Features: Fly; 2-zipper closure; rear screened window; fire retardant.

Manufacturer: Camp Trails
Model No.: 733 Sahuaro
Base Size: 7′ 6″ x 6′ 6″
Height (highest point): 4′ 2″
Material: Nylon
Weight: 7 lbs. 4 oz.
Color(s): Bark brown, ivory
Floor: Nylon bathtub
Frame: Aluminum
Sleeping Capacity: 3
Features: Fly; rear screened window; insect net door; fire retardant.

Manufacturer: Coleman
Model No.: 838 Peak 1
Base Size: 7′ x 5′
Height (highest point): 44″
Material: Breathable nylon taffeta
Weight: 5 lbs. 9 oz.
Floor: Coated rip-stop nylon
Frame: Aluminum
Sleeping Capacity: 2

Browning Model No. 1160

Features: Flame resistant; waterproof fly and floor; adjustable spreader bar; storm flaps and insect netting on door.

Manufacturer: Coleman
Model No.: 8401-803 Compact III
Base Size: 7′ 3″ x 7′
Height (highest point): 4′ 6″
Material: Duck
Color(s): Blue
Floor: Double vinyl-coated nylon
Frame: Aluminum
Sleeping Capacity: 3
Features: Moisture and flame resistant; push-pin, pole assembly; nylon mesh screens.

Manufacturer: Coleman
Model No.: 8401-804 Compact IV
Base Size: 9′ x 7′ 6″
Height (highest point): 6′ 3″
Material: Duck
Color(s): Blue
Floor: Double vinyl-coated nylon
Frame: Aluminum
Sleeping Capacity: 4
Features: Moisture and flame resistant; push-pin, pole assembly; nylon mesh; screen flaps.

Manufacturer: Coleman
Model No.: 8428-800
Type: Mountain
Base Size: 7′ x 5′
Height (highest point): 3′ 6″
Material: Drill
Color(s): Green
Floor: Sewn-in, vinyl-coated nylon
Frame: Aluminum
Features: Moisture and flame resistant; out-side-erection; adjustable poles; nylon mesh screening; inside zip storm flap.

Manufacturer: Coleman
Model No.: 8455-823 Villa Del Mar
Base Size: 12′ x 9′
Height (highest point): 8′
Material: Canvas
Color(s): Gold/khaki
Floor: Double vinyl-coated nylon
Frame: Metal
Features: Moisture and flame resistant; self-supporting; outside frame with adjustable pole; 2 Mediterranean-style windows.

Manufacturer: Coleman
Model No.: 8471-812 Compact Oasis
Base Size: 10′ x 8′
Height (highest point): 7′ 6″
Material: Canvas
Color(s): Green
Floor: Double vinyl-coated nylon
Frame: Metal
Sleeping Capacity: 4
Features: Moisture and flame resistant; adjustable poles; drill top; nylon mesh screen.

Manufacturer: Coleman
Model No.: 8471-822 Family Oasis
Base Size: 12′ x 9′
Height (highest point): 7′ 6″
Material: Canvas
Color(s): Green
Floor: Double vinyl-coated nylon
Frame: Metal
Sleeping Capacity: 5
Features: Moisture and flame resistant; adjustable poles; drill top; zipped-in, nylon mesh screen.

Manufacturer: Coleman
Model No.: 8471-832 Deluxe Oasis
Base Size: 13′ x 10′
Height (highest point): 7′ 6″
Material: Canvas
Color(s): Green
Floor: Double vinyl-coated nylon
Frame: Metal
Sleeping Capacity: 6
Features: Moisture and flame resistant; adjustable poles; drill top; zipped-in, nylon

Camp Trails Model No. 723

Camp Trails Model No. 733

Coleman Model No. 838

Coleman Model No. 8471-832

Coleman Model No. 8491A835

mesh screen; 2 double doors; window awnings.

Manufacturer: Coleman
Model No.: 8481A830 Compact Olympic
Base Size: 10′ x 8′
Height (highest point): 6′ 6″
Material: Canvas
Color(s): Blue
Floor: Double vinyl-coated nylon
Frame: Metal
Sleeping Capacity: 4
Features: Moisture and flame resistant; duck roof; cross bar and spreader with 2 upright poles.

Manufacturer: Coleman
Model No.: 8481A840 Olympic
Base Size: 11′ x 10′
Height (highest point): 7′
Material: Canvas
Color(s): Blue
Floor: Double vinyl-coated nylon
Frame: Metal
Sleeping Capacity: 5
Features: Moisture and flame resistant; duck roof; cross bar and spreader with 2 upright poles.

Manufacturer: Coleman
Model No.: 8491A815 American Heritage Compact
Base Size: 9′ 8″ x 7½″
Material: Canvas
Color(s): Green
Floor: Rope-reinforced, vinyl-coated nylon
Frame: Metal
Sleeping Capacity: 4
Features: Moisture and flame resistant; self-supporting outside frame; drill top; 2 nylon-screened windows.

Manufacturer: Coleman
Model No.: 8491A825 American Heritage Family
Base Size: 11′ 2″ x 8′ 2″
Material: Canvas
Color(s): Green
Floor: Rope-reinforced, vinyl-coated nylon
Frame: Aluminum
Sleeping Capacity: 5
Features: Moisure and flame resistant; self-supporting outside frame; drill top; nylon-screened windows on 3 sides.

Manufacturer: Coleman
Model No.: 8491A835 Vacationer
Base Size: 9′ 8″ x 7′ 2″
Height (highest point): 6′ 6″
Material: Nylon
Color(s): Red
Floor: Rope-reinforced, vinyl-coated nylon
Frame: Metal
Sleeping Capacity: 4
Features: Moisture and flame resistant; semi-dry finish, drill top; double-Dutch front door.

Manufacturer: Coleman
Model No.: 8491A845 Vacationer
Base Size: 11′ 2″ x 8′ 2″
Height (highest point): 6′ 6″
Material: Nylon
Color(s): Red/burgundy
Floor: Rope-reinforced, vinyl-coated nylon
Frame: Metal
Sleeping Capacity: 5
Features: Moisture and flame resistant; double-Dutch front door; semi-dry finish, drill top.

Manufacturer: Coleman
Model No.: 8551-814
Type: Backpacker
Base Size: 7′ 9″ x 5′
Height (highest point): 42″
Material: Nylon taffeta
Weight: 5 lbs.
Color(s): Blue
Sleeping Capacity: 2

Features: Moisture resistant; waterproof fly; roof-top vent; insect netting and storm flap on zippered side door; carrying bag.

Manufacturer: Colorado Tent & Awning
Model No.: Standard Wall
Base Size: 8′ x 10′, 10′ x 12′, 12′ x 14′, 14′ x 16′, 14′ x 20′, 16′ x 20′
Height (highest point): 6′ 8″, 7′ 0″, 8′ 3″, 9′ 2″, 9′ 2″
Material: Single filling white duck, camper cloth, army duck
Color(s): Assorted
Floor: Detachable, vinyl-coated nylon
Frame: Wood
Features: Water repellent and mildew resistant; overlap door flap with tire; carrying storage bag; poles and floor not included.

Manufacturer: Colorado Tent & Awning
Model: Western Wall
Base Size: 10′ x 10′, 10′ x 2′ 6″
Material: Camper cloth, army duck
Color(s): Light tan, pearl grey
Floor: Detachable, waterproof vinyl-coated nylon
Frame: Wood
Sleeping Capacity: 4
Features: Water repellent and mildew resistant; full screen and fabric door; screened rear window with flap; carrying bag; floor not included.

Manufacturer: Colorado Tent & Awning
Model: Colorado De Luxe
Type: Umbrella
Base Size: 7′ x 7′, 7′ x 9′, 9′ 7″ x 9′ ″7, 9′ x 11′
Material: Camper cloth
Color(s): Light tan
Floor: Built in
Frame: Aluminum
Features: Water repellent and mildew resistant; zippered screen and fabric doors, with awning; nylon screen rear window with flap; carrying bag.

Manufacturer: Colorado Tent & Awning
Model: Colorado Range
Base Size: 6′ x 8′, 8′ x 8′, 9′ 6″ x 9′ 6″
Height (highest point): 7′, 7′ 3″, 7′ 6″
Material: Single filling white duck
Floor: Sewn-in, single filling white duck
Frame: Wood
Features: Outside supports; 12″ door sill; steep sides; jointed poles.

Manufacturer: Colorado Tent & Awning
Model: Herder
Base Size: 7′ x 7′, 8′ x 8′, 9′ x 9′, 10′ x 10′
Height (highest point): 6′ 3″, 6′ 6″, 7′ 3″, 8′ 9″
Material: Single filling white duck
Frame: Wood
Features: Single center pole; steep pitch; tie strings at door.

Manufacturer: Colorado Tent & Awning
Model: Backpacker
Base Size: 5′ x 7′
Height (highest point): 4′
Material: Breathable, water-repellent nylon
Weight: 7 lbs.
Color(s): Dark brown ends and wall, sand tan top, orange fly
Frame: Aluminum
Features: Waterproof fly; zippered, screened-in entrace and rear window; pull-out sidewalls; nylon stuff bag.

Manufacturer: Colorado Tent & Awning
Model: Whelen Lean-To
Base Size: 6′ x 7′
Material: Urethane-coated nylon, camper cloth
Weight: 6½ lbs.
Color(s): Orange, light tan
Sleeping Capacity: 2
Features: Water repellent and mildew resistant (camper cloth); no poles; carrying bag; floor.

Manufacturer: Colorado Tent & Awning
Model: Lean-To Pole Kit
Weight: 2 lbs.
Frame: Aluminum
Features: Collapsible poles; nylon guy lines with tighteners; carrying bag.

Manufacturer: Colorado Tent & Awning
Model: Wall Tent Fly
Material: Camper cloth, vinyl-coated nylon
Features: Water repellent and mildew resistant (camper cloth); nylon webbing reinforced perimeter.

Manufacturer: Colorado Tent & Awning
Model: Tar
Type: Tarpaulins
Material: Single filling white duck; olive drab waterproof chexflame; olive dyed duck; vinyl-coated nylon; Neoprene-coated black and black/aluminum nylon

Manufacturer: Dickey
Model No.: DCT-767 Chalet
Base Size: 7′ 6″ x 7′
Height (highest point): 6′
Material: Nylon
Weight: 25 lbs.
Color(s): Orange
Floor: Washable vinyl
Frame: Aluminum
Sleeping Capacity: 4
Features: Self-adjusting, outside frame; drill canvas roof; fiberglass screening; nylon carry bag.

Manufacturer: Dickey
Model No.: DPT-57 Deluxe
Type: Pup
Base Size: 5′ x 7′
Height (highest point): 42″
Material: Canvas drill
Weight: 12 lbs.
Color(s): Tan
Floor: Washable vinyl
Frame: Aluminum
Sleeping Capacity: 2
Features: Adjustable ropes; fiberglass screening in nylon-zippered door; storm flaps.

Manufacturer: Dickey
Model No.: DSH-1012
Type: Screen house
Base Size: 12′ x 10′
Height (highest point): 8′
Material: Nylon
Weight: 38 lbs.
Color(s): Orange/tan
Frame: Metal
Features: Adjustable, outside frame; fiberglass screening; nylon-zippered door; sod cloth.

Manufacturer: Dickey
Model No.: DST-1016-F Screen
Base Size: 10′ x 8′
Height (highest point): 8′
Material: Drill sidewalls, canvas drill roof
Weight: 85 lbs.
Color(s): Tan
Floor: Washable vinyl
Frame: Steel
Sleeping Capacity: 9
Features: Flame retardant; adjustable, outside frame; fiberglass screening; rear picture window; screened patio; window flaps; tent and frame bags.

Manufacturer: Eureka
Model: Lakeside
Base Size: 16′ x 10′
Height (highest point): 9′
Material: Poplin
Weight: 65 lbs.
Color(s): Pearl grey
Floor: Vinyl-coated nylon
Frame: Aluminum
Features: Flame retardant; net windows with outside awning flaps or inside zip flaps; nylon divider curtain; tent and pole bags; 2 rooms.

Manufacturer: Eureka
Model No.: SH 1210
Type: Screen house
Base Size: 10′ x 12′
Height (highest point): 7′ 8″
Material: Nylon net
Weight: 32 lbs.
Color(s): Tan
Frame: Aluminum
Features: Flame retardant; poplin roof; bad weather poly curtain; internal ridge; rot-resistant, vinyl-coated nylon splash and sod cloth.

Manufacturer: Eureka
Model No.: Space 10
Type: Umbrella
Base Size: 10′ x 10′
Height (highest point): 8′
Material: Poplin
Weight: 53 lbs.
Color(s): Tan, pearl grey
Floor: Vinyl-coated nylon
Frame: Metal
Features: Flame retardant; water and mildew resistant; door awning.

Manufacturer: Eureka
Model No.: Holiday 10
Type: Umbrella
Base Size: 9′ 6″ x 9′ 6″
Height (highest point): 7′ 6″
Material: Poplin
Weight: 29 lbs.
Color(s): Desert tan
Floor: Waterproof, vinyl coated
Frame: Aluminum
Features: Flame retardant and water resistant; adjustable poles; roof vent; lantern snap; interior rings; carrying bag.

Manufacturer: Eureka
Model: Mountain
Base Size: 6′ x 9′
Height (highest point): 5′
Material: Poplin
Color(s): Tan, pearl grey
Floor: Vinyl-coated nylon
Frame: Aluminum
Sleeping Capacity: 3
Features: Flame retardant; sectional poles; pullouts; dry finish; net and storm doors.

Manufacturer: Eureka
Model: Mt. Katahdin
Base Size: 8′ 9″ x 6′
Height (highest point): 60″
Material: Breathable rip-stop nylon
Weight: 4 lbs. 2 oz.
Color(s): Orange/blue, green/gold
Floor: Waterproof, rip-stop K-Kote
Frame: Aluminum
Sleeping Capacity: 3
Features: Hooded; flame retardant; net door and rear window; map pocket.

Manufacturer: Eureka
Model: Expedition Alpine
Base Size: 8′ x 5′
Height (highest point): 49″
Material: Urethane-coated rip-stop nylon
Weight: 10 lbs. 10 oz.
Color(s): Orange/blue, green/gold
Floor: Urethane-coated rip-stop nylon
Frame: Aluminum
Sleeping Capacity: 2
Features: Flame retardant; self-supporting; mosquito netting; snow tunnel; cook hole; roof vent.

Manufacturer: Eureka
Model No.: ACC 77 Adirondack Cabin Camper
Type: Wall
Base Size: 7′ 3″ x 7′ 3″
Height (highest point): 6′
Material: Poplin
Weight: 22 lbs.
Floor: Waterproof, vinyl-coated nylon
Frame: Aluminum

Features: Flame retardant; self-supporting; water and mildew repellent; inside ridge; 3 windows, 2 with awning flaps.

Manufacturer: Eureka
Model: Aleutian
Type: Backpacker
Height (highest point): 52″
Material: Breathable rip-stop
Weight: 9 lbs. 12 oz.
Color(s): Willow green/gold
Floor: K-Kote waterproof rip-stop
Frame: Fiberglass
Features: Flame retardant; 2 A-type doors; netted roof vent; igloo-type entrance.

Manufacturer: Eureka
Model: Mt. Marcy
Type: Backpacker
Base Size: 5′ x 8′
Material: Urethane-coated rip-stop nylon
Weight: 4 lbs. 13 oz.
Color(s): Green, orange
Sleeping Capacity: 2
Features: Flame retardant; 3 pullouts/side; net door; 2 side windows with flaps; zippered rear window; carrying bag.

Manufacturer: Eureka
Model: Nu-Lite
Type: Backpacker
Base Size: 5′ x 7′ 4″
Height (highest point): 3′ 6″
Material: Taffeta
Weight: 4 lbs. 10 oz.
Color(s): Assorted
Frame: Aluminum
Features: Flame retardant; mosquito netting door; side pull-outs; storm door.

Manufacturer: Eureka
Model: Alpine Drawtite
Base Size: 5′ x 7′ 9″
Height (highest point): 48″
Material: Combed poplin
Weight: 13¼ lbs.
Color(s): Tan, pearl grey
Floor: Sewn-in, waterproof vinyl-coated nylon
Frame: Corrosion-proof aluminum alloy
Sleeping Capacity: 2
Features: Flame retardant; dry tent finish; rear window rain and overhanging front hoods; storm door; tent and pole bags.

Manufacturer: Eureka
Model: Lightweight Tarp
Material: Poplin, drill
Color(s): Pearl grey
Features: Dry finish.

Manufacturer: Holubar
Model No.: 107078A
Type: Backpacker
Base Size: 8′ x 8′
Height (highest point): 6′
Material: Breathable, rip-stop nylon canopy; urethane-coated nylon sidewalls
Color(s): Blue canopy, avocado sidewalls, forest green or orange fly
Floor: Urethane-coated nylon
Frame: Aluminum
Sleeping Capacity: 4
Features: Flame retardant; polymer-coated rip-stop nylon fly; mosquito netting; rear tunnel door; stuff sack.

Manufacturer: Holubar
Model No.: 107110A
Type: Backpacker
Height (highest point): 5′ 6″
Material: Breathable, rip-stop nylon canopy; urethane-coated nylon sidewalls
Color(s): Blue canopy, avocado sidewalls, forest green fly
Floor: Urethane-coated nylon
Frame: Aluminum
Sleeping Capacity: 3
Features: Flame retardant; polymer-coated rip-stop nylon fly; outside frame; mosquito

Eureka Mt. Katahdin

Holubar Model No. 107110A

netting; tunnel and side window vents; door flap.

Manufacturer: Hoosier
Model No.: 50-160
Type: Backpacker
Base Size: 5′ 8″ x 7′
Height (highest point): 46″
Material: Taffeta nylon
Weight: 3¾ lbs.
Color(s): Royal blue
Sleeping Capacity: 2
Features: Flame retardant; eave projections; rear, inside-zip window; nylon carrying bag.

Manufacturer: Hoosier
Model: Dry Finish Tarp
Color(s): Pearl grey
Features: Dry water repellent and mildew resistant finish.

Manufacturer: Hoosier
Model: Vinyl-laminated Nylon Tarp
Features: Waterproof; mildew and fire resistant.

Manufacturer: Margesson's
Model No.: Superlight Mark IV
Base Size: 9′ x 7′
Height (highest point): 4′ 6″

Material: Nylon
Weight: 10 lbs. 15 oz.
Floor: Rip-stop nylon
Sleeping Capacity: 4
Features: Fire restardant; waterproof walls; "A" and tunnel doors; mosquito netting; cook hole; pockets and interior rings.

Manufacturer: Margesson's
Model: Camponaire II (Gerry)
Base Size: 7′ x 6′ 6″
Height (highest point): 5′ 3″
Material: Rip-stop nylon
Weight: 9 lbs. 8 oz.
Color(s): Blue
Floor: Taffeta, with K-Kote
Sleeping Capacity: 3
Features: Fire retardant; waterproof walls; rip-stop fly, with K-Kote; rear windows; nylon mesh screening.

Manufacturer: North Face
Model: Morning Glory
Base Size: 168″ x 96″
Height (highest point): 72″
Weight: 13 lbs. 8 oz.
Color(s): Gold, taupe/gold, navy
Floor: Tub design
Frame: Metal
Sleeping Capacity: 5

Margesson's Camponaire II (Gerry)

Features: Waterproof; flame retardant; coated, rip-stop fly; mosquito netting; adjustable vents; cookhole; stuff sacks.

Manufacturer: North Face
Model: St. Elias
Type: Mountain
Base Size: 94″ x 56″
Height (highest point): 56″
Weight: 8 lbs. 6 oz.
Color(s): Green, taupe/gold, navy
Floor: Tub design
Frame: Metal
Sleeping Capacity: 2
Features: Waterproof; flame retardant; coated, rip-stop fly; mosquito netting; adjustable vent; pull-outs; frost liner; cookhole; snow flaps; tunnel and zippered doors.

Manufacturer: North Face
Model: Tuolumne
Base Size: 50″ x 84″
Height (highest point): 56″
Weight: 5 lbs. 8 oz.
Color(s): Gold, navy/royal, taupe
Floor: Tub design
Frame: Alloy
Sleeping Capacity: 2
Features: Waterproof; flame retardant; coated, rip-stop fly; mosquito netting; adjustable vent; tunnel door; stuff sack.

Manufacturer: Outdoor Venture
Model No.: 142 Promo
Type: Mountain
Base Size: 5′ x 7′
Height (highest point): 38″
Material: Nylon taffeta
Color(s): Green
Floor: Poly
Frame: Aluminum
Sleeping Capacity: 2
Features: Flame retardant; nylon taffeta roof; zippered screen door.

Manufacturer: Outdoor Venture
Model No.: 225
Type: Dining canopy
Base Size: 11′ 6″ x 11′ 6″
Height (highest point): 8′
Material: Poly
Color(s): Blue
Frame: Metal
Features: Flame retardant; adjustable center pole.

Manufacturer: Outdoor Venture
Model No.: 274
Type: Poly Screenhouse
Base Size: 12′ x 12′
Height (highest point): 7′ 6″
Material: Polyester screening
Color(s): Grey
Frame: Metal
Features: Flame retardant; woven poly roof; outside, adjustable frame; 4″ splash cloth.

Manufacturer: Outdoor Venture
Model No.: 544 Glenstone
Type: Cabin
Base Size: 9′ x 12′
Height (highest point): 6′ 6″
Material: Nylon taffeta
Color(s): Green/white
Floor: Poly
Frame: Metal
Sleeping Capacity: 5

North Face Tuolumne

Features: Flame retardant; fiberglass screening; canvas drill roof; storm flaps.

Manufacturer: Outdoor Venture
Model No.: 565 Sunrise
Type: Cabin/Screenhouse
Base Size: 10′ x 14′
Material: Coated nylon wall; cotton drill roof
Color(s): Blue
Floor: Poly
Frame: Metal
Sleeping Capacity: 4
Features: Flame retardant; fiberglass screening; cotton drill roof; screened patio.

Manufacturer: Outdoor Venture
Model No.: 576 Mt. Lodge
Type: Cabin
Base Size: 10′ x 15′
Height (highest point): 7′
Material: Nylon taffeta
Color(s): Red
Floor: Poly
Frame: Metal
Sleeping Capacity: 8
Features: Flame retardant; fiberglass screening; adjustable frame; canvas drill roof; storm flaps.

Manufacturer: Ski Hut
Model No.: T110C Fitzroy
Type: Mountain
Base Size: 60″ x 102″
Height (highest point): 51″
Material: Nylon
Weight: 8 lbs. 12 oz.
Color(s): Green, orange
Floor: Waterproof, urethane-coated nylon
Frame: Metal
Features: Self-supporting; sectional poles; mosquito screening; pullouts; rear vent; tunnel and "A" doors; fly; pockets.

Manufacturer: Ski Hut
Model No.: T105 Trailwise Ultimate
Type: Tube
Height (highest point): 44″
Material: Urethane-coated nylon
Weight: 44 oz.
Frame: Aluminum
Features: Sectional poles; mosquito netting; floor; pullouts.

Manufacturer: Springbar
Model No.: 711Z Leisure Port
Height (highest point): 7′ 6″

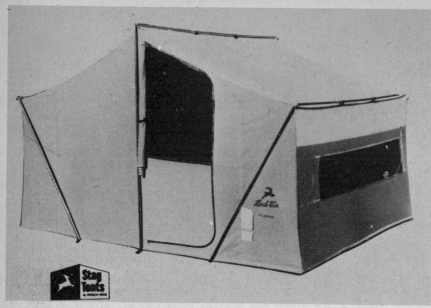

Stag Model No. 20041

Stag Model No. 21022

Material: Shelter duck
Weight: 16 lbs.
Color(s): Pearl grey
Features: Water repellent; army duck top; outside frame; attachable to module bedroom(s) and other leisure part(s).

Manufacturer: Springbar
Model No.: 1055 Supr-Lyt
Type: Backpacker
Base Size: 7′ 9″ x 5′
Height (highest point): 4′
Material: Rip-stop nylon
Weight: 6 lbs. 15 oz.
Color(s): Tan, light blue, international orange, forest green or brown fly
Floor: Flame-retardant coated nylon
Features: Double wall and roof; flame-retardant, coated taffeta fly; twin doors; ventilated roof; usable as single wall; tent and pole bags.

Manufacturer: Springbar
Model No.: 8140 Vacationer
Base Size: 10′ x 14′
Height (highest point): 87″
Material: Army duck
Weight: 65 lbs.
Color(s): Pearl grey
Floor: Vinyl-coated nylon
Sleeping Capacity: 7
Features: Interior frame; window screens and awnings; skylight; outdoor patio canopy; tent and pole bags.

Manufacturer: Springbar
Model No.: 852 3-Man Compact
Base Size: 8′ x 6′ 4″
Height (highest point): 76″
Material: Shelter duck
Weight: 20 lbs. 4 oz.
Color(s): Pearl Grey
Floor: Vinyl-coated nylon

Sleeping Capacity: 3
Features: Internal frame; tent and pole bags.

Manufacturer: Springbar
Model No.: 9110 Deluxe Family Traveler
Base Size: 10′ x 11′
Height (highest point): 7′ 3″
Material: Shelter Duck
Weight: 51 lbs.
Color(s): Pearl grey
Floor: Vinyl-coated nylon
Sleeping Capacity: 5
Features: Rear screened and zippered window; front patio awning; tent and pole bags; army duck roof.

Manufacturer: Springbar
Model No.: MC712 Module Screen Fabric Closure
Material: Polyurethane-coated nylon
Weight: 25 lbs.
Color(s): Yellow, blue, coral
Features: Nylon screen; 8″ sod cloth flap; attaches to Leisure Port, Module Bedroom and Fly.

Manufacturer: Springbar
Model No.: MB713 Module Bedroom
Base Size: 7′ x 7′
Height (highest point): 6′
Material: Shelter duck
Weight: 16 lbs.
Color(s): Pearl grey
Floor: Sewn-in, waterproof, vinyl-coated nylon
Sleeping Capacity: 3
Features: Water repellent; army duck top; carrying bag; attachable to Leisure Port(s); nylon netting; window flap.

Manufacturer: Springbar
Model No.: MF714 Module Fly
Material: Polyurethane-coated nylon
Weight: 3 lbs.
Color(s): Yellow, blue, coral
Features: Attaches to Leisure Port, Module Bedroom and Fly.

Manufacturer: Stag
Model No.: 20041 Oakwood
Type: Wall
Base Size: 11′ 10″ x 8′ 10″
Height (highest point): 7′
Material: Cotton
Color(s): Brush tan
Floor: Double-coated, waterproof rip-stop poly
Frame: Aluminum
Features: Flame retardant; fiberglass netting; storm flaps on door and 2 windows.

Manufacturer: Stag
Model No.: 21022 Yellowstone
Type: Cabin
Base Size: 11′ 10″ x 8′ 8″
Height (highest point): 7′
Material: Waterproof synthetic oxford duck
Color(s): Brown
Floor: Double-coated waterproof rip-stop poly
Frame: Aluminum
Features: Flame retardant; breathable cotton roof; door storm flap; 2 inside-zip-side windows and 1 in door.

Manufacturer: Stag
Model No.: 22018 Overnighter
Type: Umbrella
Base Size: 8′ 11″ x 8′ 8″
Height (highest point): 6′ 9″
Material: Breathable cotton
Color(s): Green
Floor: Double-coated, waterproof rip-stop poly
Frame: Aluminum
Features: Flame retardant; fiberglass netting; breathable cotton roof; storm flaps; rear window; outside frame.

Manufacturer: Stag
Model No.: 24030 Explorer
Type: Backpacker
Base Size: 7′ 4″ x 7′ 3″

Height (highest point): 6' 2"
Material: Polyester
Weight: 11 lbs.
Color(s): Blue
Floor: Sewn-in, waterproof nylon
Frame: Aluminum
Sleeping Capacity: 3
Features: Flame retardant and water repellent; nylon netting; breathable cotton roof; ventilator; storm flaps; carrying bag.

Manufacturer: Stag
Model No.: 24023 Arctic Circle
Type: Backpacker
Base Size: 5' 9" x 6' 8"

Height (highest point): 3' 6"
Material: Polyester
Weight: 7 lbs.
Color(s): Green
Floor: Sewn-in, waterproof nylon
Frame: Aluminum
Features: Flame restardant and water repellent; nylon netting; carrying bag.

Manufacturer: Stephenson's
Model No.: 2R Warmlite
Material: Urethane-coated rip-stop nylon
Color(s): Assorted
Floor: Urethane-coated rip-stop nylon
Sleeping Capacity: 2

Features: Aluminized reflective fabric tent liner; waterproof; nylon mosquito netting; vents.

Manufacturer: Upland
Model: Fastent
Type: Poleless
Height (highest point): 47"
Material: Coated rip-stop
Weight: 6 lbs. 8 oz.
Frame: Spring steel
Features: Fire retardant; coated rip-stop fly; air vents; cookhole; 2 doors; stuff sack; supported by continuous coil of spring steel.

Stag Model No. 24030

Trailers

Manufacturer: Bethany Fellowship
Model No.: Citation 46
Type: Hitched
Dimensions: Body, 9' 9" x 84"; road height, 45"; total open length, 18' 6"
Material: Thermo-core top
Weight: 1325 lbs.
Accomodations: 6
Kitchen: Sink, 3-burner range, ice box
Features: Low profile; three double beds.

Manufacturer: Bethany Fellowship
Model No.: Citation 48XL
Type: Hitched
Dimensions: Body, 12' x 6' 10"; road height, 46"; total open length, 19' 9"
Weight: 1475 lbs.
Accomodations: 8
Kitchen: 3-burner gas range, sink, gas-fired furnace, ice box (optional)
Features: Electrical hookup and water connection; low profile; hydraulic brakes.

Manufacturer: Bethany Fellowship
Model No.: Citation 86
Type: Hitched
Dimensions: Body, 12' x 84"; road height, 51"; total open length, 20'
Material: Thermo-core top, canvas sidewalls
Weight: 1778 lbs.
Accomodations: 6
Kitchen: Sink, counter top, storage, range with oven, refrigerator (optional), gas furnace (optional)
Features: Hydraulic brakes.

Manufacturer: Bethany Fellowship
Model No.: Citation 88
Type: Hitched
Dimensions: Body, 12' x 84"; road height, 51"; total open length, 20'
Material: Thermo-core top, canvas sidewalls
Weight: 1723 lbs.
Accomodations: 8
Kitchen: Sink, refrigerator (optional), range with oven (optional), gas furnace (optional)
Features: Hydraulic brakes.

Manufacturer: Bethany Fellowship
Model No.: Compact 540
Type: Hitched
Dimensions: Body, 10' 4½" x 6' ¼"; road height, 44"; total open width, 9' 11"
Material: Thermo-core top, canvas sidewalls
Weight: 1000 lbs.
Accommodations: 4
Kitchen: Sink, 2-burner range, counter, ice box (optional), gas furnace (optional)
Features: Low profile.

Manufacturer: Bethany Fellowship
Model No.: Compact 560
Type: Hitched
Dimensions: Body, 10' 4½" x 6' ¼"; road height, 44"; total open width, 13' 6"
Material: Thermo-core top, canvas sidewalls
Weight: 1100 lbs.
Accommodations: 6
Kitchen: Sink, 2-burner range, counter, ice box (optional), gas furnace (optional)
Features: Low profile.

Manufacturer: Bethany Fellowship
Model: Bethany Teepee
Type: Hitched
Dimensions: Body, 8' 6" x 6'; road height 44"; total length, 11' 7"
Material: Thermo-core top
Weight: 879 lbs.
Accomodations: 4
Kitchen: 2-burner stove, sink, porta-potti (optional), gas furnace (optional)
Features: Low profile.

Bethany Citation 46

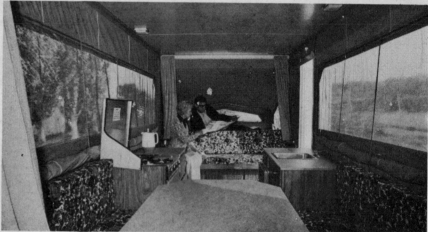

Bethany Citation 86

Bethany Teepee

Manufacturer: Bethany Fellowship
Model: PickUpper
Type: Pick-up
Dimensions: Head room, 6' 3"
Weight: 800 lbs.
Accomodations: 4
Kitchen: 2-burner gas range, sink, ice box
(optional)
Features: Low profile; fits any standard width,
8' or longer pickup box.

Manufacturer: Coleman
Model: Concord
Type: Hitched
Dimensions: Closed, 6' 8" x 10' 11"; open,
6' 8" x 15' 10"
Material: Aluminum roof
Weight: Less than 1000 lbs.
Accomodations: 5
Kitchen: 2-burner range, sink, ice box, water
tank
Features: Screen door; city-water hookup.

Manufacturer: Coleman
Model: Gettysburg
Type: Hitched
Dimensions: Closed, 6' 8" x 12' 6"; open,
6' 8" x 9' 4"
Material: Aluminum roof

Coleman Yorktown

Coleman Gettysburg

Coleman Brandywine

Coleman Lexington

Coleman Valley Forge

Accomodations: 6
Kitchen: 2-burner stove, 5-gallon water system, 38 quarts Poly Lite cooler
Features: 4 stabilizer jacks; city-water hookup.

Manufacturer: Coleman
Model: Valley Forge
Type: Hitched
Dimensions: Closed, 6' 8" x 12' 6"; open, 6' 8" x 19' 4"
Material: Aluminum roof
Accomodations: 6
Kitchen: 3-burner cook top, sink, ice box
Features: Screen door; city-water hookup.

Manufacturer: Coleman

Model: Brandywine
Type: Hitched
Dimensions: Closed, 6' 8" x 14' 6"; open, 6' 8" x 21' 4"
Material: Aluminum roof
Accomodations: 6
Kitchen: Range, sink, 2-way faucet, ice box
Features: Electricity and water hookups; 12V solid state converter.

Manufacturer: Coleman
Model: Yorktown
Type: Hitched
Dimensions: Closed, 6' 8" x 14' 6"; open, 6' 8" x 23' 4"
Material: Aluminum roof

Accomodations: 7
Kitchen: Ice box, range, sink, 2-way faucet
Features: Removable dinette; city-water hookup.

Manufacturer: Coleman
Model: Lexington
Type: Hitched
Dimensions: Closed, 6' 8" x 14' 6"; open, 6' 8" x 23' 4"
Material: Aluminum roof
Accomodations: 8 to 9
Kitchen: Ice box, range, sink, 2-way faucet
Features: Screen door with sliding privacy panel; city-water hookup.

Coleman Concord

Manufacturer: Starcraft
Model: Camelot (Venture)
Type: Fold-down
Dimensions: Closed (exterior), 14' 4" x 6' 11" x 4' 6"; open (interior), 19' x 6' 4" x 6' 5"
Weight: 1480 lbs.
Accommodations: 6
Kitchen: Ice box, 2-burner stove, sink, storage
Features: Swing-out kitchen; power converter.

Manufacturer: Starcraft
Model: Chalet (Venture)
Type: Fold-down
Dimensions: Closed (exterior), 11' 5½" x 6' 3¾" x 3' 5½"; open (interior), 7' 2" x 13' 6½" x 6' 3"
Weight: 980 lbs.
Accommodations: 6
Kitchen: 2-burner portable stove
Features: Power converter.

Manufacturer: Starcraft
Model: Windsor (Venture)
Type: Fold-down
Dimensions: Closed (exterior), 16' 8" x 6' 11" x 4' 8½"; open (interior), 21' x 6' 4" x 6' 6½"
Weight: 1690 lbs.
Accommodations: 7
Kitchen: 3-burner stove, sink, demand water, 2 dinettes
Features: Power converter.

Manufacturer: Starcraft
Model No.: Galaxy 6
Type: Fold-down
Dimensions: Closed (exterior), 16' 8" x 6' 11" x 4' 8½"; open (interior), 21' x 6' 4" x 6' 6½"
Weight: 1695 lbs.
Accommodations: 6
Kitchen: Convertible dinette, 3-burner stove, sink
Features: Fold-down wardrobe; optional shower; power converter.

Manufacturer: Starcraft
Model No.: Starlight 7
Type: Fold-down
Dimensions: Closed (exterior), 12' 4" x 6' 11" x 4' 6"; open (interior), 16' x 6' 4" x 6' 5"
Weight: 1035 lbs.
Accommodations: 7
Features: Power converter.

Manufacturer: Starcraft
Model: Galaxy Swinger

Type: Fold-down
Dimensions: Closed (exterior), 16' 8" x 6' 11" x 4' 8½"; open (interior), 21' x 6' 4" x 6' 6½"
Weight: 1745 lbs.
Accommodations: 6
Kitchen: 2-burner stove (LP power), sink
Features: Swing-out kitchen; power converter.

Manufacturer: Steury
Model No.: M400S
Type: Hitched
Dimensions: Closed, 12' 8" x 82½"; open, 12' 1" x 82½"
Material: Fiberglass roof
Accomodations: 4
Kitchen: 75-lb. ice box

Manufacturer: Steury
Model No.: M600C
Type: Hitched
Dimensions: Closed, 12' 8" x 82½"; open, 16' 1" x 82½"
Material: Fiberglass roof
Accomodations: 6
Kitchen: 50-lb. ice box, enameled sink, 2-burner removable range
Features: City-water hookup; inside electrical outlet.

Manufacturer: Steury
Model No.: S600
Dimensions: Closed, 14' 6" x 84"; open, 19' 4" x 84"
Material: Fiberglass roof
Accomodations: 7
Kitchen: 75-lb. ice box, enameled sink, 3-burner removable range
Features: City-water hookup; inside and outside electrical outlets; rear gaucho.

Manufacturer: Steury
Model No.: S600R
Type: Hitched
Dimensions: Closed, 14' 6" x 84"; open, 19' 4" x 84"
Material: Fiberglass roof
Accomodations: 4
Kitchen: 75-lb. ice box, enameled sink, 3-burner removable range
Features: City-water hookup; inside and outside electrical outlets.

Manufacturer: Steury
Model No.: D700
Type: Hitched

Dimensions: Closed, 14' 6" x 84"; open, 19' 4" x 84"
Material: Fiberglass roof
Accomodations: 7
Kitchen: 75-lb. ice box, enameled sink, 3-burner fixed range
Features: City-water hookup; inside electrical outlet; side gaucho; fold-down galley.

Manufacturer: Steury
Model No.: M700C
Type: Hitched
Dimensions: Closed, 12' 8" x 82½"; open, 16' 1" x 82½"
Material: Fiberglass roof
Accomodations: 6
Kitchen: 50-lb. ice box, enameled sink, 2-burner fixed range
Features: City-water hookup; inside electrical outlet; gaucho.

Manufacturer: Steury
Model No.: S1300D
Type: Hitched
Dimensions: Closed, 17' 6" x 89"; open, 22' 2" x 89"
Material: Fiberglass roof
Accomodations: 8
Kitchen: 75-lb. ice box, stainless steel sink, 3-burner removable range
Features: City-water hookup; inside and outside electrical outlets.

Manufacturer: Steury
Model No.: S1300G
Type: Hitched
Dimensions: Closed, 17' 6" x 89"; open, 22' 2" x 89"
Material: Fiberglass roof
Accomodations: 8
Kitchen: 75-lb. ice box, stainless steel sink, 3-burner removable range
Features: City-water hookup; inside and outside electrical outlets; rear gaucho.

Manufacturer: Steury
Model No.: S1500
Type: Hitched
Dimensions: Closed, 19' 6" x 89"; open, 24' 2" x 89"
Material: Fiberglass roof
Accomodations: 8
Kitchen: 75-lb. ice box, stainless steel sink, 3-burner removable range
Features: City-water hookup; inside and outside electrical outlets; rear gaucho.

Specifications: Accessories

Air Pillows

Manufacturer: Irving/Weather-Rite
Model No.: 1515
Size: 15″ x 15″ (deflated)
Color(s): Assorted

Manufacturer: Kelty
Model No.: Air Pillow
Size: 11″ x 16″
Material: Vinyl
Color(s): Green
Features: Snaps to attach air mattress.

Manufacturer: Recreational Equipment
Model No.: B13-042
Size: 15″ x 18″ (flat)
Material: Coated nylon
Weight: 6 oz.

Manufacturer: Ski Hut
Model No.: S340 Stebco Air Cushion
Size: 15″ x 18″
Material: Inflatable nylon
Weight: 5 oz.
Color(s): Green

Stebco Model No. S340

Axes

Manufacturer: Academy
Model No.: 880
Handle: Hardwood

Manufacturer: Academy
Model No.: 892
Handle: Steel; rubber grip
Features: Sheath.

Manufacturer: Compass
Model No.: 270
Size: 15″ handle, 3½″ cutting edge
Weight: 2 lbs.
Handle: Wood
Features: Leather sheath.

Compass Model No. 270

Manufacturer: Moor & Mountain
Model No.: 525
Size: 26″ handle
Weight: 2.95 lbs.
Handle: Hickory
Features: Leather sheath.

Manufacturer: Recreational Equipment
Model No.: B33-100
Size: 12″ handle
Weight: 1¾ lbs.
Handle: Hickory
Features: Sheath.

Manufacturer: Springbar
Model No.: 3330
Size: 36″
Weight: 5 lbs.
Blade: Carbon forged steel
Handle: Hickory

Manufacturer: Springbar
Model No.: 3332
Size: 24″ handle
Weight: 2½ lbs.
Blade: Carbon forged steel
Handle: Hickory

Manufacturer: True Temper
Model No.: 11002
Size: 13¼″ handle, 3⅛″ blade
Weight: 1¼ lbs. head
Handle: Chrome-plated steel, cushion grip
Features: Sheath slotted to hang on belt.

True Temper Model No. 11002

Manufacturer: True Temper
Model No.: 11004
Size: 14″ head, 3⅜″ blade
Weight: 1¼ lbs. (head)
Blade: Steel
Handle: Fire-hardened hickory
Features: Sheath.

True Temper Model No. 11004

Manufacturer: True Temper
Model No.: 11014
Size: 28″ handle, 4″ blade
Weight: 2¼ lbs. (head)
Blade: Forged steel
Handle: Fire-hardened hickory
Features: Cowhide sheath.

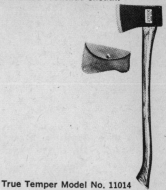

True Temper Model No. 11014

Cabinets

Manufacturer: Arco
Model: Penderie
Dimensions: Folded, 25½″ x 17¾″ x 4⅓″; erect, 25½″ x 17¾″ x 45″
Features: Zipper door; rod for coat hangers; frame of tubular steel; assembled.

Manufacturer: Arco
Model: Placard Junior
Dimensions: Folded, 23½″ x 15″ x 3″; erect, 23½″ x 15½″ x 26″
Features: Zipper door; 3 shelves; frame of tubular steel; assembled.

Manufacturer: Arco
Model: Placard Pliant
Dimensions: Folded, 23½″ x 10¼″ x 4⅓″; erect, 23½″ x 10¼″ x 41⅓″
Features: Zipper door; 4 shelves; frame of tubular steel; assembled.

Manufacturer: Arco
Model: Placard Senior. Same as Model Placard Pliant except:
Dimensions: Folded, 23½″ x 15¾″ x 4″; erect, 23½″ x 15¾″ x 41⅓″

Camp Tables

Manufacturer: Arco
Model: Gimbourra
Dimensions: Folded, 25½″ x 15¾″ x 5½″; erect, 49″ x 15¾″ x 40½″
Features: Windshield; metal cabinet with 2 shelves; converts into trunk or folds into suitcase.

Manufacturer: Arco
Model: Pistou
Dimensions: Folded, 27½″ x 16″ x 4″; erect, 54⅓″ x 16″ x 26⅓″
Features: Windshield; shelf; drawer; cabinet; folds into suitcase.

Manufacturer: Arco
Model: Pitchoun
Dimensions: Folded, 18″ x 16″ x 3″; erect, 35½″ x 14½″ x 26⅓″
Features: Windshield; 2 side shelves; cabinet; folds into suitcase.

Manufacturer: Arco
Model: Pusse
Dimensions: Folded, 22″ x 14½″ x 2⅓″; erect, 22″ x 14½″ x 26⅓″
Features: Windshield; cabinet; shelf; sink, water tank and extension are optional.

Canteens

Manufacturer: Academy
Model No.: 7
Material: Aluminum
Capacity: 1 qt.
Features: Side spout opening; cap closure with safety chain; canvas carrying case; adjustable shoulder strap.

Manufacturer: Academy
Model No.: 80
Capacity: 1 qt.
Features: G.I. style; safety chain cap; canvas cover.

Manufacturer: Academy
Model No.: 277
Material: Rustproof steel
Capacity: 2 qts.
Features: Covered with blanket lining; screw cap with safety chain; adjustable shoulder strap.

Manufacturer: Palco
Model No.: 510
Material: Plastic
Capacity: 2 qts.
Insulation: Polystyrene
Features: Large mouth opening; screw cap with retainer ring; adjustable and removable strap.

Palco Model No. 510

Manufacturer: Springbar
Model No.: 3122
Weight: 3 lbs.
Capacity: 4 qts.
Insulation: Polyethylene
Features: Covered with blanket.

Manufacturer: Springbar
Model No.: 3124
Weight: 4 lbs.
Capacity: 2 qts.
Insulation: Galvanized steel
Features: Covered with blanket.

Cord Tighteners

Manufacturer: Moor & Mountain
Model No.: 106
Weight: .03 lb.
Features: Holds in high winds; good on all lines; 1/4" hole.

Moor & Mountain Model No. 106

Manufacturer: Recreational Equipment
Model No.: B21-320
Material: Aluminum
Weight: 1 oz.
Features: Accepts 1/8" cord; bent and grooved; package of 8.

Manufacturer: Stag
Model No.: 30418
Material: Plastic
Features: Accepts up to 1/8" cord.

Manufacturer: Stag
Model No.: 30419
Material: Heavy-duty plated spring wire.

Stag Model No. 30418   Stag Model No. 30419

Cups

Manufacturer: L. L. Bean
Model No.: 5461C
Material: Stainless steel
Weight: 1/2 oz.
Features: Snaps open; folds flat.

Manufacturer: Camp-ways
Model No.: 252
Color(s): Assorted
Features: Collapsible; 4 per pack.

Manufacturer: Coghlan's
Model No.: 933
Material: Plastic
Weight: 5 to 12 oz.
Features: Snap-off cover; built-in pill compartment; 6 in 1.

Coghlan's Model No. 933

Manufacturer: Coghlan's
Model No.: 7625BP
Material: Stainless steel
Features: Stay-cool rim.

Manufacturer: Mirror
Model No.: S2-2206-53
Size: 4 1/2 oz.
Material: Aluminum
Features: Collapsible.

Fire Extinguishers

Manufacturer: BernzOmatic
Model No.: FE5A

Range: 8 to 10 ft.
Features: Dial-type pressure gauge; all types of fires; meets DOT requirements; refillable.

Manufacturer: BernzOmatic
Model No.: FE10G
Size: 14 3/4"
Diameter: 3"
Range: 8 to 10 ft.
Features: 1 1/2" dial pressure gauge; meets DOT requirements.

Manufacturer: BernzOmatic
Model No.: FE18-UL
Range: 10 ft.
Features: Shoots foam; effective on gasoline, grease, oil and any liquid fire.

Manufacturer: BernzOmatic
Model No.: FE21R
Size: 9 1/2"
Diameter: 3"
Range: 8 to 10 ft.
Features: Compact size; push-button activator.

Fuel Sticks/Tablets

Manufacturer: Academy
Model No.: 4690
Duration: 10 hrs.
Features: Solid fuel charcoal; fits all fuel heaters.

Manufacturer: Champion Industries
Model No.: 31-FT
Type: Tablets
Duration: 12 minutes
Features: Start under any conditions.

Champion Industries Model No. 31-FT

Manufacturer: Ski Hut
Model No.: U718
Type: Tablet
Duration: 2- or 4-hour supply

Manufacturer: Speaker
Model: Heattab
Duration: S, 5 minutes; L, 10 to 12 minutes
Features: Light with match; smokeless; odorless; reuseable.

Gaiters

Manufacturer: L. L. Bean
Model No.: 3674C
Size: 16" tall
Material: Urethane-coated nylon
Weight: 9 oz.
Color(s): Navy, green
Closure: Zipper front, Velcro flap
Features: Waterproof, lace hook and boot cord hold gaiter in place.

Manufacturer: Holubar
Model No.: 105023
Size: 6 1/2" tall
Material: Polyester/cotton
Weight: 5 oz.
Color(s): Navy
Closure: Zipper, snaps with storm flap
Features: Eyelets for lacing under instep; water repellent.

Manufacturer: Holubar
Model No.: 105049A
Material: Two layers of polyester/cotton

Weight: 11 oz.
Color(s): Orange, navy
Closure: Zipper, snaps with overflap
Features: Reinforced bottoms of Ply-suede; water repellent.

L. L. Bean Model No. 3674C

Manufacturer: Moor & Mountain
Model No.: 604
Size: 15″
Material: Urethane-coated nylon
Weight: 30 lbs.
Closure: Zipper, Velcro tab at top

Moor & Mountain Model No. 604

Manufacturer: Recreational Equipment
Model No.: C45-020
Material: Urethane-coated nylon
Weight: 4¼ oz.
Color(s): Red, sage
Closure: Zipper, snap
Features: 7″ high; elastic at top and bottom; hook in front to hold laces; instep cord.

Manufacturer: Recreational Equipment
Model No.: C45-200
Material: Rip-stop nylon
Weight: ⅝ lb.
Color(s): Navy, red
Closure: Zipper, snap over flap, drawstring at top
Features: Water resistant; elastic ankle; lacing.

Hand Warmers

Manufacturer: Academy
Model No.: 469

Material: Felt-covered case, fiberglass insulated
Fuel: Charcoal sticks
Duration: 10 hrs.
Features: Ignites with match; velveteen bag.

Manufacturer: Academy
Model No.: 667
Material: Nickel-plated steel
Fuel: Lighter fluid
Duration: 24 hrs.
Features: Flameless; also a cigarette lighter; velveteen bag.

Hatchets

Manufacturer: Academy
Model No.: 892
Blade: Forged polished steel
Handle: Steel forged to blade, rubber grip
Features: Sheath.

Manufacturer: Irving/Weather-Rite
Model No.: 109
Blade: Forged steel
Handle: Rubber grip
Features: Sheath.

Manufacturer: Springbar
Model No.: 3352
Blade: Forged head
Handle: Hickory
Features: Sheath.

Manufacturer: True Temper
Model No.: 12007
Size: 14½″
Handle: Fire-hardened hickory
Features: Single right-hand bevel.

True Temper Model No. 12007

Hoods

Manufacturer: L. L. Bean
Model No.: 1413C
Size: S-M ,L-XL
Material: Goose down filled
Color(s): Navy, tan
Closure: Drawstring around face
Features: Snaps to collar.

Manufacturer: L. L. Bean
Model No.: 1443C
Size: One size fits all
Material: Rip-stop nylon, Polarguard polyester fiberfill
Weight: 7 oz.
Color(s): Royal blue, burnt orange
Closure: Drawstring around face; snap at throat

L. L. Bean Model No. 1443C

Manufacturer: Holubar
Model No.: 103135A Expedition II
Material: Rip-stop nylon, goose down filled
Weight: 7 oz.
Closure: Drawstring and Velcro front
Features: Snaps to Expedition II Parka.

Manufacturer: Recreational Equipment
Model No.: C24-600
Size: Medium
Material: Rip-stop nylon, goose down filled
Weight: ¼ lb.
Closure: Snaps to collar
Features: 1⅜ oz. of down with average loft of 1¾″.

Lighters

Manufacturer: Coghlan's
Model No.: 502A
Size: 9½″
Features: Lights camp stove; uses lighter flints; automatic press release action.

Coghlan's Model No. 502A

Manufacturer: Coghlan's
Model No.: 503A
Features: Lights gas lanterns; uses lighter flints.

Manufacturer: Moor & Mountain
Model No.: 434
Features: Lights fires; flint set in wood holder; steel blade for striking flint and scraping tinder in holder.

Manufacturer: Moor & Mountain
Model No.: 490
Size: 1¾ oz. tube
Weight: .17 lb.
Features: Preheats gasoline or kerosene stoves; burns without flaming; replaces use of liquid fuels.

Matches

Manufacturer: Coghlan's
Model No.: 700
Material: Wooden
No. per Box: 25
Features: Waterproof striker surface; cannot light accidentally; windproof; 3 boxes in poly bag.

Coghlan's Model No. 700

Manufacturer: Compass
Model No.: 434
Material: Chrome-plated brass box
Features: Waterproof box.

Manufacturer: Kelty
Model: Waterproof, windproof matches
Material: Wooden
No. per Box: 25

Kelty

Manufacturer: Moor & Mountain
Model No.: 560
Size: 1¾"
Weight: .05 lb.
No. per Box: 25
Features: Waterproof.

Manufacturer: Ski Hut
Model No.: E506
Material: Plastic
Weight: 1½ oz.
Features: Waterproof; cork gasket; striking flint.

Pack Rain Covers

Manufacturer: Kelty
Model: Rain Cover
Size: S, M, L, XL
Material: Urethane-coated nylon
Weight: 7 oz.
Color(s): Red, olive green
Closure: Snaps, bottom drawstring
Features: Covers any pack; extra long to cover sleeping bag.

Manufacturer: Recreational Equipment
Model No.: B07-050
Size: M, L

Material: Coated nylon
Weight: ¼ lb.
Color(s): Green
Closure: Drawstring at bottom with toggle lock

Pot Grippers

Manufacturer: Coghlan's
Model No.: 7760
Features: Opens like pliers; clamps to any size pot.

Coghlan's Model No. 7760

Manufacturer: Mirro
Model No.: M-3475-53
Size: 5¾" x 4¼" x 6"
Material: Aluminum
Features: Clamps to pots or pans.

Manufacturer: Moor & Mountain
Model No.: 422
Size: 5½"
Weight: .18 lb.
Features: Spring jaw grip and lifter.

Manufacturer: Ski Hut
Model No.: U906
Size: 4¾"
Material: Aluminum
Weight: 3¾ oz.

Manufacturer: Ski Hut
Model No.: U907
Size: 6"
Material: Steel
Weight: 3¼ oz.
Features: Spring-loaded grip; for use on heavy pots.

Ski Hut Model No. U-907

Rope Tips

Manufacturer: Coghlan's
Model No.: 7701
Diameter Range: ⅜" to ⅝"

Coghlan's Model No. 7701

Manufacturer: Moor & Mountain
Model No.: 94
Diameter Range: ½" to ¾" (13 mm to 19 mm)
Length of Tip: 1"

Manufacturer: Moor & Mountain
Model No.: 96
Diameter Range: ¼" to ⅜" (7 mm to 9 mm)
Length of Tip: ¾"

Manufacturer: Moor & Mountain
Model No.: 98
Diameter Range: 1/16" to ⅛" (2 mm to 3 mm)
Length of Tip: ⅝"

Saws

Manufacturer: L. L. Bean
Model No.: 6133C
Weight: 1 lb.
Blade: Steel
Handle: Aluminum
Features: Blade folds into handle.

Manufacturer: Margesson's
Model: Sven Saw
Features: Blade collapses into handle.

Manufacturer: Moor & Mountain
Model No.: 513
Size: Folded, 1½" x 23"
Weight: .75 lb.
Blade: Steel
Handle: Aluminum
Features: 3 pieces; folds.

L. L. Bean Model No. 6133C

Manufacturer: Moor & Mountain
Model No.: 526
Size: 24″ blade
Weight: 1 lb.
Blade: Steel
Handle: Red oak
Features: Saw folds to enclose blade.

Moor & Mountain Model No. 526

Manufacturer: Recreational Equipment
Model No.: B33-330 Bandsaw
Size: 17″
Weight: ¼ oz.
Blade: Twisted toothed wire
Features: Ring at each end.

Recreational Equipment Model No. B33-330

Sealers

Manufacturer: L. L. Bean
Model No.: 3667C Bean's SuperDry
Weight: 5-oz. bottle

L. L. Bean Model No. 3667C

Manufacturer: Recreational Equipment
Model No.: B22-918 Gard
Weight: 15 oz.
Features: Silicone weatherproofing; aerosol spray.

Recreational Equipment Model No. B22-918

Manufacturer: Recreational Equipment
Model No.: B22-923 K-Kote Seam Sealer
Weight: 2 oz.
Features: Same material as used to coat nylon.

Manufacturer: Recreational Equipment
Model No.: B22-924 Pliobond
Weight: 3-oz. bottle
Features: All-purpose cement for bonding porous and non-porous material.

Sleeping—Bag Liners

Manufacturer: L. L. Bean
Model No.: 5796C
Size: 35″ x 79″
Material: DuPont's Tyvek Olefin outer shell, aluminum lining
Weight: 7 oz.
Features: Machine washable.

Manufacturer: Moor & Mountain
Model No.: 315
Size: 82″ x 34″
Weight: .25 lb.
Features: Disposable; one size fits all.

Manufacturer: Recreational Equipment
Model No.: B10-750
Material: Cotton flannel
Weight: 17 oz.
Features: Rectangular.

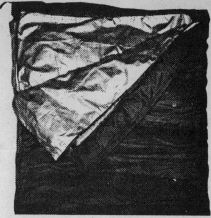

L. L. Bean Model No. 5796C

Manufacturer: Recreational Equipment
Model No.: B10-763
Size: Short, regular, long
Material: Flannel
Weight: 13 oz., 15 oz., 1 lb.
Features: Backpacker style.

Manufacturer: Stag
Model No.: 12002
Material: Flannel
Weight: 1 lb.
Features: 10 Velcro fastener tabs; stick-on matching tabs for sleeping bag.

Socks

Manufacturer: Academy
Model No.: 15 Electric Hot Socks
Material: Wool, nylon
Color(s): Gray with red trim top
Features: Operates with D-size battery for each sock; plastic battery case; 14″ height.

Manufacturer: Holubar
Model No.: 450155B
Size: 9, 10, 11, 12, 13
Material: Worsted wool
Color(s): Gray with red top, heel and toe
Features: 12″ long; 3-dimensional stitch pattern; thermal.

Manufacturer: Moor & Mountain
Model No.: 645
Size: 9, 10, 11, 12, 13
Material: Silk
Weight: .06 lb.
Color(s): Natural
Features: Inner sock; 9¼″ height; thermal.

Manufacturer: Moor & Mountain
Model No.: 675
Size: 9, 10, 11, 12, 13, 14, 15
Material: Worsted wool
Weight: .07 lb.
Color(s): White
Features: Inner sock; 10″ height; ribbed top; nylon reinforced heel and toe.

Manufacturer: Moor & Mountain
Model No.: 913
Size: One size fits all
Material: Worsted wool
Weight: .28 lb.
Color(s): Assorted
Features: Over the knee stirrup type; snowflake pattern with black elastic under arch.

Manufacturer: Moor & Mountain
Model No.: 937
Size: 9, 10, 11, 12, 13
Material: 85/15 wool-nylon
Weight: .26 lb.
Color(s): Gray
Features: 11″ height; raggsock design.

Stuff Bags

Manufacturer: Academy
Model No.: 169
Material: Nylon
Closure: Drawstring
Feature: Water repellent.

Manufacturer: Camp-ways
Model No.: 537
Dimensions: 10″ x 18″
Material: Nylon
Weight: 1½ oz.
Color(s): Assorted
Closure: Drawstring

Manufacturer: Holubar
Model No.: 108183
Dimensions: 9¾″ x 18″
Material: Urethane-coated nylon
Weight: 2¼ oz.
Features: Waterproof.

Manufacturer: Kelty
Model: Stuff Bag
Size: S, 9″ x 17″; M, 10″ x 18″; L, 11″ x 19″
Material: Nylon
Weight: 3½ oz., 4 oz., 4½ oz.
Color(s): Red, olive green, blue
Closure: Drawstring with top flap
Features: Water repellent; seams double stitched.

Manufacturer: Recreational Equipment
Model No.: B06-332
Dimensions: 14″ x 24″
Material: Coated nylon
Color(s): Red
Closure: Drawstring top

Tarps

Manufacturer: Camp-ways
Model No.: NT 79
Size: 7′ x 9′
Material: Nylon
Weight: 20 oz.
Color(s): Assorted
Features: Double stitched around edges; reinforced grommets.

Manufacturer: Holubar
Model No.: 658609
Dimensions: 55″ x 93″
Material: Rip-stop nylon
Weight: 14 oz.
Features: Grommets at corners and in middle of each side.

Manufacturer: Kelty
Model: Ground Sheet
Size: 4½′ x 8′
Material: Vinyl
Weight: 12 oz.

Manufacturer: Moor & Mountain
Model No.: 105
Dimensions: 43″ x 96″
Material: Coated-nylon taffeta
Color(s): Royal blue
Features: Grommets at corners.

Manufacturer: Moor & Mountain
Model No.: 150. Same as Model No. 105 except:
Dimensions: 60″ x 96″

Manufacturer: Recreational Equipment
Model No.: B19-230
Dimensions: 11½′ x 13½′
Material: Coated nylon
Weight: 3⅝ lbs.
Color(s): Blue
Features: 8 reinforced grommets; 5 reinforced pull-offs on flat open surface.

Manufacturer: Sunshine
Model No.: FR-912-1
Dimensions: 9′ x 12′

Weight: 2 lbs.
Features: Flame retardant; grommet kit.

Sunshine Model No. FR-912-1

Manufacturer: Sunshine
Model No.: FR-957-1. Same as Model No. FR-912-1 except:
Dimensions: 5′ x 7′
Weight: ¾ lb.

Tent Cords

Manufacturer: Kelty
Model: Tent Cord
Dimensions: 36′ long; ⅛″ thick
Material: Braided nylon
Color(s): Yellow

Manufacturer: Outdoor Venture
Model No.: 70-960
Weight: 5 lbs.
Dimensions: 10′ each.
Features: 4 per pack.

Manufacturer: Paul Petzoldt
Model No.: M14
Weight: 3½ oz.
Dimensions: 10 yds.
Material: Nylon

Manufacturer: Recreational Equipment
Model No.: B21-330
Weight: ¾ oz.
Features: Figure-8 shape to keep tension.

Tent Poles

Manufacturer: Camp-ways
Model No.: 603
Size: 42″ tall
Material: Aluminum
Weight: 11 oz.
Features: Pop-up design; locks automatically; 3 per pack.

Manufacturer: Camp-ways
Model No.: 610
Material: Aluminum
Weight: 1½ lbs.
Features: Socket locking connector; pop-up design; 3 pieces.

Manufacturer: Holubar
Model No.: 657106
Size: 11½″, 12″, 14½″
Weight: 1½ oz., 1½ oz.
Features: Makes either A-frame or vertical poles; any length pole possible by stacking more than one.

Manufacturer: Moor & Mountain
Model No.: 162
Size: 5′ 3″ to 6′ 10″
Material: Aluminum
Weight: 1.15 lbs.
Features: Adjustable; telescopes for easy packing.

Manufacturer: Recreational Equipment
Model No.: B21-100
Size: ⅝″ x 48″
Material: Aluminum
Weight: 7 oz.
Features: 3 sections connected with ¼″ shock cord.

Manufacturer: Recreational Equipment
Model No.: B21-165
Size: 16″ (collapsed)
Weight: 1½ lbs.
Features: 4-pole set with top elbow connectors.

Manufacturer: Stag
Model No.: 30307
Size: 3′ 6″
Weight: 5 oz.
Features: Telescoping 3-piece pole.

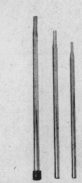

Stag Model No. 30307

Manufacturer: Stag
Model No.: 30308
Size: 3′ 6″
Weight: 5 oz.
Features: Non-telescoping 2-piece pole.

Stag Model No. 30308

Tent Stakes

Manufacturer: Camp-ways
Model No.: SKS7
Size: 7″
Material: Steel
Weight: 8 oz.
Features: 14 per pack.

Manufacturer: Eureka
Model: Alpine Tent Stakes
Size: 7″

Manufacturer: Eureka
Model: Tent Stakes
Size: 9″, 12″
Material: Plastic

Manufacturer: Holubar
Model No.: 657023
Size: 11¾″
Material: Aluminum
Weight: 1½ oz.
Features: Corrosion-resistant; semi-circular; rolled lip at top.

Manufacturer: Kelty
Model: U Tent Stakes
Size: 6″, 10″
Material: Aluminum
Weight: ⅝ oz., 1 oz.

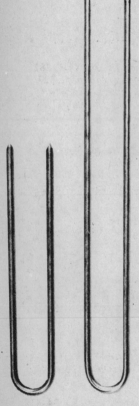

Kelty

Manufacturer: Moor & Mountain
Model No.: 129
Size: 12″
Material: Lexan plastic
Weight: .09 lb.
Color(s): Orange

Manufacturer: Recreational Equipment
Model No.: B21-265
Size: 9½″
Material: Aluminum
Weight: 1 oz.
Features: 6 holes.

Manufacturer: Stag
Model: 30416
Size: 12″
Material: Plastic
Weight: 1½ oz.

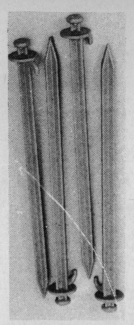

Stag Model No. 30416

Water Jugs

Manufacturer: L. L. Bean
Model No.: 5487C
Size: 3½″ (folded)
Material: Transparent polyethylene
Weight: 7 oz.
Volume Capacity: 2½ gal.
Features: Folds when empty; crack resistant; spigot for easy pouring.

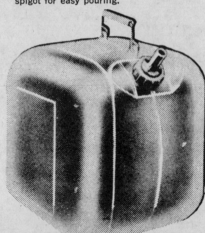

L. L. Bean Model No. 5487C

Manufacturer: L. L. Bean
Model No.: 5496C
Size: 3½″ (folded)
Material: Translucent Polyethylene
Weight: 10 oz.
Volume Capacity: 5 gal.
Features: Crack resistant; spigot for easy pouring, folds flat.

Manufacturer: Moor & Mountain
Model No.: 505
Material: Polyethylene
Weight: .05 lb.

Volume Capacity: 2.5 gal.
Features: Spigot; folds flat.

L. L. Bean Model No. 5496C

Manufacturer: Recreational Equipment
Model No.: B30-210
Size: 12¾″ x 8¾″
Material: Polyethylene
Weight: 1¾ lbs.
Volume Capacity: 2½ gal.
Features: Reversible spout; 1¼″ opening; vent.

Manufacturer: Recreational Equipment
Model No.: B30-220. Same as Model No. B30-210 except:
Size: 15″ x 11″
Weight: 2¾ lbs.
Volume Capacity: 5 gal.

Manufacturer: Recreational Equipment
Model No.: B30-300
Size: 6″ x 6″ x 6″
Material: Polyethylene
Weight: 2 oz.
Volume Capacity: 1 gal.
Features: Collapsible; plastic screw cap; 1¼″ opening; cube shaped.

Manufacturer: Recreational Equipment
Model No.: B30-330
Size: 7½″ x 7½″ x 7½″
Weight: 5 oz.
Volume Capacity: 1½ gal.
Features: Plastic handle; spigot.

Manufacturer: Reliance
Model No.: 100101
Material: Polyethylene
Volume Capacity: 3 gal.
Features: Folds for storage; handle; tapered design to eliminate splash.

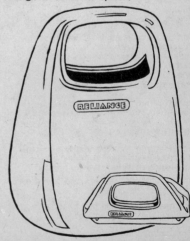

Reliance Model No. 100101

Index

"Once you have discovered solitude—the gigantic, enveloping, including, renewing solitude of wild and silent places—and have learned to put it to creative use, you are likely to accept without a second thought such small additional dangers as the solitude imposes. Naturally, you are careful. You make darned sure that someone always knows where you are, and when you will be 'out.' You leave broad margins of safety in everything you do: hurrying (or not hurrying) over rough country to make up time; crossing (or not crossing) the creek on that narrow log; inching past (or not inching past) that perilously perched boulder. And when it comes to the all-important matter of luck, you keep firmly in mind the Persian proverb 'Fortune is infatuated with the efficient.'

"But if you judge safety to be the paramount consideration in life you should never, under any circumstances, go on long hikes alone. Don't take short hikes alone either—or, for that matter, go anywhere alone. And avoid at all costs such foolhardy activities as driving, falling in love, or inhaling air that is almost certainly riddled with deadly germs. Wear wool next to the skin. Insure every good and chattel you possess against every conceivable contingency the future might bring, even if the premiums half-cripple the present. Never cross an intersection against a red light, even when you can see that all roads are clear for miles. And never, of course, explore the guts of an idea that seems as if it might threaten one of your more cherished beliefs. In your wisdom you will probably live to a ripe old age. But you may discover, just before you die, that you have been dead for a long, long time."

—Colin Fletcher in *The Complete Walker*

A selection of antique camping and backpacking catalog pages has been reproduced on the inside front and back covers to capture the flavor of a past which is gone but not forgotten.